ISBN 978-0-265-61663-5
PIBN 10152039

EALTH CARE REFORM

ial No. 103-...

HEARINGS

BEFORE THE

COMMITTEE ON HEALTH

OF THE

EE ON WAYS AND MEANS

OF REPRESENTATIVES

HUNDRED THIRD CONGRESS

VOLUME XII

Health Care Reform Proposals:
n Providers and Consumers

26; NOVEMBER 15, 1993; FEBRUARY 1 AND 4, 1994

PART 3 OF 3

FEBRUARY 1 AND 4, 1994

Serial 103–91

ie use of the Committee on Ways and Means

HEALTH CARE REFORM

HEARINGS

BEFORE THE

SUBCOMMITTEE ON HEALTH

OF THE

COMMITTEE ON WAYS AND MEANS

HOUSE OF REPRESENTATIVES

ONE HUNDRED THIRD CONGRESS

VOLUME XII

President's Health Care Reform Proposals: Impact on Providers and Consumers

OCTOBER 7, 21, 22, 26; NOVEMBER 15, 1993; FEBRUARY 1 AND 4, 1994

PART 3 OF 3

FEBRUARY 1 AND 4, 1993

Serial 103–91

Printed for the use of the Committee on Ways and Means

U.S. GOVERNMENT PRINTING OFFICE

83–037 CC   WASHINGTON : 1994

For sale by   .S. Government Printi
Su rintendent of Documents   oressional Sales Office   20402

COMMITTEE ON WAYS AND MEANS

DAN ROSTENKOWSKI, Illinois, *Chairman*

SAM M. GIBBONS, Florida
J.J. PICKLE, Texas
CHARLES B. RANGEL, New York
FORTNEY PETE STARK, California
ANDY JACOBS, JR., Indiana
HAROLD E. FORD, Tennessee
ROBERT T. MATSUI, California
BARBARA B. KENNELLY, Connecticut
WILLIAM J. COYNE, Pennsylvania
MICHAEL A. ANDREWS, Texas
SANDER M. LEVIN, Michigan
BENJAMIN L. CARDIN, Maryland
JIM McDERMOTT, Washington
GERALD D. KLECZKA, Wisconsin
JOHN LEWIS, Georgia
L.F. PAYNE, Virginia
RICHARD E. NEAL, Massachusetts
PETER HOAGLAND, Nebraska
MICHAEL R. McNULTY, New York
MIKE KOPETSKI, Oregon
WILLIAM J. JEFFERSON, Louisiana
BILL K. BREWSTER, Oklahoma
MEL REYNOLDS, Illinois

BILL ARCHER, Texas
PHILIP M. CRANE, Illinois
BILL THOMAS, California
E. CLAY SHAW, JR., Florida
DON SUNDQUIST, Tennessee
NANCY L. JOHNSON, Connecticut
JIM BUNNING, Kentucky
FRED GRANDY, Iowa
AMO HOUGHTON, New York
WALLY HERGER, California
JIM McCRERY, Louisiana
MEL HANCOCK, Missouri
RICK SANTORUM, Pennsylvania
DAVE CAMP, Michigan

JANICE MAYS, *Chief Counsel and Staff Director*
CHARLES M. BRAIN, *Assistant Staff Director*
PHILLIP D. MOSELEY, *Minority Chief of Staff*

SUBCOMMITTEE ON HEALTH

FORTNEY PETE STARK, California, *Chairman*

SANDER M. LEVIN, Michigan
BENJAMIN L. CARDIN, Maryland
MICHAEL A. ANDREWS, Texas
JIM McDERMOTT, Washington
GERALD D. KLECZKA, Wisconsin
JOHN LEWIS, Georgia

BILL THOMAS, California
NANCY L. JOHNSON, Connecticut
FRED GRANDY, Iowa
JIM McCRERY, Louisiana

(II)

CONTENTS

FEBRUARY 4, 1994

WITNESSES

SUBMISSIONS FOR THE RECORD

PRESIDENT'S HEALTH CARE REFORM PROPOSALS: IMPACT ON PROVIDERS AND CONSUMERS

TUESDAY, FEBRUARY 1, 1994

House of Representatives,
Committee on Ways and Means,
Subcommittee on Health,
Washington, D.C.

The subcommittee met, pursuant to call, at 10 a.m., in room 1310, Longworth House Office Building, Hon. Fortney Pete Stark (chairman of the subcommittee) presiding.

[The press releases announcing the hearing follow:]

FOR IMMEDIATE RELEASE
THURSDAY, SEPTEMBER 30, 1993

PRESS RELEASE #18
SUBCOMMITTEE ON HEALTH
COMMITTEE ON WAYS AND MEANS
U.S. HOUSE OF REPRESENTATIVES
1102 LONGWORTH HOUSE OFFICE BLDG.
WASHINGTON, D.C. 20515
TELEPHONE: (202) 225-7785

THE HONORABLE PETE STARK (D., CALIF.), CHAIRMAN,
SUBCOMMITTEE ON HEALTH,
COMMITTEE ON WAYS AND MEANS, U.S. HOUSE OF REPRESENTATIVES,
ANNOUNCES HEARINGS
ON
HEALTH CARE REFORM:
THE PRESIDENT'S HEALTH CARE REFORM PROPOSALS

The Honorable Pete Stark (D., Calif.), Chairman, Subcommittee on Health, Committee on Ways and Means, U.S. House of Representatives, announced today that the Subcommittee will hold a series of hearings on issues relating to the President's health care reform proposals.

The hearings will begin on Thursday, October 7, 1993, at 10:00 a.m. in the main Committee hearing room, 1100 Longworth House Office Building. They will continue on Tuesday, October 12, 1993, in the main Committee hearing room, 1100 Longworth House Office Building, beginning at 10:00 a.m. Subsequent hearings will be announced at a later date.

In announcing the hearings, Chairman Stark said: "The President's health care reform plan presents a comprehensive response to the nation's most pressing problem. The plan would commit the nation to universal health coverage and to cost containment -- goals we have been seeking for many years. The President's proposals are complex, and we want to explore this plan and the alternatives to it, thoroughly, before proceeding to mark up a bill. We, therefore, expect to hold hearings to examine various aspects of the proposals throughout the fall of 1993."

Oral testimony will be heard from invited and public witnesses during the course of the Subcommittee hearings on the President's proposals.

BACKGROUND:

The first hearing, scheduled for October 7, will include testimony from representatives of affected groups, including labor unions, health care providers, and health insurers.

Testimony from Administration experts on various aspects of the President's proposals, including benefits, coverage, low-income subsidies, cost containment, governance, and Medicare proposals, will be heard by the Subcommittee at the next two hearings. The first day of Administration witnesses will be held on October 12, and the second day will be announced in a later press release.

At subsequent hearings the Subcommittee will receive testimony from Members of Congress and from representatives of other affected groups, including consumer and employer groups.

Testimony will be heard at additional hearings to focus on a series of priority health reform issues, including:

    (1) Role of State governments and the Federal Government, including the role and functions of the proposed National Health Board, the Department of Health and Human Services, and other Federal agencies;

    (2) Role and functions of the proposed health alliances;

    (3) Health cost containment, including premium caps and alternative mechanisms;

    (4) Proposed insurance reforms and their impact, risk selection, and risk adjustment;

(MORE)

(5) Impact of the plan on underserved inner-city and rural areas;

(6) Impact of the plan on low-income populations generally;

(7) Medicare savings proposals;

(8) Impact of the plan on the structure and future of the Medicare program, including the proposed Medicare drug benefit;

(9) Alternatives to the plan, including single-payer options, and other managed-competition options;

(10) Administrative simplification under the plan;

(11) Quality assurance;

(12) Fraud and abuse measures;

(13) Retiree health benefits;

(14) Long-term care benefit;

(15) Proposed standard health benefit package;

(16) Graduate medical education and academic medical centers;

(17) Impact of the plan on other affected groups and individuals.

Hearings also will be scheduled by the full Committee on Ways and Means to consider financing issues (other than Medicare savings proposals) and other tax-related matters.

DETAILS FOR SUBMISSION OF REQUESTS TO BE HEARD:

Members of Congress, individuals and organizations interested in presenting oral testimony before the Subcommittee must submit their requests to be heard by telephone to Harriett Lawler, Diane Kirkland or Karen Ponzurick [(202) 225-1721] no later than the close of business on Friday, October 15, 1993, to be followed by a formal written request to Janice Mays, Chief Counsel and Staff Director, Committee on Ways and Means, U.S. House of Representatives, 1102 Longworth House Office Building, Washington, D.C. 20515. The staff will notify by telephone those scheduled to appear as soon as possible after the filing deadline and after additional hearings have been scheduled.

Individuals and organizations must specify in their requests to testify on which topic they would like to be heard. Given the limited time for the Subcommittee to hear from public witnesses, it is likely that witnesses will be restricted to one scheduled appearance before the Subcommittee. Additional comments on other aspects of the President's proposals may be submitted for the printed record of the appropriate hearing.

It is urged that persons and organizations having a common position make every effort to designate one spokesperson to represent them in order for the Subcommittee to hear as many points of view as possible. Witnesses are reminded that the Subcommittee has held extensive hearings on various health reform issues earlier this year. To the extent possible, witnesses need not restate previous testimony heard by the Subcommittee.

Time for oral presentations will be strictly limited with the understanding that a more detailed statement may be included in the printed record of the hearing. In addition, witnesses may be grouped as panelists with strict time limitations for each panelist.

(MORE)

In order to assure the most productive use of the limited amount
of time available to question hearing witnesses, all witnesses
scheduled to appear before the Subcommittee are requested to submit
300 copies of their prepared statements to the Subcommittee office,
room 1114 Longworth House Office Building, at least 24 hours in
advance of the scheduled appearance. Failure to comply with this
requirement may result in the witness being denied the opportunity to
testify in person.

WRITTEN STATEMENTS IN LIEU OF PERSONAL APPEARANCE:

Persons submitting written statements for the printed record of
the hearing should submit at least six (6) copies of their statements
by the close of business on the last day of the hearings, to
Janice Mays, Chief Counsel and Staff Director, Committee on Ways and
Means, U.S. House of Representatives, 1102 Longworth House Office
Building, Washington, D.C. 20515. An additional supply of statements
may be furnished for distribution to the press and public if supplied
to the Subcommittee office, room 1114 Longworth House Office
Building, before the final hearing begins.

FORMATTING REQUIREMENTS:

Each statement presented for printing to the Committee by a witness, any written statement or exhibit submitted for the
printed record or any written comments in response to a request for written comments must conform to the guidelines listed below
Any statement or exhibit not in compliance with these guidelines will **not** be printed, but will be maintained in the Committee
files for review and use by the Committee.

1 All statements and any accompanying exhibits for printing must be typed in single space on legal-size paper and may not
   exceed a total of 10 pages.

2 Copies of whole documents submitted as exhibit material will not be accepted for printing Instead, exhibit material should
   be referenced and quoted or paraphrased All exhibit material not meeting these specifications will be maintained in the
   Committee files for review and use by the Committee

3 Statements must contain the name and capacity in which the witness will appear or, for written comments, the name and
   capacity of the person submitting the statement, as well as any clients or persons, or any organization for whom the witness
   appears or for whom the statement is submitted

4 A supplemental sheet must accompany each statement listing the name, full address, a telephone number where the witness
   or the designated representative may be reached and a topical outline or summary of the comments and recommendations
   in the full statement This supplemental sheet will not be included in the printed record.

The above restrictions and limitations apply only to material being submitted for printing. Statements and exhibits or
supplementary material submitted solely for distribution to the Members, the press and public during the course of a public hearing,
may be submitted in other forms

FOR IMMEDIATE RELEASE
WEDNESDAY, OCTOBER 6, 1993

PRESS RELEASE #19
SUBCOMMITTEE ON HEALTH
COMMITTEE ON WAYS AND MEANS
U.S. HOUSE OF REPRESENTATIVES
1102 LONGWORTH HOUSE OFFICE BLDG.
WASHINGTON, D.C. 20515
TELEPHONE: (202) 225-7785

THE HONORABLE PETE STARK (D., CALIF.), CHAIRMAN,
SUBCOMMITTEE ON HEALTH,
COMMITTEE ON WAYS AND MEANS, U.S. HOUSE OF REPRESENTATIVES,
ANNOUNCES ADDITIONAL HEARINGS
ON
HEALTH CARE REFORM:
THE PRESIDENT'S HEALTH CARE REFORM PROPOSALS

The Honorable Pete Stark (D., Calif.), Chairman, Subcommittee on Health, Committee on Ways and Means, U.S. House of Representatives, announced today that the Subcommittee will continue its series of hearings on issues relating to the President's health care reform proposals with two hearings focusing on testimony from Administration witnesses.

The hearing previously announced for Tuesday, October 12, 1993, in the main Committee hearing room, 1100 Longworth House Office Building, beginning at 10:00 a.m., will begin at 10:30 a.m. All other details for this hearing remain the same. (See Subcommittee press release #18, dated September 30, 1993.)

The Subcommittee will continue its hearings on Friday, October 15, 1993, in the main Committee hearing room, 1100 Longworth House Office Building, beginning at 10:00 a.m. The dates, times, and rooms for subsequent hearings will be announced at a later date.

In announcing the hearings, Chairman Stark said: "The President has put forward a comprehensive and complex plan to address the critical goals of universal coverage and cost containment. As a follow-up to full Committee hearings with the First Lady and Secretary Shalala, the Subcommittee will hold two hearings with additional Administration officials to explore the proposed health plan in detail."

Oral testimony will be heard from invited and public witnesses during the course of the Subcommittee hearings on the President's proposals. For further details about these hearings, see Subcommittee press release #18, dated September 30, 1993.

BACKGROUND:

On October 12, the Subcommittee will receive testimony from the Administrator of the Health Care Financing Administration, the Honorable Bruce C. Vladeck. Mr. Vladeck's testimony will focus on various aspects of the President's proposal, including the methodology for controlling the rate of growth in public and private health care spending, the employer and individual mandates, subsidies for firms with fewer than 50 employees, subsidies for low-income individuals, retiree health benefits, the Medicare prescription drug benefit, and more generally, the future of the Medicare program.

Judy Feder, Ph.D, Principal Deputy Assistant Secretary for Planning and Evaluation, Department of Health and Human Services, will appear before the Subcommittee on Friday, October 15th. Dr. Feder's testimony will cover issues of governance under the Administration's health care reform plan, including the role of the States, various Federal agencies, the National Health Board and the alliances. She will also focus on essential providers, insurance reforms and long-term care.

* * * CHANGE IN SCHEDULE * * *

FOR IMMEDIATE RELEASE .
FRIDAY, OCTOBER 8, 1993

PRESS RELEASE #19-REVISED
SUBCOMMITTEE ON HEALTH
COMMITTEE ON WAYS AND MEANS
U.S. HOUSE OF REPRESENTATIVES
1102 LONGWORTH HOUSE OFFICE BLDG.
WASHINGTON, D.C. 20515
TELEPHONE: (202) 225-7785

THE HONORABLE PETE STARK (D., CALIF.), CHAIRMAN,
SUBCOMMITTEE ON HEALTH,
COMMITTEE ON WAYS AND MEANS, U.S. HOUSE OF REPRESENTATIVES,
ANNOUNCES SCHEDULING CHANGES FOR HEARINGS
ON
HEALTH CARE REFORM:
THE PRESIDENT'S HEALTH CARE REFORM PROPOSALS

The Honorable Pete Stark (D., Calif.), Chairman, Subcommittee on Health, Committee on Ways and Means, U.S. House of Representatives, announced today scheduling changes for the hearings on issues relating to the President's health care reform proposals with testimony from Administration witnesses. (See Subcommittee press release #19, dated October 6, 1993.)

The hearing previously announced for Tuesday, October 12, 1993, in the main Committee hearing room, 1100 Longworth House Office Building, beginning at 10:30 a.m., will be held on Thursday, October 14, beginning at 10:00 a.m.

On Thursday, October 14, Judy Feder, Ph.D., Principal Deputy Assistant Secretary for Planning and Evaluation, Department of Health and Human Services, will appear before the Subcommittee. Dr. Feder's testimony will cover issues of governance under the Administration's health care reform plan, including the role of the States, various Federal agencies, the National Health Board and the alliances. She will also focus on essential providers, insurance reforms and long-term care.

The Administrator of the Health Care Financing Administration, the Honorable Bruce C. Vladeck, originally scheduled to appear on Tuesday, October 12, 1993, instead will appear before the Subcommittee on Friday, October 15, 1993, at 10:00 a.m. in the main Committee hearing room, 1100 Longworth House Office Building.

Mr. Vladeck's testimony will focus on various aspects of the President's proposal, including the methodology for controlling the rate of growth in public and private health care spending, the employer and individual mandates, subsidies for firms with fewer than 50 employees, subsidies for low-income individuals, retiree health benefits, the Medicare prescription drug benefit, and more generally, the future of the Medicare program.

For additional information about these hearings and other Subcommittee hearings, see Subcommittee press releases #18, dated September 30, 1993, and #19, dated October 6, 1993.

FOR IMMEDIATE RELEASE
FRIDAY, OCTOBER 15, 1993

PRESS RELEASE #20
SUBCOMMITTEE ON HEALTH
COMMITTEE ON WAYS AND MEANS
U.S. HOUSE OF REPRESENTATIVES
1102 LONGWORTH HOUSE OFFICE BLDG.
WASHINGTON, D.C. 20515
TELEPHONE: (202) 225-7785

THE HONORABLE PETE STARK (D., CALIF.), CHAIRMAN,
SUBCOMMITTEE ON HEALTH,
COMMITTEE ON WAYS AND MEANS, U.S. HOUSE OF REPRESENTATIVES,
ANNOUNCES ADDITIONAL HEARINGS
ON
HEALTH CARE REFORM:
THE PRESIDENT'S HEALTH CARE REFORM PROPOSALS

The Honorable Pete Stark (D., Calif.), Chairman, Subcommittee on Health, Committee on Ways and Means, U.S. House of Representatives, announced today that the Subcommittee has scheduled two additional hearings as part of its series of hearings on issues relating to the President's health care reform proposals.

The Subcommittee will hold a hearing on Thursday, October 21, 1993, in the main Committee hearing room, 1100 Longworth House Office Building, beginning at 10:30 a.m., with testimony from representatives of consumer groups.

On Friday, October 22, 1993, the Subcommittee will hear testimony from provider groups beginning at 10:00 a.m. in the main Committee hearing room, 1100 Longworth House Office Building.

Witnesses for these hearings will include both invited witnesses and individuals and organizations who have requested an opportunity to testify before the Subcommittee. All witnesses who will appear at these hearings, however, will be notified in advance by the staff.

The dates, times, and rooms for subsequent hearings will be announced at a later date. Oral testimony will be heard from invited and public witnesses during the course of the Subcommittee hearings on the President's proposals. For further details about the hearings, see Subcommittee press release #18, dated September 30, 1993.

FOR IMMEDIATE RELEASE
WEDNESDAY, OCTOBER 20, 1993

PRESS RELEASE #21
SUBCOMMITTEE ON HEALTH
COMMITTEE ON WAYS AND MEANS
U.S. HOUSE OF REPRESENTATIVES
1102 LONGWORTH HOUSE OFFICE BLDG.
WASHINGTON, D.C. 20515
TELEPHONE: (202) 225-7785

THE HONORABLE PETE STARK (D., CALIF.), CHAIRMAN,
SUBCOMMITTEE ON HEALTH,
COMMITTEE ON WAYS AND MEANS, U.S. HOUSE OF REPRESENTATIVES,
ANNOUNCES ADDITIONAL HEARINGS
ON
HEALTH CARE REFORM:
THE PRESIDENT'S HEALTH CARE REFORM PROPOSALS

The Honorable Pete Stark (D., Calif.), Chairman, Subcommittee on Health, Committee on Ways and Means, U.S. House of Representatives, announced today that the Subcommittee has scheduled additional hearings as part of its series of hearings on issues relating to the President's health care reform proposals.

The dates, times, rooms, and topics for the additional hearings are as follows:

Tuesday, October 26	9:00 a.m.	1100 Longworth	Provider groups
Thursday, October 28	10:00 a.m.	1100 Longworth	Labor representatives
Tuesday, November 2	10:00 a.m.	1100 Longworth	Long-term care issues
Thursday, November 4	11:00 a.m.	1100 Longworth	Impact on the economy and jobs
Friday, November 5	10:00 a.m.	1100 Longworth	Role of State governments and health alliances
Tuesday, November 9	10:00 a.m.	1310A Longworth	Issues relating to risk selection and adjustment by health plans
Monday, November 15	10:00 a.m.	1310A Longworth	Health care cost containment

· Witnesses for these hearings will include both invited witnesses and individuals and organizations who have requested an opportunity to testify before the Subcommittee. All witnesses who will appear at these hearings, however, will be notified in advance by the staff.

The dates, times, and rooms for subsequent hearings will be announced at a later date. Oral testimony will be heard from invited and public witnesses during the course of the Subcommittee hearings on the President's proposals. For further details about these hearings, see Subcommittee press release #18, dated September 30, 1993.

* * * CHANGE IN ROOM AND TOPIC * * *

FOR IMMEDIATE RELEASE
MONDAY, NOVEMBER 8, 1993

PRESS RELEASE #21-REVISED
SUBCOMMITTEE ON HEALTH
COMMITTEE ON WAYS AND MEANS
U.S. HOUSE OF REPRESENTATIVES
1102 LONGWORTH HOUSE OFFICE BLDG.
WASHINGTON, D.C. 20515
TELEPHONE: (202) 225-7785

**THE HONORABLE PETE STARK (D., CALIF.), CHAIRMAN,
SUBCOMMITTEE ON HEALTH,
COMMITTEE ON WAYS AND MEANS, U.S. HOUSE OF REPRESENTATIVES,
ANNOUNCES A CHANGE IN ROOM AND TOPIC FOR THE HEARING ON
THE PRESIDENT'S HEALTH CARE REFORM PROPOSALS**

The Honorable Pete Stark (D., Calif.), Chairman, Subcommittee on Health, Committee on Ways and Means, U.S. House of Representatives, today announced that the Subcommittee hearing on the President's health care reform proposals scheduled for Monday, November 15, 1993, at 10:00 a.m. in room 1310A Longworth House Office Building, will be held instead in the main Committee hearing room, 1100 Longworth House Office Building, beginning at 10:00 a.m. (See press release #21, dated Wednesday, October 20, 1993.)

The topic of this hearing will not be health care cost containment. Testimony will be heard instead from public witnesses on issues relating to benefits under the President's health care reform proposals.

The Subcommittee hearing on health care cost containment will be rescheduled at a later date.

FOR IMMEDIATE RELEASE
FRIDAY, JANUARY 14, 1994

PRESS RELEASE #23
SUBCOMMITTEE ON HEALTH
COMMITTEE ON WAYS AND MEANS
U.S. HOUSE OF REPRESENTATIVES
1102 LONGWORTH HOUSE OFFICE BLDG.
WASHINGTON, D.C. 20515
TELEPHONE: (202) 225-7785

THE HONORABLE PETE STARK (D., CALIF.), CHAIRMAN,
SUBCOMMITTEE ON HEALTH,
COMMITTEE ON WAYS AND MEANS, U.S. HOUSE OF REPRESENTATIVES,
ANNOUNCES ADDITIONAL HEARINGS
ON
HEALTH CARE REFORM:
THE PRESIDENT'S HEALTH CARE REFORM PROPOSALS

The Honorable Pete Stark (D., Calif.), Chairman, Subcommittee on Health, Committee on Ways and Means, U.S. House of Representatives, announced today that the Subcommittee has scheduled two additional days of hearings to receive testimony from the public, as part of its series of hearings on issues relating to the President's health care reform proposals.

The first hearing will be held on February 1, 1994, in room 1310A Longworth House Office Building. This hearing will begin at 2:30 p.m. or, if necessary, upon completion of the earlier full Committee hearing.

The second hearing will be held on Friday, February 4, 1994, beginning at 10:00 a.m., in the main Committee hearing room, 1100 Longworth House Office Building.

Witnesses for these hearings will be individuals and organizations who have previously requested an opportunity to testify before the Subcommittee, in accordance with Subcommittee press release #18. All witnesses who will appear at these hearings will be notified in advance by the staff.

WRITTEN STATEMENTS IN LIEU OF PERSONAL APPEARANCE:

Persons submitting written statements for the printed record of the hearings should submit at least six (6) copies of their statements by the close of business on the last day of the hearings, to Janice Mays, Chief Counsel and Staff Director, Committee on Ways and Means, U.S. House of Representatives, 1102 Longworth House Office Building, Washington, D.C. 20515. An additional supply of statements may be furnished for distribution to the press and public if supplied to the Subcommittee office, room 1114 Longworth House Office Building, before the final hearing begins.

FORMATTING REQUIREMENTS:

Each statement presented for printing to the Committee by a witness, any written statement or exhibit submitted for the printed record, or any written comments in response to a request for written comments must conform to the guidelines listed below Any statement or exhibit not in compliance with these guidelines will not be printed, but will be maintained in the Committee files for review and use by the Committee

1 All statements and any accompanying exhibits for printing must be typed in single space on legal-size paper and may not exceed a total of 10 pages

2 Copies of whole documents submitted as exhibit material will not be accepted for printing. Instead, exhibit material should be referenced and quoted or paraphrased All exhibit material not meeting these specifications will be maintained in the Committee files for review and use by the Committee

3 Statements must contain the name and capacity in which the witness will appear or, for written comments, the name and capacity of the person submitting the statement, as well as any clients or persons, or any organization for whom the witness appears or for whom the statement is submitted

4 A supplemental sheet must accompany each statement listing the name, full address, a telephone number where the witness or the designated representative may be reached and a topical outline or summary of the comments and recommendations in the full statement This supplemental sheet will not be included in the printed record

11

FOR IMMEDIATE RELEASE
MONDAY, JANUARY 24, 1994

PRESS RELEASE #23-REVISED
SUBCOMMITTEE ON HEALTH
COMMITTEE ON WAYS AND MEANS
U.S. HOUSE OF REPRESENTATIVES
1102 LONGWORTH HOUSE OFFICE BLDG.
WASHINGTON, D.C. 20515
TELEPHONE: (202) 225-7785

THE HONORABLE PETE STARK (D., CALIF.), CHAIRMAN, SUBCOMMITTEE ON HEALTH, COMMITTEE ON WAYS AND MEANS, U.S. HOUSE OF REPRESENTATIVES, ANNOUNCES A TIME CHANGE FOR HEARING ON HEALTH CARE REFORM: THE PRESIDENT'S HEALTH CARE REFORM PROPOSALS

The Honorable Pete Stark (D., Calif.), Chairman, Subcommittee on Health, Committee on Ways and Means, U.S. House of Representatives, today announced that the Subcommittee hearing on the President's health care reform proposals previously scheduled for Tuesday, February 1, 1994, at 2:30 p.m. in room 1310A Longworth House Office Building, **will begin instead at 10:00 a.m.**

All other details for the hearing remain the same. (See Subcommittee press release #23, dated January 14, 1994.)

Chairman STARK. Good morning. The Subcommittee on Health continues its hearings on health care reform, and as we have already learned, the President's plan is rather complex and deals with just about every issue in the health care arena.

Because of this, it is not surprising to find that the plan has drawn mixed reactions. I hope this morning will provide an opportunity for members and organizations to comment on various aspects of the President's plan, and I would encourage comments on the various alternatives to the President's health care reform plan.

Due to the number of witnesses testifying today, I intend to keep the hearing moving along in order to allow members to explore those issues about which they have particular questions and concerns.

I would like to recognize Mr. Thomas.

Mr. THOMAS. Mr. Chairman, briefly, I think that complex plan of the President's was pre-State of the Union. Post-State of the Union, he mentioned one item. I assume that some of the others may be up for grabs, so I look forward to all the alternatives that are going to be offered. Thank you.

Chairman STARK. We will begin with testimony from the following members of the House of Representatives. Before we go ahead, I would a apologize to my colleagues, both on the committee and those who have come to testify, and ask Mr. Thomas if he has seen Mrs. Doubtfire; and through the computer, I seem to be chairing two simultaneous meetings both in rooms starting with 1300.

Mr. Cardin has agreed to Chair the meeting while I see if I can quickly change my costume and go back and forth. I will ask Mr. Cardin if he would take the gavel and I will try and return to hear some of the summary of the testimony. I hope you will forgive me.

Mr. CARDIN [presiding]. Without objection, the entire statements of all of our witnesses today will be included in the subcommittee record, and I would ask that all witnesses please try to summarize their comments.

Today we do have a rather long list of people to testify, an opportunity for the public to have input in the public hearing process; so I would ask everyone to be mindful of the time problems that we have.

We are pleased to have our colleagues testify before the committee. We always welcome your views. You have been very actively involved in health care reform, and we appreciate your willingness to directly participate with the work of this committee.

We will start with Hon. Rosa L. DeLauro from the State of Connecticut.

STATEMENT OF HON. ROSA L. DeLAURO, A REPRESENTATIVE IN CONGRESS FROM THE STATE OF CONNECTICUT

Ms. DeLAURO. Thank you very much. I thank the chairman in absentia, thank the Acting Chair and ranking member Mr. Thomas for the opportunity to be here this morning. I know you have worked very hard over the past several months. I appreciate arranging the schedule so I could speak this morning.

I believe the President's State of the Union address crystallized the debate between those who believe we have a major health care problem and those who believe that things are just fine. The President clearly and forcefully restated the case for reform, and I firmly agree with his call for the Congress to pass meaningful health care reform legislation this year. Those who don't believe that there is a health care crisis, have not been talking to the people that I see in my district every week. I do not want to hold any more office hours in my hometown and listen to their heartbreaking stories about their need for health insurance. So this is an opportune moment. We must make sure that no American will lose his or her health care because they change jobs or get sick. We must also make sure that if you are fortunate enough to survive a serious illness that, subsequently, you cannot be denied health care coverage. I believe if we fail to address this, we will have squandered a tremendous opportunity.

I believe the final product should reflect the President's health care bill's principles, including guaranteed universal health care coverage; a comprehensive benefits package that includes preventive services and addresses the special needs of women, children, the chronically ill and disabled; assuring high quality care; and reducing waste, fraud and abuse in the system to keep costs down. We have to devote the resources necessary to aggressively go after those who commit fraud in the system, which amounts to $80 billion a year. We need to build in safeguards against abuses.

But in addition to these general principles, there are a few specific concerns that I want to mention this morning. A major concern that I have is that health care reform should address mental health care. It is an important and too long overlooked element of health insurance. The President's plan would improve mental health coverage, but it does not go far enough. On the other hand, his plan is better than most of the competing proposals. While I am fully aware that any expansion of covered services has budgetary implications, I also believe that we can be penny wise and pound foolish in continuing to give mental health treatment second class status. In fact, according to the National Institutes of Mental Health, equitable insurance coverage for severe mental disorders would yield $2.2 billion annually in net health care savings through decreased use of general medical services and decreased social costs.

If you determine that it is not possible to provide full coverage for all mental health services right away, I would encourage your subcommittee to consider taking one small additional step beyond the President's plan by providing full coverage for neurobiological disorders in the initial benefits package. In the same manner in which they have limited coverage for all mental health problems, insurance plans have discriminated against these disorders, which include Tourette's syndrome, autism, and obsessive-compulsive disorder, because they have been classified as "mental health" disorders. However, recent advances in science document that many severe mental illnesses are actually physical illnesses—neurobiological disorders—that are characterized by significant neuroanatomical and neurochemical abnormalities. Legislation that I have introduced, the Equitable Health Care for Neurobiological Disorders Act, would ensure that health insurance plans would have to provide equitable coverage for neurobiological disorders on a par with the manner in which they cover other "physical" diseases.

Another issue I am concerned about is graduate medical education. I represent a congressional district which is fortunate to have one of the finest academic health centers in the country and a first-rate health care professional community. However, I also represent an area which the Department of Health and Human Services says is a primary health care shortage area. We must make sure that whatever approach to graduate medical education we take in health care reform that we wind up with adequate numbers of primary care and specialist physicians in our underserved urban and rural areas and that everyone has proper access to them.

The President's proposal calls for a dramatic increase in the number of primary care physicians we train versus specialists. While there seems to be a consensus that we need to move in that direction, there is a lot of concern about how we achieve the proper physician mix. I believe that we have to carefully consider what incentives we use to attract medical students into primary care practice, how we determine the number of specialists that we will need in the future, and how residency slots will be distributed and funded. The Federation of Pediatric Organizations, representing the community of practicing and academic pediatricians, has developed a graduate funding proposal which you may wish to consider in your subcommittee's deliberations in this matter. In short, the proposal calls for the creation of a national health care workforce commission, akin to the Base Closure Commission, that would determine the appropriate national number and allocation of residency slots. Funding, derived from all health payers, would be allocated directly to programs, regional or local consortia, or given to medical students as proposed in the Commonwealth Fund task force report on academic health centers. With your permission, I would like to submit for the record copies of this proposal and the Commonwealth Fund report.

The final matter that I would like to touch on affects senior citizens in my State. It is a glitch in Medicare reimbursement for services provided on voluntary ambulances.

When Connecticut seniors call for an ambulance, they often are billed hundreds of dollars for paramedic services that Medicare will not cover. Medicare will cover paramedic services when a commercial ambulance answers the call for help, but not when a volunteer ambulance takes a senior to the hospital.

A community-sponsored ambulance is often qualified to provide only basic life support services because they don't have the highly trained paramedics necessary to perform advanced life support services. When necessary, community ambulances borrow paramedics from commercial ambulances and because the paramedic services are performed aboard this voluntary or basic life support ambulance, neither the volunteer ambulance services nor the paramedic can bill Medicare for reimbursement. Unless this technicality in Medicare law is changed, volunteer ambulance services may soon disappear and lives will be endangered. If communities give up their volunteer ambulances, they will be forced to rely on commercial ambulance services that often must travel longer distances to pick up patients, wasting precious minutes that can mean the difference between a senior's life and death.

I have introduced legislation that would allow "intercept" paramedics providing emergency life support aboard nonprofit ambulances to apply directly for Medicare reimbursement. These "intercept," which is what they are called, paramedics would be covered at the same rate under part B of the Medicare program, as they would be when they bill for services on commercial ambulances. Intercept service will only be billable to Medicare if transportation services are provided by a town-sponsored noncommercial ambulance corps. The paramedic providing these services must meet the same qualifications Medicare currently requires for paramedics as part of full ALS services.

I would submit that legislation and ask you to give serious consideration to rectifying this situation as you deliberate health care reform legislation.

Thank you for providing me this opportunity to talk with you today. A tremendous task is ahead of you, and I know that there is a long witness list this morning. I look forward to talking with you further about some of these issues.

Mr. CARDIN. Thank you.

[The attachments to the statement follow:]

THE
COMMONWEALTH
FUND

REPORT OF THE TASK FORCE
ON ACADEMIC HEALTH CENTERS

GRADUATE MEDICAL EDUCATION PROGRAMS IN THE UNITED STATES

ACKNOWLEDGEMENTS

This report was commissioned by The Commonwealth Fund Task Force on Academic Health Centers and is one in a series of Task Force reports on issues facing academic health centers. The report was prepared under the direction of a committee of the Task Force chaired by Merlin K. DuVal, M.D. Other members included David R. Challoner, M.D.; Arthur J. Donovan, M.D.; Clifton R. Gaus, Sc.D., and Katherine W. Vestal, R.N., Ph.D.

The Task Force acknowledges the assistance and consultation of Steven A. Schroeder, M.D.; Barbara Gerbert, Ph.D., and staff at The Institute for Health Policy Studies, University of California, San Francisco, in the research used in preparation of this report.

Special thanks are also extended to Barbara Culliton and Wallace Waterfall for their expert and skillful writing and editing assistance.

In all cases, the statements made and the views expressed are those of The Commonwealth Fund Task Force on Academic Health Centers and do not necessarily entirely reflect those of individual Task Force members, The Commonwealth Fund, Dr. Schroeder or The Institute for Health Policy Studies.

PROBLEM AND OPPORTUNITY — A SUMMARY

High costs, high technology and high expectations have created pressures to change and restructure the American health care system.

The Commonwealth Fund Task Force on Academic Health Centers was formed to help the nation's leading medical institutions find ways to accomplish the changes needed in these times of rising costs; declining public support for medical services, education and research, and a growing supply of medical personnel and facilities. As part of its effort, the Task Force is issuing reports that examine the effects of public policy decisions on the performance of academic health centers.

An academic health center consists of a medical school and a teaching hospital as its main components and may also include schools of nursing, dentistry and other health professions. The teaching hospital is the principal site of graduate medical education.

Medical education in the United States today begins in medical school and continues intensively for as many as eight years of graduate medical training. In medical school, future physicians study the basic biologic sciences and have their first contact with patients. But not until the new M.D.s enter a program of graduate medical education, a "residency," is their training for the care of patients fully under way.

Most states require one year of graduate medical education (the year that formerly was called an internship but now is part of the residency) before licensing a physician. The medical profession regards three years of graduate (residency) training as the minimum needed to practice medicine.

The physician in graduate medical education not only learns the skills needed by a practitioner, but also takes care of patients, serves as an instructor for medical students and conducts clinical research. These multiple functions of the education process are indispensible to quality health care in this country. However, now they are threatened from both outside and within the system.

Externally, a widespread and growing concern over the cost of health care has attracted unprecedented scrutiny of graduate medical education. Internally, fragmented organizational influences have diffused controls of the education process to a point that the functions of such education can be preserved only by decisive action.

The cost of graduate medical education is quite small in comparison with total health care expenditures — hardly two percent. In the present national mood of economy, however, every component of health care costs is subject to close examination, and the training of new physicians is no exception.

The problem of funding graduate medical education offers an opportunity to correct the problem of its disjointed organizational structure. The creation of a successful funding mechanism should force the various auspices under which the education is conducted to realign themselves and assume appropriate shares of responsibility for the enterprise.

This Task Force report views the size, content and cost of graduate medical education. The report presents principles, policy options and recommendations that the Task Force believes can set a direction for constructive and significant change in the academic health center. Among the questions facing medical educators and public policymakers are whether we are training too many or too few doctors for the services most needed, such as primary care. The Task Force makes these suggestions consonant with its view that graduate medical education is a national resource that must be supported by all payers for health care.

It suggests that limits be set on numbers of residencies or length of training. It recommends that formal connections be established between the organizations that have decision-making powers over residencies and the hospitals who, with revenues from patient care, support residency training. It recommends that training be broadened to include more exposure to ambulatory outpatients. And it recommends a voucher system for more equitable distribution of funds for graduate medical education.

GRADUATE MEDICAL EDUCATION IN THE U.S. — HOW THE SYSTEM WORKS

The physicians in graduate medical education are called residents; they make up a teaching hospital's house staff. Both terms* connote the historical closeness of young doctors to the teaching hospital where they are receiving their advanced clinical training. The residency prepares a physician for practice in a medical specialty; there are now 24 specialties (listed in Appendix I). In a period ranging from three to eight years, depending on the specialty, the residency imparts the knowledge and experience required for certification of the physician by one of 23 medical specialty boards.

Further time in residency can lead to certification in a subspecialty, of which there now are 42. For example, graduate training in the specialty of internal medicine can lead to any of 11 subspecialties, such as gastroenterology or nephrology. Training beyond that required for board certification is often achieved in a fellowship, which typically emphasizes a path of research toward subspecialty expertise.

Teaching hospitals range from smaller affiliates of academic health centers, with only a few residency programs, to major institutions that offer training in almost all of the specialties. Of the approximately 7,000 hospitals in the United States, about 1,500 have some residency programs, and thus meet the definition of teaching hospitals. But 46 percent of all residents in the United States are trained in only 100 hospitals, which is to say that hardly more than one percent of all the hospitals in the country handle

*A glossary of terms used in describing the organizations and processes of graduate medical education is in Appendix I of this report.

the graduate training of almost half of all medical residents (Smith and Stemmler, 1984).

Graduate medical education began early in this century as apprenticeship programs in a few institutions or offices of established physicians. For many years, the majority of physicians trained to be general practitioners. Specialty boards, which certify physicians appropriately prepared to practice a specialty, originated in 1917 with ophthalmology. Otolaryngology was next, in 1924, and then a flood of specialty boards rose—13 in the next decade. (Specialties and subspecialties are listed in Appendix II.) By the 1960s, the Federal government was developing a concern that the country had too few physicians for its future needs. Existing medical schools were encouraged to expand, and new ones were founded. Specialty training programs were opened up to receive the influx of newly graduated M.D.s. The new Medicare and Medicaid programs included provisions to pay their share of graduate medical education. Not surprisingly, the number of medical graduates seeking specialty training surged from 29,000 in 1950 to 66,000 in 1973, and then to 72,000 in 1983.

The growth of graduate medical education over the years has brought a number of organizational participants into the process, but they have never integrated into a coherent system of control. Instead, a complex arrangement of partial controls variously affects the accreditation of residencies, the certification of specialists and the conduct of the programs themselves. The effects of these fragmented controls are described in the following sections.

Accreditation of
Residency Programs

The American Medical Association (AMA) established a body in 1927 to oversee graduate medical education. During the next fourscore years the body's name was changed several times, but it remained solely under AMA control. In 1972, the body's participation was enlarged to include the American Hospital Association, the Council of Medical Specialty Societies, the American Board of Medical Specialties and the Association of American Medical Colleges. That body is now called the Accreditation Council for Graduate Medical Education (ACGME). It delegates its accreditation responsibilities to 24 Residency Review Committees (RRCs), one for each of the specialties. The members of RRCs are appointed by the AMA and the relevant specialty boards; in some instances, appointments also are made by a specialty society, for instance, the American College of Surgeons appoints to surgical RRCs. Appendix I defines specialty boards and societies; Appendix III lists RRCs and their sponsoring organizations.

The ACGME lays down general requirements for residency programs, and each RRC draws up particular requirements, tailored to its specialty, that follow the ACGME guidelines for faculty, administration, program content and the like. RRCs also set the minimum length of program and may further stipulate the educational procedures and the number of residents that may be in each year of training.

The RRCs make alterations in their requirements as circumstances warrant. These alterations are subject to ACGME approval, but they are rarely countermanded. The five parent organizations of the ACGME and the specialty boards may review rules established by the RRCs, but they cannot modify or veto them.

Certification of Specialists

Apart from the system that accredits residency programs is the system that certifies specialists. Twenty-three specialty boards—independent bodies — set the educational requirements whose fulfillment is necessary for a physician to be certified in a specialty. To be eligible for certification by a specialty board a physician both has to meet the education criteria and successfully complete an accredited residency program. The distinction between those two attainments is hazy but serves to establish some connection between an RRC and a specialty board. A board-eligible physician must pass the certification examination in a specialty to become board-certified. See Appendix IV for certification requirements by specialty.

A physician does not have to be board-eligible or board-certified to practice a specialty, but the incentives are considerable. Some RRCs see rates of certification of graduates as indicative of the quality of residency programs; physicians in those programs are encouraged to become certified. Some hospitals demand that physicians be board-eligible before they can admit patients, or have operating room privileges, or use such facilities as coronary care units. Also, professional fee reimbursement rates both vary with individual specialties and are higher for subspecialists as compared with physicians in primary care. And a new development is one insurance company's* reduction of malpractice insurance premiums for board-certified physicians.

*Cooperative of American Physicians/Mutual Protection Trust

The projected trend into the next century is for more physicians to become board-certified, probably to the extent that specialists in surgery, internal medicine, radiology and anesthesiology are now—which is about 78 percent. Another trend is toward *recertification*, intended to ensure a specialist's continued competence. This was first required by the American Board of Family Practice; six other boards now issue time-limited certificates and 12 more have approved plans for recertification.

Control of GME in the Academic Health Center

Influences on graduate medical education are expressed at a number of levels in the academic health center.

Hospital directors often determine the number of residents needed to fulfill the hospital's needs, including staffing of such services as intensive care units. Thus, the director influences the experience and education of residents. The director also establishes controls, such as mandatory supervision of surgical residents by senior staff, to ensure quality care and to minimize malpractice exposure.

Medical school deans sometimes exert influence to make the resident's experience meet the criteria for good education. Deans also are interested in the function of house staff in teaching medical students; the deans are concerned that the quantity and quality of residents in each service will maintain good teaching.

Program directors in an academic health center have the basic responsibility for the quality of graduate medical education. Often a program director also is a medical school department chairman and chief of a service in the teaching hospital.

I/10

The clinical faculty in a medical school can have some influence over the number of residents in their departments and the content of education experience by expressing their opinions to the program directors. Such faculty members probably have the most influence when they are part of a practice plan that contributes from its pool of funds, earned by caring for patients, to support residency programs.

The residents themselves can affect residency programs by what they believe are the best experiences and conditions for learning. Programs often are developed with consideration of the residents' views. Additionally, although the National Labor Relations Board has ruled (223 NLRB 251) that residents are students rather than employees, residents in many hospitals have organized to affect the educational experience through higher wages, fewer work hours and less time on call.

Funding of Graduate Medical Education

Not until after World War II did the cost of graduate medical education begin to be noticeable. Before about 1950, faculty volunteered time for the supervision of residents, and the residents lived on small stipends that often included room and board and perhaps uniforms.

Today, the situation is vastly different. First-year residents earn an average of $20,800 (COTH, 1984) and receive increases each year after that. Residents' stipends are only part of the *direct costs* of graduate medical education; other parts are fringe benefits, pay for faculty time spent in teaching house staff, and overhead expenses attributable to having a house staff, such as food service, laundry and administration. Altogether the direct costs have been estimated at $3 billion a year.

1/11

In addition, *other costs* are associated with residency training, largely
the extra costs of patient care because teaching is involved. They include a
greater use of diagnostic services for educational purposes even when treatment will not be modified by the findings, and the increased availability of
the highest technology in testing and therapy. These other costs of education are *not* the same as Medicare's "indirect medical education adjustment" described in the following pages. Extra costs of graduate medical
education have not been quantified and Medicare's estimate of indirect
costs clearly overstates what can actually be attributed to medical education.

Most of the costs of graduate medical education are paid as part of the
patient's hospital bill, much as labor training costs in industry become part
of the product price to the purchaser. Estimates ranging from 81 to 87 percent of residency training costs have been identified as being covered by
hospital patient care revenues (AAMC, 1983; Hadley and Tigue, 1982).
The rest of the cost is supported variously by state and local graduate medical education funds, the Veterans Administration, physician fee revenue,
grants from foundations or the National Institutes of Health and gifts to
hospitals and medical schools (Appendix V).

Until recently, hospitals routinely added the costs of graduate medical
education to their other expenses in figuring how much to charge patients.
Third-party payers for health care, whether Medicare or commercial insurance companies, accepted these costs as an appropriate part of the patient's
bill going for support of graduate medical education.

Medicare—As the nation's single largest payer of hospital bills, Medicare also has been the biggest supporter of graduate medical education (projected at one-third of the total bill for GME) and the strongest influence on its funding patterns. At the onset in 1965, Medicare reimbursed hospitals on the basis of their costs, and explicitly included the Medicare share of salary, benefits and related support costs of house staff. In addition, Medicare covered its share of what the hospital paid for teaching services by physicians (Institute of Medicine, 1976).

In the early 1970s, however, Medicare put limits on what it would pay for all routine services per patient day. That daily rate also was supposed to cover the direct costs associated with graduate medical education, but hospitals whose teaching costs pushed beyond the rate were allowed to apply for an annual adjustment. So many teaching hospitals had to seek adjustments in the first several years of the new program that Medicare changed the regulations again in 1975. The situation was eased by making the direct costs of education a "pass-through," reimbursable outside the daily rate. That process continues as part of the 1983 legislation that established the Medicare Prospective Payment System.

But even when the direct costs of education became a pass-through, teaching hospitals continued to have costs that were exceeding the daily rate, because they performed more functions—teaching, research, etc.—as they engaged in patient care. They were much more likely to be penalized by the per diem limit than were other hospitals.

Seeking some way to adjust for these additional costs of teaching, Medicare chose as a measure of graduate medical education the ratio of a hospital's residents to its beds. When a statistical procedure was applied to

1/13

that ratio, it yielded an estimate of added expense that the presence of residents contributed to the cost of admitting a patient to the hospital. In 1980, Medicare began paying an "indirect medical education adjustment" based on those figures. The resident-to-bed ratio continues in use today, although subsequent study indicates the adjustment it specifies is related less to medical education expenses than it is to patient services. Medicare's handling of graduate education costs is discussed in the Task Force report, "The Future Financing of Teaching Hospitals."

Other Payers—Insurers such as Blue Cross historically have paid for graduate medical education by allowing its direct and indirect costs to be included with the hospital's other costs, as Medicare used to do. On the other hand, Medicaid, the state-federal program to care for the poor, reimburses only a portion of hospital costs. A survey of teaching hospitals (Hadley and Tigue, 1982) found that 5.8 percent of them had been turned down by Medicaid on reimbursement for house staff stipends.

Commercial health care insurers and other third-party payers who simply remunerate according to hospital charges have given scant attention to costs of education. That situation is changing as everyone becomes more aware of all contributions to the increasing costs of health care.

The Veterans Administration is supporting about 12 percent of all the full-time equivalent house staff positions in the United States, with a graduate medical education budget of about $200 million a year. The size of the VA's education financing would give it a strong voice in specialist training policies were it to seek changes.

ISSUES IN GRADUATE MEDICAL EDUCATION

The Issue of Cost

The prominence of the issue of cost of graduate medical education is an outgrowth of public concern about costs in the entire health care enterprise The concern over education costs may be misplaced, considering that the largest estimate of yearly education costs is hardly two percent of the $400 billion spent nationally for health. However, there is a growing unwillingness simply to accept the cost of education—or the cost of anything else, for that matter—as an unidentified part of the overall hospital bill. Itemizing the bill may show where costs can be controlled. Such teasing apart o the costs gives a new visibility to the funding of graduate medical education and portends changes.

Although Medicare is now paying explicitly for the direct and indirec costs of education, potential alterations are in the offing. The Social Secu rity Advisory Council has recommended that other payment sources be identified by 1987, a move that will, it is hoped, save the Medicare Trus Fund some $41 billion by 1995 (Aiken and Bays, 1984). Also, the Sena Finance Committee's subcommittee on health is proposing to put limits the Medicare pass-through of education's direct costs.

As these nationwide changes are being debated, pressures also are becoming evident at state and local levels:

- State budget cuts prompted the University of Washington to reduc state-supported residency slots by 31 percent.

- In each of the past three years, California legislators have reduceu funding for all graduate-level medical education except primary c residencies.

- Blue Cross and Blue Shield of Maryland have instituted a "Select-Care" program that directs patients to hospitals that charge less, thus bypassing some hospitals where costs are boosted by education expenses.

- Employers seeking to control costs of health benefits are inducing employees to get their care from low-bid providers, which constitutes a refusal to pay the costs of education.

The Issue of Size

The size of graduate medical education programs has been determined largely by the demands of newly-graduated medical students and the service needs of teaching hospitals. Individual institutions, either hospitals or medical schools, have not taken responsibility for producing the amounts and types of physicians to match the nation's medical manpower needs (Tarlov, 1983).

Some observers are predicting an oversupply of physicians in the United States before the turn of the century, but projections that were stated in firm numbers hardly more than a year ago now are couched in less certain terms. Reasons for uncertainty include a shrinking number of students enrolling in medical schools, which will mean fewer new M.D.s seeking residencies a few years from now.

In any event, the planners of graduate medical education programs in the future will have to take into account not only the costs of those programs but also the obligations that will result from the number of physicians trained.

The Issue of Control

The size and design of graduate medical education programs are influenced, to a greater or lesser extent, by many agents, as was described in detail earlier: the Accreditation Council on Graduate Medical Education and its five parent organizations, 24 residency review committees, 23 specialty boards, 24 specialty societies, hospital directors, medical school deans, program directors, training directors, faculty and house staff.

Some of these can be grouped coherently, as shown in Figure 1. The ACGME and the RRCs, for instance, are responsible for accrediting residency programs, whose size and operating characteristics are affected by the hierarchy of people in the teaching hospital, from director to house officer. Playing in a separate ring are the specialty boards, which set up educational criteria for certification of physicians and do the certifying, but have little say in the rest of the action. In yet another ring are the specialty societies, some of which nominate members to some RRCs and some specialty boards—and some of which do not. The main interest of the specialty societies is that graduate medical education produce highly skilled physicians.

The lack of dependable and constructive relationships among the players in the three rings is readily apparent. But something else is missing: None of the players is in the chain of funding for graduate medical education. This funding is anchored in the reimbursement of teaching hospitals for patient care. The teaching hospitals have the responsibility of providing graduate education but have little influence on the decisions made elsewhere in the system that determine costs.

Two problems arise when separate players can make decisions independently of each other and apart from considerations of funding. One is that,

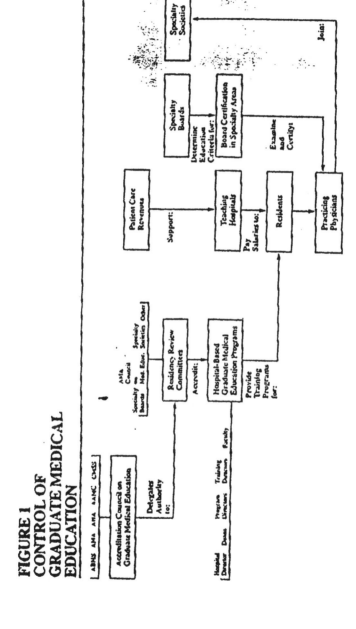

**FIGURE 1
CONTROL OF
GRADUATE MEDICAL
EDUCATION**

if the players disagree, there is no built-in mechanism to settle their differences. The other is that decisions about program or certification can be made without knowledge of their costs to the teaching hospital.

An example of the first problem is the recent decision of the American Board of Pathology to increase from four to five years the training required for certification. The board acted in the belief that knowledge in the discipline had greatly expanded and that longer training was necessary. However, members of the pathology RRC and many academic pathologists disagreed with the decision or objected that it was made without consulting them. At this writing, the RRC has not changed its accreditation requirements to conform with the board decision, and some program directors have declared that they will not offer the fifth year that the board now requires for certification.

Unilateral changes in training requirements by specialty boards are not novel—14 boards have made such changes since 1976—but they introduce dispute into a system that cannot be certain of accomplishing reconciliation. When specialty boards flex their autonomy in establishing educational standards, something else has to give way. The RRCs ostensibly are independent bodies, operating with the authority delegated by the ACGME, an authority that includes rights to disapprove changes in the length or content of training programs. But seldom has the ACGME or an RRC gone against edicts of a specialty board.

The second problem inherent in the current disjointed system of control also can be illustrated by the pathology situation. The added fifth year of training in pathology has been estimated to pose an added cost of $21.3 million nationwide (Colloton, 1983). In simpler days, a decision to extend a training program would mostly affect the residents in that program.

1/19

Today, however, the impact of such a decision is pervasive in the teaching hospital. Hospital directors must decide whether to increase financial support for the program, to reduce the size of the program and offset the cost of its greater length, or to discontinue one or another program altogether. The one thing the hospital director cannot do is passively accept decisions that require more funding for education, when payers for medical care already are questioning the high expense of teaching hospitals. It is increasingly likely that a hospital director today would have to drop entire educational programs in order to become more price competitive.

The Issue of Program Content

The medical service rendered during residency training and the required educational experience have never been a perfect fit. What the hospital needs from the resident in the way of patient care is not congruent with the content of an ideal training program. A long-standing incongruency, for example, exists in the commitment of many academic health center hospitals to provide graduate medical education in every specialty, although a hospital seldom needs such a depth of service in every specialty. The result of this lack of fit is inefficiency.

Basic differences in aims between service and education are now being overlaid with new disparities as the means and functions of hospital care change because of cost considerations and technologic advances. A few examples make the point.

Shorter Hospitalizations. Both financial pressures and changes in clinical practice are reducing hospital length-of-stay. Some of the consequences are greater patient turnover, more admission work-ups, and more paperwork for discharges. The effect of this on the education process was recently described in the case of a fairly healthy patient needing a subtotal thyroidectomy (Rabkin, 1984). Not so long ago, the patient would have been admitted to the hospital the day before surgery and would stay several days afterwards. Residents could evaluate the patient before surgery, review the relevant anatomy, physiology and pathology, and then follow the patient's surgery and postoperative course. Traditional hospital-centered education precludes resident contacts with patients at home, either before or after surgery. Today, the resident's first contact may be in the surgical suite, and the patient may be discharged the following morning, leaving very little time for the resident to appreciate the natural history of the disease, the recovery process and the effect of medical and surgical treatments.

Life-supporting Technologies. The ability of well-equipped and well-trained physicians to sustain life in today's hospital settings is widely attested. Nowhere is this ability more evident than in the academic health center hospital, which can bring together the variety of disciplines and state-of-the-art equipment necessary for the task. But these advantages threaten to turn teaching hospitals into overlarge intensive care units, offering excellent experience in care of the very sickest patients, but unbalancing the education of the resident, who is deprived of experience with more customary diagnostic and therapeutic procedures.

More Specialized Care. The high-technology expertise in the example above also is perturbing to graduate medical education in another way; it is self-perpetuating as a market strategy. Competing against nearby community hospitals, the teaching hospital offers services that the community hospital cannot. And those services largely involve very specialized care. As a result, residents can be overexposed to patients with problems seldom seen in the usual medical practice.

Missing the Action. Hospital residents once were in a position to participate in the full range of diagnoses and pharmacotherapies, because the great majority occurred in the hospital. Today, much in the way of diagnostic imaging, biochemical testing and drug therapy for cardiac dysfunction, metabolic abnormalities and infectious disease is available in ambulatory clinics. Only the more seriously ill patients or those in the end stages of severe chronic disease may be admitted to a hospital and come to the attention of the residents. Even then, the decisions about care may already have been made outside the hospital. And yet, current estimates are that only 10-15 percent of the internal medicine resident's time, and only 20 percent of the pediatric resident's, is spent in out-of-hospital care.*

The Issue of Specialty Distribution

High-level commissions, professional associations and knowledgeable educators have predicted that by the year 1990 the ratio of medical specialists to generalists will be out of the proportions needed. (*Physicians of the Future*, 1976; Graduate Medical Education National Advisory Committee, 1980; Association of American Medical Colleges, 1981; Petersdorf, 1983.) Although some observers may quarrel about the specific estimates of oversupply in each specialty, few dispute that the predictions have caught the trend.

---

*These estimates do not include federally-supported programs that have more ambulatory care experience. However, in 1984 those programs accounted for only four percent of all internal medicine residencies and 12 percent of pediatric residencies. (Primary Care Graduate Medical Education Branch, 1984).

Academic health centers have not faced this problem directly and continue to develop training programs according to service needs, specialty slots and research activities. Aside from small, federally-supported residency programs with a primary care emphasis that exist in some academic health centers, family practice training at the centers is uncommon. Most medical schools sponsor family practice residencies, but the slots are largely in affiliated hospitals, many of them rural.

Widespread acknowledgement that specialties are moving into oversupply has not prevented increasing specialization over the past five years. Before this increase is halted, some powerful social, economic and academic forces will have to be dealt with:

- Rapid advances in knowledge and its application attract physicians to ever-narrower subspecialities.

- Physician use of technology-intensive methods of diagnosis and therapy is more financially rewarding than methods of practice employed in primary care.

- Hospitals gain a market advantage by having specialty services for patient care, abetted by residents in training.

- Academic prestige accrues more plentifully to faculty in specialist rather than generalist education.

- Neither teaching methods nor financial compensation have been developed adequately for graduate medical education in an ambulatory setting that might encourage more primary care training.

PRINCIPLES FOR
THE FUTURE OF GME

The entire health care enterprise is undergoing a change, largely because of increasing costs. As a consequence, each part of the enterprise is being examined anew and none more thoroughly than graduate medical education. Academic health centers, and particularly their teaching hospitals, must work with government, business and industry to come to a better understanding of what teaching hospitals produce.

This Task Force report was commissioned to provide a sound basis for fashioning policies that will lead graduate medical education through these times of change to a stable future.

This examination has convinced the Task Force that (1) benefits of graduate medical education to society are plentiful and substantial, (2) the costs of such education are relatively small, (3) problems with graduate medical education are related less to cost than to program content, specialty distribution and program control, and (4) emerging economic forces will adjust the future supply of trained physicians that graduate education produces.

The Task Force urges that both in the public and private sectors the shapers of policy, who will be considering revisions in the structure and funding of graduate medical education, preserve the benefits of the education, remove its outdated features and ensure that its cost is reasonable.

The following four principles can serve as a framework for the public debate and a basis for the Task Force's subsequent descriptions of policy options and recommendations.

Principle #1: Support for graduate medical education
should continue to be included in the dollars spent for health
care by all payers.

Graduate medical education benefits our society by ensuring the availability of quality practitioners in whatever numbers are needed. Its support
is both a sound investment on the part of society and, when provided by all
payers for health care, is consistent with other enterprises in which appren-
tice training is part of the price to consumers. In health care, the consumers
largely are represented by third-party payers—Medicare, Medicaid, Blue
Cross, commercial insurers and self-insured businesses. These, then,
should also be the payers for graduate medical education; for any one of
them to reject participation in its support not only would be unfair, but also
would be detrimental to the future quality of medical care in the United
States.

Graduate medical education is vulnerable to shifts in financial support,
because so much of the training is concentrated in so few hospitals. Some
7,000 hospitals of all kinds exist in this country, but nearly half of all graduate physicians are trained in only 100 of them — the major teaching hospitals. These hospitals also provide a wealth of special services to patients,
serve as the acute care resource for entire regions, and foster the clinical
research that ensures continual improvement in care. To jeopardize their
support would be against the public interest.

Principle #2: Financial support for graduate medical education should be limited to preclude over-specialization of
physicians.

1/25

The public perception of the worth of graduate medical education will depend on that education's success in meeting the public requirements for health care. Teaching hospitals should not produce physicians whose numbers and training fail to match the nation's present and future needs. Many predictions have been made that physicians in the subspecialties will be too numerous before the end of the current decade, while the number of primary care physicians will continue to be in short supply.

Incentives to heighten the specialization of graduate medical education are powerful, but they are not beyond the influence of the system of financial support for education. That system should favor the training of physicians for whose services there is the greatest demand.

> Principle #3: Decisions about the size, content and design
> of graduate medical education programs should remain in
> the private sector, but decisions affecting the cost of educa-
> tion should not be made in isolation from the source of fund-
> ing for that education.

A resort to governmental regulation for reshaping the system of graduate medical education would deny what the Task Force sees as emerging market forces that will determine the future supply of physicians. These forces, in the best tradition of our economic system, should be allowed to work. Moreover, governmental regulation of such an historically private sector enterprise as medical education would run counter to today's direction in all Federal policies.

Keeping control of graduate medical education in the private sector, however, must be accompanied by the establishment of connections between the funding of education, which relies on the patient care revenues of teaching hospitals, the accrediting of education programs, and the certification process that establishes education criteria. As described earlier, teaching hospitals are responsible for providing funding for graduate education but have little influence on decisions that determine its costs.

> Principle #4: Allocation of funds for graduate medical education should encourage training in all clinical settings, ambulatory as well as hospital-inpatient.

The financing of residency training today encourages greater specialization and less attention to primary care because it emphasizes services to hospital inpatients. Hospital inpatient care is becoming increasingly technologically specialized, which deprives residents of experience with the more customary problems of medical practice that are being seen in ambulatory clinics. The structure of financing can be altered so as not to favor some practice settings over others. New emphasis is needed on training for the primary care specialties of internal medicine, family practice, and pediatrics—and on ambulatory outpatient settings for care.

POLICY OPTIONS AND
RECOMMENDATIONS

On the Issue of Cost

Continuation of the current financing practices for graduate medical education is unlikely. Changes, which have been described here, are already underway and furnish strong indication of more to come. The Task Force has developed policy options and recommendations that take into account both the likelihood of change and the importance of the preceding four principles.

> Payers for medical care should continue to support graduate medical education, but the funds for education should be separated from the price of inpatient hospital care.

Funds for education could be raised through taxes on the health care industry, such as on admissions to hospitals, on the net revenues of hospitals or on all health insurance premiums. However, taxing net hospital revenues would penalize hospitals that have higher costs, and a tax on health insurance would be difficult to levy on employers who self-insure.

A tax on hospital admissions, although superficially resembling a "sick tax," has the advantage of distributing costs of education across all users of hospital services. It would be paid primarily through health insurance, which is funded by premiums paid by sick and well alike, including users of primary care.

Funding of graduate medical education, by whatever means, should be limited to three years or first eligibility for certification in a general specialty.

The three-year limit coincides with board eligibility in four primary care specialties—internal medicine, pediatrics, family practice and emergency medicine. The Task Force recognizes that other specialties require training beyond three years and that reasonable arguments can be made for funding them to completion under current requirements of eligibility for general certification (e.g., five years for surgery). Further training in subspecialties can be supported in other ways, such as professional fees, faculty practice plans and scholarships.

Funding of graduate medical education should not be limited to fewer than three years.

The Task Force believes that three years is the minimum period of supervised practice that is needed to ensure that physicians are qualified before entering private practice. The Task Force does not favor proposals that would fund through health care revenues only the first year of training. That is a year in which residents are not yet licensed and cannot bill independently for their services. Under the one-year proposals, residents would charge for their services after the first year; teaching hospitals would neither pay nor be reimbursed for residents' salaries after licensure.

Billing by residents early in their training has several difficulties. It would preclude billing by an attending physician if his or her services overlapped those of the residents. Also, the likelihood of residents earning enough to support their education is fading as more people join prepaid health groups and as more surplus specialists enter primary care.

Funds for graduate medical education should support the indirect cost of resident training.

The indirect cost of education comprises many expenses that arise solely because of teaching programs, such as more diagnostic procedures or the maintenance of a broader range of services. They should be supported through education funding. They should not be confused with the Medicare Prospective Payment System's "indirect medical education adjustment," which is a formula payment not necessarily associated with functions of graduate medical education.

On the Issue of
Distributing GME Funds

If money for graduate medical education is generated by means of a tax, several options are available for distributing the funds.

- Aggregated at the Federal level, the funds could be disbursed as grants. However, if the government made much of a change in dollar amounts from year to year, it would gain control of graduate medical education; hospital administrative and education planning would be delayed until success in obtaining a grant was assured.

- A block grant program could be implemented to transfer funds from the Federal government to the states. That would avoid the establishment of a large Federal bureaucracy to administer the grant program, but it would necessitate the creation of state-level offices of disbursement and, more importantly, would give states discretion in allocating funds for graduate medical education.

- If the funds initially were aggregated at the state level, state government would have virtually complete control of their disbursement. The difficulty with this, and to some extent with a block grant program, is the possibility that state control of education funds would mean more support for residency training in state and municipal hospitals than in private academic health centers.

The following option for distribution of funds is the choice of the Task Force.

A voucher system should be developed to distribute graduate medical education funds among individual residents.

The Task Force believes that a voucher system would bring to the distribution of graduate medical education funds a combination of desirable elements not fully available in the disbursement options described above. Medical school graduates would be entitled to receive vouchers with which to purchase their graduate education. They could choose from among accredited residencies offered by hospitals on the basis of what the hospital wished to provide to match its service needs, faculty, patient mix and other considerations.

Vouchers could be financed by a combination of Federal, state and private sector funds in the relative proportions that they now support the direct costs of graduate education. The money value of a voucher would be held approximately equal to the cost of resident stipends, fringe benefits and other direct education costs. Disbursements of vouchers could be accomplished through any number of arrangements ranging from purely governmental to a voluntary private sector organization.

Whatever system is put in place, the Task Force emphasizes that contributions by the private sector are crucial for preservation of graduate medical education. Although Medicare is the single largest payer of health services, the entire Federal government accounted for less than one-third of expenditures for personal health care in 1982. Most of the remainder of those expenses were paid by insurers, by businesses, and directly by patients—all in the private sector.

On the Issue of Size

The number of vouchers for first-year positions in graduate medical education should be limited to the number of graduates from accredited medical schools in the United States in the most recent year.

This recommendation, when coupled to the three-year-or-first-board eligibility recommendation stated earlier, would limit voucher support to little more than three times the number of graduates in the index year from schools accredited by the Liaison Committee on Medical Education and schools of osteopathic medicine. On the basis of 1983 graduates (15,885), the total number of vouchers offered would be 47,655 (not counting the extra-time slots for surgery and other first-board eligibility periods of more than three years). This is significantly fewer than the 59,176 occupied by United States medical graduates in 1983. Also in 1983, another 13,221 positions were held by foreign medical graduates (FMGs). In the proposed system, vouchers would not go to FMGs, but they would be free to seek other funding sources for training in the United States. The Task Force rec-

ognizes that exclusion of FMGs from a voucher system could pose detrimental effects for some public hospitals that have traditionally relied on
FMGs. One solution would be the allocation of some vouchers to those
hospitals most affected by the loss of FMGs so that the hospitals could
recruit residents to meet their service needs.

On the Issue of
Program Content

Principle #4 summed up the Task Force's strong opinion that funds for
graduate medical education should no longer tie a resident exclusively to
the teaching hospital or hospital-based services. The tertiary care training
received in the high-technology hospital does not match the majority of
cases seen in typical practice. There are many ways in which the discrepancy could be reduced. Teaching hospitals could establish satellite clinics
in the communities, thereby giving residents more ambulatory care experience and perhaps enlarging the hospital referral base. Or hospitals could
affiliate with group practices at non-hospital sites. Or residents could be
encouraged to accept rotations in offices of physicians in private or group
practice, as the University of Iowa does in family practice programs. However, these and other possibilities of more appropriate clinical experiences
for residents depend on separating funding for education from payment for
hospital care.

On the Issue of
Specialty Distribution

Academic health centers must become engaged in efforts to slow and
ultimately reverse the trend toward specialty maldistribution in the United
States. One reason is that an oversupply of specialists logically has some

connection with the functions of academic health centers, where most specialists are trained.

Another reason is that academic health centers are positioned to encourage change in a system that oversupplies specialists by virtue of the centers' many memberships on bodies that accredit specialist training programs, bodies that certify specialists and organizations of national scope in medical education. A third reason is that academic health centers are discovering that an oversupply of specialists can become intense competitors against the centers' teaching hospitals.

There are several direct actions that could be taken or encouraged by academic health centers. They could, for instance, subsidize the primary care specialties with funds taken from the professional and hospital fees of the higher-earning subspecialties and services. Residency review committees (RRCs) could limit the time spent by primary care trainees in high-tech units, as the pediatric RRC has been doing. Conversely, RRCs could mandate that an appropriate number of hours be spent in ambulatory care settings.

A change in the supply of specialists may be aided by market forces as prepaid health care plans increase. Such plans have greater need for primary care physicians than for subspecialists. However, the market forces may have to be speeded by the addition of reimbursement formulas biased toward primary care, such as making reimbursement neutral as between technological procedures and time-consuming activities like history-taking.

CONCLUSION

The mounting pressures on graduate medical education come at an opportune time for the future health of residency training. The system has undergone little in the way of basic alteration since shortly after World War II. Its principal change has been to produce greater numbers of physicians, more specialized than is warranted by the medical needs of U. S. citizens. The organizational structure of almost any human enterprise seldom goes seriously unchallenged for as long as half a century, and it is neither surprising nor unsettling that graduate medical education is now in possible need of revamping. The Task Force was formed to consider alternatives for policymakers and academic health centers to preserve the virtues of graduate medical education and yet accommodate the changing contexts of cost consciousness, physician supply and specialty distribution.

The Task Force regards graduate medical education as a national resource and seeks to keep its proven benefits intact. The Task Force recognizes that GME's financing will become more explicit, its capacity will be reduced for the production of highly specialized physicians, its organizational framework must become more rational, and its base should be broadened beyond the traditional emphasis on exposure to hospital inpatients.

No better opportunity is likely to present itself for graduate medical education to undergo the inevitable realignments that can help it move into the next century, continuing to produce future generations of physician practitioners, teachers and researchers.

REFERENCES

1. Aiken, L., Bays, K. The Medicare debate—Round one. (Special Report) N Engl J Med, 311:1196-1200, 1984.

2. Association of American Medical Colleges. Report of the Task Force on Graduate Medical Education. Washington, D.C. AAMC, 1981.

3. Cole J. W. Health Services and Postgraduate Medical Education in the United States. Chapter on The Impact of Health Services on Medical Education: A Global View, John C. Bowers and Elizabeth F. Purcell, eds. New York.: Josiah Macy Jr. Foundation, 1978.

4. Colloton, J. Where will the resources for the fifth year come from? Presentation at the Sixth Conference of Pathology and Residency Program Directors at 1983 Fall Meeting of the American Society of Clinical Pathologists and College of American Pathologists. St. Louis. Mo., Oct. 16, 1983.

5. COTH (Council on Teaching Hospitals. Association of American Medical Colleges) survey of teaching hospitals. Washington, D.C. 1984.

6. Graduate Medical Education National Advisory Committee. Summary report to the Secretary. Department of Health and Human Services. DHHS publication number (HRA)81-656. Health Resources Administration. 1980

7. Hadley J., Tigue. P. Financing graduate medical education: An update and a suggestion for reform. Health Policy and Education, 2:157- 71, 1982.

8. Institute of Medicine. Medicare-Medicaid Reimbursement Policies. Washington, D.C.: Nation Academy Press, 1976.

9. Petersdorf, R. G. Is the establishment defensible? (Sounding Boere) N Engl J Med. 309:1053-1057, 1983.

10. Physicians for the Future: The Report of the Macy Commission. New York. Josiah Macy Jr. Foundation 1976

11. Rabkin, M. T. The teaching hospital and medical education: One-room schoolhouse, university, dinosaur? Presented at the 95th annual meeting, Association of American Medical Colleges, Chicago, Ill., Oct. 29, 1984

12. Tarlov, A. The increasing supply of physicians, the changing structure of the health services system, and the future practice of medicine. (Shattuck Lecture) N Engl J Med, 308.1235, 1244, 1983b.

The Task Force will issue future reports further defining the variations in teaching hospitals and the part they play in meeting their major responsibilities.

In Society's Interest

The Task Force wants to underline that its recommendations are aimed at preserving the functions of academic health centers that are essential to society. The Task Force fully recognizes that academic health centers must adjust to changing circumstances in society. However, these changes must preserve society's vital interests in retaining the most technologically advanced and most effective system of medical education, research and patient care in the world.

In relation to the cost of our entire health system, the amount of money required to deal constructively and effectively with the problems of academic health centers is relatively small. But failure to solve these problems will be a disastrous error. These reports are aimed at helping to conserve and improve what is best in America's system of academic health centers.

Robert M. Heyssel, M.D.
Chairman

FEDERATION OF PEDIATRIC ORGANIZATIONS

NOVEMBER 1993

GRADUATE MEDICAL EDUCATION AND PEDIATRIC WORKFORCE ISSUES
PRINCIPLES

The following draft principles were crafted by a special Task Force on GME convened by the American Academy of Pediatrics to develop policies and principles concerning GME and pediatric workforce issues. The Task Force met in the Washington office of the Academy on September 4, 1993. These principles have been reviewed at a meeting on September 9, 1993, revised and approved by the Federation of Pediatric Organizations. The Federation component organizations include: the Ambulatory Pediatric Association; American Academy of Pediatrics; American Board of Pediatrics; American Pediatric Society; Association of Medical School Pediatric Department Chairmen; Association of Pediatric Program Directors; and Society for Pediatric Research. These principles represent the consensus opinion of the American pediatric community comprising both academic and practicing physicians and residents.

OVERVIEW:

The United States is presently poised to enact a national health care insurance program that could include the coverage of an additional 12 million children and adolescents. The passage of such a proposal might eliminate financial barriers to needed health care for many children and generate an increase in demand for primary care physicians. These children and adolescents will need quality health care, the provision of which is very complex. Pediatricians are the most appropriate providers of primary care for infants, children and adolescents. Today, nearly two-thirds of office (physician) visits made by children aged 5 years and younger are to pediatricians.

There is presently a national shortage and geographic maldistribution of pediatricians the effects of which could be acutely aggravated by health care reform. The federated pediatric community agrees that there is a need for increased support for primary care specialties as a whole, and pediatrics in particular. In contrast to adult medicine and surgery, the overwhelming majority of pediatricians practice primary care medicine; less than 20 percent of certified pediatricians are certified in subspecialties and even fewer are practicing subspecialties exclusively. Currently, and for the past decade, over 60 percent of graduating pediatric residents still choose to enter primary care.

It is important to recognize the need for training of pediatric generalists and pediatric subspecialists to meet the unique clinical, research and educational needs of child and adolescent populations in the next century. There will be an increased demand for subspecialists (in the face of existing shortages) due to the complex illnesses faced by children and adolescents--congenital anomalies, pediatric AIDS, derivatives of substance abuse, etc. Some pediatric fellowship training --such as general academic pediatrics, adolescent medicine, behavioral pediatrics, developmental pediatrics --is often undertaken to enhance the pediatrician's ability to provide optimal primary care services and many graduates of such programs actually practice primary care.

Population and incidence of disease limit the numbers of pediatric subspecialty patients and, because of this, the number and distribution of subspecialists the country needs. There is currently an acute shortage of certain pediatric subspecialties (i.e., pediatric gastroenterologists, pediatric hematologist/oncologists and pediatric endocrinologists). In contrast to adult specialists, pediatric subspecialists are not usually found in private practice.

NATIONAL HEALTH CARE WORKFORCE COMMISSION:

The federated pediatric community recommends that an independent National Health Care Workforce Commission be established, insulated from the political process and with broad representation from the primary care community, including pediatrics. This National Health Care Workforce Commission would be responsible for:

- projecting the aggregate need of the medical care workforce for the health care delivery system;

- determining the necessary number of residency positions on a national basis (including the number of International Medical Graduates (IMGs)) and maintaining the appropriate number of generalists and subspecialists;

- allocating residency positions by specialty and subspecialty with regard to medical personnel and population needs;

- implementing appropriate incentives to reinforce the selection of primary care;

- conducting on-going research that will ensure the availability of appropriate data on which to base workforce decisions;

- evaluating and monitoring the efficacy of all recommendations and their implementation; ensuring that the process allows for flexibility, particularly during the transition period; and reevaluating recommendations as appropriate.

The federated pediatric community recommends that this independent and autonomous National Health Care Workforce Commission have features of both the Federal Reserve Board and the Defense Base Closure and Alignment Commission. The statute creating this National Workforce Commission would require that its recommendations be sent to the President for approval or disapproval, and then require the Congress to take an "up" or "down" vote on its package of recommendations without amendment. Its decisions, if accepted in this manner, are binding as statute.

The composition of the National Commission should be balanced and should reflect the entire primary care community as well as include representation from non-primary care disciplines. Its membership should include practicing physicians, medical educators, allied health professionals, i.e., nurse practitioners and physicians assistants, hospital administrators and consumers.

The federated pediatric community believes that training and service needs should be disconnected. Therefore, distribution of residency training positions should be based on the quality of the training program. However, until there is appropriate distribution of training positions based on quality and primary care/specialty needs, we recognize that some service issues must still be considered.

The federated pediatric community believes that the ACGME and the RRC should maintain their current function and focus on quality, and should not be involved in the allocation of residency training positions.

ALLOCATION OF GME SLOTS:

The principal goal of the federated pediatric community is to increase the number of primary care pediatricians. We support the need to prepare more generalists. Accordingly, whatever mechanism for allocating residency positions is selected must assure that there are at least as many residency positions in pediatrics as currently exists. We recognize the need to decrease the total number of GME training slots overall, while simultaneously increasing the number of primary care slots. However, reliable data for projecting future physician need are not available, particularly the need for pediatric generalists and subspecialists.

While the goal of limiting the number of filled first year resident positions to 110 percent of the number of US medical school graduates may be a reasonable initial target, the federated pediatric community believes that the National Health Care Workforce Commission should ultimately establish the total number of residency positions, including IMGs.

The federated pediatric community supports the limitation of residency positions only if it is implemented subsequent to the allocation of slots across specialties and pursuant to the recommendations of the National Health Care Workforce Commission.The pediatric community is deeply concerned that, in some parts of the country, IMGs currently provide a significant portion of pediatric care especially in urban hospitals in under-served communities. In these communities, ImGs may provide more than 50 percent of care. The health of children in these communities must not be compromised by the reduction of residency positions while awaiting alternative health care providers.

The federated pediatric community believes the phasing in period, accompanied by transition funding, is vitally important to hospitals that lose a larger percentage of their residency positions through the allocation process or with the assignment of residents to ambulatory care sites.

PAYMENT FOR GME:

The federated pediatric community concurs with the Physician Payment Review Commission's (PPRC) 1993 Annual Report to Congress in its support of the concept that "all payers should share the costs of graduate medical education."

Within the limits of the national goals established by the National Commission, the pediatric community is in favor of maintaining as much flexibility of choice by resident applicants as possible. Operating under the allocation of residency slots established by the National Health Care Workforce Commission, the federated pediatric community supports a continuation of the current matching system.

One option to assist in assuring a distribution of residency specialties that will meet the future health needs of the nation is to explore the use of a voucher/certificate system given to medical students in conjunction with the National Resident Matching Program as suggested in a 1985 Report by the Task Force on Academic Health Centers of The Commonwealth Fund. Alternatively, funds could be allocated directly to programs or to regional or local consortia as proposed by the PPRC and the Council on Graduate Medical Education. Any one of these proposals would help assure that monies for medical education are used for that purpose.

Whatever the mechanism, it is preferable that the funds are allocated in a manner that facilitates the training of primary care physicians, including expanding the training venues outside of the hospital setting.

INCENTIVES, INCLUDING WEIGHTING OF PRIMARY CARE POSITIONS:

The federated pediatric community believes that primary care residents should receive total compensation that is equal to or greater than other residency positions in the institution.

The federated pediatric community believes that the use of differential weights in calculating payments for primary care residency positions could provide an incentive for teaching institutions to increase the number of primary care residency positions. However, these weights must be large enough to encourage the development of additional primary care positions and education sites outside of the teaching hospital. Funding must be specifically designated for this purpose.

This short term strategy must be accompanied by long term incentives for medical students, residents, and physicians (especially under-represented minority groups) to choose primary care. A full array of support for primary care should be considered including: expansion of the National Health Services Corp; continuation and expansion of primary care training programs, such as Title VII; loan forgiveness in return for practicing in identified under-served areas; loan repayment based on a percentage of earnings; forbearance and deferment of low interest loans for entering primary care; development and implementation by all payers of a pediatric RBRVS and increased payment for pediatric services; increased funding for primary care research and other system-wide supports for pediatric and other primary care specialties including the reduction in administrative burden to primary care physicians.

RETRAINING:

Unlike adult medicine and surgery, retraining for pediatricians is not a significant issue because all pediatricians are initially trained as generalists and some take additional training in a subspecialty. Renewal of subspecialty certification in pediatrics also requires recertification in general pediatrics. However, the pediatric community strongly believes that the setting of standards for retraining other specialists in fields which include the care of children must involve the federated pediatric community. This is to ensure that the same quality of care is provided to all children and adolescents.

CONCLUSION

The Federation of Pediatric Organizations supports designing a program to ensure quality health care to all children by developing appropriate guidelines and funding for GME.

11/15/93

Mr. CARDIN. I want to welcome our colleague from the State of Idaho, Hon. Larry LaRocco.

STATEMENT OF HON. LARRY LaROCCO, A REPRESENTATIVE IN CONGRESS FROM THE STATE OF IDAHO

Mr. LaROCCO. Thank you, Mr. Chairman. I appreciate having the opportunity to bring an Idaho perspective to this hearing on health care.

I represent the people of Idaho's First Congressional District. It is the eighteenth largest district in the Nation, stretching some 500 miles from Nevada to Canada and, by any measure, one of the most rural. Idahoans have a tradition of self-reliance and personal responsibility. They like to have good tools, make their own choices, and have the freedom to solve their own problems.

As we consider the challenge of reform, we are faced with a confusing mixture of facts and figures. For instance, the cost of care in Idaho is the lowest in the Nation, per capita; in fact, it is even lower than it is in Canada! But at the same time, thousands of working Idahoans are without health insurance. We are doing some things right, but there are some significant problems that remain.

Idaho has consistently ranked as the most underdoctored State in the Nation, and despite intense community recruiting and a State-level loan repayment program, that condition continues. There are only 150 doctors for every 100,000 people, and the residual impact of this situation in Idaho's rural areas is impossible to overstate. In Idaho, access to health care means more than having insurance; it means being able to locate and get to a health care provider when you need one. The situation in Idaho is unique in many ways, and a "one size fits all" approach to the problem is not likely to solve many of our problems.

Idaho hospitals also reflect the unique nature of the rural and frontier State health care landscape. While they deliver health care services at very low cost when compared to the rest of the Nation, many struggle to keep their doors open. Some Idaho hospitals are small, and their potential patient base is spread across great distance. In order to build cost-effective community networks of care, they need the ability to work more closely with one another.

Nonetheless, throughout my district, I have encountered considerable apprehension about health care reform. When I visited "Becky's Burgers," a small restaurant in Orofino, Idaho, last month, Becky herself told me that health care reform would put her out of business. In response to Becky's challenge, I arranged for Health and Human Services Secretary Donna Shalala to do an indepth study of this Idaho small business. With factual information of this kind, I believe that we will be able to keep Becky in business, and cover her employees with affordable health insurance.

My own bill, H.R. 237, the Rural Health Care Access Improvement Act, outlines several ideas that I believe will promote solutions to many of the health care delivery problems in rural America. It outlines a series of Medicare incentives for physicians and other care providers who practice in rural areas. It alters the formula which determines physician placements through the National

Health Service Corps, and provides for administrative simplification and paperwork reduction.

In addition, it provides grants for primary care nursing facilities and telecommunications demonstration programs in rural areas. It revises some current Federal antitrust provisions to enhance the development of cost and resource effective networks in rural areas.

In addition, I have introduced H.R. 3070 to support the development of electronic telemedical networks in rural areas. I have a personal interest in seeing that we support and enhance the development of telemedicine in this country, because this field holds enormous potential for increasing access, for delivering service, and reducing costs, especially in rural areas.

The widely distributed study by Arthur D. Little and Co. suggests that significant savings could be achieved throughout our system by applying this technology to health care delivery. However, in order to speed the development, distribution and application of this technology, the Health Care Financing Administration will have to join the effort and develop reimbursement procedures to support "telemedicine."

In conclusion, Mr. Chairman and colleagues, I urge the committee to examine quickly the wide range of legislative options for health care reform, so that we retain what is best about our current system and create the kind of flexibility for the future that maintains individual choice, improves access and controls costs for all concerned. Our goal as Members of Congress should be the guarantee of private health insurance for every American, insurance that cannot be taken away. This is a tall order, but I am optimistic that history will record health care reform as the most important accomplishment of the 103d Congress.

Thank you.

Mr. CARDIN. Thank you, Larry.

[The prepared statement follows:]

The Honorable Larry LaRocco

Testimony before the Health Subcommittee of
the Committee on Ways and Means

U.S. House of Representatives

February 1, 1994

Thank you Mr. Chairman. I appreciate having the opportunity
to bring an Idaho perspective to this hearing on health care.

I represent the people of Idaho's First Congressional
District. It is the 18th largest district, stretching some 500
miles from Nevada to Canada. It contains the largest wilderness
area in the lower 48 states, and by many measures, it is one of
the most rural districts in the House. The physical geography of
Idaho is on a scale often difficult to grasp. Divided by 12,000
foot high mountain ranges and deep river gorges, Idaho is a vast
landscape where travel is difficult, and where simple access to
health care is by no means a certainty.

Idahoans have a tradition of self-reliance and personal
responsibility. They like to have good tools, make their own
choices, and the freedom to solve their own problems.

As we consider the challenge of reform, we are faced with a
confusing mixture of facts and figures. For example, the cost of
care in Idaho is the lowest in the nation, per capita; in fact,
it is even lower than it is in Canada! But at the same time,
160,000 Idahoans are without health insurance, and 80 percent of
these uninsured have jobs and pay taxes. We are doing some
things right, but there are significant problems that remain to
be solved.

Idaho has consistently ranked as the most under-doctored
State in the nation, and despite intense community recruiting and
a state-level loan repayment program, that condition continues.
There are only 150 doctors for every 100,000 people, and the
residual impact Idaho's rural areas is impossible to overstate.
In Idaho, access to health care means more than having insurance;
it means being able to locate and get to a health care provider
when you need one. The situation in Idaho is unique in many
ways, and a "one-size-fits-all" approach to the problem is not
likely to solve many of our problems.

Idaho hospitals also reflect the unique nature of the rural
and frontier state health care landscape. While they deliver
health care services at very low cost when compared to the rest
of the nation, many struggle to keep their doors open. Some
Idaho hospitals are small, and their potential patient base is
spread across great distance. In order to build cost-effective
community networks of care, they need the ability to work more
closely with one another.

Nonetheless, there is considerable apprehension about what
the health care future may hold. When I visited "Becky's
Burgers" in Orofino, Idaho, last month, Becky herself told me
that health care reform would put her out of business. In
response to Becky's challenge, I arranged for Health and Human
Services Secretary Donna Shalala to do an in-depth study of this
Idaho small business. With factual information of this kind, I
believe that we will be able to keep Becky in business, AND cover
her employees with affordable health insurance.

Throughout my first term, I held hearings and town meetings throughout my district to hear what Idahoans had to say about health care reform. In all of these forums, my constituents told me that they wanted to see changes in our system that would improve access to health care in rural areas. They expressed concern that many proposals they has heard about or read would do little or nothing for access to care in Idaho.

After listening to my constituents, I introduced H.R. 237, the Rural Health Care Access Improvement Act. This bill outlines a moderate agenda that I believe will promote solutions to many of the health care delivery problems in rural America. Doctors and other health care providers will be encouraged to practice in rural areas through a combination of financial incentives and administrative simplification. To increase the number of rural and frontier physician placements through the National Health Service Corps, the bill changes the current allocation formula. In addition, it provides grants for primary care nursing clinics in medically underserved areas, and telecommunications demonstration programs in rural areas. It revises some current federal anti-trust provisions to enhance the development of cost and resource-effective networks in rural areas, and provides for system-wide paperwork reduction.

In addition, I introduced H.R. 3070, to support the development of electronic telemedical networks in rural areas. I have a personal interest in seeing that we support and enhance the development of telemedicine in this country, because this field holds enormous potential for increasing access, for delivering service, and reducing costs, especially in rural areas. The widely distributed study by Arthur D. Little and Company suggests that significant savings could be achieved throughout our system by applying this technology to health care delivery. However, in order to speed the development, distribution and application of this technology, the Health Care Financing Administration will have to join the effort, and develop reimbursement procedures to support "telemedicine."

Before I introduced H.R. 3070, I spent time thinking about underlying principles that can move us forward quickly and reliably. There is no need to wait for some super-high-tech development. We merely need to use some common sense.

In constructing a rural telemedicine infrastructure, we should use as many off-the-shelf components as possible. The constituent pieces of a telemedicine delivery system already exist, to a large extent. We need a policy structure that allows for the use of current technologies without committing large amounts of capital to the latest theoretical innovation that will be obsolete in the near future. We cannot wait for the perfect high tech development. We need to be trying and demonstrating. We need to be building modest networks that work and that have the latent ability to fit together. We need to put the little pieces together right, and then begin connecting them. Putting pieces together is what "rural" is all about.

An information infrastructure to support telemedicine, but with the capacity and architecture to permit expansion, can provide the link between rural providers of all kinds. In Idaho, in health care, that provider may be a clinic, not a hospital; it may be a nurse practitioner or a physician's assistant, or even an emergency medical technician, rather than a doctor. In each case, an information infrastructure can make access a promise we can deliver; in the health care field over the near term, and eventually in areas and applications we cannot even imagine today.

The networks would give patients, doctors, and health care facilities in rural areas and small towns instant access to other doctors, specialists, and state-of-the-art medical equipment located hundreds, or even thousands, of miles away. These linkages will allow patients to receive care in their community and will ease the burden on specialists already in underserved areas. These links will also support efforts in underserved rural communities to recruit and retain physicians by helping to increase education and training opportunities.

Doctors could participate in lectures and conferences without leaving home. Electronic medical school libraries could provide access to books, journals, and graphics describing medical protocols. Digitized videos of surgical procedures could help educate medical staff and students.

The fundamental purpose of the Rural Telemedicine Development Act would be to begin -- now -- constructing linkages between health care providers of all levels, right down to the emergency medical technicians. It would be to begin constructing them in sufficient numbers with sufficient coherence that they evolve into compatible networks. We need networks to keep the health care professionals we have in place, with support, so that they can live "out there" and work "out there," and keep the edge that comes from knowing one is doing a good job delivering top-rate health services. We need to ensure that they can stay involved in rural health care but not lose touch with the cutting edge of their profession.

The Rural Telemedicine Development Act offers federal support for building telemedicine networks. It uses three grant programs to encourage their development in rural areas. The first provides seed money for rural hospitals and other facilities seeking to benefit from the cost savings and access to specialists that telemedicine can provide. The second would help strengthen the link between existing rural health networks, allowing interactive video consultation, shared educational services, and greater efficiency in administrative activities. The third would provide grants for networks of rural hospitals and other providers to link to existing fiber optic telecommunication systems.

In conclusion, Mr. Chairman, I urge the committee to examine quickly the wide range of legislative options for health care reform, so that we retain what is best about our current system, and create the kind of flexibility for the future that maintains individual choice, improves access and controls costs for all concerned. Our goal should be the guarantee of private health insurance for every American that cannot be taken away. This is a tall order, but I am optimistic that history will record health care reform as the most important accomplishment of the 103rd Congress. Thank you.

Mr. CARDIN. We will now hear from Hon. Bernard Sanders from the State of Vermont.

STATEMENT OF HON. BERNARD SANDERS, A REPRESENTATIVE IN CONGRESS FROM THE STATE OF VERMONT

Mr. SANDERS. Thank you, Mr. Chairman. We have already submitted written testimony, so I will summarize.

There are some debates in this country as to whether or not we are in a health care crisis or whether we need patchwork to deal with some of the more obvious problems. The people that I talk to in the State of Vermont suggest to me that our entire system is out of whack, and we need fundamental reform. The only way that we are going to address the issue of comprehensive health care, universal health care and doing it in a cost-effective way is through a Canadian-style, single-payer national health care system, administered at the State level, in my opinion—only a single-payer system which eliminates the private insurance companies, whose only function in life is not to provide health care but to make as much money as they can for themselves—only a single-payer can save substantial sums of money through elimination of the private companies, through simplification of the system. The single-payer system is, by definition, the simplest, least complicated system for doctors, hospitals and patients.

Several national studies have suggested that there are enormous savings and that, in fact, the single-payer approach is the most cost-effective approach to universal health care. Only the single-payer approach, in my judgment, can stand up to the pharmaceutical industry, which is ripping off the American people. It is a national disgrace that we pay twice the price for prescription drugs that they do in Europe and 30 percent more than they do in Canada.

Only a single-payer system can effectively control the cost of medical procedures and doctors' fees. It is very interesting—we border on Canada; Canada coronary bypasses, appendectomies are 50 percent of the cost that they are in the United States. Somebody has to stand up to the specialists and to the surgeons of America, some of whom are making enormous amounts of money. We cannot control health care costs until we begin to stand up to them.

When we talk about universal health care, the word "universality" means nothing unless we are talking about deductions and copayments. We have universal access to our local Cadillac dealer. The problem is many of us can't afford the $40,000 it costs to purchase the automobile. So unless we are talking about eliminating deductibles and copayments, we are not truly talking about universal access.

One of the concerns that I have is understanding the power of the insurance companies and the AMA and the pharmaceutical companies and the people who are making billions off the current health care system. I am not confident nor are the American people that Congress is going to fully deal with those institutions and organizations and do the right thing and pass single-payer.

The major aspect about the President's plan that I feel most comfortable with is not managed competition or managed care, which I happen not to believe in, and which I think for a small State like

Vermont is irrelevant. We don't have competing hospitals. We have one major hospital in the State of Vermont. It is absurd to divide our State up into five HMOs. We have 560,000 people. But the major aspect of the President's plan which I like is that it at least gives the States the option to go forward with a single-payer plan. I must confess I find it somewhat humorous or not so humorous that some people in Congress, especially conservatives, who day after day tell us how much they dislike the big, bad Federal Government and how they want the States to be a laboratory for change, that there is now a concerted effort on the part of the insurance companies and some Members of Congress to take away the option and the freedom of those States that want to go forward with single-payer to do so.

I hope you will pay attention to that because if you don't have an option for States to go forward with a single-payer plan, I think the President's health care approach for rural America is not terribly significant.

In my State of Vermont, the single-payer movement is very, very strong. A recent poll done by our largest paper indicated that while there are many plans out there, single-payer has more support within our legislature than any other; physicians and small business support it. What we are proposing is, we have concluded based on a task force that I appointed that we can save $270 million in a small State with a $1.8 billion health care budget by going the route of single-payer.

Second of all, what we are doing now is seeing that many physicians, senior citizens coming forward, trade unions, low-income people coming forward in support of the single-payer concept.

My hope, Mr. Chairman, is that as the debate unfolds, that this committee be very, very strong in making sure that States are allowed to go forward with single-payer, because I believe that ultimately this country will be single-payer, and the way it will move in that direction is through the success shown State by State.

Thank you, Mr. Chairman.

Mr. CARDIN. Thank you, Bernie.

[The prepared statement follows:]

February 1, 1994

TESTIMONY OF REP. BERNARD SANDERS ON NATIONAL HEALTH CARE
HOUSE WAYS AND MEANS COMMITTEE, HEALTH SUBCOMMITTEE

Mr. Chairman and Members of the Committee:

I appreciate the opportunity to testify today on the vital subject of national health care. Like many of my colleagues, I have been very impressed by the President's initiative on this issues. For the first time in decades, a President of the United States has said clearly that all Americans should be guaranteed the health care they need, and that health care is a basic human right of all our citizens.

The President has correctly diagnosed the ills of our current wasteful system, which costs far more per capita than any other in the world, overwhelms doctors and patients in paperwork, and yet still leaves 40 million of our people without health insurance. The President and the First Lady deserve a great deal of credit for bringing the crisis in our national health system to the fore, and for starting a national debate about the fundamental reforms that are necessary.

As you may know, I do not agree with the specific solution that the President has proposed, or with the concept of "managed competition" on which it is based. I believe that, particularly in a small state like my own state of Vermont, the only way to provide universal, comprehensive, cost-effective health care coverage is through a Canadian-style single-payer system, administered by the states.

Only a single-payer system can save substantial amounts of money by eliminating the bureaucracy inherent in both the present system and the managed competition system.

Only a single-payer system can stand up to the pharmaceutical industry and get skyrocketing drug prices under control.

Only a single-payer system can effectively control the costs of medical procedures and doctor's fees.

Only a single-payer system will allow Americans to go to any doctor or hospital they choose, without out-of-pocket expenses.

And finally, the single-payer system is the only one which will treat all Americans alike, whether rich and poor, eliminating deductibles and copayments and making health care a right of every citizen.

The national health care bill which I am cosponsoring, H.R. 1200, the American Health Security Act, provides for comprehensive, universal coverage for all Americans. The federal government would provide 85% of the financing. States would administer the system and negotiate reimbursement rates with providers in their state.

The system would function without copayments and deductibles. In addition, the single payer system would allow for lower negotiated manufacturer prices for pharmaceuticals and for medical supplies and equipment.

Administrative and bureaucratic savings from this system are estimated to be $60 to $100 billion, enough to provide comprehensive coverage to all Americans without increasing overall health spending in the nation.

To cite just a single example of the savings of a Canadian-style system: there are more than 6800 people administering Blue Cross/Blue Shield in Massachusetts, more than required to administer the _entire_ Canadian health insurance plan. This is despite the fact that Canada covers all its 26 million people, while Massachusetts Blue Cross/Blue Shield covers less than 3 million. We simply can't afford to continue with a system which wastes so much of our health care dollar on paper-pushing.

The U.S. General Accounting Office (GAO) has estimated that implementing a single-payer, Canadian style system would save about 10% of total health spending (more than $90 billion in 1993) by eliminating much of the paperwork and bureaucracy of the current U.S. system. This $90 billion is more than enough money to cover all the uninsured and improve the insurance of millions who now have only partial coverage.

The Canadians, who provide all of their citizens with a card entitling them to all the health care they need without out-of-pocket expense, spend 11 cents of every health care dollar on administration. The U.S., with its myriad of private companies, public insurers, deductibles, co-payments, regulations, complicated billing forms, profiteering, and easily hidden fraud, spends over twice as much.

Let's be clear. The current U.S. health care system is by far the most expensive and wasteful in the world. Despite the fact that 80 million Americans are either uninsured or underinsured, we spend far more per capita than any other country. In 1989, the U.S. spent $2354 per capita; Canada spent $1683, Sweden $1376, Germany $1232, Japan $1035 and the United Kingdom $836. We don't need to spend more money on health care. We need a new system.

I'm very pleased that the President's proposal will give the states the option to go forward with single-payer systems. It is important to preserve, and indeed to expand this option, as the bill is debated in Congress.

My hope is that Vermont can lead the nation and become the first state in our country to adopt a single-payer system and achieve real national health care reform.

As you go through the difficult process of developing a national health care bill, you will more and more find it necessary to choose between human needs and the profits of insurance companies, drug companies, hospitals, medical equipment suppliers and certain groups of physicians -- between the interests of our people, and the special interests of those who profit from our present wasteful system. I urge you to opt for the interests of all Americans, and choose a single-payer system.

Thank you very much.

Mr. CARDIN. We will now hear from Hon. Earl Pomeroy from the State of North Dakota.

STATEMENT OF HON. EARL POMEROY, A REPRESENTATIVE IN CONGRESS FROM THE STATE OF NORTH DAKOTA

Mr. POMEROY. Mr. Chairman and members of the House Ways and Means Health Subcommittee, in years past I have addressed this committee as a State insurance commissioner, as the president of the National Association of Insurance Commissioners, and more recently as a member of this body representing the State of North Dakota.

During these prior hearings over the last several years your interest has focused on the undeniable signs that our health care delivery and financing systems were in trouble due to spiraling costs and the growing numbers of uninsured.

As we meet this morning, costs have never been higher. The number of uninsured in this country is also the highest in recent history. I personally don't care whether our present situation is called a crisis or a severe aggravation; one thing is absolutely certain, the present system will continue to deteriorate in terms of cost and people's access to health care if meaningful health care reform is not enacted. Our health care system is not on solid ground. It is on quicksand and the longer nothing is done the worse is gets.

I agree wholeheartedly with the two stated goals of H.R. 3600, the President's health care reform proposal. Universal coverage and cost containment should be the ultimate goals of any meaningful reform effort.

On the other hand, I have deep reservations about the bill before you which, in my opinion, relies to an inappropriate degree on the Federal Government to regulate, administrate and shape the health insurance marketplace of tomorrow. In other instances, H.R. 3600 preempts existing market-based activity which is directed at managing health care costs. The bill jettisons considerable private sector effort and investment in managed care in favor of the great health care alliance experiment.

You will hear a great deal about the most pronounced features of this bill—the role and structure of alliances, global budgeting through premiums caps, and mandatory employer-based coverage. I have concerns about each of these issues and will closely follow your deliberations.

Two issues of lesser magnitude included in this bill may not receive as much discussion, and it is to these areas I will direct my comments this morning.

With the challenge of health care reform being daunting enough, I am disappointed in those who inserted into this bill extraneous but significant issues not central to the task at hand.

Section 5501 relating to the partial repeal of the McCarron-Ferguson Act, and sections 2301 through 2304 and 2321 through 2326 relating to the regulation of long-term care insurance should not be included in their present form in this legislation.

I will briefly describe these issues and will be happy to provide any of you with further information as you request.

The McCarron-Ferguson Act was enacted 49 years ago and has survived without amendments ever since. This act codified the

States' historic regulatory jurisdiction over insurance and granted an antitrust exemption which has facilitated the market participation of thousands of smaller insurance companies throughout the country.

The McCarron-Ferguson Act has not been without its critics and legislative proposals to change this longstanding framework for insurance appear perennially and are carefully considered in the House Judiciary Committee. I personally have testified on the topic in at least three different sessions of Congress. To date, McCarron-Ferguson reform proposals have never made it to the House floor. I am confident, if the issue was simple and clear-cut, it would have been addressed long ago.

To include McCarron-Ferguson reform in this legislation is at direct cross-purposes with loosening the antitrust treatment of medical providers elsewhere in the bill. In short, those who generate bills have greater leeway and those who pay bills have new uncertainties as to the proper scope of their activities. This is counterproductive for effective cost containment.

The section would generate considerable litigation given its vague wording and is utterly unnecessary in light of the comprehensive regulation and premium caps envisioned in the bill.

I am also concerned about the total overhaul of private long-term care insurance provided in the bill. The sections at issue write into Federal statute detailed specifications for this emerging line of insurance. I have not evaluated fully the reasonableness of each requirement offered, but even if every section addressees in an appropriate way a legitimate concern, they do not belong carved in granite in the Federal code without benefit of independent hearing and careful evaluation. This is the stuff of regulation, not new Federal law as part of an omnibus bill.

Even if Congress would determine more comprehensive Federal standards are necessary for long-term care insurance, new requirements can be provided within the structure of our existing legislative formate as has been accomplished with Medicare supplement insurance. H.R. 3600 scraps the proven Federal-State relationship whereby the NAIC implements regulation as directed by Congress. In the place of elected and appointed State Insurance Commissioners, the bill creates a new council appointed by the Secretary of Health and Human Services and staffed to the tune of $2 million per year with new bureaucrats.

Mr. Chairman, for several years I served as chair of the NAIC's Long-Term Care Insurance Task Force when minimum product and marketing standards were developed and expanded. In addition, I have chaired the NAIC's Medicare Supplement Task Force while we implemented the mandates of the catastrophic care extensions to Medicare and OBRA 1989 and 1990. I invite you to assess the track record of the NAIC effort. There is no need for H.R. 3600 to sweep such broad, ill-considered changes as the long-term care insurance section represent into this omnibus reform proposal.

There was not sufficient time in these few minutes to comment on other areas, large and small, rolled into this proposal. As you go to markup, I urge you to take this bill page by page. The central question I hope you ask is whether every section is closely directed at the central challenge of health care reform or represents extraneous material thrown onto this legislative vehicle.

The law of unintended consequences seems to apply even more ferociously to health care issues than other legislative areas. The task at hand is formidable enough. Move a reform proposal, but give H.R. 3600 a badly needed pruning in the process.

Thank you.

Mr. CARDIN. Thank you for your testimony.

[The prepared statement follows:]

Testimony by Congressman Earl Pomeroy
before the
Ways and Means Subcommittee on Health
February 1, 1994

Mr. Chairmen and members of the House Ways and Means Health Subcommittee.

In years past I have addressed this committee as a State Insurance Commissioner, as the President of the National Association of Insurance Commissioner, and more recently as a member of this body representing the state of North Dakota.

During these prior hearings over the last several years your interest has focused on the undeniable signs that our health care delivery and financing systems were in trouble due to spiraling costs and growing numbers of uninsured.

As we meet this morning costs have never been higher and the number of uninsured in this country is also the highest in recent history. I personally don't care whether our present situation is called a crisis or a severe aggravation, one thing is absolutely certain the present system will continue to deteriorate in terms of cost and people's access to health care if meaningful heath care reform is not enacted. Our health care system is not on solid ground. It is on quick sand and the longer nothing is done the worse is gets.

I agree wholeheartedly with the two stated goals of HR 3600, the President's health care reform proposal. Universal coverage and cost containment should be the ultimate goals of any meaningful reform effort.

On the other hand I have deep reservations about the bill before you which is in my opinion relies to an inappropriate degree on the federal government to regulate, administrate and shape the health insurance marketplace of tomorrow. In other instances HR 3600 preempts existing market-based activity which is directed at managing health care costs. The bill jettisons considerable private sector effort and investment in managed care in favor of the great health care alliance experiment.

You will hear a great deal about the most pronounced features of this bill -- the role and structure of Alliances, global budgeting through premiums caps, and mandatory employer basted coverage. I have concerns about each of these issues and will closely follow your deliberations.

Two issues of lesser magnitude included in this bill may not receive as much discussion and it is in these areas I will direct my comments this morning.

With the challenge of health care reform being daunting enough, I am disappointed in those who inserted into this bill extraneous but significant issues not central to the task at hand.

Section 5501 relating to the partial repeal of the McCarron Ferguson Act, and Sections 2301 through 2304 and 2321 through 2326 relating to the regulation of Long Term Care Insurance should not be included in their present form in this legislation.

I will briefly describe these issues and will be happy to provide any of you with further information as you request.

Section 5501 repeals the McCarron Ferguson Act for the business of insurance related to the provision of health benefits. The McCarron Ferguson Act was enacted 49 years ago and has survived without amendments ever since. This act codified the states historic regulatory jurisdiction over insurance and granted an antitrust exemption which has facilitated the market participation of thousands of smaller insurance companies throughout the country.

The McCarron Ferguson Act has not been without its critics and legislative proposals to change this long standing framework for insurance appear perennially and are carefully considered in the House Judiciary Committee. I personally have testified on the topic in at least three different sessions of Congress. To date, McCarron Ferguson reform proposals have never made it to the House floor. I am confident if the issue was simple and clear cut it would have been addressed long ago.

To include McCarron Ferguson reform in the legislation is at direct cross purposes with loosening the antitrust treatment of medical providers elsewhere in the bill. In short, those who generate bills have greater leeway and those who pay bills have new uncertainties as to the proper scope of their activities. This is directly counterproductive for effective cost containment.

The section would generate considerable litigation given its vague wording and is utterly unnecessary in light of the comprehensive regulation and premium caps envisioned in the bill.

I am also concerned about the total overhaul of private Long Term Care Insurance provided in the bill. The sections at issue write into federal statute detailed specifications for this emerging line of insurance. I have not fully evaluated the reasonableness of each requirement offered, but even if every section addressees in an appropriate way a legitimate concern they do not belong carved in granite in the federal code without benefit of independent hearing and careful evaluation. This is the stuff of regulation not new federal law as part of an omnibus bill.

Even if Congress would determine more comprehensive federal standards are necessary, new requirements can be provided within the structure of our existing legislative format as has been accomplished with medicare supplement insurance. HR 3600 scraps the proven federal state relationship whereby the NAIC implements regulation as directed by Congress. In the place of elected and appointed State Insurance Commissioners the bill creates a new Council appointed by the Secretary of Health and Human Services and staffed to the tune of $2 million per year with new bureaucrats.

Mr. Chairmen, for several years I served as Chair of the NAIC's Long Term Care Insurance Task Force when minimum product and marketing standards were developed and expanded. In addition I have chaired the NAIC's medicare Supplement Task Force while we implemented the mandates of the Catastrophic care extensions to medicare and OBRA '89 and '90. I invite you to assess the track record of the NAIC effort. There is no need for HR 3600 to sweep such broad ill considered changes as the long term care insurance section represent into this omnibus reform proposal.

There was not sufficient time in these few minutes to comment on other areas -- large and small -- rolled into this proposal. As you go to mark up I urge you to take this bill page by page. The central question I hope you ask is whether every section is closely directed at the central challenge of health care reform or represents extraneous material thrown onto this legislative vehicle. The law of unintended consequences seem to apply even more ferociously to health care issues than other legislative areas. The task at hand is formidable enough. Move a reform proposal, but give HR 3600 a badly needed pruning in the process.

Mr. CARDIN. Once again, let me thank all four of our colleagues for being here. I would like to make an observation about your testimony: The bill before us, the President's bill, is complex but all here seem to agree that the national legislation should provide the wherewithal to make sure that there is universal coverage and the Federal Government has a direct role to make sure that is done and financed appropriately.

Second, there needs to be effective enforcement of cost containment, as I understand from your testimony. I agree with the comments made by several of you that the States must have the flexibility to implement the system that is best for their communities and that we want to minimize the Federal Government's intrusion as to how the States operate.

I need to clarify this point because I served on the Judiciary Committee and participated in many of the hearings on McCarron-Ferguson. There seems to be general agreement that the medical insurance field needs some national guidance.

I think most of the reform bills, if not all, provide for Federal legislation that will regulate health insurance carriers as far as underwriting practices, preexisting conditions, et cetera. You did not directly comment about that in your statement. Do you oppose the Federal Government moving into this area to establish national regulation for health insurance carriers as it relates to preexisting conditions and community rating?

Mr. POMEROY. Mr. Chairman, I do believe many of those insurance reforms are central to meaningful health care insurance reform. I do not oppose them. I am not saying that I blanket-endorse every single one of the reforms proposed, but when I was president of the National Association of Insurance Commissioners, we began an exercise that dealt with this at a regulatory level, and many States have enacted model legislation that we move forward.

I don't mind where necessary due to policy concern the Federal Government specifying what shall be the regulation of the insurance industry. That has been done several times with Medicare supplement insurance. That can be done irrespective of the McCarron-Ferguson Act. You don't need to touch the McCarron-Ferguson to specify how the States should regulate insurance or even what is permitted within the insurance marketplace. They are separate and distinct issues.

Mr. CARDIN. Long-term care, I don't quite understand the distinction here between long-term care insurance policies and basic insurance policies from the point of view of Federal regulation. If you can philosophically go along with the national government moving toward regulating basic health care insurance, why shouldn't we establish a policy for long-term care in order to try to give greater consumer involvement in pricing and obtaining long-term care insurance?

Mr. POMEROY. That is a policy issue that I don't automatically oppose. Congresswoman Johnson has a bill in to set standards for long-term care insurance, and that is the appropriate vehicle to consider that policy question, not part of a 3,600-page bill, the essence of it, which is alliances and mandates and what not. Don't sneak in a little section that throws an enormous amount of detail on regulation of this emerging insurance industry and creates a new council, funded to the tune of $2 million a year for staff support, appointed by the Secretary of Health and Human Services, to do what in other areas Medicare supplement in particular the States have provided, the hands-on regulatory administrative detail as directed by Congress. So if the policy question would be determined that there ought to be more Federal guidance on long-term care standards, do it—follow the precedent; use the NAIC to ultimately implement the standards.

Mr. CARDIN. Mr. Thomas.

Mr. THOMAS. Thank you, Mr. Chairman. I share your concerns, Earl. It is kind of like a continuing resolution in which everybody thinks this is the only train and they have to get on it. I cannot reconcile all the subsections and the new time line this has been given is to move some kind of a product out of this subcommittee by as soon as the end of March. No way are we going to be able to give all these druthers, goals and desires that have been pent up for some time to change a number of areas, added to the fundamental focus.

I think I can help you by saying that it is my belief in trying to read members of the committee—and we will speak and vote for ourselves—that one of the areas of the President's plan, the alliances and that structure I think it has been proven through testimony already, and will continue to be, that it doesn't work. It doesn't make sense and it is probably not going to be in a package.

So we are going to pare some of those pages away on some of the core stuff. What we substitute, I don't know yet. I am concerned about the druthers in terms of not just the education of members of the subcommittee as to what is in the bill, but members of the House itself as we move forward. There will be a lot of things in this bill that most people are not fully aware of, and I appreciate your testimony.

Having said that, I would tell my colleague from Connecticut, I wish we would take more time in looking at the kinds of changes that are long overdue, and a key one is defining mental health and a clear separation between physical causes of mental health. I think once you complete all the investigations that will be going on for years, that neurobiological and chemical reasons are going to explain an enormous number of chemical imbalances versus those that we know right off as not having a physical base.

We will have to move forward with an imperfect product. That is a battle I will join with you in moving forward over the next few years in terms of trying to get people to understand what is going on.

One of the biggest problems we have had is the ignorant consumer and the fact that the only question they ever ask is, does my insurance cover it, and that is all they want to know. That is why, Bernie, when you say that universal coverage has to eliminate deductibles and copayments, most of us I think have come to the conclusion—and we can screen out on a dollar amount those at the lower end so it would not be a barrier to sitting in the Cadillac and twisting the steering wheel—that more for most people who can afford it, it is a positive, useful thing on an educational basis.

It is important to get people to understand partially the costs of what we are dealing with and to use it as, frankly, a "prioritizer" in terms of what you do and when you do it. I know there is a downside to that, but I think there is a positive; and I think the President is correct in talking about deductibles and copays as part of a necessary structure for clearinghouse and educational purposes.

I have a hunch the groups that you get invited to talk to about health care are slightly different than the groups that I get invited to talk to about health care, and your profile of what is out there might be slightly different than mine.

Larry, I understand your concern. I was born in the panhandle, still got a lot of folks in Bonners Ferry. I represent an area not unlike yours. Even though it says California, I am up against the Sierra Nevadas. We talk about hundreds of miles of distances with very small towns. Frankly, one size could never fit all. It won't now. And I will at least concede this, Bernie, that the private sector probably cannot in any kind of a competitive model meet the needs of all Americans in terms of health care. That is why we have to look at a number of innovative components like clinics and other s r c r s that we use now to make sure that system is delivered.t u tu e

I want to thank you all for your testimony and resensitizing us to the concerns that you have, and they are legitimate.

Thank you, Mr. Chairman.

Mr. CARDIN. Mr. Stark.

Chairman STARK [presiding]. I want to thank my colleagues for their contribution and their interest in this, because we are going to get down in the next 6 or 8 weeks to having to do something that will bring us together on one sort of a plan.

Rosa, I share your concern. I just looked through your testimony, of providing increased mental health benefits and substance abuse benefits. We are going to be faced in all of these areas, whatever the types of benefits, with a cost constraint. And it is difficult for the subcommittee to even begin to think what we will do until we get numbers.

I hate to say that we are slave to those numbers, but indeed when I talk to Larry next, and we deal with Becky's Burgers, it is one thing. Becky has been in business awhile?

Mr. LAROCCO. A couple of years. Not more than four. Since 1991.

Chairman STARK. She hasyhad two kicks in the minimum wage, which is probably all she is paying, two 45-cent-an-hour increases. So she survived the 90-cent increase in our minimum wage and so did all her competitors.

I think you have to make the case that there is not a small business in the country—one was a 14 percent increase, the other was a 12 percent increase—can't handle something in that order as a minimum to their fair contribution to health care costs. We have to say, Becky, you have got to do it; some minimum contribution we have to ask from those people in addition to the individuals. But we won't know how much that is and whether we can include any benefits that you want to include until we see the numbers.

I am inclined to think that the President's first veto, the pen, the lightning rod in the form of that veto pen is, we get everybody in the system. I then suspect, politically it will be easier for us to increase the benefits because we have a lot of support—seniors, middle-aged and young people. If everybody is in the system, it is going to be easier for us to increase. We don't have the luxury of having Henry Waxman on our committee who can sneak these things in. If you—my good friends who have testified before us so often in different guise, I think you have to address the idea of sneaking things into legislation to Henry, because if we don't do it, he will; and I usually try to learn from him.

So your concerns fall on rather deaf ears here. You come from an area of concern. It is a different committee that does all of this. But on McCarron-Ferguson, if we eliminate medical underwriting, you don't have a concern if we also eliminate McCarron-Ferguson, no sharing medical information if there is no medical underwriting. If the law says you won't have medical underwriting, then you can't gather the information and share it under the umbrella of McCarron-Ferguson. If we should say that we will not allow companies to medically underwrite, does it not make sense that we can't let them gather the information and share it.

Mr. POMEROY. You can address certain concerns without touching McCarron-Ferguson.

Chairman STARK. If we go to community rating, then I don't care if they share rating, premium information. So I think that if McCarron-Ferguson is symbolic—and I suspect it is—or becomes more symbolic, I think we could make a deal. It is of more concern that we get the end result of open enrollment and the rest, so I don't see a problem in—and I think, for my distinguished colleague from Vermont, the committees will be driven by Mr. Cardin, if no one else, to see that every opportunity exists for Vermont having a single-payer system, perhaps Hawaii to have one.

And I guess my question to all of you who talk about and say these words, is whether or not you agree we will have guaranteed rights to private insurance. I assume that none of you have any objection to the public nature of Medicare. So for those 35 million people you are content to let the public plan be part of that guarantee. Are there any witnesses who want to see us privatize Medicare?

Mr. SANDERS. I don't believe that the private insurance companies should continue to play a role.

Chairman STARK. The President used that word. It has a lot of adherence I am saying that I don't want to fight over that one; I am just saying that I don't know that we want to eliminate some good public plans by such strict adherence to that.

Mr. LaRocco. I don't want to privatize it. We will continue to fight for proper reimbursements in rural areas, where they have been a problem.

Chairman STARK. We have not had on our full committee or subcommittee the rural representation that we would have liked. I think given the fact working in cooperation with the rural caucus and understanding that sometimes we will get upped by the Senate with a more rural tilt, I think we have done pretty creative things to fulfill our responsibility. We are not going to have a plan if it is a big city—New England/West Coast/big city plan. We know that.

We appreciate your concerns, and I hope that as we go along we will fulfill our obligation to your constituents, Bill Thomas' and—

I don't have any rural constituents where I am, but we have them in California as we have them in Wisconsin, as we have them in Maryland. Although most of us are not from those particular districts, almost all of our States have that concern and I hope that whatever we come out with here will not only not disadvantage but will help the unique problems of the rural communities.

Mr. LaRocco. That is why this opportunity is very important to me and rural America, Mr. Chairman. The reason I have focused on my two pieces of legislation is because it is a laser beam that is focused on rural America. I appreciate the opportunity to bring it to your attention, because we are a bit outgunned and if we are going to have this shake-up in our system, we don't want to get left behind. It is too important for all of America.

Chairman STARK. I want to get you psyched for the Rotary Club when Becky raises her hand and be able to say, It ain't free, Becky. That is the message. If we can define her share that is reasonable and doesn't break her and doesn't unfairly disadvantage whoever else may have been paying something for health insurance, that is where I think we have to come to fulfill the President's concern that everybody contributes fairly. That is going to be a really political problem.

NFIB is not going to endorse anything. They don't want a plan if they have to pay anything for it. That is a very difficult position to compromise with. So we hope we can give you a package and a message so you can go back and say—they say, it is a tax; OK, call it a tax, but it is a fair sharing of the burdens to get something we all want, which is guaranteed coverage.

Mr. SANDERS. If I could say a word on that point, Vermont is very heavily small business and the single-payer funding mechanism that we developed was an 8 percent payroll tax with a $50,000 deduction, which would be of significant help to the small businesses that have a payroll of $200,000.

Chairman STARK. Did you hear the Governor of Hawaii today? In Hawaii, they have a mandate on small businesses. They set up a million dollar fund and they said, any small business that can show that it will go out of business because of the increased cost of health insurance, we will pay that business's health insurance.

In the 8 or 10 years, they paid $100,000 out of that fund. The Governor said he has earned more in interest on the fund than he has had to pay out to honor that commitment.

We can say, if you can prove that you are so marginal in your operation that doing what every other business in the country has to do—maybe we ought to.

Mr. LaRocco. Studies have shown that in Oregon, small businesses pay the same amount for health insurance, but their benefits are less. That is part of the inequities as well. Idaho passed a small business reform, but it only makes available the pools, and I believe we need private insurance that is guaranteed to everyone that can't be taken away. I still will maintain that is our goal.

Chairman STARK. What about the fallback? What do we do for in an unnamed State that either cannot or will not or does not put in a plan? Is it not reasonable to say, if there is nothing else there, we will provide it to the poor or where location makes insurance unavailable? I think we have to—rather than just say if a State does it, we are going to fine them; that only compounds the problem of a poor State.

I would say at some point we have to be willing for those States—it won't include Vermont, it won't include North Dakota, and it won't include Idaho, won't include California or Hawaii—but some State may say, we can't do it, or they gridlock. It seems to me if we are going to make that promise and fulfill the President's pledge, we have to be prepared with something as a fallback.

We may contract it out, we may have to buy a universal plan from Blue Cross or provide some form of a Medicare-type plan, but something in the final analysis that if it ain't there otherwise, there is a safety net.

Mrs. Johnson.

Mrs. JOHNSON. Thank you, Mr. Chairman. It is a pleasure to hear from some of my colleagues on such an important matter, and I appreciate your testimony; and I agree with you, Earl, that long-term care ought to be separated off.

Actually, there is a better job we can do on some aspects of encouraging and rewarding people for buying long-term care insurance, and certainly some of the problems we have created in the real world for ourselves have been the consequence of not actually holding hearings specifically on issues like these standards, and then when they are promulgated, they have a devastating impact and cannot be reversed. I hope we will be able to separate that issue and focus on it.

Another aspect of your testimony I would like to ask you about, Eark—and then there is a comment, Larry, that I would like to discuss with you—you say this bill jettisons all the efforts that the private sector has made and the capital investment that the private sector has made to control cost.

We won't change the delivery system in a way that will control costs without capital investment. It is interesting that the pace of that investment and the pace of those efforts in the private sector have now brought medical inflation down in the private sector to 4.4 percent in the last quarter. In the public sector, it has stayed up because we are not making investments in cost control.

It concerns me that the President's plan would entirely eliminate those investments and the effort that the private sector is making, and shift the responsibility for cost control entirely to the public sector. Because when you go to a payroll tax then you eliminate any incentive to invest.

If you are going to pay 7.9 percent of payroll—whether you invest in wellness programs, whether you invest in physicians onsite in your factory, whether you invest in family nights where there are inoculations and family wellness or family illness clinics—if your health care costs are the same, whether you make those investments or not, you cannot in good conscience, in responsibility to your stockholders or to your workers, continue to make that kind of health and wellness investment. If that is not made on the frontline on a company-by-company basis, there is no way government can substitute for it and the medical inflation rates in public programs versus private programs indicates that.

I thought your statement that the bill jettisons all this was a very important statement, and it is not being understood by members because we are hearing that this bill builds on the current employer mandate. It doesn't. It deeply transforms the way employers participate in this, and the effect is to eliminate any private sector involvement and cost control. Would you agree?

Mr. POMEROY. I agree with a great deal of what you say. I think the present lower inflation rate shows also long-overdue provider self-restraint that we haven't seen. Cost containment is achieved through one of two strategies: Sheer brunt of budget, like they have done in the United Kingdom, where they say this much is available for your health care, you sort it out, and we see a system that has got dramatically lower standards of medical technology, quality of care, than we might find in most of this country; or you do it on a case management basis, no shortcuts, carefully evaluating the needs of the patients and trying to match them with the best, most cost-effective medical care. That is what, because they haven't had other tools, much of the private sector efforts has been devoted to, and they have developed technologies and business plans that are accomplishing that objective, I think, and to an unhealthy degree it is wiped out.

I wanted to raise the issue of Worker's Compensation reform. In this area, the company paying the claims is removed absolutely from managing the care of the people they are paying the claims for. If you have a company paying claims, they have a strong incentive to move the Worker's Comp claimant into rehabilitation, to get them back to work as soon as possible. There is no market structure that has a bigger cost containment incentive than on that Worker's Comp carrier. They are wiped out from their cost-containment role altogether.

I think, as you mention, rather than build on the cost containment forces that have developed in the private sector, it wipes out a lot of them and throws them into some new alliance experiment.

Mrs. JOHNSON. As a member from a State that has extraordinarily high Worker's Comp costs and is just now moving into this kind of case management, there is a lot of concern that this bill will destroy the growing ability to deal constructively with those costs in a way that is really better for people, too.

Larry, back to the issue of Becky because more than 50 percent of the small businesses in America are being founded by women, because women don't find a level of opportunity in established business that men do and they are not willing to wait any more. So whether or not you can expand a small business is of particular interest to women. I maintain that our society has a far greater interest in allowing a small business with its new product or its new invention to hire those next marginal people because until you get up to 40 or 50 employees, you are not going to be exporting.

We need invention, products and market expansion. If you keep small businesses at four or five—and I do every year two conferences on how to set up and expand small business; I see where the break points are between being very small, moderately small, and the next step—if we make it harder to grow, we do fundamental damage not only to opportunity for women in our society but also to the vitality of our economy.

Becky's problem, I think, is far better solved with a combination of an individual mandate and an outright voucher or subsidy to expand the wage to ensure affordable insurance.

We grew up with fuel assistance. We recognize some people don't make enough to pay their fuel bills and so we give them the wherewithal. If we did an honest job of subsidizing premiums up to 250 percent of poverty income, we could have health care for everyone as a solid social policy, which is what it is, without having the heavy-handed consequences on our economy, which in small towns is going to be great. Even if you fix her so that she stays alive, she is not going to a expand her business.

This is of enormous concern to me because Connecticut is losing its big producers, big companies are downsizing and they are not going to grow very soon. The small businessmen, the people who come through my office now, who have figured out that you could make tiny air conditioners instead of big air conditioners, it is their growth that is going to matter to America's future.

Every time we increase the marginal costs of hiring someone by several thousand dollars, we make a difference in the vitality of our economy. So I hope that you will work with some of us who are looking for universal coverage and that absolute access, that all Americans deserve but are looking for a far more flexible, locally oriented system.

I also strongly support your interest in electronic telemedical networks. You ought to be concerned with how slow Congress has been to fund EACHs and RPCHs. We have not put our money where our mouth is for 3 to 5 years now. To think health care reform is going to somehow fund the very resources that have to create the network we are talking about is high risk, and I am really interested in a system where we can see far more visibly how we are going to move the resources to create the system that is going to guarantee universal access; and I would rather raise the taxes for the vouchers and see it than try to push it into the invisible arena of small business where we won't be able to see the jobs we don't create.

In Hawaii, there is clear evidence that while many businesses have survived, they don't hire; and they say that themselves. So I appreciate your testimony and I think the variety of concerns that you have brought to our attention has been very fruitful for us. As Vermont will have its opportunity, I hope Connecticut will have an opportunity to do something equally different from the President's proposal.

Thank you, Mr. Chairman.

Mr. CARDIN. Congressman McDermott.

Mr. MCDERMOTT. Thank you, Mr. Chairman. I am sorry I did not hear your testimony. I was in the Energy and Commerce Committee testifying about what I think is a better health care plan than the ones presented here, except by Mr. Sanders, the single-payer system.

I am sorry Mrs. Johnson left because I wish to follow up on the issue she raised.

The State of Washington has adopted a health care reform plan very much like what the President is proposing. It is going to be very instructive to talk about whether you want to have a payroll deduction premium or this individual premium that people are talking about setting up for people.

The Washington State experience has been that the most difficult problem to solve is to figure out an individual premium for 5.2 million people in the State of Washington, because they are all going to have a different one, depending on who they work for and what kind of company and how big it is and how much money they make. And these are the friends of this plan who are putting it together. There are five different committees operating, trying to get a handle on a system that you can efficiently, year by year, decide individual premiums on the basis of where you work and how much you work, and so forth, simply because they want to avoid using the income tax structure and a payroll deduction for accumulating the premium.

It is, in my opinion, an absolute Rube Goldberg nightmare. We are not going to be able to foist that on the American people because of the complications of setting premiums and deciding the way in which people are going to pay.

I think, Mr. Chairman, that is one of the most difficult problems we have to solve. How do you deal with the fact that people have different abilities to pay for their health insurance and how do you do it in a fair way in a democracy? I think that the individual premium issue is simply a nightmare that we are going to have to avoid as a Congress.

Mr. CARDIN [presiding]. This will not be the last word on this issue. Thank you for your testimony.

The next series of witnesses are in a panel. First, representing the Federation of State Medical Boards of the United States, Dr. James Winn, the executive vice president. We have Dr. Dennis O'Leary, president of the Joint Commission on Accreditation of Healthcare Organizations; Margaret O'Kane, National Committee for Quality Assurance, president; Dr. David Nash, member, board of directors, the American Medical Peer Review Association; and Dr. Paul Kerschner, chair of the Consumer Coalition.

Welcome. As I indicated at the beginning of the hearing, your entire statements will be made part of the committee record. You may proceed as you so desire, starting with Dr. Winn.

STATEMENT OF JAMES R. WINN, M.D., EXECUTIVE VICE PRESIDENT, FEDERATION OF STATE MEDICAL BOARDS OF THE UNITED STATES, INC.

Dr. WINN. Thank you and good morning. I am Dr. James Winn, the executive vice president for the Federation of State Medical Boards of the United States. The Federation is a national organization composed of State boards empowered to license and discipline physicians within the United States. The mission of the State medical boards is to protect the public from unqualified practitioners and the Federation assists their State boards with this mission by acting as a clearinghouse for the latest information on licensure and discipline and to assist the credentialing process in the maintenance of a comprehensive database on board actions involving physician disciplinary matters.

We are very concerned about the somewhat ambiguous confusing and cryptic references in the Health Security Act with regard to

State licensure. Particularly, we are concerned about section 1161, which reads that "No State may, through licensure or otherwise, restrict the practice of any class of health professionals beyond what is justified by the skills and training of such professionals."

We are concerned that, if allowed to stay in the act, this section has the potential to create an upheaval of the health provider regulatory system. The section appears to imply that State laws unreasonably and improperly restrict the practice of certain classes of providers who are otherwise skilled in providing medical services to the public. It would also appear to override current laws that are in fact already assessing the skill and training of individuals who apply for licensure.

The true criteria for judging competency to perform a certain function in the delivery of health care should be qualifications and training. In fact the three elements—education, training and examination—form the basis for physician licensure in this country. If there is to be some other method for evaluating competency under this act, we would ask that it be brought to light at this time so it may be carefully examined.

Who would determine limitations of skill and training? I would submit that the objective measures already in place in the State licensure process are both adequate and appropriate.

We are also concerned that all although the act gives the States responsibility for establishing the regional health alliances, for certifying health plans and for processing consumer complaints about plans, it remains unclear what role the licensure and discipline practitioners will play in this new system. We believe that this is an important function and that it is properly placed at the State level with State regulatory boards.

With regard to quality assurance, the act would create a large and ambitious bureaucracy. However, there appear to be few, if any, direct references to the actual methods of monitoring and enforcing provider quality standards. State licensure with its attendant disciplinary authority continues to be the best tool to enforce such standards. The quality management program should build on existing structures at the State level rather than create new national and regional ones.

Time does not permit me this morning to review with you the many areas where State medical boards are already filling the quality assurance role with regard to physicians, but I submit to you that much has been done by boards in the realm of quality assurance.

Medical boards are already experts in investigation and prosecution of consumer complaints about the quality of care delivered by a physician. Health care reform measures should instruct States to adequately fund medical board activities.

Health care reform should also mandate reporting of physician misconduct to State boards by peer review organizations, government agencies and any other entity involved in peer review. New instruments are constantly being developed for use by State boards to assess the competency of questionable and problem physicians. We would urge that the Congress encourage the development of such instruments, and we would also urge that the government encourage and support programs which remediate the incompetent physician and again allow the contribution of his or her skills and training to the health care system.

I would ask you to consider the following:

Congress should recognize the important role of State medical boards as the proper agencies to license and discipline physicians and to assure the delivery of quality medical care.

Congress should take appropriate steps to assure that States adequately fund State medical boards so that they may carry out their role with increased effectiveness; and

Congress should maintain the role of the States in licensing health care professionals through the medical boards and not include any provisions in legislation to override States' licensure laws or to call into question their validity.

Mr. Chairman, thank you for the opportunity to appear before you today with these concerns. At the appropriate time, I would be happy to answer any questions that you may have.

Mr. CARDIN. Thank you.

[The prepared statement follows:]

STATEMENT OF THE
FEDERATION OF STATE MEDICAL BOARDS
OF THE UNITED STATES, INC.
TO THE
SUBCOMMITTEE ON HEALTH
COMMITTEE ON WAYS AND MEANS
UNITED STATES HOUSE OF REPRESENTATIVES
PRESENTED BY

JAMES·R WINN, M D
EXECUTIVE VICE PRESIDENT

FEBRUARY 1, 1994

Good morning, Mr Chairman and Members of the Subcommittee I am Dr James R Winn, Executive Vice President of the Federation of State Medical Boards. The Federation is a national organization, the members of which are the state medical broads empowered to license and discipline physicians in the United States. The mission of the state medical boards is to protect the public from unqualified practitioners of medical services, through enforcement of standards established by state laws The Federation assists boards with this mission, acting as a clearinghouse for the latest information on licensure and discipline, and assists in the credentialling process through maintenance of a comprehensive database of board actions involving physician disciplinary matters, that is available for query by state boards and other credentialling agencies.

I appreciate this opportunity to address the implications of Section 1161 of the Health Security Act and the disruptive impact this simple statement could have on the existing system of professional regulation in this country. Section 1161 reads

"Section 1161. Override of Restrictive State Practice Laws"
"No State may, through licensure or otherwise restrict the practice of any class of health professionals beyond what is justified by the skills and training of such professionals "

We oppose the inclusion of this language in the Health Security Act or any other health reform legislation considered by the Subcommittee. This statement, if allowed to stay in the Act, will likely cause a complete upheaval of the health provider regulatory scheme The section's title implies that state laws unreasonably and improperly restrict the practice of classes of providers who are otherwise skilled in providing medical services to the public, it seeks to override current laws that in fact quite reasonably assess the skill and training of individuals who apply for a license to practice in that jurisdiction as a practitioner of any of the numerous health professions regulated in the system

The true criteria for judging competence to perform a certain function in the delivery of health care should be "qualifications and training". An individual's qualifications to be licensed as a particular type of practitioner are based on education, examination and training. These are the three basic elements used by state medical boards to evaluate physicians for licensure.

It is unclear under Section 1161 if some other method for evaluating competence would be instituted. The Health Security Act does not actually describe any other process by which "skill" is to be assessed, nor does it describe what "training" is necessary to adequately assure the public is protected from providers who are unqualified to do what they claim they can do. If methods other then existing processes are to be instituted, they must be discussed and debated. These important decisions cannot be left to individuals or practitioner groups asserting adequate "skill and training", but must be made by properly constituted regulatory boards. I submit that the objective measures already in place in the state licensure process are appropriate and adequate.

The Federation is also very concerned with other sections of the Health Security Act which contain confusing and cryptic references to licensure and scope of practice laws Section 1112, where "health professional services" are defined, appears to acknowledge the authority of states to establish criteria for the various types of practice, but cannot easily be reconciled with Section

1161. These two sections seem to say that states may make distinctions between groups, but cannot enforce the differences through licensure laws. Although the Act gives the states many responsibilities for establishing the regional health alliances, the certification of health plans, and for processing consumer complaints about plans, it is unclear what role the licensure and discipline of practitioners will play in the new system. This is a vital role and is properly placed at the state level, with state regulatory boards

As currently drafted the Health Security Act's approach to licensing and scope of practice will surely lead to a variety of interpretations. The language in Section 1161 may encourage individuals to sue states and their licensing boards because it puts a cloud over the appropriateness of current state licensure laws. Therefore, the Federation asks this Subcommittee to not include Section 1161 or any similar provision in health care reform legislation.

With regard to quality assurance, the Health Security Act creates a very large and ambitious bureaucracy of interwoven Federal, state, and regional agencies to carry out this function. However, very few if any direct references to the actual methods of monitoring and enforcing provider quality standards are found in the bill. State licensure, with its attendant disciplinary authority, is the best tool to enforce quality standards. The Act's quality management program should build on the existing structure at the state level

I'd like to take a few minutes to point out areas where state medical boards assume the quality assurance role with regard to physicians, a role that can be continued and enhanced under a new health care delivery system, but only if state licensure and disciplinary structures are maintained

-State medical boards have established mechanisms to investigate, and prosecute consumer complaints about the quality of care delivered by a physician.

-State medical boards are using post licensure assessment tools to assess the competence of questionable and problem physicians. Boards are experts in determining whether a physician is in need of reeducation or retraining

-State medical boards are involved with physician assistance programs, usually used in conjunction with disciplinary action, to change a physician's problem behavior so that he/she can again contribute to the health care system

If states are to be left in charge of ensuring provider quality which the Federation believes it critical to health care reform, increasing investigatory and sanctioning authority for state medical boards would of course, only enhance these processes. Currently, state boards are funded through state processes; some boards are entitled to keep all fees generated by their licensure activities and have relatively independent control over these funds. Other boards must rely on the state appropriations process and are often hampered by the inability to use the very funds they generate because this money is rolled into the general budget of the state. State boards can do a better job in quality assurance if through Federal legislation states are instructed to adequately fund medical board activities. Increased funding will allow boards to devote time ad attention to these difficult quality cases.

In considering reforms to the U.S. health care delivery system the Federation of State Medical Boards urges the Congress to:

1. Maintain the role of the states in licensing health care professionals through the state medical boards and not include any provisions in legislation to override state licensure laws or to call into question their validity.

2. Recognize the role of state medical boards as the proper agencies to license and discipline physicians and to assure the delivery of quality medical care.

Mr. CARDIN. Dr. O'Leary.

STATEMENT OF DENNIS S. O'LEARY, M.D., PRESIDENT, JOINT COMMISSION ON ACCREDITATION OF HEALTHCARE ORGANIZATIONS

Dr. O'LEARY. Thank you, Mr. Chairman. We appreciate the opportunity to appear before this subcommittee to present our viewpoint on quality issues under health care reform.

I am Dennis O'Leary, president of the Joint Commission on Accreditation of Healthcare Organizations, the Nation's largest and oldest private sector health care accrediting body. We are here to suggest the addition of several specific items to the health care reform legislation that you mark up in the subcommittee. These suggestions would, we believe, strengthen oversight, maintain public confidence in the new system, and promote continuous improvement in the delivery of health care services.

Our first recommendation addresses the basic framework necessary to ensure constructive oversight of the health plans that are emerging in response both to current changes in the health care environment and to anticipated health care reform initiatives. Quite simply, we recommend that: Congress insist on the inclusion of a core set on national quality standards for health plans as part of health care reform legislation.

We are deeply concerned that there is an apparent tendency to dismiss the need for national quality standards. For instance, the Health Security Act makes no provision for national quality standards for participating health plans. To construct a national quality management program without national standards would be to roll the dice on patient outcomes and provide only for after-the-fact review of substandard health plans.

If we fail to set standards for the new configurations of health services delivery, we may jeopardize our Nation's citizens as well as this country's leadership in providing quality care.

Recognizing that integrated networks, or health plans, are becoming a prominent feature of the reform landscape, the Joint Commission has recently designed a set of comprehensive standards for networks that consist of simple, patient-centered performance objectives. We should expect similar, state-of-the-art standards for any national quality oversight program.

We note that there are those who, instead, support the establishment of individual State certification programs for health plans. Given the limited resources and expertise across the States to establish such programs, this requirement would simply become another unfunded mandate.

Further, this would in essence create 50 different State quality programs, thereby subverting the interests of multi-State employers, multi-State providers, and consumers who, sometimes of necessity, shop across State lines for health care. We therefore believe that national standards are in the best interest of all affected parties, including the States themselves.

A second important challenge of health care reform will be the gathering and dissemination of performance information about health plans that is understandable to consumers and helpful to them in making judgments about quality. Expectations are high for the role report cards will play in educating the public and in - leveraging consumer purchasing power.

We are deeply concerned, however, that report cards, as currently conceptualized, will not serve those purposes. A basic problem is that they would usually contain self-reported data against a limited number of variables. In addition, noncomparable information in report cards will frustrate those who try to use them. These problems could eventually undermine public confidence in the new delivery system. To avoid this serious risk, we urge that Congress enhance the concept of report cards to require that: One, the Federal Government standardize all of the measures to be used for report cards; and, two, require that these report cards include information on health plan compliance with national standards.

The Joint Commission has had a long and unique experience in the development and use of performance measures. We have learned several important lessons from this experience. First, we need to keep the system simple and focused. Data should not be collected as an end in itself; otherwise, we will undermine the credibility of the system with those who must provide the data.

Second, performance measures are an effective complement to standards, but cannot supplant them. Documentation of bad outcomes is an after-the-fact reality that may guide future consumer choice, but offers little solace to those already affected; and.

Third, self-reported data must be monitored for accuracy.

If we design our quality measurement program with these specifications in mind, we will create a system that is relevant to the needs of all users.

I would like to conclude with the observation that change, particularly change of this potential magnitude, in an area as sensitive and personal as health care, will inevitably create major public anxieties. For the public, quality is every bit as major an issue as cost and access, and any reform initiative must have a sound process to address that concern. At issue is the priority which Congress must give to quality maintenance and enhancement.

We at the Joint Commission, together with others in the private sector, stand ready to assist you in this endeavor.

Mr. CARDIN. Thank you very much.

[The prepared statement follows:]

STATEMENT OF DENNIS S. O'LEARY, M.D.
PRESIDENT
JOINT COMMISSION ON ACCREDITATION OF HEALTHCARE ORGANIZATIONS

Mister Chairman:

Thank you for the opportunity to appear before this
Subcommittee to present our viewpoint on quality issues under
health care reform. I am Dennis O'Leary, President of the Joint
Commission on Accreditation of HealthCare Organizations, the
nation's largest and oldest private sector healthcare accrediting
entity. Quality measurement is our business, and has been for
over 75 years. We are recognized, nationally and internationally,
as a leader in developing standards and performance measures for
health care delivery.

Health care reform poses new, but exciting challenges for
quality oversight, particularly in providing accurate and useful
information to consumers and in ensuring appropriate
accountability for complex, managed networks of care. The Joint
Commission is poised for these challenges as a result of both its
seven-year Agenda for Change, which is now concluding, and its
new evaluation and accreditation program for health care networks
(a.k.a. health plans). We believe that both of these futuristic
Joint Commission initiatives can serve as models for the federal
government during its debate over the proper structure for
quality oversight of health plans.

We seek to shape your legislative perspective by suggesting
the addition of three specific items to the health care reform
legislation that you mark-up in the Subcommittee. These
suggestions would, we believe, strengthen oversight, maintain
public confidence in the new system, and promote continuous
improvement in the delivery of health care services.

Our first recommendation addresses the basic framework
necessary to ensure constructive oversight of the diverse array
of health plans that are emerging in response both to current
changes in the health care environment and to anticipated health
care reform initiatives. Quite simply, we recommend that:

> Congress insist on the inclusion of a core set on national
> quality standards for health plans as part of health care
> reform legislation.

In this regard, it is important to recognize that there are
two types of quality measures which are integral to the structure
for any sound national health care quality management program - -
standards and performance measures. Both are vital, and each is
complementary to the other. Performance measures are a
description and quantification of past events; while standards
are designed to predict future performance based on an assessment
of current organizational function.

We are all aware that performance measures are currently in
vogue and viewed by many as the primary substrate for Report
Cards. We take no issue with that basic premise. The federal
government should require that health plans measure performance
outcomes and report those results. However, we are deeply
concerned that there is an apparent propensity to discount the
need for national quality standards. I specifically allude to the
Health Security Act which makes no provision for national quality
standards for participating health plans. To construct a
national quality management program without national standards
would be to roll the dice on patient outcomes and provide only
for after-the-fact review of substandard health plans. Further,
the absence of standards would effectively eliminate the
availability of critical information needed to evaluate the
effects of health care reform on quality of care.

Standards for health care organizations have been around a long time, and are widely credited with significantly raising the level of quality care in the United States. This has in turn provided assurances and comfort to consumers, purchasers, and the government alike. As early as 1918, standards for hospitals were published by the American College of Surgeons, thus forming the basis of the College's Hospital Standardization Program -- the predecessor to the Joint Commission. The Joint Commission was formally established in 1951 to measure hospital compliance with standards related to quality of care. Today, we evaluate and accredit over 9000 health care organizations that include not only hospitals, but also those providing home care, nursing home care, mental health care and ambulatory care.

In the landmark Social Security Amendments of 1966, Congress established requirements for standards that would apply to hospitals wishing to participate in Medicare, and embraced a partnership between the private sector and the federal government in order to assure substantive oversight of hospital performance. Since then, the federal government has relied upon the Joint Commission to determine the performance eligibility of hospitals and other health care organizations to receive Medicare and Medicaid reimbursement.

The standards-based approach has stood the test of time, and it remains the foundation of any future quality oversight program. Application of state-of-the-art standards has steadily raised the level of quality of United States health care to the finest in the world. President Clinton acknowledged in his September 22nd speech to the nation on health care, that superior quality is now a hallmark of the American healthcare system. The President said, "We are blessed with the best health care professionals on earth, the finest health care institutions, the best medical research, the most sophisticated technology." In his recent State-of-the-Union address, he reiterated this theme by saying that we have "...the world's best health care professionals, cutting edge research and wonderful research institutions, Medicare for older Americans. None of this -- none of it should be put at risk."

We agree with the President's characterization of America's health care, but I respectfully submit that we must continue to do well what we have done well in the past. If we fail to set standards for rapidly changing configurations of health services delivery, we may jeopardize our nation's citizens and this country's leadership in quality. With the opportunity to reconfigure our nation's health care delivery system comes the solemn obligation to effectively oversee the quality of care provided through this new delivery system.

Recognizing that integrated networks are increasing in number and are a prominent feature of the reform landscape, the Joint Commission began a pioneering venture last year to develop an evaluation and accreditation program tailored to the characteristics of these new entities. Developing meaningful standards for health plans presents a more complex and unusual challenge than does the process for creating, say, home care standards. For instance, standards will need to assess factors that relate to the integration of many types of services and their accountability. These include attention to continuity of services, access to and use of patient care information, and health plan management, among others

We should expect similar state-of-the-art, standards for any national quality oversight program. We understand the concerns that some have about previous over-zealous efforts in developing federal regulations for health care facilities, but that need not, and should not, be a blueprint for the future. The art of standard-setting has now evolved to a point where it is quite feasible to design a comprehensive standards framework consisting

of simple, patient-centered performance objectives for any type
of organization, including a health plan or network, We know
this is feasible, because we have done precisely this type of
standard-setting as part of our Agenda for Change and our new
evaluation program for health care networks.

We finally note that there are those who support the
establishment of individual state certification programs for
health plans or networks, as in the Health Security Act. Given
limited resources and expertise across the states to establish
such programs, this requirement would simply become another
unfunded mandate.

Further, and more importantly, this would in essence create
50 different state quality programs, thereby subverting the
interests of multi-state employers, multi-state providers, and
consumers who, sometimes of necessity, shop across state lines
for health care. To the point, 50 different certification
programs for quality would render any meaningful comparisons
between or among states impossible. We therefore believe that
national standards are in the best interest of all affected
parties, including the states which will be expected to actually
administer the quality oversight activities within their
jurisdictions.

****

A second important challenge of health care reform will be
the provision of performance information about health plans that
is understandable to consumers and helpful to them in making
judgments about quality and in committing to important purchasing
decisions. Report Cards are being widely touted as the linchpin
for effective health care reform and as the vehicle for
empowering consumers. Expectations are high for the role they
will play in educating the public and in leveraging consumer
purchasing power, while giving providers comparative information
for quality improvement activities. We are deeply concerned,
however, that Report Cards as currently conceptualized will not
serve those purposes. Rather, they run the real risk of
containing incomplete and noncomparable information that will
eventually frustrate those who try to use them. This in turn
undermines public confidence in the new delivery system. To avoid
these serious but unnecessary risks, we urge that:

> Congress enhance the concept of Report Cards to require that
> (1) the federal government standardize all of the measures
> to be used for Report Cards and, (2) require that these
> Report Cards include information on health plan compliance
> with national standards.

The Joint Commission is firmly on record in support of
providing useful information about provider performance to the
public. We commend the President for introducing the concept of
routine collection and dissemination of performance data as part
of the Health Security Act. Such information is integral, as
well, to the promotion of accountability for sound quality
management. The availability of standardized information on
specific quality parameters would give plans the ability to
compare their performance with others and use this information in
their internal quality improvement activities. Yet, we cannot
ignore the reality that Report Cards as currently conceptualized,
would generally be self-reported data against a limited number of
variables, few of which may be sensitive measures of quality.

We believe it important that the following specific cautions
about the contemplated Report Cards be raised:

    o Self-reported data are easily misreported and
      sometimes purposefully engineered to reflect favorable

performance. Such propensities can be curtailed
through on-site evaluations and other screening
mechanisms.

o Report Cards solely containing performance measures
quantify the performance of a health care organization
on a relatively small number of important variables
(approximately 50, per the health Security Act) that
would be measured.

o Most performance measures presently being suggested
for Report Cards focus on process and access issues,
and few on clinical or functional outcomes. This
reality is unlikely to change in the near term. Thus,
it is essential that Report Cards contain information
about standards compliance to obtain a full picture of
a plan's ability to deliver high quality care.

o Report cards solely containing performance measures
will only provide consumers with a picture of past
performance, and will not predict the future
performance of the organizations which the consumer-
turned-patient must choose among for care.

The Joint Commission has had a long and unique experience in
the development and use of performance measures. We are quite
cognizant of the potential value that can be gained from the
routine collection of performance measurement data, but we are
also aware of the limitations of outcomes data when used as the
lone measures of quality. As part of our initiative to modernize
the accreditation process -- the Agenda for Change -- we began
the development of a new outcomes-based performance measurement
system called the Indicator Measurement System (IMSystem.) This
effort has placed the Joint Commission at the forefront of
developing clinical performance measures. The IMSystem will
continuously collect objective data on indicators -- our name for
performance measures -- which can be used to assess each
organization's performance on important governance, managerial,
clinical, and support functions in the context of a national
database.

We have learned several important lessons from this
ambitious, pioneering effort that are germane to the concept of
Report Cards. I would like to share these with you. First,
choosing what to measure is not a simple task. Each measure
should have real impact on, or be a direct measure of, an
important patient outcome. Determining relevance and importance
is a matter of combining consumer priorities and clinician
knowledge with a realistic assessment of the ability to collect
the desired data. Second, we need to keep the system simple and
focused. Data should not be collected as an end in itself, nor
for purposes that are to be defined at a later date. If we fail
on this point, we will undermine the credibility of the system
with those who must provide the data, and we will have created
another expensive albatross. Third, we must link performance
data to improved outcomes through a cyclical process of
continuous quality improvement. That is the ultimate objective of
this activity. Fourth, indicators (performance measures) are an
effective complement to standards, but cannot supplant them.
Documentation of bad outcomes, if they occur, is an after-the-
fact reality that may guide future consumer choice, but offers
little solace to those already affected. Documentation of failed
standards compliance creates the opportunity to make changes
before bad outcomes occur. And lastly, self-reported data must
be monitored for accuracy. If we design our quality measurement
program with these specifications mind, we will create a system
that is relevant to the needs of consumers, purchasers,
providers, and policymakers.

We would hope that the Congress will not create a large new bureaucracy to relearn the private sector's years of experience with measuring performance. Rather, Congress should insist that any federal Council, Commission, or Board given oversight responsibilities with regard to Report Cards, have the explicit charge of ensuring that Report Cards contain standardized measures of care -- for both performance measures and standards - -- that will produce comparable, useful information for consumers. Any such oversight group should borrow heavily from private sector experience and growing array of new measurement tools, in order that there be an effective transfer of knowledge on quality measurement issues and efficient use of federal resources.

****

Our third suggestion relates specifically to the need for a meaningful better public/private sector partnership concerning national quality management activities. Simply stated, it is important that the right expertise be at the table during the design of a national quality measurement and management system. We therefore believe that Congress should require that:

Any national quality management group created in legislation, such as the proposed National Quality Management Council, be required to include representation from among those entities having expertise in direct quality evaluation.

Such expertise is necessary to the creation of an efficient and sound system of performance measurement. We suggest that those of us who have labored to create and implement national quality monitoring programs have a special perspective and set of skills that could constructively be brought to bear on creating the architecture for and making operational the goals of a national quality measurement system. We do understand first-hand the technical issues and difficulties that attend such a formidable undertaking.

One of the major challenges that such a group would face is selecting and refining measures that will produce useful performance information across health plans. Comparable, risk-adjusted, accurate and understandable information products also will be essential if we are to expect providers of care to take the Report Cards seriously and commit themselves to improvement against these measures.

It is also important that the right type of expertise be immediately available to address important data issues such as standardization of data elements. The tasks of identifying appropriate performance measures that truly reflect significant patient outcomes; testing these measures for validity and reliability; and developing data specifications to ensure comparability of findings, dictate that organizations with this experience be part of any national quality committee such as the Health Security Act's National Quality Management Council.

I would like to conclude with the observation that change, particularly change of this potential magnitude in an area as sensitive and personal as health care, will inevitably create major public anxieties. For the public, quality is every bit as major an issue as cost and access, and any reform initiative that may inadvertently infuse negative incentives for quality in the delivery system, must have a sound balancing process to address that concern. Therefore, Congress must address more than structural provisions for health care reform. It must also provide credible quality measurement and oversight processes that provide ready public access to relevant information and offer assurances that attention is indeed being directed to improving health care services. At issue is the priority which Congress must give to quality maintenance and enhancement, and how best to achieve the excellence in medical care which the American people clearly desire. We at the Joint Commission, together with others

Mr. CARDIN. Dr. O'Kane.

STATEMENT OF MARGARET O'KANE, PRESIDENT, NATIONAL COMMITTEE FOR QUALITY ASSURANCE

Ms. O'KANE. I am not a doctor, but thank you. My name is Margaret O'Kane.

Mr. CARDIN. I don't know whether we have promoted you or not.

Ms. O'KANE. My name is Margaret O'Kane and I am the president of the National Committee for Quality Assurance (NCQA). We are pleased to have the opportunity to testify today before the Subcommittee on the important topic of quality and health care reform.

To monitor and ensure quality, NCQA proposes a public accountability system using two complementary efforts: An accreditation process and public reporting of performance measures. This approach is consistent with President Clinton's health care reform legislation and mirrors the current efforts of NCQA. The goals of an accountability system include: Consumer protection and appropriate access to care; continuous improvement in quality; and consumer access to information on quality NCQA believes that both an accreditation process and the performance measures are critical to ensuring the delivery of quality care and service.

The accreditation process ensures that minimum standards are met and that the plan is continuously pursuing quality improvement. For the first time, the report card provides the opportunity to compare health plans on specific aspects of their performance.

We recommend that national entry requirements be established for all health plans, indemnity and managed, and that the requirements be increased each year.

Implementation should be continuous, with more measures to be added as our ability to measure improves and as health plans develop the information systems that need to produce the data.

The President's plan embodies a number of the principles NCQA believes are necessary for a strong quality component in a health care reform environment. First, the proposal makes an important and crucial change—it moves away from the punitive "find the bad apple" approach and moves to a systematic, performance-based system for measuring and encouraging improvement in quality. Then, consumers will be given information on specific health plans so that they can make informed decisions about quality and cost.

An area that is virtually unexplored is the information needs of consumers. We do not know either the types of technical quality information that will be compelling to consumers or how the information should be represented so that it is understandable. We are currently working with consumers to find out what they want to know.

NCQA strongly believes that all health plans should be accountable for quality, regardless of their financing and delivery structure. With both managed and fee-for-service health plans operating in the proposed system, minimum quality elements should be in place to monitor all services and medical delivery.

Our accreditation program evaluates the extent to which a health plan has a delivery system which supports high quality patient care, and is continuously improving. The process also ensures that basic protective and monitoring systems are in place for the problems which do arise.

Another important goal of the accreditation program is to consolidate multiple review processes which health plans often must undergo. Eliminating the duplication will free time and resources at the health plan for real quality improvement.

We look at an organization's quality improvement program, credentialing activities, utilization management, preventive health services, medical records, and systems for ensuring member rights. We also include physician review of medical records in order to assess the quality of care being delivered by the health plan.

A framework for assuring the accountability of health plans should also include the public reporting of comparable data on various aspects of performance.

The President's plan appropriately reflects the dynamic nature of this area and requires that Federal boards set priorities and annually make changes to the national performance standards as necessary.

The development of such measures is an ongoing process. The performance measures that already exist, have high consensus in the medical community and a strong scientific base. This is not true, however, for a broad range of other procedures and services.

In November, NCQA released HEDIS 2.0, a core set of performance measures that were defined by a combined group of major employers and health plans. The components include quality, access, patient satisfaction, utilization and finance.

Based on our experience with the HEDIS and other projects, involving modest numbers of health plans, NCQA believes that a carefully thought-out implementation strategy, with goals and a phasein schedule, must be established for any kind of national initiative. We also hope you will look at work already done, for example, HEDIS 2.0.

The Clinton health care proposal correctly shifts to a systematic performance based system with national standards.

We have a few concerns: The timetable for implementing a performance system might be unrealistic. We are also concerned that the Clinton proposal appears silent on the role of accreditation. The first goal of the quality component should be to protect consumers.

The Clinton plan proposes multiple layers of bureaucracy, creating potential for a burdensome program which has conflicting or duplicative quality requirements. The result might be a process which diverts resources from delivery of services.

We recommend the following:

A public/private approach that builds on current work;

An accountability system using accreditation and performance measures;

Establishment of national standards for all health plans managed care and fee for service indemnity plans;

An implementation strategy with realistic short term goals and a phasein period for long-term goals;

A system that is uniform, streamlined and avoids duplication; and

A medical research system that works to inform what is effective in medical care and how to measure quality. Health care reform is necessary, and NCQA is committed to working with the members of this subcommittee, the administration, health plans, employers, consumers, and regulators to assure that the quality component of any reform proposal meets the goals that we all agree on—assuring quality, continuous quality improvement, and accountability.

Thank you.

[The prepared statement and attachment follow:]

My name is Margaret O'Kane and I am the President of the National Committee for Quality Assurance (NCQA). We are pleased to have the opportunity to testify today before the Subcommittee on the important topic of quality and health care reform.

NCQA promotes improvements in the quality of patient care provided by managed health plans through development and application of specific, detailed principles for continuous quality improvement and measures of performance for health plans. NCQA is committed to providing information on quality to the public, consumers, purchasers, health plans, and state and federal government. Governed by a Board of Directors of managed-care executives, purchasers, independent quality experts, and union and consumer representatives, NCQA represents a unique collaborative partnership through which to implement effective mechanisms to monitor and improve the quality of care and services.

To monitor and ensure quality, NCQA proposes a public accountability system using two complementary efforts: an accreditation process and public reporting of performance measures. This approach is consistent with President Clinton's health care reform legislation and mirrors the current efforts of NCQA. The goals of an accountability system include:

- Consumer protection and appropriate access to care
- Continuous improvement in quality
- Consumer access to information on quality

The accreditation process assesses how well a health plan has established management structures and processes to monitor the quality of patient care and member service, and verifies that the structures and processes are functioning to deliver an acceptable level of quality and to continuously improve it.

Public reporting of performance measures or "report cards" will give consumers and purchasers more information on specific aspects of health plan performance in order to make informed choices about health plans. This information will also give policymakers the means to gauge progress towards public health priorities. Performance measures address medical care processes and outcomes, accessibility and service, and member satisfaction. Comparable data from health plans will be compiled into report cards to facilitate health plan comparisons by consumers and purchasers. The report card concept is being piloted by NCQA in 21 of the country's largest and most prominent health plans using a core set of Health Plan Employer Data and Information Set (HEDIS 2.0) measures.

NCQA believes that both the accreditation process and the performance measures are critical to ensuring the delivery of quality care and service. The accreditation process ensures that minimum standards are met and that the plan is continuously pursuing quality improvement. The report card provides for the first time the opportunity to compare health plans on specific aspects of their performance.

We recommend that national entry requirements be established for all health plans, indemnity and managed, and that the requirements be increased each year until all plans are subject to a full range of accreditation standards. We also recommend that initial reporting on performance measures begin. Implementation should be continuous, with more measures to be reported on as medical research supports their validity, and as health plans develop the information systems needed to produce the data. Let me discuss these points in more detail and describe what NCQA activity has been in these areas.

Quality and Health Care Reform

The Clinton health care reform proposal embodies a number of the principles NCQA believes are necessary for a strong quality component in a health care reform environment. (Please see the NCQA principles which are attached).

First, the proposal makes an important and crucial change -- it moves away from the punitive "find the bad apple" approach and moves to a systematic, performance-based system for measuring and encouraging improvement in quality. Then, by requiring health plans to collect and report comparable data on performance, consumers will be given information on specific health plans so that they can make informed decisions about quality and cost.

Consumer Needs

NCQA believes that consumers and purchasers have the right to make informed choices among health plans and that these decisions should be based on quality as well as cost. That is why NCQA has devoted so much time to HEDIS 2.0 -- a report card developed with health plans and purchasers. However, an area that is virtually unexplored for both accreditation and report cards is the information needs of consumers. We do not know either the types of technical quality information that will be compelling to consumers or how the information should be represented so that it is understandable to consumers. A dialogue with consumers must be initiated and pilot testing must be performed to determine what consumers want to know in order to guarantee that the goals of public reporting are accomplished. Specifically:

- What information do consumers want and need in order to select among competing health plans?
- What is the most consumer-friendly way to present this information?

NCQA believes that no one -- neither consumers nor health care experts -- currently has the answers to these questions. Although minimal work has been done to determine what consumers want to know, significant progress has been made in producing information for purchasers, particularly when it comes to performance-based report cards. NCQA has received support from the Commonwealth Fund to initiate a major consumer-focused research project.

The receipt of The Commonwealth Fund planning grant is a first step toward a larger project that will help NCQA to develop more consumer-focused report cards, thereby helping to foster greater public accountability within the health care system. Accountability is a theme echoed by most, if not all of the various health care reform proposals which envision consumers choosing among competing plans based on cost and quality.

The research for the planning grant has involved a literature review, interviews and a focus group with consumers to test methodology and develop an initial list of consumer issues. These steps will enable NCQA to design a proposal for the main project which would include: a methodology for producing, prioritizing, and validating a list of consumer issues; and the steps necessary to develop, test, and produce useful, consumer-friendly information. This main project, anticipated to begin in April 1994, will allow NCQA to identify consumers' values when it comes to assessing health care, as well as to determine the information needs of particular groups such as the elderly and the chronically ill.

Requirements for all Health Plan Structures

NCQA strongly believes that all health plans should be accountable, regardless of their financing and delivery structure. With both managed and fee-for-service health plans operating in the proposed system, minimum quality elements should be in place to monitor all services and medical delivery. Even less structured delivery systems such as indemnity plans should be required to: credential their providers; monitor both insurance and health delivery complaints and grievances; implement standards for utilization management; and provide data about member satisfaction and clinical performance. All health plans must be able to provide data on quality performance, or the more structured plans that do have data will be at a disadvantage in the marketplace.

NCQA recommends establishing basic "entry" requirements for all health plans, both indemnity and managed, and increasing these requirements annually until all accreditation standards can be applied to all plans. This will serve as a mechanism to encourage indemnity health plans to make a transition towards more effective management. In addition to basic 'entry" requirements, NCQA recommends establishing standard quality reporting requirements to be used by all health plans. These requirements must be phased in gradually to allow health plans to develop the necessary internal information system capabilities. The implementation of information systems in health plans to collect the data needed to produce performance measures is an ongoing process. Many health plans will require some years to establish these systems.

Policy makers must strike a balance between the desired types of quality measurement and the ability of health plans to meet these requirements. If the requirements are too minimal, quality will be compromised. However, quality requirements that lack practical applicability may undermine a reformed systems's likelihood of success.

Quality oversight systems and measures will drive health plan behavior. It is essential to carefully consider the incentives in potential monitoring strategies in order to make successful quality performance consonant with public health priorities. Performance requirements should hold health plans responsible for appropriate care to their entire population. Quality requirements should be based on indicators that emerge from the efficient functioning of effective delivery systems.

As previously mentioned, NCQA believes that to monitor and ensure quality under any reformed health care system, there must be a public accountability system using two complementary efforts: an accreditation process and public reporting of performance measures. We are concerned, however, that the Administration proposal appears silent on the role of accreditation.

Both the accreditation process and performance measures are critical to ensuring the delivery of quality care and service. As stated in the Physician Payment Review Commission's (PPRC) draft chapter on quality, "information from report cards alone may not drive plans that provide inferior quality out of the market; external monitoring and controls may be necessary." Accreditation is vital to ensuring that a given health plan thoroughly investigates its providers, is responsive to member grievances, has a system that ensures appropriateness of care and performs other critical functions.

The Accreditation Process

Evaluation of the effectiveness of a health plan's internal systems, through external review and accreditation, provides information on the extent to which a health plan has created an environment supportive of high quality patient care, and the ability of the health plan to continuously improve its performance. The process also ensures that basic protective and monitoring systems are in place for the problems which do arise. Such information is crucial as consumers and purchasers make choices among competing health plans.

Another important goal of the accreditation program is the consolidation of multiple review processes which health plans often must undergo. Eliminating the duplication of efforts caused by repetitive external reviews will free time and resources at the health plan for substantive quality improvement activities. This also decreases the total cost of federal, state and employer reviews. We would caution that under a "reformed" system where there are potentially separate federal, state and alliance quality requirements, that care must be taken so these not be substantially different, nor duplicative and burdensome.

NCQA's accreditation review process includes a structured survey of an organization's quality improvement program, credentialing activities, utilization management, preventive health services, medical records, and systems for ensuring member rights. The accreditation process also includes physician review of medical records in order to assess the quality of care being delivered by the health plan. The standards are not "entry level." The survey is conducted by a team of highly qualified managed-care professionals using NCQA standards. Upon successful completion of the NCQA accreditation program, a managed-care organization receives a three-year accreditation. Alternatively, a plan which receives provisional accreditation is reviewed again within one year. NCQA provides detailed recommendations to provisionally accredited plans to help them move to full accreditation. Approximately 77 percent of the health plans reviewed to date received provisional status, 18 percent have been fully accredited, and five percent were denied.

At present, a number of major national employers require NCQA accreditation for all the HMOs they offer, including Allied-Signal, Ameritech, GE, GTE, Pepsico, Procter & Gamble, UPS, and Xerox. Many other employers like General Electric, IBM, Mercantile Stores, and USAir strongly recommend that their health plans become NCQA accredited.

In addition to major employers, the states of Kansas, Florida, Pennsylvania, and Oklahoma now require external review for all their HMOs and have approved NCQA as an external reviewer. Other states are evaluating the NCQA accreditation program and may accept its review process in addition to, or in place of their own.

While our accreditation program is new, having begun in 1991, by the end of 1993 we completed accreditation reviews of over 150 managed care organizations nationally. More than 90 new reviews are scheduled for 1994.

Performance Measures

In addition to an accreditation program, a framework for assuring the accountability of health plans should include the public reporting of comparable data on various aspects of performance, as previously mentioned. Such a system will serve to: 1) provide health plans with "benchmarking" information to identify areas of improvement; and 2) provide consumers, purchasers and regulators with information to assess health plan performance.

The Clinton health care reform proposal appropriately reflects the dynamic nature of this area and requires that the National Health Board and the National Quality Management Council annually make changes to the national performance standards as necessary. The proposal also rightly directs that a five-year priority list of performance measures be established and that federal dollars be spent to support research that focuses on the area of measuring quality of care.

It is important to note that the development of such measures is an ongoing process. The performance measures that already exist, such as those for most preventive health services, have high consensus in the medical community and a strong scientific base. However, measures of a range of other procedures and services have not yet achieved the level of validity and consensus which should be attained before being included as national standards for performance. Quality indicators for cardiac care are one example. Implementing comprehensive measures of quality for a broad array of acute and chronic conditions is a goal for the next several years. We expect to see an increased focus on outcomes measures as medical research establishes more linkages between the delivery of care and its outcomes.

Let me describe NCQA activities in this area. In November, NCQA released the final version of HEDIS 2.0, a core set of performance measures that were defined by a combined group of major employers and health plans. This effort began in 1992, when NCQA was asked to coordinate the project.

Specific components within HEDIS 2.0 are:

- Quality - measuring the health plan's performance in the delivery of certain selected services. These include:
  1. Preventive Services
  2. Prenatal Care
  3. Acute and Chronic Disease
  4. Mental Health
- Access and Patient Satisfaction - measuring performance in member access to care and satisfying members;
- Membership and Utilization - measuring performance regarding membership stability and demographics as well as resource allocation within the plan; and
- Finance - measuring performance in achieving financial stability.

As HEDIS 2.0 gains widespread acceptance, it will assist health plans in their quest for a common set of reporting standards that will satisfy the needs of multiple users. Standardized definitions and specific methodologies for deriving performance measures, as outlined in HEDIS 2.0, will enable plans and employers and others to accurately trend health plan performance, and as the measures are refined, use them in a comparative manner.

HEDIS is only the first step toward the development of a system of comparable performance measures on health plan quality. As future improvements in methodologies and underlying data systems are made, plan data will become more reliable, and more measures will be developed for report cards on health plans.

We have also been involved in the Michigan Project, a collaborative effort involving Ford, GM, Chrysler, the United Auto Workers' Union, nine southeastern Michigan HMOs, and NCQA. This project is the first effort to collect standardized, comparable data, use a consumer satisfaction survey and accreditation. The data includes information on mammography, pre-natal care, childhood immunizations and access. The project's goal is to produce comparable performance data on each participating HMO for use by external customers such as the auto companies. The auto companies will use the information to ascertain the quality of care and service delivered by their participating managed-care organizations. The information will be used to establish baseline data and benchmarks for HMO quality improvement, enhancing opportunities for HMOs to demonstrate to their major employer groups their successes in improving the quality of their care and service.

The Administration's proposal requires that the National Health Board "establish a performance-based program of quality management and improvement designed to enhance the quality, appropriateness, and effectiveness of health care services and access to such services" not more than one year following enactment. As we have discussed, the whole area of quality measurement is a relatively new one and certainly dynamic. While NCQA is on the cutting edge in terms of what we're doing with managed care organizations, our projects with HEDIS 2.0 and the Michigan Project are relatively new.

Based on our experience with these projects, which involve modest numbers of health plans, NCQA believes that a very carefully thought out implementation strategy, with goals and a careful phase-in schedule, must be established for any kind of national initiative. Further, whichever body is ultimately responsible for establishing national quality standards or requirements, we strongly suggest that advantage be taken of the work already done. You may want to direct them to look at and use HEDIS 2.0, for example.

The National Quality Management Council under the Clinton plan is also responsible for periodic consumer surveys. Where the survey is to deal with access, use of health services, health outcomes, and patient satisfaction, we would suggest that there are already excellent surveys in use which address these areas.

<u>Conclusion</u>

The Clinton health care proposal makes the important and necessary step of moving to a systematic performance-based system with national standards. The criteria cited in legislation for selecting the standards are sound.

We don't question the need to establish goals and appropriate time schedules, but we are concerned that the timetable for implementing a performance system might be unrealistically rapid. The first goal of the quality component should be to protect consumers. As mentioned, whatever federal body is ultimately responsible for establishing a quality management program, it should look at work already done such as HEDIS 2.0 and consumer surveys. We are concerned that the Clinton proposal appears silent on the role of accreditation. Also, with the multiple layers of bureaucracy under the Clinton plan with the National Health Board, the National Quality Management Council, the states, the alliances and the corporate alliances, there is potential for a burdensome program which has either conflicting or duplicative quality requirements. The result might be a process which diverts resources from delivery of services.

We recommend the following:

- A public/private approach that builds on current work
- A quality accountability system using accreditation and performance measures
- Establishment of national standards
- Quality requirements for all health plans -- managed care and fee-for-service indemnity plans
- A carefully structured implementation strategy that provides a quick time frame for reasonable, short term goals and a priority list and phase in period for long term goals
- A system that is uniform and streamlined and avoids duplication and burdensome requirements resulting from multiple sets of requirements.
- A medical research system that works to inform what is effective in medical care and how to appropriately measure quality

Everyone agrees that there are flaws in our current health care system and that some reform is necessary. NCQA is committed to working with the members of this subcommittee, the Administration, health plans, employers, consumers, and regulators to assure that the quality component of any reform proposal meets the goals that we all agree on -- assuring quality, continuous quality improvement, and accountability.

NCQA

NCQA PRINCIPLES ON QUALITY AND HEALTH CARE REFORM

The National Committee for Quality Assurance (NCQA) believes that consumers and purchasers have a right to make informed choices among competing health plans based on cost *and* quality. Cost is relatively easy to assess while gauging quality is a more difficult undertaking NCQA supports responsible evaluation and reporting about health plan quality.

Specifically, NCQA believes that quality and health care reform should be guided by the following five principles:

I. *Public Reporting*

Health plans and outside organizations have a responsibility to publish meaningful, accurate and consumer-friendly quality information.

II. *Accountability*

Accreditation reviews and performance measures are inter-related, standard tools that purchasers and consumers should require to make health plans accountable for the quality of care and services they deliver.

Such standard accountability tools must be rigorously tested for reliability, and implemented and/or validated by an objective, outside organization.

These tools must be dynamic to respond to changes in the science and practice of medicine.

III. *Continuous Improvement*

Accreditation reviews must give purchasers and consumers information about a plan's quality infrastructure, and provide a mechanism for the plan's self assessment and continuous improvement.

IV. *Comparability*

Performance measures must be standardized to allow consumers, purchasers and regulators to make comparisons between health plans.

These measures should evaluate high volume, high impact processes which serve as indicators of health plan quality.

V. *Stakeholder Involvement*

Physicians and allied health professionals, as well as purchasers, consumers, regulators and health plans should be involved in generating ways to evaluate and measure quality.

Mr. CARDIN. Dr. Nash.

STATEMENT OF DAVID B. NASH, M.D., MEMBER, BOARD OF DIRECTORS, AMERICAN MEDICAL PEER REVIEW ASSOCIATION

Dr. NASH. Good morning. Thank you for the privilege and the opportunity to come and talk to you this morning.

I am David Nash, a board-certified practicing primary care general internist, the kind of doctor the President likes. I also am a full-time medical school faculty member at the country's largest private medical school, Jefferson Medical College in Philadelphia, but I am here today in my capacity as a member of the board of the American Medical Peer Review Association and our research affiliate, the American Medical Review Research Center, both here in Washington. We represent an organization of national independent quality oversight groups.

I really only have three main points I would like to make this morning. Before starting, I want to recognize Chairman Stark, for his role in support of the Mediplan Act which recognizes the importance of one of the issues you have already heard a lot about this morning, namely making quality oversight as an important part of any reform proposal.

My three main points are as follows:

One, we must recognize that quality is not a byproduct of any of the proposed systems. It ought to be recognized as an essential tenet of what we do. We see within managed competition certain incentives and the potential for a serious conflict of interest. If you are involved in trying to cut costs, offer the best price possible, gain enrollees and compete with other health plans, how can those organizations also be responsible in part for policing their own affairs and evaluating the quality of the care they deliver? So we see again a potential conflict of interest inherent within the managed care model.

I would also point out that there is no published evidence anywhere or experiments anywhere in our country that managed competition can work.

My second point and you have heard from Peggy and Dennis, regards consumerism and report cards. We support collecting and evaluating quality-of-care information, but are concerned about who is going to audit this information, where will it come from, who will make sure that it is collected in a standardized way that everybody can have equal access to? Are consumers really that discerning about the value of this information?

How does a consumer know if they are getting overtreated or undertreated? How does a consumer know whether a practice guideline is being followed or not?

So while we support consumerism and report cards we need some system for evaluating these report cards if you are looking at the integrity and accuracy of the quality information.

My third point is our group, AMPRA, and our sister organization, AMRRC, support the creation of a national federation, a national network of State-based health quality foundations. These independent health quality foundations will have three major roles. They will provide objective information to consumers, information that has been audited, evaluated and been implemented in a way that makes sense to the average American citizen. There will be ways to protect consumers against poor quality with an auditing function as well, and these organizations, these health quality foundations, will improve quality by doing research in these arenas, helping to foster practice guidelines and—most importantly as a practicing doctor—feed information back to us so we can improve our daily performance.

There is definitely a Federal role here in terms of a national database, standardization of this approach and continuing to support research in all the areas we have been talking about this morning.

Let me summarize my three principal points:

One, quality is not a toxic byproduct of what we are here talking about this morning. It ought to be the central tenet of any reform proposal;

Two, we have to help consumers. It is unbelievable to me that my patients know enough about what is going on in the hospital or the office to always make the right decision, and we know that they are going to walk based on price, accessibility and affability of the providers with whom they are used to working; and

Three, let's draw on the strengths of the programs we already have to help us to create this national network of State-based health quality foundations.

Thank you very much.

Mr. CARDIN. Thank you.

[The prepared statement and attachment follow:]

Written Statement
of the
American Medical Peer Review Association

Introduction

Mr. Chairman and members of the Subcommittee on Health, of the Committee on Ways and Means, my name is David B. Nash, M.D., M.B.A, F.A.C.P. I am a board certified practicing internist. I am currently Director, Office of Health Policy and Clinical Outcomes at Thomas Jefferson University and Clinical Associate Professor of Medicine at Jefferson Medical College in Philadelphia. I am here today to testify before this Committee in my capacity as Board member of the American Medical Peer Review Association (AMPRA), the national association of independent quality evaluation organizations, including the federally designated Peer Review Organizations (PROs). I am also chairperson of AMPRA's research and education affiliate, the American Medical Review Research Center (AMRRC). I appreciate the opportunity to participate in today's hearing as we discuss the future of quality of care in health care reform.

In addition to this prepared written statement, I submit for the record a just released AMPRA policy report entitled *Health Reform and the Quality Imperative*. Our following written statement highlights the primary recommendations contained in this policy report.

Health Reform and the Quality Assurance Imperative

A decade ago, called to action by unrelenting medical care cost pressures, Congress enacted a radically new prospective payment system (PPS) for the Medicare program. Fixed payments for hospital admissions were introduced based on Diagnosis Related Groups (DRGs). Overnight, financial incentives for hospitals were altered with hospitals rewarded for tight management of inpatient days and operating costs. Congress, concerned about the impact of these new financial incentives on patient care, enacted a comprehensive quality monitoring system through Peer Review Organizations (PROs). The potential for undertreatment, premature discharges, gaming of the DRG coding system, and inappropriate hospital admissions were closely monitored as an active and ongoing safeguard against compromises to patient care quality.

Ten years later, the debate on health reform is raging with the prospects never better for enactment of some form of comprehensive legislation before the mid-term elections of 1994. As before, medical cost pressures are driving much of the debate and new reimbursement mechanisms are being sought to promote increased efficiencies in the delivery system. Under both President Clinton's proposed Health Security Act and the plans being promoted by the Senate Republican Task Force on Health and the House Conservative Democratic Forum, medical care received by Americans will be delivered by competing health plans receiving fixed per capita payments from regional and corporate alliances. The downward pressure on plan revenues exerted by a capitated reimbursement system, competition with other plans, and the potential for explicit premium price controls provides rich incentives for undertreatment that parallel the prospective payment system for Medicare. Only this time around, the financial incentives will be on a more far reaching basis touching all health care services and the entire patient population.

Mr. Chairman, there can be little doubt in my mind that such a reformed health care delivery system will need an active and ongoing quality monitoring and assurance system. In a recent policy pronouncement, the Institute of Medicine writes:

...the paradigm shift calls for health plans to provide needed services to a population in the face of stringent resource constraints, and the incentive will likely be to underserve people. These changes make monitoring the quality of care imperative, especially for the sickest individuals and other at-risk populations. (The *Journal of the American Medical Association*, October 27, 1993, p. 1911)

In a managed competition system, health plan profits will depend upon how much or how little they spend on delivering care. Checks and balances are crucial to managing quality for the nations most vulnerable -- the sick, disabled, chronic and terminally ill, and poor urban and rural populations. The transition to managed competition must support quality of care protection for consumers, promote provider and practitioner continuous improvement, and provide community/state quality information about performance in this dramatically different health services delivery system.

Mr. Chairman, I believe we must commit to assuring and improving the quality of care to all Americans as an explicit goal of health reform. But meeting this goal represents a formidable task that demands an equal commitment to a national quality monitoring and improvement system.

The Clinton Prescription for Quality Assurance

Mr. Chairman, designing a national quality oversight and improvement program to match up effectively against the new incentives that would be created under health reform based on managed competition is a major challenge. In its blueprint for health care reform, the Clinton

Administration begins to build a national framework through the design of a "National Quality Management Program." The plan has a number of positive features: the policy principle that health care plans are responsible for the improved health of the populations served; creation of a national health care information database that will serve as the foundation for quality related activities; enshrining the principle of meaningful consumer choice by promising consumers a "report card" that compares plans and providers within plans not merely on costs, but also on specific performance measures; the establishment of a state based patient complaint office to permit redress for consumers that feel their benefits have been curtailed by competing health plans; a renewed national commitment to patient outcome research and national practice guidelines.

However, the Clinton plan falls short of an active quality monitoring system that holds health plans and participating providers and practitioners publicly accountable for improved performance. In philosophy, the Clinton plan is too reliant on a theoretical construct that health care plans, given proper incentives, will compete on the basis of quality and that individual health care consumers, armed with meaningful quality data, will be discerning in their choice of plan, provider and treatment. While an elegant goal that needs to be aggressively pursued, I do not believe, Mr. Chairman, that we are close to protecting consumers through a quality based competitive marketplace. For some time to come, most consumers will select a health care plan based on other factors, like price or which plan their own doctor joined, and will not be "walking with their feet" based on reading and comprehending performance measures in a consumer report card. Surely, it is hard to believe that the average health care consumer with a complicated condition is knowledgeable enough to realize that he or she is not being treated according to the accepted practice guidelines or that a patient admitted to the hospital for an acute illness will be fully cognizant of all the treatments he or she receives or should have received during an episode of care. Appealing to "medical professionalism" and establishing a consumer report is not enough to ensure a comprehensive national quality management program.

For this reason, Mr. Chairman, AMPRA strongly endorses the quality assurance and oversight provisions contained in the health care reform proposal you have sponsored, HR 200, The Mediplan Act of 1993. Your proposed legislation would extend Medicare's existing quality oversight and consumer protection infrastructure, including the Peer Review Organization Program, across the entire population. As you fully appreciate, a comprehensive, on-going, independent quality oversight mechanism is imperative in the context of reform of our health care system.

The latest version of the Clinton plan also substantially weakens the quality management function itself by penciling out the "state-based technical assistance foundations" which in the original proposal had been assigned with designing and implementing quality measurement and management systems. Instead, this state-based infrastructure was replaced with "Regional Professional Foundations" whose mission would be to develop programs in "lifetime learning" for health professionals. It is difficult to understand why a state-based, broadly representative quality monitoring and management system close to local markets, consumers and practicing health professionals was abandoned in favor of an academically led, continuing medical education and research initiative based at the regional level. Absent are any provisions for: data analysis and quality monitoring; external auditing of data self-reported by health care plans; community-based quality improvement initiatives for health plans and, within plans, to areas of greatest need; measuring, documenting and holding plans accountable for subsequent quality improvement on an ongoing basis; supporting the compilation of quality related performance measures in a consumer report card; and most importantly, monitoring rates of adherence to national practice guidelines.

Monitoring Adherence to Practice Guidelines

Most would agree that the current state-of-art in medical quality assurance circles lies with national practice guidelines. The science of risk adjusted outcomes measurement is still in infancy and frustrated by the difficult search for consensus. Guidelines based on clinical trials, outcome research and expert clinical consensus are generally more positively received by practicing physicians. By clarifying major areas of medical ambiguity, practice guidelines and their diffusion into medical practice should go a long way towards reducing practice variations and improving overall quality of care. What is all too rarely mentioned, however, is the need to develop and routinely apply guidelines-based quality review criteria to monitor whether they are being observed. With the increased incentives for undertreatment, the mere existence of a guideline will not ensure broad compliance.

Past research has shown that passive dissemination techniques are inadequate for transferring the scientific knowledge codified within practice guidelines into actual clinical practice. The collaborative medical review, research and clinical communities extensive experience in this arena has demonstrated that to sustain profiling and feedback activities it is necessary to have a central organizational structure with management expertise and responsibility as well as quantitative, outreach, education and clinical skills. The expectation for continuous attention to quality improvement should have a concrete structure. This experience includes the development of numerous behavioral techniques (e.g. opinion leader education, small area analysis data feedback). Interactive CME in which different medical specialties review their own performance rate analysis and that of their peers in assessing their compliance to practice guidelines[1] is needed in order to implement self-initiated quality improvement. Continuous feedback and reinforcement of appropriate practice patterns are all methods and techniques which review organizations are presently managing and facilitating to measure the successes of guideline implementation processes. They are working with medical specialty groups, large multi-specialty group practices, Area-wide Health Education Centers and others.

Performance measures for assessing and evaluating the impact of several specific practice guidelines (Urinary Incontinence (in females), Acute Post-Operative Pain, and Benign Prostatic Hyperplasia) are presently being implemented by the American Medical Review Research Center in collaboration with academic researcher, public health, and medical review organizations. The recently re-tooled Peer Review Organizations (PROs) now have staffs of biostatisticians, analysts, practicing physicians with advanced public health and quantitative degrees, evaluation experts and other experienced clinical professionals. They are serving as the "local intelligence, engine," and administrative mechanism within the community. These state-based groups have been uniformly trained for quality improvement work and for working with academicians and large groups practices. Historically academic centers and health services researchers have not embraced program operation ventures.

Monitoring and evaluating practice guideline adherence has been shown to require careful translation, validity and consistency checks to assure the guideline content is completely and accurately represented. It would be unfair for a health plan to suggest elimination of procedures on the basis of their cost, when a portion of the guideline indicates its positive impact on quality. On the other hand if the evaluative exercise linked to outcomes demonstrates that in fact quality is not enhanced -- this is important information that needs to be fed back to the National Health Board, Alliances, and health plans.

AMPRA Recommendations

In the marathon race from health care reform proposal to enactment, vocal consumers will work tirelessly to ensure that quality of care will be closely monitored on their behalf. Here is what is needed at a minimum:

1. Quality monitoring and improvement activities should be integrated and coordinated through a nationally-directed but state-based network of independent Health Quality Foundations. As currently written, the Clinton proposal fragments the responsibility for conducting quality activities among various federal, state and regional entities: Regional Alliances (report cards); state government (health plan certification and consumer complaints); the Regional Professional Foundations (continuing medical education and research); and the Quality Councils under the National Health Board (practice guideline dissemination, consumer surveys). While ultimate responsibility for quality needs to be shared by government, purchasing, and health delivery entities, the Clinton proposal lacks an identified infrastructure that can integrate and coordinate community-based quality monitoring and improvement activities. It would make far more sense to establish for this purpose a national network of state-based Health Quality Foundations, broadly representative of consumer, purchaser and medical professional interests, with close communication and formal linkages to regional/corporate alliances, state government and the National Health Board.

Primary responsibilities of Health Quality Foundations would be to: monitor quality through data analysis and national practice guideline adherence; protect quality through holding plans and providers accountable for improved performance, through reporting findings and conclusions to appropriate purchasing and regulatory bodies (e.g. alliances, state government, National Health Board), and through providing medical consults to support the state patient complaint office; improve quality through the feedback of comparative performance data to health plans and participating providers; inform consumers about quality through developing a community-based resource for medical treatment alternatives and through the support of purchasing alliances in development of the quality related aspects of a consumer report card; assure data integrity by conducting external audits of the accuracy and reliability of the data self reported by health plans.

2. Rates of adherence to practice guidelines should be monitored. Established research

---

[1] Three State medical review organizations (MD, AL, IA) have completed this work in collaboration with three academic centers led by the Center for Quality of Care Research and Education at Harvard. This unique quality evaluation CME was coordinated by the American Medical Review Research Center.

and experience suggests that health plans and physicians will not conform their practice behavior to practice guidelines merely because they exist. Although the experience of the PRO program in monitoring practice guidelines is recent, early experience suggests that the application of review criteria based on practice guidelines can serve as both an effective quality monitoring tool while providing a catalyst for plan and practitioner self-examination and improvement. PROs have the only existing infrastructure and increasingly the expertise in appropriate sampling, abstracting, and feedback methodologies to ensure that the process is scientifically-based, streamlined and non-intrusive to health plans and physicians.

   3. Quality management and oversight should be separated from, but closely coordinated with Regional and Corporate Alliances. As the chief purchasing agents on behalf of purchasers and consumers, Alliances clearly hold whatever clout exists in a managed competition system to negotiate with health plans on the basis of quality. Under the currently proposed system in which the federal government would limit costs through budget caps and alliances through premium price controls, it poses a conflict of interest for a single entity to regulate both price and quality. Ideally, the quality measurement, monitoring, and improvement functions would be conducted by a Health Quality Foundation explicitly devoted to that purpose but working closely with the Alliance if sanctions, penalties, or cancellations of health plan contracts should become necessary.

Conclusion

   In the past decade, medical oversight and quality assurance methodology has evolved dramatically in response to changes in payment incentives and in response to advances in the field of quality evaluation. As the dominant reimbursement mechanism changed from per diem to per case under DRGs and, as it now moves towards fully capitated systems, medical review is less concerned with excessive use and is focused now on adherence to guidelines, technical quality and the creation of safeguards against underutilization. PROs have been leaders in forging expansions in technical capability: moving away from contentious retrospective individual case review with its reliance on the vagaries of peer judgement to the effective manipulation of large quantities of data and toward increasingly sophisticated modeling of medical practice variation, patient outcomes, and practice guideline compliance.

   In the exciting decade to come in medical care delivery, an independent quality monitoring system will be needed to hold the health care delivery system publicly accountable for assuring and improving the quality of care for all Americans. AMPRA and its membership look forward to participating in this critical component of national health care reform.

   Thank you, Mr. Chairman, for the opportunity to testify.

Health Reform and the Quality Imperative

A POLICY REPORT

Prepared by

American Medical Peer Review Association

JANUARY 1994

Table of Contents

This policy report of the American Medical Peer Review Association (AMPRA) recommends the establishment of a **National Quality Management Program (NQMP)** to complement any health reform legislation enacted by Congress. The program's mission would be to preserve and improve the quality of health care for all Americans. Special attention would be focused on identifying barriers to access and underuse of appropriate services as health reform legislation encourages the spread of prepaid systems of health care delivery

A National Quality Management Program would be responsible for the following functions:

Consumer Protection -- To safeguard against health care delivery of potential harm to patient health and welfare, the NQMP would establish:

* *An independent quality monitoring system that holds plans accountable for improved performance;*
* *Authority by regulatory bodies to penalize consistently poor quality care;*
* *A consumer complaint and appeals system;*
* *A licensing and accreditation system for health plans, institutional providers and medical professionals.*

Quality Improvement -- To ensure the diffusion and transfer of new medical knowledge and to share comparative performance information among competing health care plans and participating providers, the NQMP would establish:

* *A community-based feedback and education program that creates a safe environment for provider self-examination and acts a catalyst for quality improvement at all levels in the delivery system.*

Informed Consumer Choice - To ensure that consumer selection of competing health plans is guided by objective and scientifically-based measures and to ensure that consumers have adequate information in making treatment decisions, the NQMP would establish:

* *Comparative performance reports on health plan price, quality, service and consumer satisfaction;*
* *A community-based information resource on treatment alternatives.*

These important functions would be distributed within a federal, state, and local framework that take advantage of existing organizational structures, require a minimal degree of additional bureaucracy and insist upon coordination and active communication among all entities.

The Federal Government would be responsible for establishing a national health care information database, setting quality standards and performance expectations based on emerging medical knowledge, and monitoring the impact of the delivery system on the quality of care, particularly for the most vulnerable populations. Participating federal entities would include:

* *A National Quality Management Council;*
* *A national network of state-based, independent Health Quality Foundations;*
* *State-based Data Networks.*

State Government would take the lead role in the administrative and regulatory oversight of the health care delivery system. Participating state entities would include:

* *State Insurance Commissioners Office;*
* *State Licensing Boards;*
* *State Ombudsman Program;*
* *State Consumer Complaint and Appeals Office.*

Value purchasing and the provision of high quality health care services would be the responsibility of the **Local Marketplace.** Local entities would include:

* *Health and Corporate Alliances, responsible for organizing the consumer choice function and negotiating health plan contracts on the basis of quality;*
* *Health Plans and Participating Providers, accountable for the improved health status of their enrolled population.*

HEALTH REFORM AND THE QUALITY IMPERATIVE
An AMPRA Policy Report

INTRODUCTION

The prospect for enactment of comprehensive health care reform has never been better. The emerging constellation of public opinion, motivated legislators, and an ambitious Clinton Administration augurs for a lively national debate on the topic. Not only is there consensus on the need for comprehensive reform, but there is also significant bipartisan support for some version of the "managed competition" approach, first articulated by the Jackson Hole Group, championed by President Clinton during his campaign and then drafted into proposed legislation by the Administration and other lawmakers. This model envisions a medical marketplace dominated by prepaid health plans competing on the basis of price, quality, service, and consumer satisfaction.

> *"Nevertheless, it is quality and the public's perception of whether or not it will be jeopardized under the new plan, that will help decide the fate of health reform legislation."*

The success of any health care reform agenda rests on its ability to master the basics: cost, access, and quality. Incentives and controls must be designed that can tame rising costs and provide universal coverage while preserving and improving quality of care. The public discussion of the problem has been lopsided. The cost of health care has become a huge concern as it consumes an ever larger share of the gross domestic product with no real abatement in sight. The perception of unfairness regarding inadequate access to care and coverage has also grown dramatically as recession robbed millions of middle class Americans of their job-related health benefits. Quality -- for those who do have adequate coverage -- has been a relative non-issue in the public debate over health care reform.

Nevertheless, it is quality and the public's perception of whether or not it will be jeopardized under the new plan, that will help decide the fate of health reform legislation. Health Maintenance Organizations (HMOs), which would be encouraged as the dominant delivery system under managed competition, have not been preferred by most consumers of health care in most parts of the country, despite their lower out-of-pocket costs, and efforts to be consumer-responsive. Persistent fears about undertreatment and the incentives inherent in pre-payment to cut costs at the high end have frightened many into opting for more expensive fee-for-service alternatives that allow patients more direct control over their choice of physicians, and preserving what they perceive as a wider range of treatment options in the case of serious illness.

Q

The various legislative proposals for health care reform based on managed competition share a collective weakness: the inadequacy of provisions to ensure quality under the powerful new incentives it gives providers to curb expenditures. In fact, nowhere is there to be found a structure capable of performing basic, ongoing, independent quality monitoring that would logically seem to be at the heart of any quality program. The Institute of Medicine (IOM) in a recent policy pronouncement articulated the need succinctly:

" ... the paradigm shift calls for health plans to provide medical services to a population in the face of stringent resource constraints, and the incentive will likely be to underserve people. These changes make monitoring the quality of care imperative, especially for the sickest individuals and other at-risk populations "[1]

> *"Effective quality assurance and improvement must complement vigorous cost containment and expanded access -- it is the essential third component of a sound health care system."*

The purpose of this document is to examine the basic elements of the managed competition bills in Congress and to propose a National Quality Management Program that is accountable, dedicated, efficient, effective, and logically organized across federal, state and local jurisdictions. It is critical that quality and consumer protection be built into the system from the outset Effective quality assurance and improvement must complement vigorous cost containment and expanded access -- it is the essential third component of a sound health care system

Q

DEFINING MANAGED COMPETITION

It is important to first outline the framework of the new health care delivery system that has been proposed before the quality requirements of the system can be discussed The Clinton plan and several of the other congressionally sponsored plans for health reform are modeled on the managed competition proposals of the Jackson Hole Group, some in combination with global expenditure budgets. Managed competition restructures the market for health services into competing prepaid health plans, giving providers built-in incentives to offer the standard package of benefits at the lowest premium price.

National Health Board — Under managed competition, the locus of health system design and control would be with a National Health Board comprised of presidentially appointed members Its primary functions would be to determine the standard benefit plan; to establish global and statewide budgets (Clinton Plan), to set up rules of fair play for competing health plans, and to oversee the state Health Alliances. The National Health Board would also be responsible for establishing a uniform data reporting system that would serve as the basis for measuring the performance of competing health plans and the new system's impact on the quality of care.

> *"Managed competition restructures the market for health services into competing prepaid health plans, giving providers built-in incentives to offer the standard package of benefits at the lowest premium price."*

State Flexibility — Generally speaking, the federal government can be expected to establish the rules of the game, with administrative and regulatory control of the health care delivery system concentrated at the state level Recognizing that many states have already taken steps toward health care reform, the Administration has signaled its willingness to allow states to experiment and design alternative approaches To that end, Medicare and Medicaid waivers will be encouraged and monitored, presumably creating variations and adaptations to local circumstances, including single payer systems.

Health Alliances — In every state, at least one Health Alliance would operate as a collective purchasing agent for small to medium (proposals range up to 5000 employees) employers, and would be organized as not-for-profit membership organizations governed by employers and consumers Alliances would be subsidized by federal, state, employer (an employer mandate is proposed by Clinton) and individual contributions. In addition to small employers, Alliances would act on behalf of self-insured and uninsured individuals The state-administered Medicaid program would also be folded into Alliances. Large employers would be permitted to opt out, acting as their own Corporate Alliance but under similar rules of operation

Health Plans — Each year, Alliances in each state would organize rosters of integrated delivery systems, called Health Plans Although all types of delivery systems would be allowed to participate (i.e , HMO, PPO, indemnity), it is expected that indemnity plans will quickly be phased out of operation because they will not be able to compete on premium price Health plans would be required to report uniform price, quality and service

4

Q

information under the national data reporting system mandated by the National Health Board.

Each year, Alliances would administer open-enrollment periods allowing Alliance members to select the health plan of their choice. A health plan would not be able to prevent an Alliance member from enrolling, even if the individual was a poor medical risk.

Medicare — Under the managed competition proposals, Medicare would continue as a stand-alone program although beneficiaries would be allowed to opt out of Medicare by joining a local Health Alliance. Several proposals would add additional coverage for home and community-based long term care and coverage of prescription drugs.

The Context for Quality Management Under Managed Competition

The Institute of Medicine (IOM) has identified three broad categories of potential concerns with regard to health care quality: use of unnecessary or inappropriate care ("too much care"); underuse of needed and appropriate care ("too little care"); lapses in the technical and interpersonal aspects of care ("inferior care").[2] To these, one might add another category, service or consumer responsiveness.

> *"The IOM has identified three broad categories of potential concerns with regard to health care quality: use of unnecessary or inappropriate care; underuse of needed and appropriate care ; lapses in the technical and interpersonal aspects of care."*

One can reasonably assume that health plans would, by themselves, strive to improve service quality, i.e., waiting times, amenities, convenience, etc., in order to increase their enrollment Similarly, the restructuring of incentives in the direction of managed competition will improve quality to the extent that it virtually eliminate quality concerns that directly result from overtreatment. No longer will there be any need for external utilization review or any real concern that patients will be encouraged toward inappropriate or marginally needed surgeries

Apart from the natural motivation of professionals towards excellence, technical quality should not be affected by managed competition incentives. Technical quality is thought to be protected by the opportunity for patients to bring malpractice suits in the event of serious problems. While the threat of malpractice may indeed provide consumers with a degree of assurance of medical competence, it has long been recognized that the threat of malpractice can itself distort clinical judgement. Even in fully capitated managed care environments, in which financial incentives strongly discourage overtreatment, physicians point to a degree of unnecessary diagnostic testing that is conducted purely as a defense to potential malpractice suits

Any concerns about technical quality will be greatly ameliorated by the increased dissemination, application, and use of practice guidelines which clearly define the best practices for treating specific medical conditions The Clinton health reform plan would encourage pilot programs in which documented adherence to a practice guideline could confer protection to a provider against malpractice litigation Widespread development of and adherence to practice guidelines will work to minimize variations in practice that have been documented to currently exist between geographic regions As such, health reform can be seen as making a concrete contribution to improving standards of care across the board

As the IOM has pointed out, the most significant quality concern that a managed competition model must address is the incentives for undertreatment Managed competition purists claim that by simulating conditions for a free market in health care services, quality will emerge as a natural byproduct of informed consumer choice and competition between plans for consumer favor as in other service industries The flaw in this reasoning, however, is that much of the health services enterprise remains a "black box" for consumers who must trust that at any given time for a particular disease or condition, physicians and other health professionals are using commonly accepted best practices and professional standards in their treatment decisions It is extremely difficult for a consumer to identify a treatment, screening, or referral that may have been medically indicated but withheld, or even to identify when a treatment has been poorly performed.

> "Consumer empowerment, however, in no way relieves the system of its responsibility to implement an ongoing monitoring mechanism capable of identifying patterns of undertreatment and poor technical care."

Clearly, the issue of patient perception of quality must be separated by not divorced from the issue of quality standards for medical practice Certainly the Administration and other health reform architects are to be commended for their emphasis on an informed consumer Patients must be educated to the understanding that when it comes to health services "more" is not synonymous with "better " The proposed consumer "report cards" in health reform plans will flag some important indicators of quality and differences among providers. Consumers should also be provided with direct user-friendly access to resource information to guide their decision-making about the pros and cons of various elective procedures

Consumer empowerment, however, in no way relieves the system of its responsibility to implement an ongoing monitoring mechanism capable of identifying patterns of undertreatment and poor technical care. Using existing population-based data analysis capabilities, broad patterns of care must be analyzed to monitor risk-adjusted rates of practice utilization and health outcome Particular attention must be focused on low utilization rates for specific diagnostic and treatment interventions as potential markers for undertreatment High rates of unexpected poor outcomes must be monitored as potential markers for plan deficiencies in the technical provision of care.

Additionally, capability is emerging to monitor rates of adherence to practice guidelines for treating specific conditions. Not only does practice guideline monitoring have potential to improve technical quality and malpractice driven overtreatment, it is a powerful tool against undertreatment. Subtle deviations from acceptable procedures that may be undetectable at the level of the individual case can become apparent when large amounts of data are examined Aberrant plans or providers thus identified can be provided with appropriate feedback on which to change behavior.

It is critical, however, that monitoring and oversight activities be designed to facilitate and not impede the momentum that has finally started to build around the continuous quality improvement movement Plans need access to quality standards and comparative performance and compliance data so as to appropriately target their own internal quality improvement activities Such data can also foster collaboration among competing plans and the conduct of community-based quality improvement initiatives Penalties or sanctions should only be imposed after the information has been provided and ample opportunity for improvement has been extended The encouragement of a "safe" environment for quality improvement also suggests that enforcement authority be separated from the data analysis and monitoring function

Ultimately, the quality of a health system and the performance of a health plan should be measured largely on the degree to which it improves the health status of its population. Sensitive, risk-adjusted, population-based outcome measurements will allow us to give credit to health system efforts at prevention, education, and early diagnosis in addition to its capabilities in treating illness. Unfortunately, these outcome measurement instruments are still their infancy. Until that time, a national system of quality assurance and improvement must take advantage of existing process measurements, and must encourage the continuous evolution of consensus regarding practice guidelines so that consumers can be assured that they are receiving the right treatment, performed the right way, leading to the right outcome.

> *"This report recommends that a comprehensive, National Quality Management Program be established for the purpose of preserving and improving the quality of health care for all Americans under health reform."*

A NATIONAL QUALITY MANAGEMENT PROGRAM

This report recommends that a comprehensive, National Quality Management Program be established for the purpose of preserving and improving the quality of health care for all Americans under health reform.

The program must be fashioned after the model of continuous quality improvement, that is, it must ensure that its "customers" i e. consumers, providers, and health professionals, will in fact be able to help shape it to suit their needs. Local providers and consumers must provide essential input about such issues as variations in patterns of care and the monitoring and evaluation of local and regional epidemiologies. Quality review and monitoring data should be used to support medical professionals in refining and improving clinical practice based upon emerging new standards of care.

Accomplishing these objectives requires a program of national design with flexible, strong local applications; one that can take health care information from all sources and use it to empower health professionals and consumers to define the outcomes they would like to achieve, while assisting them in working toward those goals The program would assure all purchasers and consumers that health care services are being monitored for quality and

Q

would coordinate principles of epidemiologic surveillance, quality improvement, health services research and interactive education directed at both the medical community and the public.

Such a plan would stand in dramatic contrast to present oversight activities, which are perceived as evaluating individual clinical decisions rather than patterns of care; relying on subjective reviewer judgments, lacking statistical and clinical probability measures; and, employing punitive measures to enforce compliance with undefined standards. A nationally coordinated public/private enterprise of this kind would supersede the multitude of external review activities presently financed by purchasers of care and reduce and redirect the high level of expenditures that existing efforts require.

Functions

The model proposed is built upon four interlocking sets of functions that can be broadly characterized as consumer protection, quality improvement, informed consumer choice, and national database development Each of these elements is essential to the overall performance of the system and to continued consumer confidence that their interests are being protected.

> *"A nationally coordinated public/private enterprise of this kind would supersede the multitude of external review activities presently financed by purchasers of care and reduce and redirect the high level of expenditures that existing efforts require."*

Consumer Protection

As discussed, consumer protection under managed competition must include effective safeguards against undertreatment, must empower the consumer with rights of redress, and must ensure the fiscal and professional integrity of the system's components. Federal legislation enacting health reform must require:

* *Ongoing monitoring and feedback of clinical behavior and practice patterns with the goal of holding competing health plans and providers accountable for improved clinical performance;*

* *Authority by which regulatory bodies can monetarily penalize, sanction or terminate health plans and providers for consistently poor care,*

* *An independent patient complaint and appeals mechanism capable of swiftly addressing consumer concerns regarding access or denial by a plan of specific treatments;*

* *Independent ombudsman that can operate as an unrestricted consumer advocate,*

* *Accreditation and licensure of health plans, institutional providers, and health professionals. Plan certification must be based on detailed information concerning*

Q

fiscal solvency, governance, internal quality management and overall organizational adequacy, at both a plan and facilities level;

• Conduct of surveys for individuals who have chosen to disenroll from a plan Such surveys will yield valuable information on perceived plan weaknesses leading to opportunities for quality improvement and/or disciplinary action

Quality Improvement

To ensure the diffusion and transfer of new medical knowledge among competing health care plans and medical professionals, a community-based infrastructure for quality improvement must be established that creates a safe environment for plan and provider self-examination. Such an infrastructure must include an interactive program of feedback and education to support and complement internal quality improvement initiatives while creating a context for collaborative community-wide efforts.

"Organizations responsible for quality monitoring must walk a fine line between encouragement of these laudable self-improvement exercises and insistence on agreed upon standards of care."

While it can be persuasively argued that specific external controls are still needed in a capitated system, it is also critically important to encourage and facilitate the enthusiasm that is already building regarding the organized self-examination and self-improvement activities represented by the adoption of continuous quality improvement management practices by health care organizations. Organizations responsible for quality monitoring must walk a fine line between encouragement of these laudable self-improvement exercises and insistence on agreed upon standards of care.

Classic quality improvement is a data driven organizational exercise that has typically focused on improvements in cycle times, process efficiency and productivity both in hospitals and other industries Currently, the dearth of comparative data emerging from capitated systems limits the overall systemic improvement that might be possible if such data were routinely captured, analyzed and then reported back to plans by an independent quality monitoring system. Health plans can clearly benefit from access to the comparative performance information that will be produced from the uniform data reporting system that will be mandated under all of the legislative options currently being considered. Benchmarking strategies that identify industry best methods can be used as models for quality and productivity improvement for all plans. In addition, the disseminated results of targeted peer review can identify opportunities for improvements in the processes of care leading to better outcomes.

External quality organizations should actively support health plans in their pursuit of clinical (as opposed to operational) quality improvement by encouraging their participation in practice guideline development, and by facilitating an ongoing learning process to continuously update professionals regarding evolving medical consensus that integrates new research developments.

To ensure that internal quality improvement initiatives are both facilitated and validated, federal legislation enacting health reform must require:

- *Organized feedback and education to competing health plans and participating providers of the comparative clinical performance information made possible by population based data analysis, risk-adjusted outcome measurement and monitoring rates of adherence to practice guidelines;*

- *Organized feedback and technical assistance to competing health plans and participating providers regarding dissemination and applied use of new research and development in the field of practice guidelines and outcome measurement;*

- *Community based quality improvement initiatives that foster collaboration among health plans and participating providers.*

Informed Consumer Choice

Informed consumer choice is the engine that drives the managed competition model. The ability of a consumer to choose between two or more competing health plans based on objective measures of plan value is at the heart of the incentive-based market reforms envisioned by the Jackson Hole Group

> *"Informed consumer choice is the engine that drives the managed competition model."*

To ensure that consumer selection of competing health plans is guided by objective and scientifically-based measures, comparative performance reports on price, quality, service, and consumer satisfaction must be generated and disseminated to the public. The quality components of that "consumer report card" must be developed and validated according to rigorous standards These quality components should change from year to year, serving an educational as well as a consumer choice function

In addition, consumers should be provided with a community-based resource for information on treatment alternatives to help guide consumer choice of medical treatment. No matter how refined practice guidelines become, there will always be conditions for which there are a number of treatment alternatives. In these instances, patient preference based on the value and expectations of the individual must direct treatment decisions. User-friendly patient information systems have been proven to greatly facilitate patient choice in these commonly occurring medical situations.

To ensure that informed consumer choice is encouraged, health reform legislation must require.

- *Generation of performance reports on competing health plans to be distributed to all consumers during each open-enrollment period. These reports must contain information comparing health plan price, quality, service and consumer satisfaction and will help guide plan selection. These reports must also outline an enrollee's rights and responsibilities in joining each health plan,*

Q

- *Creation of a consumer information resource that uses the most accessible educational formats available to help guide decisions about treatment alternatives*

National Database Development

To ensure the viability and ultimate success of a National Quality Management Program, a national health information database must be created. Health plans and participating providers must be required to report health information, including minimum data elements for every patient encounter and detailed data for measuring performance across specific conditions or disease categories. Such data will support both internal management and external monitoring functions.

> *"At minimum, it is recommended that a uniform data reporting system capture common data for each patient encounter in each care setting."*

The task at hand in building a knowledge base from data is a formidable one. Although each of the major health reform proposals do mandate uniform reporting, it will require political courage to preserve the mandate for this costly data and analysis infrastructure. It will require innovative applications of emerging technologies and educational strategies in the fields of quality evaluation and behavioral science to get the quality message out and understood by the public. It will require patience and a belief in the virtues of incrementalism to allow the marketplace time to mature.

The experience to date in generating a common database on prepaid health plan services is lamentable. While fee-for-service payment mechanisms require providers to report patient encounter information on a relatively uniform claim form in order to trigger reimbursement, no such claims based system is needed under capitated arrangements.

This situation should improve as managed competition marches closer to enactment. Given the importance of informed choice and health plan accountability, every managed competition proposal mandates the creation of a uniform data reporting system for competing plans. The ensuing debate will now turn on questions relating to the specific data elements to be collected and the magnitude and administrative cost of the data collection effort.

The scope of this report does not permit a thorough discussion of these data related issues. At minimum, it is recommended that a uniform data reporting system capture common data for each patient encounter in each care setting. Specific data elements must include measures of patient risk, diagnosis, treatment and outcome (including functional status). Data describing a health plan's delivery system and organizational structure must be routinely collected -- from the roster of participating doctors and hospitals to the organizational protocols employed to direct patients through the prepaid system.

To ensure that informed consumer choice becomes a reality, federal legislation enacting health reform must require.

- Establishment of a uniform data reporting system for all eligible health plans,

- Independent validation of the accuracy and completeness of data reported ;

- Technical assistance and training of health plan personnel in data collection procedures particularly the reliable abstraction of clinical data from medical records;

- Health plans to submit additional data and information as may be needed to participate in quality monitoring and community-based quality improvement activities

Guiding Principles

A national quality assurance and improvement program must be guided by a set of principles The principles that follow are a distillation of basic tenets of good government, practical regulatory and organizational experience, in addition to a growing body of theory and practice on quality improvement methodologies in health care and private industry. These basic principles include:

> *"It is also important that quality oversight be independent of payor and provider organizations and thus free from conflict of interest."*

Independent Oversight - It is critical that a national quality program be perceived by all parties as a neutral, independent and unbiased system of quality evaluation Competing health plans and providers must be as convinced as consumers and regulators that standards and measurement systems are reliable and fairly enforced It is also important that quality oversight be independent of payor and provider organizations and thus free from conflict of interest concerns.

Public Accountability -- A national quality assurance and improvement program must hold health plans and participating providers accountable for improved performance.

Public/Private Partnership -- Just as the larger health care delivery system is characterized by a mix of public and private enterprises, so too should quality of care be protected through a public-private partnership. Wherever possible, private sector organizations and expertise should be relied upon as long as there is public accountability for the services provided.

Focus on Scientific Measurement and Educational Feedback -- Quality assurance and improvement must begin from valid, objective measurement of performance, and as such, is profoundly data-dependent. Entities responsible for quality evaluation in a universal health care system will be largely in the business of designing and implementing data collection and analysis tools and feeding back actionable information to its customers, be they consumers, purchasers, or providers. Of particular focus, in the absence of reliable risk-adjusted outcome measures, is the development, use and monitoring of compliance with practice guidelines.

Q

Anticipation of Likely System Disorders -- It is axiomatic that any system involving the exchange of large amounts of money provides its own particular opportunities for individuals or organizations to game the system. It is also widely accepted that managed competition and its reliance on capitated reimbursement invites undertreatment and careful risk selection by health care plans. A quality assurance mechanism for managed competition should anticipate, monitor, and have a mechanism for correcting predictable problems that will occur as a result of managed competition incentives.

Utilize Existing Resources -- Designing an optimal system should not necessitate reinventing the wheel. Federally supported research on outcomes and practice guidelines as well as the cumulative experience of the Medicare Peer Review Organization Program and private accreditation efforts can and should be applied to the quality measurement, assurance and improvement needs of a reformed health care system.

> *"Just as Congress created a statewide structure of PROs to safeguard quality when introducing the new incentives of the Medicare PPS ... a similar quality oversight structure will be needed to accompany a universal coverage system in which capitation and managed care are the norm."*

Minimal Bureaucracy -- Quality improvement and consumer protection activities should be housed in as few organizational entities as possible, consistent with avoiding conflict of interest. The flow of funds and data should be streamlined and efficient.

Separation of Powers/Checks and Balances -- Entities responsible for health care purchasing and premium price controls should not be primarily responsible for quality assurance due to conflict of interest concerns. Similarly, within a national quality assurance and improvement program, a system of checks and balances should be created that separates organizational entities responsible for regulatory, licensing and disciplinary action from entities responsible for quality improvement and monitoring.

Funding through Health Premium Dollar -- Funding for the national quality program must not be subject to the whims and vicissitudes of the annual appropriations process. Rather, funding should be accomplished as a direct draw from the premium dollar. A fixed percentage of that dollar should be applied to the accomplishment of specific quality functions. The net cost should be significantly less than that of the current plethora of private and public review and surveillance mechanisms.

Structure

There is little reason to believe that the public will support passage of a health care reform package that lacks an explicit and independently accountable mechanism for quality assurance and improvement. Just as Congress created a statewide structure of Peer Review Organizations (PROs) to safeguard quality when introducing the new incentives of the Medicare prospective payment system in the early 1980's, a similar quality oversight structure will be needed to accompany a universal coverage system in which capitation and managed care are the norm.

The question remains -- what is the most effective way to structure the quality oversight mechanism needed to sell health reform based on managed competition to the public and to provide it the best chances for success? It is axiomatic that any system designed to control health costs and expand access will create perverse incentives -- new ways to game the system and to maximize profits at the expense of quality. Fortunately, the methodologies of quality evaluation have advanced in recent years and provide the basis for a dedicated National Quality Management Program.

Health care is a service that is provided and purchased locally. Many regulatory structures and professional associations are organized at the state level. At the same time, new clinical knowledge, drug and technology approval, health professional education, services for the elderly, and clinical consensus building take place on a national stage. The design of a National Quality Management Program should complement existing and proposed mechanisms for the purchasing and delivery of health services, the dissemination of clinical knowledge, and existing regulatory and professional organizations.

Figure 1 (see page 15) illustrates the following organizational model that effectively coordinates federal, state and local roles and responsibilities.

> *"Significant variations in clinical practice, based on nothing more than local tradition or geography are a national concern and should be aggressively addressed."*

Federal Government

Clinical quality standards and practice guidelines should be established and disseminated nationally. The mobility of both consumers and health professionals demands that there be a high degree of consistency nationwide with regard to best practices, acceptable treatments and covered benefits. Significant variations in clinical practice, based on nothing more than local tradition or geography are a national concern and should be aggressively addressed. This goal can best be accomplished through the creation of a single organization with authority to mediate top clinical expertise and research into continuously evolving standards of care, to disseminate those standards to clinicians and to create the context by which those standards can be monitored for compliance.

It is to be expected that this national entity would draw heavily on existing clinical consensus mechanisms to arrive at its conclusions, including professional associations and academic medical centers. This role would fall to a **National Quality Management Council** organized within the National Health Board responsible for establishment of a national health information database, support and conduct of outcome research and practice guideline, setting quality standards and performance expectations for health plans and providers, ongoing monitoring of quality to reenforce standards and performance expectations, overall assessment of the health status impact of the reformed health system.

It would be highly impractical to attempt to implement the huge task of disseminating and monitoring national quality standards from a single central location. Therefore, it is necessary to create state-based networks to carry out both the quality management functions and data collection/analysis activities that would be specified by the National Quality

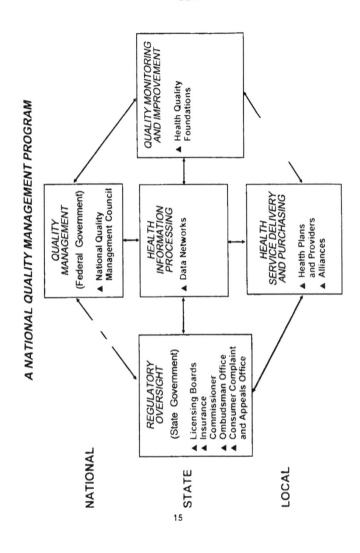

A NATIONAL QUALITY MANAGEMENT PROGRAM

Q	*Anatomy of a Health Quality Foundation*	Q
Name:	Health Quality Foundation	
Structure:	National network of state-based organizations	
Contracting Basis:	Competitive grants with the National Quality Management Council	
Governance:	An alliance of consumers, purchasers and health care professionals	
Key Functions:	Quality monitoring and community-based quality improvement activities	
Corporate Status:	Private sector, independent, not a payer or provider organization	
Staff:	Biostatisticians, epidemiologists, quality improvement specialists, data analysts, peer reviewers, behavioral science experts, communication specialists	

The most significant point of departure between this report's National Quality Management Program and that of the other managed competition proposals including Clinton's Health Security Act is its recommendation to create a state-based network of Health Quality Foundations under contract with the National Quality Management Council These organizations would be independent private sector organizations funded through a direct draw on the premium dollar Their primary mission would be to provide ongoing system-wide quality monitoring and to act as a convener for community-based quality improvement initiatives Health Quality Foundations would be governed by an alliance of consumers, purchasers and health care professionals and they would employ a highly skilled staff of biostatisticians, epidemiologists, quality improvement specialists, data analysts and medical professionals

Given the incentives of managed competition towards undertreatment, this program would focus on such quality indicators as rates of appropriate screening, rates of referral to specialists, rates of compliance with federally approved practice guidelines, and other risk-adjusted outcomes and health status measurements The evolution of sampling, screening and focusing methodologies currently in use by the Medicare Peer Review Organization program make it feasible to project that meaningful surveillance of all provider-consumer interactions across all venues of care could be achieved in a highly cost-effective manner

By making comparative performance information available to health plans, a Health Quality Foundation would support quality improvement – not only by those plans whose rates of compliance or clinical adequacy is demonstrably at the low end, but by all providers and plans It would support and preserve the necessary "safe" environment in which such quality improvement should optimally take place while providing an incentive for decisive and immediate action on problem areas It would foster collaboration between plans and guide the conduct of community-based quality improvement programs It would also facilitate ongoing professional learning pursuant to new practice guidelines and provide input to the research and development of future practice guidelines and performance measures

Although the sentinel effect in support of quality improvement activities should be expected to resolve the vast majority of variations, persistent failure to improve identified problems would ultimately result in consequences to plans and providers At a minimum, consistent quality concerns would be reported to Alliances for use in their contract negotiations Flagrant and continued violations would be referred to licensing or accrediting bodies for redress The Health Quality Foundation would also serve as a resource for state regulatory bodies, including the ombudsman and the consumer complaint and appeals authorities to provide independent medical consultation regarding clinical appropriateness and technical quality

A Health Quality Foundation would be responsible for creating an independent community information and resource center for consumers regarding treatment alternatives It would provide independent, unbiased "user friendly" information to consumers to help inform those choices

Additionally, a Health Quality Foundation would be responsible for compiling, validating, and providing to the Alliance the quality components of its annual Consumer Report Card Each Health Quality Foundation would also publish an annual "State of the Quality Report" to include state aggregated health status measures and a summary of quality improvement initiatives

Management Council. State-based, independent, **Health Quality Foundations** (see page 16) would provide the Council with the arms and legs to carry out critical functions such as ongoing quality monitoring, feedback and interaction with plans and providers, interactive educational programs for professionals and consumers, support of state regulatory and enforcement mechanisms, communication with state professional organizations, and, annual reports to the National Quality Management Council on state-aggregated health status indicators

Data Networks, responsible for data collection and aggregation, should also take place as a nationally managed, state based program -- in order to take advantage of existing data collection and analysis mechanisms that currently exist in most states, and to facilitate the data organization's close interaction with the Health Quality Foundation

State Government

"These state regulatory mechanisms are expected to be heavily dependent on the Health Quality Foundation for information and expertise regarding medical quality and clinical effectiveness."

There is an important role for state government in the overall design of a National Quality Management Program Building on existing structures wherever feasible, states should be directly responsible for administrative/regulatory control of the delivery system This would include continued reliance in most states on the state **Insurance Commissioner's Office,** various state **Licensing Boards,** an expanded state **Ombudsman Program,** and a new state **Office of Consumer Complaints and Appeals**

The apparatus for licensing health plans, providers and professionals already exists at a state level. Health departments issue professional licenses, insurance commissioners oversee the rules regarding the formation of health maintenance organizations and other health insurance plans These programs are already well-disseminated statewide and could be re-engineered to work within existing state authorities Likewise, a patient complaint and appeals process could be administered through the state judicial system with relative ease States currently are required to oversee an ombudsman program for long term care, this could easily be expanded to include health plans

These state regulatory mechanisms are expected to be heavily dependent on the Health Quality Foundation for information and expertise regarding medical quality and clinical effectiveness. Likewise, Health Quality Foundations will be dependent on these state regulatory and enforcement mechanisms to impose penalties on plans and providers in the event of persistent non-compliance with standards and failure/refusal to self-correct

Local Marketplace

Health care delivery and purchasing takes place at a local level so to a significant degree, quality can be affected by local markets and conditions The **Health and Corporate Alliances** have an important role to play in the overall design of the National Quality Management Program They are responsible for purchasing and negotiating with plans on quality and for organizing the consumer choice function, including the preparation and distribution of consumer report cards. The Alliance should expect to rely on the Health Quality Foundation for the quality information to be published in these consumer reports and for additional quality findings that may assist it in its negotiations with plans. Likewise, Health Quality Foundations will depend on the Alliances to contractually reward or punish plans based on quality determinations.

It must not be forgotten that the primary responsibility for quality rests with **Health Plans and Providers** themselves. Through their own internal management, communication and quality improvement mechanisms, they must be active participants in all aspects of quality. Participation in community-based quality activities of the Health Quality Foundation should be contractually mandated.

CRITIQUE OF
LEGISLATIVE PROPOSALS

How do the quality provisions of the managed competition bills compare with the principles and structure outlined above? All of the proposals currently under consideration place too much reliance on market mechanisms to achieve and maintain the consistently high standards of quality Americans should and do expect. The theory is that, given proper incentives, health care plans will compete on the basis of quality and that individual health care consumers, armed with meaningful quality data, will be discerning in their choice of plan, provider and treatment

> *"The theory is that, given proper incentives, health care plans will compete on the basis of quality and that individual health care consumers, armed with meaningful quality data, will be discerning in their choice of plan, provider and treatment."*

While it can be expected that health plans (in regions capable of supporting multiple alternatives) will compete on visible measures of consumer satisfaction, e.g., service quality, there is little reason to think that plans or providers will compete on technical and difficult to extract measures of clinical quality. Even assuming that some comparative quality indicators are made available to the consumer through the consumer report card, consumers are much more likely to be influenced by price, or to choose the plan their own doctor joined than to "vote with their feet" based on that information. Once having chosen, a consumer is extremely unlikely to be able to detect or adequately document clinical deficiencies — especially care that should have been but was not provided.

All the current legislative proposals are to be commended, however, for their political courage in mandating a national database that includes reporting on all patient encounters as well as comprehensive data that correlates with performance measures for specific conditions or disease categories. . No meaningful evaluation of system quality or performance would be possible without such data. It is anticipated that the rapid movement to computerized medical records keeping will greatly reduce the administrative burden associated with this requirement in addition to enhancing internal quality improvement activities.

Q

Of the legislative proposals currently on the table, Clinton's Health Security Act goes the farthest in spelling out the functions and framework of a comprehensive quality management program and provides the starting point on which the foregoing discussion is based. In particular, the plan succeeds in the following respects.

- *Affirms the policy principle that health care plans are responsible for the improved health of the populations served, that ultimately, improved health status should be the outcome of a health care plan,*

- *Creates a national health care information database that serves as the underpinnings for quality assessment and improvement activities;*

- *Enshrines the principle of meaningful consumer choice by promising consumers a "report card" that compares plans and providers within plans not merely on costs, but also on specific performance measures,*

- *Establishes a state-based complaint and appeals office to permit redress for consumers that believe their benefits have been curtailed by competing health plans;*

> *"The latest version of the Clinton plan substantially weakens the quality management function by penciling out the state based 'Technical Assistance Foundations' which in the original proposal had been assigned the role of designing and implementing quality measurement and improvement systems."*

- *Reaffirms a national commitment to patient outcome research and national practice guidelines.*

The greatest failing of the Health Security Act with regard to quality is the conspicuous absence of an ongoing monitoring and quality improvement function To that end, Health Quality Foundations are proposed, the chief purpose of which would be to provide ongoing system-wide surveillance of quality indicators, with organized feedback and education to providers and practitioners.

There is obviously some ambivalence on this issue within the Administration itself The latest version of the Clinton plan substantially weakens the quality management function by penciling out the state based "Technical Assistance Foundations" which in the original proposal had been assigned the role of designing and implementing quality measurement and improvement systems Instead, this state-based infrastructure was replaced with "Regional Professional Foundations" whose mission it would be to develop programs in "life-time" learning for health professionals.

While academic medical centers might usefully play a role in helping drive medical consensus on practice guidelines and providing targeted education to physicians and other health professionals, it is unreasonable to think that an academically-based regional organization could be expected to implement an administratively efficient process for system-wide quality monitoring In any event, such a role would present an extreme conflict of interest for an academic medical center which is, itself, a health care provider whose

Q

performance should be monitored. A better model would be for academic health centers to work actively with the proposed independent Health Quality Foundations to assure that their expertise and skills are utilized effectively.

The original plan to create a state-based entity, broadly responsible for quality monitoring and improvement, close to local markets, consumers and practicing health professionals would appear to make a good deal more sense. This report advocates that it be reinstated as health reform makes its way towards law.

There are a number of other points on which this proposed plan for national health quality management differs from the Clinton proposal:

- *There appears to be a need for only a single National Quality Management Council at the national level Recognizing that schools of medicine and academic medical centers should be encouraged to take leadership roles in helping frame and research clinical quality research, the addition of the National Quality Consortium would appear to have little functional value;*

- *It would appear sensible to locate the data networks at the state level to take advantage of existing local data collection and analysis apparatus,*

- *It would also appear to be administratively easier and provide less appearance of a conflict of interest to house the Ombudsman program within state government rather than within Alliances. Existing state Ombudsman programs for long term care could be expanded to accommodate this function.*

> *"A better model would be for academic health centers to work actively with the proposed independent Health Quality Foundations to assure that their expertise and skills are utilized effectively."*

Q

SUMMARY AND CONCLUSIONS

The United States is on the verge of major health care reform based on the managed competition model As a necessary complement to health reform legislation, this policy report proposes a comprehensive national program to evaluate and monitor the quality of care provided to all Americans regardless of payer, provider, consumer, or site of care The program must rely on federal mandates for the reporting of health care information and nationally driven policies on clinical consensus, but should be implemented through a statewide infrastructure of Health Quality Foundations interacting with other appropriate regulatory mechanisms. The goals of the program will be to: empower consumers with health care information that can help guide their decision making at all levels in the system, protect consumers from compromises to quality that a managed competition system invites, and facilitate provider quality improvement initiatives through an active program of quality monitoring accompanied by education and feedback

---

[1] Institute of Medicine, *The Journal of the American Medical Association,* October 27, 1993, p. 1911

[2] Institute of Medicine, Assessing Health Care Reform, National Academy Press, Washington, DC. 1993, p. 35-36

AMPRA - THE ORGANIZATION

The American Medical Peer Review Association (AMPRA) is a national membership association dedicated to improving the quality of health care delivery in the United States for all consumers through the creative application of quality evaluation programs and services.

AMPRA's current membership includes the federally designated Peer Review Organizations (PROs) under contract with the Medicare program. AMPRA works with its members and other interested parties to promote quality evaluation programs at the local level.

To link AMPRA's practicing review community with the work of health services researchers, AMPRA is affiliated with the American Medical Review Research Center (AMRRC), a non-profit, 501 (c)(3) public benefit, research and education organization dedicated to advancing the art science of quality assurance and quality medical peer review. AMRRC is a national information, evaluation, testing, and analysis resource for practical tools, methodologies, and programs in quality evaluation. AMRRC is presently working under contract with the Agency for Health Care Policy and Research to develop practice guideline-based review criteria and performance measures.

For further discussion or additional copies please contact:

Andrew Webber
Executive Vice President
American Medical Peer Review Association
810 First Street, NE, Suite 410
Washington, DC 20002
(202)371-5610 or Fax (202)371-8954

Mr. CARDIN. It is always nice to welcome a friend to the President. Dr. Kerschner.

STATEMENT OF PAUL KERSCHNER, PH.D., CHAIR, COALITION FOR CONSUMER PROTECTION AND QUALITY IN HEALTH CARE REFORM

Mr. KERSCHNER. Thank you, Mr. Cardin. Until 1 month ago, I was one of your very satisfied constituents.

Mr. CARDIN. Did you move or are you just not satisfied now?

Mr. KERSCHNER. I got tired of 15 years of commuting and moved into the District to flee the crime in Maryland.

I am the executive director of the Gerontological Society of America and chair of the Coalition for Consumer Protection and Quality in Health Care Reform. The Coalition applauds the President's all-out effort to reform the Nation's health care system. Our job now is to recommend specific improvements where necessary.

Mr. Chairman, the Coalition's members know what it is like for health care consumers under the current system. They are vulnerable to losing benefits or being denied coverage. The managed care model relies on competition between health care plans and providers to drive down the cost of care and drive up the quality of care. But there are obvious incentives for plans to contain costs while providing less service, so we believe a systematic approach to protecting consumers must be implemented. Allow me to summarize our recommendations.

Under quality improvement and public accountability, the Health Security Act provides an excellent foundation for independent monitoring of quality. However, the Coalition strongly believes there is a missing component. The bill does not satisfy our basic principle that there must be an external quality review entity independent of the payer-based alliance and provider-based plan, systems to monitor and improve quality in each State.

The Coalition also believes that what we call "quality improvement foundations" should be created in each State by the National Quality Management Council through competitive grants. The QIFs would be governed by a consumer majority board which would also include experts in a variety of health and quality research fields. Each QIF would perform quality monitoring and improve functions such as development of and support for quality improvement activities, practice guidelines, adherence monitoring and profiles of the database for low rates of utilization. This would ensure that quality improvement activities, which are currently very successful in some hospitals and with some health care professionals, will be used consistently across the Nation.

The QIF also will ensure that information regarding consistently poor care and poor plans will be forwarded to the appropriate entities. Under consumer representation, public accountability depends greatly on consumer representation on advisory boards, including the advisory boards for regional and corporate alliances, the National Quality Management Council and the State-located quality improvement foundations. In fact, Coalition members would argue that consumers must have a majority on these advisory boards since they are both the recipients of care and the ultimate source of financing.

Licensing and certification: Rigorous professional licensing and accreditation and planned certification is needed to ensure quality of care. Licensing boards and other regulatory bodies must sanction those that fail to provide acceptable care. We believe that the subcommittee should address ways to mandate sufficient financial support for licensing boards and mandated at the national level, at least minimum functions to assure consistency from State to State.

Ombudsman: We are pleased that the Health Security Act calls for the creation of ombudsman offices to serve as consumer advocates and help negotiate the system, resolve complaints and problems with the quality of services and facilities. However, we request that you provide greater detail about this program and how it can be used by consumers.

For example, the ombudsman program must have a stable source of financing not only one of voluntary contribution. We strongly believe that corporate enrollees should have the same access to an ombudsman as regional alliance enrollees; they currently don't. Also, ombudsman offices must be independent of plans and alliances to protect from conflicts of interest. Under any new system, consumers will need easy access to unbiased information to help them make meaningful choices between plans, providers and coverage options.

I should mention that consumers will benefit greatly by the inclusion of point-of-service options. A managed care system's competitive success depends greatly on the quality of information provided to consumers. Therefore, we request that you define more precisely the kinds of information that will be available to consumers.

For example, the Consumer Handbook should include the results of the consumer satisfaction survey conducted by the National Quality Management Council, enrollment and disenrollment figures collected by the Health Care Information System. Consumers will also need information such as physician certification and repeated disciplinary actions, and they will need condition-specific information to be able to choose between doctors and hospitals when they face major surgery.

The Coalition believes that due process rights are essential in any national health care plan and is quite pleased with the appeals process provided in the Health Security Act. We would, however, like to offer several refinements. Most importantly, we believe that Congress must clarify the circumstances for providing notices to patients when decisions to deny, reduce or terminate a service or payment have occurred in order to protect patients who may not know their benefits or options. These are all from low-income or less-educated consumers.

Notices should, one, state the specific reasons for the decision and describe the appeals process; and two, be triggered automatically whether certain benefits have been denied reduced or terminated.

It also appears that the burden falls too heavily on the consumer to provide a necessity for treatment and places the responsibility and cost of purchasing second opinions on the beneficiary.

Mr. Chairman, the Coalition is grateful to you for holding this hearing, and we look forward to working with you and your colleagues.

Mr. CARDIN. Thank you.

[The prepared statement and attachments follow:]

STATEMENT OF PAUL KERSCHNER, PH.D.
CHAIR
COALITION FOR CONSUMER PROTECTION AND
QUALITY IN HEALTH CARE REFORM

Mr. Chairman, members of the Committee, my name is Paul Kerschner. I am the Executive Director of The Gerontological Society of America and the Chair of the Coalition for Protection and Quality in Health Care Reform, a coalition of more than 25 organizations

We thank you for providing us with the opportunity to testify today. Chairman Stark, we commend you for your longtime support of critical health care system reforms for all Americans.

The Coalition applauds the President's all-out effort to reform the health care system. Specifically, we are pleased with the attention to consumer empowerment through an extensive system of data collection, analysis and dissemination. For the first time ever, consumers will base their plan selection on comparative information. We are delighted that the plan recognizes the importance of choice through requiring the offering of point-of-service options. Included in the plan is an ombudsman program, a vigorous appeals procedure and a separate grievance procedure, and a sound foundation for quality improvement and public accountability. The language in the bill sends the strong signal that consumer protection and quality are important to this Administration Our job now is to flesh out the intent of specific consumer and quality provisions and to suggest specific improvements where necessary.

I would like to briefly outline our vision of consumer protection in the new health care system. This new system relies on competition between health care plans and providers to drive the cost of care down and the quality of care up. But there are obvious incentives for plans to contain costs by providing less service.

Under any new system consumers will need easy access to unbiased information to help them make meaningful choices between plans, providers, and coverage options. They will need an advocate or ombudsman to help them understand and navigate through the system and assist with resolving complaints. They will want a grievance procedure for patient complaints. They will need an appeals process to address the denial, reduction, or termination of benefits, and quality issues quickly and fairly

The system will need independent quality improvement organizations and quality assurance and public accountability through improved licensing, certification, and accreditation systems, and consumer control of governance structures. There must be guaranteed funding for these programs.

These are the elements of a health care system that is sensitized to the basic fact that the system -- physicians, nurses, pharmacists, other health care professionals, hospitals, and health care plans -- is there to serve those who need care, the consumers.

We do not promote red tape or over regulation, but the burden to ensure consumer protection and prevent poor quality of care falls on the President and Members of Congress. Please do not miss this opportunity to design a consumer-focused system or you will be hearing from your constituents when the system fails.

Today, I would like to address four areas of particular interest to consumers:

1.   Quality improvement and public accountability;

2.   The financing, location, and additional details for the ombudsman program;

3.   Information that should be provided to consumers through the consumer report card and other means; and

Quality Improvement and Public Accountability

The Consumer Coalition believes that consumer information, consumer protection, and quality improvement programs must be accountable to the public, independent of providers and payers of health care, and free of potential conflicts of interest.

Health Security Act Quality Provisions. As I mentioned, we believe with great conviction that quality oversight must be independent and external of providers The Health Security Act provides an excellent foundation for independent monitoring of quality in the following ways. First, the National Health Board would establish a National Quality Management Program (NQMP) designed to oversee a performance based quality management and improvement program.

Second, the National Quality Management Council would manage the NQMP and develop a set of national measures of quality performance. These will be used to assess health care services in relation to access, appropriateness, effectiveness, outcomes, health promotion, prevention, and consumer satisfaction.

Third, the Council will conduct periodic surveys of health care consumers based on a standard design and administered to all plans. This information will be of great importance to other consumers and should be used by plans for quality improvement.

Fourth, the performance reports that each alliance will publish and that the Council will provide to Congress, and the practice guidelines and utilization protocols will serve consumers and providers with information to improve quality and provide consistency throughout the system.

Quality Improvement Foundations. The aforementioned approach in tandem with the data collection system provides a foundation for quality improvement. However, the Coalition strongly believes that there is a missing component in the Health Security Act's quality improvement system. The elimination of the technical assistance foundations from the September 7th draft of the Administration's plan exacerbates this problem. We had considered the technical assistance foundations as a possible location for the independent, external entity to monitor and improve the quality of care. The bill currently does not satisfy our basic principle that there must be an external quality review entity, independent of the payer-based (alliance) and provider-based (plan) systems to monitor and improve quality in each state.

For lack of a better name, we will call these entities "Quality Improvement Foundations." They are needed to ensure that the consumer information, due process, advocacy, and other quality related aspects of our new health care system function properly. Each entity must be free from potential conflicts of interest. It must have as a primary goal the protection of consumers from providers who would create barriers to quality care.

Let me take this opportunity to describe how Quality Improvement Foundations (QIFs) would fit into the new system.

The National Quality Management Council would provide competitive grants to create one QIF in each state. Funding would come from the National Health Board through an amount designated from each premium. The QIF would be governed by a consumer majority board, which includes others who are experts in a variety of health and quality research fields.

A QIF must be independent of purchasers and providers of care. Each QIF would perform the following quality monitoring and improvement functions:

*   Data analysis and data quality testing;

* Dissemination of information on successful quality improvement programs;
* Technical assistance to plans and alliances;
* Development of and support for quality improvement activities;
* Consumer information beyond the report card;
* Practice guidelines adherence monitoring/feedback;
* Profiles of database for low rates of utilization (immunization, infection rates, voluntary surgery); and
* Quality assurance:
  -by providing information to consumers
  -feedback to licensing, certification, and accrediting entities and the National Quality Management Council.

We believe that all health care plans should be required to participate in the quality improvement activities of the QIF. This will ensure that quality improvement activities which are currently very successful in some hospitals and with some health care professionals will be used consistently across the nation. The QIF also will ensure that information regarding consistently poor care and plans that do not implement successful quality improvement programs will be forwarded to the appropriate licensing, and other regulatory entities, so that they can take appropriate action.

The Coalition believes that the QIF has an integral role to play in ensuring the quality of care for consumers. Given the current structure of the Administration's quality program, this independent entity would be in an ideal position to assist health care plans to learn from nationally collected and analyzed data Outcomes data could be used by plans for quality improvement and by the QIFs for examining plans compliance with national practice guidelines and health services utilization protocols. As I mentioned, when plans do not meet standards or deviate from best practices, this information will be provided to the appropriate entities. This will lead to improvements in the quality of care for consumers and sanctions for those plans or providers that do not improve quality appropriately.

Along these same lines, the quality of care under the Medicare program must not be reduced as a result of a merger with the new system and its yet to be tested quality programs In fact, until the new system can demonstrate equal or better quality improvement and consumer protection systems, it does not make sense to merge the two. The Coalition opposes the Health Security Act provisions which terminate the Medicare Peer Review Organizations.

Consumer Representation. One of the most effective ways to ensure public accountability is to mandate consumer representation on advisory boards, including the advisory boards for regional and corporate alliances, the National Quality Management Council, and state-located Quality Improvement Foundations. In fact, Coalition members would argue that consumers must have a majority on these advisory boards since they are both the recipients of care and the ultimate source of financing. The Administration's legislation does not yet provide adequate representation for consumers on these and other boards. Consumers are in a unique position to advocate for a system that delivers high quality care -- unlike payers or providers of care, they are immediately affected by any changes in the quality of care delivered and are free from potential conflicts of interest.

The Coalition is pleased that the Health Security Act recognizes the importance of consumer involvement by providing for consumer representation on some of the boards and advisory councils specified in the bill. However, we believe that the consumer role in the governance of the health care system must be strengthened. Consumers should have control of the boards of the regional alliances. With respect to the corporate alliances, we did not find any provision for consumer representation. We recommend that corporate alliances and Quality Improvement Foundations be governed by a board or council that is controlled by consumers, as well We are also concerned that there is currently no provision for consumer representation on the National Quality Management Council or on the National Long-Term Care Insurance Advisory Council among others. We envision significant consumer representation on these and other councils and boards. Consumers have the greatest stake in assuring and improving quality in the new health care system and must be adequately represented.

In addition, for consumers to have a real impact on these various boards, funds must be made available for training and technical assistance. Adequate staff and resources must also be provided to enable consumers to effectively fulfill there roles. The Coalition believes that the health care legislation should specify that consumers should be generally representative of the ethnic, geographic, and socio-economic demographics of the people served.

Licensing and Certification. One area of quality assurance for which the Coalition has not yet completed its analysis, is improving the effectiveness of professional licensing and accreditation, and plan certification entities. They will play critical roles both in establishing that providers and plans will provide quality care and in sanctioning those that fail to provide acceptable care.

For example, we believe that the Subcommittee should address ways to mandate sufficient financial support for licensing boards to enable them to effectively carry out their functions. It would also make sense for at least minimum functions to be determined at the national level to ensure consistency from state to state. Of course, consumers should also be represented on the boards of these entities. Furthermore, we suggest that you consider incentives and penalties to make licensing boards fulfill their missions and improve public protection.

Ombudsman

We are pleased that the Health Security Act calls for the creation of ombudsman offices. We believe it is important to have ombudsman programs to assist consumers with their questions and concerns about the quality of services and facilities and in obtaining information about grievance and appeals options. The ombudsman should serve as a consumer advocate and should help him or her negotiate the system when necessary and resolve complaints if possible. We believe, however, that the Health Security Act should provide much greater detail regarding how this program will be designed, how it can be used by consumers, and what kinds of consumer information about the program will be provided.

For example, a major function of the ombudsman would be to work with individuals in (a) securing necessary information and assistance (including obtaining representation -- information and referral -- in filing a claim under sec.5201-5243 of the Health Security Act) and (b) providing information and assistance in filing grievances within a plan. This type of detail should be added to the Act.

If we are to take the ombudsman program seriously -- and consumers have every intention of doing so -- it must have a stable source of financing, not one of voluntary contribution. We think it would make sense to determine the cost of this and other quality improvement and consumer protection systems within the Health Security Act and mandate that a percentage of premiums collected be set aside to cover their costs. The Health Security Act includes the option for alliance eligible individuals to designate one dollar of their premium towards an ombudsman program. This approach puts the program in jeopardy from the beginning. Our concern is that not every enrollee will be aware of the value of an ombudsman until they have a problem and need such services. For the ombudsman system to be effective, it needs a trained, full-time staff. Without an assured financial base, it will be unable to plan from year to year Under the current framework it is unlikely to become a successful advocacy program for consumers We recommend that this important program be assured dependable financing.

The Administration's legislation states that "each regional alliance must establish and maintain an office of an ombudsman to assist consumers in dealing with problems that arise with health plans and the alliance." To whom does the corporate alliance enrollee turn? These enrollees should have the same access to a consumer advocate or ombudsman.

Further, the Health Security Act locates the ombudsman offices in the alliances, which creates a clear conflict of interest. We agree that the ombudsman must assist with both plan and alliance-related problems, but it is unrealistic to expect the ombudsman to effectively deal with problems that arise within the alliance if it is located there and receives its funding from it. We understand that some hospitals, newspapers, and other organizations serving the public employ their own ombudsman. However, this is not the model consumers have in mind. Rather, we believe that the program should be modeled after the State Long-Term Care Ombudsman Program mandated by the Older Americans Act that serves consumers in nursing homes, and other programs which attempt to avoid such potential conflicts of interest. We have seen this model work quite successfully. It is the consensus of the Long-Term Care Ombudsmen that the program is most effective when it is housed independent of the organization(s) whose services it has a mandate to monitor

The following is a list of issues that we believe should be specifically addressed regarding the ombudsman its relationship to the State Long-Term Care Ombudsman Program; ensuring nationwide consistency; conflict of interest protections; eligibility requirements; procedures for access by ombudsman to facilities, patients, records, etc.; a uniform system to collect and report data regarding complaints; confidentiality and disclosure procedures; and access to legal counsel for the ombudsman. We ask the Subcommittee to consult with the National Association of State Ombudsman Programs and the National Association of Protection and Advocacy Systems for addition input on this important issue.

Consumer Information

The Administration plan calls for easily understood, useful, comparative, consumer information published annually. The National Health Board will decide the type of information, but it is to include at a minimum: first, cost of plan; second, characteristics and availability of health care professionals and institutions in the plan; third, any restrictions on access to providers and services, fourth, a summary of quality performance standards. Consumers will need basic educational information to use the new health care system In addition, some clarification and expansion is needed in the area of consumer information.

Comparative Information. Congress should consider adding to the consumer handbook the following items: 1) the results of the consumer satisfaction survey conducted by the National Quality Management Council, 2) enrollment and disenrollment figures collected by the Health Care Information System to inform consumers about plan size and percentage of enrollees leaving the plan; 3) the ratio of complaints to enrollees; 4) the cost or implications of using services outside the plan, 5) premium increase trends to let consumers know which plan has the slowest rate of increase, 6) benefits covered beyond the standard benefit package; 7) how long the plan has been in operation; 8) ratio of primary care practitioners to enrollees; 9) ratio of board certified physicians to non-board certified; 10) names of participating hospitals and other providers; 11) the financial health of the plan; 12) phone numbers for information specialists who can explain plan details and the ombudsman; 13) any limitations on prescription drugs or procedures for each plan; and 14) any financial incentives that health care providers have regarding the services they provide. I refer you to our White Paper, "Minimum Requirements for Consumer Information," which I would like to request permission to submit for the record, for additional suggestions.

Plan-Specific Information. Once a person has chosen a plan, he or she should have access to further details about the plan's health care professionals to help select a physician. This information should be provided by the plan itself or by the health alliance. Fact sheets on each of the physicians in the plan, their training, years of practice, board certification, faculty responsibilities, and confirmed disciplinary actions such as repeated malpractice payments should be provided in this documentation. Fact sheets on individual hospitals, home health agencies, laboratories, pharmacies, and other contracted health providers with lists of services and other details should be available upon request.

Condition-Specific Information. Condition or treatment-specific information is important to the person who faces a major operation or health care decision and should be available upon request. This information includes both hospital and physician specific practice profiles and outcomes data on a particular procedure or condition. This is similar to what has been done for coronary artery bypass graft surgery in both Pennsylvania and New York. The information could be presented on either a nation-wide, region-wide, or state-wide basis and could be available from the National Quality Management Council or its state-located Quality Improvement Foundations - which I will discuss later. The data should be appropriately adjusted for severity to avoid skewing outcomes for surgeons and hospitals serving a more vulnerable population. For a particular condition, this data could include:

* number of surgeries performed (by hospital and by surgeon);

* death rates within a certain time period,

* infection rates and readmissions for the same condition, and

* patient satisfaction survey results.

We believe that this committee should add these details to the Health Security Act which currently leaves too much of the consumer information up to chance and may promote inconsistency across the nation.

Consumer Due Process Protections

The Coalition believes that consumer notice, appeal, and grievance rights -- collectively referred to as consumer "due process" rights -- are essential in any national health care plan. Under a managed care system, health plans and the utilization review systems work to keep the cost of care down. In some instances this will be done at the expense of the health of the enrollee who seeks services. Therefore, access to an independent and timely appeals process is critical to maintaining quality care for consumers.

Appeals Process. The Coalition is quite pleased with the review structures envisioned by the Health Security Act, "Subtitle C -- Remedies and Enforcement " Its basic approach is consistent with our White Paper, "Consumer Due Process Protections," which we request be inserted in the record. We would, however, like to raise several concerns that should be addressed as refinements to the Health Security Act.

First, we believe that Congress must clarify the circumstances for providing notice to patients when decisions to deny, reduce, or terminate a service or payment have occurred. We have concern for patients who may not know their benefits or options - these are often low-income or less educated consumers. This notice should state the specific reasons for the decision and describe the appeals process available to the patient. We would argue that notices should be triggered automatically when certain benefits, such as hospital, nursing home and home health care, have been denied, reduced, or terminated Other circumstances triggering automatic notice should be defined in regulations.

It should be clarified that a "claim" under the Health Security Act, includes the review of a decision to terminate services. Proper notice to patients is particularly important in this situation. We have concern for patients who may not know that their benefits or options have been reduced or that certain options are not being made available to them. We suggest that you also consider using periodic notices to remind consumers of their rights.

Another issue that the Subcommittee may consider is whether under the Administration's proposal the burden of proving the necessity for a particular treatment or service is the consumer's It appears to us that the burden falls too heavily on the consumer and could prove to be a great obstacle, particularly for low-income beneficiaries. Similarly, the current bill places the responsibility and costs of purchasing second opinions on the beneficiary. This places an unacceptable burden of proof on the beneficiary For low-income individuals in particular, this burden will negate the appeal right

Grievance Process Each alliance should assure that its plans initiate and maintain a grievance process for patient complaints about problems other than denial, reduction, or termination of service or payment. We believe the grievance process should have the following components:

(a)   initial investigation of oral and written complaints from patients shall be performed by a patient advocate, who will prepare a written report for the plan and the consumer within 15 days;

(b)   action in response to the patient advocate's report shall be recommended by a grievance committee within the insurer or health plan within 30 days; copies of the complaint and recommended response shall be available to members of the insured group or health plan and appropriate regulatory agencies; and

(c)   beneficiaries who are dissatisfied with the grievance committee action shall be able to lodge further review with the Complaint Review Office, which is created by the Health Security Act.

We would also like the Subcommittee to consider the role played by the Early Resolution Program or alternative dispute resolution mechanisms. We mention this because it is our belief that although these mechanisms should be available to consumers and can be helpful in some instances in resolving grievances and complaints, not all grievances and complaints are suitable for the alternative dispute resolution process.

Other issues that we believe are important for you to consider are· 1) shortening to 15 days the time-period for plans to make decisions on claims; 2) removing jurisdictional amounts as a barrier to litigation about coverage policy and Constitutional issues, particularly for low-income beneficiaries; 3) requiring uniform appeals rights under all plans and alliances; 4) further details on what this system will address (e.g. refusal by gatekeeper to refer to a specialist, out-of-plan emergency disputes); and 5) whether consumers will have access to utilization review criteria information.

We will submit any further recommendations on due process issues to the Subcommittee in writing.

Conclusion

Mr. Chairman, We believe that those who would like to protect the status quo in our health care system will distort the facts and attempt to scare consumers into believing that quality will suffer under the Health Security Act. We believe the improvements that we are recommending will protect quality further and provide consumers with the information, advocacy, due process rights, quality improvement, and public accountability that will make this reform better for American consumers of health care

Chairman Stark, the Coalition is grateful to you for holding this hearing and focusing your attention and the work of this Subcommittee on these critical issues. We look forward to working in the future.

Coalition For Consumer Protection And Quality
In Health Care Reform

White Paper On
Consumer Due Process Protections

November 30, 1993

Executive Summary

This white paper identifies and examines key consumer notice, appeal, and grievance rights -- collectively referred to as consumer "due process" rights -- essential in any national health care legislation and consistent with the Clinton Health Bill. Section I, the Executive Summary, provides an outline of these rights. Section II is an analysis of the key principles arising under federal statute, case law, and constitutional law that a impact on the nature and scope of due process in the delivery of health care services.

I. **EXECUTIVE SUMMARY: Outline of Necessary Due Process and Consumer Protection Elements In National Health Care Reform**

A. **Broad Societal Interests In An Appeals Process That Is:**

- **Fair**

- **Accountable**

- **Timely**

B. **Specific Due Process and Consumer Protection Elements**

1. Appeals Process. An appeals process shall be established for patients for whom health care services or payments have been denied, reduced, or terminated. The appeals process shall have the following components:

   o Written notice shall be given to the patient by the insurer or health plan for:

      a) any decision to deny or reduce requested services;

      b) all terminations of institutional care, such as hospital, nursing home, home health care;

      c) failure to provide specified services, such as rehabilitation services and home health services for the improvement/or prevention of deterioration of a patient's condition.

[Regulations should be developed to specify the circumstances under which written notice of appeal rights is required and the relevant time periods for the receipt of notice.]

o   Posted Notice of the right to appeal denials, reductions, and terminations of coverage are to be appropriately displayed in public areas of all health plan facilities.

o   A "Plain Language" Explanation of appeal rights shall be provided to individuals upon enrollment in health plans.

o   Expedited review of the correctness of the denial, reduction, or termination of urgently needed services must be available as follows --

> a)   the patient attests that services are urgently needed and the failure to provide them promptly or the failure to continue them may impair or retard improvement or cause deterioration of the patient's health status.
>
> b)   expedited review must be performed by an independent hearing officer, as defined below, who shall issue a written decision to the patient within two (2) days of the request for review.
>
> c)   services or payment by the insurer or plan must continue until an expedited review decision has been issued.

o   Review by an independent hearing officer for all other services shall be governed by the following administrative process --

> a)   review of its denial, reduction, or termination decision must be provided by the insurer or health plan, which shall issue a written decision within 15 days of the request for review.
>
> b)   hearing by an independent hearing officer must be available with 30 days of a review decision. An independent hearing officer is an individual who is not an employee or designee of the insurer or health plan;

c) written decision setting out the hearing officer's rulings on issues of fact and law must be issued within 30 days of the hearing;

d) beneficiary coverage of services in place before the insurer's or health plan's initial adverse decision shall continue pending a hearing decision when requested by the beneficiary, unless the continuation would be harmful to the beneficiary as documented in writing by the treating physician;

e) beneficiaries shall have the right to present favorable evidence, including out-of-plan second opinions in cases challenging plans' service denials, the right to review and present information from their medical records, and the right to compel the attendance at hearings of decision-makers whose actions are under challenge;

f) hearing officers shall have a duty to assist claimants in developing the factual record, including ordering out-of-plan second opinions.

o   Judicial review shall be available in state or federal court in cases involving at least a specified threshold amount of charges, including the aggregation of claims to meet the threshold amount. Such threshold requirements can be waived for low-income persons at the discretion of the courts. Relief for prevailing consumer-claimants should include reasonable costs and fees.

o   A Private Right of Enforcement shall be available to plan enrollees to maintain an action for damages and for any other relief, including injunctive and declaratory relief, for acts or omissions of a Health Plan, Health Alliance, State, or Federal Government which deprive such an enrollee of any right or benefit created or established to implement the provisions of the Act.

o   Penalties should be set by a national health board for plans and alliances that do not meet appeal rights standards and time-lines.

2.   Grievance Process. A grievance procedure shall be established within each health plan for the resolution of complaints of individuals about problems other than denial, reduction, or termination of service or payment, including, but not limited

to, delays in scheduling appointments, rude or undignified treatment at health plan facilities, the physical conditions of facilities, or enrollment and disenrollment disputes. The components of the grievance process are as follows --

> o   The right to complain orally or in writing to a
>   Patient Advocate or other independent ombudsman who
>   shall investigate the facts, seek to resolve the
>   problem in a way suitable to the patient, and
>   prepare a written report for the individual and for
>   the plan within 15 days.
>
> o   The right to have the complaint referred to a
>   Grievance Committee of the health plan that will
>   recommend action in response to the complaint and
>   report to the individual and to the plan within 30
>   days.
>
> o   The right to have still unresolved grievances
>   reviewed by Health Alliances or other independent
>   monitoring entities authorized to investigate and
>   respond with a full range of sanctions including
>   corrective action, civil monetary penalties, and
>   termination of health plan status.
>
> o   Penalties should be set by the national health
>   board for plans and alliances that do not meet
>   grievance procedure standards and time-lines.

C.   **Health Plan Governance.** Individual health plan beneficiaries shall have the right to substantial and meaningful participation as consumers of care in all levels of governance and decision-making in the operation of health plans, health alliances, and state and federal oversight organizations.

D.   **Protection of Existing Rights.** Rights afforded under any Federal health reform plan should not invalidate or limit any other federal or state law or any law of any political subdivision of any state that provides greater protection for the rights of beneficiaries under health plans.

E.   **Alternative Dispute Resolution (ADR), Including Mediation.** The use of ADR under appropriately defined circumstances can augment an appeals process. We stress, however, that ADR is not effective in situations where the only solution is "yes" or no," or in a determination of which side wins.[1] Disputes

---

[1].   See, L. Singer, M. Lewis, A. Houseman, E. Singer, "Alternative Dispute Resolution and the Poor Part II: Dealing with Problems in Using ADR and Choosing a Process, " 26 Clearinghouse Review 288, 290 (July 1992).

over whether a particular service is covered under the plan,
whether a participant meets the eligibility criteria for
particular services (such as long-term care or home health
services) would not be appropriate for ADR.

There is also a concern about the unequal bargaining power of
the parties to ADR and that ADR not become a vehicle for
delay. Plans are likely to control the review forum, its
location and setting, as well as medical and other information
relevant to decision-making. In addition, ADR can have the
harmful affect of deflecting consumer energy -- making them
give up -- and in the process, consuming time and financial
resources that could be used more appropriately.

ADR works where multiple outcomes are possible, where the
parties want to maintain an on-going relationship, and where
the parties want to help develop a settlement. Grievances
concerning service, such as long waits, difficulties in
getting appointments, rudeness and undignified treatment, may
lend themselves to ADR.

II. STATUTORY DUE PROCESS PRINCIPLES AND PRECEDENTS

The Medicare and Medicaid programs[2] have served as the primary
laboratories of experience in shaping due process rights in
government sponsored health care programs. Because Medicare has
followed a social insurance model, it offers a useful analog to the
types of national health plans under consideration. In 1982, the
Congress changed the structure of Medicare payments to allow and
encourage Health Maintenance Organizations (HMOs) to enroll
Medicare beneficiaries. HMOs receive a monthly capitated at-risk
payment for each Medicare enrollee. By 1992, Medicare enrollment
in HMOs had climbed to about 1.5 million persons, or about three
(3) percent of total Medicare enrollees.[3] This growing segment of
the Medicare program represents an even closer analog to the models
of managed competition being considered for national health reform.

The Medicaid program likewise provides a useful analog,
although in a different respect. Medicaid represents a
Federal/State collaborative program with substantial state control

---

[2].   42 U.S.C. §1395 et seq. (Medicare); 42 U.S.C. 1396 et
seq. (Medicaid). Medicare eligibility is not based on an
applicant's financial status. See, 42 U.S.C. §1395c. Eligibility
for Medicaid, however, is based on state income and resource
requirements and status, i.e., disability. 42 U.S.C §1396a.

[3].   Nancy De Lew, et al., "Special Report: A Layman's Guide
to the U.S. Health Care System," 14 Health Care Financing Review
151, 162 (Fall 1992).

over specifics of the program within federal standards. The principle of Federal/State collaboration and State flexibility are characteristic of national health reform proposals to date.

Finally, the Employee Retirement Income Security Act (ERISA) establishes federal statutory protections for participants in private employer-sponsored group health plans.[4] Due process rights under ERISA are not as extensive as the rights under Medicare and Medicaid. National health reform proposal based on the current model of employer-provided health insurance may, however, look to ERISA as the underpinning for its due process provisions.

A. Medicare Hearing Rights

With respect to denials, terminations, or reductions of services, due process for Medicare beneficiaries has been approached primarily from a constitutional protection model as outlined originally in the 1970 Supreme Court case, Goldberg v. Kelly.[5] In Goldberg, the opportunity to be heard is identified as the fundamental requisite of due process.[6] Due process is further defined as including the right to adequate notice;[7] to appear personally (with or without counsel) before an impartial decision maker; to present evidence; and to confront or cross-examine adverse witnesses.[8] Courts have recognized at least three public policy interests that favor due process hearings to mediate claims and disputes with respect to entitlements: "the desire for accuracy, the need for accountability, and the necessity for a decision making procedure which is perceived as "fair" by the citizens."[9]

Due process principles also underlie the concept of

---

[4]. The primary focus of ERISA is on pension plans. However, its disclosure and fiduciary duty rules, as well as its causes of action, are applicable to all employee benefit plans, including health plans.

[5]. Goldberg v. Kelly, 397 U.S. 254 (1970).

[6]. Id., at 267.

[7]. David v. Heckler, 591 F. Supp. 1033 (E.D.N.Y. 1984).

[8]. Id., at 268-69. See also, Bowen v. Michigan Academy of Family Physicians, 476 U.S. 667 (1986); Kraemer v. Heckler, 737 F.2d 214 (2nd Cir. 1984).

[9]. Gray Panthers v. Schweiker, 652 F.2d 146, 161-162 (D.C.Cir. 1986) (Gray Panthers I). The court reiterated this position in Gray Panthers II, 716 F.2d 23 (D.C.Cir. 1993), at 28.

pre-termination review. As the Court noted in Goldberg, "termination of aid pending resolution of a controversy over eligibility may deprive an eligible recipient of the very means by which to live while he waits."[10] Unfortunately, with respect to the Medicare program, pre-termination review as a legal concept is not uniformly developed. Pre-termination review, however, has been recognized to some extent in the areas of Medicare covered home health, and skilled nursing facility (SNF) care, and hospital care.[11] Even there, the precise nature and scope of pre-termination review is not established.

The Supreme Court, in Morrissey v. Brewer, noted, "[D]ue process is flexible and calls for such procedural protections as the particular situation demands."[12] In Matthews v. Eldridge, the Supreme Court established a three-pronged balancing test for evaluating whether a hearing procedure meets due process standards for Social Security Act cases:

> First, the private interest that will be affected by the official action; second, the risk of an erroneous deprivation of such interest through the procedures used, and the probable value, if any, of additional or substitute procedural safeguards; and finally, the Government's interest, including the function involved and the fiscal and administrative burdens that the additional or substitute procedural requirement would entail.[13]

Medicare hearing rights are codified at 42 U.S.C. §1395ff. The Hearing is to provide the same procedural rights as provided to Social Security Title II beneficiaries. 42 U.S.C. §1395ff(b)(1). Title II hearing rights, including review in the federal district courts, codified at 42 U.S.C. §405(b)-(g), require reasonable

---

[10]. 397 U.S. at 264.

[11]. See, Martinez v. Sullivan, 874 F.2d 751 (10th Cir. 1989); Kraemer v. Heckler, 737 F.2d 214 (2d Cir. 1984); Martinez v. Richardson, 472 F.2d 1121 (10th Cir. 1972); Martinez v. Bowen, 655 F. Supp. 95 (D.N.M. 1986). See also, Sarrassat v. Sullivan, (N.D. Calif. 1989) [1990] Medicare and Medicaid Guide, ¶38,504)(Skilled nursing facilities must use uniform denial notices to inform residents of their right to request facilities to submit claims to the intermediary for initial decision. The notice must also state that a facility cannot bill the resident until the intermediary makes a formal determination).

[12]. Morrissey v. Brewer, 408 U.S. 471, 481.

[13]. Matthews v. Eldridge, 424 U.S. 319, 334-35.

notice and opportunity for a hearing. These hearings are non-adversarial.[14] Attorneys fees are available pursuant to 42 U.S.C §405(g) and through the Equal Access to Justice Act (EAJA), 42 U.S.C. §2412 et seq., (federal district court review).

Medicare beneficiary hearing and appeals rights are urther defined in 42 C.F.R. §405, Subpart G (Reconsiderations and ppeals Under Medicare Part A); 42 C.F.R. §473, Subpart B (Peer Review Organizations Reconsiderations and Appeals); 42 C.F.R §405, Subpart H (Review and Hearing Under the Supplementary iedical Insurance Program -- Part B); 42 C.F.R. §417, Subpart C HMO/CMP Beneficiary Appeals). While these appeals procedure: /ary in specifics, they all include, at a minimum: (1) an init:.. review and/or "reconsideration" by the original decision-making entity or someone else; (2) review in the form of a hearing before an independent hearing officer; and (3) recourse to the judicial system if a threshold amount of money remains in controversy. Medicare beneficiaries who have been successful in judicial appeals can recover their attorneys' fees under two provisions of the law.[13]

Circumstances requiring expedited appeals are illustrated by the Peer Review Organization (or PRO) hearing procedures. These apply, for example, when a Medicare beneficiary is a hospital inpatient and the doctor and hospital agree that the patient should be discharged. If the patient requests PRO review before noon of the first working day after the denial notice was delivered to the inpatient, then the hospital must provide the patient's record to the PRO by the close of that first working day. The PRO must issue a review decision within one full working day after the date the PRO received the review request and the records. In such cases, the hospital may not charge the patient for any charges incurred before noon of the day following the day on which the PRO review decision is received by the patient. If the patient is still dissatisfied with the decision, the regular process of reconsideration, hearing, and judicial review remain available.

Due process rights have been the subject of beneficiary litigation involving HMOs. For example, Medicare beneficiaries who use HMOs have claimed that they have been denied due process because HMO appeals procedures were not clearly defined and made known to them. Problems have included the lack of notice or a clearly defined procedure for review (including timely review by the HMO and access to external review such as Administrative Law

---

[14]. See, e.g., Richardson v. Perales, 402 U.S. ?89, 403 (1971).

[13]. 42 U.S.C. §405(g) (concerning judicial review of the Secretary's decisions under the Social Security Act); and the Equal Access to Justice Act, 28 U.S.C. §2412.

Judge and court review).[14] Empirical studies of Medicare HMO operations by the General Accounting Office and Medicare advocacy groups have confirmed the existence of substantial problems in claims approval and payment, processing beneficiary appeals, and quality assurance systems.[15]

Experience with statutory changes in Medicare Part B appeals highlights the need for Congress to act with clarity in writing review and adjudicatory rights into statutes. In extending Part B benefits to Medicare beneficiaries in the Omnibus Budget Reconciliation Act of 1986, Congress did not make explicit the procedural steps leading to administrative law judge review.[16] This resulted in additional layers of claims review and considerable delays in obtaining relief for beneficiaries. The experience further led to Congressional studies of the problems created and to protracted litigation.[17]

B.   Medicaid Hearing Rights

Medicaid hearing rights are found in federal law at 42 U.S.C. §1396a(a)(3) and in the regulations at 42 C.F.R. §431, Subpart E, as mandated by Goldberg v. Kelly and its progeny.[18] They include an opportunity for an appeal of any action or inaction harmful to the Medicaid beneficiary. Notice and hearing protections are triggered by a broad range of adverse actions, including denials of

---

[14].   See, e.g., Levy v. Sullivan, (C.D. Calif. 1989) [1989-2] Medicare and Medicaid Guide ¶37,809 (Settlement calling for the processing of HMO reconsideration requests pursuant to a 30-day timeliness standard and the issuance of a new HMO manual setting out a 30-60 day standard for the HMO stage of reconsideration decision-making.)

[15].   General Accounting Office, HCFA Needs to Take Stronger Actions Against HMOs Violating Federal Standards, HRD-92-11 (November 12, 1991); Medicare Advocacy Project, Inc., Medicare Risk-Contract HMOs in California: A Study of Marketing, Quality, and Due Process Rights (January 1993); E. Hallowell, Challenging the HMO System of Incentives. Philadelphia Inquirer, (March 28, 1989).

[16].   Omnibus Budget Reconciliation Act of 1986, §9341, codified at 42 U.S.C. §1395ff

[17].   See, Isaacs v. Bowen, 865 F.2d 468 (2nd Cir. 1989); Abbey v. Sullivan, 785 F.Supp. 165 (S.D. N.Y. 1992).

[18].   Goldberg, supra note 2.

eligibility [19] or services;[20] claim denials for "technical reasons," such as form errors;[21] and imposition of copayments.[22] Related rights include the requirements that the agency issue and publicize its hearing procedures; that applicants and recipients receive notice of an adverse agency action, generally in advance of the action (with aid and services continued pending the appeal); and that applicants and recipients have the right to see case files, to review documents used by the state, to present witnesses, to cross-examine adverse witnesses, and to receive a decision on the record within a specified time.

Medicaid recipients must receive notice from the Medicaid agency of provider claims that have been denied. The agency must provide recipients with written certification that they are not liable for denied claims,[23] and recipients are entitled to limited notice and hearing rights regarding denied provider claims.[24]

Under Medicaid, consumers may sue in federal court to vindicate their rights, without jurisdictional dollar minimums.[25] Attorneys' fees and experts' fees are available to consumers who prevail.[26] Jurisdiction is also available in many state courts.[27]

---

[19]. See, e.g., Phillips v. Noot, 728 F.2d 1175 (8th Cir. 1984).

[20]. See, e.g., Eder v. Beal, 609 F.2d 1175 (8th Cir. 1984).

[21]. See, e.g., Easley v. Arkansas Dep't of Human Services, 645 F. Supp. 1535 (E.D. Ark. 1986).

[22]. See, e.g., Claus v. Smith, 519 F. Supp. 829 (N.D. Ind. 1981); Becker v. Blum, 464 F. Supp. 152, 155-57, 156-57 n. 5 (S.D.N.Y. 1978).

[23]. Easley v. Arkansas Depart. of Human Services, 645 F. Supp. 1535 (E.D. Ark. 1986).

[24]. Daniels v. Tennessee Depart of Health and Environment, (M.D. Tenn. 1985)[1985] Medicare and Medicaid Guide, ¶34,562.

[25]. 42 U.S.C. §1988; and see also, Suter v. Artist M., 112 S.Ct. 1360, 60 U.S.L.W. 4251 (March 25, 1992), raising questions about the standing of consumers under current law.

[26]. 42 U.S.C. §1988.

[27]. One example of a discrete issue in the Medicaid program is Medicaid estate recoveries. Numerous state court decisions have shaped the development of this law. See, e.g., Estate of Burke, 443 N.Y.S.2d 1003, 111 Misc. 2d 196 (N.Y. Surr. Ct. 1981), aff'd,

C. **ERISA Consumer Experience**

ERISA was enacted to safeguard the rights of workers and beneficiaries in employee benefit plans, including employer provider health insurance. Nonetheless, the protections available under ERISA are much less extensive than those available under Medicare and Medicaid. In fact, in some instances the limited appeals provisions of ERISA actually cause harm to individuals.

ERISA explicitly provides that "disclosure be made and safeguards be provided with respect to the establishment, operation, and administration of [employee benefit] plans."[28] The disclosure provisions are especially important for participants and beneficiaries in employer-sponsored group health plans. The required disclosure documents explain eligibility to participate in health plans, coverage amounts, co-payments and deductibles, and describe grievance and appeal rights. Congress felt so strongly about the need to provide information to participants and beneficiaries that it established a cause of action and penalty for plan administrators who fail to comply with a request for documents within thirty days.[29]

In addition to the disclosure requirements, ERISA and its implementing regulations and case law establish a notice and review process for any participant or beneficiary whose claim for benefits has been denied.[30] Adequate written notice must be provided in language calculated to be understood. The notice must contain the specific reasons for the denial, reference to the health plan provisions upon which the denial is based, a description of any additional information needed to perfect the claim and the reasons why the information is necessary, and an explanation of the steps for submitting the claim for review.[31]

Failure to comply with the notice provisions can result in liability to the health plan. Thus, a health maintenance organization whose notice did not adequately inform the participant of the reasons for denial of coverage and of the need to obtain a second opinion was required to reimburse the participant for the

---

57 N.Y.S.2d 382, 456 N.Y.S.2d 716 (1982); In re Estate of Hanson, 451 N.W.2d 364 (Minn. Ct. App. 1990); Shelton v. Fresno Community Hosp., 174 Cal. App. 3d 39, 219 Cal. Rptr. 722 (1985).

[28]. 29 U.S.C. §1001(a).

[29]. 29 U.S.C. §§1132(a)(1)(A), (c).

[30]. 29 U.S.C. §1133.

[31]. 29 C.F.R. §2560.503-1(f).

medical expenses he incurred.[32] A plan whose denial notice was not specific enough about reasons for the denial of benefits and about the appeals process could not claim that the participant's appeal was untimely filed, and was required to pay the participant's attorneys fees.[33]

Participants whose claims have been denied must be given a reasonable opportunity for a "full and fair review by the appropriate named fiduciary of the decision denying the claim."[34] Although ERISA does not require claimants to pursue remedies through the plan's internal appeals procedure, courts have established a federal common law requirement that participants exhaust plan remedies before going to court.[35] An exception may be made and exhaustion not required in cases where serious procedural violations are shown or where exhaustion would be futile.[36]

Each health plan must establish a time period during which a claimant may file a request for review of a denied claim. Department of Labor regulations require that decisions on review be made "promptly," generally within 60 days. Plans may extend the time period for response to 120 days after receipt of the request for review if there are special circumstances, such as the need to hold a hearing or to wait for a meeting of the board of trustees. A request for review that is not acted upon within 120 days is deemed to be denied, and the claimant may seek judicial review.[37]

Participants and beneficiaries have hurt by the restrictions in the ERISA claims procedure. Unfortunately, many plans do not comply with the regulatory time frames, and some do not respond to requests for review. Claimants who have received inadequate notice concerning the appeals procedure have literally spent years waiting for the plan to act on their appeals.

---

[32]. Bellanger v. Health Plan of Nevada, 814 F.Supp. 918 (D.Nev. 1993).

[33]. White v. Jacobs Engineering Group, 896 F.2d 334 (9th Cir. 1989).

[34]. 29 U.S.C. §1133(2).

[35]. See, e.g., Amato v. Bernard, 618 F.2d 559 (9th Cir. 1980).

[36]. See, e.g., Schwartz v. Interfaith Medical Center, 715 F.Supp. 1190 (E.D.N.Y. 1989); Gavalik v. Continental Can Co., 812 F.2d 834 (3d Cir. 1987).

[37]. 29 C.F.R. §2560.530-1.

The Department of Labor regulatory time frame also is problematic. A health plan participant can be made to wait four months for a decision whether a plan will cover needed medical treatment, thus delaying the treatment or the payment of expenses already incurred. There is no provision for expedited review in emergency situations; the most that the claimant can hope for is that a court will agree to waive the exhaustion requirement. Finally, too many plans view the claims procedure as a rubber stamp of the initial determination. There may be no independent evaluation of the dispute; the review is performed by the same person who made the initial determination.

Unlike Medicaid, and unlike Medicare to a certain extent, there is no right under ERISA to pre-termination review. Coverage under a private employer-sponsored group health plan is not an entitlement. Nothing in ERISA requires employers to offer health insurance to their employees and retirees, or to continue providing benefits at a constant level of coverage. Rather, ERISA gives employers and plan sponsors flexibility to create, alter, or terminate a health plan. Courts have cited the voluntary nature of ERISA health plans in upholding the right of plan sponsors to reduce coverage for a specific illness such as AIDS.[38] If, however, an employer has promised employees or retirees a specific level of benefits or benefits for a specific amount of time, courts may under a contract analysis require the employer to provide the health benefits that were promised.[39] While the court case is pending, however, the claimant is not entitled to the medical benefits in question.

An on-going case exemplifies the difficulties with ERISA. An insurance company notified a beneficiary, who uses both a gastrostomy tube and a jejunal tube, that it would no longer cover the nursing services he requires in order to reside at home. Coverage will terminate before the ERISA appeals process is complete, and there is no requirement that benefits continue pending appeal. Thus, even if the beneficiary receives a favorable decision from the claims process, his condition may deteriorate so much during the period in which his nursing needs are not covered that he will be forced into a nursing home anyway.

III. CONSTITUTIONAL UNDERPINNINGS OF HEALTH CARE ACCESS AND DUE PROCESS

A review of the constitutional underpinnings of health care access starts with the question of whether a "fundamental right" to

---

[38]. McGann v. H & H Music, 946 F.2d 401 (5th Cir. 1991); Owens v. Storehouse, 984 F.2d 394 (11th Cir. 1993).

[39]. See, e.g., International Union v. Yardman, 716 F.2d 1476 (6th Cir. 1983); Owens v. Storehouse, supra at 398.

health care exists in this country. This question is at the heart of constitutional equal protection analysis. As will be shown below, the absence of a firm positive answer to the fundamental right/equal protection question shifts the epicenter of constitutional analysis to the principles of procedural due process under the Fifth and Fourteenth Amendments.

A. A "Fundamental Right" To Health Care?

Legal commentators have frequently acknowledged the sad fact that the United States Constitution neither mandates nor creates a general or universally applicable "fundamental" right to health care.[40] Such a right has been recognized only in circumstances involving incarceration or commitment. For example, courts have reasoned that to put someone in prison where he or she is stripped of the ability to have access to care, and subsequently not to provide care, can result in "cruel and unusual" punishment which the Eighth Amendment prohibits. Inmates, therefore, have a right to care, and correctional officials have a duty to provide care that does not manifest a "deliberate indifference to the serious medical needs" of inmates.[41] Similarly, persons with mental retardation who are involuntarily committed possess a constitutional right to liberty, which includes rights to adequate food, shelter, clothing, and medical care:

> When a person is institutionalized-- and wholly dependent on the State[,] ... a duty to provide certain services and care does exit.[42]

The Supreme Court has refrained from explicitly recognizing a general right to treatment for all institutionalized persons. However, numerous lower courts and state legislatures have formalized this basic entitlement.[43] For the public at large, however, the lack of a recognized fundamental right to health care virtually eliminates a key constitutional avenue in advocacy for health care-- that of "equal protection."

---

[40]. See, e.g., Nancy N. Dubler & Charles P. Sabatino, "Age-Based Rationing and the Law: An Exploration," in Too Old For Health Care? - Controversies in Medicine, Law, Economics, and Ethics (Robert H. Binstock & Stephen G. Post eds., 1991).

[41]. Estelle v. Gamble, 429. U.S. 97,106 (1976).

[42]. Youngberg v. Romero, 457 U.S. 307, 317 (1982); see also, DeShaney v. Winnebago County Department of Social Services, 109 489 U.S. 189 (1989).

[43]. Barbara A. Weiner, "Treatment Rights," in The Mentally Disabled and the Law (S.J. Brakel, J. Parry, & B.A. Weiner, 1985).

B. **Equal Protection Analysis**

The Fourteenth Amendment provides that "no State shall ... deny to any person within its jurisdiction the equal protection of the laws." While this clause is not applicable to the federal government, it has been held that most acts by the federal government that would deny equal protection constitute a "deprivation of liberty" within the Fifth Amendment's due process clause.[44]

Generally, equal protection analysis has been used to determine the validity of classifications used in legislation. Most legislation imposes responsibilities on, or grants or denies benefits to, some classes of people-- whether they be taxpayers, parents, sport fishermen, pickle producers, employees, older persons, low income persons, high income persons, able bodied persons, or persons with disabilities. Normally, any such classifications will be upheld by the courts if "rationally related" to a proper state interest.[45] This test is highly deferential to legislative discretion. However, a higher standard -- a "strict scrutiny" test -- will apply if either of two conditions are met: (a) the legislative classification interferes with the exercise of a fundamental right, or (b) the classification operates to the particular disadvantage of a "suspect class".[46] Under this more rigorous test, a classification will be held to violate equal protection unless found to be necessary to promote a "compelling" state interest. Challenges to legislative classifications have a relatively high likelihood of success under the strict scrutiny test. While some justices have argued regularly for intermediate versions of this test, the dichotomous approach remains the official analytic approach of the Supreme Court. A right of the public at large cannot, of course, rely on a "suspect class" claim. Consequently, the non-recognition of a fundamental right to health care extinguishes viable constitutional claims based on equal protection.

Despite the lack of a general and legally enforceable right to health care in the United States, there may be some notion of a "right to life-sustaining care," based, paradoxically, on two growing bodies of cases: one establishing the right to refuse

---

[44]. _Bolling v. Sharpe_, 347 U.S. 497 (1954).

[45]. Ronald D. Rotunda, _et al._, 2 _Treatise on Constitutional Law: Substantive and Procedure_, (1986).

[46]. _See_, _e.g._, _Massachusetts Board of Retirement v. Murgia_, 427 U.S. 307, 312 (1976).

life-sustaining treatment or a so-called "right to die,"[47] and the
other addressing the concept of a "right to life," first
popularized in the abortion debate. These lines of cases
acknowledge a state's "interest in the protection and preservation
of human life" in the case of treatment refusals,[48] and the state's
"interest in protecting potential human life" in the abortion
cases.[49] The policy consequences of these two lines of cases have
led some commentators to conclude, wryly, that the federal
government is interested in children "from conception to birth" and
in adults "from sickness to death," but only if life itself is
imperiled.

Unfortunately, even within these limited contexts, the
existence of a state interest in protecting and preserving human
life has not led to the recognition of a fundamental constitutional
right to life-sustaining health care. Therefore, equal protection
analysis in this context ultimately fails. Instead, these cases
focus on an analytically different but related constitutional
principle, that of procedural "due process" under the Fifth and
Fourteenth Amendments.

C.   **Procedural Due Process Analysis - The Constitutional
     Cornerstone**

Applied to the federal and state governments, respectively,
the Fifth and Fourteenth Amendments mandate that no person shall be
deprived "of life, liberty, or property, without due process of
law." As stated earlier, equal protection analysis is used to
determine   the   constitutional   validity   of   legislative
classifications. In contrast, due process analysis is most
relevant in adjudicating alleged deprivations of existing property
or liberty interests. Of key importance is the fact that the
existing liberty or property interests do not have to be
constitutionally created. They may be rights created by statute or
those recognized in the common law.

The due process clause is essentially a "limitation on the

---

[47].   The line of cases starting with In re Quinlan, 355 A.2d
64, 70 N.J. 10 (1976), cert. denied, 454 U.S. 858 (1976) eventually
led to the U.S. Supreme Court's first decision on the right to
refuse life-sustaining treatment in Cruzan v. Director, Missouri
Department of Health, 497 U.S. 261 (1990).

[48].   Cruzan, supra note 47, at 261.

[49].   Webster v. Missouri, 492 U.S. 490, 519 (1989).

State's power to act."[50] It was intended to secure the individual
from the arbitrary exercise of the powers of government and to
prevent "unwarranted government interference,"[51] but it does not
create an affirmative general obligation upon the government to
provide any particular form of aid. The Supreme Court has been
quite clear on this point, particularly in abortion cases, most
recently reaffirming this proposition in Webster v. Missouri where
it stated:

> ...the Due Process Clauses generally confer no
> affirmative right to government aid, even where such aid
> may be necessary to secure life, liberty or property
> interests of which the government may not deprive the
> individual.[52]

The Court applied similar reasoning in a case contemporaneous
to Webster, holding that the due process clause imposed no duty on
the state of Wisconsin to provide adequate child protective
services.[53]

Even though the due process clause provides no affirmative
assurance of health care access, its procedural implications are,
nevertheless, extremely significant for any national system of
health care in two respects. First, to the extent that health
reform legislation creates or controls statutory entitlements to
benefits, procedural due process protections against deprivations
of these benefits will apply. Statutory entitlement to a benefit
is a property interest to which due process rights attach.[54] For
example, state statutes establishing Medicaid and other indigent

---

[50]. DeShaney v. Winnebago County Department of Social
Services, 489 U.S. 189, 195 (1989).

[51]. Id., at 196; see also, Parratt v.Taylor, 451 U.S. 527,
549 (1981).

[52]. Webster, supra note 49, 492 U.S. at 507; see also,
Harris v. McRae, 448 U.S. 297, 316 (1980), in which the Court said:
"Regardless of whether the freedom of a woman to choose to
terminate her pregnancy for health reasons lies at the core or the
periphery of the due process liberty recognized in Roe v. Wade, 410
U.S. 113 (1973), it simply does not follow that a woman's freedom
of choice carries with it a constitutional entitlement to the
financial resources to avail herself of the full range of protected
choices."

[53]. DeShaney, supra note 50.

[54]. See, e. g., Atkins v. Parker, 472 U.S. 115 (1985); Logan
v. Zimmerman Brush Co., 455 U.S. 422 (1982).

care programs have been held to engender property interests protected under procedural due process.[55]

Second, any rationing of care under such a system will likewise be scrutinized under principles of due process, since rationing may be functionally equivalent to a deprivation for those groups adversely affected. The following sections examine the nature and extent of procedural protections that may be constitutionally necessary in any government mandated or sponsored universal health care system. The rationing of health care is not addressed in this paper.

IV. QUALITY ASSURANCE AND CONSUMER PROTECTION

The duty to provide an adequate level of quality in the provision of health care is deeply rooted both in common law principles of tort and contract and in manifold state and federal administrative laws regulating health care providers. For certain vulnerable populations, such as those involuntarily institutionalized, poor quality of care may also result in a deprivations of a patient's constitutional rights.[56]

All states license individual and institutional health care providers, setting standards for practice and services. States commonly set additional standards for state-funded health and long-term care services. On top of all this, Medicare and Medicaid set extensive standards, primarily through "conditions of participation," on all participating providers.[57]

The central role of the individual with respect to his or her own health care is rooted in the common law right of self determination. In the oft-quoted 1914 case of Schloendorff v. N.Y. Hospital, Justice Cardozo succinctly articulates this right:

> Every human being of adult years and sound mind has the right to determine what shall be done with his own body.[58]

---

[55]. See, e.g., Daniels v. Woodbury County, 742 F.2d 1128 (8th Cir. 1984); Griffeth v. Detrich, 603 F.2d 118 (9th Cir. 1979); Eder v. Beal, supra; Kimble v. Solomon, 599 F.2d 599 (4th Cir. 1979); Jones v. Blinziner, 536 F. Supp. 1189 (N.D. Ind. 1982).

[56]. Estelle v. Gamble, supra note 41; Youngberg v. Romero, supra note 42, 457 U.S. at 317.

[57]. See, generally, Medicare & Medicaid Guide, ¶12,305 (CCH).

[58]. Schloendorff v. Society of New York Hosp., 105 N.E. 92, 93 (N.Y. 1914).

The other common law root of consumer control arises from the common law offense of battery which made any offensive, unwanted touching an actionable wrong. From this common law action evolved the right of "informed consent" and the corollary right to refuse treatment. A constitutional basis for personal control over health decisions is now well established in a substantial line of cases from the 1976 Karen Ann Quinlan (recognizing a privacy interest)[59] decision to the Supreme Court's opinion in Cruzan v. Director, Missouri Department of Health (recognizing a liberty interest).[60]

From these foundations has developed a body of patient/client rights and protections concepts that have been articulated most extensively in the area of nursing home care pursuant to the 1987 nursing home reform amendments.[61] While the depth and breadth and detail of these rights is specific to a targeted, highly vulnerable group of patients, they are, nevertheless, instructive as a high water mark of patient/client rights and as an affirmation of basic consumer protection elements establishing: the right to notice and information necessary to make informed decisions; the right to protections against abuse; the right to complain through effective grievance mechanisms without fear of retaliation; and the right to personal preferences and privacy.

V.   The Administrative Procedures Act (APA) (5 U.S.C. §§554-557)

The formal adjudication sections of the APA apply to cases which by statute must be reviewed on the record after a hearing. While not directly applying to Medicare or Medicaid beneficiary appeals, these adjudicatory sections, consistent with constitutional norms of due process, provide the following:

1.   A clear statement (notice) of the right to a hearing. Generally, this includes a statement that a hearing is available, the applicable time periods for requesting the hearings, and the steps necessary to obtain that hearing. §554(b).

2.   An opportunity to participate in the hearing. This includes the right to be physically present at the hearing. §554(c).

---

[59].   In re Quinlan, 355 A.2d 647, cert. denied sub nom. Garger v. New Jersey, 429 U.S. 922 (1976).

[60].   Cruzan, supra note 47.

[61].   Omnibus Budget Reconciliation Act of 1987 (OBRA), Pub. L. No. 100-203, Title IV, Subtitle C, §§4201-4206, 4211-4216, 42 U.S.C. §§1395i-3(a)-(h), 1396r(a)-(h), Medicare and Medicaid, respectively.

3. **An opportunity to appear before an impartial hearing officer.** The hearing officer should be free to make an independent judgment of the facts at issue. §554(d) and 556(b).

4. **The right of parties to be represented by counsel at hearings.** Parties should be free to have either a lawyer or other representative present at hearings. §555(b)

5. **The right to present oral and written evidence and to conduct cross-examination.** This includes the right to see and examine all relevant documents prior to the hearing. §556(d).

6. **The right to submit proposed findings of fact, conclusions of law, or to note exceptions.** This includes the right of parties to submit oral and written legal arguments in support of their respective positions. §557(c).

7. **The right to a written record or transcript of the hearing.** This includes the right to have access to the transcript of the proceedings in a timely fashion and at affordable costs. §556(3).

Coalition for Consumer Protection and Quality in Health Care Reform

White Paper on Minimum Requirements for Consumer Information

Washington, D. C.
July 31, 1993

Introduction

Consumer information is an important dimension in any reform of the health care system, whether the reform is based on managed competition or a single payer system. Managed competition assumes that well-informed consumers will stimulate plans to provide high quality care at low costs. Under a single payer system, consumer information is important for much the same reason—information about practitioners and providers allows consumers to shop for the best care at reasonable prices. For this to happen, consumers must have access to comprehensive, uniform and comparable information. Under either type of reform, the data collected by the health plans must be verified on an ongoing basis by state entities independent of the health plans, health alliances or other purchasers of care.

A national entity such as a National Health Board should be responsible for 1) establishing uniform data formats, 2) setting standards for collecting and analyzing data and 3) distributing the data on the national, state and plan levels. It is essential that the data and information be accurate, reliable, comparable, timely, and easy-to-understand. It must also be available in different languages and formats for people with special challenges such as the visually or hearing impaired.

With the increase of data collection and dissemination through the electronic media, the protection of consumer confidentiality becomes increasingly important. National standards should be established to protect consumers from unauthorized disclosure of any personal and individually identifiable information.

We want to make it clear, however, that even good consumer . information will not eliminate the need for appropriate grievance and appeals procedures, internal and external quality assurance and external, independent quality oversight and monitoring of the health care system.

Summary

We believe that information available to consumers must be more than a "report card." A more appropriate description for what is needed is a "Consumer Guidebook" for plan selection and use. National standards should mandate what specific information will be provided in this guidebook, which should be readily available to every consumer.

The data should also be utilized to assist health care professionals in providing appropriate and effective care and to enable policy makers to fine tune the system to increase quality and reduce costs.

We envision four main categories of information:

1) plan-specific descriptions including general information about the health alliance, the health care system and where to get help

2) plan-specific quality report cards—quality indicators reflecting a common set of performance measures and enrollee satisfaction

3) provider and practitioner-specific descriptions to help discriminating consumers choose a plan based on the background of specific practitioners or services of a hospital

4) condition-specific provider and practitioner quality report cards to help guide the consumer to the best specialist or the best hospital for treatment of a specific condition.

1) Plan-Specific Description Information

If consumers are going to make informed choices, they need good understandable information describing plan configurations, how the health care delivery system works, how to use the consumer guide, how to appeal a health care decision, how to resolve complaints, and how to contact a health ombudsprogram or counseling program. Next, they will need to know the prices, benefits, and services of each plan option. The goal is to enable the consumer to compare health care plans in a given health alliance. The information should include descriptive and practical summaries presented in a comparative format.

Price, benefit and plan operation information could include:

Price Information for individuals and families:

- premiums, deductibles and co-payments
- cost or implications of using services outside the plan
- cost of coverage beyond the basic plan
- premium increase trend

Benefits, Plan Description and Policies:

- benefits covered
- services not covered by the plan
- time in operation
- membership size and percent in certain age groups
- number of practitioners and their areas of specialization
- ratio of membership to primary care physicians

- ratio of physician to non-physician primary care practitioners
- specialists available within the plan; outside the plan
- ratio of board certified physicians to non-board certified
- names of participating hospitals, home health agencies, laboratories, diagnostic facilities, pharmacies
- contractual relations between plans and providers
- plan policy regarding scheduling of routine annual physical exams, pre-natal visits, well-baby visits, immunizations
- plan policy regarding promptness of access for evaluation of symptoms
- plan policy regarding urgent care, hospitalization, length of hospital stays, specialist referrals, diagnostic procedures, mental health services, laboratory services, home health services, prescriptions
- plan policy regarding care management and long-term care
- plan policy regarding second and third opinions
- phone numbers for information specialists who can explain plan details

2)   Plan-Specific Quality Report Cards—quality indicators reflecting a common set of performance measures and enrollee satisfaction surveys

The "report card" or quality measures and consumer satisfaction section of the consumer guidebook should compare the plans, providers, and practitioners in a given health alliance and, when appropriate, provide national averages for comparison. Areas that should be covered include enrollee access to care, quality of care, appropriate use of medical care, utilization rates, and the effectiveness of specific treatments and patient outcomes by diagnosis or procedure. Information about where to get assistance in interpreting the information and data should be provided to the consumer.

Performance Measures

Use of a common set of performance measures will not only provide consumers with good decision-making information, it will also enable health plans and providers to identify the best practices. The national health board created to oversee the new health care system should also use the quality measures in the development and dissemination of clinical practice guidelines, the updating of the benefit packages, and the analysis of the cost-effectiveness of the health care provided.

It is expected that quality and its indicators will improve and evolve based on information from outcomes research. Required reporting of patient care encounters (presenting problem, diagnosis and treatment), and uniform patient identifiers to allow longitudinal records, should be considered. In addition, reporting of complications and hospital acquired injuries in the clinical record should be required. Clinical information will provide far more useful data than data extracted from billing codes (notably not available from managed care programs). Outcomes research studies should be conducted to evaluate patients' health status after specific treatments, including physiological measurements, functional status, and well-being/quality of life. This information should be made available to consumers, providers, and policy makers. These measures are essential for competition to succeed in improving and/or maintaining quality of health services.

The following types of information could be included in this section of the guidebook:

Preventive Care

Percentage of enrollees of certain age groups for whom appropriately timed preventive measures were provided or recommended, such as:

- health history interview and record
- annual physical and functional status assessment; urinalysis; blood hemoglobin, cholesterol (adult)
- childhood immunizations and boosters
- seniors: flu vaccination annually; pneumococcal vaccination one-time; boosters for tetanus and diphteria
- hepatitis b vaccine (for those with high exposure risk)
- tuberculosis screening
- colorectal screening
- mammogram screening
- gynecological exam and Pap smear annually (adult and/or sexually active females)
- prenatal care during 1st, 2nd, 3rd trimesters
- routine eye exams for seniors and diabetics

Indicators of undesired or unplanned occurrences, such as:

- inappropriate use of medications
- re-admissions within 30 days of post-surgery hospital discharge
- location-of-service acquired infections
- pressure ulcers occurring in patients confined to bed.
- injuries sustained at location-of-service: e.g., fractures, muscle contractures, harmful medication and treatment errors

Utilization of services related to service policy, such as:

- average time between first report of acute illness and examination
- average time between diagnosis and treatment of acute illness
- percent follow-up visit or phone call after acute illness

- average length of hospital stay: surgery, normal delivery, C-section, rehabilitation, mental health acute care
- number of referrals to specialists per primary practitioner
- number of referrals for diagnostic-procedures
- average time between diagnosis and various kinds of elective procedures

Consumer Satisfaction

A standard survey should be developed that will measure satisfaction among health plan participants. It could have some regional or otherwise appropriate individualized characteristics, but the main body of the survey should be consistent across the country so that it can be used for national comparisons. The survey should be short and clear and contain questions related to acceptability, availability and accessibility. It could include:

- overall satisfaction with care received
- degree to which questions were answered
- adequacy of treatment information
- did treatment alleviate symptoms
- convenience of location of doctors and hospitals
- number of specialists from which to choose
- number of primary care physicians from which to choose
- ease of obtaining desired referral
- degree to which plan follows through on referrals to medical services
- attitude of staff and of physician
- length of time between making appointment and visit for symptoms or for preventive care
- length of time "on hold" before getting through to the plan
- length of time spent in the waiting room
- length of time spent with practitioner
- length of time between diagnosis and treatment
- availability of advice over the phone
- excessive paperwork or bureaucratic hassles
- willingness to recommend this plan to a friend

It should be mentioned that the New England Medical Center, Health Institute has developed an "Employee Health Care Value Survey" as part of the Health Plan Employer Data and Information Set, HEDIS, which looks promising.

Membership statistics

Membership statistics can also be indicative of consumer satisfaction and should be listed:

- number of new enrollees and dis-enrollees per year
- number of enrollee complaints

3)   Provider and Practitioner-Specific Descriptive Information

Further details on plans and their health care professionals should be provided on a per request basis. For example, if a consumer is trying to decide between Plan A and Plan B, he or she may want to review the detailed plan descriptions, which would be written in a standardized format with the plan's unique features set apart from items that the plans must contain. Information such as fact sheets on each of the physicians in the plan, their training, years of practice, board certification, faculty responsibilities, and documented disciplinary actions, including repeated malpractice payments, should be provided in this documentation. Fact sheets about home health services, hospitals, laboratories and other contracted health facilities could also be developed. The health alliances or individual plans could supply this information under supervision and monitoring of the state quality assurance entity.

Hospitals

Types of services provided, bed capacity and nursing services staffing of each type of unit:

- emergency department
- intensive care unit
- cardiac care unit
- general medicine and specialty units
- rehabilitation therapies
- surgery general and specialties
- obstetrics: delivery room, birthing room, operative procedures
- newborn care: normal newborn and intensive care nurseries
- radiology treatment and diagnostic capacity
- laboratory
- social services and discharge planning

Home Health Services

- skilled nursing and rehabilitative care
- hospice care services
- personal care aides
- home care equipment (e.g. oxygen, suction, special beds)

Out-patient Services

- urgent care

- diagnostic and follow-up care
- pharmacy services
- laboratory services

Nursing home skilled care

- routine practitioner visits
- diagnostic services

4) **Condition-Specific Provider and Practitioner Report Cards including Enrollee Surveys**

Condition or treatment specific information is important to the person who faces a major operation or health care decision and should be available upon request. This information is different from the plan specific report card in that it includes both hospital and physician specific practice profiles and outcomes data on a particular procedure or condition.

For example, a consumer may want to know which hospital in the region (or the country) has the most experience in kidney transplants; which surgeon has the lowest mortality rate within that particular hospital or within a region; which hospital has the lowest mortality rate; which has the lowest post-surgery complication rates, and other factors. This is similar to what has been done for coronary artery bypass graft surgery in both Pennsylvania and New York. The information could be presented either on a nation-wide or a region-wide basis and could be available from the national health board or its designees. The data should be appropriately adjusted for severity to avoid skewing outcomes for surgeons and hospitals serving more vulnerable populations. Also, health counselors should be available for answering questions regarding this and other consumer information.

Information obtained through the enrollee satisfaction surveys which address condition-specific provider and practitioner quality and outcomes should also be available as part of this report card.

Confidentiality of Personal Information

With more emphasis on data collection and improved electronic data interchange, the risk of violating a person's right to privacy increases. Health care information often contains very personal information about physical and mental medical history, conditions and treatments.

The collection, storage, handling, and transmission of individually identifiable health care data should in no way infringe upon a person's right to privacy and to keep certain information confidential. National uniform standards should delineate very specifically what type of individually identifiable information may or may not be released without the person's authorization. Such standards should also delineate to whom confidential data may be released and for what purposes it may be used.

Conclusion

Consumer information must be developed with consumers' needs in mind and with active consumer participation. Information should be available in written, verbal and electronic forms, and in Braille and other languages to reach all populations. The success of health care reform is largely dependent on the ability of consumers to make wise choices and influence the quality and cost of health care. Therefore, the plan must provide the consumer with the necessary tools for good decision-making. Consumers need to know which provider offers the best services at the least costs, which practitioners have the most success with which treatments, and which hospitals are most likely to send the patient home without further complication. They also need protection against misuse of their personal records; and information about how to file complaints, appeal decisions or get outside assistance by a health ombudsprogram or counselor. This will require resources, but it will cost a small fraction of the cost of not implementing an effective health care monitoring and reporting system from the start. Good information and decisions alone will not ensure quality care. Quality assurance measures, grievance and appeals procedures, and independent, external entities must be in place to monitor quality and enforce standards.

Mr. CARDIN. I think this has been one of the most informative panels that we have had on health care reform, because if we cannot deal with quality issues, cannot make consumers more intelligent in the selection of health care providers or plans, then we are not going to succeed.

We need to develop ways in which we can judge the standard of outcome by providers and plans, and we don't have that today.

I was trying to reconcile your testimonies and had a little bit of difficulty because there is a problem as to how much should be established at the national level, how much should be delegated to the States in developing the standards and enforcing the standards. There seem to be some differences, at least among the panelists, as to how much should be spelled out and detailed in the national legislation, how much should be left for future developments through some boards or through delegation to the States. We haven't quite come to grips with this.

One or two questions I would like to get your comments on:

Practice guidelines today have been developed in several of the fields. I am curious as to your assessment as to what proportion of physicians currently use some form of practice guidelines and how effective that has been.

Dr. NASH. Mr. Chairman, our group has a large grant from the Federal Agency for Health Care Policy and Research in Washington to, in part, evaluate how we can use practice guidelines. If our hospital is any indication, I think practice guidelines are a step in the right direction, but we have a very long way to go to get doctors to pay attention to what are involved in the guidelines, how to implement them and then to see whether following the guidelines does, in fact, improve or make a difference in patient outcomes.

We support them and think there is a way to apply them, but we know very little about what motivates and helps to change patient behavior in use of the guidelines.

Mr. CARDIN. What are the obstacles?

Dr. NASH. There is always a distrust of expert opinion coming from very far away. There is a sense that all practice is really local in nature, and they may not understand the types of patients, the types of resources we have. There is the doctor's complaint that my patients are different than the ones displayed in the guidelines.

Dr. O'LEARY. I will add a brief, additional comment. I think that part of this problem helps define the issue of why you need to standardize your measurement system. You have lots of practice guidelines, but no mechanism for determining which are good or not good.

We have conflicting guidelines. There is no point at which we have defined which are the guidelines that we should be using, and until somebody steps forward——

Mr. CARDIN. Should they be national or should they be done by the States?

Dr. O'LEARY. Whether we are talking about organization-based standards, whether we are talking about performance measures, whether we are talking about practice guidelines, the Federal Government could play a useful role in standardizing the measurement system; and measurement itself should take place at the local level.

Mr. CARDIN. Practice guidelines would be established nationally, but enforced locally?

Dr. O'LEARY. Yes. There should be some mechanism for evaluating them and they can be adapted locally and used locally. I would say the same thing for standards and performance measures.

Ms. O'KANE. We have reviewed about 150 managed care organizations in the couple of years accreditation program has been in existence. One of our standards is that the organization adopts practice guidelines and encourages the providers to use them. We have seen them widely adopted in the area of preventive services and the area of pediatric care and in OB–GYN.

I think it reflects a fact that is the major obstacle, which is the lack of a science base for a lot we do in medical care. I think that is part of the reason for the attitude of physicians. There is a fear that practice guidelines will get ahead of the science and be used to contain costs.

There is an attitude of distrust in the provider community, partly because of the culture of medicine and independent practice, but partly perhaps justified by the idea that practice guidelines might be used to contain costs rather than enhance quality.

Mr. KERSCHNER. One twist: The consumer also needs to be educated about outcome measures and what outcomes. If we are talking about looking at an outcome-based system, we need to tell the consumer—I disagree with Mr. Thomas who said the only question consumers ask is, is insurance paying for it? Consumers ask, is my father going to walk again, is my child going to be viable again.

We need to educate, and the Federal Government needs to provide consumer education so the health care system is better understood by those using it.

Mr. CARDIN. I can understand practice guidelines being established on a national basis, but it seems to me it would be extremely difficult to develop standards on quality and outcome at a national level for the different plans that are going to be developed by the States.

Dr. NASH. There are what we call benchmarks or best performance measures that can be established at a national level, that we can strive and work toward in our various quality improvement programs. It is a difficult job, but there is lots of good activity happening around the country. So there are things we would like to compare ourselves to.

At a local level, there are certain places we want to be compared to and we want to achieve that particular level of outcome and performance. We are willing to put that information out publicly if it helps us and assists in improving quality and outcomes for our patients.

Mr. CARDIN. Dr. McDermott.

Mr. MCDERMOTT. Thank you, Mr. Chairman. I was listening to the testimony, and I thought of Tip O'Neill, who said that all politics is personal. It is interesting that there are only the chairman and a small number of members here to talk about quality, which is probably the toughest issue in all of health care reform. People who want to talk about malpractice and how to deal with that must come to grips with the difficulties of what we are doing here. There are two levels; one is the level of the practitioner.

I was a PSRO physician and pulled charts off lots of shelves in hospitals and looked at quality of care all over the State of Washington for a number of years. So I understand the issue at the professional level, but I also understand it at the consumer level.

With regards to the issue of report cards, there is a belief that somehow you can put a report card together that will help the consumer. When I go out to buy a refrigerator, I know it has to be 32 inches wide because it has to fit in a slot in my wall; and I want it to be self-defrosting, but I don't know much more beyond that.

My father had a stroke this week and he went to the university hospital. I have worked in university hospitals in a number of cities, and it is hard for me to imagine a report card that would ever explain to a consumer whether going to a university medical center was better than going to the fancy hospital up the street, because all the worst cases get sent to the university hospital and all their statistics are difficult to explain.

I would like to hear you talk about what kind of relevant information you think a report card could have that would be really useful to a consumer to decide, am I going to take the Aetna plan or the Blue Cross plan or the whatever plan. Since Blue Cross has all these hospitals, how do you decide? What do you put in there that isn't 5,000 pages thick?

Ms. O'KANE. Let me start. I think what we need to think about is a diverse strategy for providing information to consumers. We should not assume that there is a single type of consumer that we are trying to find and address their needs. There are many different types of consumers. Some will want more information on some things and others may want an overall opinion on whether this is a good health plan, a rating or something.

I think it ought to be viewed like a Russian doll where you can get a small amount of information or more if you want it. But it needs to be a process that is very open to the public and that gives information as you need it.

When you get into issues of tertiary care and trying to evaluate that, it is kind of a puzzle that you would want to know about the outcomes of the hospitals and have the severity systems to be able to give valid outcome data that accurately reflects performance of the organization rather than the population that it is serving.

So there are many difficult issues to sort out here, but I think it is very exciting to start down this road, because to date we haven't given the consumer much credit.

Mr. McDERMOTT. I agree that it has to be an open system. Does anybody else have ideas about what information——

Dr. O'LEARY. I agree. I think that all of us are in support of the concept of report cards, but are urging caution about the complexity of the task we are talking about.

I think you have put your finger on key issues. It is going to take time to put these things in place. You have a variety of dimensions of quality, ranging from efficacy to effectiveness, efficiency, timeliness, continuity; we can go on. There are also different tiers. You may be measuring a big health plan, its components or you may be looking at Dr. Jones and Dr. Smith and Dr. Brown, and the amount of information that you could present is huge. And all of that ignores what I thought was your basic question; and that is, how do you risk adjust or assure that data are comparable from one entity to another. We are talking about a very complex process.

I believe—and we have worked in this area as have others—it is becoming increasingly possible to do this from a technical standpoint. I think we need to be able to produce encyclopedic information for people who like encyclopedias and bottom line information saying, trust me, that this is the bottom line. If you don't trust me, there is an encyclopedia.

When will we be able to produce this? Maybe by the end of this century, realistically.

Ms. O'KANE. I don't think we should think about a little card. I think it should be an interactive system. Technology is going to enhance our ability to communicate.

Mr. MCDERMOTT. So my 88-year-old father will have to sit down——

Ms. O'KANE. We figure your 88-year-old father goes to you for advice. It may not be the patient that is actually the user of the information. There is usually someone in the family that is the broker.

Dr. NASH. In the Commonwealth of Pennsylvania, as you know, we have one of the leading data collection and dissemination efforts on outcomes for medical care in the country, in something we call the Health Care Cost Containment Council. I serve on a Statewide committee that helped put this thing together. We spent 4 years just trying to figure out how to create a report card for one procedure, open heart surgery, and tens of millions of taxpayer dollars. It is very complicated.

I agree with Dr. O'Leary, slow and steady is going to win this race. Not everybody wants to see a detailed report on open heart surgery on a physician-by-physician basis with severity adjustments. They want to know what hospital is closest to my home and is my primary care doctor connected with that hospital in anyway.

Mr. MCDERMOTT. That is on the consumer level, but on the professional level, I assume that you were asked to look at other bills. I understand the national peer review organization looked at H.R. 1200 and thinks that it is the best way to develop practice guidelines.

How long do you think it is going to be before we have a system of reports on more than just the simple issues, such as whether or not you should give immunization to children under the age of one, which are fairly single dimensional and you can do them very quickly? How about treating the ulcer or treating back pain? How long are we talking, in your mind, before we are able to develop practice guidelines that would be of any use whatsoever, either in malpractice situations or in cost containment to decide whether you have outliers or not.

If everybody that comes to me for back pain gets a back x ray and a handful of pills, and the next guy never uses a x ray, those outliers will be simple, but then you have to start looking at the nuances. How long is it going to take you to do that?

Dr. NASH. You have raised a critical issue, Congressman, and I think it is going to take quite some time. The good news is we are making progress on the issue you raised, low back pain. There is a Federal—effort out of AHCPR called the Patient Outcome Research Team. These projects are looking at the bread-and-butter, primary care issues—what we ought to be doing, what we ought not to be doing—and we have learned a lot which says that lower back spine films aren't worth anything.

It is going to take time, and I think you are hearing today that we have to make progress in all of these arenas in a parallel way; but we have to recognize that there is no easy answer to any of these issues, and we have to involve the profession, too. I can't help but think about many of my clinical colleagues that don't know anything about practice guidelines, and when they hear about them they are resistant to the whole notion and view it as a dangerous potential erosion of professional autonomy. I don't personally share that view, but I think we are up against an important cultural problem here as well as a technical one.

Dr. O'LEARY. I think you need to set the climate right.

Consistent with a comment I made earlier, some of this is not time dependent as it is on creating some mandate that we have a system for evaluating and proclaiming practice guidelines as good, as being scientifically based, et cetera, that is really more a matter of whether you sit down and say we are going to have the mechanism for doing this rather than letting it play out over time.

We have a problem of people getting the word. I made a presentation last year to a group of PRO medical directors, a couple of hundred people in the room and Jarrett Clinton made a presentation and asked the people who had seen the practice guidelines, which had been out for a couple of months, to hold up their hands. One physician held up his hand in the room.

Now, that should worry us. They hadn't seen it to know whether they agree with it or disagree with it. We have to think about mechanisms for information transmission and translation to the people who are going to use it.

Forget consumers for 1 minute; we have to talk about people who are practicing medicine.

Dr. NASH. One issue that I think you will hear something about this afternoon is, you know, I am already over the hill in a lot of respects in terms of my medical knowledge. What we really need to focus on, in my opinion, is the younger doctors that are coming up through the ranks in the medical education process.

As a teacher at a big medical school, I can tell you pretty confidently that we are not doing what we ought to be doing in this arena in terms of preparing physicians to practice in a world of consumer report cards, practice guidelines, standards, accreditation. The average well-meaning, well-educated, hard-working medical student, intern and resident has no idea what we are talking about today.

Mr. CARDIN. Let me thank the entire panel for their contribution. It is an area that we will be looking at your testimony and reading it carefully and working with you in order to develop the necessary guidelines nationally to bring this new component into health care reform. That will complete the testimony of this panel. Some of us need to be on the floor, but our Chairman is here, so we will continue the hearing.

Mr. CARDIN. The next panel consists of Dr. Ralph Snyderman, chancellor for health affairs, Duke University Medical Center, another one of my former constituents, Dr. Spencer Foreman, immediate past chair of the Association of American Medical Colleges, and president of the Montefiore Medical Center, Bronx, N.Y.; Suzanne M. El-Attar, M.D., American Medical Student Association legislative affairs director; Geraldine Bednash, Ph.D., R.N., and executive director of the American Association of Colleges of Nursing; and Olen E. Jones, Jr., Ph.D., chairman, Board of Governors, American Association of Colleges of Osteopathic Medicine, and president of the West Virginia School of Osteopathic Medicine in Lewisburg, W. Va.

I regret that I need to leave the hearing. I will turn the chair back to our distinguished chairman.

Chairman STARK [presiding]. Please proceed.

STATEMENT OF RALPH SNYDERMAN, M.D., CHANCELLOR FOR HEALTH AFFAIRS, AND DEAN, SCHOOL OF MEDICINE, DUKE UNIVERSITY MEDICAL CENTER, DURHAM, N.C.

Dr. SNYDERMAN. Good morning, Mr. Chairman and distinguished members of this committee. My name is Ralph Snyderman; I am the chancellor for health affairs and dean of the School of Medicine at Duke University. I am pleased to offer my perspective on the future of medical education in the context of health care reform.

In 1924, James B. Duke directed that part of his resources be used to create Duke University Medical Center to provide health care for the citizens of rural North and South Carolina. While the urban area around Duke has developed rapidly, our service region is still largely rural, and Mr. Duke's challenge remains a key component of our mission.

As chancellor, I am responsible for the operations of a thousand-bed hospital, the training of 900 residents, the operations of a complete clinical service, and one of the Nation's largest medical research institutions. As dean, I am responsible for the training of 400 future physicians and a graduate school of nursing. From this perspective, I would like to offer a few observations.

The health care delivery system must be reformed to assure all citizens access to the highest quality of health care at an affordable price. To achieve this, we must alter health care financing; we must produce a health services workforce trained to provide cost-effective health care; we must affirm support for biomedical and clinical research; and we must expand the utilization of preventive and value-oriented care. We and all other academic health centers are committed to this.

To provide more generalists, we are instituting a new curriculum to develop leaders in generalist medical practice. We are training nurse practitioners and physicians' assistants to enhance the corps of nonphysician primary care providers. Medical students are being taught the concepts of cost-effectiveness and how to work with other providers to form effective health care teams.

We have recently formed the Duke Health Network, which integrates community physicians throughout our region as full members of our health system, working closely with students and faculty. We will expand these programs in even more creative ways, but to do this—and this is the major point of my message—we must continue to receive a level of funding for medical education that is at least equivalent to the current system.

Even after substantial cost reductions, academic health centers will still have higher intrinsic operating costs than other providers whose sole mission is to provide patient care. In addition to our role in education, which materially adds to our cost, the citizens of this Nation have come to expect academic health centers to provide a full range of complex services not always available elsewhere. Moreover, these services are available 24 hours a day, 365 days a year.

Academic health centers are currently funded for these additional services through a public private partnership rather than by Medicare supplements alone. Virtually every academic health center is bringing its resources and creative energies to the task of successful reform of our health care system. However, I want to assure you that without the continuation of the current level of funding of the academic health center, the Nation's goals for continued improvements in its health care system will not be achieved.

My second major concern is with the number and distribution of providers caring for our patients. We agree that the number of primary caregivers should increase. However, the magnitude of that need is simply unknown at the present time. For example, certain primary care functions may well be performed by nurse practitioners and physician assistants. In addition, specialists are already retraining to practice primary care medicine. Thus, the need for primary care physicians could be less than currently anticipated.

We believe that no decision on exact numbers and percentages of primary caregivers should be made without more information; and I urge you to set general goals for primary care, but to remove the mandate of a specific number that has little basis in fact.

The academic health centers of this Nation have the capacity and the will to improve the value of care and the excellence of the American health care system, but these goals cannot be achieved without appropriate support. Our health care system depends on a vibrant, effective network of academic health centers.

Thank you for inviting me to testify, and I am happy to answer any questions you might have.

Chairman STARK. Thank you.

[The prepared statement follows:]

STATEMENT OF RALPH SNYDERMAN, M.D.
CHANCELLOR FOR HEALTH AFFAIRS
DEAN, SCHOOL OF MEDICINE, DUKE UNIVERSITY
DUKE UNIVERSITY MEDICAL CENTER

Good Morning Mr. Chairman and Distinguished Members of This Committee.

My name is Ralph Snyderman, and I am the Chancellor for Health Affairs and Dean of the School of Medicine at Duke University. I am pleased to appear today to offer my perspective on the future of medical education in the context of the proposed health care reform. As I approach this task, I want to tell you about the nature of the institution I represent and exactly what my job responsibilities encompass because I believe the structure under which we operate is representative of a number of the nation's academic health centers and, thus, affords me an important perspective from which to view the issue of reform.

James B. Duke directed that part of his resources be used to create Duke University Medical Center to provide a total health care service for those individuals living in the rural areas of North Carolina. While the urban area around Duke has developed rapidly in the last 30 years, the major component of our service environment remains rural, and Mr. Duke's challenge remains a key component of the mission of Duke University Medical Center which is amongst the nation's leading academic health centers that serve both rural as well as urban populations.

As Chancellor for Health Affairs, I am responsible for the operations of an 1100 bed hospital, the education and training of 900 residents in our graduate medical education programs, the operations of a complete clinical service, the operations of a physician practice, and the operations of one of the nation's largest medical research programs. As Dean of the School of Medicine, I am responsible for the training of 400 future physicians. From this perspective, let me offer a few observations on the issue of health care reform.

The health care delivery system must be reformed to assure all citizens access to the highest quality care at an affordable cost. To achieve this goal as a nation we must: alter health care financing; produce an appropriate health services workforce; affirm support for biomedical and clinical research; and expand the utilization of preventive, cost-effective care and treatment of disease.

Many opinions are being voiced by interested parties, but those who have traditionally been central to medical progress and innovative health care -- the nation's Academic Health Centers -- are in an ideal position to identify the long-term solutions that will result in needed reform without sacrificing quality. Because academic health centers are central to medical progress and innovation, they are willing to bring their considerable resources and creative energies to the task of contributing to the successful reform of our health care system.

Consisting of medical schools, other health professional schools, and affiliated teaching hospitals, academic health centers serve a critically important role in our nation's health care system. They are centers of excellence and provide the foundation of quality and innovation in the health care system. They educate and train most of the nation's medical manpower, and they are centers of lifelong learning where all are learners and all are teachers. Academic health centers perform the vast majority of biomedical and clinical research which leads to new technology and improved care. And through their teaching hospitals, they provide a larger portion of the nation's inpatient care, including for the severely ill, the under- and uninsured and other vulnerable populations.

In spite of the tremendous contributions of and advances made by academic health centers, their traditional core missions of education, research and health care delivery have not historically been directed toward such practical issues as cost-effectiveness, outcomes research, and preventative medicine.

Well before serious discussions of national health care reform began, Duke University Medical Center recognized the need for fundamental changes in the way medicine is taught and practiced and started implementing changes several years ago. In 1992, it took the bold step of adding a new overarching mission statement:

To the maximum extent possible, we will apply our core missions in education, research and health care delivery to develop the means to solve regional and national health care problems, including providing accessible, cost-effective health care of measurable quality.

The future viability of Duke University Medical Center and, indeed, all academic health centers may well depend on our ability to respond to societal needs while maintaining and benefitting from our academic principles. We must integrate this mandate into each of our core missions. Reorienting the institutional ethos to utilize our academic resources to meet societal needs, especially in the provision of value-based health care, has evolved over several years.

I would like to share with you some of the major changes that are being instituted at Duke University Medical Center. These may serve as models for other academic health centers that are also rapidly redirecting their efforts to address pressing society health needs.

Providing more cost-effective, broadly applicable health care will require a complete reevaluation of the way the medical education system is currently structured. At the Duke Medical School, we have examined all facets of the medical education process: admission criteria, curriculum design and educational tracks; medical student and resident training; continuing medical education; education and integration of allied health professionals into the health team; and retraining of specialists for generalist practice and the teaching and practice of cost-effective medicine.

We established a task force whose sole purpose it is to design a curriculum in cost effectiveness, not only for the medical students throughout their four years, and not only for the residents during their training, but more importantly for our entire faculty who will be the cost-effective teachers of tomorrow. Changes already implemented include the "Clinical Arts" course for first-year students which introduces them to problem-based learning. This course has been modified to include instruction on access and cost-effectiveness. In 1994, cost-effectiveness will be formally integrated into the second-year clinical curriculum. The traditional third year of independent research has been amended to allow students the opportunity to pursue health policy research as well as traditional laboratory research. Health services research, health policy analysis and health systems analysis and epidemiology are of special interest to our primary care medical students and their training should produce a new cadre of leaders in primary care and population medicine.

We would agree that the nation does not have enough primary care physicians to meet society's needs. Duke has had a long and distinguished commitment to generalist training There are more Duke-trained family physicians practicing in the state than those from any other program; however, a 1992 report from the Association of American Medical Colleges showed that only 19.1% of our graduates chose residencies in family medicine, general internal medicine and general pediatrics for the years 1987-1989. It is clear that more must and can be done.

A new, primary care track has been established to identify medical students committed to generalist careers. Once admitted, these students are provided with special support and mentoring services to nurture their interest throughout their medical school experience, and their curriculum modified to include studies in clinical epidemiology and public policy. Duke's program is unique because it produces a generalist with educational experiences in epidemiology and public policy. This knowledge will allow generalist physicians to both provide care for their individual patients and apply this knowledge to serving societal needs.

If our nation is to have a more effective and efficient health care system, then academic medical centers must continue to make medical discoveries and find potential applications for research but also establish and improve both the standards of care and the cost-effectiveness of care through prospective outcomes research. Focusing upon which treatments work best, outcomes research seeks to determine the effectiveness and efficiency of various alternative treatment strategies for a particular medical disorder.

In this critically important new arena of research, Duke University Medical Center has already established an enviable record of leadership, particularly in assessing various approaches to heart disease. The Duke Databank for Cardiovascular Diseases, for example, is a national resource for assessing outcomes for patients with cardiovascular disease. Established in 1969, the Databank is the world's largest cardiovascular disease database and has played an instrumental role in numerous studies determining which treatments provide maximum benefit to patients. Using such detailed historical information from the Databank, Duke researchers recently reported that the treadmill exercise test, which costs from $200 to $300, is just as effective in diagnosing heart disease in most patients as the more invasive angiogram, which costs several thousand dollars to administer.

As the nation's attention focuses on the problems of health care delivery, we believe it critical that we continue our strong commitment to excellence throughout the spectrum of research. While numerous examples can be cited illustrating the link between basic research and patient care, few are more powerful than the work being conducted at Duke University Medical Center's Joseph and Kathleen Bryan Alzheimer's Disease Research Center. Beginning almost a decade ago with the most basic research into the brain chemistry of deceased Alzheimer's patients, a team of Duke researchers is rapidly unraveling the genetic influences on Alzheimer's disease. This group has already identified the genetic markers for Alzheimer's and now believes that possible therapies are on the horizon.

As the need for primary care has increased, we have developed and are putting into practice the Duke Health Network which will consist of close affiliations between Duke, other hospitals and a large number of primary care practitioners. As students and residents require more and more training in non-hospital settings, the Duke Health Network will provide an optimal setting for this training as well as comprehensive, cost-effective and accessible health care for our region..

We at Duke are proud of the efforts we began several years ago, not in anticipation of legislation but because it was the right thing to do. We plan to continue these efforts and to redouble them. However, there are two issues that bring us at Duke major concern that I would like to share with you. The first is the funding of the academic health center.

Funding for the academic health center is a public-private partnership that subsidizes not only the educational and clinical research efforts of the academic health center but more importantly pays for the disproportionate share of critically ill patients and those who have unusual diseases. I like to think of one component of the academic health center as a fire or police station that is always open, 24 hours a day to handle any medical need that comes along, such as severe, complex illnesses or unusual diseases. For example, our coronary artery bypass team, trauma team and burn team all are available 24-hours a day, 365-days a year whether needed or not. Our bone marrow transplantation unit provides cures for breast cancer not previously available. This level of care cannot be obtained in a community hospital. This care is not only expensive, it is also inefficient (because of the firehouse phenomenon); however, it is absolutely necessary. Therefore, even with the streamlining of our processes and our teaching of cost effectiveness, we will not be able to provide such levels of care at a competitive price.

If we now add the cost of educating our students, our residents, and communicating this knowledge to our community as well as the costs for the broad range of research conducted to improve the care we deliver, it is obvious that the academic health center is more expensive and requires appropriate subsidies for its societally needed services. These subsidies, at present, are provided by increased charges to private insurers and by payments from Medicare under the rubric of GME, direct graduate medical education payments and indirect medical education adjustments. These payments help to fund the core missions of the academic health center. Managed competition (the premise upon which the Health Security Act [HSA] is based) could unravel academic health centers' entire financing system of cross-subsidization but would make accommodation for only a portion of the needed compensation by replacing it with two smaller funds.

I am pleased that the HSA recognizes that academic health centers are unique national resources and that they fulfill special societal needs in the health care system. I strongly support the need to fund separately the spectrum of costs associated with an academic mission including the costs of graduate medical education and other health professionals, and the special and unique patient care costs that make it difficult for these institutions to compete in the current environment. I agree that all payers should contribute to the financing of both accounts.

However, I am concerned about the level of the financing of the two accounts and how the funds are distributed. Overall, the amount available to fund these costs is insufficient. Proponents of the HSA have argued that, if enacted, teaching hospitals would be better protected and more adequately financed than if the current situation were maintained. They compare the current level of Medicare payments for direct graduate medical education and indirect medical education costs--nearly $6 billion in FY 1994 to the $9.6 billion total amount that teaching hospitals would receive in the year 2000 under the HSA. In addition, many HSA-proponents believe that teaching hospitals will be able to "make up the difference" by commanding premium prices in the delivery system based on their service offerings and reputations.

While the total of these set-aside funds would exceed current Medicare spending for direct graduate medical education costs and the indirect medical education (IME) adjustment, this premise indicates an apparent misunderstanding of the current competitive environment and the level of support that the academic mission requires. The Medicare program supports only a portion of the academic mission. Data from hospitals belonging to the AAMC's Council of Teaching Hospitals show that Medicare payments cover only about 20-33 percent of the costs associated with the academic mission. The other 67 to 80 percent must be obtained from public and private payers who provide the balance of funding for these additional costs, primarily through increased charges for services.

Historically, teaching hospitals have financed their multiple functions through cross-subsidization. For example, patient service revenues have supported graduate medical education and other academic activities; routine service revenues have supported tertiary care patients; revenues from high volume services have supported low volume services; and payments from paying patients have supported charity care patients. However, during the past few years, as the overall costs of medical care have risen sharply, private health care payers have adopted payment systems--such as capitation, aggressive contacting and discounting--that restrict their payments to cover only goods and services they believe are necessary and of identifiable benefit to their enrollees. Costs associated with the education and research missions of teaching hospitals are not generally recognized by these payers.

In the newly price competitive environment, there is pressure to identify the cross-subsidized products of teaching hospitals. I believe that teaching hospitals will no longer be able to "make up the shortfall" to fund the costs associated with their academic missions through higher charges to patients. Therefore, the overall financing of the two funds must be adequate to ensure the continued financial viability of these institutions.

Notwithstanding my specific comments on the funding of the workforce and AHC proposals, there is another issue of major concern to the academic community. Managed competition, the fundamental premise on which the HSA is based, would not only unravel medical schools' entire financing system of cross-subsidization, and replace only a portion of it. My colleagues and I are concerned about the ability of medical schools to continue to support physician education, particularly at a time when medical schools and teaching physicians are being called upon to transform the medical education system from one that focuses on specialist training in hospital inpatient settings to a more inexpensive system of generalist training in ambulatory, non-hospital sites.

For several reasons, medical schools will have difficulty sustaining this elaborate system undergirding the education and research missions. Federal support is increasingly constrained with medical schools expected to accept a greater share of the costs. Pressures brought to bear on medical service costs will likely lead to declining income from the faculty clinical practice, and less money available to support educational and research efforts. In order to preserve the patient base critical for medical education and research, faculty physicians are being drawn into developing networks with affiliated teaching hospitals and are being asked to accept capitated or discounted payments from private payers. As community physicians are forced to align with various health plans in integrated networks, their willingness to "contribute" teaching services are being threatened.

Undergraduate medical education in the clinical setting, directed by the medical schools, is not recognized explicitly by any payment system, but like other academic costs, it has been financed indirectly. The shift to a more explicit financing system threatens the ability of medical schools and teaching hospitals to fund this activity through other sources of support. Funds from physicians' clinical incomes cannot be expected to maintain their current levels. Fundamental forces are causing the traditionally cross-subsidized products to rise to the surface, yet only in two arenas has the HSA provided assistance. My colleagues and I believe that a complete and adequate financing system for academic medicine must be provided, and we would be pleased to work with members of Congress and the Administration to remedy the situation.

My second major concern is with the number and distribution of individuals caring for our patients. There is a general notion that the number of primary care givers should increase, and we agree with that premise. However, the exact magnitude of that need is simply unknown at this time. Additionally, as it becomes clear that certain primary care functions can and should be performed by nurse practitioners and physician assistants, the need for primary care physicians will not be as great.

Similarly, assessing the need for specialty care is extremely complex. The methodology for determining exactly how many and what kind of specialists is not perfected. While it is likely that there are too many of some, are we to believe that there are too many of all? This problem becomes further complicated by the welcome addition of 37 million currently uninsured Americans. To assume that we should change our residency programs to achieve the mandate for 55 percent primary care physicians is premature. I urge the Congress to enact legislation that would create a National Health Professional Workforce Advisory Board.

This Board should be empowered to develop the methodology to assess the needs in primary care and specialty care throughout this nation. I urge you to set general goals for an increase in primary care but to remove the mandate of a specific number that has little basis in fact.

In return, I can assure this committee and the American people that their investment in the critical functions of the academic health centers will be rewarded many times over by the contributions these centers make to improve the quality of care and the excellence of our still-evolving American health care system.

Thank you.

Chairman STARK. Dr. Foreman.

STATEMENT OF SPENCER FOREMAN, M.D., IMMEDIATE PAST CHAIR, ASSOCIATION OF AMERICAN MEDICAL COLLEGES, AND PRESIDENT, MONTEFIORE MEDICAL CENTER, BRONX, N.Y.

Dr. FOREMAN. Mr. Chairman, I am Spencer Foreman, the president of Montefiore Medical Center in the Bronx, N.Y., and immediate past chairman of the Association of Medical Colleges; and I am here to speak on their behalf.

The Nation's teaching hospitals and medical schools recognize their great responsibility in the health care system and are confident that, given the necessary tools, they can provide a competent, properly balanced physician workforce. The AAMC appreciates the administration's leadership in proposing comprehensive, high quality, cost-effective coverage for every American, and is particularly pleased that the Health Security Act has as an underlying policy requirement all payer support of the academic mission. The principal portions of my written testimony focus on the workforce and academic health center provisions of the act. My oral comments will, as well.

With respect to manpower development, the AAMC agrees with the need to train more physicians in generalist disciplines and supports an overall national goal of having at least 50 percent of graduating physicians entering generalist careers. However, we are concerned that the act's timetable for achieving that goal may be overly ambitious and that the government will move too quickly to a regulatory approach to accomplish it. We strongly urge allowing time for the new incentives now coming into play in the marketplace to work.

Managed care and revised fee schedules are reducing the demand for specialists and shrinking their income, while the same forces are enhancing the status of generalists and improving their income. We are already seeing significant shifts in specialty preference among graduating medical students. Furthermore, the AAMC is very concerned that a national physician manpower regulatory body would have a great deal of difficulty making the thousands of equitable allocation decisions required to regulate 82 specialties and 7,000 training programs.

I call your attention to tables 3 through 7 in my written statement, which attest to the complexity of the problem and the need for flexibility. Nevertheless, the AAMC is prepared to support a more regulatory approach if there is insufficient progress toward meeting the national goal.

With respect to financing workforce development, the AAMC enthusiastically endorses all-payer support of physician training, but is very concerned that the funding proposed in the Health Security Act is inadequate. The workforce account, which is designed to support the operating costs of graduate medical education, uses as a basis for payment a cost-finding methodology which omits real and presently recognized costs of training including those now covered by Medicare in its direct graduate medical education payments. Furthermore, payments from this fund are to be made based on the national average cost of training.

We are very concerned that moving to an average payment will cause a marked and unwarranted redistribution of support among training programs and will have very serious consequences for those programs which lose substantial amounts of funding.

Chairman STARK. Back up on that 1 minute. Just before the average payment, the preceding paragraph.

Dr. FOREMAN. The workforce account which is designed to support the operating costs of graduate medical education uses as a basis for payment a cost-finding methodology which omits real and presently recognized costs of training, including those now covered by Medicare in its direct medical education payments. Furthermore, payments for this fund are proposed to be made on the basis of national average cost of training.

We are concerned that moving to an average payment will cause a marked and unwarranted redistribution of support among training programs and will have very serious consequences for those programs which lose substantial amounts of funding.

Chairman STARK. In the aggregate institutional support and in programs within the institution?

Dr. FOREMAN. In the aggregate institutional support and in programs within the institution. That is, presently those costs are paid on a cost-finding basis, which is institution specific. If you move to an average, the ones that get high amounts of reimbursement will lose it and those that are low will be unanticipated winners.

Chairman STARK. It is not a popular program in New York?

Dr. FOREMAN. No, sir, it is not. Finally, the AAMC does not support payments being awarded directly to training programs. The Association believes that payments from the workforce account should be made to the entity that incurs the cost.

The second major fund is the academic health center account, and while the AAMC is pleased that the act would create a stream of support for academic health centers, the pool is seriously underfunded at $3.8 billion. Preliminary results from an analysis conducted by Lewin/VHI indicates that the real 1991 inpatient and outpatient cost difference between teaching and nonteaching hospitals, excluding the direct costs of education, was between $9 and $11 billion.

Looking back at that 1991 period, Medicare's $4.2 billion in indirect medical education expenditure served as a proxy payment for those costs. The balance was obtained by cross-subsidization from other payers or in rate regulated States, explicitly as payment adjustments. But with managed competition shrinking payments from other payers, it becomes increasingly difficult to sustain a cross-subsidy system. If the Medicare indirect medical education adjustment is eliminated October 1, 1995, as is proposed in the act, without a substantial enhancement of the academic health center adjustment, there will be a huge hole in the funding required to assure that Medicare beneficiaries and others have access to services provided by teaching hospitals.

The final concern of the academic community is that managed competition is likely to unravel the system of cross-subsidization through which faculty professional services income helps to underwrite medical education. Note on table 2 of my testimony that

America's medical schools rely on clinical faculty professional services income for one-third of their overall revenue.

Clinical faculty operate in the same markets and on the same terms as other physician providers and are subject to the same price pressures. Managed care organizations are aggressively using discounted price arrangements and utilization controls to reduce their costs at the expense of providers, which will inevitably result in less medical service plan money being available to support educational efforts.

The AAMC believes that a complete and adequate financing system for academic medicine must be provided and would be pleased to work with Members of the Congress and the administration to remedy this last situation.

Thank you.

[The prepared statement and attachments follow:]

STATEMENT OF SPENCER FOREMAN, M.D.
PRESIDENT, MONTEFIORE MEDICAL CENTER
IMMEDIATE PAST CHAIR, ASSOCIATION OF AMERICAN MEDICAL COLLEGES

Mr. Chairman and members of the subcommittee, I am pleased to appear before you today to comment on two proposals of particular interest to academic medicine in the Health Security Act, HR 3600 (HSA). I am Spencer Foreman, M.D., Immediate Past Chair of the Association of American Medical Colleges (AAMC) and President of Montefiore Medical Center, Bronx, New York. The AAMC represents the nation's 126 accredited medical schools, 400 major teaching hospitals, the faculty of these institutions through 92 constituent academic society members, and the more than 140,000 young men and women in medical training as students and residents.

The AAMC appreciates the administration's leadership in initiating legislation to extend universal comprehensive health coverage while improving quality and constraining growth in health care costs. Mr. Chairman, the association commends your commitment to these goals as well. As early as 1969, the AAMC called for universal access to health care, and since then has advocated a number of other positions on reform of the overall system, including the need to: balance the provision of a basic benefits package with available resources; provide access to primary, preventive, and specialty care; support pluralistic financing systems with appropriate beneficiary cost sharing mechanisms; and develop planned community health care programs.

In June 1993, the association adopted a set of five goals and supporting principles that should guide health care reform. These goals are: 1) giving all Americans the chance for a healthy life; 2) providing universal access to health care; 3) recognizing that once health care excellence is achieved, the necessary resources must be provided so that quality and capacity are maintained; 4) instituting cost containment measures that do not compromise health care quality; and 5) supporting the essential roles of medical and other health professional education and of biomedical, behavioral and health services research. (Appendix A provides a complete list of goals and principles.)

Health care reform will test the entire health care system, and academic medicine in particular will face special challenges. These institutions and their faculties constitute the cornerstone of the health care system, as educators of physicians and other health professionals, creators and evaluators of scientific knowledge and its transfer into practice for the benefit of society, and major providers of primary, secondary and tertiary care in their local communities--often to indigent patients--and on regional, national and international levels. These special responsibilities are highly interdependent in both their missions and financing, and increase the costs, and therefore the price that teaching physicians and teaching hospitals must charge for their services, making it difficult or impossible for them to compete in a price conscious environment. Additionally, the contributions of academic medicine depend on multiple sources of financing, each of which is increasingly constrained. If medical schools and teaching hospitals are to sustain their roles as ultimate guarantors of the effectiveness of the health care system, health care reform must recognize the special roles these institutions play in society.

The AAMC is interested in many issues in the proposal, ranging from broad areas such as anti-trust, to more narrow concerns, such as the provision for contracting with academic health centers. There are many policies in the HSA that deserve enthusiastic support, ranging from reforming the Medicaid program to altering the malpractice system. The AAMC is particularly pleased that the HSA recognizes the critical missions of teaching physicians and teaching hospitals in the health care system: educating physicians, research scientists and other health professionals; developing new medical technology; treating rare and unusually severe illnesses; providing specialized patient care; and caring for special populations. However, the association must call to the attention of this committee and others that the HSA, as proposed, represents a severe threat to the financial viability of the nation's medical schools. Medical school financing is based on a fragile structure of internal cross-subsidies; a very substantial portion of medical school expenses are borne by revenue derived from patient services provided by medical school faculty members. Managed competition, by creating a medical care market highly sensitive to price, will tend to reduce revenues available for this purpose. Simultaneously, it will demand radical shifts in educational emphasis, from specialist to generalist, from hospital to ambulatory focused care. Thus, traditional revenue generating activities will be curtailed or become less rewarding while revenue consumptive activities will increase. Faculty income promises to be reduced, while greater reliance for educational purposes must be placed on community physicians. The income of community physicians will be constrained and medical schools will be without income to compensate them for the additional contributions to professional education asked of them.

Currently, the HSA makes no provision for revenue lost to medical schools, no provision for supporting costly new activities that must be undertaken and makes no allowance for a transition to a new and highly uncertain future. Thus, as a medical school dean, I and my colleagues anticipate health care reform with considerable trepidation.

The legislation's provisions for physician workforce priorities, academic health centers (AHCs), health research initiatives, health programs of the Department of Veterans Affairs (VA), and hospitals serving vulnerable populations give the association an opportunity to continue a dialogue in these areas. They are of special concern to academic medicine and are crucial to the overall viability and quality of the health care system. Today I will focus my comments on two specific provisions in the legislation: the health professions workforce and the academic health center proposals. I will then return to the theme of the financial viability of medical schools.

The HSA has an underlying policy requiring support for the missions of academic medicine from all insurers or sponsors of patient care programs. The level of financial support, the purposes for which the funds are intended, and how money is allocated are all matters that will be subject to debate. However, the AAMC wishes to emphasize the fundamental importance of the principle that all payers must support education and the training of the workforce as well as providing an environment in which education and clinical research can flourish. Our commitment to this principle will not waiver.

The Health Security Act: The Workforce Planning and Allocation Provisions

Summary of the Act. The HSA would establish a national council on graduate medical education within the Department of Health and Human Services (DHHS) to designate annually the total number of residency training positions in each specialty and allocate positions to approved training programs. The national council, to be appointed by the Secretary of the DHHS, would include consumers, medical school faculty and other practicing physicians, and officers or employees of regional and corporate alliances and health plans.

The national council would make its first annual designation of training positions in each specialty for the three-year period beginning July 1, 1998, notifying programs of their approval no later than July 1, 1997. At least 55 percent of the class entering residency training in July 1998 (and classes thereafter) must, in the aggregate, complete training in the primary care specialties of family medicine, general internal medicine, general pediatrics and obstetrics/gynecology. Thus, 55 percent of the physicians starting their graduate training in 1998-99 would complete their training at the end of the 2000-01 academic year as generalists.

For each of the academic years 1998-99 through 2002-03 (a five-year period), the national council also would adjust the total number of positions by a percentage that it would determine. The HSA states that the annual number of positions should bear a relationship to the number of U.S. allopathic and osteopathic medical school graduates in the preceding academic year.

In making its annual designation of the number of positions, the council would consider the need for additional practitioners in each specialty based on the incidence and prevalence of diseases and disorders with which the specialty is concerned; the number of practicing physicians in the specialty currently and five years from the start of the academic year; and the recommendations of physician specialty and consumer groups. The council would allocate positions based on the historical distribution and quality of training programs; the extent to which programs train under-represented racial and ethnic minorities; and the recommendations of private physician specialty and consumer organizations.

AAMC Comments on Workforce Planning and Allocation Provisions.

The Need for Generalists. The AAMC agrees with the need to train more physicians in the generalist disciplines, one of the basic principles underlying the HSA. Increasing access to the health care system for all Americans will require more generalist physicians. In 1992, the association called for a national goal of a majority of graduating medical students committing to generalist careers in family medicine, general internal medicine, and general pediatrics. However, the AAMC believes that a regulatory approach to physician workforce training might not be necessary. Changes in market forces already are shifting the balance of generalist and specialist physicians as incentive systems are restructured, and it appears likely this trend will continue. Changes in the practice environment, namely the increase in managed care arrangements, increases in physician reimbursement for cognitive services, and mitigation of the "hassle factor" are also likely to affect medical students' career choice.

Although data on medical students' career choice from as recently as the graduating class of 1989 show a declining selection of the generalist specialties, more recent data give the AAMC and the academic medical community signs that 1993 medical school graduates have noticed the changes in the environment. This year, for the first time in more than ten years, the percentage of medical school graduates indicating their intention to pursue certification in one of the generalist disciplines increased. Of graduating medical students, 19.3 percent indicated an intent to choose a generalist career in 1993 compared to 14.9 percent in 1991 and 14.6 percent in 1992.

If, on the other hand, an all-payer fund for the costs of training the physician workforce is created and analysis has shown that market forces have not been effective in shifting the balance of generalist and specialist physicians and in achieving appropriate goals for the total number of residency positions, then the AAMC would support a regulatory approach to physician training. A national commission or council could assume responsibility for authorizing payment from the fund for the costs of graduate medical education to assure that national goals are met.

The Need for a Planning Process. The AAMC recognizes the need for a permanent and continuous physician workforce planning process at the national level. The successful implementation of health care reform rests upon an adequate supply of well-trained health professionals in an appropriate specialty mix that addresses the needs of the population.

The association supports the creation of a national physician workforce council or commission, authorized in statute, that would be composed predominantly of private citizens representing various constituencies with interests in physician education. However, we strongly support the addition of medical school deans and teaching hospital executives to the membership of the HSA's proposed national council. The administration's proposal does not now include these categories for representation.

We also believe that the national council should be independent of the DHHS and funded separately from the workforce account. The AAMC is currently considering options for how the council or commission could be structured and organized. Our concerns are whether this body would be advisory or the locus for all responsibility concerning graduate medical education and whether the council would be insulated appropriately from attempts to influence its decisions. Additionally, the council would need sufficient funding and staff to permit its effective operation.

The AAMC is concerned that the timetable for making the council operational may be too ambitious. The HSA requires that training programs would have to be notified of their approval by July 1, 1997. If the HSA were signed into law in August 1994, the national council would have less than three years to establish and organize itself, adopt broad principles and policies for change, and make thousands of allocation decisions.

Determination of the Number and Allocation of Residency Positions. As in the HSA, the association endorses no specific number or limit on the total number of positions, but expects training capacity to relate to projected physician need and the number of U.S. allopathic and osteopathic medical school graduates. The AAMC believes that the commission should assess physician workforce needs and provide guidance for setting goals for the total number and specialty mix of residency positions. We agree with the administration that in designating the annual number of positions, it would be desirable to consider the current and future distribution of practicing physicians, and the incidence and prevalence of diseases associated with particular specialties, among other factors.

The AAMC believes that implementing the achievement of the 55/45 ratio by the year 2001-02 is much too aggressive. As currently described in the HSA, the national council would adjust the specialty mix of first-year positions for the 1998-99 entering residency class, which would be required, in the aggregate, to complete their training in a 55/45 generalist-to-specialist ratio by 2001-02.

The AAMC also is concerned that the timetables for allocating positions by specialty and for adjusting the total number of residents are poorly coordinated and are too rapid to permit institutions to adjust their training program size and mix. At the same time the council would adjust the specialty mix of first-year positions to a 55/45 generalist-to-specialist ratio, the council also would begin to reduce the total number of residents in 1998-99 for the first reduction over a five-year period (through 2002-03). Assuming a policy of first-year positions equal to 110 percent of U.S. allopathic and osteopathic medical school graduates, the national council would be placed in the position of advocating or directing an increase in the number of generalist positions, only to have to eliminate some of them later to achieve a reduction in the overall number of first-year residency positions.

Table 1 below uses current (1992-93) data to demonstrate how the number of generalist and specialist first-year positions would change if this limit were placed on the total number of residency positions. In this example, the overall limit is 18,660 positions, roughly the number of graduates of U.S. allopathic and osteopathic medical schools plus ten percent. The number of first-year generalist positions would have to be increased dramatically in 1998-99, but then would have to be decreased to limit the overall number of positions to 110 percent, while maintaining the 55/45 generalist-to-specialist ratio. This example assumes that the 110 percent goal of 18,660 first-year positions would be reached in 2002-03 through a gradual, annual reduction of about 850 positions over a five-year period beginning with the 1998-99 entering residency class.

Table 1
An Example of Adjusting Total First-Year Residency
Training Positions: Reducing the Total Number to 110 Percent of 1992-93 Graduates
While Maintaining a 55/45 Ratio of Generalists to Specialists

	Current (1992-93) Filled First-Year Positions	--	1998-99	1999-2000	2000-01	2001-02	2002-03
Total	22,905	--	22,056	21,207	20,358	19,509	18,660***
Generalists*	7,817**	--	12,131	11,664	11,197	10,730	10,263
Specialists	15,088	--	9,925	9,543	9,161	8,329	8,397
LCME + Osteo Grads + 10%	18,662	--					

*Generalists include residents in family medicine, general internal medicine, general pediatrics and obstetrics/gynecology.
**AAMC estimate of PGY-1 trainees likely to complete training as generalists; proportion applied to current PGY-1 data based on experience of recent years, i.e, outcomes at the conclusion of residency training.
***18,660 total positions in 2002-03 used in this example as the target reflect the recommendations of the Council on Graduate Medical Education and the Physician Payment Review Commission that the total number of positions be reduced to 110 percent of graduates of LCME and AOA approved medical schools.

Source: Association of American Medical Colleges Tracking Survey, SAIMS Database, 1993.

Although the AAMC recognizes that there is an immediate need to adjust the size and specialty mix of the physician workforce, the training period for physicians is long. Any adjustments in aggregate and in specialty-specific training capacity should be carefully planned and coordinated so that the quality of the educational experience will not diminish and that teaching hospitals and training programs will be able to adapt to the requirements of the new system. One way to limit the number of residents and shift the specialty mix would be to encourage voluntarism among the specialties. The national council, early in its operations, could designate national goals or targets for each specialty. The private sector would then be able to determine its own methods for reaching the goals. Whether the specialties could meet these targets in a hostile legal environment, however, is unclear. Particularly in the area of workforce planning, and in many other areas as well, where societal needs might be better and more efficiently met by a coordinated effort among academic institutions and health care organizations, the watchful eye of the antitrust enforcers of the Federal Trade Commission and the Department of Justice casts a pall over the potential for joint endeavors. Wherever institutions, professionals, or professional societies might be regarded as actual or potential economic competitors, the current state of the law, perversely, precludes private sector efforts, and forces constructive initiatives to be the sole province of government. Thus, to accomplish its objectives, the HSA must address legislatively the boundaries of antitrust law and its enforcement in the health care arena.

If an allocation methodology is necessary, however, the AAMC proposes that the timetable as described in the earlier draft version of the HSA is more reasonable, providing institutions with the opportunity to adjust their training program size and mix and allowing time for market forces to shift the balance of generalists and specialists. As described in the earlier draft version of the HSA, 55 percent of the class that enters residency training in academic year 2002-03 would be required to complete their training in generalist disciplines. The council would reduce the total number of residents by a percentage for each of the academic years 2003-04 through 2007-08. The provision of a transition period from 1998 until 2002 would give institutions the flexibility to determine how to achieve the phase-down or closure of a training program as long as they achieved the goal by the end of the three- to seven-year time period depending on the specialty.

The national council could inform institutions and training programs of the size and mix targets that should be met by the end of a determined period, rather than annually, so that they could devise and implement their own strategies for adjusting training program size and mix. A series of annual decisions over a five-year period would cause significant disruption and uncertainty by requiring institutions to respond incrementally. While adoption of the timetable in the earlier draft would mean aggregate changes in the number of residents would not be completed until 2007-08, compared to 2002-03 in the current version, we believe this method would be a better approach than the current version of the HSA, both for the nation's workforce planning process and for current sponsors of training programs.

If an all-payer fund has been established and the academic medical community agrees to accept an allocation process because market forces have not had an adequate impact on shifting the balance of generalist and specialist physicians, the AAMC would support a process in which allocation decisions by specialty would be based on a variety of factors. Among the factors in the HSA are the historic geographic distribution of training programs, quality, underrepresented minority groups, and the recommendations of private health care and consumer organizations. The AAMC believes that educational organizations and associations, which often collect and analyze data on graduate medical education and other relevant topics, could make meaningful recommendations to the council concerning the allocation of residency positions.

Even so, an equitable allocation system will be difficult to achieve. The structure of graduate medical education is complex. Graduate medical education is the period of formal education in clinical practice that begins with graduation from medical school and ends with the fulfillment of the requirements for certification in specialty or subspecialty practice. The training period for physicians is long. Each of 82 specialties and subspecialties has its own training requirements, and there are nearly 7,000 training programs. Any allocation system must be flexible. For example, some specialties or programs require residents to enroll first in a broad-based clinical year of training, often in internal medicine or pediatrics, before entering specialty training. Other trainees, about 6.5 percent of all first-year residents in 1992-93, may enter a first-year residency experience, often referred to as a transitional year, to obtain a broad-based clinical year because they may be undecided about their future discipline. How to count the first, and in some unusual cases a second, transitional year will become an important issue in how positions get allocated by specialty. Other trainees may not complete their training within the minimum required time because they train part-time, share a residency position, interrupt their training for childbearing or other reasons, or change the discipline in which they train. The allocation system must be designed to accommodate these factors.

Another issue of concern to the association is the length of period for which the Council would approve residency training positions in each specialty. The HSA would require the Council to determine which slots would be approved for a three year period. While this is the length of training for initial board eligibility in internal medicine, pediatrics, and family medicine, there are many programs which are longer than 3 years. For example, initial board eligibility in general surgery requires 5 years of training. Longer training programs would be disrupted if a program were notified in the third-year of a resident's training, that the program would no longer be funded. Therefore, the Council should designate positions, at a minimum, until at least the period of initial board eligibility in each specialty.

A review of the concentration of specialties and location of training reveals some important points which can be understood by reviewing Tables 3-7 at the end of this testimony. While the majority of residents are concentrated in a relatively small number of specialties and states, the remaining residents are widely distributed. Residents, training in 25 specialty and 57 subspecialty areas, are concentrated in a relatively small number of specialties. Table 3 shows that nearly one-half of all physicians in training are in the specialties of internal medicine, pediatrics and surgery. Residency training programs are unevenly distributed across the nation. Table 5 shows that while 48 states have some residents in training, one-half of all residents are trained in seven states. With this heavy concentration but broad dispersion of residents, policy makers will have to consider carefully the impact of proposed policies on both the large concentrations as well as the broader distribution in designing an allocation system.

While the AAMC concurs that quality should be a major factor in the allocation process, the association has several concerns about the process for stratifying training programs by quality. One is that there would have to be a process in place by which new training programs could enter the system. In addition, there would need to be a process to address fluctuation in individual program quality across years. Educational quality is dynamic. The process and incentives must be in place to motivate the program to improve its quality continuously, rather than simply taking a snapshot of educational quality. Finally, one must make the distinction between the significant reductions in positions that are likely to occur in the first five years after the proposed legislation is passed compared to the continuous monitoring of educational quality that will be needed in later years. The decision of whether to eliminate a training program entirely or whether merely to reduce the size of the existing program may require very different approaches.

A large number of professional organizations participate in graduate medical education to provide control over the quality of the training. They determine the standards to be met by each type of specialty training program and assess whether or not individual programs meet the standards. The Accreditation Council for Graduate Medical Education (ACGME) accredits nearly 7,000 graduate medical education programs in the United States. It is sponsored by five parent organizations, including the AAMC. The ACGME relies on residency review committees (RRCs) to perform the actual review of each training program. A RRC consists of representatives from the specialty appointed by the appropriate specialty board, and in some cases, a national specialty society, and the American Medical Association. Residency programs are accredited either by the ACGME upon recommendation of the RRC or by the RRC itself, if the ACGME has delegated authority to it.

Some policy makers have suggested that the ACGME or the American Osteopathic

Association's Committee on Post-doctoral Training, which would be separate from the proposed national council, should assume the additional and sole responsibility of allocating positions on the basis of measures of educational quality. The association believes that the medical profession should judge the quality of its training programs, but it has several concerns about the ACGME's ability to differentiate and stratify training programs by educational quality. For example, it is unclear whether the ACGME has the information systems or methodology to quantify educational quality objectively beyond established minimum criteria. To rank training programs would be highly subjective. In addition, the structure and resource level of the ACGME may be inadequate to undertake this role. Developing and implementing a mechanism to stratify programs by quality certainly would require more staff and financial resources than the ACGME currently has at its disposal. It is also clear that, if the ACGME were to take on the role of ranking training programs by quality, it and its five sponsoring organizations would need significant legal protection. The ACGME relies almost wholly on contributed professional time. Thus, it is not structured to command the resources to deal with the inevitable legal challenges to a ranking process that will accumulate over time. The role of quality in the allocation process and the method of measuring program quality are difficult issues. While the AAMC's current position is that the ACGME should not assume responsibility for allocation or ranking, the association also recognizes that there are strong arguments favoring some greater level of participation by the ACGME in an allocation process. The AAMC, along with other sponsors of the ACGME, is currently evaluating an ACGME proposal on how the ACGME could effectively and appropriately participate in allocation activities.

The AAMC strongly supports considering underrepresented minority groups in position allocation decisions. The association has implemented an initiative aimed at increasing the number of underrepresented minorities who apply to medical school. Called 3000 X 2000, our goal is to have 3,000 individuals in underrepresented minorities apply to U.S. medical schools in the year 2000.

The AAMC believes there are a variety of allocation approaches to study. We hope that the HSA provides the national council with the flexibility to examine a number of national, regional and local approaches. Staff to the Public Health Service (PHS) in the DHHS have been very gracious in consulting with the AAMC on this and other workforce issues. We have provided data on residency training to PHS and hope to continue working PHS representatives to help them refine their proposals. Before I comment further on the workforce provision, I would like to address the overall financing adequacy of the workforce and academic health center provisions.

The Health Security Act: Summary and General Comments on Financing Provisions for the Workforce and AHC Accounts

Summary of the Act. The HSA would recognize the critical roles of academic medicine in the health care system by creating two funds. The physician workforce account would assist in the funding for the institutional costs of graduate medical education; the academic health center (AHC) account would assist these institutions and teaching hospitals in covering the special costs they incur as part of their academic mission. Both funds would be separate from patient care revenue and, according to the administration's December 1993 analysis of the HSA, three sources--the Medicare program, regional health alliances and corporate alliances-- would be required to contribute to both funds.

AAMC Comments on Overall Financing.

The AAMC is pleased that the HSA recognizes that teaching hospitals and teaching physicians are unique national resources and that they have added societal responsibilities in the health care system. The association strongly supports the need to fund separately the spectrum of costs associated with an academic mission, including the costs of graduate medical education and other health professionals, and the special and unique patient care costs that make it difficult for these institutions to compete in the current environment. We also agree that all payers should contribute to the financing of both accounts.

However, the AAMC is concerned about the level of the financing of the two accounts and how the funds are distributed. Overall, the amount available to fund these costs is insufficient. Proponents of the HSA have argued that, if enacted, teaching hospitals would be better protected and more adequately financed than if the current situation were maintained. They compare the current level of Medicare payments for direct graduate medical education and indirect medical education costs-nearly $6 billion in FY 1994-to the $9.6 billion total amount that teaching hospitals would receive in the year 2000 under the HSA. In addition, many HSA-proponents believe that teaching hospitals will be able to "make up the difference" by commanding premium prices in the delivery system based on their service offerings and reputations.

While the total of these set-aside funds would exceed current Medicare spending for direct graduate medical education costs and the indirect medical education (IME) adjustment, this premise indicates an apparent misunderstanding of the current competitive environment and the level of support that the academic mission requires. The Medicare program supports only a portion of the academic mission. Data from hospitals belonging to the AAMC's Council of Teaching Hospitals show that Medicare payments cover only about 20 to 33 percent of the costs associated with the academic mission. The other 67 to 80 percent must be obtained from public and private payers who provide the balance of funding for these additional costs primarily through increased charges for services.

Historically, teaching hospitals have financed their multiple functions through cross-subsidization. For example, patient service revenues have supported graduate medical education and other academic activities; routine service revenues have supported tertiary care patients; revenues from high volume services have supported low volume services; and payments from paying patients have supported charity care patients. However, during the past few years, as the overall costs of medical care have risen sharply, private health care payers have adopted payment systems--such as capitation, aggressive contracting and discounting--that restrict their payments to cover only goods and services they believe are necessary and of identifiable benefit to their enrollees. Costs associated with the education and research missions of teaching hospitals generally are not recognized by these payers.

In the newly price competitive environment, there is pressure to identify the cross-subsidized products of teaching hospitals. The AAMC believes that teaching hospitals will no longer be able to "make up the shortfall" to fund the costs associated with their academic missions through higher charges to patients. Therefore, the overall financing of the two funds must be adequate to ensure the continued financial viability of these institutions.

Notwithstanding these comments on the overall adequacy of the two provisions, the AAMC has several specific comments about the financing of the workforce and academic health center (AHC) accounts and about the need to address some technical issues.

The Health Security Act: Financing of the Health Professions Workforce Account

Summary. Payments for operating a residency training program and transitional payments to institutions that lose residency positions would be made from a federal health professions workforce account. The account would be funded at $3.2 billion in Calendar Year (CY) 1996, the first-year of implementation; $3.55 billion in CY 1997; $4.8 billion in CY 1998; and $5.8 billion in CY 1999 and CY 2000. In subsequent years, that amount would be increased by the general health care inflation factor. Medicare payments for the direct costs of graduate medical education would terminate for cost report periods beginning on or after October 1, 1995. Beginning in Federal FY 1996, Medicare would contribute to the workforce account: $1.5 billion in FY 1996; $1.6 billion in FY 1997 and FY 1998; and after 1998 the $1.6 billion would be increased by the consumer price index. According to the administration's December 1993 analysis of the HSA:

> after the level of Medicare payments is determined, corporate and regional alliances pay the balance needed in the annual health professions workforce account, with such payments coming from the 1 percent corporate alliance assessment (under section 7121) and the 1.5 percent regional alliance assessment (under section 1353). For 1996 and 1997, one-half of such regional alliance payments are available for the annual health professions workforce account, with the remainder made available from

payments by corporate alliances. In subsequent years, payments into the annual health professions workforce account are made in proportion to the total payments to corporate and regional health plans by corporate and regional alliances, respectively (Page 112).

Workforce payments in any year would be pro-rated if necessary on the basis of available funds. Starting in CY 1996, training programs that have applied and have been approved for payments would receive them directly from the Secretary of the DHHS. Calendar years 1996 and 1997 would be transitional years during which some states would not participate in the HSA. All states would be participants by CY 1998. In 1996 and 1997, the Secretary would first make payments to those programs located in participating states. Programs in non-participating states would receive pro-rated payments from the remaining funds in the workforce account.

Training programs would have to apply and be approved for payment and then would receive funds directly. Programs would submit applications to the Secretary of the DHHS for approval. Programs must agree to spend workforce funds only for the purpose of physician training. The institution within which the program operates would be required to agree that payments would be made directly to the program by the Secretary.

Payments would be calculated using the national average cost for training residents multiplied by the number of full-time equivalent residents in the program. The national average cost would be determined using the 1992-93 academic year, trended forward by the consumer price index (CPI) for each year, and adjusted to reflect regional differences in wages and wage-related costs. The national average cost of training would consider the national average salary of residents and the national average cost of providing faculty supervision and related activities.

Beginning in CY 1997, "transitional payments" to assist institutions that lose residency positions would be made from the health professions workforce account, subject to the availability of funds. The payment would be determined by multiplying the aggregate number of full-time equivalent positions lost by the national average salary of residents in 1992-93, updated by the CPI and adjusted for regional variation. The payment would be available for a four-year period, starting in the year in which an institution has fewer positions than during the 1993-94 academic year. Institutions may apply only once to receive the funds. For the first-year in which an institution would be eligible, the payment would be 100 percent of the national average salary, and would be reduced by 25 percent in each of the three subsequent years.

AAMC Comments on Workforce Financing

The AAMC has adopted the position that all payer financing of graduate medical education must accompany the establishment of a regulatory process for allocating residency positions if a national commission determines that market forces have failed to shift the balance of generalists and specialists. Upon creation of an all-payer fund for the costs of graduate medical education, the national commission would determine whether the medical education community has made adequate progress toward achieving its goals. If adequate progress has been made, there would be no need for the national commission to control the allocation of positions through a regulatory process, but a mechanism for distributing payments from the all payer fund would still be needed. However, if adequate progress has not been made upon establishment of the all payer fund, the commission could assume responsibility for authorizing payments for the costs of GME, and could develop and implement strategies to assure that the national goals are achieved.

The AAMC is concerned that the amount of money in the workforce account is not adequate. This account does not include financing for the 8,500 residency positions which are currently funded by the Department of Veterans Affairs. It also appears to exclude payments for podiatry, oral surgery or general dentistry residents, for whom the Medicare program currently pays its proportionate share. In addition, the dynamics of how the regional and corporate alliances would participate in financing these costs are not well understood, including how these entities contribute to both the workforce and the AHC accounts and at what level.

Even more troubling is that the overall level of the fund--$5.8 billion in CY 2000 (which has not been adjusted for inflation to the year 2000)--is determined using a national average per resident amount which includes no overhead costs. It is our understanding that the aggregate funding needed for this account was estimated using only the national average resident's stipend and fringe benefits and an average salary and fringe benefit amount for faculty supervision.

The AAMC believes the level of payment should recognize all types of costs, including direct overhead costs, such as malpractice costs, classroom space and clerical support, and is concerned about the adequacy of the proposed national average payment which excludes overhead costs. The AAMC also is concerned about the use of a national average payment methodology and its redistributional effect across institutions. The overall financing of teaching hospitals and medical schools often is driven by historic circumstances, which have led to certain costs, especially faculty costs, being borne by the medical school, or in some cases, the teaching hospital. The diversity of faculty costs is probably the most important reason for the variation in Medicare per resident payments. Additionally, there are legitimate differences in educational models depending on the specialty and the institution. Residency programs also may have unique histories and differences in the funding available to them, such as state or local government appropriations. While the HSA requires the national average payment to be adjusted to reflect regional differences in wages and wage-related costs, these other structural factors would not be reflected in the HSA's proposed national average payment methodology, creating winners and losers inappropriately.

At its January 20, 1994 meeting, the Prospective Payment Assessment Commission (ProPAC) discussed recommendations on graduate medical education financing for its March 1994 report. Commissioners reviewed a staff analysis of graduate medical education costs and payments and noted the complexity of the distribution of these payments to hospitals. Chairman Stuart H. Altman, Ph.D., cautioned those who prefer moving to a national average payment methodology for residency costs without incorporating a number of adjustments in the payment system. Pointing to the commission's eleven-year experience with the prospective payment system--the first attempt by the federal government to standardize payments based on national averages--Dr. Altman noted how many adjustments had been added to the PPS over the years to achieve payment equity. ProPAC's preliminary analysis of graduate medical education costs found significant positive relationships between per resident costs and hospital size; its share of full-time equivalent residents in the outpatient setting; its share of costs related to faculty physicians' salaries; geographic region; location in a metropolitan statistical area; and area wages.

The AAMC believes that since the HSA imposes an overall limit on the amount available for workforce funding, other payment policy options, which would distribute the funds more equitably among training sites, should be explored. The AAMC intends to pursue the development of alternative payment proposals that would recognize the significant diversity across institutions that participate in graduate medical education. We would be pleased to share our payment policy proposals with members of the committee and with the administration.

The AAMC believes that some institutions may be unduly harmed financially during the transition years of 1996 and 1997, when some states would not yet be participating in the HSA and would therefore receive pro-rated payments from the balance in the workforce account. It would be possible for the entity to receive a smaller payment in 1997 than it did in 1996. The AAMC believes that language should be added to the bill so that training entities would not receive less than they did in 1996, or less than they would have received from the Medicare program.

The AAMC understands that there is an error in the bill regarding the funding level of the workforce account in CY 1998. At $4.8 billion, it is funded at $1 billion less than it should be funded. CY 1998 would be the first-year in which all states would participate in the new system. Thus, a fully-funded workforce account of $5.8 billion in CY 1998, and updated for inflation in CY 1999, would be essential.

Another correction needs to reflect the transition between the end of Medicare payments for direct graduate medical education costs and when payments from the workforce account would begin. As currently written, Medicare payments for these costs would terminate for cost reporting periods beginning on or after October 1, 1995. There may be a gap in available funding depending on the timing of the contributions. The AAMC does not support payments being awarded directly to training programs. The association believes that payments from the workforce account should be made to the entity that incurs the cost. Recipients of payments could be teaching hospitals, medical schools, multi-specialty group practices or organizations that incur training costs. The AAMC strongly encourages the formation of formal associations, or graduate medical education consortia, to assure the continuity and coordination of medical education and to serve potentially as the fiscal intermediary in distributing payments across various training sites.

The AAMC agrees that transition payments should be available to institutions that lose residency positions. However, the association is concerned about their timing and their adequacy. To encourage institutions to adjust the size and mix of their training programs, transition funds should be made available as soon as the national council is operative. The HSA now states that these payments would not be available until CY 1997. Additionally, there should be some flexibility in how these payments are used so that institutions could try different approaches. The AAMC also is concerned that because an institution could apply only one time to receive payments, it would be locked into a four-year period during which it could become even more disadvantaged if further reductions in positions were imposed after the institution's application. Additionally, because these payments would be determined using only the national average salary of a resident, they will not provide enough relief. Some hospitals may still be unable to attract highly skilled non-physician practitioners or community physicians as substitutes for residents, particularly in inner city areas. Further, highly skilled non-physician practitioners are paid more than residents and will require physician supervision. These additional costs are not included in the transition payment amount. If a hospital replaces residents with non-physician practitioners, the salaries and supervisory costs of these non-physician professionals become permanent costs to the institution.

We support the funding for other health professionals-nursing and allied health-through the continuation of Medicare hospital payments and through other authorized programs. How the costs of training general dentists, oral surgeons and podiatrists are paid under the HSA's plan is not clear. Currently the Medicare program pays their costs through the physician per resident payment amount. We believe the HSA language should be clarified as to how these trainees are funded.

The Health Security Act: The Academic Health Center Account

Summary of the Act. The HSA would require the federal government to make payments to academic health centers and teaching hospitals to "assist eligible institutions with costs that are not routinely incurred by other entities in providing health services, but are incurred...by virtue of the academic nature of such institutions."

The HSA defines an "academic health center" as an entity that operates a school of medicine or osteopathic medicine; operates or is affiliated with one or more other health professional training schools or programs; and operates or is affiliated with one or more teaching hospitals. A "teaching hospital" is a hospital that operates an approved physician training program. To be "eligible" for payments from this account, institutions must apply each year to the Secretary of the DHHS and be "qualified" AHCs or "qualified" teaching hospitals. A "qualified" AHC operates a teaching hospital; a "qualified" teaching hospital is any teaching hospital other than one operated by an AHC. Payments could be in the form of a grant, contract or a cooperative agreement.

Total available amounts for payments would be $3.1 billion in CY 1996; $3.2 billion in each of CYs 1997 and 1998; $3.7 billion in CY 1999; and $3.8 billion in CY 2000, after which that amount would be updated by the general health care inflation factor in each subsequent year. As in the workforce account, AHC funds would be derived from three sources: Medicare, regional and corporate alliances. On October 1, 1995, Medicare indirect medical education payments under the prospective payment system would terminate and the program would contribute $2.1 billion to the AHC account. In each of Federal Fiscal Years 1997 and 1998 the Medicare program would transfer $2.0 billion to the AHC account, and in each subsequent year that amount would be increased by the CPI for all urban consumers and transferred to the account. As in the workforce account, regional and corporate alliances would make up the balance in the annual AHC account. For CYs 1996 and 1997, one-half of the 1.5 percent regional alliance assessment would be available with the remainder to be made available from payments by corporate alliances. The alliance contribution would increase based on the proportion of the population assumed to be in the new system.

Funds would be distributed among AHCs and teaching hospitals in proportion to the product of the institution's annual gross receipts for inpatient and outpatient care and the indirect teaching adjustment factor applicable to patients discharged from the center in the preceding year or in CY 1997. No later than July 1, 1996, the Secretary must submit a report to Congress with recommendations for modifying the allocation policies to eligible institutions. In making recommendations, the Secretary is to consider the costs incurred by eligible institutions.

AAMC Comments on AHC Financing and Technical Issues

While the AAMC is pleased that the HSA would create a separate fund for the costs associated with the academic mission, the legislative language in the bill causes confusion regarding the purpose of the funds and creates expectations that are not forthcoming in terms of which entity gets the payment. Much of the confusion arises from comparing this fund and its rationale with the indirect medical education (IME) adjustment and its purpose in the Medicare prospective payment system. The confusion is only compounded because the Medicare program eliminates the IME adjustment beginning in Federal FY 1996 and then contributes funds to the academic health center account. However, the purpose of the academic health center account—reduced productivity of faculty, uncompensated costs of clinical research and exceptional costs of specialized treatment—differs from the broad rationale behind the Medicare IME adjustment for inpatient hospital costs:

> This adjustment is provided in light of doubts...about the ability of the DRG case classification system to account fully for factors such as severity of illness of patients requiring the specialized services and treatment programs provided by teaching institutions and the additional costs associated with the teaching of residents...the adjustment for indirect medical education is only a proxy to account for a number of factors which may legitimately increase costs in teaching hospitals (House Ways and Means Committee Report, Number 98-25, March 4, 1983. Senate Finance Committee Report, Number 98-23, March 11, 1983).

The AAMC suggests that the complete range of purposes of the AHC fund as described in the bill, which we assume to be examples rather than definitions of academic costs, along with the spectrum of costs associated with the academic mission, should be studied and incorporated in the Secretary's report to Congress. The AAMC believes that the due date as specified in the HSA, July 1, 1996, is too early, given the ambitious nature of the study, and should be changed to July 1, 1998.

A second point of confusion surrounds the definitions in the bill and the issue of what entity receives the AHC payment. Some definitions, such as the use of the term "operates," need further clarification. As stated in the bill, hospitals must "operate" training programs to receive payments from this account, but hospitals that participate in affiliated programs assumedly would not receive payments. There is no definition of "affiliated with" in the bill.

The AAMC has major concern that the AHC pool is seriously underfunded at $3.8 billion (unadjusted for inflation) in the year 2000. While the intent of this fund is to provide assistance to academic health centers and teaching hospitals in "leveling the playing field" so that they may compete on a price basis with non-teaching providers, the size of the fund is insufficient to narrow the gap to a level where teaching hospitals and teaching physicians could expect to compete reasonably. Teaching physicians and hospitals recognize that, like all other providers, they will need to become more efficient in a competitive delivery system. However, an analysis of hospitals' costs per case in the eighth-year of the Medicare PPS (1991), conducted for the AAMC by Lewin-VHI, Inc., showed teaching hospitals on average were 32 percent more costly (excluding direct graduate medical education costs) relative to non-teaching hospitals. Lewin-VHI estimated that a level playing field between teaching and non-teaching hospital inpatient costs per case would have had to be funded at $7.0 to $8.3 billion in 1991, depending on the regression model used in the analysis.

However, the HSA requires payments to be calculated using inpatient and outpatient "gross receipts." Preliminary results from Lewin-VHI's analysis showed that an all-payer fund for the inpatient and outpatient costs of teaching hospitals would have been funded at $9.0 to $10.6 billion in 1991, significantly more than the $3.8 billion planned for CY 2000, to address adequately the costs associated with the academic mission. The AAMC would be pleased to share the results of this analysis with the members of this subcommittee as the models and data are refined.

The AAMC has serious concern that the Medicare contribution to the AHC account would be lower than statistical analysis of the differences in inpatient hospital costs warrants. The HSA would reduce substantially the current IME payment formula to a rate of about 3.0 percent for every 0.1 percent increase in a hospital's intern and resident-to-bed ratio (IRB) beginning October 1, 1995, when the program would contribute $2 billion to the AHC fund. Current Medicare IME payments are expected to be about $4.2 billion in Federal FY 1994. The AAMC is unaware of any analysis that justifies the proposed level of reduction in the operating cost IME adjustment. The association views the proposed reduction in the IME adjustment as simply a mechanism for lowering Medicare's contribution to the AHC fund.

The AAMC also is concerned about using the Medicare resident-to-bed formula to allocate the fixed amount of money on a pro-rated basis to eligible institutions, which in effect pays institutions at a lower rate than 3 percent. Analysis presented by ProPAC staff at the commission's January 20 meeting found the distribution of AHC funds using the Medicare IME formula on a proportional basis to the maximum allowed by the bill resulted in an IME adjustment of 1.4 percent.

The AAMC is very concerned about the elimination of the IME adjustment as of October 1, 1995. These Medicare funds, which are essential to assuring that Medicare beneficiaries and others have access to services provided by teaching hospitals, would be reduced and removed from the PPS and then redistributed without knowing the impact on teaching hospitals' financial status. The AAMC urges the Congress to reflect carefully on this consequence when considering any change in the level of the IME adjustment, particularly until a new system is fully operational and the effect of the new system on the financial viability of teaching hospitals can be determined.

The AAMC believes that the methodology of using the IRB to distribute AHC dollars unfairly penalizes a teaching hospital that is exempt for the prospective payment system. Presumably its IRB is zero. One remedy to this oversight may be to calculate IRBs for these hospitals as if they were subject to the PPS.

Medical School Financing in an Era of Health Care Reform

Notwithstanding our specific comments on the workforce and AHC proposals, there is another issue of major concern to the academic community about which policy makers should be aware. Managed competition, the fundamental premise on which the HSA is based, would unravel medical schools' entire financing system of cross-subsidization, but would make accommodation for only a portion of the system by replacing it with two funds. The Health Security Act recognizes only academic costs that are already paid in the Medicare payment system, but fails to address the financial cross-subsidies of medical schools by offering no substitution for lost funds. The AAMC is concerned about the ability of medical schools to continue to support physician education, particularly at a time when medical schools and teaching physicians are being called on to transform the medical education system from one that focuses on specialist training in hospital inpatient settings to a more expensive system of generalist training in ambulatory, non-hospital sites.

Like teaching hospitals, medical schools, to a significant degree, finance educational and research activities through a complex system of cross-subsidization. Education, research and patient care exist as joint products. Undergraduate medical education is supported partially and directly by tuition and fees and state appropriations (primarily at public institutions). Table 2 on the following page shows that these sources of support accounted for 4.1 percent and 11.5 percent, respectively, of total medical school revenues in 1991-92.

Research is supported partly by federal and local grants and contracts. Philanthropic support supplements these sources, but by themselves these funds remain insufficient. The current educational and research output of the nation's medical schools relies on significant revenues from the delivery of medical services by the faculty of the school. Revenue from the clinical faculty practice plan constituted 32.4 percent of total medical school revenue in 1991-92; in 1980-81, medical service revenue contributed only 15.7 percent of the total. Hospitals also support medical schools for activities conducted in the hospital. Reimbursements from hospitals have increased from 6.2 percent in 1980-81 to 11.4 percent in 1991-1992. Grants and contracts for medical services represented about 3.3 percent of total medical school revenue in 1991-92. Education also benefits from an elaborate system of nonpaid voluntary faculty drawn from the community.

For several reasons, medical schools will have difficulty sustaining this elaborate system undergirding the education and research missions. Federal support is increasingly constrained, with medical schools expected to accept a greater share of the costs. Pressures brought to bear on medical service costs will likely lead to declining income from the faculty clinical practice, and less money available to support educational and research efforts. In order to preserve the patient base critical for medical education and research, faculty physicians are being drawn into developing networks with affiliated teaching hospitals and are being asked to accept capitated or discounted payments from private payers. As community physicians are forced to align with various health plans in integrated networks, their willingness to "contribute" teaching services may even be threatened.

Undergraduate medical education in the clinical setting, directed by the medical school, is not recognized explicitly by any payment system, but like other academic costs, it has been financed indirectly. The shift to a more explicit financing system threatens the ability of medical schools and teaching hospitals to fund this activity through other sources of support. Funds from physicians' clinical incomes cannot be expected maintain their current levels. Fundamental forces are causing the traditionally cross-subsidized products to rise to the surface, yet only in two arenas has the HSA provided assistance. The AAMC believes that a complete and adequate financing system for academic medicine must be provided and we would be pleased to work with members of Congress and the administration to remedy the situation.

Conclusion

Society must understand that supporting academic medicine ensures its vital role as an international leader in education, research and patient care. Medical schools and their faculties educate fully trained physicians to meet the nation's health care needs. Teaching hospitals provide an environment for the conduct of biomedical clinical research, serve as educational sites, and with their staff, work with academic physicians to deliver sophisticated patient care to all who need it. But academic institutions also need support to maintain their essential role in the health care system.

The AAMC is pleased that the HSA recognizes the important functions of these institutions. However, we must give considerable thought and attention to ensuring that these proposed changes, if enacted, would be implemented effectively and financed adequately. While we have some concerns about the two proposals, the AAMC shares in their overall objectives. We look forward to working with this subcommittee and the administration to ensure the future of academic medicine and the nation's health care system. We can afford to do no less.

TABLE 2
REVENUES
U.S. MEDICAL SCHOOLS
(DOLLARS IN MILLIONS)

	1980-81		1991-92	
Fully Accredited Schools	116		126	
Number of Schools Reporting	123		126	
	Amount	% of Total	Amount	% of Total
GENERAL OPERATING REVENUES*				
Federal Appropriations	57	0.9%	105	0.5%
State & Local Government Apropriations	1,351	20.8%	2,662	11.5%
Appropriations	1,252	19.3%	2,523	10.9%
Subsidies	99	1.5%	139	0.6%
Recovery of Indirect Cost	445	6.9%	1,516	6.5%
Federal Government	409	6.3%	1,309	5.7%
State & Local Government	10	0.2%	32	0.1%
Non-Government	26	0.4%	175	0.8%
Medical Service Plans	1,020	15.7%	7,505	32.4%
Tuition and Fees	348	5.4%	955	4.1%
Endowment (1)	110	1.7%	401	1.7%
Gifts (2)	46	0.7%	509	2.2%
Parent University Funds	113	1.7%	208	0.9%
Reimbursements from Hospitals	404	6.2%	2,640	11.4%
Miscellaneous Sources	172	2.7%	957	4.1%
Total General Operating Revenues*	**4,066**	**62.7%**	**17,458**	**75.4%**
GRANTS AND CONTRACTS				
Research	1,340	20.7%	3,705	16.0%
Federal Government	1,098	16.9%	2,787	12.0%
State & Local Government	21	0.3%	101	0.4%
Non-Government	221	3.4%	817	3.5%
Teaching & Training	397	6.1%	533	2.3%
Federal Government	277	4.3%	317	1.4%
State & Local Government	35	0.5%	67	0.3%
Non-Government	85	1.3%	149	0.6%
Service & Multi-Purpose	491	7.6%	763	3.3%
Federal Government	124	1.9%	181	0.8%
State & Local Government	265	4.1%	362	1.6%
Non-Government	102	1.6%	220	1.0%
Research & Teaching/Training Programs at Affiliate Institutions	188	2.9%	688	3.0%
Total Grants and Contracts	**2,416**	**37.3%**	**5,689**	**24.6%**
TOTAL REVENUES	**6,482**	**100.0%**	**23,147**	**100.0%**

(1) Includes unrestricted and restricted endowment   * Detail may not add due to rounding.
(2) Includes one provisionally approved school

SOURCE: LCME Questionnaire, Part I-A, Section for Operational Studies.

TABLE 3
NUMBER OF RESIDENTS AND FELLOWS
RANKED BY TOTAL TRAINEES BY SPECIALTY
1993

Specialty	No. of Residents	No. of Fellows	No. Physician in GME	% of Total	Cumulative %
Internal Medicine	19,962	10,581	30,543	30.9%	30.9%
Pediatrics	6,600	2,389	8,989	9.1%	40.0%
Surgery	7,832	886	8,718	8.8%	48.8%
Family Practice	6,925	539	7,464	7.6%	56.4%
Psychiatry	5,138	912	6,050	6.1%	62.5%
Anesthesiology	5,078	896	5,974	6.0%	68.6%
Obstetrics-Gynecology	4,665	620	5,285	5.3%	73.9%
Radiology	3,606	1,478	5,084	5.1%	79.0%
Orthopedic Surgery	2,752	583	3,335	3.4%	82.4%
Pathology	2,222	734	2,956	3.0%	85.4%
Emergency Medicine	2,024	354	2,378	2.4%	87.8%
Ophthalmology	1,476	332	1,808	1.8%	89.6%
Neurology	1,355	444	1,799	1.8%	91.5%
Transitional	1,589	--	1,589	1.6%	93.1%
Otolaryngology	819	403	1,222	1.2%	94.3%
Urology	911	246	1,157	1.2%	95.5%
Physical Medicine/Rehab.	993	118	1,111	1.1%	96.6%
Dermatology	708	261	969	1.0%	97.6%
Neurosurgery	630	224	854	0.9%	98.5%
Plastic Surgery	161	362	523	0.5%	99.0%
Thoracic Surgery	--	345	345	0.3%	99.3%
Preventive Medicine	235	57	292	0.3%	99.6%
Allergy/Immunology	--	169	169	0.2%	99.8%
Nuclear Medicine	90	45	135	0.1%	99.9%
Colon & Rectal Surgery	--	64	64	0.1%	100.0%
TOTAL	**75,771**	**23,042**	**98,813**	**100.0%**	

Source: Association of American Medical Colleges, Medical Education Census, SAIMS Database, 1993

TABLE 4
NUMBER OF FMGs IN GME
RANKED BY PERCENTAGE OF FMGs OF TOTAL TRAINEES BY SPECIALTY
1993

Specialty	No. of FMGs	No. Physician in GME	% of Total	% of Total FMGs
Nuclear Medicine	52	135	38.5%	0.2%
Internal Medicine	10,402	30,543	34.1%	49.8%
Pediatrics	2,787	8,989	31.0%	13.3%
Allergy/Immunology	52	169	30.8%	0.2%
Neurology	526	1,799	29.2%	2.5%
Pathology	819	2,956	27.7%	3.9%
Psychiatry	1,534	6,050	25.4%	7.3%
Family Practice	1,396	7,464	18.7%	6.7%
Transitional	293	1,589	18.4%	1.4%
Colon & Rectal Surgery	11	64	17.2%	0.1%
Anesthesiology	862	5,974	14.4%	4.1%
Preventive Medicine	36	292	12.3%	0.2%
Physical Medicine/Rehab.	110	1,111	9.9%	0.5%
Surgery	849	8,718	9.7%	4.1%
Neurosurgery	83	854	9.7%	0.4%
Thoracic Surgery	31	345	9.0%	0.1%
Plastic Surgery	37	523	7.1%	0.2%
Obstetrics-Gynecology	369	5,285	7.0%	1.8%
Ophthalmology	107	1,808	5.9%	0.5%
Radiology	269	5,084	5.3%	1.3%
Urology	59	1,157	5.1%	0.3%
Dermatology	43	969	4.4%	0.2%
Emergency Medicine	101	2,378	4.2%	0.5%
Otolaryngology	25	1,222	2.0%	0.1%
Orthopedic Surgery	49	3,335	1.5%	0.2%
TOTAL	**20,902**	**98,813**	**21.2%**	**100.0%**

Source: Association of American Medical Colleges, Medical Education Census, SAIMS Database, 1993

204

TABLE 5
PHYSICIANS IN GME RANKED BY STATE, 1993

State	No. Physician in GME	% of Total	Cumulative %
New York	14,805	15.0%	15.0%
California	9,004	9.1%	24.1%
Pennsylvania	7,236	7.3%	31.4%
Texas	5,859	5.9%	37.3%
Illinois	5,530	5.6%	42.9%
Ohio	4,728	4.8%	47.7%
Massachusetts	4,433	4.5%	52.2%
Michigan	3,904	4.0%	56.2%
New Jersey	2,603	2.6%	58.8%
Maryland	2,491	2.5%	61.3%
Florida	2,413	2.4%	63.8%
Missouri	2,233	2.3%	66.0%
North Carolina	2,211	2.2%	68.3%
Minnesota	2,193	2.2%	70.5%
District of Columbia	2,179	2.2%	72.7%
Connecticut	1,878	1.9%	74.6%
Georgia	1,826	1.8%	76.4%
Tennessee	1,798	1.8%	78.3%
Virginia	1,751	1.8%	80.0%
Wisconsin	1,583	1.6%	81.6%
Louisiana	1,504	1.5%	83.1%
Washington	1,415	1.4%	84.6%
Indiana	1,162	1.2%	85.8%
Colorado	1,130	1.1%	86.9%
Alabama	1,002	1.0%	87.9%
Arizona	997	1.0%	88.9%
Kentucky	986	1.0%	89.9%
South Carolina	908	0.9%	90.8%
Iowa	846	0.9%	91.7%
Puerto Rico	779	0.8%	92.5%
Kansas	702	0.7%	93.2%
Oklahoma	683	0.7%	93.9%
Oregon	648	0.7%	94.5%
Rhode Island	576	0.6%	95.1%
Utah	560	0.6%	95.7%
Arkansas	534	0.5%	96.2%
Nebraska	499	0.5%	96.7%
West Virginia	496	0.5%	97.2%
Mississippi	432	0.4%	97.7%
Hawaii	430	0.4%	98.1%
New Mexico	386	0.4%	98.5%
Vermont	265	0.3%	98.8%
New Hampshire	238	0.2%	99.0%
Maine	214	0.2%	99.2%
Delaware	195	0.2%	99.4%
North Dakota	120	0.1%	99.5%
Nevada	112	0.1%	99.7%
South Dakota	85	0.1%	99.7%
Idaho	39	0.0%	99.8%
Wyoming	38	0.0%	99.8%
Montana	0	0.0%	99.8%
Alaska	0	0.0%	99.8%
Unidentified Military	17?	0.2%	100.0%
TOTAL	**98,813**	**100.0%**	

Source Association of American Medical Colleges Medical Education Census, SAIMS Database, 1993

TABLE 6
PHYSICIANS IN GME PER THOUSAND POPULATION BY STATE, 1993

State	No. Physicians in GME	Population	Phys. in GME per 1,000 population
District of Columbia	2,179	589,000	3.70
New York	14,805	18,119,000	0.82
Massachusetts	4,433	5,998,000	0.74
Pennsylvania	7,236	12,009,000	0.60
Rhode Island	576	1,005,000	0.57
Connecticut	1,878	3,281,000	0.57
Maryland	2,491	4,908,000	0.51
Minnesota	2,193	4,480,000	0.49
Illinois	5,530	11,631,000	0.48
Vermont	265	570,000	0.46
Missouri	2,233	5,193,000	0.43
Ohio	4,728	11,016,000	0.43
Michigan	3,904	9,437,000	0.41
Hawaii	430	1,160,000	0.37
Tennessee	1,798	5,024,000	0.36
Louisiana	1,504	4,287,000	0.35
New Jersey	2,603	7,789,000	0.33
Texas	5,859	17,656,000	0.33
Colorado	1,130	3,470,000	0.33
North Carolina	2,211	6,843,000	0.32
Wisconsin	1,583	5,007,000	0.32
Nebraska	499	1,606,000	0.31
Utah	560	1,813,000	0.31
Iowa	846	2,812,000	0.30
California	9,004	30,867,000	0.29
Delaware	195	689,000	0.28
Kansas	702	2,523,000	0.28
Washington	1,415	5,136,000	0.28
Virginia	1,751	6,377,000	0.27
West Virginia	496	1,812,000	0.27
Georgia	1,826	6,751,000	0.27
Kentucky	986	3,755,000	0.26
Arizona	997	3,832,000	0.26
South Carolina	908	3,603,000	0.25
New Mexico	386	1,581,000	0.24
Alabama	1,002	4,136,000	0.24
Arkansas	534	2,399,000	0.22
Oregon	648	2,977,000	0.22
New Hampshire	238	1,111,000	0.21
Oklahoma	683	3,212,000	0.21
Indiana	1,162	5,662,000	0.21
North Dakota	120	636,000	0.19
Florida	2,413	13,488,000	0.18
Maine	214	1,235,000	0.17
Mississippi	432	2,614,000	0.17
South Dakota	85	711,000	0.12
Nevada	112	1,327,000	0.08
Wyoming	38	466,000	0.08
Idaho	39	1,067,000	0.04
Montana	0	824,000	0
Alaska	0	568,000	0
Puerto Rico	779	--	--
Unidentified Military	174	--	--
TOTAL	**98,813**	**255,052,000**	**0.39**

Source: Association of American Medical Colleges, Medical Education Census, SAIMS Database 1993
Population Data: U.S. Bureau of the Census, Current Population Reports 1992

TABLE 7
FMGs IN GME, RANKED BY % OF PHYSICIANS IN GME BY STATE, 1993

State	No. Physicians in GME	No. of FMGs	% FMGs of	% of Total FMGs in U.S.
New Jersey	2,603	1,377	52.9%	6.6%
North Dakota	120	50	41.7%	0.2%
New York	14,805	6,168	41.7%	29.5%
Nevada	112	40	35.7%	0.2%
Puerto Rico	779	269	34.5%	1.3%
Illinois	5,530	1,797	32.5%	8.6%
Michigan	3,904	1,154	29.6%	5.5%
Connecticut	1,878	549	29.2%	2.6%
West Virginia	496	121	24.4%	0.6%
Rhode Island	576	123	21.4%	0.6%
Pennsylvania	7,236	1,419	19.6%	6.8%
Wisconsin	1,583	306	19.3%	1.5%
Maryland	2,491	479	19.2%	2.3%
Ohio	4,728	908	19.2%	4.3%
District of Columbia	2,179	411	18.9%	2.0%
Florida	2,413	417	17.3%	2.0%
Missouri	2,233	367	16.4%	1.8%
Massachusetts	4,433	722	16.3%	3.5%
Oklahoma	683	107	15.7%	0.5%
Tennessee	1,798	275	15.3%	1.3%
Minnesota	2,193	323	14.7%	1.5%
Texas	5,859	845	14.4%	4.0%
South Dakota	85	11	12.9%	0.1%
Georgia	1,826	222	12.2%	1.1%
Indiana	1,162	139	12.0%	0.7%
Kentucky	986	113	11.5%	0.5%
Virginia	1,751	185	10.6%	0.9%
California	9,004	943	10.5%	4.5%
Iowa	846	81	9.6%	0.4%
Vermont	265	25	9.4%	0.1%
Nebraska	499	47	9.4%	0.2%
Maine	214	20	9.3%	0.1%
Delaware	195	18	9.2%	0.1%
Alabama	1,002	91	9.1%	0 4%
Kansas	702	63	9.0%	0.3%
Arkansas	534	45	8.4%	0 2%
Arizona	997	77	7.7%	0.4%
Hawaii	430	33	7.7%	0.2%
Mississippi	432	31	7 2%	0.1%
South Carolina	908	63	6.9%	0.3%
North Carolina	2,211	152	6.9%	0.7%
Louisiana	1,504	95	6.3%	0.5%
Utah	560	32	5.7%	0.2%
New Mexico	386	20	5.2%	0.1%
Idaho	39	2	5.1%	0.0%
Colorado	1,130	57	5.0%	0.3%
New Hampshire	238	12	5.0%	0.1%
Oregon	648	30	4.6%	0.1%
Washington	1,415	65	4.6%	0.3%
Wyoming	38	1	2.6%	0.0%
Montana	0	0	--	
Alaska	0	0	--	
Unidentified Military	174	2	1.1%	0.0%
TOTAL	**98,813**	**20,902**	21.2%	100.0%

Source. Association of American Medical Colleges, Medical Education Cens s, SAIMS Database, 1993

GOALS AND PRINCIPLES FOR HEALTH CARE REFORM

The Association of American Medical Colleges proposes and advocates the following goals and supporting principles for health care reform in the 1990s:

Any health care system must strive to achieve five goals: (1) giving all Americans the chance for a healthy life; (2) providing universal access to health care; (3) recognizing that once health care excellence is achieved, the necessary resources must be provided so that quality and capacity are maintained; (4) instituting cost containment measures that do not compromise the quality of health care; and (5) supporting the essential roles of medical and other health care professional education and of biomedical, behavioral, and health services research.

- Any health care reform plan must include not only diagnosis and treatment for existing illness, but also health-promotion and disease-prevention efforts so that each American has the opportunity for a healthy life.

- Health insurance must be transportable, affordable, and continuous.

- Any health care reform plan must guarantee access to a specified set of basic services, including preventive care.

- Even in a system that guarantees universal access, some individuals may lack health insurance, either by choice or by circumstances beyond their control. To eliminate the possibility that some individuals would choose not to participate in an available health insurance program, the health care system should be designed to require eligible individuals to participate. For those individuals who lack insurance because of circumstances beyond their control, alternative mechanisms to assure payment for the services they use must be maintained and funded.

- Existing public and government programs serving defined populations should not be terminated or significantly changed unless an alternative system has the ability to adequately replace them.

Efficient, effective, and comprehensive health care must be of consistent high quality. The criteria for assessing these factors should be continually re-evaluated and updated through the results of research efforts.

In areas where the current infrastructure is inadequate to meet the needs of underserved and disadvantaged populations, the health care delivery system must be improved and expanded to assure high-quality care and support systems.

Reforms should be phased in over a reasonable time frame that allows the health care system adequate time to adapt to the demands of expanded coverage while ensuring that high quality care continues to be delivered.

Appropriate cost control mechanisms must be incorporated into the health care system without creating barriers to expanding access and promoting quality and should reflect broader societal objectives and economic needs.

Cost containment efforts should: (1) ensure efficient and effective health care delivery; (2) not become an impediment to individuals seeking care; and (3) not place an unreasonable financial burden on the providers of care.

The health care financing system should recognize and support the additional costs that are incurred by those institutions that accept responsibility for the essential activities of medical and health care professional education, health-related research, and technology development.

ACADEMIC MEDICINE: THE CORNERSTONE
OF THE AMERICAN HEALTH CARE SYSTEM

Medical schools, teaching hospitals, and their faculty members and staff are valuable resources that serve national as well as local and regional health care needs. Their education, research, and patient care activities are the cornerstone on which the American health care system is built.

These academic institutions house much of the nation's biomedical, behavioral, and health-related research; and teaching hospitals make available treatments that may be unavailable elsewhere, provide the highest quality care, and are places of last resort for many who need care but do not have the wherewithal to pay for it.

The restructuring of the national economy underway as part of the president's economic plan, when combined with changes that are part of the health care reform proposal. may have serious and unintended consequences for academic medicine, which is the cornerstone of the American health care system.

Change will be counterproductive if reforms in the health care system do not protect and strengthen all of the essential elements of our system:

- Education of excellently prepared physicians and other health care workers;

- Medical research producing scientific advances that translate into prevention of disease and the cure or alleviation of human suffering; and

- Innovation, evaluation, and development of new treatments and procedures that have made American medical care the best in the world.

Medical schools and teaching hospitals have unique and valuable roles in the nation's health care system. Their contributions depend on multiple sources of financing, each of which is increasingly constrained. This simultaneous challenge to all sources of support jeopardizes the ability of medical schools and teaching hospitals to meet their societal commitments.

If health care reform constrains the flexibility that has existed within the patient care payment system to support academic medicine's other missions, then the reformed health care system must make explicit provision for new and dedicated funding mechanisms for these missions. Support must be provided to allow academic medicine to continue:

- Educating the world's best physicians and assuring that the physicians in training, as well as those now in practice, are prepared for the nation's evolving health care needs;

- Conducting research that will determine the most cost-effective and efficacious of present therapies, thus arming future physicians with the tools to reduce human suffering and lower the costs of health care even further;

· Providing much needed specialized services such as trauma care, burn units, and transplantation centers; and

· Caring for those who remain uninsured during a transition period to universal coverage or for those who may never be adequately incorporated into the health system.

The synergism between research and education, especially biomedical research and medical education, is readily apparent: medical school curricula depend heavily on biomedical research findings, and medical school faculty typically conduct such research in addition to teaching. Until recently, the link between traditional health services research and medical education has been less apparent for two reasons: traditional health services research was perceived as less relevant, and the research projects were smaller and often located in schools of public health and other health professions schools rather than medical schools. The relevance of health services research to medical education is increasing with the growth of outcomes research and an increased awareness of medical students' and residents' need to understand the health care delivery system.

SUPPORT FOR BIOMEDICAL, BEHAVIORAL, AND HEALTH SERVICES RESEARCH

The vitality and success of the U.S. health care system has depended, and will continue to depend, upon the ongoing generation of new basic biomedical and behavioral information. The federal government and other organizations must maintain their respective investments in a balanced and stable program of support for the acquisition of new basic knowledge and clinical applications that will improve the effectiveness of the health care system. The quality of this endeavor can only be ensured through continued reliance upon an effective peer-review system for the allocation of resources targeted to biomedical and behavioral research. Such funds must not be commingled with funding for other purposes.

- Appropriate public and private organizations, including the Association of American Medical Colleges, should consider the evolving requirements and implications of health care reform initiatives in developing future policy positions on biomedical and behavioral research that assure a responsive and vigorous research enterprise.

- Initiatives for health care reform should increase the funding and sponsorship of peer-reviewed health services research because of its importance to overall reform strategies. While a variety of funding sources are possible, funding for health services research should be separate from funding for biomedical research.

- Organizations such as the Association for Health Services Research, the Institute of Medicine, and/or other appropriate organizations should convene public and other private organizations concerned about health services research to: (1) develop a clearinghouse for health services research projects and findings; (2) propose appropriate expansion of funding for outcomes and other health services research; and (3) recommend a time period during which the increased resources, including manpower and funding, should be phased in.

As is true of our current health care system, whatever reformed system may be adopted will strive to provide health care that is beneficial in terms of both outcome and cost. It is through health-related research -- biomedical, behavioral, and health services -- that advances in diagnosis and treatment are discovered, evaluated, and, finally, made available to those who need them. Only by ensuring adequate and stable funding for all types of health-related research will it be possible to provide Americans with the most appropriate and effective care available.

GRADUATE MEDICAL EDUCATION

To encourage medical students to choose careers that meet national physician supply goals, incentive programs aimed at individuals throughout the medical education and practice continuum should be created and/or maintained. Individuals' behavior in choosing certain careers in influenced best by offering sets of incentives that affect them directly and personally as medical students, resident trainees, and practicing physicians.

Because graduate medical education is an integral component of educating physicians to provide all Americans with high-quality and cost-effective health care, it should continue to receive broad-based societal support. All public and private payers of health care services should be required to contribute to a national fund separate from payments for patient care services, to finance graduate medical education.

To assure that the financial support for graduate medical education is used to promote and improve the nation's health, a National Physician Resources Commission (NPRC) should be established. The NPRC would be an independent body, recognized by the federal government, with broad representation from the health care sector and other relevant societal groups. The NPRC would be responsible for:

* projecting the aggregate supply of physicians needed to support the nation's health care delivery system;

* setting national goals for both the total number of graduate medical education positions and for the appropriate mix of residency positions that would be dedicated to the education of generalist and other specialist physicians;

* reviewing the availability and appropriateness of incentive systems to assure that they reinforce national goals; and

* providing a linkage between the work force planning activities for physicians and other health professions.

Upon the establishment of an all-payer national fund and a determination that significant progress is not occurring in achieving the appropriate specialty redistribution, the NPRC could assume responsibility for authorizing payment for graduate medical education costs. The NPRC also could establish guidelines for the circumstances under which other funding could be used for graduate medical education activity.

In addition, the national commission could assist in the optional development of decentralized planning bodies for the physician work force to assure that regional, state, and local needs, objectives, and characteristics are recognized. Functioning under the auspices of the NPRC, these independent bodies would have broad public and private representation from the health care sector and other communities. The scope and role of these bodies would be determined by the NPRC.

Medical schools, teaching hospitals, and other organizations currently -- and potentially -- involved in graduate medical education should strongly consider the creation of formal associations, or "graduate medical consortia." Such consortia could provide enhanced mechanisms to assure the continuity of medical education and to develop centralized support, direction, and coordination for member institutions so that they function collectively to meet changing work force requirements.

The Accreditation Council for Graduate Medical Education (ACGME) or the American Osteopathic Association's (AOA) Committee on Post-doctoral Training should continue to accredit programs solely on the basis of whether the programs meet established educational criteria. The accreditation process should remain separate from physician work force planning, allocation, and financing activity.

The level of payments for graduate medical education should recognize all costs, including residents' stipends and benefits, salaries and benefits related to faculty supervision, allocated overhead, and costs related to the infra-structure overhead inherent in the graduate medical education process. The payments should be made to the organization or entity that incurs these costs.

Transitional relief funds should be made available to teaching hospitals that lose residency positions as part of the fundamental changes that may occur in the structure and financing of graduate medical education. Changes in the number and specialty mix of residents and their sites of training would be disruptive to teaching hospitals and their service activities and could have a particularly profound impact on some institutions. In these cases, relief funds would mitigate the effects of graduate medical education reform.

Because of its public role and responsibilities, the Medicare program should continue to recognize and support the costs of graduate medical education. In addition, the special and unique patient care costs of teaching institutions should continue to be recognized and paid through the indirect medical education (IME) adjustment in the Medicare prospective payment system. As changes are made in the overall health care delivery system and within the Medicare program, it may be appropriate to re-examine the purpose and level of Medicare payment mechanisms. Until such changes and/or alternative payment mechanisms have been developed, however, the payment structure and level of funding provided by the Medicare program for graduate medical education costs and the special costs of teaching hospitals should remain unchanged.

214

Chairman STARK. Dr. El-Attar.

STATEMENT OF SUZANNE M. EL-ATTAR, M.D., LEGISLATIVE
AFFAIRS DIRECTOR, AMERICAN MEDICAL STUDENT
ASSOCIATION

Dr. EL-ATTAR. Thank you, Mr. Chairman, for allowing me to participate in this discussion on health care reform. I am Suzanne El-Attar, the legislative affairs director for the American Medical Student Association. I am also a 1993 graduate of the University of Pittsburgh School of Medicine, and am currently applying for a residency in family practice.

The American Medical Student Association (AMSA) is the oldest and largest independent medical student organization in the country. With over 30,000 physician in training members at nearly every allopathic and osteopathic medical school, AMSA is the voice of medical students.

Because of our great commitment to primary care, AMSA is very encouraged by the recent attention and emphasis the Nation is giving to primary care. We support the efforts to increase the primary care physician workforce and improve access to primary care for all our citizens. Specifically, we support the goal of achieving a workforce composed of at least 50 percent generalists.

The reasons for lack of primary care physicians are many and complex and are rooted in the undergraduate and graduate medical education systems as well as the physician practice environment. Some of the well-documented deterrents are medical education environment and curricula. The hospital-based tertiary-care focus and biomedical research emphasis at most medical research schools results in few generalist-position role models and few required primary care experiences.

Income: Expected income for generalist positions can be two to three times less than their subspecialist colleagues. With the debt burden of today's medical students averaging $59,000 and often reaching higher than $100,000, future income is a great concern.

Prestige: Generalism is implied to require less knowledge and clinical skills than subspecialty professions. I am speaking from experience when I say it is very discouraging to constantly be defending a career decision to fellow classmates and medical school faculty. I have been asked why I would want to waste a good education on family practice and if my grades weren't good enough to enter a subspecialty field.

Although AMSA supports many of the things being proposed to increase the number of generalists, we are very concerned with the fervor with which our government is addressing the graduate medical education system while placing much less emphasis on needed reforms in undergraduate medical education and the practice environment. Focusing only on residency training will never succeed in creating long-term solutions to the problems with primary care.

AMSA urges the Federal Government and the medical community to address all aspects of physician training and practice from medical school admissions criteria to physician reimbursement. To increase the number and improve the quality of primary care physicians in this nation, I would like to remark on a few of AMSA's recommendations. A more detailed discussion of our recommendations can be found in the written testimony.

One, rotations in family practice general internal medicine and general pediatrics should be a required part of each medical school curricula.

Two, more generous faculty should be hired and maintained by each medical school to act as mentors and role models for aspiring primary care physicians in training.

Three, efforts must be made to increase education and training in ambulatory and community settings at every medical school.

Four, scholarships, low-interest loans and loan repayment programs must be created for medical students interested in primary care careers.

Five, the number of residency positions in primary care should be increased to 50 percent or more of all residency positions and the total number should be capped at 110 percent of U.S. medical graduates. We support the use and redistribution of Medicare's graduate medical education funding to accomplish this goal.

Six, the National Health Service Corps program should be revitalized and expanded. With such a great need for primary care physicians in underserved communities, there is no reason the National Health Service Corps should not have the funding to accept every qualified applicant. I am speaking as one who was denied a corps scholarship.

Primary care is well recognized as one of the most efficient ways to provide quality health care in a cost-effective manner. AMSA applauds the administration's and Congress' efforts to create a health care system with universal coverage and an increased number of primary care physicians. However, graduate medical education cannot be reformed as if it exists in vacuum. As long as undergraduate medical education continues to get the message that primary care is not worthwhile, it will be very difficult to create the physician workforce we all know this country needs.

Let's stop giving medical students mixed messages and begin addressing the entire system of medical education. Thank you.

Chairman STARK. Thank you.

[The prepared statement follows:]

216

STATEMENT OF SUZANNE M. EL-ATTAR, M.D.
LEGISLATIVE AFFAIRS DIRECTOR
AMERICAN MEDICAL STUDENT ASSOCIATION

Thank-you for allowing me to participate in this discussion on heath care reform. I am Suzanne El-Attar, the Legislative Affairs Director for the American Medical Student Association. I am also a 1993 graduate of the University of Pittsburgh School of Medicine, and am currently applying for a residency in family practice.

The American Medical Student Association (AMSA) is the oldest and largest independent medical student organization in the country. With over 30,000 physician-in-training members at nearly every allopathic and osteopathic medical school, AMSA is the voice of medical students. For over forty years AMSA members have been active in medical education reform, health care policy debates and community service.

AMSA has a productive history of providing opportunities for students to experience primary care medicine in underserved communities. Through the summers of 1969-75, AMSA members developed and directed massive community health projects in the core Appalachian states, Native American nations and migrant workers' communities. Since 1975, AMSA has worked closely with the National Health Service Corps to introduce medical students to health care in underserved areas through our Health Promotion Disease Prevention project. Furthermore, a number of student efforts initiated by AMSA's chapters and task forces have grown into comprehensive, inner-city health clinics. While providing much needed services, students have received positive exposure to primary care practice in these areas, and many have returned to practice in underserved communities.

In 1992, AMSA initiated a national Generalist Physicians In Training (GPIT) project. GPIT is a medical student organized and administered program, designed to produce a forum for the exposure of AMSA members to generalism and encourage the pursuit of generalist careers. This is accomplished through the use of mentors, the development of primary care projects, and the exposure of our membership to community-based primary care.

Because of our great commitment to this issue, AMSA is very encouraged by the recent attention and emphasis the nation is giving to primary care. We support the efforts to increase the primary care physician workforce and improve access to primary care for all our citizens. Specifically, we support the goal of achieving a workforce composed of at least 50% primary care physicians. AMSA acknowledges the importance of primary care to the improvement of health and health care in the U.S.

AMSA defines primary care, or generalism, to include medical care delivery which incorporates and emphasizes the four principles of: first contact, ongoing responsibility, comprehensiveness of scope and overall coordination of the patient's health problems, be they biological, behavioral or social. The medical specialties that best encompass these four principles are family practice, general practice, general internal medicine, general pediatrics and obstetrics-gynecology.

Currently, there are too many sub-specialty trained physicians and too few generalists to enable the delivery of quality, cost effective health care in the U.S. Primary care physicians amount to approximately 30% of all practicing physicians. In contrast, only 19% of the graduating class of 1993, my own class, chose generalist careers. The shortage of generalist physicians is even more severe in many inner-city and rural areas of this nation.

There are two compelling reasons for increasing the number of primary care physicians in the U.S. First, primary care physicians provide quality health care at less cost to our nation than sub-specialists. With the cost of health care in this country reaching $1 trillion per year, or over 14% of our gross domestic product, significant measures must be taken to diminish this spending rate. It is known that sub-specialists perform more tests, prescribe more medications and hospitalize more frequently than generalists resulting in more costly care. Yet, there is no evidence supporting that care provided through generalists will decrease quality. Greater access to primary care physicians may actually improve the health status of our nation by resulting in greater utilization of health promotion and disease prevention services.

Second, increased numbers of primary care physicians are needed because they choose to work in underserved communities at greater rates than sub-specialists. Our rural and inner-city communities have a significant need for all types of physicians, especially generalists. The health status of some of these communities is embarrassingly poor. Over the past 30 years, the ratio of generalists to sub-specialists has decreased from 50:50 to the current 30:70. During this same period, the number of designated Health Professions Shortage Areas has doubled. The U.S. will be better poised to address the problems of the growing number of underserved communities with a workforce that emphasizes primary care.

The reasons for our nation's lack of primary care physicians are many and complex and are rooted in the undergraduate and graduate medical education systems as well as the physician practice environment. Some of the well documented deterrents are:

- Medical school curricula and environments are overtly biased towards sub-specialty training. The hospital-based, tertiary-care focus and biomedical research emphasis of most medical schools attracts sub-specialty oriented faculty, resulting in few primary care physician role-models and mentors for medical students. Many students are never exposed to a primary care rotation or a rotation located in an ambulatory or community setting. There are still medical schools that do not have departments of family medicine.

- Expected salaries for generalist physicians can be two to three times less than their sub-specialist colleagues. With the debt burden of today's medical students averaging $59,000 and sometimes reaching higher than $100,000, future income is a great concern for physicians-in-training.

- Careers in primary care are both overtly and subtly depicted as less prestigious than sub-specialty professions. Generalism is implied to require less knowledge and clinical skills. I am speaking from experience when I say, it is very discouraging to constantly be defending a career decision to fellow classmates and medical school faculty. I have been asked why I would want to waste a good education on family practice, and if my grades weren't good enough to enter a sub-specialty field.

Although AMSA supports many of the changes being proposed to increase the number of generalists, we are very concerned with the fervor to which our federal government is addressing the graduate medical education system, while placing much less emphasis on needed reforms in undergraduate medical education and the practice environment. Focusing only on residency training will never succeed in creating long-term solutions to the problems with primary care. AMSA implores the federal government and the medical community to devise a plan for reform which addresses all aspects of physician training and practice. Only through comprehensive medical education reform, can we ensure significant and long-lasting improvements in our physician workforce.

To increase the number and improve the quality of primary care physicians in this nation, the American Medical Student Association recommends the following.

Undergraduate medical education:
1. Medical school admissions policy, structure and function should reflect the need to recruit and admit more qualified applicants who demonstrate a commitment to primary care.

2. Every medical school should have a mission statement and strategic plan to address the social needs of our country and the school's community, including increasing the number of primary care physicians and fostering interest in practice in medically underserved areas.

3. Each medical school should be required to have a department of family practice, equivalent in status and financial support to other major clinical departments of that school. Third year rotations in family practice, general internal medicine and general pediatrics should be a required part of each medical school curriculum. Title VII funding under the Public Health Service Act must be increased and redistributed to address these needs.

4. More generalist faculty should be hired and maintained by each medical school to act as mentors and role-models for aspiring primary care physicians-in-training. One way to affect this is to shift NIH funding from pure biomedical research to more outcomes, population-based research and increase funding for the Agency for Health Care Policy and Research.

5. Efforts must be made by the government and medical schools to increase education and training in ambulatory and community settings. This should include increased funding and expansion of already existing programs such as Area Health Education Centers.

6. Generalist interest groups should be formed, by students and faculty, to maintain and stimulate interest in primary care careers.

7. Scholarships, low interest loans, and loan repayment programs must be created for medical students interested in primary care careers. These scholarships and loans must be available to all students interested in generalism, and should not target one group in society. AMSA is concerned with the current trend of the federal government to attach primary care qualifiers to loans formerly designated solely for students from disadvantaged backgrounds. Loan repayment programs must also be available for those students, like myself, who made the decision to become a generalist later in their medical school career.

Graduate medical education:
1. The number of residency positions in primary care should be increased to 50% or more of all residency positions.
2. The total number of residency positions should be capped at 110% of all U.S. medical school graduates. The issue is not only increasing the number of primary care physicians in the country. The total number of physicians must be maintained or reduced to help address the currently over-saturated markets for certain sub-specialists.

3. Medicare's graduate medical education (GME) funding should be redirected to favor primary care residency training. This includes allowing funding for non-hospital based training sites.

4. Medicare GME payments should fund primary care residency programs located in medically underserved communities at higher rates.

5. Incentive salaries should be established for primary care resident physicians.

Practice environment:
1. Income disparities between primary care and sub-specialist physicians must be reduced.
2. The National Health Service Corps' programs should be revitalized and expanded, and more state funded service programs should be created. With such a great need for primary care physicians in underserved communities, there is no reason the NHSC should not have the funding to accept every qualified applicant. I am speaking to you as a NHSC scholarship reject.

3. Medicare and Medicaid reimbursements should be restructured to more equitably pay for primary care services. AMSA supports the intent of the Resource Based Relative Value Scale (RBRVS) system, but believes this intent was distorted and diminished upon implementation of the program. AMSA encourages improvements in the RBRVS system and the creation of other programs to enhance primary care physician reimbursement.

4. The voluntary retraining of sub-specialist physicians should be encouraged to meet the primary care needs of the community. Hospitals who have lost sub-specialty residencies, through the redistribution of residency positions, could take advantage of the opportunity to create generalist training positions to specifically address the needs of sub-specialists desiring to increase their generalist skills.

Primary care is well recognized as one of the most efficient ways to provide quality health care in a cost effective manner. AMSA applauds the administration's and Congress' efforts to create a health care system with universal coverage and an increased number of primary care physicians.

However, graduate medical education can not be reformed as if it exists in a vacuum. As long as undergraduate medical education continues to give the message that primary care is not worthwhile, it will be very difficult to achieve the physician workforce we all know this country needs. Let's stop giving medical students mixed messages, and begin addressing the entire system of medical education.

If the recommendations of the current physicians-in-training are supported, the future of primary care is bright and the goal of producing 50% generalist physicians in the United States is achievable. We appreciate your interest in receiving AMSA's perspectives and recommendations regarding the current problems in primary care and medical education. We offer our continued input and support in addressing this issue.

Chairman STARK. Ms. Bednash.

STATEMENT OF GERALDINE BEDNASH, PH.D., R.N., EXECUTIVE DIRECTOR, AMERICAN ASSOCIATION OF COLLEGES OF NURSING

Ms. BEDNASH. Good morning, Mr. Chairman. I am Geraldine Bednash, executive director of the American Association of Colleges of Nursing. We represent over 450 senior colleges and universities in this country with baccalaureate and graduate nursing education programs. The primary mission of our association is to improve the health of the public by improving the quality of nursing education and research.

One group of nursing clinicians prepared in our member institutions, advanced practice nurses, are increasingly recognized as an important resource for expanding access to health care.

Mr. Chairman, AACN has for some time had concerns about the adequacy of funding for graduate nursing education, especially in this time of exploding demands for these practitioners. In order to educate adequate numbers of highly skilled, expert, advanced-practice nursing clinicians, such as nurse practitioners, nurse midwives, nurse anesthetists and clinical nurse specialists, a reliable revenue stream that is not subject to the uncertainties of the annual appropriations process must be available.

Frankly, the fastest way to expand the number of advanced practice nurses in this country would be to eliminate the barriers to practice and reimbursement which prevents these nurses from practicing to their fullest capabilities. Therefore, AACN supports strongly removal of these barriers. Due to time restrictions, however, I will limit my statement to the need for stable funding for graduate nurse education.

President Clinton's Health Security Act, as presently introduced, includes language that authorizes funding for graduate nurse education through a program modeled on the current graduate medical education funding strategy. Under the Clinton plan, all users of the health care system properly would also be required to contribute to the costs of health professionals education separate from reimbursement for patient care. AACN supports this all-payer initiative, and further, is supportive of the proposed graduate nurse education initiative.

In particular, AACN believes that the cost of clinical training and a stipend support for these students should be made an element of any efforts to expand production of these clinicians. Graduate nursing education support would expand enrollments and increase the rate at which these students are completing their studies.

Currently, the costs of graduate nursing education are almost entirely borne by the academic institutions and by the students themselves, despite the fact that the clinical service sector benefits heavily from the skills and capabilities of these advance practitioners. We believe that all entities that incur clinical costs for support of advanced practice nursing education should have access to this funding. This funding would allow the allocation of resources for additional clinical faculty to expand the number of advance practice nurses in training.

Moreover, with health care delivery evolving beyond acute care to community-based sites, it is imperative that the clinical training sites be broadly defined to include a variety of ambulatory care delivery sites.

In addition to the proposal for graduate nurse education funding, the Health Security Act recommends the establishment of a national council for graduate nurse education with responsibility for allocation of funding priorities in nursing training programs. AACN supports the establishment of this national advisory body, but recommends that this be an independent nursing council appointed by the Secretary and comprised of a group of experts who would review the supply of and demand for advanced-practice nurses and project the workforce needs for graduate-prepared nurses to inform logical funding decisions.

The advanced practitioner is a vital component in increasing access to quality health care services in a reform system. In order to quickly expand the numbers of these expert clinicians, we need your help and we ask for your support. Investment in graduate nursing education will ensure that nursing education will remain viable and allow continuation of its unique contribution to the health of the nation. The time is right for an increased commitment to graduate nursing education.

Mr. Chairman, thank you for the opportunity to testify and look forward to working with you and the subcommittee in making this a reality, and I would be pleased to respond to any questions.

Chairman STARK. Thank you.

[The prepared statement follows:]

Before the House Ways and Means Committee
Subcommittee on Health

Testimony of the American Association of Colleges of Nursing
on
Graduate Nurse Education and the Health Security Act, H.R. 3600

Presented by Geraldine Bednash, PhD, RN, Executive Director
February 1, 1994

I am Geraldine Bednash, PhD, RN, FAAN, Executive Director, American Association of Colleges of Nursing (AACN) representing 456 baccalaureate and graduate nursing education schools. The primary mission of AACN is to serve the public through the promotion and improvement of higher education for professional nursing, leading to better delivery of health care services. Mr. Chairman, AACN has had a longtime interest in graduate nurse education funding, and I am pleased to note that at least one of the proposed health care plans - the Administration's - has addressed this issue.

President Clinton's Health Security Act, as presently introduced, includes a provision in sections 3061 and 3062 for funding for graduate nurse education. This would provide a stable, on-going revenue source to expand the production of advanced practice nurses (APNs), a vital resource to meeting health care needs. Advanced nurse education includes the training of nurse practitioners, nurse midwives, nurse anesthetists, and other clinical nurse specialists. These APNs are prepared as expert clinicians to deliver primary care and other services vital to America's health care needs.

AACN members have 211 master's programs, 103 NP programs, 59 doctoral programs, 70 nurse anesthetist programs, and 24 nurse midwife programs. Also, 78 academic health centers house schools of nursing with graduate programs (See Table L)

The cost of nursing graduate education is that of any student receiving a master's degree. The Economic Investment in Nursing Education, published by AACN in 1989, found that based on 1988 dollars, it would cost a graduate nursing student $36,837 without financial aid to receive a master's degree. Please note that it includes net income foregone. This is because these students are registered nurses who are giving up employment to go to graduate school. It is assumed that the average debt burden is low because graduate nursing students go to school part time on the "pay as you go" plan, and do not accumulate large debts. Converting these students to full time as GNE would do, would eliminate much of their opportunity and need to work.

I will briefly describe the APN student. She goes to graduate nursing school part-time for an average of 3.9 years and is a primary earner for the family. She does not go to school to earn a significantly higher income, but rather goes to become an expert practitioner and a stable health care resource in the community. Stipend support from GNE would provide opportunities for the APN student to attend school full-time, eliminate the need to work while going to school, and allow the completion of a graduate degree on the average of 18 months. Currently the Health

Care Financing Administration is funding five demonstration projects on graduate nurse education. The projects are in their fifth and final year and are producing outcomes that demonstrate that with student stipends and clinical faculty support, students are graduating in 12 to 24 months, are better prepared clinically, and remain employed at the clinical training site. This helps to retain high quality staff, lowers costs of recruitment/orientation, and substantially decreases turnover rates.

Frankly, the fastest way to expand the number of APNs in this country would be to eliminate the barriers to practice and reimbursement which prevents these nurses from practicing to their fullest capabilities. Therefore, AACN strongly supports removal of these barriers. Due to time restrictions, however, I will limit my statement to the need for stable funding for graduate nurse education.

In order to educate adequate numbers of skilled APNs who provide high quality, and cost-effective services, there must be a reliable revenue stream that is not subject to the uncertainties of the annual appropriations process. Under the Clinton plan, all users of the health care system properly will be required to contribute to the cost of health professions education, separate from reimbursement for patient care. Other components of the Health Security Act include the establishment of a National Council for Graduate Nurse Education, allocation of primary care and specialty slots, the inclusion of training programs in ambulatory settings, and formula payments for operating costs. AACN supports this GNE initiative, because it will increase the number of students and the rapidity with which they can be produced.

AACN supports the establishment of an independent nursing council, appointed by the Secretary, which is comprised of a group of experts who will deal with the supply and demand of practitioners for the future. It would project, on an annual basis, the workforce needs for graduate prepared nurses. The establishment of this council would provide broad recommendations regarding supply and demand for APNs to inform logical funding decisions. With health care delivery evolving beyond acute care to community based sites, ambulatory care facilities, as well as tertiary care sites, should be reimbursed for costs incurred for clinical training of APNs. Ambulatory care facilities should be defined broadly to encompass facilities without links to acute care settings, such as school clinics, nurse managed centers, school of nursing administered health care delivery sites, HMOs, public health settings, and home care services. A broad definition of eligible training facilities is necessary to facilitate clinical training of the largest number of APNs in those sites that have the greatest need for these providers

AACN also supports the proposed formula for payments of operating costs: the product of the number of full-time training participants and the national average cost of the programs, determined by the national average salary of the participant and the average cost of programs providing supervision of trainees. Currently, most nursing schools pay their own faculty or make arrangements with preceptors at clinical sites to provide clinical training at patient care sites outside the school's academic facilities. The costs of faculty at the clinical site and costs of preceptorships for advanced nursing students are part of the costs of providing patient care, because patients receive the benefit of the care delivered by graduate students and their faculty.

In a 1988 cost study on nursing education by AACN, a majority of participating clinical service agencies indicated that the presence of nursing students in the clinical service agencies and the agencies' participation in nursing education had a positive influence on the standards of care and on patient satisfaction. Nurses enjoyed working with nursing students and liked the challenge of remaining current with nursing theory and technological advances. Students and faculty also served as resources for the staff relating to updates in nursing.

We believe that all entities that incur clinical costs for support of APN education should have access to GNE funding. GNE funding would allow the allocation of resources for added clinical faculty to expand the number of APNs in training. This would help eliminate the waiting lists which all graduate nursing programs are experiencing, with an average of 21.1 qualified applicants per program. Support of preceptors in the clinical sites would allow them to provide teaching and direct clinical supervision to the APN students as a planned component of their job responsibilities, rather than as an additional responsibility to their current workload. GNE support would also provide incentives to the practice sites to agree to take on students for clinical training. It would allow the clinical site to focus on training activities without having adverse input on patient care.

Due to limited resources at a typical clinical site, most can only take on one or two APN students at any one time. This forces schools of nursing to contract with numerous sites in order to provide clinical training for students. Reimbursement to clinical sites for clinical faculty would allow the concentration of groups of APN students, reducing the need for APN students to be placed in numerous sites by the academic institution. In addition, reimbursing clinical sites for training APN students would reflect the value of their services to patient care. With the number of specialty resident physicians likely to be reduced, APNs will be delivering many of the services formerly performed by resident physicians. In fact, this is already occurring in a number of clinical sites.

The APN is a vital component in increasing access to quality health care services in a reformed system. The cost of preparing the APN are borne almost entirely by schools of nursing and the students themselves, each with very limited resources. In order to quickly expand the numbers of these expert clinicians, we need your help. We ask for your support. Investment in GNE will ensure that nursing education will remain viable and allow continuation of its unique contributions to the health of the nation. The time is right for an increased commitment to GNE.

Mr. Chairman, thank you for the opportunity to testify and I look forward to working with you and the subcommittee in making GNE funding a reality. I would be pleased to respond to questions.

Table 1. Enrollment[1] and Graduations[2] by Type of Nursing Program in 79 Institutions that are Part of Academic Health Centers Compared to All Institutions[3] in the American Association of Colleges of Nursing Database.

TYPE OF PROGRAM	Number of Schools	ENROLLMENT			GRADUATIONS
		Full-time	Part-time	Total	
Generic Baccalaureate					
All Schools	418	75,530	11,431	86,941	19,245
AHCs	68	17,716	2,855	20,571	5,886
(% of All Schools)	(16.3%)	(23.5%)	(25.0%)	(23.7%)	(30.6%)
RN Baccalaureate (RN Completion)					
All Schools	501	6,492	25,676	32,168	9,221
AHCs	72	863	3,901	4,764	1,933
(% of All Schools)	(14.4%)	(13.3%)	(15.2%)	(14.8%)	(21.0%)
Master of Nursing					
All Schools	239	7,047	19,507	26,554	6,881
AHCs	78	4,100	8,760	12,860	3,854
(% of All Schools)	(32.6%)	(58.2%)	(44.9%)	(48.4%)	(56.0%)
Generic Master's					
All Schools	12	632	60	692	179
AHCs	5	363	33	396	143
(% of All Schools)	(41.7%)	(57.4%)	(55.0%)	(57.2%)	(79.9%)
Doctoral					
All Schools	54	1,200	1,597	2,797	374
AHCs	39	932	1,013	1,945	249
(% of All Schools)	(72.2%)	(77.7%)	(63.4%)	(69.5%)	(66.6%)
Doctor of Nursing (ND)					
All Schools	3	123	46	169	31
AHCs	3	123	46	169	31
(% of All Schools)	(100%)	(100%)	(100%)	(100%)	(100%)

[1] Fall 1992.
[2] From September 1, 1991 to August 31, 1992.
[3] 521 institutions in enrollment database (81.9% response rate) and 522 institutions in graduation database (82.1% response rate).

Table 2

RECOMMENDATIONS FOR FACULTY COSTS AND STUDENT SUPPORT

Based on an average faculty-student ratio of 1:4.

1. Clinical faculty cost $45,000 (clinical faculty salary)
                            +
                            $14,850 (33% benefits)
                            +
                            $ 7,500 (1/4 FTE support staff)
                            =
                            $67,350 for every 4 students

                            _____

                            =$16,837 per student year + $8,418
                            per 1/2 year (for 18 month program)

                            =$25,256 faculty/staff cost per graduate

2. Student support:
   average RN salary @ $28,000 per year = $42,000 (18 month program)

                            Total = $67,225 (18 month program or yearly average of
                            $44,800

* According to 1990 HCFA data, the average annual cost per medical resident was $85,000. A
three year residency will cost $255,000.

Chairman STARK. Dr. Jones.

STATEMENT OF OLEN E. JONES, JR., PH.D., CHAIRMAN, BOARD OF GOVERNORS, AMERICAN ASSOCIATION OF COLLEGES OF OSTEOPATHIC MEDICINE, AND PRESIDENT, WEST VIRGINIA SCHOOL OF OSTEOPATHIC MEDICINE, LEWISBURG, W. VA.

Mr. JONES. Good morning. I am Olen E. Jones, Jr., president of the West Virginia School of Osteopathic Medicine. I am privileged to appear as the board chair of the American Association of Colleges of Osteopathic Medicine to share our views about medical education reform.

Although some of the ideas in my statement may fall outside the traditional jurisdiction of this committee, we want to share our experience with you and encourage the members to think broadly and creatively about ways to increase the number of primary care physicians.

Our experience has shown that because students must choose to enter primary care before they graduate from medical school, the best time to influence their career decisions is at the undergraduate level. To focus only on the period of residency training is to miss most of the educational opportunities that have real impact on influencing physician manpower policy. Before I proceed, however, I want to provide some background to illustrate the special interest osteopathic medical education has in primary care.

Osteopathic physicians are an important resource in meeting the primary care needs of the Nation. They are physicians, fully licensed to provide comprehensive health care. Like their M.D. counterparts, they work in hospitals, clinics, private offices, Federal agencies and many other health care settings. What sets osteopathic medical care apart is the more than century-old tradition of training family doctors.

The commitment of osteopathic medicine to family and community care is reflected in its colleges' curricula. Clinical training most often occurs in community hospitals, clinics and physician offices rather than in large metropolitan teaching hospitals. Although osteopathic physicians can earn certification in the same medical specialties as allopathic physicians, most D.O.s have chosen primary care practice. If I may, I would like to use my school as an example of this commitment to primary care.

The very first sentence of our school's mission statement states we are "committed to providing family physicians for rural West Virginia and Appalachia." We emphasize family practice and primary care in our recruitment and admission strategies. Our students come to our school knowing we train primary care physicians with a special emphasis in family practice.

Although osteopathic medical colleges have done a unique job in producing primary physicians, I would be remiss if I did not speak of the recent shift in career preferences among our students. For example, of all 1992 seniors, only 32 percent said they plan careers in primary care, down from 41 percent the previous year. AACOM believes we can reverse this trend with Federal assistance. We support the initiative in the President's health care reform package to increase the supply of primary care physicians.

Turning now to specific recommendations, AACOM supports the President's proposal requiring at least 55 percent of all graduate training positions in the Nation be in primary care fields, provided that this 55 percent figure applies to both osteopathic and allopathic residence positions, individually and jointly. In addition, AACOM believes that it is crucial that a representative from the osteopathic medicine profession be included on the national board that will allocate residency positions.

It is important to recognize, Mr. Chairman, that changing the distribution of graduate training is but one of a number of educational changes needed to produce an adequate primary care workforce. Therefore, it is crucial that attention and resources be paid to the undergraduate medical education level. AACOM recommends that a two-prong approach should be utilized to ensure that there is a sufficient primary care workforce to provide increased access to health care.

First, AACOM recommends increased appropriations for loans and scholarships to assist students with a commitment to a primary care career. AACOM also supports the health education lending program introduced by you, Mr. Chairman, which addresses our concerns of increased borrowing limits and providing income-contingent repayment.

Second, AACOM recommends establishing a new Federal capitation program for medical schools to maintain and enhance the capacity to educate students in ambulatory primary care settings. AACOM believes that a capitation approach would allow schools flexibility to address those aspects of primary care education needed to ensure more adequate production of primary care physicians.

Mr. Chairman, on behalf of our schools, the students we train and the parents we serve, thank you for this opportunity for us to share AACOM's views with the subcommittee. At the appropriate time, I will be happy to respond to questions.

[The prepared statement follows:]

STATEMENT OF OLEN E. JONES, JR., PH.D.
PRESIDENT, WEST VIRGINIA SCHOOL OF OSTEOPATHIC MEDICINE
CHAIRMAN, BOARD OF GOVERNORS, AMERICAN ASSOCIATION OF COLLEGES OF
OSTEOPATHIC MEDICINE

Good Morning, Mister Chairman and Members of this Subcommittee. I am Olen E. Jones, Jr., Ph.D., and I am President of the West Virginia School of Osteopathic Medicine. I am also privileged to be the current Chairman of the Board of Governors of the American Association of Colleges of Osteopathic Medicine, or "AACOM." We represent all of the colleges of osteopathic medicine.

I am appearing before you this morning as AACOM's Board Chairman. And before I proceed, I want to express my sincere thanks to you and to the Members of this Subcommittee for giving AACOM the opportunity to place in the public record the important contributions to primary health care made by our member schools.

This Committee, and Congress generally, has tried to influence physician manpower policy through manipulation of the Medicare payments to hospitals for the costs of residency training programs. Changes in the payments for the direct expenses associated with interns and residents, as well as the indirect medical education adjustment, have been made in order to alter the ratios of primary care physicians to specialized physicians. I think it is clear that the effectiveness of these moves on physician manpower policy and physician career choice is limited. Changes are certainly needed at the graduate medical education (GME) level in order to make sure that there are appropriate numbers of training slots in primary care for medical school graduates, but these are not enough.

Unfortunately for the success of these financial policy changes, students must choose to enter primary care training before they graduate from medical school. Thus the best time to influence their career goals is at the undergraduate level. In fact, the point of greatest influence may come before entry to medical school. The colleges of osteopathic medicine have learned that recruitment of particular types of students is an important aspect is the choice of a primary care career. We have learned that the career of the physician is influenced by a spectrum of educational experiences. To focus only on the period of residency training is to miss most of the opportunities to have real impact.

Although some of the ideas in my statement may fall outside the traditional jurisdiction of this committee, we want to share our experience with you and encourage the members to think broadly and creatively about ways to increase the number of primary care physicians. We urge you to examine the entire physician educational spectrum to find innovative ways to enhance primary care.

AACOM supports a reconfiguration of Medicare payments for graduate medical education that will promote primary care education. We encourage reimbursement systems that support primary care providers adequately and adjust the imbalances in physician payment that now exist.

Let me turn to the other areas of our experience that may be helpful to the committee as it determines how best to influence physician career choices.

The 16 colleges of osteopathic medicine have together close to 7,500 students enrolled in four-year programs leading to the degree of Doctor of Osteopathy, or D.O. At the close of the academic year, in June 1994, they expect to confer close to 1,800 D.O. degrees. As you know, the D.O. degree is recognized as the equivalent of the M.D. degree throughout this country -- licensed to provide comprehensive medical care in all 50 states.

Our oldest member school, Kirksville College of Osteopathic Medicine, was founded in Kirksville, Missouri, in 1892 by Dr. Andrew Taylor Still, the originator of the osteopathic discipline. Our youngest member school, Lake Erie College of Osteopathic Medicine was founded last year in Erie, Pennsylvania (and has just applied for membership in AACOM). Ten of the osteopathic medical schools were established within just the past three decades.

There are several reasons for this sharp growth curve in recent years, but the most significant reason is the American people's increasing demand for quality primary medical and health care. And primary care has been and continues to be the foundation-stone of the osteopathic discipline.

The curricula of our member schools reflects the four over-arching principles of osteopathic medicine, principles which embody the primary care ethic. These principles are:

First, that the human body is a unit. Good medical practice is concerned, therefore, with doing more than merely curing a particular disease condition or repairing a specific disability; good medical practice, we believe, must be concerned with helping the whole human body recover and maintain total health.

The **Second** principle is that the human body, on its own, tends toward being healthy and whole; the physician's role, therefore, is mainly to assist the body's own normal mechanisms for self-regulation and self-healing.

The **Third** principle of osteopathic medicine states that the human body is an integrated organism. Hence, when the nervous system and the circulatory system are able to work successfully together with -- and in support of -- other systems, then we say that person is "in good health."

The **Fourth** principle is that rational therapy is based upon an understanding of the three principles I just mentioned: body unity; self regulatory mechanisms and the inter-relationship of structure and function.

I've provided this little preamble, Mr. Chairman, in order to illustrate the special interest we have, as osteopathic medical educators, in the issue before us; that is, the great national need for more and better trained primary care health and medical care providers.

By training and by tradition, osteopathic physicians practice "hands-on" medicine and place a high value on maintaining close and interactive physician-patient relationships. In fact, almost *30 percent* of the full-time faculty in all 16 schools teach family medicine, pediatrics, and internal medicine, the three specialties that are at the heart of primary medical care. That emphasis is even more pronounced among the volunteer or adjunct faculty of our schools; roughly *half* of all volunteer faculty teach in one or another of these three departments. Since volunteers comprise about two-thirds of all our faculties, it is apparent that students at schools of osteopathic medicine receive a strong and, we believe, an appropriate bias in favor of the practice of primary care medicine.

If I may, Mr. Chairman, I would like to use our own West Virginia School of Osteopathic Medicine as my first illustration of how we carry out this commitment to primary care.

The very first sentence of the mission statement of our school states that we are "committed to providing family physicians for rural West Virginia and Appalachia". Consistent with that mission statement, we emphasize family medicine and primary care in our recruitment and admission strategies. For example, we specifically look for men and women who have experienced rural life -- and who *love* rural life -- and who want to share our commitment to bringing quality primary care to the citizens of rural West Virginia. Because of our mission statement our students come here knowing that we train primary care physicians with a special emphasis on family practitioners.

We receive about 1,400 applications for the 65 spaces in our freshman class. Most are young men and women who want to live in and serve the rural areas of our State. But we also encourage applications from non-traditional students as well, individuals who have already experienced life as teachers or miners or possibly as nurses. We respect their decision to want to start a new career in osteopathic medicine, and we value their first-hand understanding of the great need for primary health and medical care in rural America.

Eighty percent of our student body is drawn directly from among the good people of West Virginia. But so is most of our excellent clinical faculty. Many are osteopathic physicians who themselves have had a primary care practice in rural West Virginia. They personally have known both the trials and joys of being the only doctor taking care of the health and medical needs of dozens of families scattered throughout several hundred square miles of West Virginia's forested mountains and hollows.

Our students learn osteopathic medicine from faculty who have this kind of experience, knowledge, and dedication. I should also note, Mr. Chairman, that our students do not learn about primary care entirely in the classroom. The average student at West Virginia School of Osteopathic Medicine will spend 13 of his or her final 24 months studying primary care specialties on-site in community-based, primary care settings, such as solo practitioners' offices, community clinics, or regional or area-wide community hospitals.

I am, of course, very proud of our record of service to the people of West Virginia. But it is the kind of record you will find repeated by all of AACOM's member schools.

Mr. Chairman, in your own state of California at the College of Osteopathic Medicine of the Pacific, or COMP, in Pomona, the average student spends his or her first two years in the Department of Family Medicine learning the essentials of anatomy, biochemistry, pharmacology, being exposed to a number of family practitioners -- those same volunteer teachers I spoke of earlier. These faculty teach important aspects of clinical practice, but they are also very effective mentors and role models to young and impressionable medical students.

I should add that about 50 percent of the required third- and fourth-year clinical training at COMP is in the primary care disciplines.

Across the continent, in Biddeford, Maine, the University of New England College of Osteopathic Medicine, or UNECOM, uses local practicing generalists to help select the members of each incoming freshman class.

In UNECOM's first- and second-year program, students are placed in community-based primary care settings to work as team members with family medicine practitioners, physician assistants, nurse practitioners, therapists, and social workers in order to understand, be comfortable with, and eventually choose primary care as a career.

And it seems to be working. More than 60 percent of UNECOM's graduates choose primary care postgraduate placements, and 40 percent of all UNECOM's graduates are practicing primary care medicine today in rural communities with less than 10,000 people.

My final illustration, Mr. Chairman, is the College of Osteopathic Medicine and Surgery at the University of Osteopathic Medicine and Health Sciences in Des Moines, Iowa.

The College's largest clinical department is Family Medicine. The College requires a minimum of four months in family practice rotations and an additional four months in another primary care medical rotation, such as pediatrics or internal medicine.

The College of Osteopathic Medicine and Surgery has also begun an innovative second track which not only emphasizes primary care but also reduces the traditional four-year program to three years of study and clinical training for obtaining the degree of Doctor of Osteopathy. Persons wi'·h advanced degrees in basic sciences, for example, are eligible for this accelerated program.

Finally, the State of Iowa has made funds available to the College of Osteopathic Medicine and Surgery to reduce or buy out the education loans incurred by those students who agree to practice in rural Iowa after graduation. Loan forgiveness, of course, is another very powerful incentive for convincing young osteopathic physicians to choose a primary care specialty and practice it in a medically underserved area.

Mr. Chairman, I am happy to bring these few examples before this Subcommittee. I hope the point has been made that all our colleges of osteopathic medicine share a fundamental commitment to primary care.

But I would be remiss, Mr. Chairman, if I did not speak of a recent and very serious phenomenon, and that is the first evidence of the weakening of resolve among our students to pursue a postgraduate career in primary care.

While many schools have outstanding records in the production of primary care physicians, I must add that a significant number of our former students are not in primary care.

For example, of all 1991 seniors from schools of osteopathic medicine, 41 percent planned careers in primary care. However, of all *1992* seniors, *only 32 percent* said they were heading into primary care.

Several factors are at work here. One is the overall ability of the specialty organizations -- cardiology, radiology, psychiatry, orthopedics, and so on -- to reach students with a powerful story of careers larded with prestige and high incomes. They have been very convincing in the past and I should point out, the Federal Government itself, through its policies for medical education and services reimbursement, has been an ally of these specialties.

Of course we need their expertise, and it is certainly true that the medical specialties in America have made this country the envy of the rest of the world, with regard to cutting-edge medical technologies and so-called "medical miracles". And I should add that some 70 percent of the permanent faculty in our colleges of osteopathic medicine are men and women who have distinguished themselves across the spectrum of specialties and subspecialties.

However, we, as a Nation, have come to realize that most Americans do not need -- and will *never* need -- the skills of such specialists: we know that most Americans need basic primary care. We in osteopathic medicine continue to believe that and will continue to emphasize primary care in our schools, despite the swings in student response.

It is because of our commitment to primary care that we support the broad outlines of the President's health care reform package.

AACOM applauds the President's initiative to reform health care and supports: (1) universal access, (2) universal insurance coverage, (3) comprehensive benefits package, and (4) incentives for providers to practice primary care.

The President proposes a new system to reduce the supply of specialty training for physicians. A total of 55% of new physicians are to be trained in primary care at the end of a five-year phase-in period. Primary care is defined to include family medicine, general internal medicine, general pediatrics, and obstetrics and gynecology.

Although the precise number of residency slots to be maintained is not specified in the President's health care reform proposal, limiting the number of graduate medical education positions "to the number of U.S. allopathic and osteopathic medical school graduates plus 10%" (i.e., 110% of U.S. graduates) is a proposal which the current Council on Graduate Medical Education (COGME) recommends and is implicit in the Health Security Act. COGME would also use 1993 as the base year for the computation.

We recommend: (1) the 110% figure be applied to the number of allopathic and osteopathic school graduates separately; and (2) no base year be established.

Based on the recommendations of the National Council on Graduate Medical Education and according to the President's proposal, the Secretary of Health and Human Services would determine the number of training positions in each specialty. Although medical educators would be represented on the National Council, there is no specific mention of representation by osteopathic medical educators. Consequently, we seek statutory mandates requiring substantial representation by osteopathic physicians/educators on the National Council on Graduate Medical Education.

The President's Health Care Reform proposal envisions payment of graduate medical education funds directly to the residency program. Adopting such a proposal could eliminate COGME's suggestion that consortia with at least one medical school joining with hospitals providing graduate medical education be formed. Under COGME's proposal, the medical school would be the recipient of GME funds and would be responsible for the quality of graduate medical education.

We recommend the adoption of the COGME consortia model for graduate medical education thus making the osteopathic medical school responsible for the quality of GME and for receiving GME funds.

The National Council, in determining the total number of positions for each medical specialty, would be required to take into account, among many other factors, the quality of training programs. We are concerned about how quality would be measured and who would measure quality. To assure equitable treatment of osteopathic graduate medical education programs, we recommend that the National Council on Graduate Medical Education be required to consult with the American Osteopathic Association concerning the osteopathic residencies to be approved and the number of positions to be retained.

The Health Security Act makes minimal reference to undergraduate medical education. However, implementation of reform may have a profound impact on undergraduate medical education indirectly. Health plans must operate efficiently if they are to compete effectively with other plans. Educating medical students does not enhance the cost-effectiveness of service delivery. Therefore, special consideration needs to be given to assuring that clinical settings will be available for educating undergraduate students. Special consideration has been given to funding graduate medical education. Special provisions also need to be made for clinical settings used to educate undergraduate medical students.

We recommend that special reimbursement be provided to clinical settings which are used for the education of undergraduate medical students.

AACOM supports measures in the health care reform proposals that would increase the authorization levels for existing Title VII health professions training programs. Increased funding in these programs would enhance primary care medical education in the nation. These programs, including Family Medicine, Health Careers

Opportunity Programs, Area Health Education Centers, Health Education and Training Centers, and the various student loan and scholarship programs have been highly useful to our member schools in maintaining their traditional primary care emphases.

AACOM agrees that extending graduate medical educational funding to ambulatory settings that are not owned and operated by teaching hospitals should enhance the effectiveness of primary care graduate training.

We are concerned, however, with the potential impact of proposed changes in health care financing on ambulatory training in undergraduate medical education. Osteopathic medical schools have relied heavily on the use of volunteer [let me emphasize, unpaid] primary care practitioners to provide community-based ambulatory training experiences for our students. This emphasis on community-based, ambulatory clinical education has played a major role in maintaining our students' interests and competencies in primary care. The dedication of our volunteer primary care faculty preceptors to the osteopathic medical education process would be in danger of contracting as health care reform encourages practitioners to enter the managed care sector.

Health maintenance organizations and similar managed care arrangements have not shown a great interest in undergraduate medical education because it would reduce the number of patients that a preceptor could see during a working day. Ironically, just as the nation has begun to recognize the value of community-based medical education that has been at the heart of osteopathic medical education, the economic forces generated by reform may be a barrier to community-based participation in undergraduate medical education. As more and more attention is paid to the "bottom line", colleges will be forced to utilize hospitals and tertiary care centers for almost all of their clinical education, losing the benefits of ambulatory training; or, the costs of that education would substantially increase as a significant number of primary care preceptors drop out of the volunteer faculty network.

With the above concerns in mind, AACOM recommends that a two-pronged approach should be utilized to insure that there is a sufficient and prepared primary care workforce to provide increased access to health care: 1) loans and scholarships to assist students with a commitment to a primary care career to finance the costs of their medical education; and 2) new direct support to medical schools to maintain and enhance their capacity to educate students in ambulatory primary care settings.

1) Additional Support for Student Financial Assistance Programs Geared to Primary Care -AACOM recognizes that Federal financial assistance programs for health professionals are now organized to achieve two goals: increasing student access to a primary care medical career and enhancing the socio-economic and ethnic diversity of the medical workforce in the United States. As osteopathic medical schools continue in their efforts to recruit and retain more underrepresented minority students and to produce more primary care physicians, current funding for Federal loans and scholarships is inadequate to meet student demands for assistance and this is intensified because of the instability of Federal loans and scholarships. For example, the HPSL program was changed to the Primary Care Loan program without any new monies appropriated. The student demand for support from this program has exceeded the funds our schools have available.

Increased appropriations for the Primary Care Loan program and the scholarship and loan programs for disadvantaged students, as well as the National Health Service Corps Scholarship and Loan Repayment programs, are needed. AACOM recommends that increased appropriations be provided for those scholarship and loan programs tied to primary care service; however, we note our concern with attaching additional eligibility requirements to all of these programs.

In addition, AACOM supports the Health Education Lending Program (H.R.2077), introduced by you, Mr. Chairman, which addresses our concerns of increasing borrowing limits and income contingent repayment in order to meet the needs of many of our students.

2) Support of Community-based Undergraduate Primary Care Medical Education -Additionally, AACOM recommends establishing a new Federal capitation program for medical schools that would use a formula involving the number of the medical school's graduates entering a primary care practice, the proportion of the undergraduate clinical curriculum conducted in ambulatory settings, and the size of the medical school class. These funds would then be allocated by the school to support the community based training network.

Assuming a base level of support of $100,000 as an adequate, but modest, public investment in the education of a medical student, the annual appropriation to a particular medical school would be obtained by multiplying this base by the number of entering medical students. This total amount would then be pro-rated by the percentage of that school's graduates who enter practice in the U.S. as primary care physicians (as measured at a point four years after graduation) and further pro-rated by the percentage of required clinical training time that is spent in ambulatory, community-based primary care settings. Thus, for a medical school with an entering class of 100 students which has 50% of its graduates of four years earlier entering primary care practice and requires 25% of its undergraduate clinical training curriculum to occur in ambulatory primary care settings, the funding level for that year would be 100 x $100,000 x 0.50 x 0.25 = $1,250,000. Under this ambulatory primary care formula approach, medical schools and ambulatory care settings would have strong incentives to enhance community-based medical student training and the development of new primary care graduate training programs for their alumni.

AACOM believes that a capitation approach, rather than traditional competitive granting mechanisms, would provide schools with predictable funding levels for use in educational planning, would reduce the need to employ a large group of Federal administrators to staff these programs, and would allow schools flexibility to address those aspects of primary care education needed to insure a more adequate production of primary care physicians.

One approach that bridges the gap between undergraduate and graduate medical education in the primary care disciplines would be to establish primary care track programs for medical schools as a means to increase their production of primary care practitioners, as a few of our member schools are experimenting with now.

Such tracks would include a separate application and admissions procedure to fill a fixed number of entering class seats. With admission to the primary care track, assurance of admission to an affiliated primary care residency program would be offered, provided that the student demonstrates acceptable progress during his or her medical school education.

Such a program would remove the traditional "shopping for a residency" component of the senior year of undergraduate medical education; give primary care residency programs greater involvement in the selection and education of students enrolled in this track; and, better integrate primary care curricula to produce a true continuum of primary care medical education. While such an approach may not work well at every medical school, flexible authorization language would allow interested medical schools to address simultaneously curricula at the undergraduate, graduate, and practitioner levels.

Mr. Chairman, it has been a pleasure for me to testify here today and share with you AACOM's views on medical education reform. I would be pleased to answer any questions.

Chairman STARK. I want to thank Dr. Jones for that unsolicited endorsement of our proposed legislation to figure out a more sensible way to fund medical education. Although we didn't initially direct it toward graduate medical education, arguably that would be the next step.

I would point to Dr. El-Attar and suggest that the complaints of many students about large loans tends to fall on deaf ears. I am prepared, with you, to become one of the two richest people in America; and you and I could do that by offering to purchase every nickel of debt that every person graduating from medical school has on their dossier in exchange for our receiving the difference between their earnings and the average earnings of, say, an engineering or legal graduate for the next 10 years. We would make a fortune. I have gone to the trouble of extrapolating that.

So the debt, while it may be higher than my children's, who are lawyers, has resulted in a lot higher earnings, I am not sure it is not a very good investment and am prepared to purchase that debt on those terms, if you know anybody who would like to sell it to me.

But thinking of a better way, perhaps, to help—and I would hopefully extend this to all forms of graduate or post-secondary education as is done in Germany, for example; and that is to give anyone that can matriculate a grant that approximates the reasonable cost for a semester in exchange for which they would be burdened for life with a higher tax payment, like an extra quarter percent on gross income forever, so the more they make, the more they pay back into the pot. In time, it would become self-funding. We might be able to try something like that because medical education is so focused in this bill.

We have had some support from student organizations and some of the medical teaching fraternities, so that we would like to find a way to not make that a concern, and I appreciate both of your interest in that.

I share the concerns of Drs. Foreman and Snyderman that there is going to be a problem in this present bill, as it is structured, for academic centers; and I just think you can't get to where you want to stay from here. You may be in the same sort of trouble regardless of whether or not we pass any legislation.

There was a recent supplement in the Sun Sentinel or some such paper in Florida, which was a 10-page tribute to HMO operators like Humana, figuring out how not to provide specialist service to their beneficiaries, which seems to be what managed care is all about, and that is how to deliver less care, particularly when it is expensive.

That doesn't even come close to sending people to graduate medical centers. It just says, we ain't going to send them to a specialist for a relatively expensive procedure, much less send them to a center of excellence. I have a hunch that with the growth of people pushing managed care down the throats of companies that have to provide plans, you have another plan having nothing to do with the government, and that is how to continue to receive your reasonable allocation of patients who might like to come to a center if they knew about it and could get there.

But it seems to me if you were going to design a way to deny patients access to your centers, I think the alliance system is a textbook case on how to do it. The good news is that I don't think that alliances will see the light of day, so there is no sense talking about it because I think that those won't happen. Therefore, whatever system we find to provide coverage for everyone will arguably allow them to seek you out in whatever way they do now, either through referrals or through their own searching for the best treatment for their particular problem.

As to specialization versus primary care, first of all, I come from the prejudice that this committee should never have been in the business of funding medical education in the first place. It was, if one studies the legislative history, an afterthought in the Medicare program in 1965; and somebody in the waning hours of the legislation said, my goodness, what do we do with medical education, and they threw it into Medicare.

It is a leap of faith as to why seniors or taxpayers representing only 35 million of Americans should pay for medical education. I make no argument, it should be assisted and subsidized and helped as a matter of social policy; but the Medicare system, there is no logic as to why it should be put there. It seems to me we might have a chance to do it more fairly and sensibly in any legislation that we pass.

My guess is that the way you have more primary care people is either pay them more or pay specialists substantially less. I suppose the most highly paid specialists are often on the faculties of academic centers—making hundreds and hundreds of thousands of dollars on the side, as it were, or in their special little partnerships that the school was subsidizing by providing the structure and not participating in the profits. That again is a matter of no concern to me.

You all have to operate your schools and staff them as best you can and pay for them. I do think that the end result will probably not mandate any kind of quotas, that the only thing I can think of is that the payment structure may tend to begin to favor primary care. That may make it more attractive for people.

On the other hand, the gatekeeper system will make it more difficult for people to get the specialists and, therefore, for specialists to earn the differential that they earn. I am relatively content to watch that happen. I think you guys have to figure out how to educate people.

The non-M.D. providers I have supported for a long time. I believe that in this room we wrote the first bill in the early 1970s to allow physicians' assistants to exist in the District of Columbia. I thought it was a good idea then, and I do now.

I would make one statement to the nurses whose issues I have supported for a long time, that those of us who oppose featherbedding by those above us on the technical scale often forget those below us, so that we will leave the physicians alone for 1 minute; but as the nurses have been after me for years to get comparable pay for comparable service, when they provide that service, I have always been receptive to that. But when they won't let the candystripers deliver the meals because they don't have an R.N. degree,

I say, wait 1 minute; if you are going to move up the scale, remember those down the scale because this is a two-way street.

I think we are making great progress with nurses' groups and letting them be more concerned for finding assistants for them. If we can't provide better and more care through having more work done by nonmedical providers, then we have to look to fill some of the duties that R.N.s have reserved unto themselves, and we will work it out.

We are trying to figure out right now what is going to evolve, and I have had a concern for some time that the graduate medical groups can't exist under this plan. I think I feel fairly certain, just because I can count votes, that we are not going to have that kind of structured alliance or mandated number of slots; we will do something else. But I don't think any of us know, at this point, what; and we will appreciate your reasoning with us as we try to figure it out. It will evolve.

Dr. Foreman.

Dr. FOREMAN. The concern that we have is that with or without the implementation of a system as now envisioned in the alliances, the market is moving rapidly to a competitive one in precisely the way that you have described, and that that competitive market is putting tremendous pressure on those institutions whose price is above the average, even if the cause for that excess is paying for the special byproduct of medical care called education. It is the reason that the AAMC has advocated moving the payment for education away from payment for patient care, into special pots.

Now, special pots obviously bring special dangers. And this proposal does create two special pots. The notions behind those pots are correct; the funding in them is inadequate.

With respect to looking at this problem from the viewpoint of the faculty versus the hospital, we can parse it apart in two ways. The hospitals can be made whole, I believe, or at least placed on a level playingfield if their special educational costs can come to them in an assured nonpatient care-related flow. With respect to the specialty faculty, they are prepared to take their chances in the marketplace.

The problem, however, is that we should understand that presently, a portion of faculty income is being taxed explicitly, often by the dean or by some functionary within the education system, and those dollars are being reapplied to an educational function. If those extra dollars disappear in a competitive marketplace, they must be found somewhere else, and if they are not found, there will be consequences to the medical education enterprise.

Chairman STARK. I agree. I mean, of course, the argument is going to be how you separate it and how you allocate the costs of the medical education, some of which provides service, some of which costs. And whether Dr. El-Attar has to pay more to cover the actual cost of her education, and then how, if we fund her, how she pays us back. Unless that goes on patients in your hospitals, I am not sure, but I figure you guys can figure that out a lot better than Members of Congress.

So somehow, I don't think that the President's commitment to provide universal coverage for every American in the next 5 years, say, hinges on whether or not we completely revise the way medical education operates. I am perfectly willing to see that evolve, but I don't know that that has to be on exactly the same track.

Mr. SNYDERMAN. Mr. Chairman, I am really pleased to hear that you understand so clearly some of the problems we are facing in academic health centers. I think it is important to go one step further from what Dr. Foreman indicated, beyond the important concern of funding medical education, to the funding of the dynamic nature of medical improvement over time.

The last portion of this session dealt with standards of care, and the question came up, when will we be finished with standards of care and have them? Well, the answer to that is never, but the good news is that we are constantly improving them. Our health care system is changing over time more rapidly than any other area of industry that I can think of, including the computer industry. It is a dynamic system.

The concern that we have in academic health centers is as we go into a cost-sensitive environment, there is a tremendous disincentive to invest in centers of excellence. Indeed, if you look—as you stated, where the wisdom is in investing in health care, one would want to have an affiliated health plan that did not have centers of excellence so that you would accumulate the healthiest individuals in you place such as 22- to 26-year-old men who were not married and who had very little use of health care at that time in their lives. Our institutions attract individuals in need of our special services. Ultimately, people will need the unique services that we provide. They may develop cancer, they may——

Chairman STARK. I am afraid so.

Mr. SNYDERMAN. Unfortunately, that is the case with all of the prevention that we are going to put into the system. What we need to figure out is how we appropriately provide that access to large populations and pay for that margin of excellence appropriately. And I feel very comfortable in knowing that you will figure it out.

Chairman STARK. Do we pay for it adequately now in Medicare?

Mr. SNYDERMAN. No. It is a very important question.

Chairman STARK. How bad is it?

Mr. SNYDERMAN. The word in the street is that Medicare pays roughly about a third, maybe a little bit less than that, and the rest is in the private payer sector. I think that is a very important concept.

Chairman STARK. Wait 1 minute. I am saying in an individual patient who comes to Duke—nobody pays full sticker, OK, anymore for medical care.

Mr. SNYDERMAN. That is right.

Chairman STARK. So either they are coming in on some kind of a preferred provider gimmick by those generous people at Aetna or wherever, or they are coming in through a charity-Medicaid sort of combination, or they are coming through, say, Medicare.

Now, how much different are all of those in terms of what you recover from your population?

Mr. SNYDERMAN. Let me give you a very rough rule of thumb. With Medicaid, we recover roughly—in terms of our own costs, maybe 75 cents on the dollar. With Medicare, it may be closer to 85 or 90 cents and we make it up with the private payer.

Chairman STARK. Then you are saying what I am saying. I have said that if you got the Medicare rate for everybody who came through your door, no bad debts, no charity, that you could probably survive.

Mr. SNYDERMAN. Yes. We would have to change, and I think we are changing. We are going to become very cost competitive.

Chairman STARK. Which is why I want to stay in an indemnity plan until I qualify for Medicare so I can come in to see you guys. Because if I don't, if I get into one of these managed plans, they aren't going to let me get 2 blocks away from home.

Dr. FOREMAN. Just one comment on Medicare. Medicare is a better payer for some organizations than for others. Medicare is an outstanding payer for academic health centers, because it explicitly recognizes the special cost needs of those institutions. It is a poorer payer in nonacademic medical centers, poorer, and in some States it is arguable as to whether the basic Medicare payment pays full costs of care. But it doesn't——

Chairman STARK. It is arguable as to what costs are. Because if you put into the cost the uncompensated care, the bad debts and the shifting, it doesn't. But as Dr. Snyderman said, I don't think you are going to find an appendectomy in a small hospital with no academic attachments where it pays a whole hell of a lot less as a percentage than it does for Johns Hopkins or Duke or any of the centers.

That is not to say that it is perfect, believe me. But it is one of the reasons that when we got this trouble in Florida is that what you are finding is that after people are in these deals and they suddenly say, Oh, my God, they go back to Medicare. And why it is very popular, quite frankly, is that there is that choice factor in which the physician community keeps talking about, but I don't think they illustrate it as well as they might. It isn't the fact that they can continue to control the patients; it is that those patients who are closer to my age and the stories you see about people who aren't 26 any more, who suddenly say, Uh-oh, if this happens, I want to go there, and rightly so.

That is one of the great things that I have always felt about Medicare is that that choice is limited only by the cost of a plane ticket.

I am sorry. Mr. Levin.

Mr. LEVIN. Thank you.

Let me just ask a quick question to go back to what the chairman and some of you were discussing before, and that relates to the training of physicians, because at some point a basic decision is going to have to be made.

Dr. Foreman, you say on page 7, "if an allocation methodology is necessary," and then you go on. Let me just ask you point-blank. Forgetting for a moment about what form it might take, let's assume a reasonable "allocation" methodology could be found. Is it necessary or isn't it?

Dr. FOREMAN. Permit me to spend a moment talking about the surfeit of specialists, because a little background information I think throws some light on this. If one compares the number of specialists in each specialty to some reasonable projection of need for those specialties, it turns out that the surfeit of specialists is not uniform across the board. There is no reason to believe, for instance, that we are producing too many general surgeons or too many orthopedic surgeons or too many neurosurgeons, or in fact, virtually all of the surgical specialties. The production of those specialists has been in balance with the needs for those specialists over the last 10 years more or less.

There are some exceptions. More or less. Where the surfeit has developed is in what are called subspecialists, particularly in internal medicine and pediatrics, but much more so in internal medicine. That is, people pursue a training program which leads them to a complete education in general internal medicine, and then decide they want to go on to become a subspecialist: Cardiologists, gastroenterologists, endocrinologists, pulmonologists. It is those subspecialists in both medicine and in pediatrics that constitute the largest proportion of the extra specialists.

Now, it is important to recognize two things about that. First, before one decides to become a subspecialist one has to be a complete generalist at the outset. What moves people to go beyond the well-trained generalist career to become a subspecialist are a whole bunch of complex incentives: Lifestyle, income, recognition, prestige, practice pattern, all of that.

It is now apparent that the emerging competitive economy is not going to support the surfeit of specialists it has in the past. Managed care is reducing the demand for specialists and the income for specialist.

What we are seeing now is two trends. Young internists saying, I am not going to go on and take two additional years to become a gastroenterologist because the demand for my services is falling and the income associated with them is falling.

The second thing is, among our practicing subspecialists, we are seeing more and more open their offices to general internal medicine particularly and general pediatric patients that they previously would not have had to see, because there was enough demand for their subspecialty time that they didn't open their practice to generalist time.

So the bottom line on that is, I believe that the market is already driving people to, one, not choose subspecialties as they used to, and two, for those people in the practice of subspecialty medicine, to go back to their primary specialty and practice in that area. And I believe that incentives in the market place may tip us in that direction over the next 5 years without large interventions by the Federal Government, although we are prepared to support them if the incentives don't work.

Dr. EL-ATTAR. I agree that the marketplace is actually shifting and we are seeing some great changes, but it is very difficult for a medical student to feel some of those changes. It takes a lot longer for us to actually reach a point in our training where we see the impact of some of the market forces, and a lot of the decisions required are made long before that.

I actually feel, and AMSA feels, that if there are some significant changes made in the way undergraduate medical education is done today, we will see some significant changes in medical student choice, without any changes in the graduate medical education system.

And I want to acknowledge our osteopathic colleagues sitting here, for their training exemplifies what good primary care emphasis and basis in undergraduate medical education can produce from medical students. Their numbers are falling, and I think the numbers of the students in osteopathic medicine are falling because of some of the other factors that influence medical students, such as prestige and income. But they have a good foundation in the 4 years of medical school to primary care.

I could have gone through 4 years of medical school and never seen and ne\ ⌄r done a primary care rotation, and it is very difficult to make a choice to become a primary care physician if you never see one or never experience that.

Ms. BEDNASH. Mr. Levin, one other comment that I would like to make. One of the concerns that we have had for a number of years is that there is this resistance to movement into primary care by other providers, and there is a discipline that is actively involved in primary care, and supported by other disciplines in their role as primary care providers, and that is nurses, and yet there are inadequate resources available to expand dramatically the production of these providers.

We know that in 103 of our member institutions, we have 308 nurse-practitioner programs. Over half of those programs report waiting lists of people to get into the programs, and the other half don't report waiting lists because they don't keep waiting lists.

And the primary factor that is hindering the acceptance of these students into the program is faculty, faculty who can be on board to accept those students. It is a labor-intensive curriculum but nowhere as labor intensive as other kinds of curricula that are out there. And with some additional resources through some sort of a stable funding initiative, whether or not it is a Medicare-type-based program, we can dramatically expand the production of those providers, along with removal of some of those barriers to this practice. I think we can meet some of those needs that are there.

Mr. Chairman, in response to your concern certainly about some of the resistance to using a variety of providers in the delivery of nursing care, I would like to, for the record, also let you know that the four major nursing organizations, the Tri-Council for Nursing, which includes the American Nurses Association, the American Organization of Nurse Executives, the National League for Nursing, and our organization (AACN) is on record that we accept the use of unlicensed assistive personnel, that in fact they are a vital resource in the delivery of services today. But we do believe there absolutely must be adequate supervision by professionals who can assure the quality of the care that is delivered to these patients in those settings.

Chairman STARK. That could have been written by the AMA.

Ms. BEDNASH. Wonderful. Then we are right in line, aren't we?

Dr. FOREMAN. You are absolutely right.

Mr. LEVIN. I don't want to get into that. But when you pull together what you have been saying, it seems to me that there are arguments for enhancing the incentives for trying to avoid some of the overly rigid walls, the walls among the services. But I also think, Dr. Foreman, that you are saying it might make sense to see how the market works with some enhanced incentives, but have a backstop provision there in case it doesn't work.

Dr. FOREMAN. Correct.

Mr. LEVIN. And perhaps the notion is that if there is a backstop provision, it may accelerate the working of the market? Is that an accurate description?

Dr. FOREMAN. Exactly.

Mr. LEVIN. Thank you, Mr. Chairman.

Chairman STARK. I want to thank the panel very much. We will be in touch with you, I am sure, over the few weeks ahead as we try and put Humpty Dumpty back together again. Thank you very much.

Chairman STARK. Our final panel today is comprised of Wendy Herr, who is the group executive of policy services for the Healthcare Financial Management Association; Jim Houtz, who is chairman of the Association for Electronic Health Care Transactions; Robert Peterson, who is the president of C4SI, Inc.; Linda Watson, who is the vice chair of the Joint Legislative Task Force for the Medical Library Association; and David Kreidler, on behalf of the American Society of Association Executives.

We welcome the panel, and as our previous panel and their guests move on, we will suspend for just a moment. If you would like to proceed to summarize or expand on your written testimony, which will appear in the record in its entirety, in the order in which I called you, you may proceed.

Ms. Herr.

STATEMENT OF WENDY W. HERR, GROUP EXECUTIVE, POLICY SERVICES GROUP, HEALTHCARE FINANCIAL MANAGEMENT ASSOCIATION

Ms. HERR. Good afternoon, Mr. Chairman and members of the subcommittee. My name is Wendy Herr. I am here today representing the Healthcare Financial Management Association. I have served as head of the association's Washington office for the past 3 years, and have been a personal member of the professional society for most of my health care career. Prior to joining the national staff of HFMA, I worked for over 15 years in various financial management positions, including several years as the chief financial officer of a private nonprofit psychiatric provider.

HFMA represents more than 31,000 professionals involved in the financial management of various types of health care institutions. These entities include hospitals, clinics, managed care providers and physician offices. On behalf of these individuals, I appreciate the opportunity to present our views on health care administrative simplification.

HFMA's membership is very diverse, both in terms of geography and professional affiliation. This puts us in the unique position of being able to identify problems from all angles that are associated with health care claims and patient accounting.

HFMA determined several years ago the need for uniformity and simplification. By working closely with our members, we have developed a detailed plan to achieve this goal.

From a personal standpoint as a former chief financial officer, I can tell you that administrative simplification is needed and it is needed now. I still vividly remember the choices I had to make and the tough decisions the volunteer community board had to grapple with when making spending decisions for the various clinics. Often the decisions boiled down to whether new clinical staff could be brought on board to meet the demands of an ever-growing waiting list of patients, or if more clerical personnel needed to be hired instead to move the mountains of paperwork, making the time-consuming phone calls, and to decipher the never-ending iterations of billing and claim forms.

Mr. Chairman, last May we had the opportunity to present HFMA's proposed administrative simplification process to this subcommittee. The membership has recently revisited this proposal and affirmed the approach as feasible, practical and cost effective.

The fundamental goals of administrative simplification are to simplify and standardize the health care administrative functions. Our written statement provides a detailed analysis of HFMA's seven guiding principles on administrative simplification. These principles are: Industry compliance; use of an industry commission reporting to Congress; mandated use of electronic transactions; definition of basic core transactions; maintenance of data; confidentiality and privacy protection with the use of uniform identifiers; and strategic timetables that are realistic and constructive to the transition process.

Mr. Chairman, we urge you and the members of your subcommittee to consider the HFMA proposal and these guiding principles when deliberating administrative simplification. Administrative simplification can and should be enacted with or without overall health care reform.

Mr. Chairman, while HFMA recognizes the need for comprehensive health care reform, we remain convinced that certain key elements of health care reform can be enacted quickly. Administrative simplification is one of those key elements.

HFMA supports the subcommittee's work toward enacting legislation to simplify and standardize the health care administrative process now. We are available to be of technical assistance to you in your work, and pleased to offer our expert guidance as you make decisions.

On behalf of HFMA, I appreciate the opportunity to appear before you today and present the organization's views on health care administrative simplification.

Thank you.

[The prepared statement follows:]

STATEMENT OF WENDY W. HERR, FHFMA, CMPA
GROUP EXECUTIVE, POLICY SERVICES GROUP
HEALTHCARE FINANCIAL MANAGEMENT ASSOCIATION

INTRODUCTION

Good morning, Mr. Chairman and members of the Subcommittee. My name is
Wendy Herr, and I am here today representing the Healthcare Financial Management
Association (HFMA). I have served as head of the Association's Washington Office
for the past four years, and have been a personal member of the organization for most
of my healthcare career. Prior to joining the national staff of HFMA, I worked for
over fifteen years in various financial management positions, including several years
as a chief financial officer and chief operating officer in a private non-profit psychiatric provider organization.

HFMA represents more than 31,500 professionals involved in the financial management of various types of healthcare institutions, including hospitals and clinics,
managed care providers, public accountants, consultants, insurance companies,
governmental agencies and other organizations. On behalf of these individuals, I
appreciate the opportunity to present our views on healthcare administrative costs and
to offer an approach to simplifying the processes associated with these costs.

Given the geographic and professional diversity of its members, HFMA is in a unique
position to identify the problems associated with the current healthcare claims and
patient accounting processes. Based on our analysis of the system, we have determined there is a definite need for uniformity and simplification. Moreover, administrative simplification can and should begin now. After in-depth consultation with our
members and others, we have developed a detailed plan to achieve this goal.

From a personal standpoint, I can clearly state from experience that administrative
simplification is needed, and that it is needed now. I still remember vividly the
choices that I had to make, and the tough decisions the volunteer community board
had to grapple with when making spending decisions for the various clinics. Often the
decisions boiled down to whether new clinical staff could be brought on board to meet
the demands of an ever growing waiting list of patients, or more clerical personnel
needed to be hired to move the mountains of paperwork, make the hundreds of phone
calls and decipher the never ending iterations of billing claim forms. I am proud to be
part of a dedicated, professional society of financial management executives that is
tackling this critical dilemma, a dilemma that wastes billions of dollars each year.
HFMA believes strongly that an immediate implementation of administrative simplification is needed now, and would be compatible with whatever system of healthcare
reform is passed.

HFMA PROPOSAL FOR HEALTHCARE ADMINISTRATIVE
SIMPLIFICATION AND UNIFORMITY

Mr. Chairman, last May, we had the opportunity to present HFMA's proposed
administrative simplification process to this Subcommittee. That proposal would
simplify the current healthcare administrative processes through the mandated use of
various electronic processes for all participants in the healthcare delivery system. It
has been reviewed by healthcare financial managers and others involved with these
processes. These professionals have confirmed that the concepts contained in our
proposal are feasible, practical and will meet the goals of the Congress, the Administration, the healthcare community, and most importantly, the consumer.

Very briefly, the fundamental goals of administrative simplification are to simplify and
standardize the healthcare administrative functions of enrollment, eligibility, coordination of benefits, billing, and payment for all healthcare providers and third-party
payers. This can be accomplished through two primary initiatives:

- Provide universal electronic processes for healthcare enrollment, eligibility, coordination of benefits, first report of injury, billing, claims follow-up and payment and remittance to be used by all healthcare providers and third-party payers, while allowing alternative mechanisms for smaller providers and employers.

- Form an independent healthcare administrative commission, reporting to Congress, and comprising representatives from the industry and the government. This Commission would recommend to the Executive Branch uniform standards that would permit the creation of the universal claims process system; and would provide Congress an ongoing assessment of the system.

These two primary initiatives would:

- Apply to all private and government sponsored healthcare benefit plans.

- Assure the development of an electronic system that provides a universal administrative process for the healthcare industry.

- Provide rules and information transfer mechanisms to facilitate coordination of benefits and Medicare Secondary Payer programs.

- Implement a system that will standardize the use of a nationally acceptable electronic transmission standards.

- Allow healthcare providers (including rural and small providers), payers, and sponsors unable to use the electronic transmission systems to alternatively use clearinghouses.

- Provide that these provisions would preempt any state or local laws addressing hard copy documentation of medical, healthcare benefit plan records or data, or confidentiality.

- Provide that any changes to the current system are implemented within a realistic strategic timetable.

HFMA continues to support this concept. We urge you and the members of your Subcommittee to consider this proposal when deliberating possible solutions to the current problems with the healthcare administrative process.

HFMA's concept can be broken down according to the following seven guiding principles:

I. Industry Compliance

    A. Administrative simplification will not be achieved unless all members of the healthcare community are mandated to participate.

        1. This includes governmental and private sponsors (employers, unions, government bodies), providers, payers/administrators, vendors, suppliers, etc.

    B. Any new programs, systems, mechanisms, etc., established to achieve simplification must be continually reviewed to ensure that the goals are being achieved without increasing costs.

II. Use of an Industry Commission Reporting to Congress

A. To ensure total involvement by the healthcare community, there must be an industry based commission.

1. To ensure against domination by any one segment of the community, the commission should report to Congress.

B. Commission members should include healthcare financial managers, healthcare practitioners, and third party payers, including government representatives.

III. Electronic Transactions

A. To engage the healthcare community to achieve the same level of sophistication as other U.S. industries, administrative simplification should mandate only electronic solutions.

B. The overall electronic mechanism should use existing data interface standards, such as those standards devised by the Insurance Subcommittee of the Accredited Standards Committee X12 of the American National Standards Institute (ANSI).

C. Clearinghouses and value added networks (VANs) are appropriate mechanisms to provide assistance to those members of the healthcare community that are not able to directly interface electronically.

IV. Core Transactions

A. Uniformity or administrative simplification cannot occur without uniform data definitions, data sets with maximum approved data, and integration of such definitions and uniformity requirements.

B. The Commission should *initially* address the following "core transactions:" enrollment, eligibility, billing/claims, coordination of benefits, billing follow-up, first report of injury, and payment/remittance.

V. Data Maintenance

A. There is a very important role for the Federal government in maintaining a central or shared data base.

1. Government control assures access by all and appropriate data security and privacy controls.

VI. Confidentiality, Privacy, and Preemption of State and Federal Laws Governing Electronic Data with Uniform Identifiers

A. Federal preemption of existing state requirements for privacy, confidentiality, and electronic data is essential to achieving total administrative simplification and uniformity.

B. There must be uniform identifiers for most participants in the healthcare delivery system.

VII. Strategic Timetables

    A. In recognition of limitations/difficulties in implementing adminis-
    trative simplification and uniformity, any legislation must include a
    reasonable and strategic time table to ensure against increased costs
    and/or diminished efficiency.

        1. The industry based Commission will have the best ability to
        make such implementation plans and therefore timetables for
        implementation should not be legislated.

Mr. Chairman, administrative simplification can and should be enacted with or without
overall healthcare reform. While a total overhaul of the healthcare system may be
preferable, enacting a comprehensive reform package may take longer than anticipated. Administrative simplification, in and of itself, will result in savings to the
healthcare system, thereby increasing the availability of public and private funds that
can then be directed to other essential areas of the healthcare delivery system.

DISCUSSION OF THE PROBLEM

For 25 years, healthcare providers and third-party payers have worked toward
administrative uniformity. While it is generally agreed that this is essential, our
efforts to achieve it thus far have been inconsistent, because acceptance and utilization
of the standardized formats created by various healthcare groups are voluntary.
HFMA believes that total uniformity of healthcare administrative processes and
systems will not be accomplished without changes to current Federal law requiring all
providers and third-party payers to adopt uniform, standard, electronic processes.
Without such a requirement, the administrative process will remain complex and cost
inefficient.

HFMA's analysis of the administrative burdens currently placed on the healthcare
industry can best be summarized by the following points:

- Standard uniform formats and processes for healthcare claims are readily
  available, but not used consistently by all participants of the healthcare
  delivery system.

- With most systems, any request for additional information that is not
  included on the original electronic form will result in the submission of
  paper documents, thereby negating the advantages of an electronic transmission.

- Current development of electronic data interchange (EDI) standards have
  included data transmission standards, but there is no uniform convention
  for the use of these standards. Any movement by the industry must
  require uniformity or the industry will be compelled to maintain costly
  multiple systems.

HFMA COST STUDY

It is widely held that inefficiencies in the current administrative processes are a major
contributor to the high cost of healthcare. To substantiate this theory, the Association
contracted with Lewin-VHF, a nationally recognized independent consulting firm, to
research the potential cost savings once simplification is realized. The study found:

- 1991 administrative costs totaled approximately $126 billion, or 17 percent of total health expenditures.

- Administrative costs can be broken down into three components: $45 billion was spent by hospitals; $43 billion was spent by physicians; and $38 billion was spent by payers.

- It would cost approximately $800 million per year to implement HFMA's proposed administrative simplification processes.

- *Implementation of HFMA's legislative proposal would save $3.4 to $6.0 billion annually.*

HEALTHCARE REFORM PROPOSALS PENDING IN CONGRESS

HFMA was pleased to find that administrative simplification is a prominent issue in many healthcare reform proposals pending in Congress, including the President's Health Security Act. We have worked very closely with members of the House and Senate, most notably Representatives Tom Sawyer and David Hobson and Senators Christopher Bond, David Riegle and Conrad Burns. We are very pleased to note that most of HFMA's guiding principles for healthcare administrative simplification and uniformity are included in H.R. 3137/S. 1494, The Health Care Information Modernization and Security Act of 1993 ("The Health Care Modernization Act").

The following analysis of the President's plan and the Health Care Modernization Act is based on HFMA's seven guiding principles for healthcare administrative simplification and uniformity:

Industry Compliance
Both the Health Security Act and the Health Care Modernization Act mandate annual reports to Congress outlining the healthcare community's progress in achieving simplification and uniformity. This will enable changes to be made quickly so that simplification can continue to move forward expeditiously.

The Health Security Act does not appear to mandate total compliance. Rather, it appears that certain government departments may be separate from some or all of the provisions.

The Administration also attempts to provide for state flexibility. While the Association strongly supports this overall concept, flexibility will invalidate the benefits of administrative simplification. Basically, all providers and third party payers must be required to use the same format. If states are given the flexibility to change or augment that format, then uniformity becomes thwarted. This will also occur if, as stated in preliminary documents outlining the Administration's plan, only minimum standards for administrative simplification are mandated. Minimum standards would allow third party payers to require additional input on their form. It is this additional input that causes the burden, since each payer may desire something different. This would all result in a setback for uniformity among providers and third-party payers.

The Health Care Modernization Act applies to all payers, but only mandates changes to the Social Security Act. Compliance of Federal programs is specifically outlined, as are dates for compliance. Penalties are also mandated. The bill does not allow for anyone to exceed the maximum data in an approved data set.

Use of a Industry Commission Reporting to Congress

The Health Security Act provides for the creation of two councils that would report to the National Health Board: the National Quality Management Council and the National Privacy and Health Data Advisory Council. Neither of these Councils have full industry participation and their role is limited. Of particular concern to HFMA is that there does not appear to be any preference for financial managers to be involved in the National Health Board or either of the two councils.

The Health Care Modernization Act would establish a parent "Health Care Data Panel" comprised of 12 Federal appointees and chaired by the Secretary of the Department of Health and Human Services (HHS). A separate 15 member Health Informatics Commission, comprised of industry representatives, would report to the Panel.

Electronic Transactions

The Health Security Act contains several different mandates for the use of EDI. There are some requirements for electronic transfer for "those ... that have the capacity," but there is also discussion of "uniform paper forms." Finally, there is a list of "electronic data interchange requirements for those who are automated."

The Administration's reference to the use of standardized paper forms, implies that we would continue to rely on processing via paper, as opposed to EDI. The Association strongly urges that there be a mandate for standardized *formats* thereby creating paperless billing processes. This will significantly streamline the current system and result in substantial savings.

The Health Care Modernization Act provides for an all electronic processing and the use of clearinghouses and VANs. It also suggests that existing national standards be used, including X12 EDI. Clearinghouses are to be certified. HFMA supports such a move to total EDI.

Core Transactions

The Health Security Act includes language for transactions for eligibility, coordination of benefits, claims, payments, disenrollment, enrollment, and utilization review. Specific comments on core transactions are limited,and are more directed toward monitoring, measuring and planning functions. These core transactions are not those identified by HFMA as core transactions. The Health Care Modernization Act includes language for all core transactions as identified by HFMA.

Data Maintenance

The Health Security Act specifies an "electronic data network consisting of regional centers" to be established in two years. This network would collect, compile and transmit information related to enrollment, eligibility, and coordination of benefits. Employers would be required to update enrollment information monthly.

The Health Care Modernization Act provides for a "uniform working file system" that would hold quality data. While providing for coordination of benefits, it is unclear whether eligibility and coordination of benefits data would be included.

Confidentiality, Privacy, and Preemption of State and Federal Laws Governing Electronic Data with Uniform Identifiers

Both the Health Security Act and the Health Care Modernization Act contain provisions meeting HFMA's concerns regarding confidentiality, privacy and state preemption. Uniform identifiers are also included.

Strategic Timetables

The Health Security Act outlines several time periods conditioned on other portions of reform. This may result in too much flexibility and may inhibit total uniformity. As mentioned earlier in this analysis, any apparent flexibility in the establishment of a strategic timetable could create problems if administrative simplification is left to various councils and perhaps state government.

The Health Care Modernization Act includes some very detailed, short initial time frames, especially considering the voluntary/part time nature of the panel and the commission and the extended requirements related to quality. The timetable for implementation of the Act's quality data requirements is more in keeping with a reliable strategic plan. In both cases, however, the existing timetable may not meet the healthcare community's current capabilities given the current environment.

The Association is concerned about the inclusion of waivers in the Health Care Modernization Act. We recognize, however, that there are fair safeguards to ensure that any waivers do not affect the uniformity standard.

ACTIVITIES OF THE INDUSTRY TO ACHIEVE UNIFORMITY

Over the past 25 years, HFMA participated on the National Uniform Billing Committee (NUBC), working closely with other healthcare representatives and the government. The NUBC established the UB-82, a uniform bill form and accompanying data set. The UB-82 was designed to provide a uniform format for the submission of hospital-based claims. Although the UB-82 satisfied the goals of a uniform bill, due to a variety of factors, some payers began requiring additional information that was not contained on the uniform bill.

There were about 50 different versions of the UB-82, representing the variances of each State Uniform Billing Committee. There were also as many as 420 different electronic versions of the UB-82, representing various payer versions of this data set. Hence, the uniform bill has not been used uniformly.

The voluntary UB-82 provided an official data set and format. Official formats, data sets, and standards are important, but without uniformity, there are no savings. Our members find themselves faced with hundreds of modifications to their systems each year to meet the different versions of this "uniform bill."

The UB-82, approved by the Office of Management and Budget for use in the Medicare program, has now been replaced by the UB-92. This conversion represents two and a half years of work by the NUBC. Medicare providers were given three months to initiate final conversion to this form.

In addition to the UB-92, the HCFA 1500 form also is used generally by providers for ambulatory and physician billing. Initially it was only used for Medicare, but recently others in the healthcare community have broadened its use. Since the Medicare program requires all physicians and clinics to bill using the HCFA 1500, many have found it easier to perform all of their billing on the HCFA 1500 rather than use other forms.

It should be noted that the HCFA 1500 and the UB-92 share approximately 95 percent of the same data elements. However, even with the availability of the HCFA 1500 and the implementation of the UB-92, the use of these forms is, and will continue to be, inconsistent. HCFA and other payers may require supplemental claims forms for certain healthcare services. They may also require multiple forms to satisfy the need for additional requisite information. State laws do not necessarily prevent this situation since, in many cases, the transactions are either regulated by the Federal government or are required by out-of-state payers or administrators. Additionally, ERISA based self-insurance plans are exempt from any state legislative initiatives attempting to alleviate a state-specific problem.

A provider's economic health is dependent upon the prompt payment of claims. Therefore, providers will continue to respond to payer demands for additional data in different formats. This increases the provider's administrative costs, resulting in higher overall healthcare costs.

RELATIONSHIP OF THE INDUSTRY WITH ANSI AND WEDI

In 1989, representatives of several of the nation's larger insurance companies and banks sought to eliminate the use of checks to pay for healthcare claims. Healthcare payers, including HCFA, and providers, specifically HFMA and the American Hospital Association, concerned about the problems and limitations previously noted, joined forces with the insurers and banks to form ANSI's Insurance Subcommittee of the Accredited Standards Committee X12. ANSI directed the X12 to develop standard data transmissions between business partners.

Through the X12 and other subgroups, payers and providers have suggested EDI and electronic funds transmission standards to allow for the electronic transmission of large amounts of data and funds. To date, draft standards have been developed for enrollment, eligibility, claims, claim status, payment and remittance, and first report of injury. Task groups have also undertaken projects addressing issues such as utilization review data, crossover or coordination of benefits billing, and other healthcare related data exchanges.

In late 1991, the HHS Secretary convened a summit with the leaders of several of the nation's health insurance companies. The Workgroup on Electronic Data Interchange, or WEDI, was a by-product of this summit. The WEDI group, which included a small representation of healthcare providers, was directed to evaluate the use of X12 standards in the healthcare industry. After several months of deliberating, a report was presented to HHS in July 1992. That report contained an ambitious time table to implement, with government assistance, many of the current and proposed X12 standards for all healthcare providers and payers by the fourth quarter of 1996. The report also recommended potential legislation if providers do not meet the implementation schedule.

In late 1993, WEDI released its blueprint for streamlined administration of the U.S. health care system. The report continues to support WEDI's original concepts, but calls for a tighter implementation timetable than what was originally projected. For example, WEDI recommended that the adoption and implementation of approved X12 standards be completed by the fourth quarter of 1994 for all payors with 50,000 or more claims or encounters per year, hospitals, nursing home and group practices with 20 or more physicians, and employers with 100 or more employees. All other payors, providers and employers would be required to adopt the standards by the fourth quarter of 1996. Incentives, such as higher tax credits and accelerated depreciation, should be developed to facilitate timely implementation.

While not minimizing the work of the WEDI group, it is HFMA's opinion that the group did not fully represent all necessary participants of the healthcare community. Consequently, the report's recommendations do not reflect the essential elements to establish a strategic plan for implementation of a standardized system. Furthermore, the report recommends legislative action only after it becomes apparent that voluntary compliance is not effective. HFMA contends that given the past experiences with

voluntary efforts and the need to accelerate the process toward administrative simplification, Congress must enact legislation to mandate compliance now.

CONCLUSION

Mr. Chairman, HFMA recognizes the need for comprehensive healthcare reform. We
remain convinced, however, that certain key elements of healthcare reform can be
enacted quickly. Administrative simplification is one of those key elements. We
therefore urge you and the members of your Subcommittee to enact legislation now to
simplify and standardize the healthcare administrative processes and not wait for a
complete reform package. The concept we have outlined for you today can be effectively integrated into the current system, yet it will also function within any new
system. The time to begin moving toward change is now.

On behalf of HFMA, I appreciate the opportunity to appear before you today and
present the organization's views on healthcare administrative costs. With more than
31,500 members engaged in the management of healthcare financial operations, we are
available to provide guidance to you as decisions are made on simplifying the system.
We look forward to working with you, as well as other members of the Congress and
the Clinton Administration and, of course, our partners in the healthcare community.
Together we must plan the steps necessary to create a national standard, thereby
improving our industry, lowering the administrative burdens of health care, and
controlling the unnecessary costs brought about by duplication of efforts and paper
processing. Thank you.

ABOUT HFMA

- HFMA is the nation's leading personal membership organization for more
  than 31,500 financial management professionals involved in the financial
  management of various types of healthcare institutions, including hospitals
  and clinics, managed care providers, public accountants, consultants,
  insurance companies, governmental agencies and other organizations.

- Members' positions include chief executive officer, chief financial officer,
  controller, patient accounts manager, accountant, and consultant.

- Given the geographic and professional diversity of its members, HFMA is
  in a unique position to identify the problems associated with the current
  healthcare claims and patient accounting processes.

Chairman STARK. Thank you.

Mr. Houtz.

STATEMENT OF JIM H. HOUTZ, CHAIRMAN OF THE BOARD, ASSOCIATION FOR ELECTRONIC HEALTH CARE TRANSACTIONS, AND PRESIDENT, CYDATA SYSTEMS, INC., SCOTTSDALE, ARIZ.

Mr. HOUTZ. Mr. Chairman, my name is Jim Houtz and I chair the Association for Electronic Health Care Transactions. Thank you for inviting us, and per your request, I will summarize my comments.

AFEHCT is an association comprised of companies who are engaged in building that portion of the electronic highway that will be used to transmit and process health care data, both financial and clinical, and a list of our member companies has been attached to our testimony. The companies that comprise AFEHCT believe that they have and are in the process of developing the tools and the systems that will enable the health care industry to better manage the delivery of care, reduce redundant and unnecessary or ineffective services, and eliminate much of the paperwork hassle that today comprises a significant portion of the system. Without the tools and the systems being developed by AFEHCT members, meaningful health care reform will be virtually impossible to accomplish.

Our association mission is to promote innovation, cooperation, and open competition within the EDI health care industry, and to improve the quality of health care and to achieve administrative cost savings. We have several principles which we would hope would be included in any health care reform legislation. One pertains to the networks and data systems that is covered in several of the bills.

We believe that any legislation in this area should avoid dictating any single system or proposing a limit on the size or number of competing data systems. AFEHCT believes that the Nation and the health care delivery system will be best served by open competition among vendors and suppliers of such services.

Chairman STARK. Excuse me.

Mr. HOUTZ. Yes, sir.

Chairman STARK. You say system. Are you suggesting that the standards shouldn't be such that all of the systems are completely compatible, one with the other?

Mr. HOUTZ. We are suggesting in a subsequent position, position on standards, and we do believe that standards should be utilized and standards should be mandated throughout the industry to expedite the EDI process throughout health care. Yes, we are.

Chairman STARK. Well, let me state it another way.

Mr. HOUTZ. Yes.

Chairman STARK. There are standards now for banking transactions.

Mr. HOUTZ. Yes, sir.

Chairman STARK. So that there is, for all practical purposes, no terminal in the world which won't accept and use my Visa card, if in fact they are on the Visa system, and the same thing is true with Dr. McDermott's American Express card. I mean, the system is absolutely transparent. And approvals are uniform and transactions are automatically transmitted and updated.

Is there anything in what you are suggesting that would prevent that same interchange of information from happening?

Mr. HOUTZ. None whatsoever. We advocate very strongly the usage of standards, the ANSI standards within the industry so that the transmission protocol——

Chairman STARK. So nobody is precluded from being in the system because they bought system A rather than system B.

Mr. HOUTZ. Absolutely not. But when they transmit from system A to system B, we are asking that they use a same type of transmission and industry protocols which is consistent with——

Chairman STARK. Wouldn't that be best accomplished by having the Federal Government just pick one and say this is what everybody would use?

Mr. HOUTZ. Yes, it would. It would expedite it by about 4 or 5 years.

Chairman STARK. Thank you. I didn't quite understand what you meant by dictating—I mean, the technical words here between standards. So go ahead.

Mr. HOUTZ. In some of the legislative proposals we have read, they have talked about regional data centers or so many centers per State, and we are concerned about that really adversely impacting what you are trying to accomplish.

We support universal identification of——

Chairman STARK. Social Security number?

Mr. HOUTZ. That would be adequate we feel for patients, but we need universal numbers for payers and providers.

We support the use of electronic cards if used as an identification card as opposed to the smart card approach. We support the development of an open network access system with all payers and employers participating, and we also——

Mr. McDERMOTT. Please clarify for me the difference between a smart card and any other kind of card?

Mr. HOUTZ. I think the position of AFEHCT and the position of WEDI is that if identification cards are to be used——

Mr. McDERMOTT. That is a card with a picture?

Mr. HOUTZ. Whatever is on it, like a bank card.

Chairman STARK. Let me try this one. The card identifies you in the machine and therefore, if somebody has the code to get your record someplace else, but it doesn't carry your own record in the card itself, all right?

Mr. McDERMOTT. All right.

Chairman STARK. Is that a fair characterization?

Mr. HOUTZ. Right.

Mr. McDERMOTT. You favor the former; that is, that you put that card in and you could get the data right then.

Mr. HOUTZ. We feel that the only thing the industry could handle right now is the identification card, because before you can use smart cards you need identification systems installed in all physicians' offices, and we are a decade away from that happening, or maybe two decades.

We support the privacy and confidentiality aspects of the system, and probably, if I left here with one thought that I could share with you, we strongly support the ANSI standards. That is the American—I am sorry, the American National Standard Institute, and it is a standard that all of us in health care are really working toward.

When people talk to you about standards, there is currently a pharmacy standard, which is good; there is a national standard format, which is good, and used by Medicare. But beyond that, for the other EDI transactions, we support the ANSI standards.

I have a red light on here, but I will make one final comment, if I may.

In conclusion, we think there are two things that are utmost of importance in the bill. First of all, the system must be universal, allow all participants to compete and enter, and utilize standardized data. And second of all, it must be open. For example, if a participant can meet the standards and pass the accreditation, we feel they should be allowed to compete.

With that, I would like to thank you for being here and appreciate it very much.

[The prepared statement and attachment follow:]

STATEMENT OF ASSOCIATION FOR ELECTRONIC HEALTH CARE TRANSACTIONS (AFEHCT)

February 1, 1994

"Information Transfer Technology, Administrative Simplification and Health Care Reform"

Mr Chairman, Ladies and Gentlemen of the Subcommittee. My name is Jim H Houtz and I chair the Association for Electronic Health Care Transactions (AFEHCT) Thank you for inviting us here today and for this opportunity to offer our thoughts and suggestions as to how the information transfer technology industry may support the nation's effort in simplifying the administrative processing of health care.

AFEHCT is a membership association comprised of companies who are engaged in building that portion of the "electronic highway" that will be used to transmit and process health care data -- both financial and clinical. A list of our member companies is attached to the printed version of my testimony which has been filed with the Subcommittee.

Sometime this year, at a moment and time that perhaps will sneak by uncommemorated and virtually unnoticed except by those whose job it is to track these esoteric figures, spending on all aspects of health care in the United States will pass the annualized threshold of One Trillion Dollars ($1,000,000,000,000 00) By some estimates, as much as 30% of this is being spent on a combination of administrative overhead, duplicated and unnecessary services and administrative waste, fraud and abuse.[1] The companies that comprise AFEHCT believe that they have and are in the process of developing the tools and the systems that will enable the health care industry better manage the delivery of care, reduce redundant and unnecessary or ineffective services, and eliminate much of the paperwork hassle that today comprises a significant portion of that waste

We are here today to both applaud the efforts that have been underway to promote these efficiencies and administrative simplifications and to encourage the continued support for this activity which has been accelerating in recent years. *Without the tools and the systems being developed by AFEHCT members, meaningful health care reform will be virtually impossible to accomplish.* Our major concern is that the initiatives already underway not be curtailed by the placing of artificial limits on the private sector or by any decision in structuring the network for information transfer and technology that would somehow stifle the private sector or inhibit free and open competition for new technology and new services.

AFEHCT has adopted as its Mission Statement a basic commitment to the competitive process and to the private sector playing a key role in building this electronic network and processing system. Our companies have already made substantial headway in developing the system and designing the tools to make this vision a reality -- and we have done so entirely without a government mandate and without the "big stick" of government being waved over our heads. We stand ready and are prepared to make the even greater investment in capital equipment and

---

[1]   Lewin/VHI UCLA Study

in the development of computer software that will be necessary to make the future vision of an electronic highway for health care a reality -- but we need to know that the role of the private sector will be preserved and stimulated.

Our Mission: *To promote innovation, cooperation and open competition within the EDI health care industry and to improve the quality of health care and to achieve administrative cost savings* -- can only be fulfilled if we approach the matter of health care information transfer technology and administrative simplification as a joint and cooperative effort between the government and the private sector

With these principles in mind, we have been closely monitoring the national debate over health care reform and have looked at not only the plan that has been proposed by President Clinton (the Health Security Act), but also at the other proposals that have so far been out forth, including the suggestions offered by the Chairman, and the outlines for Administrative Simplification contained in the plans suggested by Senator Chafee, incorporating the work in this area done by Senator Bond and his staff, Representative Cooper and Senator Breaux, and the suggestions put forward by several other organizations including the Work Group on Electronic Data Interchange (WEDI) and by others.

The following are the guiding principles which we would hope will be included in any health care reform legislation:

Governance and Regulation

AFEHCT does not believe that an additional regulatory bureaucracy needs to be established in order to assure that the electronic highway for health care information can be safely navigated. While the Health Care Financing Administration (HCFA) and the Secretary of Health and Human Services have had considerable experience in these areas, we believe that any legislation should require the Secretary to continue to work with the industry and with those who have expertise in health care EDI and in privacy and confidentiality matters in establishing the standards and the guidelines needed for implementation. We suggest that any "Board," "Advisory Panel," or "Commission," established by legislation or by the Secretary, include at least one, but preferably more, representatives from the health care EDI industry.

Networks and Data Systems

In reviewing the several pieces of pending legislation now before this Subcommittee, AFEHCT is concerned that there has been a lack of clarity and specificity regarding the number and operation of the networks, clearinghouses and suggested "regional" data centers and operational systems that may be established or which will be permitted to compete. AFEHCT believes that any legislation in this area should avoid dictating any single system or proposing a limit on the size or number of competing data processing systems. AFEHCT believes that the nation and the health care delivery system will be best served by a freely competitive marketplace wherein each EDI vendor and supplier is allowed to compete openly -- hospital by hospital, physician by physician, payer by payer, employer by employer, to provide such services -- competition that will assure both the latest technology and the lowest prices. The Subcommittee should maintain oversight authority and continuously monitor how the health care EDI industry is meeting the nation's need for innovation and value of services.

Universal Identification

AFEHCT supports and encourages the development of a unique -- but consistent -- numbering system to identify patients, payers and providers of care

Electronic Cards

AFEHCT suggests that the issuance of "cards" and the content and control of the information contained thereon needs to be fully evaluated and the cost and feasibility of maintaining electronic records through such a medium and the cost of maintaining a back-up central system, needs to be considered.

Health Care Information Transactions

AFEHCT supports the development of an *open network access system*, with all payers and employers working with EDI network vendors and suppliers to foster interconnectivity for all health care EDI transactions -- administrative, financial and clinical. Payers and employers must make this information available to providers and their support systems without separate fees and charges and this must be made a condition of their participation in the network.

Privacy and Confidentiality

AFEHCT supports the development of comprehensive safeguards for personally-identifiable patient care records and calls for strong compliance assurances from all participants in the communication network.

We caution, however about controls and limitations which would unnecessarily burden the electronic process by requiring redundant paper back-up and notifications to individuals. The development of standards and protocols for the delivery of health care offers the best hope for improving both the quality of such care and the needed control over utilization and potential waste and duplication of care. A balance between personal privacy protection and the need for collecting and measuring such data needs to be established. This will not be an easy task and it is one where the government needs to play a pivotal role.

There must be a fail-safe system for the privacy of individuals -- but at the same time some protection to participating EDI companies to encourage system developers to continue their work in electronic communications. Proposals for civil monetary damages must be tempered by allowing vendors and service agents to establish as an affirmative defense that they have complied with all disclosure requirements.

ANSI Standards

AFEHCT endorses the use of those standards that have been and are being developed by the X.12 Committee of the American National Standards Institute for implementation throughout the health care information transfer technology industry. While the industry is moving to adopt these standards on its own, there have been roadblocks in this development that may be appropriately addressed by the government. AFEHCT's major concern here is that there may be a tendency to make any initially-adopted standard, a rigid and unchanging mandate. Any mandate for standards needs to allow for their periodic review and revision so that the standards in use may also evolve in tune with new technology and with the innovations and inevitable changes in the EDI networks.

Standards Implementation

While supporting ANSI standards for the industry, AFEHCT suggests to the Subcommittee that merely "proclaiming" a standard does not go far enough and that some oversight needs to be maintained to assure uniformity both in the timing of any standard throughout the whole industry and in the protocols and edits that are incorporated by all of the players into their electronic systems.

Accreditation

AFEHCT supports and has set on the design and implementation of an industry accreditation program for all suppliers, vendors, clearinghouses and value-added network operators Our members are funding the development of quality and utilization for the network standards and are working with both payers and providers in devising a program to apply these standards to the industry.

Dynamic Software

AFEHCT supports the use of private sector-developed and supplied software to meet the continuously changing and growing requirements of the health care industry in

Pre-Emption of State Laws

Currently a myriad of state laws exist which in many cases impede the development of electronic networking and administrative simplification   Many of these laws, known as "quill-pen" laws, currently require handwritten documents and signatures on most medical records   These must be pre-empted by new Federal legislation.   We support the development of national rather than regional or state standards that would promote the development of electronic authorizations and alternatives for maintaining and verifying such records.

CONCLUSION

AFEHCT applauds the effort of this Subcommittee and supports the initiative included in virtually all the health care reform proposals now before you to simplify the administrative process and to begin the process of implementing standards and protocols by which the latest in computer networking and communication systems may be utilized to help in not only reducing the costs of administering the day-to-day operations of the health care system, but in developing new management tools, utilization controls and cost/outcomes evaluation measurements.

The system that must be promoted will incorporate at least the following:

System must be UNIVERSAL and utilize STANDARDIZED electronic processing and communication protocols.

• It will use a single national system of standards for processing of claims, including a universal billing form, common eligibility (*i.e.*. "swipe" card) inquiry and "coordination of benefit" standards, common managed care authorization and pre-certification protocols, uniform claims adjudication processes, simplified claims tracking and payment review procedures, including electronic funds transfer

• It will incorporate common audit review and utilization control mechanisms and standardized record-keeping coupled with medical records privacy controls.

• It will enable program managers to see on a real-time basis actual trends in the delivery of care and to identify cost efficiencies as well as inefficient delivery capabilities.

System must be OPEN, permitting all players who are capable of meeting the STANDARDS of the UNIVERSAL system to freely COMPETE for market share.

• Present system of closed competition and federally-supervised monopolies in administration of government health care programs has stifled innovation and has not encouraged the maximum use of technology.

• Suppliers of technology and services will compete on the open market not only for price but for "bells and whistles," technology advances and improved systems.

I thank you once again for the opportunity to present the vision that our members have for the industry and we look forward to seeing this vision fulfilled as part of the nation's efforts toward health care reform.

ASSOCIATION FOR ELECTRONIC
HEALTH CARE TRANSACTIONS
MEMBERSHIP

Advacare, Inc.
Advantis
Ameritech Health Connections, Inc.
Blue Cross-Blue Shield of Georgia
Blue Cross-Blue Shield of Maine
Blue Cross-Blue Shield of Rhode Island
Blue Cross of California
BT of North America, Inc. (MCI)
CIS Technologies, Inc.
Comprehensive Technologies, Int'l.
Context Software Systems, Inc.
Cooperative Health Network (CHN)
    (Equifax)
Croghan & Associates, Inc.
CSA Provider Services
CSC Healthcare Systems
CyData Systems
Datamatic Corporation
Electronic Data Systems (EDS)
Envoy Corporation
Ethix Corporation
Exclaim
First Health Services Corporation
General Computer Corp.
GTE Health Systems
Healthcare Interchange, Inc.
Health Information Technologies
Health Management Systems, Inc.

Health Net
Integrated Systems Solutions Corp.
IVANS
John Deere Health Care, Inc.
Learned-Mahn, Inc.
Med E America, Inc.
Medical Management Resources, Inc.
Medical Review Systems
Mediquest, Inc.
Med-Systems Management, Inc.
Millenium Healthcorp
National Data Corporation (NDC)
National Electronic Information Corporation
Orion Computer Systems, Inc. (U.S. Healh
    Care)
PCS Health Systems, Inc.
PhyMed Services International, Inc.
Physician Practice Management
Professional Office Systems, Inc. (Blue
    Cross-Blue Shield of the National
    Capitol Area)
SPS Transaction Services
Teleclaims, Inc.
United Healthcare
US Facilities Corporation
Verifone
Wellmark

Chairman STARK. Can I try one more thing? We have some problem philosophically among some of my colleagues with the government mandating anything. Even to try and decide what day it is sometimes is not something for the government to be involved in. So recognizing that concern, it has seemed to me that one way to jump start this process would be to take all government payments and records and put them out in one big uniform system and start it. It would seem to me others would follow.

Somebody has got to start going to make it attractive for other people voluntarily to get into the system, and if you take the biggest membership group, as it were, the biggest chunk of money that is being spent that can be done by one piece of legislation, that we might get the program going faster. Does that——

Mr. HOUTZ. That is true, and in today's environment, everybody likes to criticize things, but in terms of electronic payers, in terms of electronic receivers of claims, Medicare does a better job than any of the other payers. They also do a better job of sending electronic remittances back to the providers, which saves the providers a fair amount of money.

So I think the fact that Medicare has gone to the national standard format for electronic claims, we currently have several hundred other payers that have also gone to the national standard format, and that has been a big help.

Chairman STARK. Let me presume on Mr. Peterson's time one more time.

I am aware that the Secretary has just promulgated regulations for doing much of this without any more legislation. Are you aware of their most recent, either proposed regulations or whatever they put forward?

Mr. HOUTZ. For Medicare we are getting a new set of regulations very frequently, and——

Chairman STARK. No. This was a form payment structure and an electronic billing system that they had. Do you know anything about it?

Ms. HERR. Yes, Chairman Stark, I am familiar with it. One of our concerns with it, and why it sounds good, is that if you voluntarily have a critical mass, that which the government is and is putting out all of these standards, one asks "Why doesn't everyone else jump on?" Essentially we already have that situation. We have a HCFA 1500 form and UB–92 form.

Chairman STARK. I am just talking about something that has happened in the past month. What I want to know is if anybody is aware of those regulations and are they all right?

Ms. HERR. Yes. They are all right, but the problem is, again——

Chairman STARK. We will get back to the problem.

Ms. HERR. OK.

Chairman STARK. I have interjected on Mr. Peterson's time, and I just let him go ahead and we will get back to questions when you have all had a chance to comment. Please proceed.

STATEMENT OF ROBERT PETERSON, PRESIDENT, C₄SI, INC., CHICAGO, ILL.

Mr. PETERSON. Good afternoon, Mr. Chairman. I am Bob Peterson, the president of the C₄SI, Inc. We are a small Midwestern firm that specializes in advanced management information systems.

I would like to take this opportunity to describe to you very briefly the kind of work we have done, and encourage you to consider that the very latest technology will allow us all of the flexibilities we need to implement literally any kind of system you legislate and handle anything that you either choose to mandate or choose not to mandate.

I will describe one system as I see it. And that is, first of all, there are several components. One component being a smart operating system which would be in the medical provider's office itself. A system that would be so inclusive and so universal in nature that it would be the only system that they would have to use to operate their office.

I know this is possible because we have done this to operate schools and school districts; an extremely difficult type of situation to operate. The system would handle their payroll and their purchasing and their medical records, their correspondence, keep in touch with their patients. But in order to be operational, this would have to be an extremely user-friendly system, one that does not take a great deal of time to learn, one that makes extensive use of pop-up menus, point-and-click type of selections.

To communicate with this system, I would envision a card, an optical memory card. This optical memory card would be sufficient to store emergency medical information which could be used by emergency medical units as well as hospitals, emergency rooms and so on; it would be able to contain somewhere in the neighborhood of 1,200 pages of text information if that were necessary. It could also include pictures, identification information, who to contact in the case of emergency, and so on.

I would see this as a dual-use card. The card would have on the back of it a magnetic strip. The magnetic strip would carry communication between one care provider and another. For instance, a physician's prescription would be encoded on the magnetic strip; it would then be inserted into a computer at the pharmacy; the pharmacist would no longer do any input of his own. In other words, the card would communicate directly to his database, eliminating a second input. That has been one of our primary concerns in developing our systems, that information goes in only once. You should never have to re-input a piece of information.

There would have to be a database somewhere to back up the patient's card. This database could be anywhere—anything from a massive central database, a regional database or a database maintained by certain primary care physicians who would become the gatekeepers of the information. I think a policy issue would impact on where this database were maintained.

The final issue that I think is very important here is training and public education. In order for a system to be used, the public has to understand it, and the physicians and medical staff wherever they are have to understand how to use it. In such a case, I could see the use of organizations that are already in place such as the Community Learning and Information Network (CLIN), which is now developing sites at schools, the one thing that all communities have in common, they all have schools. And they are developing sites in low-income housing areas, which is where probably the first targeted group would be located and have to be educated. They would have to develop a trust in the system.

Thank you very much.

[The prepared statement follows:]

THE ROLE OF TECHNOLOGY IN HEALTH CARE REFORM
Testimony of Robert Peterson, President C₄SI, Inc.
February 1, 1994

Good morning Mr. Chairman and members of the Committee. I am Bob Peterson, President of C₄SI a small Midwestern firm that develops advanced management information systems. I am pleased to have the opportunity to appear before you today to discuss the role of information technology in health care reform. I applaud you for holding hearings on this important subject.

In the interest of time I have chosen to describe for you just one of the many ways that currently available technology can be used to modernize health care services.

C₄SI SYSTEM

Our company has developed the C₄SI software (a computer memory program) which we are prepared to tailor to meet the needs of comprehensive health care reform. I believe that technology such as this will revolutionize the health care system by enabling physicians and other health care providers to gain immediate access to medical records and insurance information. With use of technology such as C₄SI, physicians and other health care providers will have access to the information they need to provide high quality care to all Americans.

THE OPTICAL MEMORY CARD

The technology we have developed will permit doctors and other health care practitioners to store patient information on a small "optical memory card" which can be easily carried in a wallet or worn as a pendant. An optical memory card is a plastic card the size of a standard credit or ATM card. You may have seen the President display a sample card during his address last September 22, introducing his health care reform bill. Optical memory cards can be encoded with emergency health information such as a patient's allergies, blood type and medical histories. In addition, the cards can store information regarding patient insurance. The cards are essentially personal databases which are carried by individuals. The advantage of the optical memory card is that it can store all relevant health care and insurance information (including instructions for insurance claim processing) in one place which greatly simplifies the means by which physicians gain access to medical records and the way that insurers process claims for benefits. The card can store as much or as little information as one would like. It would be up to the Congress to determine what exact information would be kept on the cards, and what additional safeguards would be used to protect patient privacy and doctor-patient confidentiality. My area of expertise is in software development; I leave it to you to establish in the law whatever safeguards and standards for use of the information provided you deem necessary.

In addition to its permanent storage capability, a magnetic strip applied to the back of the card can hold temporary provider communications. For example, if a doctor or other health care provider wants to send instructions to a pharmacist, the doctor can enter information onto the magnetic strip and have the patient take the card to the pharmacist, an example of an electronic "note from the doctor," if you will. The information will be read and recorded by the receiving party, and then will be deleted from the magnetic strip, so that other providers can send notes through the same process.

This technology is available right now; there is already one card supplier in the United States who can produce at least 1 million cards per month.

THE INFORMATION NETWORK

With an understanding of how the card will be used, let me briefly describe for you the way that I envision the system could work. Essentially, a network consisting of cards and computer monitors could be established. The computers would be able to read the information stored on the cards. I call these computers "smart stations," because they would contain so much information. At least one stationary smart station would be placed in every hospital, neighborhood clinic, and physician's office. Portable smart stations would allow emergency technicians to have access to patient information right at the scene of emergencies. The portable unit would consist of a hand-held battery-operated unit for use in emergency medical service units, military field operations and health care facilities desiring fast access to patient records. It is anticipated that many physicians would purchase portable units for their own convenience.

A central database consisting of patient information would be stored at a separate facility. The central patient database would serve as the backup to the card data. The database will store each patient's health related information so that if cards become lost or unreadable, the database can replace the lost information.

I envision the process to work this way:

1.   Every insured individual will carry a memory optical card encoded with medical information.

2.   When a patient comes to a provider for care, the provider will insert the patient card into a smart station which will read the files on the card.

3.   Each time the card is scanned through the system, a new "encounter file" will be created which will keep track of health care services provided to the patient. In this way, the patient's medical records are kept up to date.

4.   At the conclusion of the encounter, the provider will initiate a computer procedure that will create a permanent record of the procedure performed, including the name of the practitioner performing the service and a description of the care given. A bill for services will be automatically generated at the end of each encounter.

5.   The physician's smart station will transmit a record of activity to a central database for permanent storage at the end of each day.

6.   In the event that the patient's optical memory card is full or missing, the provider can access patient information through the patient's social security number or other ID number and can input information regarding a particular encounter into his or her own smart station database. Information regarding each encounter will be downloaded onto a central database at the end of the day, just as if the patient had provided the memory optical card.

7.   In the event of an emergency, portable smart stations would be used. Portable stations would only be able to read patient information, no new information would be added at the actual scene of the emergency. The emergency care technicians would scan the card through the portable computer. The portable smart station would allow the emergency provider to identify the patient and the patient's medical history. The information from an emergency encounter would be entered into a smart system at a hospital or health care facility.

8. In the event that a patient in an emergency situation does not have a card, the patient's medical records will be accessible through the physician's stationary smart station. Portables can be connected to stationary stations through a modem.

9. Providers can also download patient medical records from the central database.

INFORMATION SECURITY

Unfortunately, any information system must establish a means of securing its data. For the optical memory card, I envision creating a central identification directory which will maintain an identification system for every patient information card. The identification system will enable system operators to track cards through encrypted numbers and patient social security or ID numbers. Patients will be able to report lost or stolen cards.

CONCLUSION

What I have outlined for you today is a very general description of the way in which C_4SI technology could be used to modernize our Nation's health care system. Many more details would have to be finalized before an actual plan could be put into action. My point today is not to sell you on a specific proposal, but rather to make you aware of the fact that the technology exists and, if properly designed, can be used to benefit us all. Again, we can design and implement whatever health security card system you establish, with sophisticated personal privacy protections.

Thank you again for this opportunity to appear before the Committee. With your permission, I would like to supplement this oral statement with a fuller description of some of the technologies which are currently available or in the process of being developed. I will be happy to answer any questions you may have at this time.

Chairman STARK. Thank you.

As an old slide rule user, those of you developing these high-tech systems never cease to amaze me. I will have to find out a little bit more about your system in a moment.

Ms. Watson.

STATEMENT OF LINDA A. WATSON, DIRECTOR, THE CLAUDE MOORE HEALTH SCIENCES LIBRARY, ON BEHALF OF THE MEDICAL LIBRARY ASSOCIATION AND THE ASSOCIATION OF ACADEMIC HEALTH SCIENCES LIBRARY DIRECTORS

Ms. WATSON. Mr. Chairman and members of the subcommittee, thank you for the opportunity to speak before you today. I am Linda Watson from Charlottesville, Va., where I am the director of the Claude Moore Health Sciences Library at the University of Virginia. I am appearing on behalf of the Medical Library Association and the Association of Academic Health Sciences Library Directors to present the views of these organizations on health care reform and information technology.

Our library organizations commend the efforts of the Clinton organization and administration and of Congress to improve our Nation's health care system. We believe that these efforts would benefit from attention to four important areas in which health sciences librarians and the information they provide can make a positive difference. We recommend the following actions on information technology.

First, reimbursement for information use and development. The cost of developing medical information resources and the delivery of these information resources to health care professionals and to the citizens of this country should be factored into reimbursement plans, since recent studies have shown that having access to this information has the potential to save millions of dollars.

Consumers of health care must share responsibility for their health and for their health care choices. The production and distribution of health care literature and effective access to this literature provides a knowledge infrastructure for professionals making care decisions and for patients and health care consumers. Because information systems support informed health care decision-making nationwide, the cost of maintaining and further developing these information systems should be factored into the reimbursable costs associated with optimal care.

Second, support for the national information infrastructure. The national information infrastructure and the information highway should be supported and expanded to include all libraries and all health care providers. Computerized health information networks that efficiently connect medical libraries, hospitals, clinics, pharmacies, medical schools and others will facilitate timely and accurate access to relevant medical information that support accurate diagnosis and treatment while reducing the cost of health care delivery. Health sciences librarians are leaders in applying technology and promoting its use by health care professionals, and can be called upon to make these linkages work.

Third, support for rural networks and outreach to the underserved. Librarian information services should be extended through outreach programs to health care providers in medically under-served urban and rural areas.

Access to information reduces professional isolation and improves the quality of decisionmaking. Health sciences librarians facilitate the recruitment and retention of health care providers in medically underserved areas by providing them with access to information services that help them give quality health care to their patients.

For example, from a single workstation connected to a network, a health professional in a rural area would have access to the same rich information as that available at a large university center. We ask Congress to continue to support information outreach initiatives and rural network development in the health care reform discussion.

Finally, we support the role of the National Library of Medicine. Funding for the National Library of Medicine as well as other Federal agencies involved with medical information access is an investment in information dissemination. The National Library of Medicine supports research efforts in the design, development and use of health information systems like Medline and the continued training of health sciences librarians to meet the demands of the future.

The National Library of Medicine also supports an important health services research program in cooperation for the Agency for Health Care Policy Research to develop practice guidelines for cost-effective medical care. Dissemination of these practice guidelines to the point of care through libraries and information networks also needs your support.

In closing, Mr. Chairman and members of the subcommittee, I would like to thank you for your interest and efforts on behalf of medical and health sciences librarians throughout the Nation. I appreciate the opportunity to testify regarding health care reform, and hope that you will call on medical librarians around the country to help plan a health system that works for all Americans.

Thank you.

[The prepared statement follows:]

STATEMENT OF LINDA WATSON
MEDICAL LIBRARY ASSOCIATION AND
THE ASSOCIATION OF ACADEMIC HEALTH SCIENCES LIBRARY DIRECTORS

Mr. Chairman and members of the subcommittee, thank you for the opportunity to speak before you today. I am Linda Watson from Charlottesville, Virginia, where I am the Director of the Claude Moore Health Sciences Library, at the University of Virginia. I am appearing on behalf of the Medical Library Association (MLA) and the Association of Academic Health Sciences Library Directors (AAHSLD) to present the views of those organizations on Health Care Reform.

MLA is a professional organization representing approximately 5,000 individuals and institutions involved in the management and dissemination of biomedical information to support patient care, education, and research. AAHSLD an organization composed of library directors representing medical schools belonging to the Association of American Medical Colleges. Together, MLA and AAHSLD address health information issues and legislative matters of importance to both organizations and the National Library of Medicine.

Mr. Chairman, our library organizations commend the efforts of the Clinton Administration and Congress to improve our nation's health care system. We believe that those efforts would benefit from attention to four important areas in which health sciences librarians and the information they provide can make a positive difference. We recommend the following:

Reimbursement for Information Use & Development

We believe cost containment without compromising health quality should be the principal objective of health care reform. The cost of developing information resources such as the Telecommunications and Information Infrastructure Program, and the delivery of such information programs that promote health care, research, and health professional education must be factored into reimbursement plans, since recent studies have shown that having access to this information has the potential to save millions of dollars.

In the June 1993 issue of Journal of the American Medical Association, health professionals reported that information derived from online searching of the scientific literature increased physicians' ability to provide patients with useful explanations of their specific ailments, enabling them to involve their patients in treatment decisions; this helped them motivate changes in patients' health risk behaviors.

Consumers of health care must share responsibility for their health and for their health care choices. The production and distribution of health care literature and effective access to this literature provides a "knowledge infrastructure" for professionals making these decisions, and for patients and healthcare consumers who are assuming increasing responsibility for their own health. Because information systems support informed health care decision making nationwide, even worldwide, the cost of maintaining and further developing these information systems should be factored into the reimbursable costs associated with optimal care.

National Information Infrastructure and High Performance Computing Communications

The National Information Infrastructure should be expanded to include all libraries and to ensure basic information access for all health care providers. A computerized health information infrastructure will facilitate timely, accurate access to relevant biomedical information to health care professionals thereby improving the physicians' ability to make accurate diagnosis and treatments, while reducing the cost of health care delivery. Health science librarians are leaders in applying technology and promoting its use by health care professionals. For example, from a single work station, a health professional should be able to access a computerized patient record, order tests and drugs, schedule appointments, view X-Rays, search medical databases such as MEDLINE, and request journal articles from his or her library.

The National Library of Medicine supports many High Performance Computing Communications initiatives in medical applications areas which include projects to create testbed networks that link medical libraries with hospitals, clinics, doctors' offices, medical schools, and universities. This enables health care providers and researchers to share medical data and imagery, and collaborative technology. Health care providers in rural and other remote locations using telemedicine technologies are able to provide timely treatment for patients. Health care financing agencies, insurance companies, hospitals, pharmacists, and other health care providers must be networked through outreach programs, such as MEDLINE, if health care delivery is to be successful.

Rural Networks and Outreach to Underserved

Library and information services should be extended through outreach programs to medically underserved health care providers in urban and rural areas. Access to information reduces professional isolation and improves the quality of decision-making while reducing healthcare costs. Health sciences librarians facilitate the recruitment and retention of health care providers in medically underserved areas by providing them with technical development skills for high performance computing communications and information services that help rural health care providers give quality healthcare to their patients.

Health sciences librarians organize networks to share information among their institutions so that materials needed for research, education, and patient care are available to all health care professionals, wherever they practice. The National Library of Medicine, health science librarians and medical librarians must play an important role in the improvement of the quality of networks such as MEDLINE, and continue outreach efforts to the underserved, rural and urban populations.

MLA/AAHSLD asks Congress to continue to support outreach initiatives in the upcoming health care reform discussion. The expansion of the National Information Infrastructure and High Performance Computing Communications projects are key if high quality and cost-effective healthcare is to be delivered.

The Role of the National Library of Medicine

Funding for NLM, as well as other federal agencies involved with medical information access supports efficient information dissemination. NLM's National Network of Libraries of Medicine comprises more that 3,500 libraries in hospitals and academic health sciences centers throughout the nation. It is a network of information that supports networks of health care. The NLM also maintains the world's preeminent collection of biomedical literature and provides systems and services to make it accessible. It supports research efforts in the design, development, and use of health information systems and the continued training of health sciences librarians.

For the past four years, NLM's health services research program has been conducted through interagency agreements with the Agency for Health Care Policy Research (AHCPR). The recent enacted NIH Revitalization Act authorized the creation of a National Information Center on Health Services and Health Care Technology at the NLM. These two projects enable the NLM to provide improved access to information useful to those planning and conducting health services research, and should receive your support.

It is crucial that the NLM be adequately supported and play an important role to guarantee that medical information is accessible and cost efficient if health care reform is to be successful. Some funding for NLM programs in these areas can come from discretionary sources, but some mechanism should be established that would treat medical information and technology much the same as it does any other medical commodity or supply -- it should be a reimbursable item.

In closing Mr. Chairman and members of the subcommittee, I would like to thank you for your interest and efforts on behalf of medical and health sciences libraries throughout the nation. I appreciate the opportunity to testify regarding health care reform and would be happy to answer any questions you may have.

Information contained in this testimony obtained from: "MLA/AAHSLD Statement on Health Care Reform and the Sciences Librarian: Excellence in Health through Access to Information." November 1993, Medical Library Association, 6 North Michigan Avenue, Suite 300, Chicago, Il. For copies of this statement, write this address, or call (312) 419-9094.

Chairman STARK. Thank you, Ms. Watson.
Mr. Kreidler.

STATEMENT OF DAVID B. KREIDLER, EXECUTIVE VICE PRESIDENT AND CHIEF EXECUTIVE OFFICER, EASTERN BUILDING MATERIAL DEALERS ASSOCIATION, AND CHAIRMAN, INSURANCE EDUCATION COMMITTEE, AMERICAN SOCIETY OF ASSOCIATION EXECUTIVES

Mr. KREIDLER. Mr. Chairman, my name is Dave Kreidler. I am executive vice president and chief executive officer of Eastern Building Material Dealers Association, and I currently serve as chairman of the Insurance Education Committee of the American Society of Association Executives. I have been a volunteer leader in the association community for more than 10 years.

ASAE is pleased to have this opportunity to present testimony before the Subcommittee on Health of the House Ways and Means Committee regarding the importance of association plans in health care reform.

Mr. Chairman, ASAE is a professional society of over 22,000 association executives representing more than 10,700 national, State and local associations. Most of our members work for associations with fewer than 10 employees. ASAE's members represent tax-exempt organizations, mostly under IRS Code 501(c)(6) and 501(c)(3).

The future of association-sponsored health plans is in serious doubt, as our Nation debates health care reform. Many proposals for a single-payer system or a managed care system with exclusive health purchasing alliances or cooperatives may deny a role for plans which associations now offer or operate for their members.

Associations have for many years sponsored employer group health plans as viable mechanisms for pooling risks along functional and industry lines. Associations have also increased the market leverage and buying power of small employers as consumers of health care services.

The association plans were generated by, and composed of, employers which participate directly in the decisionmaking process and management of their association health plans.

For more than 55 years, association-sponsored health plans have been providing millions of people with an effective way to protect themselves and their families against financial catastrophe. Association plans have enabled these millions of citizens to have access to quality, affordable health care, which was often denied to them through the available market. Today, thousands of U.S. trade and professional employer associations provide health coverage benefit programs to industry groups representing millions of employees and their dependents.

In an October 1992 survey of Nation's Business readers, 13 percent of the respondents polled reported they purchase their health plans through industry associations. According to a national survey of trade and professional associations conducted by ASAE and William F. Mourneau & Associates, 779 of 6,300 associations reported health premiums paid in 1991 of $6.2 billion. This amount is larger than the total annual health care premium income reported by Prudential, the largest health insurance carrier in the United

States. In addition, of the 779 associations surveyed, more than 1.9 million lives were covered.

Now, extrapolated against all associations in ASAE, this data suggests that ASAE member associations may be directly involved in the collection of approximately $21 billion in annual health care premiums—more than the 10 largest insurance companies collectively generate in premiums. When examining lives covered, the extrapolation would mean at least 10 million lives are covered by association plans.

Under the current U.S. health care system, association plans provide significant health care coverage to a substantial number of small employers throughout the Nation and in a large cross-section of U.S. industries. Many of these small employers are located in rural areas which are underserved by managed care providers. These employers have sought and received the buying power and protection of qualified association plans which provide access to quality, affordable health care.

The ASAE survey uncovered three significant facets of association-sponsored plans. One, of those associations offering plans, the average penetration of membership is a significant 27 percent. This clearly shows that this is an important service.

Two, 49 percent of the associations with plans have a trust agreement in place. This is a strong indication of the sophistication level of such plans and the degree of effort that is being made to closely manage the programs.

Three, the vast majority of plans, 86 percent, in fact, are funded on a fully insured basis, which runs counter to the common stereotype of the underfunded MEWA about to go bankrupt and leave thousands of policyholders with unpaid claims.

The importance of the widespread geographic coverage of association health plans can be seen from a study supported by a grant from the Federal Agency for Health Care Policy and Research, which concluded that reform of the U.S. health care system through expansion of governmental-managed competition is feasible in large metropolitan areas. But smaller metropolitan areas and rural areas would require alternative forms of organization and regulations. A substantial number of people live in areas that fall outside the realm of managed competition.

In 19 States, the majority of the population—well, listen, you know a lot of this, so I am just going to skip ahead, because that light is on. It is great to go last, but I don't want to make myself unwelcome.

Chairman STARK. Well, you are not.

[The prepared statement follows:]

WRITTEN TESTIMONY OF
David B. Kreidler, CAE

AMERICAN SOCIETY OF ASSOCIATION EXECUTIVES
1575 Eye Street, N.W., Washington, D.C. 20005
Telephone: (202) 626-2703

Mr. Chairman, my name is David B. Kreidler. I am the Executive Vice President and CEO of the Eastern Building Material Dealers Association, and I currently serve as Chairman of the Insurance Education Committee of the American Society of Association Executives (ASAE). I have been a volunteer leader in the association community for over 10 years.

ASAE is pleased to have this opportunity to present testimony before the Subcommittee on Health of the House Ways and Means Committee regarding the importance of association plans in health care reform.

Mr. Chairman, ASAE is a professional society of over 22,000 association executives representing more than 10,700 national, state, and local associations. Most of our members work for associations with less than 10 employees. ASAE's members represent tax exempt organizations, mostly under Internal Revenue Code Sections 501(c)(6) and 501(c)(3).

I. INTRODUCTION

The future of association sponsored health plans is in serious doubt, as our nation debates health care reform. Many proposals for a single payor system, or a managed care system with exclusive health purchasing alliances or cooperatives may deny a role for plans which associations now offer or operate for their members.

Associations have for many years sponsored employer group health plans as viable mechanisms for pooling risks along functional and industry lines. Associations have also increased the market leverage and buying power of small employers as consumers of health care services.

The association plans were generated by, and composed of, employers which participate directly in the decision-making process and management of their association health plans

For more than fifty-five years, association-sponsored health plans have been providing millions of people with an effective way to protect themselves and their families against financial catastrophe. Association plans have enabled the millions of citizens to have access to quality, affordable health care, which was often denied to them through the available market. Today, thousands of U.S. trade and professional employer associations provide health coverage benefit programs to industry groups representing millions of employees and their dependents.

In an October 1992 survey of *Nation's Business* readers, 13% of the respondents polled reported they purchase their health plans through industry associations (90% of the respondents were employers with less than 100 employees).

According to a national survey of trade and professional associations conducted by ASAE and William F. Morneau & Associates, 779 of 6,300 associations reported health premiums paid in 1991 of $6.2 billion. This amount is larger than the total annual health care premium income reported by Prudential, the largest health insurance carrier in the U.S. In addition, of the 779 associations surveyed, more than 1.9 million lives were covered.

Extrapolated against all associations in ASAE, this data suggests that ASAE member associations may be directly involved in the collection of approximately $21 billion in annual health care premiums – more than the ten largest insurance companies collectively generate in premiums. When examining lives covered, the extrapolation would mean that at least 10 million lives are covered by association plans.

Under the current U.S. health care system, association plans provide significant health care coverage to a substantial number of small employers throughout the nation and in a large cross-section of U.S. industries. Many of these small employers are located in rural areas which are underserved by managed care providers. These employers have sought and received the buying power and protection of qualified association plans which provide access to quality, affordable health care. The ASAE survey uncovered three significant facets of association-sponsored plans:

- Of those associations offering plans, the average penetration of membership (percentage of members participating in the association health plan) is a significant 27%. This is a clearly important member service at these associations.

- 49% of associations with plans have a trust agreement in place. This is a strong indication of the sophistication level of such plans and the degree of effort that is being made to closely manage the programs.

- The vast majority of plans (86%) are funded on a fully-insured basis. This runs counter to the common stereotype of the underfunded MEWA about to go bankrupt and leave thousands of policyholders with unpaid claims

The importance of the widespread geographic coverage of association health plans can be seen from a study supported by a grant from the Federal Agency for Health Care Policy and Research, which concluded that "reform of the U.S health care system through expansion of governmental managed competition is feasible in large metropolitan areas But, smaller metropolitan areas and rural areas would require alternative forms of organization and regulations..." "A substantial number of people live in areas that fall outside" the realm of managed competition, said Richard Krfonic, an assistant professor of Community and Family Medicine at the University of California at San Diego.

In 19 states, the majority of the population lives in areas of less than 180,000 persons, where hospital services must be extensively shared. In 42 states, 20% or more of the population lives in such areas. And, while 23 states and the District of Columbia have at least one metropolitan area large enough to support three HMOs, the study found, in only 10 states do the majority of people live in such areas. Association plans are active in all of these areas currently, which demonstrates their viability and market orientation.

Association plans also have extensive experience in:

- designing special plans to meet the financial needs of their members.
- pooling health risks within organized industry groups.
- gathering employee data.
- collecting and disseminating information on health care quality, cost and resource allocation.
- communicating with members and employees.
- administering of benefit programs.

All Americans should have equal access to high quality, cost-effective health care through health plans offered under a competitive market system. Employers within the U.S. employment-based system should have the flexibility and freedom to select the most effective organizational mechanisms available for delivering health services. Association plans have proven for years to be such a vehicle.

Let's consider association plans in light of the various "reform" proposals. Associations are uniquely structured to be a part of a new or revised health care delivery system. That is because they are already structured to represent their members in other areas. They possess the infrastructure, administrative mechanisms and experience to unify employers and employees into effective consumers of health services.

Employers who join purchasing groups or cooperatives organized by associations can offer employees access to high quality private health coverage at lower costs, and with an expanded number of options.

Associations already offer a wide variety of approved health plans and managed care arrangements (insured arrangements, Blue Cross/Blue Shields, HMOs, self-insured) to employers and employees. Associations can also distribute information, provide price data, and offer qualitative comparisons between health plans.

Associations also develop common statistical databases by major industry and professional groupings. This assists such plans in administering for claims, premium contributions and utilization of health care services.

Association plans also offer the best opportunity to integrate coverage and provide statistical data for work-related injuries. Many associations offer companion or side-by-side health and workers' compensation programs. Proposals to incorporate the health benefits of the workers' compensation system with traditional health plans can easily by accomplished by many associations.

In summary, qualified and functioning industry-based associations have been successfully providing comprehensive health benefit programs, as well as many other services, to their members for more than fifty years. The administrative systems, expertise in negotiation, data collection and communication are all in place and operational today, not in some theoretical planning scenario.

II.   CONSUMER ACCOUNTABILITY & ASSOCIATION HEALTH PLANS

A primary reason why health care spending is out of control is that most of the time, when we enter the medical marketplace as patients, we are spending someone else's money. Economic studies – and common sense – confirm that we are less likely to be prudent, careful shoppers if someone else is paying the bill. Association plans have been dealing with these concerns since health care costs started spiraling in the 1970's. Plan design, member education and provider involvement have been put to work to hold down health care costs. Most importantly, both employers and their employees have been able to choose between different options.

Member identity with their association, and member control of programs help educate the participants as to the costs and choices in health care, much more so than in traditional insurance coverages.

Association plans are not a "third-party" phenomenon. Members realize that association plans are, in reality, their own money and that "wellness" activities, as well as careful health care purchasing save them money directly ●

III.   STUDY TRACES HISTORY AND EXTENT OF ASSOCIATION INSURANCE PLANS

Some association executives mistakenly believe that association sponsorship of insurance programs is a new phenomenon. In actuality, many such programs have been in existence for over 55 years. The most successful association-sponsored programs are those that have continually undergone change to adapt to evolving insurance and association management trends.

The health insurance industry has been in a "hard" market for many years. Member difficulty in obtaining appropriate health insurance coverages has led many associations to adopt sponsored health insurance programs.

More than 90% of the respondents indicated "member service" as the primary reason they initiated programs.

Life and health programs appear to be generally attractive to associations with large individual memberships and/or memberships comprising a large number of companies or firms, each of which has only a few employees. The increasingly difficult health insurance marketplace has made the sponsorship of health insurance coverages particularly attractive in recent years.

Those associations reporting life or health programs offered the following coverages:

•medical insurance,	81.7%
•vision care,	8.0%
•prescription plans,	8.6%
•dental care,	30.8%
•accidental death/disab.	25.7%
•basic life,	61.7%
•short-term disability,	29.7%
•long-term disability,	32.1%
•supplemental life,	8.0%
•supplemental AD&D,	7.4%

In looking at the variety of benefit plans associations offer, it is apparent that, if empowered and encouraged by federal legislation, even more expanded programs could be offered.

Approximately 85% of those associations sponsoring insurance programs for their memberships have formal, written agreements with insurance carriers, agents, or brokers

These agreements can guarantee the association's right to continuing and complete information on the program, including loss statistics, premium income, insurer profit and expenses, and member participation, from participating insurers.

Much of this specific information, needed to design benefit plans and respond to members' needs, would not be available to employers from a governmentally operated health purchasing alliance or cooperative. Currently, association plans use this information to assist their members.

ASAE and the Aon Speciality Group's Risk Management Services consulting unit, Washington D C. are producing the *1993 Association Insurance Program Guide and Survey Report*. This publication contains how-to instructions for implementing and managing a successful program, as well as statistics from our broad survey (conducted in fall 1992) of ASAE members. ·

IV.   ASSOCIATION PLANS CAN HELP ACHIEVE THE PRESIDENT'S CAMPAIGN PLAN FOR HEALTH CARE REFORM

The health care reform plan being outlined by President Clinton contains the objective of providing universal access to affordable, high quality health care for all Americans.

His objective (often described as "managed competition with global budgets") would provide a new market structure within which competition could work to ensure efficient health care delivery and controlled costs:

- Insurance reforms would provide individuals with freer choice of plans. Group buying would drive tough bargains.
- Consumers would be given incentives to choose efficient plans.
- Systems would hold providers accountable for managing the volume and quality of care.

Association health plans now fulfill these needs for many Americans. They provide familiar, well known sources of benefits to their members. The sense of loyalty and "ownership" of members for their association plans encourages participation.

V. ASSOCIATIONS' ROLE RECOGNIZED BY HEALTH EXPERTS

The importance of association plans has been recognized by some of the members of President Clinton's Health Reform Task Force.

A preliminary work paper from their studies comments, "... groups outside of HIPCs can provide an important source of affordable [health] coverage, if they meet important solvency and other requirements. Some existing groups have strong political, historical and legal precedents, and should be permitted to continue ..."

Prohibiting existing group arrangements from continuing after health reform would, in many cases, needlessly disband arrangements that successfully provide coverage to a significant number of employees. These groups are an important source of coverage; permitting only fully insured arrangements might raise costs of coverage. These associations and similar plans are headed by plan participants or employers of plan participants, with a personal stake in successful operation. These are not entrepreneurs who create plans and market to groups of unrelated employers, a practice which has in the past created problems, such as insolvencies, that have left millions of dollars in unpaid health care claims.

VI. EXAMPLES OF ASSOCIATION SPONSORED PLANS, AND HOW THEY BENEFIT EMPLOYEES.

A. Taft-Hartley and Multi-Employer Plans.

There are thousands of Taft-Hartley multi-employer health plans covering more than eight million workers and dependents in industries as diverse as building and construction, clothing, textiles, transportation, services, retail, maritime, food, hotel and restaurant, mining, entertainment, and light manufacturing. Anywhere from two to 2,000 or more separate employers may contribute to a single plan.

These plans provide continuous health benefits coverage to workers as they change employment from one contributing employer to another. This portability or "seamless" coverage is essential for workers in mobile, seasonal industries like building and construction, entertainment, longshoremen and agriculture. Without a central plan covering all of his or her work for multiple employers, such a worker would not have health benefits coverage.

These multi-employer plans enjoy economies of scale in administration, and combined purchasing power, not available to individual or small employers. Participating employers are required to do little other than submit their periodic contributions to the plan with verifying information. All of the plan design and administrative functions are generally performed by the plan trustees with professional assistance. This eliminates any need for a participating employer to maintain its own plan administration work force.

Over the decades of their existence, these multiple employer plans have developed eligibility rules, benefit packages, and financing and collection methods tailored to meet the employment patterns, needs and practices of their particular industries.

These plans have developed industry-specific systems for maximizing coverage, given the employment patterns of the industry and the financing needs of the plan.

Many of these plans cover employers in different states. State-by-state regulation, with its threat of multiple, inconsistent rules, would adversely affect their efficient and economical operation. ERISA's preemption provisions are intended to protect these plans from such conflicting requirements.

These plans, operated by elected officers from industries and unions, are politically and directly accountable for how the plan is operating and how much it costs.

For the associations and unions which sponsor these multiple employer health and welfare plans, these plans are a proud achievement which provide health and income security benefits that would otherwise be unavailable to their members. The contributing employers function as a single employer through these plans for purposes of furnishing benefits and negotiating with health care providers. They are as concerned about the covered workers and as innovative as any single employer, if not more so, since there is more worker involvement in the design, operation and financing of these plans than in any single employer plan.

If the Clinton Administration's health care reform proposal allows large employers to opt out of the purchasing system, these plans should be given the same opportunity under the same conditions.

Association-and union-sponsored plans are really the prototypes for health care purchasing alliances, currently being discussed by the Clinton Administration. These plans are too valuable to sacrifice, for institutions that serve the same functions and solve the same problems would only have to be reinvented

B.   Coca-Cola Bottlers' Association

Founded in 1914, the Coca-Cola Bottlers' Association has operated a voluntary group health insurance program since 1937. Smaller bottlers are pooled in a group, and larger participating employers are experience rated and participate in some of the risk of medical claims.

The program now covers approximately 13,000 employees and 26,000 dependents. Approximately 93 cents of every premium dollar goes to the payment of claims. This efficiency is well above that of most insurance company or health maintenance organization plans. The association's plan includes life insurance benefits which help keep costs of medical coverage down.

The average cost per employee for the benefit plans is $2,600, well below the national average of almost $4,000 per employee per year for conventionally insured plans, or even most self-funded plans.

The association also offers an Ergonomics Program which allows employees to be assessed for their physical ability to perform necessary work-related physical tasks, and helping to avoid on-the-job injuries.

The association also provides access to HMO's, PPO's, utilization review, pharmaceutical review, individual care management, and a wellness program to improve health of their members' employees. Additionally, the association is able to negotiate performance guarantees in areas such as claims turn around time, accuracy of claims payments, and customer service.

C.   Eastern Material Dealers Association

From its humble beginnings in 1949, the Eastern Group Trust has developed the reputation for consistently good service, fair dealing, and funding stability within the scope of medical care plans.

Primarily organized to respond to the short-term disability income responsibilities under New Jersey statutes, the Group Insurance Trust has expanded its variety of coverages to include group term life, accidental death and dismemberment, weekly disability income, long-term disability income, six medical plans and a dental plan.

The major objectives of the Group Insurance Trust have been to use plan designs that are easily understood by participating employees and to provide as much stability in funding as can be obtained in a rapidly inflating market place of medical care. The program is run as an "experience rated contract" with State Mutual, with surplus funding available for reallocation to reduce future premiums paid by employers and employees.

Directed by a seven-member Board of Trustees, elected by plan participants pursuant to the requirements of Section 501(c)(9) of the Internal Revenue Code, the Group Insurance Trust is managed by staff employees. This staff is responsible for sales, installation, certificate and identification card issuance, billing and collection of premiums, payment of claims and providing Trustee and insurance carrier reports

Approximately 230 employers participate in providing innovative plans which provide $11 million per year in benefits to the industry's employees.

D. Western Agriculture

Agriculture in the Western U.S., particularly California and Arizona, is highly seasonal, with fruit, grape and vegetable production supplying over half of the entire U.S. consumers' needs, as well as providing major exports which assist the nation's international balance of trade.

Traditional insurance carriers, and all current HMO organizations, declined in the past to provide medical coverage for the 350,000 employees of this vital industry, due to their seasonal employment, wage levels, and predominantly Spanish-speaking language needs.

Four major farm organizations provide virtually all of the health benefits for these seasonal employees, using association designed and operated programs. Self funding is a critical component of these benefit plans, due to the reluctance of the usual insurance market to offer coverages.

The largest of these programs, Western Growers Association, provides benefits to 18,000 employees, offering free choice of medical provider as well as managed care plans.

Grouping the buying power of its 2,000 participating members, Western Growers has been able to negotiate discounts from hospitals which saved 46% on billed charges on 1992, and saving over $4 million dollars for farm employers and their employees. The association's plans average 20% discounts in contracting doctor's fees and elimination of "usual and customary" problems for patients using contracting physicians. WGA has contracted for 9% below-wholesale drug costs for its medical plans.

The association also operates a licensed and admitted workers' compensation company in Arizona and California, and has integrated on-the-job and off-the-job medical benefits for over 10 years, preventing "double-dipping" and making the coordination of benefits easy

The association offers flexible benefit plans, which have been very well received by seasonal farm workers. It also offers services by medical providers in Mexico for those workers near the U.S. border, and for those workers with families in Mexico.

These are but a few examples of the thousands of association-sponsored medical plans offered by nonprofit member associations of ASAE.

VII. ASAE POSITION

President Clinton has recognized the need for employers and individuals to join together in pooling their buying power. Association plans have been doing just that for over 55 years, and can provide a major service to our nation by being allowed to continue.

ASAE supports the basic goals of health care reform, which would provide quality, affordable, accessible health care for all Americans. ASAE further believes that association health care plans possess many years of proven experience in the delivery of benefits through purchasing coalitions. As such, association health care plans can lead the way to the reform goals of providing the efficient delivery of quality health care to more citizens.

Chairman STARK. Let me see, Mr. Kreidler, if we can deal with your problem here, which is somewhat different from other members of the panel, and see if I perhaps don't have this—if in fact Dr. McDermott were successful and there were a single-payer system in the country, you, the association's role in this would be gone, as would everybody else's.

If, in fact, there is a guaranteed open enrollment in every insurance plan and if, as the President suggests, there were premium controls, so you really couldn't offer anything to your members that they couldn't just walk to the corner alliance and buy, you also would be out of business.

Now, from the standpoint of the various associations, that is troublesome on several counts. One, many associations use it, and properly so as a recruiting—to get people to join up.

My daughter runs a socialworker's operation out in the West and one of the things they offer their members is health insurance. It is an incentive to join, fair game. The AARP makes money on it. I have no quarrel with that. They split the take with Prudential, a big plan.

You have somewhat the same worries that the insurance agents have, that suddenly if there is this monolithic Federal plan, you all won't have anything to do with it. I guess all I can say to you is, I don't think that is very likely very quickly. Maybe over a period of years. But I rather suspect that if nothing else, while I happen to support Dr. McDermott's single-payer plan, we are a couple of votes shy right now of overriding—well, we are working on it.

But if in fact we must provide a somewhat less generous guaranteed plan, there will basically be a role for supplemental as there is now for Medicare, is my prediction, and that will be a perfectly and logically useful place for the associations to in fact provide a service to their members, because we probably will not be able to raise the money, is my guess, to provide as generous coverage as many of your members have and want.

And so all I can say to you is that while it would be my dream to put you out of the insurance business, and you probably would share that as a social goal to say, Look, we have all got the ultimate insurance and we don't need to go to the Federal Government in my case or the materials dealers have to go to their associations in their case, but don't count on it.

So all I am going to suggest to you is I suspect there will be some role still where the associations will be able to provide a useful service to their members although it may not be as extensive as it is now.

Having said that, until we know the details of the plan it will be hard. But your interests are also supported by the insurance agents who, in a sense, want to participate and they feel, perhaps in many cases rightly so, that they provide a service. They don't want to see themselves knocked out of the ball game, and they in many States are a very potent political force and probably won't be.

I guess I can say to you, you are on the sunny side of better than 50-50 of staying very much involved, although there will be a change. If I could tell you what I thought the change was, I would. Unless Mr. McDermott and I get four votes this afternoon, then you are all out of business. Then we really will have done the right thing.

I hope that makes your trip here worthwhile, a little bit of assurance.

Dr. McDermott.

Mr. McDermott. Thank you, Mr. Chairman.

It has always been a puzzle to me as a practicing physician, but also from a broader public policy perspective, what have been the impediments to the private sector? We hear the private sector is going to fix everything in the President's plan. What have been the impediments to the private sector coming up with a database and standard forms and all the things that people use to argue that we don't want a government plan, we don't want the government intervening. The private sector for 45 years have been out there flopping around.

I practiced medicine in a small psychiatric office where we had to deal with 14 different insurance companies in Seattle. Every form was different.

You are data experts. Why hasn't it happened before they saw the club coming from us?

Mr. Houtz. I think in certain sectors it has been happening. There are several companies out there that for several years have been sending electronic claims, electronic encounters, doing some work on eligibility to various insurance companies.

The insurance companies for many years have been a bottleneck to being able to transmit electronic data back and forth to them. In today's environment there are probably less than 25 insurance companies in the United States that have the capability to provide open enrollment systems so a provider's office can call in and find out in an electronic mode which patients are eligible. That part of the industry is also starting to take off, and it will take 4 or 5 years.

Mr. McDermott. You are saying out of 1,500 insurance companies in this country, only 25 are capable of doing that?

Mr. Houtz. Twenty-five or thirty today. There is a push to begin to provide eligibility services for physicians. Although we have had a standard form for physician claims, each insurance company had different requirements of how they wanted to print data on that format; and until just recently, each insurance company had a different electronic format—an electronic claim form, procedure code and a diagnosis code, in addition to those two data elements that are 200 to 300 data elements that can go into an electronic claim, and each insurance company had different requirements.

Our company today prepares over 400 electronic formats. It has been made much easier by the national standard format because there is some consistency of information, and the rapidity with which you can bring up insurance companies has vastly improved.

When you say to the private sector, why haven't you done this, I am in the private sector and we have been trying as hard as we can. We work today with every insurance company that will accept a national standard format. We do it for them without charge.

I think insurance companies have been a tremendous bottleneck until recently.

Mr. McDERMOTT. What was the professional reason for them maintaining themselves as a bottleneck? It must have been to their advantage.

Ms. HERR. Part of the reason has been that a lot of the systems early on became homegrown systems. A lot of hospitals put together their own electronic format so they could do things through electronic transmissions. As they started investing a lot of money in these systems, it became very difficult to find money to change to another type.

Another problem, I still walk into hospitals in this country that don't have a PC to do payroll. The technology is not consistent. When you start looking at the high end of what is achievable you forget there are a lot of low-end folks who will at least need the investment funds for the hardware capability, much less the software needs. That is one of the reasons we have said the voluntary way of doing this will not work.

We support mandated standards for all of this stuff. It will not go forward without mandated standards.

Mr. HOUTZ. Our association is committed and the reason the Association was formed was a commitment to EDI and electronic data interchange. I feel that our association and others we work with, with or without government mandates, I think, will provide the leadership. And we are taking actions to make people adhere and be consistent with the formats, but it is going to take us 6 to 8 years to do that with government help. I don't know if you can get the thing passed within that time.

If you could help us with the mandates of standards, we could cut that time in half.

Mr. PETERSON. Without taking any kind of policy position, because I am a technical person, not a politician here, but I wanted to explain that with the technology that is available to us, if the impediment is one of 400 different forms or something, this is something that we have dealt with—again, with the school district administration that we have had to do. Every one of these optical memory cards could literally carry its own format, whether the filing—claim filing is to be done electronically, whether it is to be printed on a paper form, whatever, because essentially you are dealing with the same data elements. You are only talking about where you are placing them on a format.

This is almost—it takes time, but for technology purposes it is a no-brainer.

Mr. McDERMOTT. Do you accept the time line Mr. Houtz has suggested of 4 to 8 years to get the system up and running nationally? Is that too long? Could it be done before that?

Mr. PETERSON. Absolutely. From my standpoint, it is one of how quickly can the technology be moved into place, because setting up to be able to run this technology is not that long a period of time.

Mr. McDERMOTT. These are the ones that are puzzling to me because the more we try to get data, the more difficulties we face. Trying to get it manipulated in the Congressional Budget Office and in Joint Tax was absolutely the biggest bottleneck for us. The reason we haven't had figures out is because we had to wait 6 or 7 months while the CBO tried to drag together from all over the place all the bits and pieces.

It seems to me there are two types of information that we need to make sense out of. One is financial data and the other is medical data. I don't know where we are on the two systems. Are we further ahead in gathering information about financial data than we are with medical data? Is that a fair assessment?

Ms. HERR. Yes. The financial transactions have been ready to go for years. Part of the problem with the clinical data is, as we understand it, that there are still not uniform definitions of what some of the things mean. The financial transactions have been ready for years.

Mr. MCDERMOTT. Related to undefined medical events, doesn't that put a problem into your financial data if you don't have what is the dealing with an ulcer?

Ms. HERR. No. Once you know whether an encounter happened or not, the transaction can happen regardless. There is the front end of the process where you ask, are we going to charge this price or are we going to charge that price. Once you have that started, you can get the encounter paid for and the money in the bank without having to have a lot of hoopla about it.

Actually, if you don't do it that electronic way, part of our frustration is you have a lot of billing errors. Hospital errors are notorious for these errors and that happens because you have to re-key-stroke a lot of the data. If you could get standardized electronic data to do a lot of the transactions, it could be out very quickly.

Mr. MCDERMOTT. You are suggesting that that be decided by us and put out there for everybody?

Ms. HERR. Yes, only because we have been struggling for 25 years trying to do it on a voluntary basis. The government currently uses standard forms. No one uses them the same way. You can't submit things electronically if you have to staple an attachment to a claim. That is why you have to have the process mandated from the national level.

Mr. MCDERMOTT. I once did a study in medical school on psychiatric patients and looked at Scandinavian literature. The Danes can find you two left-handed plumbers living in Copenhagen if you want a matched pair.

One of our problems is how to get this done in a timely fashion. Do you all agree that we need to mandate standards from the national level?

Mr. PETERSON. If you are referring to standards as being the definitions of what we are talking about, yes, we need—anything you do with the technology does require some uniformity, so that everybody is calling a right hand a right hand instead of a right hand here, and somewhere else it is called something else.

So you do need the standard definitions. Otherwise, you can't build a database.

Mr. HOUTZ. For example, what the standard does is tell everybody we want the same width railroad track transmitting data. If you had a situation in the States now where every State could define the width of the railroad track that we had, the transportation system of America would be nonexistent.

That is the situation we have today in health care. We have nonstandard data being transmitted back and forth. We are asking for help to define the standards and that is really what the American

Institute of Standards does. They have defined standards, as you know, in every industry, and we are asking for support to adopt those standards.

It is more than just claims and encounters. It is a whole set of EDI administrative transactions, and in some cases, there are some medical transactions. But the industry is far ahead on the administrative side.

On the medical side, we really haven't had the implementation of electronic data processing systems for medical records yet within this industry. We have had that in the administration, but both sets of transactions will follow along with the EDI programs that many of our companies have under way. So we are very, very much in favor of the standards.

Mr. McDERMOTT. I recently learned that under ERISA, States are not even allowed to gather data from self-insurers. Is that correct?

Ms. HERR. That is absolutely correct. The ERISA plans have been a headache for a lot of providers for a number of years, getting information and getting claims paid. There are no State regulations.

I had an example where I had to take something up through a Pennsylvania fair hearing. I was on a psychiatric provider appealing a claim. The problem was a company that went from being Blue Cross-Blue Shield to their own self-insured plan.

I was absolutely helpless in getting any of that paid. The State commissioner said that is a self-insured plan and not covered under State rules.

The plant closed down for 2 months out of every year, and I was treating all these psychiatric patients without any reimbursement at all because they were outside the system and didn't have to follow the rules.

One of the things, as we look at health care reform and administrative simplification, as one of these pieces that can move ahead quickly, is that we want to make sure that ERISA plans are put in the scope. No matter what health care reform system we go to—it doesn't matter if it is single-payer or the President's plan—we have to get those ERISA plans in there, as well.

Mr. McDERMOTT. I actually learned something from a hearing. Sometimes you wonder whether anybody learns anything. You do if you keep asking questions.

You are saying that when the President keeps the corporate alliances and allows them to keep operating as they presently are operating, they may not be mandated into the data system?

Ms. HERR. Not unless it specifically goes into the Department of Labor laws so you are looking at all the pension funds. All those self-insured funds would have to come under the same rules for health care transmission as Medicare and Medicaid and any other payer.

You may have other types of plans, DOD, Indian Affairs—if you don't have them all standardized and all under the same health care umbrella, you don't have a standardized system.

Mr. HOUTZ. Earlier today comments were about things that the States should do, like define their own plan. That may or may not be true. If it is the way the legislation is, it may have—I learned a new word this morning—unintended consequences. If you turn everything over to the States and you think we have a problem now with electronic transmission of data, wait until all the States get in there and define their requirements.

Whatever we turn over to the States, it should only be done with the understanding and the direction that we are going to add here the mandated standards. Otherwise, you will have a mess far bigger and superior to anything we have right now.

Mr. PETERSON. The way I see it there are two sets of standards here that we have to deal with. One is the standard of data transmission and the other is the standard of definition.

The standard of definition is absolutely essential to doing any kind of comparison or analysis of a database. The standard of transmission—as our technology advances becomes less and less important, because there are very basic systems now out in the market that understand all known computer languages; you don't need to have everyone based on a mainframe type of system; unfortunately, that is where the big money still is; it is in developing mainframe systems. So with those two types of standards, it is the definition that you must maintain.

The other thing is that we have to be very concerned about the amount of time and effort it is going to take for health care providers to deal with this system. Whatever they do, we can't add to their work load. What we want to do is reduce their work load and gain more detailed information.

Mr. McDERMOTT. I have never gotten into this kind of detail before, but can you tell me what the Canadians use? I know that the doctor in his office can type into his computer and send a diskette to Ottawa and get his money back every 2 weeks. Their turnaround time is amazing.

Mr. PETERSON. They don't have to be on line, which is another thing to avoid is having to deal with on-line information.

Mr. HOUTZ. We installed 14 systems in Canada in four Provinces and several in the Ontario Cancer Research Foundation. Those systems that we installed that handle fee-for-service and the government plan, the electronic mechanisms work very similar to Medicare where you send in the disk or tape. In some Provinces they had different methodologies.

If we had the same capability here—it is not an easy task to take an individual practitioner or small group practice and bring them up on electronic claims because of the amount of data elements that go into the system. Once you get it up and running, it works pretty good. It is implementation.

Mr. McDERMOTT. How long did it take to implement it in the Canadian Provinces down to the practitioner level?

Mr. HOUTZ. Our efforts there were 4 or 5 years ago. The time in Canada was no different than time in the United States.

You have to have certain data elements and protocols that you transmit under. Whether it was an all-payer system or multiple-payer system, that wasn't what created the problem.

Mr. McDERMOTT. Are there other elements besides the ERISA, the self-insured plans, that are not in the present data system or you have trouble accessing?

Ms. HERR. Beyond the ERISA plan, you have CHAMPUS and DOD claims. You may have Indian Affairs.

Mr. MCDERMOTT. Are they not using the same definitions as Medicare?

Ms. HERR. No. They require the claim forms to look different, and they can require different information. Essentially, when you are getting eligibility information and you are trying to get a claim paid, you can sit there—a typical hospital can have all these different terminals. One may be for Veterans Affairs, one for CHAMPUS, one for an Indian reservation, one may be for all the other types of providers and insurance companies. You can have a lot that are outside of what you think are traditional health care systems and payers.

Mr. MCDERMOTT. I have exhausted my ability to ask questions here. I suspect that you will hear from us again, because this kind of hearing and information is fundamental to real reform. It is dull, it is tedious, it is not very sexy, but it is what it is all based on.

In some ways, our decisionmaking process here frightens me. We talk about Murphy's Law. Well not having the data is kind of scary when we are guessing what 250 million Americans are going to be getting out of this process. When we see this fractured data system from which we have little ability to predict, from looking at the past, what the future might be, it is scary.

I appreciate your willingness to come and spend your time before the committee. We will talk to you all again. Thank you very much.

The committee is adjourned.

[Whereupon, at 1:50 p.m., the hearing adjourned to reconvene on Friday, February 4, 1994 at 1:30 p.m.]

PRESIDENT'S HEALTH CARE REFORM PROPOSALS: IMPACT ON PROVIDERS AND CONSUMERS

FRIDAY, FEBRUARY 4, 1994

House of Representatives,
Committee on Ways and Means,
Subcommittee on Health,
Washington, D.C.

The subcommittee met, pursuant to call, at 1:30 p.m., in room 1100, Longworth House Office Building, Hon. Fortney Pete Stark (chairman of the subcommittee) presiding.

Chairman STARK. Good morning. Today the Subcommittee on Health continues the hearing it began last Tuesday with testimony of public witnesses.

The subcommittee received more than 200 requests to testify. We wanted to accommodate as many of these requests as possible. Unfortunately, due to time constraints, we were not able to accommodate everyone who wished to testify. I encourage those individuals who have not had this delightful opportunity to submit written testimony for the printed record, and without objection, it will be included in the record and the printed report of this committee.

As we have already learned, there are many diverse views on the President's plan. I hope this hearing will provide an opportunity for individuals and organizations to comment on various aspects of the plan and, indeed, recommend alternative plans to the subcommittee, should they choose.

Due to the number of witnesses testifying today, I intend to keep the hearing moving in order to allow members to explore those issues about which we have questions or concerns.

Before proceeding, I would like to recognize the ranking member, Mr. Thomas.

Mr. THOMAS. I am tempted to say, let's get on with the drawing and quartering. We had plenty of opening statements in full committee yesterday afternoon. Anybody who wants an opening statement can refer to the testimony of yesterday's full committee.

Thank you.

Chairman STARK. Our first panel will begin with testimony from Dr. William Dugan, the president of the Indiana Community Cancer Care Center; Dr. William Franklin Owen, assistant professor of medicine, on behalf of the Harvard Medical School; Kenneth Robbins, president of the Illinois Hospital Association; Dr. Howard Champion, director of trauma policy and research, The Washington Hospital Center on behalf of the Coalition for American Trauma

Care; and Ken Robinson, senior vice president of East Alabama Medical Center on behalf of the Rural Referral Center Coalition.

Before the panel begins, I recognize my distinguished colleague from Indiana, Mr. Jacobs.

Mr. JACOBS. Thank you, Mr. Chairman. I appreciate the opportunity to reminisce on my old haunts of many years ago and to welcome Dr. Dugan, my constituent, one of the outstanding oncologists in the world.

If you are an outstanding oncologist in the United States, you are outstanding in the world, so we might as well include the universe and the galaxy.

Dr. Dugan is a doctor, he is the son of a doctor, nephew of a doctor, the father of doctors and eventually, if not already, of course, will be the grandfather of doctors.

He comes here on a refreshing mission in terms of our country's hopes. He is going to tell you how to take measures to cause him to make less money. That, in my opinion, is public spirit and it might even fit the old inaugural injunction to "ask not."

Chairman STARK. My colleague has been doing the same thing in Congress for many years, telling me and my colleagues how to make less money. I hope you will be more popular in your profession with that topic than he is with his colleagues and his topic.

Mr. JACOBS. With that, I want to conclude that I am not Mr. Levin or Mr. Cardin.

Chairman STARK. Having said that, I would ask the panel, as all witnesses today, to recognize that their printed statement will appear in the record in their entirety, and you could summarize or expand on it.

Dr. Dugan, please start.

STATEMENT OF WILLIAM M. DUGAN, JR., M.D., PRESIDENT AND FOUNDER, INDIANA COMMUNITY CANCER CARE, INC., INDIANAPOLIS, IND.

Dr. DUGAN. Mr. Chairman, I am Dr. William Dugan. I have been in the private practice of hematology and oncology for 24 years in Indianapolis.

It is our strong belief that the real crisis in the U.S. health care system is the vanishing primary care doctor and that if we do not fix this problem first, we cannot possibly solve access-to-care issues, improve outcomes or decrease costs.

The problem with spending $900 billion a year is that the measurable outcomes do not justify the expenditure. How could this be when our technology and programmatic sophistication is the envy of the world? The cause is that the U.S. health care system is dominated, both in numbers and influence, by medical specialists; 75 percent of the doctors in the United States are specialists. The rest of the industrialized world has half that number.

Why is this important? The doctor's pen writes the orders that directly and indirectly spend virtually all the health care dollar. The consequence of specialty domination is that we have thousand dollar solutions for hundred dollar problems.

Why did this happen? This is not rocket science. specialists earn 5 to 10 times more than primary care doctors. Society has glorified the specialist. All this has caused primary medicine to slip down the ladder of medical prestige.

How can we fix this problem? We need to make 50 percent of the doctors or more of the practicing doctors in this country primary care doctors. No amount of good intention, government or consumer planning, Federal or third-party regulation can have a chance with the scenario of the vanishing primary care doctor.

We need to do three things. We need to create appropriate incentives to make primary care medicine the most important and attractive discipline.

There are ways to do this. We need to introduce incentives to ensure appropriate geographic distribution, and then we need to support the practicing primary physician once he is in place. We need to take the ivory tower to the trenches.

One way to do this is to implement an outreach model. This model refers to affiliations between medical specialists and hospitals that do not have access to specialty consultation.

Since 1983, Indiana Community Cancer Care has operated a data-driven, outcome-oriented cancer management program that is based on fee-for-service and continuous postgraduate medical education. This system operates in over 20 rural and underserved Indiana communities. We now have 9 years of outcome data.

In this system in 1994, 70 percent of all breast cancer was diagnosed at either the noninvasive or local stage. Nearly 80 percent of these people will be alive in 10 years. These results were achieved in Wabash, Tipton, Greencastle and other Indiana communities at an estimated 50 percent reduction in total, overall costs and with a greater than 50 percent increase in productivity with the participating oncologist.

In conclusion, Mr. Chairman, we must have more primary care doctors to achieve implementation of any health care reform plan. Once we have primary doctors in place, we must have innovative programs and systems such as the outreach model that will support local care.

Finally, it is our opinion that more hundred dollar solutions to hundred dollar problems will provide an adequate amount of money to allow all Americans to have quality health care and also provide enough money to continue leadership and research, technology and programmatic sophistication.

Mr. Chairman, thank you very much for the opportunity to present these views.

Chairman STARK. Thank you, Doctor.

[The prepared statement and attachments follow:]

STATEMENT OF WILLIAM M. DUGAN, JR., M.D.
INDIANA COMMUNITY CANCER CARE, INC.

THE REAL CRISIS IN THE U.S. HEALTH CARE SYSTEM:
THE VANISHING PRIMARY CARE DOCTOR OR
"$1000 Solutions for $100 Problems"

AN ALGORITHM

INTRODUCTION

Mr. Chairman and Committee Members - My name is William M. Dugan, Jr., M.D.
I am:
- a private practicing Hematologist/Oncologist from Indianapolis, Indiana
- a part of four generations of Indiana University Medical School trained physicians who have all practiced in Indiana (or are still in training)
- representing my patients, my associates and my family
- giving both my perception of the health care problem as well as my insights to a part of the solution

My presentation will not uncover an unrecognized problem; however it will provide an interpretation and emphasis not generally appreciated. It is our strong belief that the REAL CRISIS IN THE U.S. HEALTH CARE SYSTEM IS THE VANISHING PRIMARY CARE DOCTOR and that if we do not fix this problem first, we cannot solve access to care issues, improve outcomes, or decrease costs!

THE PROBLEM:
- The United States spends $900 billion/year (14% of GNP) on health care - as much as 25-100% more than other industrialized nations spend, e.g., Sweden, Canada, Japan, and Great Britain.
- Measurable outcomes do not justify this expenditure. For example:
  - Over 30 million Americans lack insurance coverage/access to health care.
  - Compared to many industrialized nations, the United States experiences:
    (1) higher infant mortality
    (2) lower percentage of fully immunized children
    (3) shorter average life expectancy

THE PARADOX:
- U.S. medical technology is the envy of the world.
- The programmatic sophistication found in the U.S. health care system is unequalled.

THE CAUSE:
- The U.S. Health Care System is dominated, both in numbers and influence, by medical specialists and sub-specialists.
  - U.S. Health Care System is composed of 75% specialty physicians and 25 primary care physicians. (In 1992 only 15% of graduating medical students chose primary care.)*
  - Physician distribution for most industrialized nations is 65% primary care physicians and 35% specialty physicians.

* defined as family practice, internal medicine and pediatrics

THE CONSEQUENCES OF SPECIALTY DOMINATION:

- $1000 dollar solutions for $100 dollar problems. (Over-utilization and over-reliance on high-tech, high cost diagnostic and therapeutic procedures, particularly in the last months of life.)

- Fragmentation of services and lack of continuity of care.

- Unnecessary duplication of services.

- Lack of expertise in preventive, psychosomatic and hospice medicine and care of the whole person.

- Fewer and fewer people have a primary care physician who has familiarity with the patient, his or her support system, and values.

WHY DID THIS HAPPEN?

- INCOME. In the U.S., specialists earn five to ten times more than primary care physicians. Compare these figures to other industrialized nations where specialists earn about twice as much as primary care physicians. (The following points are relevant, but income is the dominant issue.)

- MEDICAL SCHOOLS' prestige, income, grant awards, and entire infrastructure is specialty driven.

- SECONDARY AND TERTIARY HOSPITALS, with the widespread development and utilization of sophisticated technology, are increasingly dependent upon specialists.

- MEDICAL INDUSTRIES are specialty driven. Product development is carried out by specialists and focuses on specialty care needs.

- SOCIETY has glorified the specialist. Primary care medicine has slipped down the ladder of medical prestige.[1]

- PRIMARY CARE ROLE MODELS are a vanishing breed.

- SURVEYS indicate that primary care physicians are increasingly unhappy with their practices.[2]

- POST GRADUATE MEDICAL EDUCATION in the trenches is generally poor and contributes to a further widening of the techno-gap.

- Specialists dominate MEDICAL LEADERSHIP positions at virtually all levels.

- Specialists dominate REIMBURSEMENT COMMITTEES.

- SPECIALTY MEDICINE, with its limited focus, is more easily mastered than primary care medicine.

- WORKLOAD. Primary care physicians typically work more hours/week than specialists.

HOW CAN WE FIX THE PROBLEM:

A. Increase the number of primary care physicians. No amount of good intention, government or consumer planning, federal or third party regulation can have a chance with the scenario of the vanishing primary care doctor.

- Our country needs at least 50% of all doctors practicing primary care medicine.[3]

- Just as we need patrolmen on the front line of crime fighting and general medical officers in the military conflict, we need primary care doctors as the triage agents for health care.

- We need to:
  1. find mechanisms to make primary care medicine the most important and attractive discipline
  2. require two years of general medicine training before any specialty training can occur
  3. develop a plan to reduce the indebtness of graduating physicians who choose primary care medicine.[4]

---

[1] Robinson, Robert D., MD. "ReVersing the decline and fall of the general internist." Journal of Indiana Medicine, March/April 1993, Volume 86(2), p. 128.

[2] Lewis, C.E. et al. "How satisfactory is the practice of Internal Medicine? A National SurVey," Annals of Internal Medicine, 1991, Volume 114: 1-5.

[3] LeVinsky, Norman G. "Recruiting for Primary Care," New England Journal of Medicine, March 4, 1993, Vol 328 p 656.

[4] Petersdorf, Robert G,. MD. "Financing Medical Education: A UniVersal "Berry Plan" for Medical Students", New England Journal of Medicine, March/April 1993, Vol.328(9):651-654.

4. accomplish a truly fair implementation of the Harvard Resource-Based Relative Value Scale -not the current version that has been emasculated by the special interest of some subspecialty groups.
5. introduce incentives to insure appropriate geographic distribution of physicians.

B. **Take the ivory tower to the trenches.** In medically underserved and rural areas, we can:

- Implement proven Outreach Models[5] to insure broader access to state of the art medical care for patients
- Utilize proven outreach models to insure continuing clinical education and support for the primary physician

The Outreach Model refers to affiliations between medical specialists and hospitals that do not have access to specialty consultation. The elements of the Outreach Model include:

- Medical specialists travel to the community on a regularly scheduled basis to hold clinic.
- Point of need continuing medical education that gives the primary care physician the opportunity to interact with specialist.
- Registered nurses from the local community are identified to receive comprehensive

  and on-going training necessary to support specialty medicine. These individuals become a vital link in patient care and provided the continuity that avoids the duplication of services. Lack of this critical element is why most outreach programs fail.
- A data system to measure change.

Indiana Community Cancer Care:
Since 1983, we have operated a data driven outcome oriented cancer management program that is based on fee for service and continuous post-graduate medical education. This system operates in over 20 rural Indiana communities. Nine years of data documents that:

1. Breast cancer patients in the network are detected and treated as reliable as in major cancer treatment centers in this country. (Appendix A,B,C,D)
2. In our outreach network in 1993, 70% of all breast cancer was diagnosed at either the non-invasive or local stage. Nearly 90% of these patients will be alive in 10 years (adjusted survival)
3. These results were achieved at an estimated 50% reduction in total overall costs.
4. The program organization and infrastructure allows a small group of oncologists to increase productivity by over 50%

CONCLUSION
1. We must have more primary care physicians to achieve implementation of any health care reform plan. By having at least 50% of all physicians be in primary care, we can:

- Provide adequate numbers of primary care doctors for under-served urban and rural areas (access to care).
- Especially reduce health care costs in the final months of life.
- **Provide more $100 solutions to $100 problems** with a more sensible utilization of our technology and programmatic sophistication.
- Encourage better utilization of local resources.
- Reduce duplication of services by providing coordinated care.
- Increase the widespread utilization of prevention and screening. (Appendix E,F)
- Provide care to the whole person-physical, emotional and spiritual.

2. Once we have primary care physicians in place, we must have innovative programs and systems (e.g. Outreach Model) that will support local care.

3. Finally, it is our opinion that more $100 solutions to $100 poblems will provide an adequate amount of money to allow all Americans to have quality health care and also provide enough money to continue leadership in research, technology, and programmatic sophistication.

---

[5] Dugan, William M., Jr., M.D. et al. "Post Graduate Medical Education: A Cancer Management Model," 1994, to be published

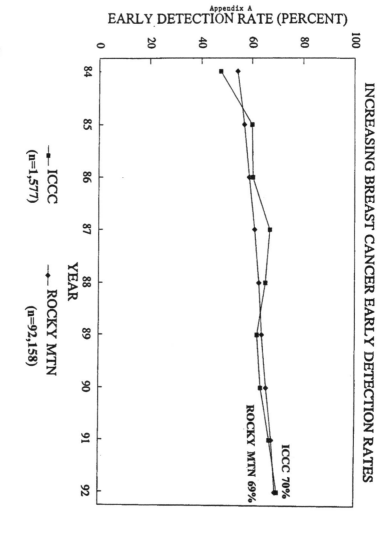

Appendix A

EARLY DETECTION RATE (PERCENT)

INCREASING BREAST CANCER EARLY DETECTION RATES

■ ICCC
(n=1,577)

◆ ROCKY MTN
(n=92,158)

YEAR

ROCKY MTN 69%

ICCC 70%

Early detection defined as insitu and local stage of disease at diagnosis.
Testing for overall difference in Early Detection Rates: p=.7132, NS.

Appendix B

ICCC '84-'92 Breast Cancer*
Observed Overall Survival by Stage**
ICCC n=1,290

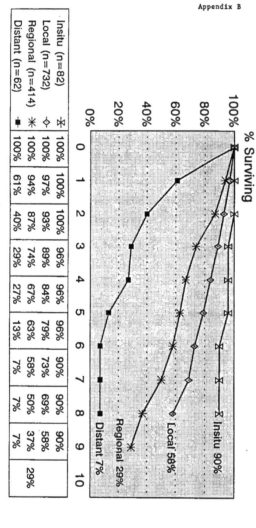

% Surviving

		0	1	2	3	4	5	6	7	8	9	10
Insitu (n=82)	⊠	100%	100%	100%	96%	96%	96%	90%	90%	90%	90%	
Local (n=732)	◇	100%	97%	93%	89%	84%	79%	73%	69%	58%		
Regional (n=414)	✳	100%	94%	87%	74%	67%	63%	58%	50%	37%		
Distant (n=62)	■	100%	61%	40%	29%	27%	13%	7%	7%	7%	29%	

Insitu 90%

Local 58%

Regional 29%

Distant 7%

Years Surviving by Stage of Disease at Diagnosis

*ICCC, Indiana Community Cancer Care Consortium
**Excluded from study are patents with multiple primaries & unknown stage at diagnosis.

Appendix C

RMCDS '84-'92 Breast Cancer*
Observed Overall Survival by Stage**
RMCDS n=70,572

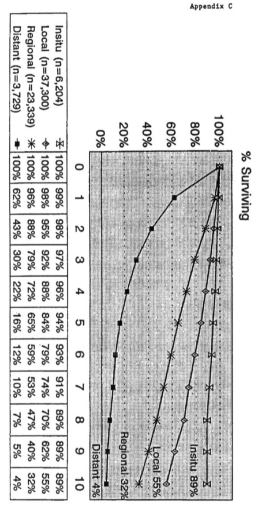

Years Surviving by Stage of Disease at Diagnosis

	0	1	2	3	4	5	6	7	8	9	10
Insitu (n=6,204)	100%	99%	98%	97%	96%	94%	93%	91%	89%	89%	89%
Local (n=37,300)	100%	98%	95%	92%	88%	84%	79%	74%	70%	62%	55%
Regional (n=23,339)	100%	96%	88%	79%	72%	65%	59%	53%	47%	40%	32%
Distant (n=3,729)	100%	62%	43%	30%	22%	16%	12%	10%	7%	5%	4%

*RMCDS, Rocky Mountain Cancer Data System
**Excluded from study are patients with multiple primaries & unknown stage of disease at diagnosis.

Appendix D

1984-1992 Breast Cancer
Observed Overall Survival Rates
All Stages

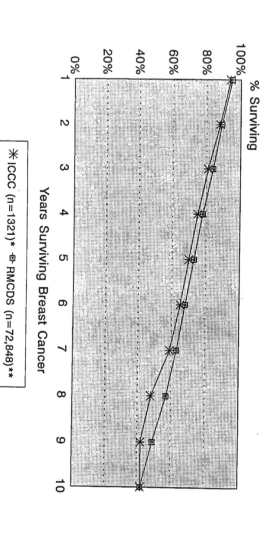

% Surviving

Years Surviving Breast Cancer

✳ ICCC (n=1321)* ⊞ RMCDS (n=72,848)**

*ICCC, Indiana Comunity Cancer Care Consortium
**RMCDS, Rocky Mountain Cancer Data System
Excluded from study are patients with multiple primaries.

301

1990 Census
ICCC Hospital County Population
vs.
Number of Mammograms Completed

Hospital	City	City Population All Persons	County Population Ages 35-84	County Population All Persons	Total Mammograms Completed & Years
Bedford Medical Center	Bedford	13,817	20,887	42,836	11,805 (87-93)
Clinton County Hospital	Frankfort	5,040	14,403	30,974	5,114 (87-93)
Columbus Regional Hospital	Columbus	31,802	30,196	63,657	58,871 (84-93)
Decatur County Hospital	Greensburg	8,644	10,529	23,645	7,863 (87-93)
Howard Community Hospital	Kokomo	44,962	38,379	80,827	21,026 (87-93)
King's Daughters' Hospital	Madison	12,006	13,906	29,797	8,172 (88-93)
Memorial Hospital & Health Care Center	Jasper	10,030	15,826	36,616	10,233 (87-93)
Memorial Hospital	Seymour	15,576	23,474	37,730	11,613 (87-93)
Mercy Hospital	Elwood	9,494	10,089*	20,864*	4,129 (89-93)
Putnam County Hospital	Greencastle	8,984	13,323	30,315	4,962 (88-93)
Tipton County Hospital	Tipton	4,751	7,839	16,119	5,362 (87-93)
Wabash County Hospital	Wabash	12,127	16,144	35,069	13,055 (84-93)
White County Hospital	Monticello	5,237	11,319	23,265	3,519 (89-93)
TOTAL:	13	182,470	226,314	471,714	165,724

*Estimated ⋆ Elwood portion of Madison County with a populatiuon of 130,669, which includes the city of Anderson with a population of 59,459.

M. Burch, CTR

1/31/94

Appendix F

Number of Mammograms Completed per Year
ICCC Consortium Hospital

Hospital	1984	1985	1986	1987	1988	1989	1990	1991	1992	1993	TOTAL
Bedford				1438	1563	1645	1697	1734	1809	1919	11,805
Clinton				120	180	753	741	1076	1114*	1130*	5,114
Columbus	2111	2848	4520	5302	6372	6340	7033	7698*	8560*	8087*	58,871
Decatur				594	733	1055	1450	1421*	1346*	1264*	7,863
Howard				1325	2261	3081	3583*	3929*	3437*	3410*	21,026
King's Daughters'					1124	1193	1374	1585	1513	1383	8,172
Memorial Jasper				651	867	1147	1251	1945	2138*	2234*	10,233
Memorial Seymour				1023	1408	1527	1688	1821	2085	2061	11,613
Mercy						651	824	829	917	908	4,129
Putnam					775	820	812	894	776*	885*	4,962
Tipton				471	593	698	689	983	961	967	5,362
Wabash	150	267	904	1302	1530	1599	1625	2035	1926*	1717*	13,055
White						497	648	1059	653	662	3,519
TOTAL:	2,261	3,115	5,424	12,226	17,406	21,006	23,415	27,009	27,235	26,627	165,724

* = Year American College of Radiology Accredited

M Burch, CTR

1/31/94

303

Chairman STARK. Dr. Owen.

STATEMENT OF WILLIAM FRANKLIN OWEN, JR., M.D., ASSISTANT PROFESSOR OF MEDICINE, HARVARD MEDICAL SCHOOL

Dr. OWEN. Thank you. Good morning. I am Bill Owen. I am, as my colleague described it, an ivory tower academic physician who does practice in the trenches. End-stage renal disease is disproportionately a malady of racial minorities, especially of African-Americans. Despite comprising only 12 percent of the American population, in excess of 35 percent of the population with end-stage renal disease are African-Americans, the remaining 5 percent in that group being Latinos and Native Americans.

The incidence of end-stage renal disease among African-Americans is the highest of any racial group, being approximately four-fold greater than for whites. Further, renal disease has culminated in end-stage renal stage occurring at significant younger ages in minority Americans.

Despite the prevalence in the demographics of the incidence of end-stage renal disease among minorities, there is apparent unequal access to kidneys for transplantation. In 1989, for example, only 20 percent of the transplant population was African-American, with waiting times for organs that were twice that of white Americans. As these trends have continued, we have seen greater numbers of minorities on dialysis for longer periods of time than their white compatriots, and morbidity and mortality are increasingly linked to the quality of care that is provided by the nephrologists and by the dialysis facility providers.

It is in this spirit that I urge the subcommittee to avoid a short-sighted global financial restructuring of the end-stage renal disease program that may effect short-term savings, but will adversely influence the delivery of adequate and appropriate care for this vulnerable population.

In 1983 and again in 1986, substantial reductions were made in the level of reimbursement to dialysis facility providers. In parallel with these reductions, we saw a progressive deterioration in patient survival, ancillary services, increased patient morbidity and diminished patient morale. Annual patient mortality prior to 1984 was consistently less than 20 percent and increased to 24 percent by 1987, a value which is greater than twofold in excess of other industrialized nations with end-stage renal disease programs.

We also must interpret these findings as evidence that the quality of care under the end-stage renal disease program has been compromised by cost-containment efforts in the setting of rampant inflation in the medical sector. These cost-containment efforts include the use of less skilled and fewer dialysis care staff, fewer socialworkers and dieticians with abbreviated hours onsite, greatly shortened dialysis time and the reuse of single-use designated equipment.

However, for minority patients, the dialysis facility has a far greater role than simply to provide equipment and staff for the performance of dialysis. Many of our patients are financially, educationally and socially disadvantaged, and therefore, the nutritionists and socialworkers are critical allies in the provision of comprehensive support and care. The declining numbers of dialysis support personnel are finding themselves performing more crisis intervention and therefore less ongoing support.

Dialysis facilities that are financially unsound cannot expend funds on new equipment and medications that improve the quality of life and, by extrapolation, patient rehabilitation. In that minority patients are the most vulnerable of the end-stage renal disease population, adverse trends in this group heralds danger for the entire American nephrologic population. To execute alterations in the end-stage renal disease program that will effect enhanced cost-containment while augmenting patient survival, minimizing morbidity and intensifying their rehabilitation, legislation should be enacted. First of all, to provide a fair inflation-adjusted reimbursement schedule for the nephrologist and the dialysis facility operators; that, second, affords adequate reimbursement to the patient and to the facility for mandatory nephrologic-directed medications; and third, assures equal access to all treatment modalities, especially renal transplantation.

Initial realization of these goals can be achieved acutely by, first of all, extending the end-stage renal disease secondary payer period to 24 months or longer to appropriately increase cost-sharing with the patients' private insurers; second, defining a precise bundle of patient care services that are to be provided by the nephrologist and incorporating a global, all-inclusive capitation payment schedule; and third, folding the funds for erythropoietin into the composite reimbursement to the dialysis facility providers.

These proposed modifications in the structure of the end-stage renal disease program will immediately enhance the quality of life for its participants, especially those of color. The disproportionate number of minorities who are captive to dialysis look to you as a voice of advocacy where previously we have had none. I hope that you will advocate a plan of fairness, a plan of equity, as you review these critical issues.

Thank you.

Chairman STARK. Thank you, Doctor.

[The prepared statement follows:]

STATEMENT OF WILLIAM F. OWEN, JR., M.D.
ASSISTANT PROFESSOR OF MEDICINE
HARVARD MEDICAL SCHOOL

Introduction

As this Subcommittee considers the reform of our troubled and often inequitable health care system, I strongly urge that Medicare's unique, disease-targeted End Stage Renal Disease (ESRD) Program be maintained in its current form, but be strengthened by a financial restructuring The Program's total annual cost of $6 6 billion (1991) poses an obvious singular target for cost savings However, I have grave concerns for the influence of further rate reductions on the morbidity, rehabilitation potential, and mortality of dialysis patients, especially for the very large number of uniquely vulnerable minority patients It is in this spirit that I urge this Subcommittee to recognize that for 20 years, this public entitlement has been a successful, albeit imperfect archetype of impartial health care.

As I assess the End Stage Renal Disease Program from my perspectives as an African-American academic nephrologist, I find that it has been exemplary of the aims for which it was championed at its inception in 1972 by Representative Wilbur D Mills (D-Ark) and Senator Vance Hartke (D-Ind) Because of a scarcity in treatment resources and a general lack of insurance coverage for this treatment modality before 1973, remarkable inequity in access to this modality was evident, the dialysis population was disproportionately composed of young, white males that were highly educated, married, and wealthy However, as a direct outcome of the End Stage Renal Disease Program, life-saving nephrologic care is now available to virtually every American However, in my more critical roles as both the Medical Director and as an active, practicing nephrologist in two large and demographically contrasting outpatient dialysis facilities--one that is suburban and serves predominantly an upper middle class, educated white population, and the other a unique inner city facility that serves a financially disadvantaged minority population--I am acutely aware of the expanding deficiencies within this Program Although neither patient population can tolerate a "cost savings" global financial restructuring of the End Stage Renal Disease Program, my minority patients are particularly susceptible to legislative actions that adversely influence the delivery of adequate and appropriate care

To execute alterations in the End Stage Renal Disease Program that will effect enhanced cost containment, while augmenting patient survival, minimizing patient morbidity, and intensifying their rehabilitation potential, legislation should be enacted that (1) provides a fair inflation-adjusted reimbursement schedule for the nephrologists and the facility operators, (2) affords adequate reimbursements to the patients and the facility for mandatory nephrologic-directed medications, and (3) assures equal access to all treatment modalities, especially renal transplantation Initial realization of these goals can be achieved acutely by (1) extending the End Stage Renal Disease Secondary Payer Period to 24 months or longer, to appropriately increase cost sharing by the patients' private insurers, (2) defining the bundle of patient care services that are to be provided by the nephrologists and incorporating a global (all-inclusive) monthly capitation payment schedule for these services, and (3) folding the funds for erythropoietin into the composite reimbursement to the dialysis facility operators These proposed modifications in the structure of the End Stage Renal Disease Program will immediately enhance the quality of life for all its participants, especially for those of color

America's ESRD Program as a Paradigm for Health Care Reform

The End Stage Renal Disease Program has been remarkably successful in several areas that are laudable goals for any model health care program The End Stage Renal Disease Program is (1) virtually universal and relatively comprehensive, (2) functions coherently for the patients, (3) quality of patient care is closely monitored and continuous improvements implemented, (4) it is structured to contain costs, and (5) the Program is paid for fairly Approximately 93% of all patients with end stage renal disease is eligible for Medicare coverage of their nephrologic care The remaining few patients who are not insured can obtain additional funding for nephrologic care through the Veterans Administration, the Indian Health Service, and state Medicaid programs An attestation to the success of the universal and comprehensive design and penetration of the End Stage Renal Disease Program is the lack of correlation between personal income and mortality secondary to renal failure Unlike most other "metaphor(s) for modern technological medicine," access to dialytic care in the United States is not compromised by poverty However, an unfortunate reality of the heavy use of medical care by end stage renal disease patients is that their average annual cost sharing amount with Medicare is approximately $4,000 -- a substantial burden for the poor of any race or ethnic group Although 80% of the costs of either dialysis or transplantation are covered, Medicare does not provide reimbursement for either the expense of transportation to and from dialysis, or the costs of the mandatory medications that supplement the dialysis treatments The latter is a particularly critical issue for patients who undergo renal transplantation, since reimbursement for immunosuppressive medications ceases after the first 18 months of transplantation For example, cyclosporine A, a critical and obligatory long term medication for renal transplant recipients is >$10,000 annually

Despite this major financial deficiency, most patients feel that in comparison to private insurance, the End Stage Renal Disease Program is a coherent system Enrollment is simple and straightforward After demonstration of medical necessity and eligibility, the provider and the patient submit a single form to the Health Care Financing Administration, and the bundle of benefits is implemented by Medicare after 18 months if the patient has been previously ineligible These patient benefits are clearly outlined to the patient and the health care provider, and their successful implementation is externally monitored Lastly, the level of health care delivery to the end-stage renal disease patient is basic and uniform In the words of the implementing law, every patient should receive a "regular course of dialysis or kidney transplantation to maintain life "

This simple stated objective of the End Stage Renal Program has been costly to achieve, but American society resists limiting expenditures that compromise access to therapies that are medically appropriate and that are life-sustaining This tacit policy is reflected in the increment in the number of participants in the End Stage Renal Disease Program and in its costs At the inception of this Program, it was extrapolated that the number of beneficiaries would be only 90,000 instead of the actual 165,000 patients The incident treatment rates for end stage renal disease in the United States is almost 4 times greater than for similarly industrialized European countries and twice that in Canada Approximately 40% of the recipients in the United States are at least 65 years old Viewed in a short-sighted financial sense alone, this 0 08 percent of the American population accounts for 0 8% of our total health care expenditure

Yet, despite the appropriate unwillingness of the health care community and the American public to achieve cost savings by the inadequate funding of such life-sustaining technologies, unprecedented cost controls have been achieved within the End Stage Renal Disease Program The monopsonist framework of the End Stage Renal Disease Program encourages competition, but attempts to ensure and implement continuous quality patient care This objective is pursued both locally and nationally. For example, on a contractual basis with the Health Care Financing Administration, the regional End Stage Renal Disease Networks have established uniform, minimal objective standards for appropriate nephrologic health care The Medical Review Boards of these Networks routinely inspect dialysis facilities, offer corrective advice in the case of medical deficiencies, sponsor educational programs for the providers and patients, and intervene in response to patient complaints In addition, the Networks routinely publish health care data for "consumers" within the End Stage Renal Disease Program The United States Renal Data System annually provides nationally derived information on the incidence, prevalence, morbidity, and mortality of end stage renal disease to patients and health care providers. Lastly, the active, working interaction between the End Stage Renal Disease Networks, the Health Care Financing Administration, and nephrology professional organizations such as the Renal Physicians Association, American Society of Nephrology, National Kidney Foundation, American Nephrology Nurses Association, permits an unprecedented level of interaction and cooperation between the patient, the provider, and the regulators

In its unique and powerful role as the major "buyer of dialysis services," the Medicare has exhibited an unprecedented capacity to control its cost per patient The reimbursement rate to the dialysis facility operators for outpatient dialysis in 1974 was $138 per treatment, and this amount was reduced to $125 in 1989 The analysis of the End Stage Renal Disease Program performed by the Institute of Medicine found that after adjustment for inflation, the 1989 reimbursement rate was only approximately $54 in 1974 dollars From 1989 to the present, the Consumer Price Index for Medical Care has increased from 149 to 186, but reimbursement to the dialysis provider has remained unchanged in current dollars Cost containment steps initiated by the dialysis facilities in response to the declining real value of Medicare payments have included the use of less skilled or fewer dialysis care staff per patient (replacing registered nurses [RN] with lower paid licensed practical nurses [LPN] or patient care technicians), fewer social workers and dietitians (smaller "ancillary services") with fewer hours on-site, greatly shortened dialysis times, and the reuse of "single-use" designated equipment (artificial kidney and lines). Because labor costs are responsible for >70% of a dialysis facility's operating expenses, the focus of cost reductions has been disproportionately expressed in this sector. And because the ancillary service professionals are erroneously viewed as the least critical personnel component within the dialysis facility, these services are disproportionately targeted for cutbacks In short, as stated by PJ Held (The Urban Institute) et al. in their analysis of the staffing practices of dialysis facilities, "if you pay more, you get more." Effectively, the dialysis providers have survived by minimizing overhead, and by spreading the capital and other fixed costs over a larger treatment base of patients Although many of the patients enrolled in the End Stage Renal Disease Program are older than at the Program's inception, and they have an increased number of comorbid conditions such as diabetes mellitus, claims that the dialysis providers have yielded to financial incentives to treat medically inappropriate patients (individuals with advanced malignancies, acquired immunodeficiency syndrome, dementia, preterminal failure of other organs) are unsubstantiated For example, fewer than 2% of the end stage renal disease population has either advanced cancer or AIDS

Over these same time intervals, the reimbursement to the nephrologists for outpatient care of end stage renal disease patients (Monthly Capitation Payment) have likewise remained fixed at a national median of $173 per month, which is reduced by approximately 35% in 1983 dollars Remarkably, despite this decline in real dollars, more nephrologists accept Medicare's reimbursement as full payment for medical services than for any other specialty or subspecialty (76.3% of the nephrologists). The Monthly Capitation Payment accounts for approximately 40% of Medicare's outlay for physician services in the care of patients with end stage renal disease In other words, most nephrologists generate the majority of their income by the inpatient care of dialysis patients This pattern of reimbursement that is biased for hospital care may encourage less attentive outpatient care, and increased patient morbidity and hospitalizations. Vexing for the physician subscribers to the current Monthly Capitation Payment system is the non-uniform definition of the physician services to be provided, a flaw that has generated unnecessary variations in reimbursement from the Medicare carriers

The largest burden of costs for the care of patients with end stage renal disease has been borne by Medicare. Despite some appropriate cost shifting by extending the period from 12 to 18 months during which Medicare is the secondary payer, the cost of this program has increased because of an escalating number of patient subscribers Because the revenue for the dialytic care of patients is significantly greater from most health insurance plans as compared to Medicare (average of 2 to 3 fold), the dialysis facility operators have readily accepted this change in policy. To the benefit of Medicare, this modest temporal cost shifting has saved Medicare approximately $56 million dollars annually

In summary, the End Stage Renal Disease Program has provided a unique opportunity to validate that a single payer, such as the Health Care Financing Administration, can control costs on a per patient basis while attempting to guarantee quality and universality.

Costs versus Quality in the ESRD Program

Despite the increased total Medicare expenditures, the stability of the End Stage Renal Disease Program has deteriorated Many within the nephrology community feel that the Program cannot absorb further reductions in the level of payments to either the dialysis facilities or the nephrologists. Considering an invalidated assumption that the payments to the dialysis providers in the early years of the End Stage Renal Disease Program were excessive, and resulted in enhanced profits without augmented patient care, substantial reductions were made in the level of reimbursement provided to dialysis facilities in 1983 and 1986 Further, adjustments for inflation were disallowed In parallel with these reductions in payments, we have witnessed a progressive deterioration in patient survival, patient well-being, and patient morale

Annual patient mortality (deaths per average enrollment in a year), which prior to 1984 was stable at 20 1%, had increased to 24 3% by 1988, and is now the highest among developed nations Further characterizing this disturbing trend, the Urban Institute examined the annual relative risk of death for dialysis patient at free-standing facilities For patients greater than 65 years of age, the risk of death during the first year of dialysis increased by 60% from 1982 (the year before the first reduction in reimbursement) to 1985 For younger patients, these trends of increased mortality became evident when the relative risk was examined over 2 to 3 years Most physicians and investigators within the nephrology community interpret these coincident trends as evidence that the quality of care under the End Stage Renal Disease Program has been compromised by excessive attempts at cost containment in the setting of rampant inflation within the medical sector The Institute of Medicine expressed concern that "rate reductions lead to unmonitored system-wide quality reductions, the lower cost of these inferior services then constitutes the basis in the rate-setting for a cut in reimbursement," thereby establishing a "vicious cycle " Arguably, attempts to derive excessive profits from a fixed fee schedule would cause patient care to suffer, hospitalizations to increase, and mortality to escalate And although 87% of the outpatient dialysis providers in 1991 were classified as independent and for-profit (60% of all outpatient providers are for-profit), this belief is not supported by objective data Using Cox's proportional-hazards model, patients treated in for-profit and not-for-profit dialysis units have the same mortality Therefore, the financial constraints that have incited these adverse patient outcomes are not simply a consequence of the facility operators attempting to derive excessive profits using the current level of reimbursement

The precise factor(s) responsible for the worsening mortality is uncertain A major contributing feature is the widespread use of abbreviated dialysis times that do not provide an adequate treatment The common practice of dialyzing patients for less than 3 hours in the United States can result in costs saving of up to 25% per treatment However, these cost effective, short treatment times are associated with a major increase in the relative mortality risk from 1 0 to 2 18 Actual and inflation adjusted reimbursement reductions have provided a negative incentive for many facilities to reduce dialysis time to the long-term detriment of patient care Recently, we observed that despite a standard that was established 10 years ago for adequate dialysis, 55% of a large cohort of hemodialysis patients received a quantity of dialysis that was associated with a greatly excessive death risk Obviously, patients that are inadequately dialyzed are costly Such patients are chronically ill, have a diminished quality of life, little rehabilitation potential, and undergo an increased number of hospitalizations.

There is little doubt that the amount and pattern of reimbursement to the dialysis facility and the nephrologists can greatly influence the length of dialysis treatments For example, in Japan, where the physician is reimbursed a greater sum if the patient is dialyzed longer, the average dialysis times are unsurprisingly >50% longer than in the United States More importantly, the annual patient mortality for a Japanese citizen on dialysis is 65% less than for an American citizen. Adjustments for case mix between the two nations does not significantly normalize this unexpectedly large discrepancy in patient survival Similar trends exist in industrialized European nations. longer dialysis times, more generous reimbursement schedules, and lowered patient mortality (mortality in Germany and France, 10 0% and 7 3%, respectively)

Another compromising reality of providing care for patients with end stage renal disease is the erosion of critical support services within the outpatient dialysis facilities The previous nationwide shortage of nurses still persists within the dialysis community, and this may contribute to the worsening patient mortality Despite a decrease in the number of RN and LPN personnel within the dialysis unit, the National Kidney Foundation Council of Nephrology Nurses and Technicians reported that the freestanding dialysis units still cannot provide salaries that are competitive with hospital wages The Council found that in some areas of the United States. it was not unusual to require 8 months to replace a staff nurse who had left the dialysis unit to pursue more profitable work for a hospital In many dialysis facilities, one nurse is responsible for coordinating the dialysis treatment of at least 8-10 patients per session, for supervising 5-8 patient care technicians, for performing patient care clerical assignments, and for administering medications before, during, and after dialysis

Another deficiency in the capacity to provide needed support to patients with end stage renal disease is in the staffing by dietitians and social workers For many units, the capacity of the dialysis facility to pay and retain a full-time renal dietitian has been compromised, resulting in fewer patient and dietitian interactions In the management of the patient with end stage renal disease, the quality of nutrition is as critical a determinant of patient outcome as is the quality and quantity of dialysis The crucial and time-intensive tasks of dynamically monitoring nutritional intake, and of offering the needed advice for the maintenance of optimal nutrition is fulfilled by the renal dietitian The critical role of this member of the dialysis support team is validated by the observation of an inverse correlation between the frequency of patient and dietitian contacts and the number of patient hospitalizations Fewer patient and dietitian interactions result in an increased number of hospitalizations Further jeopardizing the quality of patient care is the compromise in social support Many dialysis units have been unable to pay for full-time social workers The aging, financially, and educationally disadvantaged dialysis population requires far greater social and nutritional intervention Practical issues for this vulnerable population such as arranging for transportation to and from dialysis, purchasing medications and arranging for their pick-up, acquiring low cost, nutritious foodstuffs, arranging for support at home especially after dialysis treatments, and assisting with resolution of financial crises are common examples of vital socioeconomic issues that are frequently addressed by the social worker within the dialysis facility However, the declining numbers of dialysis support personnel are finding themselves performing more crisis intervention and less ongoing support In the absence of an adequate number of staff to provide such aid, it is unsurprising that patient morale is low Although these socioeconomic problems superficially seem far afield of the simple stated mission of the End Stage Renal Disease Program, the determinants of the patient's daily quality of life are inseparable from those that define rehabilitation potential, hospitalization frequency, and ultimately mortality.

Unique Issues for Minorities with ESRD

Confounding nephrologic care in America is the rapidly changing demographic composition of the End Stage Renal Disease Program Renal failure has disproportionately become a malady of racial and ethnic minorities, particularly African-Americans, Latinos, and Native Americans Although the subsequent specifics of my discourse are derived from studies based upon African-Americans, (because of the larger and older base of data), most of the trends and issues invoked are applicable to these other American minority groups Despite comprising only 12% of the population in the United States in 1990, African-Americans made up 30% of the patients with end stage renal disease Approximately 40% of the patients with end stage renal disease were non-whites Large differences exist by race in the incidence of renal failure The rates among African-American and Native Americans are approximately four times higher than rates among white patients (adjusted incidence of 424 versus 114, respectively) Further, renal diseases that culminate in end stage renal disease occur on average at a significantly younger age in African-Americans than white Americans (57 versus 63 years, respectively) Relevant to this issue, and most striking, is the race and renal disease-specific incidence of etiologies of end stage renal disease between African-Americans and white Americans The age and sex adjusted rate of hypertensive renal disease is approximately 6 times greater in African-Americans (1,533 versus 247 per 10^6, respectively, in 1988) For diabetes mellitus, the difference in rate is approximately 4-fold (1,215 versus 341, respectively) Although minorities have been clearly identified as a high risk population for severe renal disease (occurs more often and at a younger age), several investigators have demonstrated that they are referred to the nephrologist relatively late, and at such a time that their disease manifestations are more advanced and less responsive to therapy In a report from Emory University School of Medicine, patients with the worst hypertension exhibited the greatest financial constraints to pharmacological and medical care Therefore, it is unsurprising that a statistical correlation exists between finances and the occurrence of end stage renal disease For many in America, end stage renal disease may be a preventable complication of poverty

Although minority Americans and white Americans initiate maintenance dialysis with the same panel of Medicare-derived benefits, their subsequent management typically follows divergent courses For minority Americans, a disproportionately large number of patients are treated by center-based dialysis and an excessively low fraction by peritoneal dialysis Whereas 51% and 11% of white Americans receive center based and peritoneal dialysis, respectively, 75% and 7% of African-Americans with end stage renal disease are treated by these modalities This discrepancy in the use of renal replacement therapies arises from direct or indirect physician bias in referral for types of therapy, diminished health resource availability within the minority community, and the constraints of economics and living conditions for minorities However, despite the dominant percentage of minority patients with end stage renal disease being treated by center-based hemodialysis, most minorities must travel far outside their community of residence to undergo dialysis at these centers Thus, the rehabilitation and employment potential of minority patients are selectively compromised by time lost in travel to and from dialysis, and the disadvantageous dialysis modality choice exaggerates this problem.

Even greater discrepancies exist in the utilization of the preferred therapy for renal failure, renal transplantation For the minority community, there is unequal access to kidneys for transplantation In 1989, the transplant rate for African-Americans was 8 transplants per 100 patient years, whereas for white Americans, there were 17 transplants per 100 patient years This trend exists for both younger (≤44 years old) and older African-Americans and is exaggerated among older females Detailed accurate data is unavailable for the number of minorities being placed on cadaver renal transplant list However, a preliminary investigation of this issue by the Rand Corporation suggested that regional discrepancies existed in the registration of minorities as potential renal transplant recipients that could not be explained on the basis of biologic differences Despite a policy of "equal opportunity," African-Americans have a 2-fold longer waiting time than whites for cadaver renal transplants, and these differences cannot be accounted for by discrepancies in gender, age, or ABO-typing within racial groups And after renal transplantation has occurred, the survival of the transplant is compromised. In 1990, only 14% of the African-American patients had functioning kidney transplants in comparison to 33% of the whites On the basis of a proportional-hazards analysis, the presence of private insurance coverage eliminated the influence of race as a factor in renal transplant survival The apparent racial-dependent difference in transplant survival is not a function of race, but is a consequence of the financial capacity to cover the additional expenses of medications and follow-up care. In that cyclosporine A (the pharmacological mainstay of immunosuppressive therapy for renal transplantation) costs in excess of $10,000 per year, the price of medications and follow up nephrologic care is covered by Medicare for only 18 months after transplantation, and African-Americans are more sensitive to the deleterious effects of discontinuing cyclosporine A, it is unsurprising that fewer minorities have functioning transplants. Therefore, because of unequal access to alternate, better, and perhaps more cost-effective replacement therapy, minorities are trapped on dialysis at a younger age, and it is provided at geographically disadvantageous locations Thus, alterations in the end stage renal disease program will have a disproportionately great effect on the minority community

Financial Stability of the ESRD Program and Minority Nephrologic Health

In a subtle and cynical fashion, the declining economic stability of the End Stage Renal Disease Program will adversely influence the physician practice patterns in a manner likely to impact the disproportionately large number of minority patients with renal failure. As a practical reality of practicing clinical medicine, it is simpler and relatively more financially rewarding to manage large numbers of patients with less complicated illnesses that are reimbursed on a fee-for-service basis, than to manage the more intellectually and emotionally demanding, impoverished patients who are very ill with numerous comorbid conditions, little disease insight, inadequate finances, and for whom reimbursement is marginal and capitated As described earlier, a sizable portion of the end stage renal disease population within the United States fit the latter stereotype -- minorities with renal failure complicated by hypertension and (or) diabetes mellitus who are financially and educationally disadvantaged. Declining physician reimbursement complicated by increased responsibility for socioeconomic issues, generate a disincentive to care for this group, whom are the most rapidly growing segment of the end stage renal disease population. Thus, the nephrologist is forced to make a cruel choice either maintain the financial stability of his practice by excluding many such patients from his care, or increasingly compromise his livelihood by caring for the most challenging patients The unfair and inappropriate burden upon the nephrologist becomes the segregation of patient entry into this entitlement program Entry into the End Stage Renal Disease Program would be based upon an unfair appraisal of the patient's potential for the development of a time costly comorbid illness Alternatively, the nephrologists may continue to accept the responsibility for the care of such patients, but will be tempted to divert attention to hospitalized dialysis patients, to fee-for-service patients without end stage renal disease, or to perform an excessive number of fee-for-service tests or procedures (nerve-conduction studies, bone densitometry, parenteral calcitriol, etc.) on dialysis patients As expressed in the recent Institute of Medicine report "reduction in the physician's monthly rate and the absence of adjustment for inflation, when coupled with the increasing age and complexity of the patient population, have raised concerns about the effects of physician payment on patient care" Alternatively, a fair, inflation-adjusted, totally capitated physician payment for outpatient dialysis services would minimize the inequitable patterns of patient care, enhance the quality of patient care, minimize hospitalizations, and effect substantial cost savings to the Program

The dialysis facility providers play a far greater role to the minority patient with end stage renal disease than to simply provide equipment and staff for the performance of dialysis Because many such patients are financially and educationally disadvantaged, nephrologic support personnel such as the nutritionist and the social worker are critical allies in the provision of comprehensive care The legislation of decreasing reimbursements to the dialysis facility provider greatly compromises their capacity to hire these needed support staffs Dialysis providers that are financially unsound cannot expend funds on newer equipment and medications that improve the quality of dialysis, and by extrapolation, the quality of life and patient rehabilitation Provisions of dialysis machines with ultrafiltration controllers and high flux hemodialysis, the use of more costly biocompatable membranes, and the administration of optimal doses of erythropoietin are examples of costly, but appropriate dialysis innovations A critical exemplar of these issues for the minority patient with end stage renal disease is the case of erythropoietin

Most within the nephrology community feel that the development of erythropoietin is a major achievement in the treatment of renal disease Because of its capacity to improve the strength, cognition, cardiovascular function, and rehabilitation potential of patients on dialysis, >80% of the patients now receive erythropoietin However, the use of erythropoietin has added $0 5 billion annually to the direct cost of the treatment of end stage renal disease Yet despite its administration during the dialysis treatment, erythropoietin is currently paid for separately from the composite reimbursement provided to the dialysis facilities The definition of payment for erythropoietin on a usage basis only, instead of a fair standardized payment amount that is incorporated into the composite facility reimbursement, may promote inefficiency in its use. Evidence for this is that the mean dose of erythropoietin has increased from 2750 units per patient per treatment to 4000 units from 1990 to 1993; it was during this interval that the reimbursement for erythropoietin was removed from the composite rate Considering a presumption that the method of reimbursement invites overuse of this medication, the reimbursement was recently reduced by $1 00 per 1000 units In that Amgen, the manufacturer of erythropoietin, has remained unyielding in reducing its price, the financial burden of this rate reduction has fallen directly upon the dialysis facility providers These providers cannot continue to absorb increasingly harsh financial limitations imposed by the failure to provide inflation adjustments to the composite reimbursement To maintain the quality of care that is necessary in other portions of the dialysis procedure, the dialysis providers will not absorb reductions in erythropoietin reimbursement Instead they will make it less available in the dialysis facility For patients who have adequate private insurance, and (or) for affluent patients, this will be of little consequence, their physicians can write them a prescription for this costly medication that they can fill themselves In contrast, for financially disadvantaged patients, and for those with marginal or no secondary insurance coverage, erythropoietin will be unavailable. These individuals, who are predominantly minorities, will be forced to accept the risk of blood transfusions, while their more affluent counterparts are afforded the luxury of erythropoietin

We have seen these concerns come to fruition in Massachusetts, where the state has effectively discontinued payment for erythropoietin for Medicaid patients For months, the cost of erythropoietin was borne solely by the dialysis facility providers, but ultimately became so great that they were forced to discontinue it for Medicaid patients Therefore, a dichotomy of renal health care exists, with the compromise being endured by the vulnerable minorities This example also demonstrates an excessively narrow focus on the direct costs of medications within the End Stage Renal Disease Program In that approximately 40% of the Medicare expenditures for patients with end stage renal disease is for hospital care, and if erythropoietin diminishes the frequency of inpatient care and augments rehabilitation, optimizing erythropoietin use will result in an indirect cost saving Similarly, if lifelong coverage for cyclosporine A normalized the survival of renal transplants in minority patients, indirect cost savings would be minimized by the improved quality and duration of survival enjoyed by this population

Cost Effective Targets for Corrective Action

While no one can provide incontrovertible data that further rate reductions will increase patient morbidity and mortality within the End Stage Renal Disease Program, there is no support that the adverse outcomes outlined earlier will improve with such an action I am particularly concerned for our rapidly growing number of minority patients who are "captive" on dialysis The Institute of Medicine End Stage Renal Disease Committee, several key members of the Congress, and every end stage renal disease patient and professional organization have opposed the implementation of further rate reductions within the End Stage Renal Disease Program Concerns that patient care would suffer in the setting of marginal Medicare reimbursements were independently validated by the Prospective Payment Assessment Commission, that recommended that the rate for dialysis services be increased by 2.5% ($3 15 per dialysis treatment) for the 1994 fiscal year With an inappropriately narrow and excessive focus on short term cost savings, the Health Care Financing Administration turned down this recommendation Therefore, minorities with end stage renal disease, who spend a disproportionate length of time receiving center-based hemodialysis may potentially compromise their lives on dialysis because of short-sighted alterations in reimbursement

My hope is that your Subcommittee's proposal for America's health care reform will address and correct the concerns of the minority community that are a herald for the American nephrologic patient population at large As defined earlier, many of these goals can be achieved acutely by (1) extending the End Stage Renal Disease Secondary Payer Period to at least 24 months to appropriately increase cost sharing by the patients' private insurers, (2) defining the bundle of patient care services that are to be provided by the nephrologists and incorporating a global (all-inclusive) monthly capitation payment schedule for these services, and (3) folding the funds for erythropoietin into the composite reimbursement to the dialysis facility operators Further, I would suggest the following overall nephrologic care mandate

Minority Nephrologic Health Care

- To augment Federal and private funding of basic science and clinical research focused upon the prevention, pathobiology, diagnosis, and therapy of nephrologic diseases with an excessive prevalence within the minority communities of the United States,
- To enhance the funding and performance of such research at traditionally minority academic institutions or at majority institutions by minority investigators,
- To increase access to and the participation of minorities in home dialysis programs as maintenance therapy for ESRD,
- To increase the number of dialysis centers geographically located within minority neighborhoods;
- To augment the number of minorities participating in organ donation programs,
- To increase Federal and private funding of basic science and clinical research directed towards immunogenetics and transplantation immunology of minorities, and
- To improve minority access to renal transplantation as therapy for ESRD

Minority Nephrologic Professional Community

- To increase the number of minority resident physicians who pursue nephrologic careers in clinical practice or academia,
- To increase the number of minority dialysis administrators

Common Issues with Particular Impact Upon Minorities

- ♦ To assure the provision of an inflation-adjusted and fair reimbursement schedule for nephrologists,
- ♦ To assure an inflation-adjusted and fair reimbursement schedule for the dialysis facility providers,
- ♦ To enhance the retrieval and the reporting of socioeconomic data by the USRDS, and
- ♦ To educate the public and the allied professional communities to the aforementioned issues

Summary

As is true for many aspects of American life, the weakest typically pay for budgetary cuts As posed by Vance Hartke, "how do we explain that the difference between life and death is a matter of dollars? How do we explain that those who are wealthy have a greater chance to enjoy a longer life than those who are not?" A point of promise and of hope for the minority community from the current Congress and Administration is your keen recognition of the need to protect America's weaker, vulnerable citizens The End Stage Renal Disease Program was initiated with a promise to provide care for all, indifferent of their race, age, ethnicity, or finances This lofty goal is achievable within the framework of the current program Quality of life within the United States is often gauged by finances However, life and death should not be defined by dollars, as is increasingly the case in the ESRD Program The disproportionate number of minority patients "captive" on dialysis look to you as a voice of advocacy, where previously we have had none I hope that you advocate a plan of equity as you consider these critical issues during the Health Care conferences

Chairman STARK. Mr. Robbins.

STATEMENT OF KENNETH C. ROBBINS, PRESIDENT, ILLINOIS HOSPITAL ASSOCIATION

Mr. ROBBINS. Thank you, Mr. Chairman. I am here on behalf of the 200 hospitals of the Illinois Hospital Association, and I would like to share with you the conclusions of a recently completed year-long study on health reform as seen from the Illinois perspective. We support many of the principles of President Clinton's plan. Like the President, we believe that there can be no reform without universal coverage. Like the President, we believe that rational competition between accountable health plans will achieve greater efficiency while preserving consumer choice, high quality, and innovation.

Our views are very congruent with the approach of the American Hospital Association. Like the AHA, we believe that it is impossible to achieve universal coverage and keep costs under control unless the delivery system is fundamentally reorganized. We believe that integrated networks of hospitals, physicians and other providers, paid on a capitated basis, are the key to a restructured health care system.

But we have serious concerns about certain aspects of some health care proposals.

One issue that is of vital importance to us is global budgeting for health care. A formula-driven cap on health care spending linked to an unrelated factor such as the consumer price index is simply bad policy. Health care spending should be linked to the actual need for health care services.

Global budgeting implies that all health care costs are in the control of providers. It ignores such factors as labor costs, technology costs, social problems such as poverty, violence, and drug abuse, and medical disasters such as AIDS.

Global budgeting implies that if health care budgets become strained, Americans should be deprived of health services. We, in Illinois, are painfully aware of how irrational and dangerous that strategy can be.

Because our State is facing a huge shortfall in its Medicaid budget, it intends to reduce hospital reimbursement by $200 million during the next 18 months. That may balance the budget in the short run, but it does not address the real causes of escalating Medicaid costs. Instead, it will force hospitals to reduce services, to shift more costs to privately insured patients, and possibly to close their doors.

Lowering payments to providers is not the way to change the root causes of escalating health care costs. Health care costs are already moderating as providers respond to competitive pressures. Medical prices rose 5.4 percent in 1993, the smallest increase since 1973.

We believe that costs can best be restrained by changing the incentives that determine how care is provided and used. For example, providers in organized delivery systems paid on a capitated basis will conserve health resources while keeping people healthy.

We also believe that an independent national commission responsible for recommending a budget for publicly subsidized health care can help to maintain the correct balance between people's needs and the funds available to meet them.

Universal access is meaningless if we can't pay the bills for care. That is why we are deeply concerned by another element of the President's proposal: Restraining projected Medicare spending by $125 billion over 5 years. Funding universal access through Medicare cuts could threaten access to care by endangering hospitals with large Medicare populations.

We support an adequately funded Medicare program, with incentives for Medicare beneficiaries to join capitated delivery systems.

Illinois hospitals support the idea of purchasing cooperatives for small businesses and individuals, but we have serious reservations about the size and structure of the health alliances proposed by the President. We recommend that they be limited to an administrative rather than a regulatory role.

We are also concerned that a sudden influx of new patients into the current system could lead to an explosion in costs that will trigger rigid budget caps. We advocate a 6-year period for phasing in universal coverage as new incentives bring providers into integrated delivery systems and as new efficiencies are realized.

In closing, let me summarize four basic principles that Illinois hospitals support.

First is universal coverage, a guarantee that all citizens will have access to essential health care benefits;

Second, responsible health care financing, with requirements for employer and individual participation, government subsidies for low-income citizens, and a continuation of Medicare, but with some new incentives;

Third, insurance market reforms making coverage affordable and portable, with purchasing cooperatives for individuals and small businesses; and

Fourth, a restructured delivery system based on community care networks. Without this fourth goal, none of the other reforms will work.

Illinois hospitals accept the challenge of comprehensive health care reform, because we believe the goal better health for all Americans is worth it. We look forward to working with you to reach that goal.

Thank you very much, Mr. Chairman.

Chairman STARK. Thank you.

[The prepared statement follows:]

February 4, 1994

Good morning. I'm Ken Robbins, president of the Illinois Hospital Association. It is a pleasure to join you here today to support a cause that has long been a cherished goal of Illinois hospitals.

Illinois hospitals are deeply committed to comprehensive health care reform. There are still potential pitfalls and traps along the road to reform, and we would like to share with you today some of our concerns, as well as our goals. Our views are set forth in "A Healthy Future for All Illinoisans," the report of the Illinois Hospital Association's Chairman's Task Force on Health Care Reform. This blue-ribbon panel spent a year developing a comprehensive blueprint for health reform that will work for the citizens of Illinois.

We support many of the principles of President Clinton's plan. Like the President, we believe that there can be no reform without universal coverage. Like the President, we believe that rational competition between accountable health plans will achieve greater efficiency while preserving consumer choice, high quality, and innovation.

Our views are very congruent with the approach of the American Hospital Association. Like the AHA, we believe that it is impossible to achieve universal coverage and keep costs under control unless the delivery system is fundamentally reorganized. We believe that integrated networks of hospitals, physicians and other providers, paid on a capitated basis, are the key to a restructured health care system.

But we have serious concerns about certain aspects of some health care proposals.

One issue that is of vital importance to us is global budgeting for health care. A formula-driven cap on health care spending linked to an unrelated factor such as the consumer price index is simply bad policy. Health care spending should be linked to the actual need for health care services.

Global budgeting implies that all health care costs are in the control of providers. It ignores such factors as labor costs, technology costs, social problems such as poverty, violence, and drug abuse, and medical disasters such as AIDS.

Global budgeting implies that if health care budgets become strained, Americans should be deprived of health services. We in Illinois are painfully aware of how irrational and dangerous that strategy can be. Because our state is facing a huge shortfall in its Medicaid budget, it intends to reduce hospital reimbursement by $200 million during the next 18 months. That may balance the budget in the short run, but it does not address the real causes of escalating Medicaid costs. Instead it will force hospitals to reduce services, to shift more costs to privately insured patients, and possibly to close their doors.

Lowering payments to providers is not the way to change the root causes of escalating health care costs. Health care costs are already moderating as providers respond to competitive pressures. Medical prices rose 5.4 per cent in 1993, the smallest increase since 1973.

We believe that costs can best be restrained by changing the incentives that determine how care is provided and used. For example, providers in organized delivery systems paid on a capitated basis will conserve health resources while keeping people healthy. We also believe that an independent national commission responsible for recommending a budget for publicly subsidized health care can help to maintain the correct balance between people's needs and the funds available to meet them.

Universal access is meaningless if we can't pay the bills for care. That is why we are deeply concerned by another element of the President's proposal: restraining projected Medicare spending by $125 billion over five years. Funding universal access through Medicare cuts could threaten access to care by endangering hospitals with large Medicare populations.

We support an adequately funded Medicare program, with incentives for Medicare beneficiaries to join capitated delivery systems.

Illinois hospitals support the idea of purchasing cooperatives for small businesses and individuals, but we have serious reservations about the size and structure of the health alliances proposed by the President. We recommend that they be limited to an administrative rather than a regulatory role.

We are also concerned that a sudden influx of new patients into the current system could lead to an explosion in costs that will trigger rigid budget caps. We advocate a six-year period for phasing in universal coverage as new incentives bring providers into integrated delivery systems and as new efficiencies are realized.

In closing, let me summarize four basic principles that Illinois hospitals support.

First is universal coverage -- a guarantee that all citizens will have access to essential health care benefits.

Two: Responsible health care financing, with requirements for employer and individual participation, government subsidies for low-income citizens, and a continuation of Medicare, but with some new incentives.

Three: Insurance market reforms making coverage affordable and portable, with purchasing cooperatives for individuals and small businesses.

And four: A restructured delivery system based on community care networks. Without this fourth goal, none of the other reforms will work.

Illinois hospitals accept the challenge of comprehensive health care reform, because we believe the goal -- better health for all Americans -- is worth it. We look forward to working with you to reach that goal.

Chairman STARK. Dr. Champion.

STATEMENT OF HOWARD R. CHAMPION, M.D., PRESIDENT, COALITION FOR AMERICAN TRAUMA CARE, AND DIRECTOR, TRAUMA POLICY AND RESEARCH, THE WASHINGTON HOSPITAL CENTER, WASHINGTON, D.C.

Dr. CHAMPION. Mr. Chairman, I am a specialist in trauma surgery. Unlike other kinds of surgical specialists, as a trauma surgeon, I have been delivering extensive amounts of pro bono care to injured Americans. I have been in the Baltimore-Washington area doing the same for the last 20 years. I am the founding president of the Coalition for American Trauma Care and secretary of the American Trauma Society; and on behalf of those organizations, I want to thank for this opportunity to testify.

I also want to thank you, Mr. Chairman, for your longstanding support for efforts to improve the delivery and financing of trauma care services for seriously injured Americans.

The Coalition's specific comments on the Health Security Act are contained in our written statement and I will comment on the main issues. To do that appropriately, it is important to place serious injury in the public health context.

Injury is the leading cause of death for Americans from birth through age 44. For every death there are at least three or four permanent disabilities. Injury is also the leading cause of years of lost productivity—more than cancer and heart disease combined. Since it affects the young in the workforce, injury is also our most costly disease—estimated at $180 billion in lifetime costs in 1988.

The Coalition has worked to address this public health problem on many fronts. This includes community-based injury awareness and prevention efforts and university-based injury research programs. Unfortunately, even in the most effective public health models, injury can never be entirely prevented. Thus, we must focus on mitigating the consequences of injury to the greatest extent possible.

Practice guidelines for trauma care are designed to provide cost-effective secondary and tertiary prevention services so that when serious injury does occur, death and disability are prevented. When disability cannot be fully prevented, then every effort is made to restore as much function as possible.

The Coalition believes strongly that organized, regional system of trauma care are a model for reform of costly, specialized tertiary care services. The components of a trauma system are described more fully in our written statement. Let me just mention that they include prevention, 911 access, prehospital care, triage or transfer decisionmaking, specialize acute hospital care in a trauma center, and rehabilitation.

Despite the clear benefits of a regional or State trauma system, the Health Security Act does not provide any recognition of trauma care, trauma centers, or trauma systems. The Coalition believes that individuals with life-threatening injuries must not be denied access to qualified trauma care. This must be recognized in health care reform policy.

There is a concern that too much emphasis on State-based purchasing alliances could have a detrimental effect on trauma and burn centers that have catchment areas across state boundaries, as is the case in every city along the Mississippi River, leading to Balkanization of existing and effective regional trauma systems.

The Coalition is aware of instances in many areas of the country, even those with fully developed trauma care systems, where some third-party payers currently refuse appropriate transfer to a trauma center for patients subsequently determined by community hospital physicians to need the services of a qualified trauma center. Other payers have inappropriately placed financial pressures on family members for premature transfer out of a trauma center. These concerns can and should be corrected in health system reform by applying uniform treatment standards for reimbursement for qualified trauma care services.

I hasten to add, for the record, that there are many payers that specifically contract with trauma centers throughout the Nation. We need to provide an appropriate and positive environment for the growth and development of middle-aged trauma care which is extremely cost-effective, particularly when the total costs of care are assessed.

As you know, Mr. Chairman, over 100 trauma centers across the country have closed their doors since 1985, a majority of them due to chronic underreimbursement.

It has been stated to us that trauma will get relief from the burdens of uncompensated care with health care reform, but we must respond that it depends on two factors—that universal coverage proceed in concert with and not after implementation of further cuts in Medicaid and Medicare; and two, that health plans be required to contract with qualified trauma centers. Unless these things happen, we predict that further trauma center closures will occur causing further compromise to the public's access to the life-saving services of qualified trauma centers.

The Coalition strongly feels that Americans expect good care when they dial 911. Excluding critically injured Americans from qualified trauma would, in fact, violate the clinical standards of medical care and would likely result in much more completely unnecessary disability, costing State and Federal treasuries millions of dollars in lifelong support payments.

Thank you for the opportunity to share our views with the subcommittee today. The Coalition for American Trauma Care looks forward to working with you in recognizing these principles in health care reform legislation.

Chairman STARK. Thank you very much.

[The prepared statement follows:]

STATEMENT OF HOWARD R. CHAMPION, M.D.
PRESIDENT
THE COALITION FOR AMERICAN TRAUMA CARE

Mr. Chairman, and Members of the Subcommittee, I am Dr. Howard Champion, Director of Trauma Policy and Research at the Washington Hospital Center here in the District of Columbia I am also Secretary of the American Trauma Society and the Founding President of the Coalition for American Trauma Care. The Washington Hospital Center's MedSTAR trauma unit is a Level I trauma center which serves the residents of the District of Columbia and seriously injured residents in a six state area.

On behalf of the membership of the Coalition for American Trauma Care, I want to thank you for providing our organization an opportunity to testify before the Subcommittee on the vitally important issue of health care reform and how trauma care relates to this reform. We especially appreciate, Mr. Chairman, the support you have shown over the years for efforts to improve the delivery and financing of trauma care services.

The Coalition for American Trauma Care is a national, not-for-profit organization whose membership includes physician directors of trauma care, leading trauma center institutions, and national organizations with a commitment to improving the delivery of trauma care services to seriously injured individuals and a strong commitment to injury prevention. The mission and goals of the Coalition are to improve trauma care services to seriously injured individuals through universal implementation of organized regional systems of trauma care, through improved basic and clinical trauma related research, through improved reimbursement for trauma center institutions, and to improve injury prevention activities at all levels of government.

The Coalition has worked closely with the Congress, including some members of this Subcommittee, on re-authorization of the *Trauma Care Systems Planning and Development Act* (P.L. 101-590), on enactment and efforts to fund the trauma center grant program to assist trauma centers fiscally stressed due to drug related violence (Title VI, P.L. 102-321), on enactment of the trauma provisions in legislation re-authorizing the National Institutes of Health which will develop a national plan for basic and clinical trauma care research (P.L. 103-43), and in support of the newly established Center for Injury Prevention and Control and the Centers for Disease Control and Prevention.

The Coalition is now pleased to comment on *The Health Security Act,*, President Clinton's plan to reform the nation's health care system.

I would first like to state, for the record, that the Coalition genuinely applauds President Clinton and First Lady Hillary Rodham Clinton for their leadership in bringing this very important, but very difficult and complex issue, before the American people and the Congress. There is much in the President's bill that the Coalition can, and will, strongly support.

But before I discuss specific provisions in the bill, I want to place the issue of injury and the work of our Coalition and other factions of the trauma care community in an appropriate context.

Injury is the leading cause of death for Americans from birth through age 44. For every death there are at least three to four permanent disabilities. Injury is also the leading cause of years of lost productivity -- more than cancer and heart disease combined. Since it affects the young and the workforce, it is our most costly disease -- estimated at $180 billion in lifetime costs in 1988. In my opinion, injury is the nation's most important public health and social issue.

The Coalition has worked to address this public health problem on many fronts. This includes community-based injury awareness and prevention efforts and university-based injury research programs. Unfortunately, even in the most effective public health models of prevention, injury can never be entirely prevented. Thus we must focus on mitigating the consequences of injury to the greatest extent possible. The Coalition, and other members of the trauma community, have promoted organized, regional systems of trauma care which are designed to provide *cost-effective* secondary and tertiary prevention services so that when serious injury does occur, death and disability are prevented. When disability cannot be fully prevented, then every effort is made to restore as much function as possible.

The Coalition believes strongly that organized, regional systems of trauma care are a model of reform ˙ costly, specialized, tertiary care services. The regional and state programs that have been established i United States go through a rigid professional and quality assurance process.

The first step in establishing a trauma system is to determine need. This is done in conjunction wit state officials, health policy experts, and public input. Basing the trauma system on need limits the number of specialized centers that will be established within a region. **The next step** is to enact enabling legislation authorizing the state, or other entity, to establish the trauma system which include: designating trauma centers. **The third step** is to use professionally established guidelines of care in designing all components of the trauma system.

Once these steps have been taken, the authorized entity -- usually the state emergency medical service agency -- typically then allows all hospitals to participate in the designation process, recognizing that o a few will be chosen based on need, including geographic considerations, and ability to meet professic guidelines. The applications are reviewed and verified on-site by a professional review team, ideally comprised of individuals from outside of the state. Hospitals that are chosen and verified to provide trauma care services are then formally designated by the authorized state entity.

The final step is to institute ongoing needs assessment and quality assurance. This is extremely important since numerous studies document sharp reductions in preventable death rates immediately following implementation of a trauma system with even further reductions achieved in years thereafter One recent study of workman's compensation cases showed states with implemented trauma systems achieved significant direct and indirect cost savings when compared with states without trauma system Quality assurance studies show that the vast majority of even the most severely injured individuals, wl provided with timely, qualified trauma care, return to work, household, or school activities full time w one year of injury.

A state trauma system must address at least six critical components: *1) prevention* -- short and long term strategies to identify root causes of behavioral and societal factors that result in unintentional and intentional injury must be identified and implemented; *2) access to the trauma system* -- this mea 911 availability and public awareness and education to act quickly so that individuals with life-threaten injury get immediate access to expert care; *3) pre-hospital care* -- trained personnel who provide th initial resuscitation and transport by ambulance, fixed-wing, or rotor-wing aircraft; *4) triage, trans, decision-making* -- triage is a French word which means "to sort." Not all trauma patients need the expertise of a trauma center. The intent is to concentrate the critically injured in a few centers thus reducing costs while maintaining the skill level of the physician and nurses who provide care for critic injured individuals; *5) acute hospital care* -- specialized trauma care facilities where experienced surgeons and nurses and other health professionals provide 24 hour resuscitation and lifesaving surge every day of the year; *6) rehabilitation* -- rehabilitation is started within hours of the lifesaving surg The goal is to return all injured patients to lives as productive members of society.

Trauma centers are also uniquely organized to care for the seriously injured patient. The regional trauma center (Level I) has five main components: *1) pre-hospital medical control* -- pre-hospital personnel at the injury scene consult hospital-based physicians with trauma expertise and receive triage and life support direction; *2) emergency department* -- 24 hour, in-house availability of a specialized team of physicians, nurses, and other personnel that is mobilized to assess and treat seriously injured individuals upon arrival at the emergency room door; *3) operating room* -- immediate operating room availability 24 hours per day and availability of multiple surgical specialists to manage multiple life-threatening injuries simultaneously; *4) intensive care unit* -- availability of multidisciplinary state-of-the-art intensive care services coordinated by the trauma surgeon thus eliminating the need for multiple and fragmented specialty consultation;
5) rehabilitation -- early integration of rehabilitation assessment and services during the initial acute care admission with the goal of returning the patient to his or her pre-injury level of functioning.

The trauma patient requires both an organized pre-hospital response and an organized acute care and rehabilitation response to achieve the most cost-effective outcome. This is because the trauma patient, especially the individual with multi-system involvement, requires immediate, coordinated, multidisciplinary care all available in one location. This may be best illustrated by describing a multiply-injured patient. A typical example might be an individual involved in a motor vehicle crash who sustains a severe head injury (intracranial hematoma), a torn major artery (torn thoracic aorta), massive liver injury, and unstable pelvic (hip) fracture. Clearly, this individual needs immediate and simultaneous attention by those trained in neurosurgery, general surgery with trauma expertise, and orthopedic surgery, as well as expert nursing care, rehabilitation assessment and services, and specialized x-ray, and other equipment. These specialized, and very expensive, services should be concentrated in just a few hospitals to ensure they are utilized in the most cost-effective fashion possible and to ensure that professional skills are maintained. The designation of qualified trauma centers, with these characteristics, form the backbone of the trauma system.

Organized, regional systems of trauma care are a proven, cost-effective public health solution to a major public health problem. Americans expect and want safe water to drink and clean air to breathe. Americans also expect and want an environment safe from injury and a government prepared to implement primary prevention measures. But if primary prevention fails, Americans want a health care system that will save an injured loved one when death is truly preventable; a health care system that will prevent completely unnecessary disability; and a health care system that will provide the services that can make their family members productive again.

It is in the context of this public health model that the Coalition for American Trauma Care assesses the provisions of the *Health Security Act.* [1]

GENERAL COMMENTS
Availability of Qualified Trauma Care
While the various components of an organized, regional system of trauma care are covered under the benefit package there is no acknowledgement throughout the bill that serious injury, as a major public health problem, requires a system of care approach because of its time-sensitive nature and

---

[1] For the pages that follow, the "Act" denotes the Clinton Health Security Act

treatment. In addition, except for academic health centers, it is left to the discretion of states whether or not to require health plans to contract with centers of excellence, or other specialty care centers. The Coalition acknowledges that there is considerable overlap between academic health centers and qualified[2] trauma centers, but not all qualified trauma centers are teaching hospitals, or operate approved physician training programs. States often rely upon these trauma centers, usually Level II institutions, to serve major segments of their populations, particularly in smaller cities, and rural areas. The Coalition would like language added to the state responsibility section which requires health plans to contract with a qualified trauma center. The justification for this added requirement is, again, due to the unique time-sensitive nature of serious injury and the need for timely, specialized intervention which meets specific standards of care to achieve a cost-effective outcome for a major, costly public health problem.

At the same time, to facilitate the pre-hospital component of trauma care systems, it is essential that provisions in the *Act* requiring health plans to pay for medically necessary emergency medical services wherever they occur are retained in the bill. The latter should be construed to include ground and air ambulance transport as well as hospital based emergency and trauma care services.

The Coalition is aware of instances in many states and regions of states, even those with fully developed trauma care systems, where some third party payers currently refuse appropriate transfer to a trauma center for patients subsequently determined by community hospital physicians to require the services of a qualified trauma center. Other payers have inappropriately placed financial pressures on family members for premature transfer out of the trauma center. These concerns can and should be corrected in health system reform by applying uniform treatment standards for reimbursement for qualified trauma care services.

I hasten to add, for the record, that there are many payers that specifically contract with trauma centers throughout the country. Examples include trauma centers in Boston, Denver, Colorado, areas of Pennsylvania, Ohio, Minnesota, Detroit, Washington, D.C., Portland, Oregon and in many other areas where there are qualified trauma centers. We need to provide an appropriate and positive environment for the growth and development of model managed trauma care which is extremely cost-effective when the total costs of care are assessed.

Regionalization of Trauma Care
It is also important to note that many trauma centers are truly regional in nature and serve seriously injured individuals from several states. The *Act's* provisions restricting health alliances to state boundaries could interfere with the interstate triaging process for seriously injured individuals that now takes place in many areas of the country. States sometimes even designate a trauma center that is in another state. This practice should be acknowledged in the state responsibility section. States should require health plans to contract with qualified trauma centers, which may include state designated trauma centers located within another state.

The Coalition would like to see Title III of the Act, under the public health initiatives, include $20 million in funding for trauma system development as provided by the *Trauma Care Systems Planning and Development Act*. This is the minimum amount needed to fully implement the provisions of the legislation and will do much to further trauma system development. Currently, while there are qualified trauma centers in almost every state only half of the states have developed organized systems of trauma care. Requiring health plans to contract with qualified trauma centers will provide strong incentives to states to develop trauma systems; providing financial support for doing so under the Trauma Systems Act will also enhance this desirable result.

Reimbursement for Trauma Care
Finally, the Coalition feels strongly that health care reform must provide universal access to health care for the nation's uninsured in a fashion that is timed to precede, or coincide with reductions in the Medicare and Medicaid programs, as proposed under the *Health Security Act*. If the cuts precede coverage many more trauma centers may close their doors. Since 1985, over 100 trauma centers have closed across the country. Some of these closures are due to improved standards, which is a positive development. But almost all others, especially the eleven Level I trauma centers that have closed in major urban areas, have closed due to the fiscal stress caused by chronic under-reimbursement often exacerbated by outbreaks of drug-related violence.

Many officials in the Clinton Administration, including the President himself, have said to us, "Under the Clinton health plan trauma centers will finally get relief from the burdens of uncompensated care because the uninsured will be covered." We respond, honestly, that it depends. It depends on two factors: 1) that universal coverage proceed in concert with and not after the implementation of further cuts in Medicare and Medicaid; and 2) that health plans be required to contract with qualified trauma centers. It does not help the fiscal crisis facing the nation's trauma centers if the uninsured are eventually covered, but the hospital has already closed its trauma center because Medicaid and Medicare disproportionate share support and other Medicare reimbursement were significantly reduced first. Nor does it help if the trauma center survives these fiscal challenges, but health plans do not contract with it and refuse appropriate transfers to the trauma

---

[2] A qualified trauma center is a designated trauma center as defined under Title XII of the U S Public Health Service Act, and/or as verified by the American College of Surgeons Such qualified trauma centers, as defined, also include pediatric trauma centers

center or apply pressure for premature discharge from the trauma center. Under these conditions, unfortunately, we predict further trauma center closures, and further compromise of the American public's access to the life-saving services of qualified trauma centers.

OTHER COMMENTS
Coverage
While we appreciate the difficult cost considerations that led to excluding undocumented aliens from coverage under the Clinton health plan, we do not agree with this exclusion. Seriously injured individuals are admitted to the hospital and treated regardless of their ability to pay. In some areas of the country, especially along the Mexican-U.S. border, trauma centers are in serious fiscal crisis because of the great influx of undocumented aliens, a number of whom need qualified trauma care services.

Benefit Package
The *Act's* comprehensive benefit package includes most of the components of a trauma system, but the Coalition would like the following specific change. The language limiting use of air and water ambulance transport only to those instances where any other method of transport would be contraindicated by the medical condition of the sick or injured individual should be eliminated since it has no practical medical meaning for emergency care personnel and might well preclude the use, ever, of air and water ambulance transport. This wording actually works against the cost-effective regionalization of many aspects of tertiary care and cost-containment in general.

Under the section listing services that are excluded from the benefit package, cosmetic surgery is only covered if it is needed as a result of an "accidental injury." In the trauma community we never refer to any injury as "accidental" because it connotes that injury is unavoidable and akin to an "Act of God." We use the public health terms "unintentional" injury and "intentional" injury to emphasize that injury is related to personal behavior and therefore preventable. With today's unfortunate upsurge in violence, it would seem important not to exclude from coverage cosmetic surgery needed as a result of either unintentional, or intentional injury.

Academic Health Centers
Because of the strong overlap between academic health centers and Level I trauma centers, the Coalition strongly supports retention of the provisions ensuring access to academic health centers by requiring health plans to contract with them for the specialized services they provide.

Preemption of Certain State Laws Relating to Health Plans
The Coalition strongly supports retention under the section describing preemption of restrictive state laws of the exemption for emergency medical services. This permits the maintenance and fostering of trauma system development by permitting the state to retain the authority to designate trauma centers and organize pre-hospital emergency medical services accordingly.

Tax Treatment of Organizations Providing Health Care Services and Related Organizations (Title VII, Subtitle F)
The Coalition appreciates that included among the tax incentives provided to HMOs is payment for emergency care provided to an HMO member outside the member's area of residence. This provision supports the operation of trauma systems by helping to ensure that a trauma center treating a seriously injured HMO member, appropriately triaged to the center which is outside the patient's area of residence, receives payment for services.

Workers Compensation and Automobile Insurance (Title X)
The *Act* requires health plans to enter into contracts, or arrange as necessary, for the provision of workers compensation services, and automobile insurance medical services to enrollees in return for payment from the insurance carrier. The *Act* states that health plans can accomplish this through a participating provider, any other contractee, or through a specialized workers compensation provider in the case of injured workers. When defining specialized workers compensation services and automobile insurance medical services, the *Act* never mentions qualified trauma centers despite the fact that they clearly provide services that uniquely address the needs of seriously injured enrollees. The Coalition would like to see language added to Title X which includes trauma care services in qualified trauma centers in the definition of workers compensation and automobile insurance medical services.

CONCLUDING COMMENTS
Regionalized trauma care is cost-effective. Regionalized trauma systems have reduced preventable deaths, disability and have increased the chances of a seriously injured person returning to productive life. By adopting the process of trauma system development that I have described, a rational number of trauma centers are strategically located within a region. This is determined by need with input from the public, government planners, and health policy experts. Trauma systems could serve as a model for the delivery of other tertiary care.

The Coalition believes that individuals with life-threatening injuries must not be denied access to qualified trauma care. This must be recognized in health care reform policy. Just as excluding Americans with pre-existing health conditions from health insurance coverage is now recognized as counter to sound public policy, so too failure to ensure access for critically injured patients to qualified trauma care would violate accepted clinical standards of medical care. Such an omission could well erode the confidence of many Americans in the clinical standards of care they may receive when calling 911 in an emergency in a reformed health care system. Such an omission would also likely result in much more completely unnecessary disability costing state and federal treasuries hundreds of thousands of dollars per case in life-long support payments.

Thank you again, Mr. Chairman, for proving the Coalition for American Trauma Care with the opportunity to share our views on trauma care and health care reform. We look forward to working with you, and Members of the Subcommittee, in recognizing these principles in health care reform legislation.

TRAUMA CARE AND HEALTH CARE REFORM:
ESSENTIAL PRINCIPLES TO ENSURE COST-EFFECTIVE OUTCOMES

1) Cost efficiencies for the entire health care system under a privately regulated model of health system reform utilizing managed competition may be possible.(1)
2) Regulatory strategies of the 1970s and competitive strategies of the 1980s have often resulted in massive duplication of health care services and technologies, thereby driving up total health care costs while having a poorly understood effect on patient outcomes. (2)
3) Organized regional systems of trauma care, by providing early definitive interventions for the seriously injured, deliver cost-effective health care services to one of the nation's leading, and the nation's most costly, health care problems. (3,4)
4) Clinical leadership in trauma system development has led the nation in the commitment to the development of primary and secondary injury prevention strategies, utilization of patient outcome data to improve service delivery to injured individuals, and implementation of practice guidelines to improve and maintain clinical skills. (5,6)
5) Specific studies show organized regional systems of trauma care significantly reduce duplication of costly trauma care services for seriously injured individuals while also dramatically improving patient outcomes, thereby resulting in considerable direct and indirect health care and social welfare cost efficiencies. (16-33)
6) The cost efficiencies achieved by organized regional systems of trauma care can be readily compared to quality assurance programs in manufacturing. It costs less to build a product, particularly a complex product like an automobile, right the first time thereby avoiding the need for expensive recalls. (7)
7) Health system reform proposals should recognize the cost efficiencies inherent in organized regional systems of trauma care for a major public health problem, and should support universal implementation of trauma systems as specified in P.L. 101.590, the Trauma Care Systems Planning and Development Act.
8) Health system reform proposals should also recognize that access to organized regional systems of trauma care can only be ensured when reimbursement adequately covers the cost of qualified trauma care services, regardless of the source of payment. Since 1985, over 90 trauma centers have closed their doors to seriously injured Americans primarily due to uncompensated care costs. (8,9)

Basic Injury Facts
• Injury is the leading cause of death and disability for Americans from age 1 through age 44 causing 150,000 deaths and over 300,000 permanent disabilities each year. (10,11)
• Because it most often strikes the young, **injury is the leading cause of years of lost work productivity.** (10)
• Injury is the nation's most costly disease, resulting in an estimated $180 billion in lifetime costs in 1988 -- more than either heart disease or cancer. (4)
• In young children, injuries cause almost half of all deaths before age 5 and exceed all causes of deaths combined from age 5-14. (10) The most prominent causes of injury death in children are motor vehicle crashes, homicide, fires and falls. (10,11)
• When injury strikes the elderly, those over age 65 are more likely to die, have more complications and longer hospital stays than those under age 65 regardless of the severity of the injury. (12) While the elderly account for 12 percent of the U.S. population, they account for 25 percent of all hospital injury discharges and 25 percent of all hospital injury costs. (13)
• Motor vehicle crashes, which caused 43,500 deaths in 1991 are the leading cause of injury death. (10,11) Firearms are the second overall leading cause of injury death, and the leading cause of death for African-American males age 15-34. (10)
• The leading cause of non-fatal injury and of hospital admissions for trauma care is falls costing the nation only slightly less in lifetime costs than motor vehicle crashes. (10)

What is an organized regional system of trauma care?
• **Medical practice now recognizes that seriously injured individuals should not be taken to the nearest hospital for medical care without regard to the level of care available at that facility.**
• Organized regional systems of trauma care have five components:
1) *access*-- 911 availability and public awareness to act quickly to access emergency services; 2) *pre-hospital care*--ambulances, fixed-wing and rotor-wing aircraft accompanied by trained personnel who can provide initial resuscitation;
3) *triage, transport, and transfer decision-making*-pre-hospital and hospital based emergency care personnel match patient needs with the appropriate level of facility care;

4) *acute hospital care*--specialized trauma care facilities with experienced surgeons, other health care personnel and priority access to sophisticated technology and services all available 24 hours per day;
5) *rehabilitation*--access to rehabilitation services which are essential to restore injured individuals to productive lives. (5)
• Of the 2.8 million Americans who are hospitalized each year due to injury, approximately 250,000 require the services of a qualified trauma center for medical care because they are at risk of dying or permanent disability. (10,5) While small in number, acute care costs per initial trauma care admission are two to three times greater than the costs of the average acute care admission. The average U.S. acute care admission cost in 1990 was $4,946 while the average trauma care admission cost in 1990 was approximately $12,000. (14)

Organized Regional Systems of Trauma Care Save Lives and Prevent Disability.

• Death from injury occurs in a trimodal distribution: one-half of all deaths occur immediately; another 30 percent occur early, between one and three hours post-injury; the rest occur late, days or weeks post injury. (15) Organized regional systems of trauma care provide quick access to definitive care to save those at risk of early death, usually from neurological injury or various kinds of bleeding and probably significantly reduce the incidence of late deaths due to sepsis or multiple organ failure. (15)
• Studies have repeatedly shown that, when organized regional systems of trauma care are implemented, there are dramatic reductions in preventable deaths due to injury (16-20): 56% in Orange County (21), 55% in San Diego County (22), 50% in Washington, D.C. (23).
• One longitudinal study of survival outcomes at an urban hospital over a six year period found significant improvements for severely injured patients: 13.4 more survivors per 100 patients treated per year in years 5 and 6 compared with years 1 and 2. During this six year period, the hospital constructed a trauma resuscitation facility with on-site operating rooms, and the local government implemented an organized regional system of trauma care. (24)
• A recent study of 1,332 femur (thigh bone) fracture patients found that those treated in trauma centers received surgical treatment more quickly, had significantly fewer complications resulting in shorter hospital stays, and had fewer deaths than those treated in non-trauma center hospitals. (25)
• Studies also show the vast majority of even the most severely injured children and adults return to full function and productivity when treated in qualified trauma centers served by organized regional systems of trauma care. (26-29)
• One early study of severely head injured patients treated in a Level I trauma center demonstrates that aggressive, early intervention (usually within four hours) for severely head injured patients significantly increases the number of patients achieving good or moderately good (able to live independently) recovery (60 percent versus 39/40/42 percent) and significantly decreases the number of deaths (30 percent versus 52/49 percent) while the number of poor outcomes remains stable (10 percent versus 6/10/11 percent). (30)

Organized Regional systems of trauma care save health care costs.

• A recent study of worker's compensation claims for nonfatal disabling injuries and of the cost-effectiveness of organized regional systems of trauma care found 10-12 percent lower costs per hospitalized episode and a 10 percent decreased probability of hospitalization for cases treated in states with organized regional systems of trauma care. Extending trauma systems nationwide could lower annual health care costs by as much as $4 billion and perhaps by as much as $13.5 billion if preventable death and productivity loss were accounted for. (31)
• Saving young American lives and restoring them to full productivity through the provision of definitive trauma care and rehabilitative services increases the nation's wealth. Studies indicate that providing definitive trauma and rehabilitative care for one year to the typical 20 year old male trauma patient injured in a motorvehicle crash costs about $45,000 (1988 dollars). (32) One estimate indicates that, at an average annual salary of $20,000 and assuming a six percent discount rate, this individual would pay back in seven years in local, state and federal taxes the amount it cost to provide injury related health care. Across a lifetime, this individual earning the same modest salary would pay back in taxes alone 12 times more than the initial $45,000 investment in his life. (32)
• Case law examples, such as the one described below, show that further savings can be achieved through reduced legal and malpractice costs when optimal care in a qualified Level I trauma center is provided:

A 17 year old boy was helping his father trim tree branches when a large limb fell from a significant height and hit him directly on the head immediately rendering him unconscious. Emergency personnel were summoned from a nearby community hospital by family members, who requested that the boy be immediately transported to a Level I trauma center several miles away. Instead, the boy was transported to the nearby community hospital that had promoted its trauma service. Inadequate assessment of the boy's severe injury at the community hospital, and delays in transferring him to the Level I trauma center, where he was correctly evaluated and received definitive care, resulted in permanent cognitive, speech and physical mobility impairments. The family sued the community hospital. The out of court settlement amounted to $2 million. (33)

* Each year, conservative estimates indicate more than 400,000 Americans sustain head injuries and approximately 27,000 survive with moderate to severe impairment. (34) If organized regional systems of trauma care were universally available, many of these individuals could be restored to full productivity with enormous accompanying savings in direct and indirect health and social welfare costs. Reductions in potential malpractice claims alone could finance the implementation of systems. If 30 malpractice claims at an average pay out of $2 million were prevented because of the availability of definitive trauma care services, $60 million could be saved -- the amount Congress has authorized for implementation of P.L. 101-590, the *Trauma Care Systems Planning and Development Act.*

Despite evidence of their cost-effectiveness, many areas of the United States do not have fully implemented organized regional systems of trauma care, causing unnecessary death and disability particularly in rural areas.

* A 1991 study of trauma system development found that 19 states had no process for trauma center designation, 23 states had a process in place, and 9 were actively developing a process. (9) Many states do have fully implemented organized regional systems of trauma care serving major metropolitan areas, but lack a statewide system. This means many injured Americans are not getting the care they need.
* Lack of a statewide trauma system especially impacts rural areas where the death rate from unintentional injury is twice the rate for the largest cities. (10) Two of every three deaths involving motor vehicles occur in rural areas (11)
* A retrospective analysis of nearly 40 studies indicates that each year 20-25,000 lives are lost needlessly because organized regional systems of trauma care are not universally available across the United States. (32)
* Hawaii is one of the states that does not have an organized regional system of trauma care and has no process for trauma center designation currently in place. Hawaii is often looked to as the positive model for "managed competition." However, a comprehensive analysis of its emergency medical services system in May of 1991 by the U.S. Department of Transportation's Division of Emergency Medical Services found no system for responding to major trauma. (35) The state has since applied for a federal grant under P.L. 101-590 to begin the process of developing a organized regional system of trauma care. (36).
* Hawaii's basic benefit package under its State Health Insurance Program (SHIP) also does not make appropriate allowance for severely injured patients. Under SHIP, indigent beneficiaries are covered for 5 hospital days. (37) The average length of stay for all trauma patients treated in a Level I trauma center is approximately 10 days. (14) Severely head injured or spinal cord injured patients frequently require much longer hospital stays.

Managed Care and Organized regional systems of trauma care.
* Managed care clearly benefits from the cost efficiencies inherent in organized regional systems of trauma care. Promoting universal implementation of organized regional systems of trauma care and supporting universal access through appropriate payment policies can only add to cost efficiencies for managed care plans.
* Alternatively, attempts to undermine implementation and access to qualified trauma care services by providing care in facilities that do not meet national standards not only deprive injured individuals of appropriate care, but add to health and social welfare costs. Efforts to achieve short-term cost-savings at the expense of greater longer term health and social welfare cost savings must be strongly discouraged.

Organized regional systems of trauma care are an essential component of modern day health care. Any health system reform proposal that fails to ensure access to definitive trauma care and early rehabilitation services for seriously injured Americans will both fail to benefit those who are injured and will fail to realize potential cost savings.

References

1. Wallack, Stanley, S.: Managed care: Practice, pitfalls, and potential. *Health Care Financing Review*, 1991 Annual Supplement. HCFA Pub. No. 03322. Office of Research and Demonstrations, Health Care Financing Administration. Washington. U.S. Government Printing Office, March 1992: 27-34.
2. Jencks, Stephen, F. and Schieber, George, J.: Containing U.S. health care cost: What bullet to bite? *Health Care Financing Review*, 1991 Annual Supplement. HCFA Pub. No. 03322. Office of Research and Demonstrations, Health Care Financing Administration. Washington. U.S. Government Printing Office, March 1992: 1-12.
3. National Academy of Sciences: *Injury in America.* National Academy Press. Washington, D.C. 1985.
4. Rice, Dorothy, P. and MacKenzie, Ellen, J. and Associates: *Cost of Injury in the United States* : A Report to Congress. San Francisco, CA: Institute for Health and Aging, University of California and Injury Prevention Center, The Johns Hopkins University, 1989.
5. American College of Surgeons: Resources for optimal care of the injured patient. American College of Surgeons. Chicago 1990.
6. Champion, Howard, R., et al: The Major Trauma Outcome Study: Establishing national norms for trauma care. *Journal of Trauma*. November 1990; 30(11): 1356-1365

328

7. National Association of Manufacturers: Buying value in health care. National Association of Manufacturer's Industrial Relations Department. Washington, D.C. 1991.
8. U.S. General Accounting Office: Trauma care: Lifesaving system threatened by unreimbursed costs and other factors. Washington, D.C. GAP/HRD-91-57, May 1991.
9. Mabee, Marcia, S.: Summary and commentary accompanying preliminary survey of U.S. trauma centers and state-by-state analysis of trauma system development for the Eastern Association for the Surgery of Trauma, September 4, 1991, *unpublished*.
10. Baker, Susan P., et al: *The Injury Fact Book*. 2nd edition. Oxford University Press. New York, Oxford: 1992.
11. National Safety Council (1992): *Accident Facts*, 1992 edition. Itasca, IL.
12. Champion, Howard, R., et al: Major trauma in geriatric patients. *American Journal of Public Health*. September, 1989; 79(9): 1278-1282.
13. MacKenzie, Ellen, J. et al: Acute hospital costs of trauma in the United States: Implications for regionalized systems of care. *Journal of Trauma*. September 1990; 30(9): 1096-1101.
14. Mabee, Marcia S.: Financing high tech trauma care. Address before the 14th annual R. Adams Cowley National Trauma Symposium. Baltimore, March 8, 1992.
15. Trunkey, Donald D.: Trauma. *Scientific American*. August 1983; 249(2): 28-35.
16. Cales, Richard, H. and Trunkey, Donald, D.: Preventable trauma deaths: A review of trauma care systems development. *JAMA*. August 23, 1985; 254(8): 1059-1063.
17. Baxt, W., and Moody, P.: The differential survival of trauma patients. *Journal of Trauma*. Vol. 27, 1987: 602-606.
18. Shackford, S., et al: Assuring quality in a trauma system -- the medical audit committee: Composition, cost, and results. *Journal of Trauma*. Vol. 27, 1987: 8.
19. Shackford, S., et al: The effect of regionalization upon the quality of trauma care as assessed by concurrent audit before and after institution of a trauma system: A preliminary report. *Journal of Trauma*. Vol. 26: 9.
20. Rutledge, Robert, et al: Multivariate population-based analysis of the association of county trauma centers with per capita county trauma death rates. *Journal of Trauma*. July 1992; 33(1): 29-37.
21. Cales, Richard, H.: Trauma mortality in Orange County: The effect of implementation of a regional trauma system. *Annals of Emergency Medicine*. January 1984; 13(1): 15-24.
22. First year trauma system assessment: County of San Diego, August 1984-July 1985. San Diego County Division of Emergency Medical Services. November 1985.
23. National Highway Traffic Safety Administration's emergency medical services program and its relationship to highway safety. U.S. Department of Transportation Technical Report. DOT HS 806 832; August 1985.
24. Champion, Howard, R.; Sacco, William, J.; Copes, Wayne, S.: Improvement in outcome from trauma center care. *Archives of Surgery*. March 1992; 127(3): 333-338.
25. Smith, Stanley, J. et al: Do trauma centers improve outcome over non-trauma centers: The evaluation of regional trauma center care using discharge abstract data and patient management categories. *Journal of Trauma*. December 1990; 30(12): 1533-1538.
26. MacKenzie, Ellen, J., et al: Functional recovery and medical costs of trauma: An analysis by type and severity of injury. *Journal of Trauma*. March 1988; 28(3): 281-295.
27. Rhodes, Michael, et al: Quality of life after the trauma center. *Journal of Trauma*. July 1988; 28(7): 931-936.
28. Haller, Alex, J., Jr., and Buck, James: Does a trauma-management system improve outcome for children with life-threatening injuries? *Canadian Journal of Surgery*. November 1985; 28(6): 477.
29. Kivioja, Aarne, JH. et al: Is the treatment of the most severe multiply injured patients worth the effort? -- A followup examination 5 to 20 years after severe multiple injury. *Journal of Trauma*. April 1990; 30(4): 480-483.
30. Becker, Donald, P., et al: The outcome form severe head injury with early diagnosis and intensive management. *Journal of Neurosurgery*. October 1977; 47: 491-502.
31. Personal communication from Ted R. Miller, Senior Research Associate, The Urban Institute, to Marcia S. Mabee, June, 1992.
32. Champion, Howard, R. and Mabee, Marcia, S.: An American crisis in trauma care reimbursement. *Emergency Care Quarterly*. July 1990; 6(2): 65-87.
33. Hospital bypass challenge. *Emergency Department Law*. October 26, 1992; 4(18): 1.
34. Kraus, Jess F., et al: The incidence of acute brain injury and serious impairment in a defined population. *American Journal of Epidemiology*. 119(2): 186-200.
35. National Highway Traffic Safety Administration Technical Assistance Team: State of Hawaii: An assessment of emergency medical services, April 30-May 2, 1991.
36. Division of Trauma and Emergency Medical Systems, Bureau of Health Resources Development, Health Resources and Services Administration, U.S. Department of Health and Human Services: Title XII -- Trauma grant projects: FY 1992.
37. Basic benefits have many variations, tend to become political issues. *JAMA*. Medical new and Perspectives. October 28, 1992; 268(16): 2140.

Chairman STARK. Mr. Robinson.

STATEMENT OF KEN ROBINSON, SENIOR VICE PRESIDENT, EAST ALABAMA MEDICAL CENTER, ON BEHALF OF THE RURAL REFERRAL CENTER COALITION

Mr. ROBINSON. Thank you Mr. Chairman. I am Ken Robinson, senior vice president, East Alabama Medical Center, Opelika, Ala. I am pleased to appear before the subcommittee today as a representative of the Rural Referral Center Coalition. This informal coalition represents the interests of hospitals designated as rural referral centers under Medicare.

East Alabama is a large, 324-bed acute care, not-for-profit hospital with over 100 active physicians on its medical staff. We are the largest rural hospital in Alabama, one of two RRCs in the State, and a rural disproportionate share hospital.

The RRC Coalition supports guaranteed universal health insurance coverage for all Americans. We are concerned, however, that universal coverage is meaningless in rural America unless providers are geographically accessible to rural populations. As providers of primary, secondary and tertiary care in rural America, RRCs assure geographic access to residents of their immediate and surrounding rural communities. At East Alabama, 50 percent of our patients come from other rural areas out of our county. The next closest hospital is 22 miles away. We are the main referral facility for six other rural hospitals. If our services were not available, patients who use our specialty services, including obstetrics, cardiology (open heart surgery), and radiation therapy, would have to travel an additional 40 to 90 miles.

We believe that, indeed, RRCs offer both quality and cost effective care for rural populations.

A critical problem that has been identified in rural health care delivery is the lack of physicians and other professionals who are willing to locate in rural communities. Because RRCs are the larger rural health care institutions and offer a wide range of services, we are more successful than are other providers in recruiting and retaining physicians and other professionals.

In addition, RRCs are positioned to support primary care providers in outlying areas and spearhead network development and referral arrangements. For instance, East Alabama has placed the only primary care physician in an outlying rural community with a population of 15,000, even though this community actually is closer to the Columbus, Ga., metropolitan area. East Alabama also has established eight cardiology outreach clinics in underserved rural areas within a 30-mile radius.

I want to spend the rest of my time highlighting issues affecting RRCs that should be addressed under health reform.

First, while there is widespread agreement that rural America has unique characteristics that demand special consideration under health reform, pending proposals do not adequately address these circumstances. For instance, the proposals which envision a competitive marketplace do not address the widely acknowledged reality that most rural areas cannot support multiple health plans. Further, while managed care has become a significant presence in urban areas, it is barely present in most rural areas. Second, the

Clinton plan would promote incentives for urban health plans to expand to rural areas. This approach is not the answer for rural communities. Rural providers, who are stakeholders in their communities, should be the leaders in rural health care delivery. Indeed, many urban institutions are struggling to adequately serve urban populations. They are unfamiliar with and uninvested in our issues.

Third, Medicare's special payment adjustments to RRCs were designed to ensure their continued role in providing geographic accessibility to a wide range of services for rural populations. Indeed, special payment adjustments may need to be devised for rural providers under health reform, including for RRCs, to ensure that rural populations have geographic accessibility to not only primary care providers, but also specialty care providers. Fourth, the Medicare and Medicaid programs may need to be folded into reform in rural communities because their beneficiaries comprise such a high percentage of the rural patient base. East Alabama's patient population is approximately 50 percent Medicare and 10 percent Medicaid, with another 7 percent in charity care.

East Alabama presently owns and operates an emergency transport and county rescue system, but at a loss. With financial support, RRCs also would be positioned to launch managed care arrangements and innovative networking relationships.

Fifth, antitrust laws should be reexamined as applicable to rural communities to maximize cooperative relationships amidst limited resources. Many rural providers do not pursue mergers simply because the legal fees in obtaining antitrust representation are so prohibitive.

Finally, rural providers must be protected from unreasonable financial risk in order to assure that they offer geographic accessibility to rural populations. We are extremely concerned that global budgets, spending targets, fee schedules and the use of historical spending as the basis for these mechanisms could result in significant underpayments which ultimately would erode further the provider base in rural America. Fair financing must be assured under health care reform for all providers, but particular attention must be paid to designing fair financing appropriate to the rural environment, given public policy priorities of assuring geographic access to quality care in rural communities.

Lawmakers must be mindful that health care providers are a basic element of the rural economic infrastructure. Since RRCs are fundamental to this health care infrastructure, every effort must be made under health reform to assure RRC's continued role as essential providers of a broad range and depth of health care services in rural communities.

Thank you.

[The prepared statement and attachments follow:]

TESTIMONY BEFORE THE HOUSE WAYS & MEANS
SUBCOMMITTEE ON HEALTH
PUBLIC WITNESS HEARING ON HEALTH CARE REFORM
FEBRUARY 4, 1994

Introduction

I am Ken Robinson, Senior Vice President, East Alabama Medical Center,
Opelika, Alabama. I am pleased to appear before the Subcommittee today as a
representative of the Rural Referral Center Coalition (the RRC Coalition). This
informal Coalition, which has been active in the federal arena for over nine years,
represents the interests of hospitals designated as rural referral centers (RRCs) under
the Medicare Prospective Payment System (PPS). Two hundred fifty-six hospitals
currently are RRCs and receive special payment adjustments under the Medicare PPS
program in recognition of their additional costs in providing specialty care to rural
populations.

East Alabama Medical Center is a 324 acute care bed not-for-profit hospital with
over 100 active physicians on its medical staff. We are the largest rural hospital in
Alabama, one of two RRCs in the state, and a rural disproportionate share hospital
(DSH).

RRCs Are Central Players In Assuring Access To Care In Rural Areas

The RRC Coalition supports guaranteed universal health insurance coverage for
all Americans. We are concerned, however, that universal coverage is meaningless in
rural America unless providers are geographically accessible to rural populations. As
providers of primary, secondary and tertiary care in rural America, RRCs assure
geographic access to residents of their immediate and surrounding rural communities.
At East Alabama, 50% of our admissions derive from other rural areas out of our
county. The next closest hospital is 22 miles away. We are the main referral facility for
six other rural hospitals. If our services were not available, patients who use our
specialty services, including obstetrics, cardiology (open heart surgery), radiation therapy,
nephrology, orthopaedics and gastroenterology, would have to travel an additional 40 to
90 miles to receive these services. Indeed, RRCs offer both quality and cost-effective
care for rural populations who otherwise would have to travel long distances for similar
medical care. In some cases, this distance could mean the difference between life and
death. In addition, the geographic accessibility of RRCs offers the intangible benefit of
proximity to family members and saves families from costly stays in faraway urban areas.
At East Alabama, we find that many rural residents elect care at our hospital over an
urban hospital because they find rural providers to offer a more nurturing environment
and cultural affinity.

A critical problem that has been identified in rural health care delivery is the
dearth of physicians and non-physician professionals who are willing to locate in rural
communities. Because RRCs are the larger rural health care institutions and offer a
wide range of services, we are more successful than are other providers in recruiting and
retaining physicians and non-physician professionals. In addition, RRCs are positioned
to support and/or place primary care providers in outlying areas and spearhead network
development and referral arrangements. For instance, East Alabama has placed the only
primary care physician in an outlying rural community with a population of 15,000. This
community actually is closer to the Columbus, Georgia metropolitan statistical area than
to East Alabama, but the Columbus hospitals have not taken any action to place a
primary care physician in the community, because of their assumption that the rural
patients would travel to Columbus. East Alabama also has established 8 cardiology
outreach clinics in underserved rural areas within a 30 mile area, providing preventive
and specialty services.

The Prospective Payment Assessment Commission (ProPAC) recently completed an informal study of the function of RRCs in their communities. This study confirms that the RRC designation remains valid since these hospitals serve a critical role as providers of specialty care and services to vulnerable populations in rural areas. Attached is a series of charts prepared by ProPAC staff that elaborate on the role of all currently designated RRCs in their communities.

Issues Affecting RRCs That Must Be Addressed Under Health Reform

1. **Rural America is not urban America**

While there is widespread agreement that rural America has unique characteristics that demand special consideration under health reform, pending proposals do not adequately address these circumstances. For instance, those proposals which envision a competitive marketplace do not address the widely-acknowledged reality that most rural areas cannot support multiple health plans. Further, while managed care has become a significant presence in urban areas, it is barely a presence in most rural areas.

2. **Rural providers should take the lead in rural health care delivery**

The Clinton plan would promote incentives for urban health plans to expand to rural areas. This approach is not the answer for rural communities. Rural providers, who are stakeholders in their communities, who understand local politics and needs, and who must live in rural communities, should be the leaders in rural health care delivery. Indeed, many urban institutions are struggling to adequately serve urban populations. They are unfamiliar with and uninvested in our issues.

3. **Special payment adjustments may be appropriate for RRCs and other rural providers under health reform**

From the outset of Medicare PPS, Congress recognized that RRCs were critical to access to care in rural America. In 1993, Congress reaffirmed this by extending the RRC grandfather through fiscal year 1994.

Medicare's special payment adjustments to RRCs were designed to ensure their continued role in providing geographic accessibility to a wide range of services for rural populations. Even with the upcoming elimination of the standardized amount differential, RRC status still has meaning and benefit under the Medicare program. Specifically, RRCs are eligible for special access rules under the Medicare Geographic Classification Review Board (MGCRB) and receive higher DSH adjustments than do other rural hospitals. Congress must not hastily eliminate these special Medicare payment adjustments which are important to many RRCs. In the first two years of MGCRB, East Alabama qualified for a wage adjustment. The hospital now has qualified for standardized amount reclassification instead. ProPAC Chairman Stuart Altman recently reminded Congress that the Medicare payment structure includes esoteric payment adjustments in such areas as DSH and RRCs. He warned that in devising payments under health reform, a simple payment formula would not be possible.

Indeed, special payment adjustments may need to be devised for rural providers under health reform, including for RRCs, to ensure that rural populations have geographic accessibility to, not only primary care providers, but also specialty care providers. RRCs are the essential community providers in many rural communities and should be recognized accordingly.

4. **Medicare and Medicaid may need to be folded into health reform in rural America**

If Medicare remains a separate program under health reform, not only should the RRC designation be reenforced under Medicare, but also expressly recognized in health reform legislation for RRCs' central role as specialty providers. The Medicare and

Medicaid programs may eventually need to be folded into reform in rural communities because their beneficiaries comprise such a high percentage of the rural patient base. East Alabama's patient population is approximately 50% Medicare and 10% Medicaid, with another 7% in charity care. This also would ensure that hospitals would operate under the same incentives under both public and private programs.

5. **Certain financial assistance will be needed in rural America under health reform**

RRCs and other rural providers will need financial assistance to develop communication and emergency transportation linkages. East Alabama presently owns and operates an emergency transport and county rescue system, at a loss of $250,000 per year after accounting for subsidies. With financial support, RRCs also would be positioned to launch managed care arrangements and innovative networking relationships.

6. **Antitrust laws need to be reexamined as applied to rural providers**

Antitrust laws should be reexamined as applicable to rural communities to maximize cooperative relationships amidst limited resources. Many rural providers do not pursue mergers simply because the legal fees in obtaining antitrust representation are so prohibitive.

7. **Rural providers need protection from unreasonable financial risk**

Finally, rural providers must be protected from unreasonable financial risk in order to assure that they offer geographic accessibility to rural populations. The RRC Coalition is extremely concerned that global budgets, spending targets, fee schedules and the use of historical spending as the basis for these mechanisms could result in significant underpayments which ultimately would erode further the provider base in rural America. Fair financing must be assured under health care reform for all providers, but particular attention must be paid to designing fair financing appropriate to the rural environment, given public policy priorities of assuring geographic access to quality care in rural communities.

Lawmakers must be mindful that health care providers are a basic element of the rural economic infrastructure. Since RRCs are fundamental to this health care infrastructure, every effort must be made under health reform to assure RRCs' continued role as providers of a broad range and depth of health care services in rural communities.

Attachment

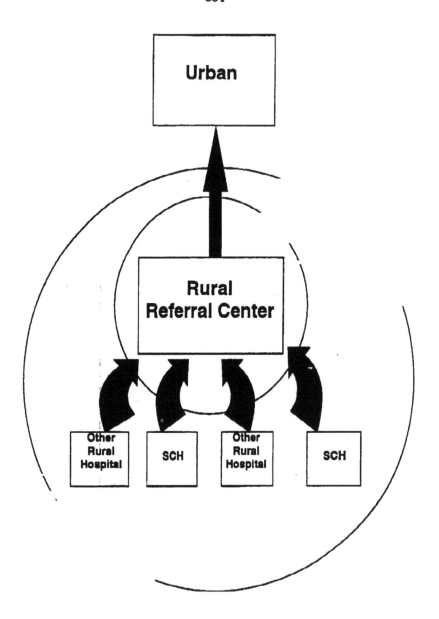

Rural Referral Center Groups

Group	Market Share for all Specialty Cases		Market Share for Vulnerable Cases	Specialty Market Area B&B Market Area Ratio	Number of Hospitals
A	>= 50%		>= 50%	>1.0	67
B(must have 2 out of 3)	>= 50		>= 50	> 1.0	26
C	> 33.33	or	> 33.33		92
D	-		-	-	71

Percent of Rural Referral Centers Providing Specialty Services

	A	B	C	D
CCU	27%	12%	26%	28%
ICU	99	92	97	99
Cardiac cath	39	38	45	61
Open heart surgery	9	4	14	25
Trauma	28	19	16	30
MRI	43	35	20	35
Radiation therapy	73	54	56	55
Outpatient surgery	99	96	100	100

County Characteristics of Rural Referral Centers

	A	B	C	D
Population density	101	106	93	102
Avg. Number of General Hospitals	1.6	2.8	1.8	2.2
Beds/1000 population	5.9	5.3	5.9	8.3
MDs/1000 population	1.5	1.3	1.5	2.3
Specialist/1000 population	0.4	0.3	0.4	0.7

Market Shares for Rural Rerral Centers

	A	B	C	D
"Bread and Butter"	77%	68%	56%	33%
Specialty Care	59	52	40	25
Vulnerable Cases	62	58	40	24

Specialty Market Area Characteristics

	A	B	C	D
Avg. number of other hospitals	1.1	1.7	3.2	6.1
Percent with:				
Teaching hospital	9%	12%	18%	31%
Other rural hospital	57	58	85	97
Another RRC	3	4	25	62
Avg. market area distance (in miles)	22.0	22.4	28.0	40.3
Avg. ratio of specialty market area to B&B market area	1.34	1.19	1.27	1.26

Financial Performance of Rural Referral Centers

	A	B	C	D
PPS margin	-6.03	-9.52	-1.69	-3.34
Total margin	5.45	6.04	6.34	6.93
Cost per case	$4374	$4509	$4231	$4766
Payment per case	4125	4117	4161	4612

RURAL REFERRAL CENTER LOCATIONS

Chairman STARK. I thank the witnesses.

Dr. Owen, I am going to come back just for 1 minute. You make reference in your written testimony and in your summary of it, I am not clear what your sense is on the proprietary operators of dialysis centers, as I refer to them. Is there anything magic about having a profit-making operator in this area?

Dr. OWEN. I do not have a problem with dialysis facility providers making a profit as long as the quality of delivered care is not just simply adequate, but is superlative.

Chairman STARK. How would the Harvard Medical School make a profit, just add to the tuition, cut their costs?

Dr. OWEN. Both. And/or.

Chairman STARK. Who would that serve besides the overseers?

In other words, what I can't quite understand is here you do have in fact, for all practical purposes, 100 percent government benefit available to 100 percent of the American people, which ought to have uniform standards if it does not. The profit element in there is not much that I can see except in there is a profit that ought to be reinvested, it seems to me, in a better standard for the patients. I really would like to—I have always felt that; I don't know why we should pay the DOD a profit.

In this particular area, we are the sole purchasers and any American figuratively qualifies to get this benefit without question; admittedly, there is some discrimination in the system. I am not sure there is anything wrong, but I don't see anything that says somehow we ought to build it into the system.

Dr. OWEN. If the impression from my statement was that it should be built into the system, I am not stating that. But a practical reality of practicing medicine in America—the practical reality of living in America is that the penetration of dialysis facility providers in this country has increased with for-profit dialysis. They are a much smaller number of nonprofit providers.

If you look at where those nonprofit providers have located their facilities, most of those facilities are unfortunately in areas that are not particularly accessible for people who are poor, for people who are of color, for people who are rural.

Chairman STARK. Mr. Robinson has the same problem.

Dr. OWEN. In my mind, if I were to reward someone modestly for doing a good job, I have no problem with it. If it serves the purpose of my patients, and someone makes a profit from it, and it is modest and not an unreasonable profit, I have no problem with that if we have overlapping agendas.

If I implied in my testimony that I have a hidden agenda of expanding profits, I do not.

I will tell you my statements are relatively controversial within the nephrology community because the restructuring I have suggested, especially with a global reimbursement, that perhaps will influence the profits of nephrologists. I think it will improve care.

Chairman STARK. Problems have come up from over utilization and fraud in the profit community; maybe your problems with quality come up in the nonprofit community.

There is no real reason that profit-making operators should be required to do the socially responsible thing. They are supposed to make a profit and do the socially responsible thing by paying their taxes and letting us redistribute that to do the socially responsible thing. It seems to me the system isn't working that way, so there is lack of access in rural and inner city communities.

I would like to work with you on what we can do. It is our program, and I think if we don't do it right, then you are going to find people come in where there is a vacuum and they can make money doing it.

I appreciate your concerns.

The reasons for the cutbacks in reimbursement—AMGEN, they are unconscionable. The AMGEN Corp., to me, is despicable.

Dr. OWEN. They bother me as well.

Chairman STARK. It is unconscionable, and they give a bad name to the pharmaceutical industry for jacking up the price. Those are the kinds of people that give us a problem and the only way we can deal with it is to cut the payment for everybody. As you say, that can really impact on people who least need it.

I appreciate your concern, and I hope we can be part of the improvement of the process and not cause problems.

Dr. OWEN. It sounds as if we have overlapping agendas, sir.

Chairman STARK. You were a lot kinder to us in your testimony than you should have been.

Mr. Thomas.

Mr. THOMAS. Thank you, Mr. Chairman.

Mr. Robinson I want to assure you that your concerns in terms of rural areas in whatever health plan passes have my complete attention. Although I am from California, I represent a portion of California without a lot of folks in it. I am up against the Sierra Nevada Mountains, and we are not only rural, we are hundreds of miles rural. We have been dealing with some of the problems you have and there is no competitive model that allows us to deliver decent health care. We have moved into some clinics, and we have been able to integrate, and we are very excited about the new electronic stuff that allows us to link up, where some of these doctors get some ongoing reward and service and assistance.

That is going to be a major component no matter what we do. In fact, that is one of the things that I think is overdue in attempting to get a handle on what we are going to do and how we are going to do it, because everybody is looking for some kind of information.

Dr. Owen, one of your points was enhance the retrieval and reporting of socioeconomic data. We need all kinds of data on all kinds of groups with all kinds of practices to be able to make rational decisions as to where to spend our money. Right now, we just throw it.

Do you have any comparative study information? Have you looked at this in terms of other societies? Is there a sufficient population of color in Canada, for example, to make comparisons?

I don't know if we can find comparable data on size and relative quality?

Dr. OWEN. A very insightful question. My immediate response is, no there isn't comparable data for populations of color. Certainly we are accumulating the morbidity and mortality data for comparable industrialized countries with ESRD programs.

One of the criticisms of studies that compare mortality in the United States as compared to Europe, where the mortalities are over half what they are in the United States, "you just put sicker patients on dialysis in the United States."

We are getting that data together, and it doesn't appear to be that simple. In our study, we looked at 10,000 patients in the United States; we have a decade-old definition of what dialysis adequately is, and over half the physicians weren't providing adequate dialysis to these people.

Mr. THOMAS. We are having heated debates now about the President's plan, and we don't have a basis to operate on.

A final comment in terms of your summary: How do we explain that those who are wealthy have a greater chance to enjoy a longer life than those who are not? My goal is to build a floor and make sure that anyone who operates in a system gets minimally adequate care, and not to put a ceiling to deny those who have the ability to get it.

This is a great quote, but if you haven't read Richard Corey in a while, by Edward R. Robinson, the rich have their problems, as well, including putting bullets through their heads. This is nice, but it doesn't advance the cause in terms of where we are trying to go very much.

Dr. Dugan, Mr. Robbins, Dr. Champion, we all focus on whether it should be the employer paying. I have an individual mandate in the Chafee-Thomas bill because I think that is a better way to go, through IRS. One of the items I am trying to get more information on is that as we talk about making what I guess are secondary changes in most of the bills—the areas of malpractice, of antitrust reform, in any of the things that you folks have been doing—either from a hospital point of view or from trying to build networks, have you bumped up against areas in the law, either antitrust or malpractice that you could offer some insight on the need to make changes because you simply bumped up against it and it didn't make sense and you had to go in a different direction?

Dr. DUGAN. Indiana has a model malpractice law which caused all physicians to have low malpractice rates.

Mr. THOMAS. How long has it been in effect?

Dr. DUGAN. Well over 10 years.

Mr. THOMAS. California just passed a malpractice law—and we are now getting some experience under it.

Dr. DUGAN. It seems to me that relative to all of these things, if we aren't able to deliver quality service because we don't have the trenches full of the doctors to do that, we can't possibly save money in order to pay for universal access to care.

Mr. THOMAS. Obviously we have got to reverse the ratio of specialists to primary care. Is there much that we can do from the other end; that is, highly skilled professionals who aren't doctors, R.N.s and others? Is there something we can do to close the gap in the middle to move those folks out as well as to redirect specialists?

Dr. DUGAN. I think that there is no question that physician's assistants are important people. I would like to preserve the doctor-patient relationship, and I want to preserve filling the trenches with quality doctors who are able to be health care tour directors for families and individuals.

I think we spend an awful lot of unnecessary money in the last years of life, and if we had these primary care doctors—not just in rural areas; the urban areas are some of the most needful places. What we have to do is find the mechanism to incentivize young men and women to go into primary care medicine, and I don't think it is all that hard.

Mr. THOMAS. Obviously, we have to begin focusing, and hopefully, with restructuring malpractice on a national basis, we can get people to focus more on the quality of life instead of pure quantity of life, because that is soaking up a lot of dollars. You folks have to do your share in terms of making choices and indicating that you won't do certain things, but that is another subject matter.

My concern is that in trying to talk with doctors, especially younger doctors, I find they are more than willing to take lower compensation for maintaining responsibility.

Frankly, it is a positive thing for me that the idea of "I don't care who makes the decisions, let the MBA run the place, let me make all the money I want," is not the thing that I am hearing from these younger folks. They are willing to take fewer dollars, but they want the responsibility of professionalism they believe they have earned. That is a trade-off and something that we can work on in terms of the legislation.

Mr. ROBBINS. I am from Illinois just to the west of Indiana. I think there is something instructive in that geographic juxtaposition. The same year that the Indiana legislature passed its malpractice reform, 1975 or 1976, Illinois did the same. Unfortunately, our law was struck down by our Supreme Court. The Indiana law was upheld by its Supreme Court. Throughout the entire eastern border of Illinois there is a real shortage of obstetricians practicing in that section of Illinois because they can just as easily move across the border to Indiana. So I think we need national standards.

Mr. THOMAS. That is a graphic example, and I appreciate that, because I did not have that available.

Dr. CHAMPION. Back to your comment with respect to limited licensed practitioners, there clearly is a substantial opportunity for lowering the overall cost by inserting them a lot more into the practice of care. We see that even in the specialized centers. But I think, ultimately, with information systems, we have got to reduce the provider-patient ratio, whether or not it is through limited licensed practitioners required to give a unit of care.

If you think about it, when you break your leg and call an ambulance and you go to a hospital, you have all the operating room staff—we are talking 150 to 200 people—required to deliver your care. It is in reducing the ratio of individuals providing the specialty care and getting the efficiencies into the system. That is where I think we will see some major economies.

That is what you will see with organized regional trauma centers. Because the efficiency is honed.

Trauma centers are a good example of how concentrating a limited number a patients into fewer centers reduces the overall regional cost of care and improves the outcome because the individuals are better at providing it, and thus it is a very cost-effective maneuver.

Mr. THOMAS. But there you have antitrust problems oftentimes where people need to communicate with each other to make sure there is no duplication, that there is an acceptance and understanding of specialization in a particular area and a willingness to direct people for that reason, because in other areas they will direct them back to you.

In California, we have had some problem with antitrust, and with not being as effective as we would like to be in creating those centers of expertise. If we dictate from the top down that people other than doctors are going to perform various functions, I think you will find that doctors are much less willing to deal with that. I am trying to figure out a way that is partly bottom up, where you folks grow into that relationship, in part not just because of a professional understanding, but of a budgetary one, as well.

If we mandate it, it ain't going to happen or it is going to happen on paper, you are not going to get the positive, interactive relationship that is going to make it work.

Mr. CHAMPION. It is also very important to protect the regional centers that exist. Centers of excellence could be undermined considerably with Balkanization of systems. Burn centers, trauma centers, specialty pediatric referral centers, specialty cancer centers like Sloan-Kettering, draw from huge catchment areas, and their role in health care reform has to be protected in some fashion.

Mr. THOMAS. A final question, partly the purpose we are here: Don't you believe that that is threatened more so by the President's alliance concept in which we fundamentally restructure everything? Isn't there a greater threat to what we have that is really working well now with that kind of a wholesale restructuring versus some kind of a voluntary arrangement in which people grow into these relationships because they make sense?

Dr. CHAMPION. I think that either way would work, provided there are Federal guidelines in place so that certain facets of care are not neglected across State boundaries. I feel that the Federal Government cannot not be involved in drawing parameters within which these relationships are refashioned.

Mr. THOMAS. Thank you very much.

Thank you, Mr. Chairman.

Chairman STARK. Mr. Kleczka.

Mr. KLECZKA. I thank the panel for their testimony. Not only do you bring forth some problems with the current health care system, but you are bold enough to bring solutions along, and that is what we are in need of here.

I wish you all could have been here yesterday. We had an all-day hearing in this room on the issue of the employer mandate. After listening to hours and hours of testimony, you would think we were talking about two different health systems or two different issues. Many of the witnesses yesterday—some with a financial stake in the status quo—came forward, and naturally ridiculed the President's proposal. They came with no solutions and indicated to the committee that if we leave the system alone, it will be better.

I agree with you that some changes need to be made, whether you call it a "crisis" or a "serious problem"; nevertheless, the national focus is on the issue. When the iron is hot, you strike; and now is the time for Congress to move on it.

Dr. Dugan, I was especially interested in your testimony because the Clinton bill does provide some movement in the area of primary care physicians. It is amazing that we have only about 20 percent primary care providers; Canada has the reverse. In the bill the President introduced, there are incentives for young men and women in med school to choose the primary care course, one of which is medical reimbursement.

You are aware of the President's proposal. Do you have any other recommendations to this committee where we could possibly strengthen that section and encourage our young people to go into primary care?

Dr. DUGAN. I think that one of the traditions in medicine reimbursement has been that cognitive skills have never been reimbursed very well. You have to do some glitzy procedure in order to make a lot of money from medicine.

What has happened is that primary care people don't get reimbursed for cognitive skills. The Harvard RBRBS system was a marvelous idea that really has not been brought to appropriate fruition. Somehow, we have to be able to reimburse cognitive skills.

I think when you do, that doctors are not going to have to own things and sell shoes and do all sorts of silly things that are probably unethical and ridiculous. If you can reimburse cognitive skills adequately, then you are not going to have these problems.

In terms of how you get more young people to go into primary care medicine, it is a money thing. You need to increase the stipend for doctors going into primary care medicine and reduce those going into specialty care a little bit. The money will dictate young people going in. If you get somebody that goes into family practice or internal medicine and they turn around and want to be a cardiologist, make them pay the money back with interest.

Once you have them into the system, incentivize the distribution all over the country with tax credits for going to Frankfort, Ind., or something like that. I don't really think it is very hard.

Mr. KLECZKA. Do you not have a current program where you go to the clinics versus the large hospital setting and retrain or train primary care physicians?

Dr. DUGAN. I think that is a waste of time. It takes 3 years to make people good primary care doctors.

Mr. KLECZKA. What is a waste of time?

Dr. DUGAN. Retraining is a waste of time. We need to make specialists more productive so that if we fill the trenches with more primary care doctors, then you have got to figure out how specialists can transfer their technology to these doctors. Specialists hold that information dearly.

They say I am the only one who can treat a person who has a heart attack or something like that. That is ridiculous. We need to support primary care doctors with our information exchanges, our technology transfer. We need to get the word to the herd so they can do a better job of taking care of their patients. If you don't do that at the point of need, it isn't ever going to happen very well.

Dr. CHAMPION. From the point of view of the specialist with respect to this, because I am a specialist——

Dr. DUGAN. I am, too.

Dr. CHAMPION. I am not entirely convinced that many of my colleagues are in the practice of medicine for money. I want to put on the record that many and most physicians are not motivated by money in going into the practice of medicine or doing primary care versus cardiology. It is the interest in technical skills that draw people into cardiology or cardiac surgery where it is possible to make a large amount of money.

I certainly believe that the cognitive skills of the primary physician need to be bolstered, and probably some of the specialists make too much money, but the most important thing is to unburden the practice of medicine in this country.

I speak with knowledge of medical practice throughout the world. The paperwork and the exposure to malpractice here is quite vicarious compared with England, Australia, Germany, anywhere——

Mr. KLECZKA. Those side issues don't determine whether doctors are going to go into a primary care or a specialty.

Dr. CHAMPION. They——

Mr. KLECZKA. In fact, if you look at the malpractice problem, which some have tried to exacerbate, if I were in med school looking at who is getting sued out there, I would go into primary care. So I don't buy the argument necessarily.

But you think our 80–20 mix—80 percent 20 percent mix in this country is smart?

Dr. CHAMPION. It certainly is, in effect, excessive compared to other countries. There is no doubt there are too many specialists here. But the amount of time an individual primary care physician spends in the enjoyable practice of medicine versus these other tasks, is also excessive. And you can make medicine a much more enjoyable practice by unburdening it, and that is why a lot of individuals like to go into organizations where all of those responsibilities are not on them as individuals but on an organization.

Mr. KLECZKA. We have a couple in the legislature here. Anyone else?

Dr. Owen.

Dr. OWEN. I am going to throw a comment in from the perspective of being at the medical schools, and I do not want to down play the role of the professors—the role models while these young people are training. Within the medical schools and the professional societies, and at the professional meetings, very often the role model is a subspecialist, the high-powered physician who is doing a procedure.

There is certainly at my medical school, at my former medical school, and at the medical schools that I visit, a tremendous bias against the primary care physician or the family practitioner. They're looked down upon—the professors look down the end of their noses at these physicians.

Certainly, we need to clean up our own shop in the medical schools. We need to impress upon young people training, that great doctors are physicians who are out in the field practicing; physicians who are doing these less glamorous specialties. How does one do that, how does one encourage the professors to do something?

You reward the medical schools that produce the most number of people who enter the primary care field.

Mr. KLECZKA. Good idea.

Thank you.

Mr. ROBINSON. I have one comment in the rural areas, not only is it hard to get doctors to enter primary care but to get doctors doing primary care in the rural areas is another issue. There are only so many doctors who want to hunt and fish. But the system has reimbursed doctors at higher levels in the urban areas. When a doctor goes to medical school in an urban area, it is much easier to stay in that urban area than to move to the rural areas, unless they have some ties to that area.

Mr. KLECZKA. We found that to be true in the State of Wisconsin when we talked about building our own veterinary school. And the hue and cry was, "we need the vet school in Wisconsin because of the number of farm animals." In fact, once it opened we found that the veterinarian who graduates does not want to live in Sobieski, Wis., getting up at 2 o'clock to do the afterbirth on a dairy cow but would rather do poodles in Greendale, Wis., or Brookfield, where it is a much nicer lifestyle.

And to follow up on that, the kids who came out of school to practice on large animals were the ones who came from rural settings. Good point.

Thank you.

We do have the vet school now, too.

Mr. THOMAS. Would the gentleman yield briefly?

Mr. KLECZKA. On the vet school?

Mr. THOMAS. One thing we found also in terms of the rural areas, we might as well be honest, when we bring in really competent people who are excited about working in rural areas, they bring along most often their wives, sometimes their husbands, and this is simply not the kind of lifestyle for a spouse, based upon their anticipation and what they thought their life was going to be. And that has been a major problem for us, especially in California, when they could move 200 miles away and be in the Bay area or down in the Los Angeles basin.

And so let's also be honest, it is the whole lifestyle structure of those folks who, although they may not want to make all that much money, they want to have cultural and artistic and other entertainment factors that are simply not available sometimes in the rural areas.

Mr. KLECZKA. The solution to that problem is to mandate in that legislation that you marry someone from the same community.

Mr. THOMAS. Or marry someone who doesn't have very expensive tastes, cultural or entertainment interests.

Chairman STARK. Mr. Hoagland.

Mr. HOAGLAND. Mr. Chairman, I don't know where this conversation is wandering, but let me tell you, in Nebraska we have avoided the med school trap. We send our students with a State subsidy to places like Champagne, or Urbana, and don't have that overhead. We went through that in the Nebraska Legislature for a couple of years.

I think those of you who have addressed it have made an excellent case for more primary care physicians.

Dr. Dugan, your statement is readable in outline form. Let me tell you, I appreciate that as well. But the issue we have to deal with here is what is the best way to get there. And I would be interested, Dr. Dugan, in your opinion as to whether we should follow the administration plan, and I am oversimplifying when I try to summarize it, and probably inaccurate, but the administration, as I understand it, would set up a national commission that would allocate to each of the medical schools around the country specialty slots and primary care slots. Places like the University of Nebraska, where we have thrived on liver transplants and bone marrow transplants, would feel the enormous competition among the medical schools for who gets the more specialty slots.

The other approach is the managed competition approach, and I want to ask Mr. Robinson about this in 1 minute, where we would help establish accountable health providers that would compete with one another based on price and quality, and the physicians and administrators of those accountable health providers would then pay salaries to physicians based on profitability. So, essentially, the market would determine how many specialists we have and how many primary care physicians we have.

It turns out we have too many neurologists in Omaha, they don't get jobs and they go someplace else.

Are you more comfortable, Dr. Dugan, with a national commission saying we are going to have so many people in this area, in that area, or would you rather see us set up a system where market forces could make those choices?

Dr. DUGAN. I would like us to have market forces dictate the distribution of doctors. I think if you get enough primary care doctors in place, that the market force will dictate how many of the specialists that you need and I think that when—I think that you can use the incentives of just money to create any kind of distribution that you want.

If you want primary care medicine, you got to pay for it. And I think that in terms of distribution, you can incentivize distribution. While it may have to do with arts and culture and everything like that, I still think it is money first, and I think that in the rural areas doctors are working hard with all the paperwork, the bureaucracy, the regulatory stuff, and they make much less money and it its very unsatisfying.

Surveys have absolutely shown that primary care doctors really don't like their lot anymore. We have got to change that. We have got to make primary care medicine No. 1 in our medical schools. And I really believe that when we can do that, and then transfer the support to the primary care doctor once he gets out there, or she, that will solve the problem. I would not like it to be regulated.

Chairman STARK. Would the gentleman yield?

Mr. HOAGLAND. Sure.

Chairman STARK. We have got market forces now, don't we? We just don't like what the market is doing. Aren't there market forces now?

Dr. DUGAN. The market forces are money and the money goes to the high-procedure specialists.

Mr. HOAGLAND. You agree with that, Mr. Robinson?

Mr. ROBINSON. Yes, we do.

Chairman STARK. You just don't have enough money to bring the doctors into the rural area.

Mr. ROBBINS. In California, there is the development of integrated health care delivery systems where primary care physicians are very much in demand.

Chairman STARK. Look, I don't want to make a case between HMOs or fee-for-service, I am just saying there is a market force out there now. Kaiser is paying $125,000 a year for a family physician, not shabby for a starting salary, and they can't get enough. They will probably have to raise the rates. The market is there, it is just that many of us don't like the results. We just don't like the fact that the market has made these decisions; right, Dr. Dugan?

Dr. DUGAN. I think that primary care doctors are second-class citizens now.

Chairman STARK. Because the market isn't paying them enough; right?

Mr. HOAGLAND. But Dr. Dugan, your point is there are a number of things we can do make the market work better, like setting up accountable health providers.

Chairman STARK. That is government regulations.

Mr. HOAGLAND. Rather than superimposing upon this market, that didn't work very well, an administrative body that says in Illinois we are going to have seven neurologists this year and we are going to have three neurologists and seven primary care physicians next year.

Dr. DUGAN. I would really take the distribution of specialists we have now and proportionately reduce all of them and then let market forces dictate if we need more emergency room doctors, which is I think a wave of the future in all of our rural hospitals, to really have good ones that are trained.

Mr. HOAGLAND. Thank you.

Mr. Chairman, I have a series of questions I would like to ask Mr. Robbins, but I see the red light is on. Might I just have 1 minute or 2?

Chairman STARK. Go right ahead.

Mr. HOAGLAND. I won't prolong this.

Mr. Robbins, I am interested in your statement. First of all, the Illinois Hospital Association position tracks the American, as I take it from your comments here.

Mr. ROBBINS. That is correct.

Mr. HOAGLAND. I see, first of all, you call for health alliances that are limited to an administrative role and don't have the heavy regulatory powers that the administration's bill would give them?

Mr. ROBBINS. Yes, sir.

Mr. HOAGLAND. The administration's plan supports cooperatives for small businesses and individuals, so would you be willing to draw the line below businesses of 5,000?

Mr. ROBBINS. No, the details of our plan would suggest that employers of 100 or more should have the opportunity to join purchasing cooperatives.

Mr. HOAGLAND. One hundred or less. Should they be required to join purchasing or can we work this in a way that the purchasing alliances are voluntary?

Mr. ROBBINS. The purchasing alliances are voluntary but we do require under our plan that every employer provide insurance to his employees just as we require that every individual obtain insurance.

Mr. HOAGLAND. Right. That sounds like the legislation Mr. Cooper has introduced. I mean, it has that provision in it.

Mr. ROBBINS. I guess I would judge on the spectrum that it is somewhere between Mr. Cooper and President Clinton's proposal.

Mr. HOAGLAND. Now, point 2 here, it looks like on page 2 of your statement, you are resisting price controls, you criticize global budgeting and indicate that you don't think that works very well. You are real concerned about continuing to cut reimbursement for hospitals for Medicare and Medicaid patients and so you are not big on price controls, it sounds like, if I read this right?

Mr. ROBBINS. You read it correctly.

Mr. HOAGLAND. Point 3, you know, I think universal coverage and particularly insurance market reforms are very important goals for us to achieve this year if we can. Can we do that without an employer mandate or does there have to be some sort of employer mandate?

And in your summary point 2, you say, responsible health care financing with requirements for employer and individual participation.

What sort of requirements? Do you mean the 80 percent the administration proposes or what are you talking about?

Mr. ROBBINS. I don't think the issue is so much in the details of whether it is 80 percent or 85 percent. But I do think that there needs to be a structure that is built on the system that we now have and the system we now have for most Americans relies on employer-based insurance, and so I think that we need to—in order to get to universal coverage, include all of those employers out there who are not currently providing it and who cause employers who do provide it to subsidize the failure of the other employers who do not provide it.

Mr. HOAGLAND. You know, presumably if we pass legislation that includes incentives to draw people into this system, tax deductibility for small businesses or sole practitioners, offer to pay the premiums for the poor and the near poor, we can cut the number of uninsureds way down, can't we, without all the negatives of the employer-mandate scheme with its subsidies and its 7.9 percent cap and everything else that is in the administration proposal?

Mr. ROBBINS. I think you can clearly improve the current situation and stop short of employer mandates. But if your goal is to achieve universal coverage, then I think an employer mandate is required.

Mr. HOAGLAND. OK. Thank you.

Thank you, Mr. Chairman.

Mr. THOMAS. Just a final comment on this business of dollars driving the process. It is a poor analogy, but nevertheless, I think it is one that is useful coming from my area in terms of academia, that it sounds a little bit like the third grade teacher, that you know they are the most important ones, and if we paid them more, the educational system would be better.

Let me tell you as far as my experience is concerned, if you paid me more as a third grade teacher than you did as doing graduate seminars, I would do the graduate seminars because of the cognitive aspects and my interest in that.

Dr. Champion's point, I think, is one that needs to be taken.

Having said that, we need to pay elementary teachers more, we need to pay primary care folk more, but that is not the complete answer. There is a degree of challenge and interest and we wouldn't want to lose those kinds of qualities either.

Dr. CHAMPION. Mr. Thomas, if I could come back on that on another issue, because the down side of this is that, and I will quote from an example: Recently in a Midwestern State where a colleague of my operated on an 11-year-old boy for a gunshot wound of the belly, and these things, as we know, are occurring on a daily basis in this country, the day after he did this specialty surgery, he was requested to transfer the patient out of the trauma center to another hospital, to the care of a pediatrician, the primary care provider. We need to protect the quality of care in this whole process and things like that, which are occurring on a daily basis, are transgressing acceptable standards of care and somehow, in some way, we need to keep a balance in this whole initiative.

Mr. THOMAS. Thank you.

Chairman STARK. I thank the panel for their testimony.

We will continue with testimony from our next panel composed of Michael Gemmell, who is the executive director of the Association of Schools of Public Health; Dr. Jonathan Fielding, on behalf of the Partnership for Prevention; Hon. Harold Hughes, former Senator from Iowa who will testify on life after a legislative career; Hon. Moses Carey, chair of the Subcommittee on Public and Environmental Health of the National Association of Counties; Dr. Martin Wasserman, health officer of Prince George's County, Md., on behalf of the National Association of County Health Officials.

Welcome to the committee, gentlemen. And we will ask Senator Hughes if he would like to lead off this morning.

STATEMENT OF HON. HAROLD E. HUGHES, FOUNDER AND CHAIRMAN, SOCIETY OF AMERICANS FOR RECOVERY

Senator HUGHES. Mr. Chairman, thank you very much for the privilege and honor of appearing before the subcommittee and the members of the committee. I am deeply grateful for this opportunity.

I would like to inform the committee that I am hearing impaired and don't hear very well, so if you make a statement to me, make sure I understand it.

Chairman STARK. Senator, let me advise you and all the other witnesses, that our committee is still in the 19th century as we approach the 21st century relative to technology. And if all of you, including the members, would remember you have to swallow these microphones before anybody in the room can hear you, so I will try and if all the witnesses would like to get very close to the microphones, it will help all of us.

Thank you.

Senator HUGHES. Thank you very much.

I am appearing here on behalf of primarily myself as a recovering alcoholic and addict and as the president of the Society of Americans for Recovery, and on behalf, through them, of the millions of Americans who suffer from addiction disease and specifically on behalf of the 7 to 10 million of us who identify ourselves as being recovered from these diseases and who have operated functionally and well for long periods of time in our society.

I am a qualified representative of each of these communities. Some of you may be familiar with my story. I was incarcerated in six States for behavior connected with my addiction and served 6 years as Iowa's U.S. Senator and three terms as Iowa's Governor. I commemorate 40 years of personal abstinence from my drug of choice, which is alcohol, on Thursday of next week.

We consider here today an opportunity of profound impact on all who suffer from chemical dependency and all Americans who are touched by the grief, the terror, and the cost of these diseases.

The nature, scale, and consequence of untreated addiction in our society can no longer be held at bay. We must face hard economic and social realities that result from these diseases.

There will be no reductions in our soaring cost of health care, in my opinion, until we attend to the nearly $300 billion annual cost we as a society tolerate from the consequences of untreated addiction disease. Untreated addiction disease in America is a major health disaster. We are the earthquake in the health care scenario.

There are 24 million alcohol and drug addicts in the United States today. Alcohol and drugs are the No.1 cause of illness, injury, and death. More than 80 percent of all incarcerated people under the age of 35 are there as a result of their alcohol or other drug use.

A rational, comprehensive, national treatment program is our key to stabilizing the economy, reducing health care costs, returning our labor force to productivity, cutting back the welfare rolls and controlling crime and violence in our communities.

The literature consistently demonstrates that treatment for alcoholism and drug addiction is enormously successful and cost-effective. Health care costs and costs to society decline significantly following treatment of alcoholism, both for the chemically dependent person and for the members of his or her family.

The average cost of alcoholism treatment can be recovered within 3 years after treatment is initiated, in medical utilization savings for the addict alone. And by 4 or 5 years after treatment, health care costs for that entire family will fall to lower than the average of other families and stay there. The most conservative studies indicate that for every dollar spent for the direct treatment of addiction, society saves nearly $10 in health care costs, crime, accidents, and job performance.

A government that shortchanges substance abuse treatment and prevention is not serious, in my opinion, about reducing health care costs. A government that shortchanges substance abuse treatment and prevention is not serious about reducing crime. A government that shortchanges substance abuse treatment and prevention loses our best shot at significant and long-term economic growth.

Congress must pass health care reform that recognizes the relationship between addiction treatment and prevention of later heart disease, liver collapse, accidents, crime and a host of other tragic and costly outcomes.

We must begin to treat addiction as the primary chronic health threat that it is and not as a moral issue or mental health problem. Require every health plan to use standard diagnosis and functional impairment criteria, removing stipulations that currently leave plan managers free to determine eligibility. Legislate a minimum benefit for substance abuse treatment that is guaranteed to be available to those who meet eligible criteria. And require all substance abuse treatment and case management decisions to be made by professionals who are licensed or certified in alcohol and other drug treatment.

We must have a benefits package that takes into account the lifelong implications of untreated addiction, the expensive deaths most of these lives entail, and the proven savings in general health care utilization that occur with high-impact, life-changing strategies for prevention, intervention, and treatment.

These are not expensive provisions. The actuarial information being used to suggest cutting addiction disease benefits is based on the potential of all current alcoholics and drug addicts using these benefits this year. We should be so lucky.

Sadly, less than 1 percent of those eligible for treatment through insurance or Medicaid actually seek medical help. If that number rose to even 30 percent, the positive impact financially on America would be tremendous.

So, please, don't be put off by misleading projections. Act instead for a stigma-free, recovery-oriented society. The actions we propose will save billions of dollars, will make genuine health care cost containment available in this century, will save millions of lives and will reduce the impact and threat on law enforcement and the necessity of spending billions of dollars in other areas of public safety.

Thank you, Mr. Chairman for this brief analysis of the testimony I presented.

Chairman STARK. Thank you very much, Senator.

[The prepared statement follows:]

352

For release 11:00 a.m. Friday, February 4, 1994

Testimony of
Senator Harold E. Hughes (Ret.)
Founder & Chairman of
Society of Americans for Recovery
Before U.S. House of Representatives
Subcommittee on Health
The Honorable Pete Stark, Chair
February 4, 1994

Mr. Chairman, I am grateful and honored to appear here today on behalf of the millions of Americans who suffer from addiction disease; on behalf of all Americans, who as taxpayers pay an extraordinary percentage of our income to support untreated addictions; and specifically on behalf of the seven to ten million Americans who today have moved beyond their personal addiction histories and enjoy new life in what we know as recovery.

I am a qualified representative of each of these communities. Many of you are familiar with my story, much of which is public record. I have experienced life at both ends of the spectrum: I was incarcerated in six states for behavior connected with my addiction, and I served six years as Iowa's United Senate Senator across the Hill here. Next week, I commemorate 40 years of abstinence from my drug of choice, which is alcohol.

We consider here today an opportunity of profound impact on all who suffer from chemical dependency, and all Americans who are touched by the grief, the terror, and the cost of these diseases. We have the opportunity to take the third and most important step in history toward conquering a plague — and demolishing a pernicious myth — that has deformed mankind since the beginning of civilization.

If we as a nation take this step, I will have lived to experience each of these historic steps.

The first major step was the founding of Alcoholics Anonymous in 1935. The ability of one alcoholic to be in service to another, thereby penetrating the wall of isolation, fear, and denial associated with the alcoholic obsession, generated a new hope for alcoholics and their families.

Alcoholics Anonymous has been called the greatest spiritual movement of the 20th Century. But equally important, the success of this movement has impacted psychology, sociology, and medicine, in broadly promoting the understanding of addiction as a primary, chronic disease, not a bad habit.

In 1970, I was happy and proud to be a channel for our nation to acknowledge for the first time the disease nature of addiction. The Hughes Act established a federal role for attention to alcohol and drug dependency. It also fostered development of treatment and prevention disciplines in the private sector. This was the second great step forward for America and its attitudes toward addiction disease.

The advent of national health care reform offers a unique and timely opportunity for America to make the third and most important step: To face addiction disease as a major public health threat and provide this nation with an appropriate public health response.

The nature, scale, and consequences of untreated addiction in our society can no longer be held at bay by programs driven by social conscience or the politics of "doing good." Instead, we must face hard economic and social realities:

> There will be no reductions in our soaring cost of health care until we attend
> to the nearly $300 billion annual cost we as a society tolerate for the conse-
> quences of untreated addiction.[1]

Let me share with you a little of the economics of addiction disease. While most Americans have ambivalent attitudes — at best — and erroneous or incomplete knowledge of addiction disease, the facts speak bluntly: Untreated addiction disease in America today is a major health disaster. We are the earthquake in the health care scenario.

- There are approximately 18 million alcoholics and 6 million drug addicts in the United States today.[2]

- Alcohol and drugs are the number-one cause of illness, injury, and death in the United States.[3] Alcohol is a factor in approximately half of all homicides, suicides, and motor vehicle fatalities.[4] Deaths from alcohol-related causes took an average of 28 years from each victim's life.[5] Alcohol abuse and dependence is the most common chronic illness between the ages of 18 and 44; drug abuse and dependence is the second.[6]

- From 25 to 40 percent of patients in general hospital beds are being treated for complications of alcoholism. Seventy-five percent of trauma victims test positive for drug use.[7]

- The majority of people in our jails and prisons today are drug abusers or addicts. The link between drugs and crime is especially clear: more than 80 percent of all incarcerated people under the age of 35 are illicit drug users,[8] and 61 percent of all federal prisoners are drug offenders.[9] Incarceration alone costs us over $7 billion. All together, alcohol and drug abuse and addiction cost us $43 billion in legal and indirect costs other than health care (see table 1).[10]

- Fetal alcohol syndrome affects nearly 2 in every 1,000 American births and as many as 25% of all Native American births. The direct cost of treating these baby victims is about $75 million. Between 350,000 and 625,000 infants are drug-exposed each year. Indirect costs for those infants, including lost worker productivity, will reach $1.4 billion by 1997[11]

- Twenty percent of all AIDS cases in the United States today, and 20 percent of the costs to care for those people (about $13 billion in 1991), are the result of intravenous drug use. And that proportion is growing.[12]

These numbers reflect only glimpses of the drain on our society that addiction in America perpetrates. A rational, comprehensive national treatment program is our key to a stable economy, the reduction of health care costs, the return of large segments of our labor force to productivity (and the related decrease in the welfare rolls), the control of crime in our communities, and the elimination of runaway violence.

This is not a job for America to face after we have solved the really big problems of health care, economic growth, and crime. It is a job that must be faced in order to reach our goals of universal health care, sustained economic growth, and safety in our homes, schools, and streets.

As a society, however, we balk at facing these facts. Why this reticence? Why this denial? Why do we Americans prefer to tolerate unbelievable costs, unspeakable behavior, and unconscionable human waste to support the most addicted society on the face of the earth?

To shed some light on these questions, consider the politics surrounding addiction disease.

While alcoholic beverages pre-date recorded history, the invention of distillation in the 14th century made possible increased concentrations of alcohol — from 14 percent to more than 50 percent. The introduction of spirits such as gin, whiskey, and scotch soon caused much higher levels of abuse and alcoholism, and the social problems that go along with them.

The stigma often associated with alcoholism was firmly enshrined in 1609 with the first attempt to legislate moderation in drinking. The English Parliament passed in that year an "Act To Repress the Odious and Loathsome Sin of Drunkenness."

Table 1.
Legal and Indirect Costs (Other Than Health Care) Due to
Alcohol and Other Drug Problems ($ millions)

TYPE OF COST	TYPE OF SUBSTANCE ABUSE	
	ALCOHOL	OTHER DRUGS
Criminal Justice System		
Police Protection	$1,338	$5,810
Legal and Adjudication	274	1,108
State and Federal Prisons	884	2,130
Local Jails	1,238	460
Total CJS	3,734	9,508
Drug Traffic Control		
Prevention		175
Law Enforcement		1,380
Total Drug Traffic Control	-	1,555
Other Legal Costs		
Private Legal Defense	342	1,381
Property Destruction	175	759
Total Other Legal Costs	517	2,140
Other Direct Costs		
Motor Vehicle Accidents	2,584	
Fire Destruction	457	-
Social Welfare Administration	88	6
Total Other Direct Costs	3,129	6
Indirect Costs		
Victims of Crime	465	842
Incarceration	2,701	4,434
Crime Careers	-	13,976
Total Indirect Costs	3,166	19,252
TOTAL	$10,546	$32,461

Source: *Rice et al*, 1990

Dr. Benjamin Rush, a signer of the Declaration of Independence and a noted American physician, made a significant medical breakthrough in 1785, though it was not recognized as such at the time. His study led him to the then-radical conclusion that once an "appetite" for spirits had become fixed, the drinker was helpless. He suggested total abstinence as a remedy.

His findings, however, were ignored by the young nation, who continued either to ignore alcoholism or to "treat" it with righteous indignation and punitive measures, while continuing to be puzzled at the lack of results.

The seeds of our current crisis, however, stem from Dr. Rush's experience. Truth will not be denied, although the trail is often treacherous and misleading. The "cure" of abstinence is such a truth.

In 1919, we as a nation adopted the cure of abstinence — not just for those afflicted with alcoholism, but for everyone. The political disaster of this experience does not need to be documented here. But let me rescue two "truths" from this history which in their proper contexts are absolutely necessary in the public policy debate of today.

The first truth is that abstinence is the current best solution for those individuals who suffer from addiction disease. While severe abuse of chemicals can result in addiction, most addiction is traceable to a biogenetic predisposition. Suffering is triggered by consumption of an addictive drug. But the condition is in place, and inherited.

The second truth is that all citizens must participate in solutions to addiction — not by participating in abstinence, but in refusing to tolerate the high costs, unsocial behavior, and archaic ignorance associated with alcoholism and other drug addictions.

The political reality and the factual reality are not in line with each other. But I believe that they are closer that most people think. And I believe that action by this Congress, based on clear, compelling, and accurate information, can create a lasting solution and hope for our nation.

I believe Americans have assimilated many of the key facts relating to addiction disease. There is great understanding of the simple fact that while millions can safely drink alcohol, approximately ten percent of our population lose any ability to control use of chemical mood changers.

I believe there is a greater climate for the reduction of the stigma associated with addiction, together with an acceptance of intervention techniques and less tolerance for antisocial behaviors resulting from abusive or addictive use.

I believe average Americans are beginning to understand wellness. More and more citizens know someone who is recovering from addiction. Just as each practicing alcoholic or addict affects an average of five other individuals, a person living in recovery also affects others in a positive way — demonstrating that wellness is achievable as well as desirable.

I believe American voters are tired of the politics of denial. They will respond to the reality of helping themselves by helping those in addiction.

The President's initiative presents the Congress with a unique opportunity to recraft health care as we know it. This recrafting will be successful to the degree that we are willing to look beyond myths and half-truths to seek solid facts.

One of the most important myths to expose is that treatment for addiction disease is an expensive and ineffective "add-on" to health care that will send taxpayer's costs sky-high. In fact, "cherry picking" by insurers and providers — the selective offloading of people who have pre-existing conditions or who simply change jobs — has obscured the reality that treatment for alcoholism and other drug addiction has been enormously successful and cost-effective. The truth is that once providers are faced with the ultimate costs of untreated diseases of any kind, prevention and early treatment will become immensely popular. This will certainly be true of addiction disease.

Virtually all the literature consistently demonstrates that total health care costs for untreated addicts are significantly higher than for non-addicts, and those costs "ramp up" at an extreme rate as the addict's untreated disease grows more severe. But health care costs and costs to society (for example, legal problems and problems on the job) also decline significantly following treatment of alcoholism, both for the chemically dependent person and for his or her family (see figures 1 and 2).

The average cost of alcoholism treatment can be recovered within three years after treatment is initiated, in medical utilization savings for the addict alone. And by four or five years after treatment, health care costs for the treated addict and family fall to lower than the average, and stay there. In other words, the initial costs of treatment are more than offset by the savings in health services not used (see figure 3).

Our opportunity is to look at these facts now and to build a public health response to addiction as we have historically done for polio, heart disease, tuberculosis, and AIDS.

This is not a feel-good or social benefit issue. At this time, and in this climate, we ask for hard-nosed, resource-based decision making.

What this means is that the benefits package for addiction disease cannot be the minimum level of care for today's symptoms and behaviors. We must have a benefits package that takes into account the life-long implications of untreated addiction, the

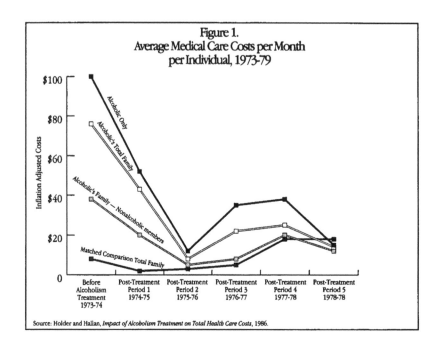

Figure 1.
Average Medical Care Costs per Month
per Individual, 1973-79

Source: Holder and Hallan, *Impact of Alcoholism Treatment on Total Health Care Costs*, 1986.

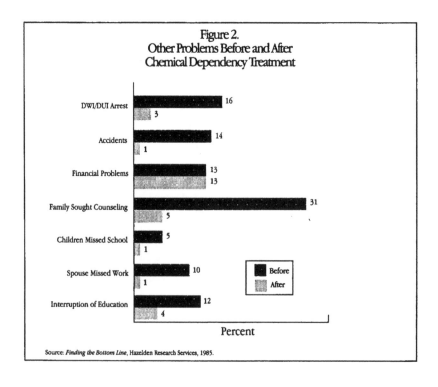

Figure 2.
Other Problems Before and After
Chemical Dependency Treatment

Source: *Finding the Bottom Line*, Hazelden Research Services, 1985.

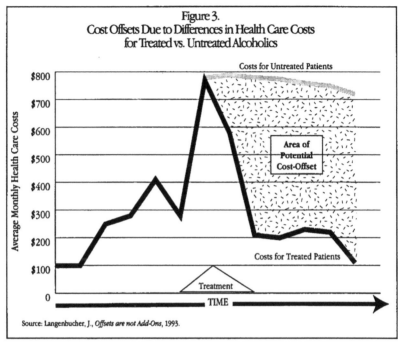

Figure 3.
Cost Offsets Due to Differences in Health Care Costs
for Treated vs. Untreated Alcoholics

Source: Langenbucher, J., *Offsets are not Add-Ons*, 1993.

expensive deaths most of these lives entail, and the proven savings in general health care utilization that occur with high-impact, life-changing strategies for prevention, intervention, and treatment.

The President's plan, though imaginative and clearly intent on broad and thorough coverage, fails to get over the barrier of fallacious actuarial considerations. The results are penny wise, but pound foolish. The most conservative studies indicate that for every $1 spent for the direct treatment of addiction, society saves nearly $10 in health care costs, crime, accidents, and job performance.[13]

A government that short-changes substance abuse treatment and prevention is not serious about reducing health care costs.

A government that short-changes substance abuse treatment and prevention is not serious about reducing crime.

A government that short-changes substance abuse treatment and prevention loses our best shot at significant and long-term economic growth.

To meet the opportunity I present today, Congress must pass health care reform which recognizes the relationship between addiction treatment and the prevention of later heart disease, liver collapse, accidents, crime, and a host of other tragic and costly outcomes. I offer you today some benchmark provisions that make that distinction. Without these provisions, we fail to connect care with ultimate savings. Without these provisions, we muddle along with band-aid cures but not substantial inroads into treating the 80 percent of our population who generate the costs but will not voluntarily look for a new way of life.

Here are the specific recommendations to strengthen the substance abuse benefit in the Health Security Act S. 1757/H.R. 3600:

1. Separate the substance abuse benefit from the mental health benefit. These are separate health issues and their treatment — and the cost of that treatment — is distinctly different. Pitting these disciplines against each other for use of benefit provisions is not in the interest of the patient.

2. Establish standard requirements for treatment, removing stipulations that currently leave plan managers free to determine eligibility. Establish standard eligibility criteria according to current standard diagnosis and functional impairment criteria.

3. Legislate a minimum benefit for substance abuse treatment that is guaranteed to be available to those who meet eligibility criteria. We recommend such a minimum to be consistent with most current health insurance and managed care health plans, i.e.,

   • 10 hours' assessment and intervention services

   • Detoxification as indicated by acute intoxication and/or withdrawal potential

   • 30 days' residential or inpatient rehabilitation (45 for adolescents)

   • 130 hours' outpatient treatment and/or aftercare

   If the scope of a national health care plan is to include prevention and long-term care traditionally funded through public sector block grants, we recommend that all limits on benefits be eliminated.

4. Treatment should be reimbursed on the level of care (i.e., inpatient, acute care, residential, outpatient) rather than on the setting.

5. Maintain funding for the Substance Abuse Block Grant and other federal programs and require states to maintain their investment in alcohol and other drug treatment. Public and private systems can be successfully integrated only when (1) universal coverage is achieved and (2) quality and outcomes data — not just costs — drive managed care decisions.

6. Eliminate cost sharing for alcohol and other drug treatment services or establish a sliding fee scale for the cost sharing requirement. Make any and all cost-sharing, co-pay, and deductible issues comparable to other diseases. Discriminatory practices to limit access under the argument that savings are achieved cannot be permitted.

7. Use the same utilization review and pretreatment authorization procedures for all services and replace the arbitrary substance abuse standards to be decided by each health plan with standard criteria, such as the Patient Placement Criteria for psychoactive Substance Abuse Disorders published by the American Society of Addiction Medicine. Without standard criteria, no comparison or study can be valid.

8. Specify uniform standards for assessment, patient satisfaction, and treatment outcome studies.

9. Require all substance abuse treatment and case management decisions, including precertification screening and utilization review, to be made by professionals who are licensed or certified in alcohol and other drug treatment.

10. Designate community-based alcohol and other drug programs as essential providers.

11. Allow for treatment outside the local health alliance at Centers of Excellence to ensure competition on the basis of quality and cost.

These are not expensive provisions. The actuarial information being used to suggest cutting addiction disease benefits is based on the potential of all current alcoholics and drug addicts using these benefits this year. We should be so lucky. Sadly, less than 1 percent of those eligible for treatment through insurance or Medicaid actually seek medical help.[14] If that number rose to even 30 percent, the positive financial impact on America would be tremendous.

So don't be put off by these misleading projections.

Act instead for a stigma-free, recovery-oriented society.

The actions we propose will save billions of dollars. It will make genuine health care cost containment achievable in this century.

It will also save lives. Millions of lives.

And it will recover our nation's collective ability to discover and seek the best in our people. We can move beyond survival. We can contemplate renewal. Of individuals. Of communities. Of nations. Of civilizations.

It is not too much to ask that we do the things which make good business sense and at the same time ensure the greatness of our country.

Notes

1. James W. Langenbucher, Barbara S. McCrady, John Brick, and Richard Esterly *Socioeconomic Evaluations of Addictions Treatment.* Piscataway, NJ. Center of Alcohol Studies, Rutgers University 1993. Prepared at the request of the President's Commission on Model State Drug Laws.

2. Center on Addiction and Substance Abuse (CASA) and the Brown University Center for Alcohol and Addiction Studies (CAAS). Recommendations on Substance Abuse Coverage and Health Care Reform. New York: Center on Addiction and Substance Abuse at Columbia University. 1993.

3. Langenbucher et al., 1993.

4. American Medical Association. Factors Contributing to the Health Care Cost Problem. Chicago, IL: American Medical Association. 1993.

5. Langenbucher et al., 1993.

6. JudyAnn Bigby, William Butynski, et al. Statement to the President's Task Force on National Health Care Reform; Alcohol, Nicotine, and Other Drug Problems. April 2, 1993.

7. AMA, 1993.

8. Bureau of Justice Statistics. *Survey of Youth in Custody.* NCJ-113365. 1987, and *1989 Survey of Jail Inmates,* and *1986 Survey of State Prison Inmates,* unpublished analyses.

9. U.S. Bureau of Prisons *Special Analysis.* February 1, 1994.

10. Dorothy P. Rice, Sander Kelman, Leonard S. Miller, and Sarah Dunmeyer. The Economic Costs of Alcohol Abuse and Mental Illness: 1985. Washington, DC: U.S. Government Printing Office. 1990.

11. Langenbucher, et al., 1993.

12. Ibid.

13. Ibid.

14. Ibid.

For further information, call Johnny W. Allem or Martha E. Rothenberg 202-347-4257 or 1-800-838-SOAR

Chairman STARK. Mr. Gemmell.

STATEMENT OF MICHAEL K. GEMMELL, EXECUTIVE
DIRECTOR, ASSOCIATION OF SCHOOLS OF PUBLIC HEALTH

Mr. GEMMELL. Good morning, Mr. Chairman. I represent the 26 schools of public health in the United States. The deans appreciate the opportunity to present our views on health reform in general and the training of public health professionals in particular.

Mr. Chairman, public health is the underlying concept of any effective health care reform system. Population-based disease prevention health promotion, which is synonymous with public health, must be the cornerstone of health care reform.

The Association of Schools of Public Health, Mr. Chairman, is on record in support of President Clinton's health care reform bill. We strongly support the public health, preventive medicine and prevention research provisions of the plan, as well as its overall principles of universal coverage, access and cost control.

However, Mr. Chairman, as experts in the public health professions education field, we believe that all health care reform proposals should place more emphasis on relieving the serious shortage of comprehensively trained professionals needed to meet health care reform objectives, especially those trained to deal with previously neglected or unidentified morbidities, such as AIDS, drugs, alcohol, violence, tobacco, and depression, among others.

State and local health department directors have reported that the lack of practical knowledge and skills in the core sciences of public health and preventive medicine have restricted the effectiveness of their agencies. In order to promote the quality of the American public health infrastructure, and therefore to properly set the stage for health care reform, we must provide adequate training, education and continuing education to the public health workforce.

We urge Congress to recognize that under health care reform the public health system would be responsible for community assessment of needed services, assurances that groups of providers are available to meet community needs, and for the administration of programs which promote health and prevent disease.

Accordingly, we recommend the following provisions to health care reform: One, recognition of the critical mass of the basic public health sciences of epidemiology and biostatistics, among others, are needed to build the prevention research capacity to rebuild the current public health infrastructure as well as to manage health care reform plans.

Two, that 3 percent of the national health care expenditures should be set aside to support the core functions of public health. We believe it is crucial to provide for a guaranteed, predictable and consistent source of funds for these functions that were identified by the Public Health Service.

And three, consolidation of current Federal academic public programs into a new entitlement that would create a Public Health Services Corps, with individuals with special skills and competency needed to function in a health care reform context.

One final recommendation, Mr. Chairman. We respectfully urge that the medical specialty of preventive medicine be included in a definition of primary care. These physicians play important roles in many health care settings where expertise in both clinical medicine and the population-based approach of public health is required.

We urge the committee to continue the precedent it set in OBRA 1993, by treating preventive medicine the same as primary care specialties for the purposes of graduate medical education.

Thank you, Mr. Chairman, and members of the committee and subcommittee, for the opportunity to testify on the need for health care reform in general and for the opportunity to present our views on the need for professionals with population-based expertise to accomplish its goals in particular.

Thank you, Mr. Chairman.

Chairman STARK. Thank you.

[The prepared statement and attachment follow:]

STATEMENT OF MICHAEL K. GEMMELL, CAE
EXECUTIVE DIRECTOR
ASSOCIATION OF SCHOOLS OF PUBLIC HEALTH

Mr. Chairman, members of the subcommittee, I am Mike Gemmell, executive director of the Association of Schools of Public Health (ASPH*). We are grateful for the opportunity to testify on our association's views on health care reform. Mr. Chairman, public health is the underlying concept for any effective health system. **Population-based disease prevention/health promotion, which is synonymous with public health, must be the cornerstone of the health care reform initiative.** A health care system that assures access to health care for all persons cannot succeed in building a healthier America unless it addresses disease prevention and health promotion in a comprehensive fashion. Population-based measures extend beyond the boundaries of any individual health provider or facility.

As such, the Association of Schools of Public Health is on record in support of President Clinton's health care reform plan (H.R. 3600). We strongly support the public health, preventive medicine and prevention research provisions of the plan, as well as its overall principles. ASPH applauds the President's vision and resolve in proposing a national health care plan and for making it a central theme of his presidency.

However, Mr. Chairman, as experts in the public health professions education field, we believe that all health care reform proposals should place more emphasis on relieving the serious shortage of comprehensively-trained professionals needed to meet health care reform objectives, especially those trained to deal with previously neglected or unidentified morbidities: HIV/AIDS, drugs, alcohol, violence, tobacco, depression, among others.

The importance of this issue was clearly outlined in the **HHS Secretary's Eighth Report on Health Personnel to Congress** in 1991. HHS listed personnel shortages in several public health occupations and stated that the problem is exacerbated by a lack of training in basic public health principles and contemporary methods. Many state/local health department directors have reported that the lack of practical knowledge and skills in the core sciences of public health and preventive medicine has restricted the effectiveness of their agencies. In order to improve the quality of the American public health infrastructure, and therefore, to properly set the stage for health care reform and prevention, we must provide adequate training, education and continuing education to the public health workforce.

Many national health groups--especially the maternal and child health agencies and state/local health officials--agree that regional shortages of adequately trained professionals present the most significant barrier to providing population-based prevention initiatives, in general and ensuring the delivery of quality health care to underserved individuals and underrepresented populations, in particular. Health professionals trained to handle the unique demands of rural and inner-city public health issues are in the shortest supply.

In order to meet the national health goals adopted as part of Healthy People 2000, as well as objectives of the President's health care reform plan, we need an adequate supply of well-trained and qualified health professionals, including public health physicians. We urge Congress to recognize that, under health care reform, the public health system would be responsible for community assessment of needed services, assurance that groups of providers are available to meet community needs, and administration of programs which promote disease prevention, healthy lifestyles and a safe environment. In addition, we encourage recognition that public health professionals will be needed to ensure the provision of necessary services not provided by other components of the proposed health care system (e.g., services to underserved populations in rural and inner city areas, including the elderly, disabled, teenaged mothers and their infants, the homeless and undocumented workers, among others).

---

*   ASPH is the only national organization representing the deans, over 2,200 faculty and over 13,000 students of the 26 schools of public health. The schools represent the primary education system that trains personnel needed to operate our nation's public health, disease prevention and health promotion programs. ASPH's principal purpose is to promote and improve the education and training of professional public health personnel. It was formed in 1959 in response to the need to give a national voice to academic public health. A list of the 26 accredited schools of public health is attached.

Mr. Chairman, lasting reform of our health care system requires a strategic (long-term) commitment to training public health personnel, shoring-up the public health infrastructure and the prevention research enterprise. But filling the current occupational voids and ensuring a supply into the next century is a priority both nationally and regionally. Therefore, ASPH recommends the following provisions to health care reform proposals be sustained or included:

- Recognition of the complementary role of community-based public health measures in health care reform; there is a need to mandate the integration of public health with medical care through community-based "networks and plans"

- Recognition that a critical mass of the basic public health disciplines of epidemiology, biostatistics, environmental health, health services administration, behavioral and social sciences, among others, is needed to build a prevention research capacity and to re-build the current public health infrastructure, as well as to manage health care reform plans

- Three percent (3%) of national health care expenditures should be set aside to support the core functions of public health including the education of the public health workforce and health professionals to accomplish these core functions. We believe that it is crucial to provide for a guaranteed, predictable and consistent source of support for core public health functions.

- Consolidation of current federal academic public health support programs into a new authorization that would earmark $50 million to train future public health professionals (a **Public Health Service Corps**) through accredited graduate public health educational programs to usher in health care reform at the federal, state and local level. Under this plan, schools of public health and accredited programs in preventive medicine, would train and educate a cadre of new public health professionals, with special skills and competencies needed to function in a health care reform environment, for careers in official public health agencies and organizations.

Expertise to provide public health services makes increased education of the existing and future public health workforce, in such disciplines as organizational management, cultural sensitivity, interdisciplinary cooperation, biostatistics and epidemiology, planning and program evaluation, and financial management, to name a few, critical to the success of health care reform.

One final recommendation, Mr. Chairman. We respectfully urge that the medical specialty of preventive medicine be included in the definition of primary care in all bills. Schools of public health pay an essential role in training physicians in public health and in the specialty of preventive medicine. They sponsor about 20 percent of all residency programs in preventive medicine, public health, and occupational medicine, and provide academic training to many more public health and preventive medicine physicians. These physicians play important roles in many health care settings where expertise in both clinical medicine and the population-based approach of public health is required. Every major study of national health workforce needs has concluded that there is a shortage of physicians trained in preventive medicine. The Third Report of the Council on Graduate Medical Education (COGME) recommended, as a national goal, increasing the percentage of physicians trained and certified in preventive medicine. We support the President's proposal and others that will enable graduate medical education funding for physicians training in settings other than hospitals. We are alarmed, however, by the proposals's exclusion of preventive medicine from the list of specialties for which training slots will be increased. If preventive medicine must compete with medical subspecialties in oversupply for a reduced number of funded training slots, we fear for its future. We urge the Committee to continue the precedent it set in OBRA 93 by treating preventive medicine the same as the primary care specialties for purposes of graduate medical education funding.

Deans of the U.S. Schools of Public Health recognize that the will to propose a plan to revitalize the health care system was lacking, until now. ASPH also recognizes that population-based approaches to disease prevention and health promotion were not given the benefit of their achievements in lowering the burden of disease and disability, not to mention delaying morbidity, until now. And ASPH recognizes that there is an opportunity <u>now</u> to make a major contribution to our society by reforming the current health care system and adopt a plan that calls for re-building of our nation's public health system (currently "in dissaray"), a plan that calls for the reduction in the burden of controllable health problems, a plan that calls for the education of comprehensively-trained public health professionals to function in a health care reform environment and a plan that calls for population-based approaches in health care reform through the application traditional public health principles and programs: assessment, policy development and assurance.

Thank you, Mr. Chairman, for the opportunity to testify on the need for health care reform, in general and for the opportunity to present our views on the need for professionals with population-based expertise to accomplish its goals, in particular.

# # #

ASPH
ASSOCIATION OF
SCHOOLS OF
PUBLIC HEALTH

ACCREDITED SCHOOLS OF PUBLIC HEALTH

School of Public Health
University of Alabama at Birmingham
305 Tidwell Hall
Birmingham, AL 35294

School of Public Health
University at Albany
SUNY
Two University Place
Albany, NY 12203-3399

School of Public Health
Boston University
80 E. Concord Street, A 407
Boston, MA 02118-2394

School of Public Health
University of California at Berkeley
19 Earl Warren Hall
Berkeley, CA 94720

School of Public Health
University of California at Los Angeles
Center for Health Sciences
Room 16.035
Los Angeles, CA 90024

School of Public Health
Columbia University
167 West 168th Street - 3rd floor
New York, NY 10032

School of Public Health
Emory University
1599 Clifton Road, NE
Atlanta, GA 30329

School of Public Health
Harvard University
677 Huntington Avenue
Boston, MA 02115

School of Public Health
University of Hawaii
1960 East-West Road
Honolulu, HI 96822

School of Public Health
University of Illinois at Chicago
Health Sciences Center
P.O. Box 6998
Chicago, IL 60680

School of Hygiene and Public Health
Johns Hopkins University
615 N. Wolfe Street
Baltimore, MD 21205-2179

School of Public Health
Loma Linda University
Loma Linda, CA 92350

School of Public Health
University of Massachusetts
108 Arnold House
Amherst, MA 02003-0037

School of Public Health
University of Michigan
109 Observatory Street
Ann Arbor, MI 48109-2029

School of Public Health
University of Minnesota
A-302 Mayo Memorial Building
420 Delaware Street, SE
Minneapolis, MN 55455-3181

School of Public Health
University of North Carolina
at Chapel Hill
Campus Box 7400 Rosenau Hall
Chapel Hill, NC 27599-7400

College of Public Health
University of Oklahoma
P.O. Box 26901
Oklahoma City, OK 73190

Graduate School of Public Health
University of Pittsburgh
111 Parran Hall
Pittsburgh, PA 15261

School of Public Health
University of Puerto Rico
G.P.O. Box 5067
San Juan, PR 00936

Graduate School of Public Health
San Diego State University
San Diego, CA 92182-0405

School of Public Health
University of South Carolina
Sumter and Green
Columbia, SC 29208

College of Public Health
University of South Florida
MHH-104
13201 Bruce B. Downs Boulevard
Tampa, FL 33612-3899

School of Public Health
University of Texas
Health Science Center at Houston
Reuel A. Stallones Building
Houston, TX 77225

School of Public Health and
Tropical Medicine
Tulane University
1430 Tulane Avenue
New Orleans, LA 70112

School of Public Health and Community
Medicine
University of Washington
SC-30
Seattle, WA 98195

Department of Epidemiology and
Public Health
Yale University
School of Medicine
P O. Box 3333
New Haven, CT 06510

School of Public Health*
St. Louis University
3663 Lindell Boulevard (4th floor)
O'Donnell Hall
St. Louis, MO 63108

* Pre-accredited

ASPH is the only national organization representing the deans, faculty and students of the 26 schools of public health. The schools represent the primary educational system that trains personnel needed to operate our nation's public health, disease prevention and health promotion programs. ASPH's principal purpose is to promote and improve the education and training of professional public health personnel.

Chairman STARK. Dr. Fielding.

STATEMENT OF JONATHAN E. FIELDING, M.D., MEMBER, BOARD OF DIRECTORS, PARTNERSHIP FOR PREVENTION

Dr. FIELDING. Thank you, Mr. Chairman.

I am from UCLA and I am testifying on behalf of the Partnership for Prevention. We are a group of more than 60 organizations, both public and private, that share one common desire: Better integrating prevention into national health policy and practice.

And we have provided written testimony from which I would like to stress six points. Our major concern is that in discussion of health system reform, the primary objective may get lost and that primary objective must be improving the health of the American people. If we don't keep this firmly in mind, we won't be successful.

Healthy People 2000 is an excellent start, but we urge that this committee use that objective as its filter for looking at all proposals.

Second, prevention works and it makes good economic sense. The tools are well-developed and proven. For many of the worst health problems, prevention is not only a good alternative, it is the only alternative, from HIV to motor vehicle injuries, from low birthweight babies to measles, and from lung cancer to handgun violence. So if prevention does not have a central role, health system reform cannot succeed.

Third, most people define prevention as one of three components. That is too narrow. They think about personal behaviors and clinical preventive services: Mammography immunization, diet.

These were very important but there are two other aspects. First, community-based interventions; if we are going to prevent violence, if we are going to reduce children bearing children, if we are going to educate our children about health, we need to have community-based interventions.

The third part is social and economic policies. We need tax incentives. There are things that providers won't do without the proper incentives, such as getting high levels of immunization or screening children for developmental disability.

Employers need incentives to continue doing work-site health promotions. Individuals need incentives. If we are going to reduce handgun availability, it is not going to be the health care system that is going to do it.

We have a specific recommendation and that is that the National Health Board look at all the potential opportunities to improve health, and from an economic and national productivity point of view, prioritize them and report to the Congress so that you can better determine where the investments should be.

Our fourth point is that the data collection and analysis systems that currently exist, particularly on the public health side, are insufficient to answer the trillion dollar question: Is our health system working? What components of it are working? Where, where not, how well, what do we do to refine it? So unless this is improved substantially, we are not going to be able to develop an efficient system and we are not going to be able to improve it.

In some States and communities today, Public Health Services don't even have computers or have the expertise to use them.

We need, therefore, a revitalized public health presence. Public health needs to be not only an equal partner but also take the lead in community programs and in social problems.

Take the issue of lead. Private providers may screen for lead, but so what? What then happens to the kids? Who is going to track them and find out what the lead sources are? Who is going to make sure the houses are deleaded? Who is going to monitor them over time?

Finally, one of the key reasons for underutilization of prevention today is 40 million Americans are without health insurance. You can make a giant step for the health of American people by passing universal, transportable, lifelong health insurance.

In the written testimony, we have provided you a public health standard, a yardstick, a measure that you can use to assess all the bills with respect to their potential to improve the health of the American people. We would be happy to answer questions about that and other aspects. And we really appreciate the opportunity to testify before you.

[The prepared statement and attachments follow:]

STATEMENT OF JONATHAN E. FIELDING, M.D., M.P.H., M.B.A.
MEMBER, BOARD OF DIRECTORS
PARTNERSHIP FOR PREVENTION

Mr. Chairman and Members of the Committee, I am Jonathan Fielding. Thank you for the invitation to testify. I am a Professor of Health Services and Pediatrics at UCLA, the past chairman and a board member of the California Wellness Foundation,[1] a former state health commissioner and former vice president of health policy for a large health-care company. I am speaking today on behalf of Partnership for Prevention, a national nonprofit organization whose more than 60 members share an interest in better integrating prevention into national health policy and practice (Appendix A lists the membership of Partnership for Prevention).

Until now, the national debate about health reform has focused primarily on access to care and controlling rising costs. "Health security" is also a recurring theme. These are important national goals and we agree that universal, transportable, lifelong insurance coverage for every American deserves to be a national priority

Based on the area of expertise and interest of our organization, we urge you to bring to center stage two issues which we feel hold the key to successful health system reform.

- First, we encourage you to adopt as an additional primary goal of any health legislation—improving the health of the American people.

- Second, we urge you to define prevention comprehensively, to include a wide array of personal/clinical preventive services, community-based interventions, and social policies for prevention that have been shown to improve health and well-being.

PARTNERSHIP FOR PREVENTION

Partnership for Prevention was founded in 1990 to provide private-sector leadership in achieving the *Healthy People 2000* national health objectives. Our mission's focus is to increase the priority for prevention among policy-makers, federal and state agencies, corporations and other nonprofit organizations. In addition to coordinating the prevention-oriented efforts of our members, we endeavor to increase the resources and incentives that will lead to general adoption of efficient, effective preventive approaches to health improvement.

Last year, Partnership conducted an analysis of national and state proposals for health reform and convened a panel of experts to discuss the inclusion of prevention in health-care reform. This work concluded that preventive services and programs offer Americans the possibility of longer, healthier, and more productive lives (the conference report describes six principles that could guide the formulation of prevention-oriented reform policy, see Appendix B).

IMPROVE THE PUBLIC'S HEALTH

Current legislative proposals are concerned with the cost of extending insurance coverage for medical care expenses to those now either under-insured or uninsured, as well as the reduction of the rate of overall cost increases for health and medical services. However, we find it disturbing that the debate thus far includes relatively limited discussion of the prospects for measurable improvement in the health status of our population. We believe that the most important objective of health reform should be the **improvement of health**. In this regard, prevention should have an integral role.

We urge that you support more emphasis on prevention not only because it is important, but because it is effective. Over the past years efficient and effective techniques have been developed to improve the public's health through preventive opportunities.

"Prevention" is a popular concept. However, many of its most promising opportunities are often overlooked because it is so narrowly defined in the eye of the public. Most often it is associated only with clinical preventive services—mammography, prenatal care, immunizations and other screening services. But even within the category of clinical preventive services are major missed opportunities. For example, there are scientifically valid ways to identify individuals with depression, the precursor of suicide. As many as 15% of Americans are victims of depression every year, with reduced personal and economic productivity and often adverse effects on family function. Yet, despite the existence of good treatment for these health problems, readily available, inexpensive and efficient screening tools to find those at risk are woefully underutilized.

Substance abuse is another serious and common problem. Experts estimate that one in four Americans is directly or indirectly affected by this disease. Perhaps even more alarming is recent data which indicate that illicit drug use is increasing again among our teenagers (Thomas, 1994). Both preventive and remediable measures are available but their use is limited. Both clinical and community settings could make better use of

---

[1] The largest foundation devoted exclusively to disease prevention and health promotion

prevention interventions, including drunk driving legislation and the use of screening questionnaires to identify the disease and refer individuals to appropriate treatment.

Therefore, prevention needs to be integrated as part of an efficient system of health services to meet the health needs of defined populations. And prevention needs to be defined comprehensively to include:

- a core set of personal/clinical preventive services,
- community-based preventive services, and
- social policies for prevention (Appendix C describes the components of prevention).

USE OF PREVENTIVE SERVICES

If health system reform is to improve the public's health it must support more effective use of proven clinical preventive services, well documented by the U.S. Preventive Services Task Force. We support the funding of a core package of clinical prevention services in any health system reform proposal. Further, we recommend that the type of process used by the U.S. Preventive Services Task Force, careful periodic assessment of all available literature on efficacy, efficiency, effectiveness and cost-effectiveness of each potential clinical preventive service, be integrated into the mechanisms to determine and revise core benefits. The process will need to

- identify specific criteria, including disease burden and efficacy and effectiveness of each intervention,
- periodically weigh the evidence, and
- prioritize, based on available funds.

However, we believe that health system reform must also support multi-sector community-based programs and services that have health objectives, and support social and economic policies when these can make a significant contribution to health.

To illustrate our view of a comprehensive approach to prevention, consider the issue of violence. Crime and related violence have become the number one concern of Americans--and for good reason. Violence took the lives of 2,428 children in 1992, 67% greater than six years earlier. A larger percentage of perpetrators of serious crime suspects are juveniles. Further, the rise in violence is mirrored by a jump in child neglect and abuse cases, which are serious risk factors for delinquency (Loose and Thomas, 1994). Some Americans are afraid to leave their homes--to send their children to school or to go to work. Clearly, violent communities are not healthy communities. Even if every person in a community with a high crime rate had good health habits and tested negative on all screening tests, their community would not be a healthy place to live.

To prevent violence requires a multifaceted approach. During my tenure as chairman of the California Wellness Foundation we initiated a program with four interactive components--a leadership program, community action program, policy program and research program. Careful evaluation of this and other violence prevention initiatives will help us to better understand the best remedies to this problem.

Community health approaches complement personal health approaches and are of equal importance. Yet most health system reform proposals do not even mention this key health issue. One opportunity is to make health plans more accountable for community health. However, while this may work to improve immunization rates and increase mammography screening, it is not sufficient to deal with many problems such as violence or adolescent childbearing.

We therefore urge the Committee to :

- build in provisions for more multi-sectoral efforts to address these and other health problems, and
- provide strong incentives for collaboration between all of those agencies and interests that can play a constructive role.

There are times when social and economic policy can have a greater impact on health than alternative preventive measures. As an example, mandatory seat belt legislation has had a much greater and faster impact than decades of media public education to "buckle up." Similarly, proposed changes in the welfare system probably contain greater potential to affect adolescent childbearing than educational campaigns promoting abstinence or contraception.

Likewise there are great opportunities to improve health through tax policy. America is the world leader in employer-sponsored health promotion programs. These programs have been shown to reduce the frequency and severity of risk factors for heart disease, cancer and other serious health problems and to reduce absenteeism. A major stimulus to these programs has been the inherent incentives for the many self-insured and other experience-rated employers to invest in health promotion to reduce their health benefit costs. If health system reform removes this incentive without a substitute, many of the 81% of worksites with some health promotion activity (U.S. Department of Health and Human Services, 1992) are likely to reduce or abandon their programming.

Another example is the relatively low taxation of tobacco products in the United States compared to other developed nations. We have ceased to make progress in reducing smoking among teenagers. Yet continued progress could be virtually assured by increasing tobacco taxes because adolescents experimenting with tobacco are more deterred by price increases than are already addicted adults. To prevent drinking, preliminary data suggest that new taxes on alcoholic beverages could reduce alcohol consumption and alcohol-related injuries and death (Chaloupka, 1993). Similarly, policy experts are considering whether a tax on handguns and assault weapons might contribute to the prevention of violence.

Most health system reform proposals under consideration rely on market mechanisms to control costs. While competition can help achieve cost efficiency, Congress has a vital interest in determining where national social policy objectives may diverge from the economic incentives to health plans under a reformed system. If a preventive procedure will not reduce health-care costs, health plans may not implement the procedure unless it is a required core benefit. For example, developmental screening of young children may not be cost-justified within a plan but should be considered essential to maximize national social productivity. Perhaps health plans should get a bit more money if they fully utilize prevention practices with proven efficacy. Similarly, since a great deal of health activity is performed outside the professional care sector, perhaps financial incentives could be designed to encourage health plans to improve the "self-care" of their members. Self-care—tooth brushing, treatment of minor injuries, etc.—is often defined as the decisions undertaken by individuals for their own or family's health benefit (Silten and Levin, 1979). Partnership for Prevention supports programs to improve informed medical decision-making by patients and their health providers.

These decisions include those pertaining to personal habits as well as utilization of appropriate health services. Some Americans have too much health care because they demand and receive unnecessary diagnostic and therapeutic procedures. As former surgeon general C. Everett Koop said, "More is not always better and may be hazardous to a patient's heath" (Russell, 1994).

Interlocking incentives can create a system of prevention with rewards for good outcomes linked to prevention. Some of these outcomes could be medical. Why not provide incentives for a low rate of complication in diabetics, a low percentage of breast cancers found beyond an early stage, a low percentage of pregnancies diagnosed after the first trimester, etc. Incentives might also be related to social outcomes such as the rate that frail elderly are maintained in an independent environment through close coordination of health-care providers and social and other community agencies, the frequency of adolescent childbearing, or suicide. A health plan that can demonstrate superior outcomes and better use of prevention should have a marketing advantage and get more subscribers.

TRACKING HEALTH STATUS

Improving health requires the data to know where the problems are, their dimensions and changes over time. Unfortunately, much essential data are lacking at all levels—national, state, community, and health plan. Data are also unavailable for many population segments defined by age, ethnicity, race or family constellation. Public health agencies at all levels are poorly equipped and staffed in health information technology. As a result, in some cases it is impossible to estimate the extent of disease burden or determine the results of preventive interventions. If we are to improve the health of Americans, these agencies must have resources to track health problems and changes in health status. Attention must also be given to assuring the privacy of individuals' medical records. Health plans should share this responsibility for their subscribers, and feed into public systems. Currently, most plans do not have the automated collection, aggregation and analysis systems and processes to develop sophisticated outcome-based report cards.

WHAT IS THE ROLE OF PUBLIC HEALTH?

What should be the role of "public health" in a new health-care landscape? We believe that public health roles need to be strengthened so that public health is not only an **equal player** in personal health-care delivery systems, but can take the lead role in community interventions and social programs and policies. Public and personal health services need to be integrated.

In the future, health plans may take over some traditional public health functions, such as lead screening. However, once an elevated lead level is found, strong linkages to an effective public health presence will allow coordination of deleading, and arrangements for temporary housing, notifying other families that their children are at high risk and arranging for them to be screened.

Many traditional core public health roles—water safety, food safety, safe sewage treatment, air quality, and control of infectious and sexually transmitted diseases—have been eroded by strained budgets and public apathy. More recently public health has taken a significant role in public education, but often without adequate resources. Improving the health of Americans requires that public health roles be buttressed and invigorated in any health system reform package (Schauffler, 1993; an executive summary of this analysis of the inclusion of health promotion and disease prevention in health reform is found in Appendix E).

THE THREE PILLARS OF PREVENTION

We recommend investment in three tactics: motivation to change personal habits and utilize preventive services; community health programming; and health-supporting social and economic policy. Let's ask whether all of these are necessary in defining health policy for Americans. The major causes of death among U.S. residents are tobacco, diet and activity patterns, alcohol, microbial agents, toxic agents, firearms, sexual behavior, motor vehicles and illicit use of drugs (McGinnis and Foege, 1993; Appendix D outlines the actual causes of death in the United States, and potential contributions to reduction).

Although many of the behaviors associated with these factors are difficult to change, reducing the toll of these would make a strong impact on the health of the public. While the health-care system, current or reformed, can contribute to this goal, greater contributions must come from elsewhere. Personal behaviors such as smoking, speeding and unsafe sex must change. Community programs must make neighborhoods safer, identify and remove toxic exposures, improve educational opportunities and reduce hopelessness. Social and economic policy must provide disincentives for tobacco use, reduce access to handguns and assault weapons, facilitate job creation, better educate the public about optimal nutrition, and continue to refine motor vehicle safety requirements.

MEETING THE PUBLIC HEALTH STANDARD

How can the Committee judge whether sufficient prevention of the right types is incorporated into the disparate health system reform proposals before you? Incorporation of effective preventive approaches should transcend system architecture. We therefore recommend that you measure each proposal against a prevention standard.

The standard has eight key components:

1. Individual/clinical preventive services in the core benefit set determined by an ongoing scientifically objective process

2. Community prevention activities of proven efficacy and efficiency

3. Social and economic policy changes that make unique contributions to health improvement

4. A revitalized public health presence with strong linkages to personal health services, and a leadership role in developing effective community interventions and recommending health policy changes

5. Data collection, analysis and reporting that show changes in population health and identify what system components and tactics work and which do not.

6. Research on how to create even more efficient and effective prevention services, programs and policies

7. Increased numbers of primary-care providers with training in personal/clinical preventive services and community-based services

8. Public awareness interventions which contribute to an improved understanding of the value of prevention in promoting good health and longevity.

CONCLUSION

In conclusion, we urge that Committee deliberations be guided by the answer to one question: What are the greatest opportunities to improve the health of the American people, overall and for specific vulnerable populations? Prevention works. Its central role in rethinking health goals and ways to achieve them is therefore not only a moral imperative but a practical imperative. Thank you very much.

372

REFERENCES

Chaloupka, Frank J. Effects of Price on Alcohol-Related Problems, *Alcohol, Health & Research World*, 17(1):46-53, 1993.

Loose, C., and Thomas, P. Spread of Violence Poisons Well-Being of Childhood, Washington, DC: *The Washington Post*, January 2, 1994: pp.1,19.

McGinnis, J. Michael, and Foege, William H. Actual Causes of Death in the United States, *Journal of the American Medical Association*, 270(18):2207-2212, 1993.

National Alcohol Tax Coalition, Saving Lives and Raising Revenue: The Case for Higher Alcohol Taxes; Raising the Excise Tax on Beer: Myths and Facts, Washington, DC, 1993.

Russell, C. Koop Seeks Taxes on Cigarettes, Guns, Washington, DC: *Health, The Washington Post*, February 1, 1994: p.5.

Schauffler, H.H. Health Promotion and Disease Prevention in Health Care Reform. Contract Report to The California Wellness Foundation, Berkeley, CA: University of California at Berkeley School of Public Health. 1993.

Silten, Robert M., and Levin, Lowell S. Self Care Évaluation, In: Lazes, Peter M., ed. *The Handbook of Health Education*, Germantown, MD: Aspen Systems Corporation, 1979: pp. 201-221.

Thomas, P. Illicit Drug Use Rises Among U.S. Teenagers, Washington, DC: *The Washington Post*, February 1, 1994: pp.1,10.

U.S. Department of Health and Human Services. *1992 National Survey of Worksite Health Promotion Activities*, Washington, DC: Office of Disease Prevention and Health Promotion, 1992.

APPENDICES

A.   Members of PARTNERSHIP FOR PREVENTION

B.   Prevention is Basic to Health Reform, A Position Paper from an Expert Panel, Washington, DC: *Partnership for Prevention*, 1993.

C.   Table: Components of Prevention

D.   Table: Actual Causes of Death in the United States and Potential Contribution to Reduction

E.   Schauffler, H.H. Health Promotion and Disease Prevention in Health Care Reform (1993): Executive Summary (Attached)

APPENDIX A

PARTNERSHIP FOR PREVENTION MEMBERS

ORGANIZATIONS

Aetna Life & Casualty

American Academy of Family Physicians

American Academy of Pediatric Dentistry

American Cancer Society

American Clinical Laboratory Association

American College of Preventive Medicine

American Council of Life Insurance

American Dietetic Association

American Medical Association

American Nurses Association

American Podiatric Medical Association, Inc.

Association of Academic Health Centers

Association of Schools of Public Health

Association for Worksite Health Promotion

Blue Cross of Western Pennsylvania

Cecil G. Sheps Center for Health Services Research

Center for Corporate Public Involvement

Central States of Omaha

Connaught Laboratories

Health Insurance Association of America

Health Management Corporation

International Business Machines Corporation (IBM)

JC Penney, Inc.

Johnson & Johnson

Lederle-Praxis Biologicals

Merck & Co.

National Association of Pediatric Nurse Associates and Practitioners

National Association of Community Health Centers

National Association of County Health Officials

National Black Nurses Association

National Association of School Nurses

Society of Behavioral Medicine

Voluntary Hospitals of America

STATES

Alabama

Arizona

Arkansas

California

Colorado

Connecticut

Florida

Georgia

Hawaii

Indiana

Kansas

Maryland

Michigan

Mississippi

Missouri

Nebraska

Nevada

New Jersey

New Mexico

North Carolina

North Dakota

Pennsylvania

Rhode Island

South Carolina

Tennessee

Washington

West Virginia

2/1/94

APPENDIX B

"PREVENTION IS BASIC TO HEALTH REFORM"

ATTACHMENT 1

[DUE TO ITS SIZE, THE ATTACHMENT IS BEING RE-
TAINED IN THE COMMITTEE FILES.]

APPENDIX C

Components of Preventive Services

Clinical Prevention	Community-Based Prevention
* Immunizations * Screening, risk evaluation, and early detection of diseases where clinical interventions are most effective * Counseling high-risk individuals and building the knowledge, skill, and motivation to establish and maintain healthy lifestyles Adapted from "The Role of Prevention in Health Care Reform: A Joint Statement by Organizations Concerned with Public Health"	* Evaluating what programs would meet the basic health needs of the community * Providing individual and community education about healthy lifestyles and good health habits * Evaluating and taking action to assure the availability of safe air, water, and food supplies * Providing the outreach and screening services to identify needy individuals or populations and linking them with the appropriate preventive services

APPENDIX D

Actual Causes of Death in the United States in 1990
and
Potential Contribution to Reduction

Causes	Deaths		Potential Contribution to Reduction			
	Estimated Number	Percentage of Total Deaths	Personal	Health Care System	Community Action	Social Policies
Tobacco	400,000	19	++++	+	+	++
Diet/Activity Patterns	500,000	14	+++	+	+	++
Alcohol	100,000	5	+++	+	+	+
Toxic Agents	60,000	3	+	+	++	++++
Firearms	35,000	2	++	+	+++	+++
Sexual Behavior	30,000	1	++++	+	+	+
Motor Vehicles	25,000	1	++	+	+	++
Illicit Use of Drugs	20,000	1	+++	+	++	++

Adapted by Jonathan E. Fielding, M.D., M.P.H.
UCLA School of Public Health and Medicine
Unpublished, February 1994

Original Chart:
McGinnis, J. Michael, and Foege, William H. Actual Causes of Death in the United States, *Journal of the American Medical Association*, 270(18):2207-2212, 1993.

Chairman STARK. Who wins?
Dr. FIELDING. Excuse me?
Chairman STARK. Who wins on the chart?
Who is at the top?
Dr. FIELDING. Who wins?
Chairman STARK. Your chart of analyzing all these bills under your assessment.
Dr. FIELDING. I am sorry. We have not done a bill-by-bill analysis, but that is something we are planning to do, Mr. Chairman.
Chairman STARK. We are, too.
Thank you.
Mr. Carey.

STATEMENT OF HON. MOSES CAREY, CHAIR, SUBCOMMITTEE ON PUBLIC AND ENVIRONMENTAL HEALTH, NATIONAL ASSOCIATION OF COUNTIES, AND COMMISSIONER, ORANGE COUNTY, N.C.

Mr. CAREY. Mr. Chairman, members of the subcommittee, I am Moses Carey.
Chairman STARK. Is that commissioner, Senator?
Mr. CAREY. Commissioner. Orange County commissioner, North Carolina, home of the Tar Heels.
Chairman STARK. All right.
Mr. CAREY. I am Moses Carey, chairman of the Orange County board of commissioners in North Carolina, and chair of the National Association of Counties Subcommittee on Public and Environmental Health. I am testifying on their behalf.

I will address the following issues: Essential community providers, jail populations, enabling services, subsidies and the regional alliance structure.

We are pleased that the concept of an essential community provider is included in the legislation but are troubled by the lack of specificity for county facility eligibility.

Automatic designation and guaranteed health plan reimbursement is given to certain recipients of Federal discretionary health funds. Since most local public health departments receive maternal and child health or Ryan White AIDS funds, we assume that many of them will receive automatic Federal designation. But that is not completely clear.

Each year, 40 million people receive personal health services from local health departments. Their potential exclusion is counterproductive to ensuring universal coverage and access. More troubling is the lack of any public hospital receiving automatic status. Clearly, they are in the business of serving the uninsured. NACo will work to ensure that the status is strengthened to provide, at a minimum, automatic designation to the highest volume providers of Medicaid and low-income care.

Hospitals such as Alameda's Highlands should be designated automatically. Some argue that this is a county turf issue. It is not. A truly reformed system should not recreate a two-tiered delivery system. Under a capitated payment, health plans have little incentive to reimburse providers that they have no contractual obligation with. Access to universal coverage must be accomplished and a short-term special status will help accomplish that principle. We support the essential community provider status through the transition to universal coverage.

Incarcerated individuals awaiting trial are denied guaranteed Federal coverage. Based on our system of justice, an individual is innocent until proven guilty. Under the President's proposal, health plans are not required to reimburse services provided to detainees in detention facilities. This provision would appear to include juveniles as well.

Over 50 percent of individuals in jails are awaiting trial. There are nearly 24,000 admissions each day. They all lose their benefits under the legislation. Multiply that by 365 days a year, and there are well over 8 million encounters a year that would result in the loss of coverage.

This issue is also important to the families of detainees. If an employer is no longer obligated to make payments to an alliance for the employee because he or she is incarcerated, then the rest of the family's current coverage is jeopardized.

The administration is committed to ensuring that health security can never be taken away. NACo will work with you to ensure that persons awaiting adjudication do not lose their health coverage because they cannot make bail.

With respect to enabling services, at the local level, services giving low-income persons access to care is a critical issue. While the President's proposal recognizes the need for nonmedical services such as outreach, transportation, and interpreting services, counties are concerned that low-income persons may be caught in a policy catch-22 under the way the proposal is currently designed.

The Clinton proposal give States the option to provide financial incentives to health plans to enroll and serve disadvantaged groups. In another section of the bill there are Federal authorizations to support enabling services and to create public or nonprofit health plans which serve significant numbers of medically underserved.

Since we see the current system in disarray at the local level, we believe that there is a potential for failing to reach disadvantaged populations under this design. Both the State and Federal Government will already be under severe fiscal pressures. Each may assume that the other will fund these services.

There must be greater assurances that enabling services will be funded and will be available to health plans or essential providers under the system.

The current State option and a possible Federal authorization leave too many chances for failure. Perhaps a specific set-aside within the regional alliance would give greater certainty that these critical services are provided.

With respect to subsidies for low-income individuals, counties are concerned about the cap on subsidies to pay for the premiums of low-income individuals. While there is a provision to give the Congress the opportunity to appropriate additional funds if the subsidies are depleted, we know from experience that too often these initiatives come to us in the form of another unfunded Federal mandate. States will not change their requirements for counties to cover the uninsured or underinsured. We will be left with the State or, in some cases, by ourselves to pick up these pieces.

With regard to employer issues and regional alliances, counties are major employers providing health coverage to about 2 million employees nationally. We are concerned about the separate treatment of public employers compared to their private counterparts.

Some counties employing 5,000 or more employees want to have the same option to become their own alliance as similar-sized corporations. They have successfully managed their own health costs or joined a State pool combining a comprehensive set of benefits. They ask to be treated the same as large businesses.

Consistent with this philosophy is county government's position that they be included in the same payroll cap as business. An employer and its employees should not be treated differently based on whether they are public servants or a part of the private sector.

Private business has been given assurances that no more than 7.9 percent of their total payroll will go toward meeting their premium contribution for the comprehensive standard benefit. Yet, public employers will not get that same treatment until the year 2002. Again, the options and flexibility given to employers and their employees should not be determined by whether they are public or private entities.

Mr. Chairman, I thank you for this opportunity to testify and will respond to any questions you may have.

Chairman STARK. Thank you.

[The prepared statement and attachment follow:]

STATEMENT OF MOSES CAREY
COMMISSIONER, ORANGE COUNTY, NORTH CAROLINA
NATIONAL ASSOCIATION OF COUNTIES

MR CHAIRMAN, MEMBERS OF THE SUBCOMMITTEE, I AM MOSES CAREY, COMMISSIONER IN ORANGE COUNTY (CHAPEL HILL), NORTH CAROLINA. I AM CHAIR OF THE NATIONAL ASSOCIATION OF COUNTIES* SUBCOMMITTEE ON PUBLIC AND ENVIRONMENTAL HEALTH AND AM TESTIFYING ON THEIR BEHALF

COUNTY GOVERNMENTS WELCOME THE HEALTH REFORM DEBATE COUNTIES ARE OFTEN THE SERVICES SAFETY NET AND ARE INCREASINGLY THE FEDERAL AND STATE FISCAL SAFETY VALVE OUR 4,500 HEALTH FACILITIES AND LEGAL RESPONSIBILITY FOR INDIGENT CARE IN OVER 30 STATES ARE JUST TWO EXAMPLES OF OUR EXTENSIVE INVOLVEMENT IN HEALTH I HAVE ATTACHED TO MY TESTIMONY A ONE-PAGE FACT SHEET OUTLINING OUR ROLE

LAST YEAR, NACo COMPLETED EIGHT REGIONAL HEARINGS ON HEALTH SYSTEM REFORM NACO OFFICIALS HEARD TESTIMONy FROM NEARLY 200 WITNESSES THE MESSAGES WERE CONSISTENT THE NATION MUST ENHANCE LOCAL DELIVERY SYSTEMS EMPHASIZING PREVENTION, PRIMARY CARE AND PUBLIC HEALTH, ADMINISTRATION OF THE SYSTEM MUST BE SIMPLIFIED AND FLEXIBLE, UNIVERSAL COVERAGE, NOT JUST ACCESS, IS IMPERATIVE, AND THE FINANCING OF THE SYSTEM MUST BE BROAD-BASED

PRESIDENT CLINTON'S PROPOSAL ADDRESSES MANY OF THESE PRINCIPLES WHILE WE HAVE CONCERNS ABOUT HIS PROPOSAL, WE BELIEVE IT IS CURRENTLY THE ONE THAT IS MOST CONSISTENT WITH NACo POLICY

I WILL NOW RAISE THE KEY SERVICE DELIVERY, GOVERNANCE AND EMPLOYER ISSUES THAT WILL DEFINE THE COUNTY ROLE AND ITS RELATIONSHIP WITH STATE AND FEDERAL GOVERNMENT

ESSENTIAL COMMUNITY PROVIDERS

WE ARE PLEASED THAT THE CONCEPT OF ESSENTIAL COMMUNITY PROVIDER IS INCLUDED IN THE LEGISLATION BUT ARE TROUBLED BY THE LACK OF SPECIFICITY FOR COUNTY FACILITY ELIGIBILITY AUTOMATIC DESIGNATION IS GIVEN TO CERTAIN RECIPIENTS OF FEDERAL DISCRETIONARY HEALTH FUNDS SINCE MOST LOCAL PUBLIC HEALTH DEPARTMENTS RECEIVE MATERNAL AND CHILD HEALTH OR RYAN WHITE AIDS FUNDS, WE ASSUME THAT MANY OF THEM WILL RECEIVE AUTOMATIC FEDERAL DESIGNATION EACH YEAR, 40 MILLION PEOPLE RECEIVE PERSONAL HEALTH SERVICES FROM LOCAL HEALTH DEPARTMENTS THEIR POTENTIAL EXCLUSION IS COUNTERPRODUCTIVE TO ENSURING UNIVERSAL COVERAGE AND ACCESS

MORE TROUBLING IS THE LACK OF ANY PUBLIC HOSPITAL RECEIVING AUTOMATIC ECP STATUS CLEARLY, THEY ARE IN THE BUSINESS OF SERVING THE UNINSURED NACo WILL WORK TO ENSURE THAT THE ECP STATUS IS STRENGTHENED TO PROVIDE, AT A MINIMUM, AUTOMATIC DESIGNATION TO THE HIGHEST VOLUME PROVIDERS OF MEDICAID AND LOW-INCOME CARE HOSPITALS SUCH AS ALAMEDA'S HIGHLAND SHOULD RECEIVE AUTOMATIC STATUS WITHOUT ADDITIONAL STATUTORY GUIDANCE, THE DEPARTMENT OF HEALTH AND HUMAN SERVICES MAY CHOOSE TO RELY UPON A HEALTH PLAN'S UNPROVEN TRACK RECORD IN PROVIDING CARE TO THE POOR

---

* The National Association of Counties is the only national organization representing county government in the United States Through its membership, urban, suburban and rural counties join together to build effective, responsive county government The goals of the organization are to improve county government, serve as the national spokesman for county government, serve as a liaison between the nation's counties and other levels of government, achieve public understanding of the role of counties in the federal system.

SOME MAY ARGUE THAT THIS IS A COUNTY "TURF" ISSUE IT IS NOT A TRULY REFORMED SYSTEM SHOULD NOT RE-CREATE A TWO-TIER DELIVERY SYSTEM UNDER A CAPITATED PAYMENT. HEALTH PLANS HAVE LITTLE INCENTIVE TO REIMBURSE PROVIDERS THAT THEY HAVE NO CONTRACTUAL OBLIGATION WITH ACCESS TO UNIVERSAL COVERAGE MUST BE ACCOMPLISHED AND A SHORT-TERM, SPECIAL STATUS WILL HELP ACCOMPLISH THAT PRINCIPLE WE SUPPORT THE ESSENTIAL COMMUNITY PROVIDER STATUS THROUGH THE TRANSITION TO UNIVERSAL COVERAGE

JAIL POPULATIONS

INCARCERATED INDIVIDUALS AWAITING TRIAL ARE DENIED GUARANTEED FEDERAL COVERAGE BASED ON OUR SYSTEM OF JUSTICE, AN INDIVIDUAL IS INNOCENT UNTIL PROVEN GUILTY OVER 50 PERCENT OF INDIVIDUALS IN JAILS ARE AWAITING TRIAL THERE ARE NEARLY 24,000 ADMISSIONS EACH DAY UNDER THE LEGISLATION AS CURRENTLY DRAFTED, THEY ALL LOSE THEIR BENEFITS MULTIPLY THAT BY 365 DAYS IN A YEAR, AND THERE ARE WELL OVER 8 MILLION ENCOUNTERS A YEAR THAT COULD RESULT IN THE LOSS OF COVERAGE UNDER THE PRESIDENT'S PROPOSAL, HEALTH PLANS ARE NOT REQUIRED TO REIMBURSE SERVICES PROVIDED TO DETAINEES IN DETENTION FACILITIES THIS OTHER PROVISION WOULD APPEAR TO INCLUDE JUVENILES AS WELL

THIS ISSUE IS ALSO IMPORTANT TO THE FAMILIES OF DETAINEES IF AN EMPLOYER IS NO LONGER OBLIGATED TO MAKE PAYMENTS TO AN ALLIANCE FOR THE EMPLOYEE BECAUSE HE OR SHE IS INCARCERATED, THEN THE REST OF THE FAMILY'S CURRENT COVERAGE IS JEOPARDIZED

THE ADMINISTRATION IS COMMITTED TO ENSURING THAT HEALTH SECURITY CAN NEVER BE TAKEN AWAY NACo WILL WORK WITH YOU TO ENSURE THAT PERSONS AWAITING ADJUDICATION DO NOT LOSE HEALTH COVERAGE BECAUSE THEY CANNOT MAKE BAIL

UNDOCUMENTED IMMIGRANTS

AS LOCAL ELECTED OFFICIALS, WE RECOGNIZE THE FEDERAL POLITICAL REALITIES OF ANY ATTEMPT TO GUARANTEE BENEFITS TO INDIVIDUALS WHO ARE IN OUR COUNTRY ILLEGALLY AT THE SAME TIME, THEY HAVE ENTERED DUE TO THE LACK OF FEDERAL ENFORCEMENT OF OUR IMMIGRATION POLICY AS PROVIDERS, COUNTIES PAY FOR THE COSTS OF THAT FAILURE

WE SUPPORT THE PRESIDENT'S PROPOSAL TO RETAIN SOME RESIDUAL PAYMENTS UNDER THE HOSPITAL DISPROPORTIONATE SHARE PAYMENT PROGRAM FOR THOSE HOSPITALS SERVING UNDOCUMENTED IMMIGRANTS AND/OR HIGH NUMBERS OF LOW INCOME PERSONS WHILE THE AMOUNT OF MONEY DOES NOT MEET THE NEED, IT IS A STEP IN THE RIGHT DIRECTION WE SUPPORT THIS USE AND THE PHASE-DOWN OF DISPROPORTIONATE SHARE ONLY WHEN THE UNINSURED TRULY HAVE COVERAGE AND PUBLIC HOSPITALS ARE RECEIVING HEALTH PLAN PAYMENTS

GOVERNANCE/INTERGOVERNMENTAL RELATIONSHIPS

THERE ARE A FEW KEY GOVERNANCE ISSUES THAT NACo HAS IDENTIFIED

COUNTY ROLE IN STATE PLAN DESIGN

FIRST, THERE IS NO RECOGNITION THAT STATES CREATING NEW HEALTH SYSTEMS MUST CONSULT WITH THEIR POLITICAL SUBDIVISIONS, PRIMARILY COUNTIES. WHICH ACTUALLY DELIVER OR ADMINISTER HEALTH CARE CURRENTLY TO UNINSURED POPULATIONS. COUNTY GOVERNMENTS MUST BE INVOLVED IN THE CREATION OF THE NEW STATE SYSTEMS IF THERE ARE SYSTEM FAILURES, WE WILL ULTIMATELY PICK UP THE PIECES WE ARE UNDER NO ILLUSION THAT ANY STATE WILL REPEAL THEIR PROVISIONS MAKING COUNTIES THE PROVIDERS OF LAST RESORT MEANINGFUL CONSULTATION MUST OCCUR BETWEEN COUNTY AND STATE OFFICIALS IN DESIGNING NEW STATE SYSTEMS

REGIONAL ALLIANCES

COUNTIES ARE ALSO INTERESTED IN THE DESIGNATION AND MEMBERSHIP OF REGIONAL ALLIANCES OBVIOUSLY, THERE ARE A NUMBER OF URBAN COUNTIES WHOSE POPULATION OR SIZE EXCEEDS INDIVIDUAL STATES THEY HAVE A GOOD UNDERSTANDING OF THEIR OVERALL HEALTH SYSTEM URBAN COUNTIES SHOULD BE GIVEN THE OPTION OF CHOOSING AN ENTITY TO ADMINISTER A SUBSTATE REGIONAL ALLIANCE

UNDER THE PROPOSAL, THE BOARD OF THE REGIONAL ALLIANCE WOULD
CONSIST OF EMPLOYERS AND CONSUMERS HEALTH PROVIDERS OR THEIR
REPRESENTATIVES ARE SPECIFICALLY EXCLUDED. AS PUBLIC SERVANTS WHO PROVIDE
HEALTH TO OUR COMMUNITIES AND ARE MAJOR EMPLOYERS, WE DO NOT BELIEVE THAT
THE LEGISLATION INTENDS TO DENY US THE OPPORTUNITY TO SERVE ON REGIONAL
ALLIANCE BOARDS WE WILL WORK TO CLARIFY THAT LANGUAGE

COUNTY ROLE IN STATE PUBLIC HEALTH GRANTS

WE APPLAUD THE PRESIDENT'S ATTENTION TO PUBLIC HEALTH. A SIGNIFICANT
NEW INFUSION OF FUNDS IS PROPOSED OUR POLICY, HOWEVER, SUPPORTED A SPECIFIC
SET-ASIDE FOR PUBLIC HEALTH WE ARE CONCERNED THAT AN AUTHORIZATION
LEAVES THIS INITIATIVE VULNERABLE, GIVEN THE FEDERAL BUDGET CAPS THE
GRANTS AVAILABLE FOR CORE PUBLIC HEALTH FUNCTIONS ARE INTENDED TO
STRENGTHEN STATE AND LOCAL PUBLIC HEALTH AGENCIES STATES WILL BID
COMPETITIVELY ON ONE OR A NUMBER OF CORE FUNCTIONS

WE URGE THAT STRONG MEASURES BE TAKEN TO ENSURE COUNTY
PARTICIPATION IN THE GRANT PREPARATION PROCESS. IF STATES ARE REQUIRED TO
IDENTIFY THE AMOUNT OF CURRENT LOCAL FUNDING SPENT TOWARDS A SPECIFIC CORE
FUNCTION, THEN COUNTIES MUST HAVE SIGNIFICANT INPUT INTO THE PROCESS THIS
PRINCIPLE ALSO HOLDS FOR THE MENTAL HEALTH AND SUBSTANCE ABUSE ACCESS
FUNDS WHICH WILL BE DISTRIBUTED BASED ON STATE APPLICATIONS WHICH MUST
DEMONSTRATE THAT NON-FEDERAL FUNDS WILL BE MAINTAINED AT CURRENT LEVELS

COUNTY ROLE IN STATE LONG TERM CARE GRANTS

STATE AND COUNTY RELATIONSHIPS NEED CLEARER DEFINITION ALSO IN THE
HOME AND COMMUNITY-BASED LONG TERM CARE PROGRAM. STATES WILL BE GIVEN
FLEXIBILITY IN SPECIFYING THE TYPES OF SERVICES AND PAYMENTS FOR THE
PROGRAM AN ADVISORY GROUP WOULD BE SET UP IN EACH STATE ESTABLISHING AND
MAINTAINING THE SYSTEM. DESPITE THE SIGNIFICANT ROLE COUNTY GOVERNMENTS
ASSUME THROUGH THEIR AREA AGENCIES ON AGING AND DISABILITY-RELATED
SERVICES, COUNTIES ARE NOT MENTIONED AS SERVING ON THE STATE ADVISORY
GROUP

ENABLING SERVICES

COUNTIES ARE CONCERNED ABOUT THE PERMISSIVE LANGUAGE GIVING STATES
THE OPTION TO PROVIDE FISCAL INCENTIVES TO HEALTH PLANS TO ENROLL AND SERVE
DISADVANTAGED GROUPS. STATES ALSO MAY PROVIDE FUNDS FOR EXTRA NON-
MEDICAL SERVICES TO ENSURE ACCESS SUCH AS OUTREACH, TRANSPORTATION AND
INTERPRETING SERVICES.

IN ANOTHER SECTION OF THE BILL, THERE ARE FEDERAL AUTHORIZATIONS
UNDER THE PUBLIC HEALTH SERVICE INITIATIVE TO SUPPORT ENABLING SERVICES AND
TO CREATE PUBLIC OR NON-PROFIT HEALTH PLANS WHICH SERVE SIGNIFICANT
NUMBERS OF THE MEDICALLY UNDERSERVED

SINCE WE SEE THE CURRENT SYSTEM DISARRAY AT THE LOCAL LEVEL, WE
BELIEVE THAT THERE IS A POTENTIAL FOR FAILING TO REACH DISADVANTAGED
POPULATIONS UNDER THIS DESIGN. STATES WILL BE UNDER TREMENDOUS PRESSURE TO
FULFILL THE NEW REQUIREMENTS OF THE SYSTEM IT IS UNLIKELY THAT THEY WILL
ACT ON AN OPTION TO PROVIDE ENABLING SERVICES SINCE THEY WILL ASSUME A
SEPARATE POOL OF FEDERAL MONEY MAY BE AVAILABLE, OR, AS A LAST RESORT,
COUNTIES WILL FILL IN THE GAPS THE CONGRESS WILL BE UNDER THE SAME SEVERE
FISCAL PRESSURES AS WELL

THERE MUST BE GREATER ASSURANCES THAT ENABLING SERVICES FUNDS WILL
BE AVAILABLE TO HEALTH PLANS OR ESSENTIAL COMMUNITY PROVIDERS THE
CURRENT STATE OPTION AND A POSSIBLE FEDERAL AUTHORIZATION LEAVE TOO MANY
CHANCES FOR FAILURE PERHAPS A SPECIFIC SET-ASIDE WITHIN THE REGIONAL
ALLIANCES WOULD GIVE GREATER CERTAINTY THAT THESE CRITICAL SERVICES ARE
PROVIDED

SUBSIDIES FOR LOW-INCOME INDIVIDUALS

COUNTIES ARE CONCERNED ABOUT THE CAP ON SUBSIDIES TO PAY FOR THE
PREMIUMS OF LOW-INCOME PERSONS WHILE THERE IS A PROVISION TO GIVE THE
CONGRESS THE OPPORTUNITY TO APPROPRIATE ADDITIONAL FUNDS IF THE SUBSIDIES
ARE DEPLETED, WE KNOW FROM EXPERIENCE THAT TOO OFTEN THOSE INITIATIVES
COME TO US IN THE FORM OF ANOTHER UNFUNDED FEDERAL MANDATE STATES WILL

NOT CHANGE THEIR REQUIREMENTS FOR COUNTIES TO COVER THE UNINSURED OR UNDERINSURED WE WILL LEFT WITH THE STATE, OR IN SOME CASES. BY OURSELVES TO PICK UP THE PIECES.

EMPLOYER ISSUES

COUNTIES ARE MAJOR EMPLOYERS, PROVIDING HEALTH COVERAGE TO ABOUT TWO MILLION EMPLOYEES. WE ARE CONCERNED ABOUT THE SEPARATE TREATMENT OF PUBLIC EMPLOYERS COMPARED TO THEIR PRIVATE COUNTERPARTS

SOME COUNTIES EMPLOYING 5,000 OR MORE EMPLOYEES WANT TO HAVE THE SAME OPTION TO BECOME THEIR OWN ALLIANCE AS SIMILAR SIZED CORPORATIONS THEY HAVE SUCCESSFULLY MANAGED THEIR OWN HEALTH COSTS PROVIDING A COMPREHENSIVE SET OF BENEFITS. THEY ASK TO BE TREATED THE SAME AS A LARGE BUSINESS

CONSISTENT WITH THIS PHILOSOPHY IS COUNTY GOVERNMENT'S POSITION THAT THEY BE INCLUDED IN THE SAME PAYROLL CAP AS BUSINESS AN EMPLOYER AND ITS EMPLOYEES SHOULD NOT BE TREATED DIFFERENTLY BASED ON WHETHER THEY ARE PUBLIC SERVANTS OR ARE IN THE PRIVATE SECTOR PRIVATE BUSINESS HAS BEEN GIVEN ASSURANCES THAT NO MORE THAN 7 9 PERCENT OF THEIR TOTAL PAYROLL WILL GO TOWARD MEETING THEIR PREMIUM CONTRIBUTION FOR THE COMPREHENSIVE STANDARD BENEFIT. YET, PUBLIC EMPLOYERS WILL NOT GET THAT SAME TREATMENT UNTIL THE YEAR 2002 AGAIN, THE OPTIONS AND FLEXIBILITY GIVEN TO EMPLOYERS AND THEIR EMPLOYEES SHOULD NOT BE DETERMINED BY WHETHER THEY ARE PUBLIC OR PRIVATE ENTITIES

THANK YOU FOR THIS OPPORTUNITY TO TESTIFY I WILL BE HAPPY TO ANSWER ANY QUESTIONS

NATIONAL ASSOCIATION *of* COUNTIES

440 First St NW, Washington, DC 20001
202/393-6226

THE COUNTY ROLE IN TODAY'S HEALTH SYSTEM

County government's broad perspective on the health system is unique due to the range and magnitude of its functions.

FUNCTIONS

1) **Public Health** - Counties work to ensure the well-being of the entire community through public health services, with a strong focus on cost-effective screening and preventive services.

2) **Provider/Administrator** - Counties administer and provide services directly to the community, including those mandated by the federal and state governments.

3) **Payor** - Counties assure access to the health care system for their employees by providing or purchasing health insurance.

4) **Purchaser** - Counties purchase health services from other providers with local tax dollars.

MAGNITUDE

- Counties are responsible for spending approximately $30 billion on health and hospital services annually.
- Counties provide care for approximately 40 million people who access local health departments.
- Counties are responsible for at least 4,500 public health facilities including hospitals, nursing homes, clinics, health departments and mental health clinics.
- Counties spend approximately $680 million annually on capital outlay for hospital construction, maintenance and equipment.
- Counties purchase health care for over 2 million employees.
- Counties are legally responsible for indigent health care in more than 30 states.
- Counties are required to pay a portion of the non-federal share of Medicaid in more than 20 states.
- Counties deliver AIDS services, including care in the majority of the 24 highest caseload areas receiving emergency funds under the Federal Ryan White CARE Act.
- Counties are often the focus of prevention services with more than 90% of county health departments active in tuberculosis screening, immunizations and child health services.
- Counties provide training for 26 % of the nation's physicians in major public teaching hospitals.

#

STATEMENT OF MARTIN P. WASSERMAN, M.D., J.D., HEALTH OFFICER, PRINCE GEORGE'S COUNTY, MD.; AND IMMEDIATE PAST PRESIDENT, NATIONAL ASSOCIATION OF COUNTY HEALTH OFFICIALS

Chairman STARK. Dr. Wasserman.

Dr. WASSERMAN. Good morning, Mr. Chairman.

I am glad that you didn't ask me to make the analysis of Dr. Fielding's plan review. However, if you accept the recommendations that we offer, I think you will come up with a winning bill in the final analysis.

I am the health officer in nearby Prince George's County Maryland and the immediate past president of the National Association of County Health Officials, affiliated with NACo, and in that capacity earlier had served as commissioner Carey's vice chair on the Public Health Subcommittee.

Today I am speaking on behalf of NACHO which is the official voice for local health officials across the country and represents more than 3,000 local health departments.

On behalf of my local health officers, I have three requests for you to consider in your deliberations as you review health care reform:

First of all, the core functions of public health identified in the President's Health Security Act should be supported through predictable, consistent, and adequate funding mechanisms. These functions are those specific activities which protect and maintain the health of entire communities. They include communicable disease and environmental protections as examples.

Second, local health departments, which currently provide direct patient care services to special disenfranchised populations, should be designated, as commissioner Carey has suggested, as essential community providers.

And third, I believe you should develop a process which assures the States consider and consult with local health officials in jointly developing their new health systems.

Let me give you some background in support of these statements and recommendations.

The eight core functions are the heart and soul of public health. Although they are not yet well known outside of our public health community, they are responsible for the many advances that have been made this century in personal health, quality of life, and longevity.

You might ask, if public health is so vital and so important, why aren't you better known and better appreciated by your public?

Our problem is that when public health works and is successful, it is largely invisible. If people stay healthy and they do not become ill, then nothing bad happens and there is no story. Thus, making a compelling argument for strengthening the public health system is often quite difficult. After all, how can you prove that you prevented something?

However, when we allow support for our preventive and public health services to erode, we then create a community crisis such as a measles epidemic, or a foodborne outbreak or the resurgence of killer tuberculosis. At this point, the need for our Public Health Services is readily apparent to everyone, but there is needless panic, which could have been avoided by practicing prevention earlier.

Let me give you an example of how the core functions work at the local level. In Prince George's County, our health department, under the leadership of our county executive Parris Glendenning, led a communitywide effort to identify public health needs in our population.

As a result, we created the Southwest Health Center, supported through a public-private partnership. It is located just 6 miles down the road off Pennsylvania Avenue. And it serves the residents in our community with the highest need for care and the fewest providers.

In addition, during this process—pardon me?

Chairman STARK. On Central Avenue?

Dr. WASSERMAN. It is on Silver Hill Road, off Pennsylvania Avenue?

Also, through this process, we garnered a commitment through community leaders to address six priority areas, including substance abuse—Senator Hughes—youth violence and infant mortality. Our efforts succeeded through the application of the core functions of data collection, leadership, policy development, disease and injury control and public education. Our public health departments, therefore, address broad community concerns.

The health care reform legislation which you enact should include provisions to assure these core public health functions exist to protect the public's health.

How can we accomplish this? First of all, we need a dedicated, consistent source of funding to ensure that core functions will always be adequately supported. In Maryland, my colleagues and I worked with our legislative leaders, just as we are trying to do here nationally, to accomplish mandated, guaranteed funding for public health. We were successful, proving it can be done.

Second, we need an adequate amount of dollars to carry out these functions. Public health leaders agree that no less than 3 percent of current total national health care expenditures is required. In Prince George's County alone, last year, we spent more than $16 million to provide the core public health functions to serve our population of 750,000, and even that amount was less than 50 percent of what we deemed satisfactory.

Third, we must all understand the necessity of providing every one of the core functions. By definition, they are essential and must be available in each community. They should not be parceled out through the competitive grant process. NACHO supports noncompetitive funding for core functions.

After we assure the availability of core functions for every community, we must guarantee health care services to special populations. Each year, 40 million Americans receive primary care services through the local health department mechanisms.

Local health departments must be afforded essential community-provider status, my second point. If we dismantle the current system, without assuring an alternate system in place for these vulnerable populations, then our common goal of universal coverage cannot possibly be met.

Finally, let me remind you that just as each of you knows your own home community, your local health official is best positioned to ensure that your community health problems are identified and that appropriate programs are developed and implemented back in your hometowns.

If States are given the sole responsibility for planning, prioritizing and apportioning resources, and the specific knowledge and expertise of local officials is lost, I ask you just how well do you think your local needs would then be targeted and met if reliance on the States alone existed? Therefore, please legislate the active participation of local health officials and local officials in the State health decisionmaking process.

Let me conclude by reminding you that local health departments have been around for more than two centuries. In September, I spoke in Congressman Cardin's home community in Baltimore, at the 200th anniversary of the Baltimore County Health Department, the oldest in the Nation. It is public health activities which have improved our current life expectancy to greater than 70 years, greatly reduced infant death, and eliminated many life-threatening infectious diseases through vaccine administration.

Let's get on with our Nation's needed health care reform, but let's be certain that we anchor our new structure on the firm foundations of public health and prevention.

Thank you, Mr. Chairman and members of the committee.

Chairman STARK. Thank you, Dr. Wasserman.

[The prepared statement follows:]

388

STATEMENT OF MARTIN P. WASSERMAN, M.D., J.D.
HEALTH OFFICER, PRINCE GEORGE'S COUNTY, MD.
NATIONAL ASSOCIATION OF COUNTY HEALTH OFFICIALS

Good morning Mr. Chairman, and distinguished members of the House of Representatives Subcommittee on Health. I am Dr. Martin Wasserman, health officer from neighboring Prince George's County, Maryland and immediate past president of the National Association of County Health Officials, also known as NACHO. I am currently president of the MD Association of County Health Officers and have served locally directing health department in Montgomery and Arlington Counties for the past 16 years. I am here today on behalf of NACHO. NACHO is the voice for local health officials nationwide, representing more than 3,000 local health departments.

On behalf of NACHO, I am pleased to have this opportunity to discuss the importance of including public health in our plans for health care reform. As you know, the discussions focus primarily on "fixing" our illness-oriented, personal health care financing system, and we are here to support and strengthen the underlying public health system which serves as the foundation for maintaining the health of and preventing illness within our communities. This is accomplished through eight core public health functions identified in the President's Health Security Act. I wish to make three points:

1. We must adequately fund core public health functions, which protect and maintain the health of entire communities, through a predictable, consistent funding stream;

2. We must explicitly designate local health departments as "Essential Community Providers;" and

3. States must consult with local officials regarding the development of new health systems and all matters of planning and funding of core functions.

1. Core Public Health Functions

Public health leaders at the federal, state and local levels are working together to achieve a common mission: to assure conditions in which people can be healthy. In order to fulfill this mission, we embrace the eight core public health functions which are enumerated in the Health Security Act. Although not well known outside of the public health community, the core functions are responsible for many advances that have been made in the health, quality of life and longevity, and are therefore critical to improving the health status of Americans. In addition, the entire public health system is responsible for monitoring and assuring progress towards the health improvement goals to be achieved in the Year 2000. A good example of this is immunization. Many immunizations are received via the private sector; however, it is the duty of the public health department to monitor the immunization rates of the community. This monitoring will be necessary regardless of the design of the health care system, in order to hold the health system accountable.

You might ask, "If public is so important, why aren't you better recognized?" Our problem is that when public health "works," it is largely invisible. People stay healthy, and do not become ill. Thus, making a compelling argument for strengthening the public health system is often quite difficult. However, when services have eroded and a public health crisis emerges, such as a measles epidemic, or a food-borne outbreak, or a resurgence of killer tuberculosis, the need for public health services is apparent to all in the community. But then there is panic . . . often needless. . . since it could have been avoided through prevention.

Let me give you an example of how the core public health functions work at the local level. In Prince George's County, shortly after I was appointed, County Executive Parris Glendenning appointed a citizen's Blue Ribbon Commission of Health and asked me to serve as Chairperson. Using health department staff, we gathered information to identify areas in the County with the highest need for care and the fewest number of service providers. We also discussed specific health problems affecting the greatest number of community residents. As a result of these efforts, the Commission was able to influence the government and the private sector to work together to place a new health center into the Suitland community - approximately 5 miles east of the Capitol just off Pennsylvania Avenue. We have been joined there by Dimensions Health Care Corporation which provides a full service primary care program alongside of our own at the Southwest Health

Center. The Commission also identified six critical areas for continued review as together we look toward improving the health of our community for the year 2000. Those six areas include the reduction of:

- infant mortality
- substance abuse
- chronic medical conditions
- youth violence
- communicable illness
- sexually transmitted diseases.

Exercising the core functions of data collection, leadership and policy development, disease and injury control, public education, and accountability and quality assurance, our public health department has facilitated broad community response to social and health problems. These problems would not be addressed without a public health system.

While NACHO is pleased to see that Section 3312 of the Health Security Act addresses the eight core functions of public health, additional provisions would greatly enhance our national ability to protect the public's health. NACHO makes the following recommendations regarding funding for these activities, and supports their inclusion in any health care reform bill:

- We need a dedicated, consistent source of funding to assure that core functions will always be adequately supported. In Maryland, my colleagues and I have worked with our legislative leaders to accomplish this exact outcome--mandated, guaranteed funding.

- Public health leaders agree that no less than three percent of current total national health care expenditures, or $27 billion, is needed to adequately support the core functions for public health, and any additional personal care services provided by public health departments should receive additional funds. (The Health Security Act does not sufficiently fund the necessary core public health functions: the authorization is only $12 million for fiscal year 1995 and reaches a peak of $750 million by fiscal year 2000.) In Prince George's County alone, we spent more than $16 million in 1993 to provide the core public health functions to a population of approximately 750,000. Even this amount is less than 50% of that deemed adequate.

- By definition, "core" functions are essential. We are concerned that competitive grants will not fund all essential services needed to keep communities healthy. Therefore, NACHO supports non-competitive funding for core functions.

2. "Essential Community Provider" Status

Each year, 40 million people receive personal health care services from local health departments. Dismantling this system of care, without assuring that other systems of care are in place to provide all necessary services, would greatly impede universal coverage.

As we progress to a new, personal care system, in the interim we must continue support of hard-to-reach and special populations by specifically designating local health departments as Essential Community Providers. Through this designation we can be assured of maintaining the efficient and effective means of providing coverage to vulnerable populations during the transition phase.

3. Local Input to Decision-Making

It seems likely that whatever health care reform legislation is passed will allow some state flexibility in designing new health care systems. States creating new health systems overall must consult with their political subdivisions, primarily counties, which actually deliver or administer health care currently to uninsured populations. County governments must be involved in the creation of the new state systems. If there are system failures, we will ultimately pick up the pieces. We are under no illusion that any state will repeal their provisions making counties the providers of last resort. Meaningful consultation must occur between local and state officials in designing new state systems.

Effectively addressing local health problems requires an understanding of the needs and resources of individual communities. Local health officials are best positioned to ensure that health problems are identified and that appropriate programs are developed and implemented at the local level. For years, leaders in public health throughout the nation, together with the Centers for Disease Control and Prevention, have been developing and testing programs of coordinated, community health priority planning and health status monitoring, which provide effective blueprints for action on a national scale. "Healthy Communities 2000: Model Standards" and "The Assessment Protocol for Excellence in Public Health (APEX*PH*)" are two of the most widely used methods for formulating and focusing local attention on health goals and objectives.

The Health Security Act, as an example, gives sole responsibility to states for planning, prioritizing, and allocating resources. The knowledge and expertise of local health officials is lost. Mandated participation of local health departments in planning, prioritizing and allocating resources would ensure that local needs are effectively targeted and met.

Let me conclude by reminding you that local health departments have been in existence for over 2 centuries. Last September I spoke during Baltimore's 200th anniversary of its health department origin . . . the oldest in the country. We have a proud an meaningful heritage. It is public health activities which have improved our life expectancy to greater than 70 years, reduced infant death rates, and eliminated many life-threatening infectious diseases through vaccine administration. Let's go forward with our nation's needed health care reform, but let's be certain we build our new structure on the firm foundations and core of public health.

Thank you for the opportunity to appear before you today. I would be happy to answer any questions.

Chairman STARK. I noticed that you have perhaps the worst of both worlds, that you are both a lawyer and a physician.

Dr. WASSERMAN. Yes, sir. People say I can sue myself.

Chairman STARK. Are you licensed to practice before the Federal Bench?

Dr. WASSERMAN. I am admitted to the Maryland Bar.

Chairman STARK. Can you plead cases in the Supreme Court?

Dr. WASSERMAN. I think so, but I don't think you would want me to.

Chairman STARK. No, but commissioner Carey does, to drum up a little business between you two guys.

Will you explain to commissioner Carey why he should retain you to sue the administration on the basis that their bill is unconstitutional relative to Article Eight, which will take care of Mr. Carey's——

Dr. WASSERMAN. Cruel and unusual punishment in the Federal prisons?

Chairman STARK. Exactly. There is no question that the President's bill denying full care to prisoners would be unconstitutional under those grounds.

Dr. Wasserman could have fame and glory. Mr. Carey could get the money for his——

Mr. CAREY. Services provided.

Chairman STARK. Is there any question in your mind that is unconstitutional?

Dr. WASSERMAN. I think my county executive would certainly support the inclusion of treatment to prisoners because it is extraordinarily expensive.

Chairman STARK. What is good enough for Haldeman, Ehrlichman and Ollie North, ought to be good enough for the rest of us.

Dr. WASSERMAN. I would support that.

Chairman STARK. Let me ask you further, Owensville is not in Prince George's, that is Anne Arundel?

Dr. WASSERMAN. I think so.

Chairman STARK. They have a community center there.

Dr. WASSERMAN. Yes.

Chairman STARK. Is that similar to the one you are mentioning in Suitland, the South County Health Clinic there?

Dr. WASSERMAN. I am not as familiar with the one in Anne Arundel County, but ours really was a public-private partnership using Dimensions Health Care Corporation to place a primary care center right indistinguishable from our center in——

Chairman STARK. You are not the only county, is what I meant. The ones I see Anne Arundel County are similarly——

Dr. WASSERMAN. Yes, sir. We can provide primary care as well as public health preventive services at the same site. What we try to create is a seamless system between the public health——

Chairman STARK. Do you see any reason that you ought to turn the services of those community centers out to public bid? Do you think you ought to have three or four or five plans competing with each other to offer those services?

Dr. WASSERMAN. Am I against competition?

Chairman STARK. No. I am just saying, would they you know, you think——

Dr. WASSERMAN. I think as I mentioned that——

Chairman STARK. Do you need two or three plans there to fulfill the mission of those centers?

Dr. WASSERMAN. I am not sure I completely understand.

Chairman STARK. OK. You have the county and a contractor—

Dr. WASSERMAN. Yes.

Chairman STARK [continuing]. Who provides care. Is there any reason you have to two or three contractors in those centers?

Dr. WASSERMAN. I don't believe so. I think that the system would save money by making sure that there was a good system, and one of the things that we would argue for as one of the core functions, is that the public health agency might be able to be in a position to assure the quality of the resultant health care from those—from that single institution.

Chairman STARK. Senator Hughes, is former First Lady Ford supportive of your position, do you know, her foundation? She is actively——

Senator HUGHES. Yes, it is. It is all cited and it is all in the information, and we are willing to furnish to the committee anything they would like to have in addition to that.

Chairman STARK. Thank you very much.

Mr. Thomas.

Mr. THOMAS. Senator, I want to thank you for your testimony, as well and congratulate you on your anniversary.

One of the frustrating things for me, at least in focusing on preventive care, everyone can talk about the usefulness, societal benefits, cost savings from prevention, but under the budgetary rules that we operate on, we can't show savings.

In your testimony, you have both in graph form and in written form, a window of 3 to 5 years which fits into the budgetary pattern of a clear return on investment in dealing with alcohol abuse. And I am going to work on that in terms of seeing if there isn't something within that window that we can use to get savings. Many other preventive services, obviously, go over a longer period of time. Sometimes even a lifetime, when we can't get savings. But yours is the first example that I have seen which fits within the ridiculous 5-year window that we have to operate off of on preventive care.

So I appreciate your testimony. It focused me on one area that is very helpful.

Dr. Fielding, it is clear that some folks think that health care reform is going to be an engine to pull a lot of other changes in the law which secondarily will benefit us in the health care arena, like gun control and other things. What we need, and I have not seen, are some folks to prioritize. As you indicated, you need some additional assistance. But, frankly, we will like to preload it in the legislation if we can, rather than set up a structure to get it. Prioritize some of the benefits from prevention in a narrow health care field definition. Then we could—and, clearly, the broader of field areas, corollary savings, if we did this in this area, if we did that in this area, if we did that in this area, so if people are looking at savings, you have a separate area in which other legislation would need to be passed, but could clearly be promoted, and education be carried on on the savings, that would be corollary, but would spill over into the health care area.

I don't know if you folks have done any work on that at all, but even if it is on a regional or a county basis, or even a State basis from California, we have got to begin showing what we could be doing if we were able to count it from the core preventive health care areas, obviously, immunization and those sorts of things, but then the secondary areas as well.

Do you have anything on that at all?

Dr. FIELDING. Well, we would be happy to provide you with some additional information. It is, unfortunately, difficult to put in it such categorical terms because it depends on the population, the setting, the frequency those types of things.

Mr. THOMAS. And that is why we can't score the savings, because they are behavioral changes.

Dr. FIELDING. On the other hand, there are plenty of examples of effective programs. Take the issue of reduction of adolescent childbearing. We know that can—we know we are spending tens of billions of dollars a year as a result of that and we know there are a bunch of effective community programs—now I am not in the middle of health care system, I am talking about the second leg of that stool—that work, as an example.

There are a number of violence prevention programs that are reducing the total firearms. We know that those can work. So I think there are good models that can be used. Whether one, in fact, can score specific savings is more difficult in a way that there would be agreement on. But I think we can provide you that additional information.

[The following was subsequently received:]

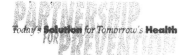

The Honorable Richard S Schweiker, *Chair*
Glenna M Crooks Ph D., *Vice Chair*
Gilbert S Omenn. M D., Ph D. *Secretary*
John R Seffrin, Ph D *Treasurer*

Karen A Bodenhorn, R N M P H *Executive Director*

November 30, 1994

Allison Giles
Office of Congressman Bill Thomas
2209 Rayburn House Office Building
U.S. House of Representatives
Washington, D.C. 20515

Dear Allison:

Last February, *Partnership for Prevention* had the priviledge of testifying before the Health Subcommittee of the Ways & Means Committee. Following the testimony presented by Jonathan Fielding, MD, MPH, MBA, the Subcommittee requested that *Partnership* provide additional information concerning the savings derived from prevention activities. We hope the enclosed materials will be helpful in understanding why prevention is essential to our health-care system and why disease prevention and health promotion programs should be included in health-care reform legislation.

To respond to the Subcommittee's general question regarding whether prevention saves more than it costs, the enclosed reports indicate that sometimes it does; for example, estimates suggest that $69 billion in medical care system spending could be averted by the year 2000 by targeting just six health problems. Other times, prevention saves lives at a reasonable cost. What is clear is that preventive services and programs offer Americans the possiblity of longer, healthier, and more productive lives.

The enclosed materials also provide information concerning the definition of prevention and explanation of its three components: clinical services, community-based services, and economic and social prevention-oriented policies and numerous success stories illustrating the benefits of a strong public health system.

Enclosed please find the following:

Prevention: Benefits, Costs, and Savings is a report prepared for *Partnership for Prevention*, which details the "bottom line" on the benefits, costs, and savings from the three components of prevention: community-based prevention, clinical preventive services, and prevention-oriented social and economic policies.

Partnership for Prevention is a
non-profit national organization
committed to increasing visibility
and priority for prevention within
national health policy and practice

1220 19th Street, NW
Suite 405
Washington, DC 20036
(202) 833-0009
(202) 833-0113 Fax

Although, as our report indicates, cross-cutting economic analyses of prevention strategies have not been completed, a body of research on the cost-effectiveness and efficacy of prevention is emerging. *Prevention: Benefits, Costs, and Savings* draws from this research and offers some general principles about the best prevention buys.

For A Healthy Nation: Returns on Investment in Public Health is a report prepared by the Office of Disease Prevention and Health Promotion. The report reviews public health activities as they are carried out at national, state, and local levels.

Five-Hundred Life-Saving Interventions and Their Cost-Effectiveness is a Harvard University study supported by a research grant from the National Science Foundation. The report gathers information on the costs and effectiveness of life-saving interventions in the United States from publicly available economic analyses. Cost-effectiveness ratios and bibliographic references for more than five-hundred life-saving interventions are provided. The study reflects that, as with medical care, the cost-effectiveness of preventive interventions vary tremendously.

Thank you for the opportunity to provide the Subcommittee with additional information. We look forward to working with you on improving the health of the public. If you have any questions or need additional information, please do not hesitate to call me at 202-833-0009.

Sincerely,

Mila N. Roschwalb
Director of Public Policy

Enclosures

[THE REPORTS REFERRED TO ARE BEING RETAINED IN THE COMMITTEE FILES.]

Mr. THOMAS. It is difficult but without that it is also difficult to educate in terms of your complaining about costs here. This is at least a relatively potential savings. We need to do some of that as we move forward, because there are real savings.

Dr. WASSERMAN, your examples were good and, obviously, civilization is a clearing in the jungle, and when we forget that, the clearing gets smaller.

Dr. WASSERMAN. I just wanted to comment, earlier this week I made a presentation to our local board of health, and one of the concerns that they had was homicide, Prince George's had about 156 homicides last year. We talked about gunshot wounds because our commission on health also had some of our local surgeons.

The night before the presentation, he had served in the ER and had two gunshots come in. We averaged the costs. For every gunshot wound, there were in direct medical care costs $16,000. That is not saying—this is not just for people who die, this is just the treatment in intensive care and the subsequent regular hospital stay, anesthesia costs, and IV costs, et cetera. So when you talk about cost savings, and we also looked at the number of firearm deaths in males aged 15 to 19, it leaves you with very compelling arguments that if you got rid of the accessibility, say, of handguns or you did something on the front end, prevention, you would save countless thousands locally, which translates into millions and billions, as Dr. Fielding suggests.

So when you talk about prevention, and we have multiple charts, you either pay now or you pay later. And when you pay now, you pay a fraction, either $1 on $10, or to give the example——

Mr. THOMAS. There is no question. The problem is when we put preventive care into a basic guaranteed benefit package, regardless of whoever's model it is, we pay now and we can't collect later, so it is pure cost for us to put those programs in. We are going to do them because we know clearly that they pay off, but from a budgetary point of view, it is very frustrating.

And if we could have some corollary examples so we could talk about how if you passed other legislation, you do make savings as well, it makes it easier for us to defend the preventive that we put in, even though we don't get the cost savings in the bill.

Dr. WASSERMAN. When Jonathan mentioned, if you prevent a teenage pregnancy in this year, 9 months later, if we put programs in our schools, and we just opened the Northwestern High School Health Center, if we prevent one pregnancy, then next year, we will save the costs and then we will save countless—

Mr. THOMAS. Some welfare savings, perhaps, on a corollary structure there as well so we can do that. But we need to have that, otherwise we are going to have to defend the total cost package, which I think is not fair, because we clearly will not spend as much as we are spending because the preventive will give us a return on our investment but we just can't score it.

Dr. WASSERMAN. Let me just ask, then, because I think we can get you the information you need. If we put certain dollars up front this year, then we can show you that you can make savings in this year's budget.

Mr. THOMAS. Did you do any look-backs, if you can say 5 years ago this was done, and therefore today, with hard savings, where you have some profiles that will allow us to extrapolate, that would be very, very helpful, because, frankly, it is frustrating as we move forward.

Dr. WASSERMAN. And we have to keep it within the $900 billion health care budget both ways or can we give you some savings in other parts of your budget?

Mr. THOMAS. As I said, I would like to have it narrowly within the health care area but then corollaries in others, so that clearly what you do in other areas will feed back into the health care system.

My time is up.

Mr. Carey, I can assure you that in your testimony, all your concerns about the difficulty of the local structures with the alliances and the rest, I feel fairly comfortable you won't have to worry about that.

Mr. CAREY. I appreciate that, Mr. Thomas.

Chairman STARK. Mr. Kleczka.

Mr. KLECZKA. Thank you, Mr. Chairman.

While I would not like to get Dr. Fielding or Dr. Wasserman in trouble with either Senator Moynihan or the NRA, I am sure you gentlemen wouldn't mind that conflict.

One of the proposals floating out in thin air is a proposition to help fund the health care reform bill by increasing the tax on ammunition.

Now, clearly there would be additional dollars coming in, so I don't think that is in dispute. Do you see an effect on the current crisis of handgun violence and injuries that end up in the emergency room by an increase in the tax on ammunition?

Dr. FIELDING. I am not sure how much information is available on that. I am not an expert in that area. I have looked a lot at the availability of handgun issues.

Let me answer it in this——

Mr. KLECZKA. I would assume that the same would be true, if in fact we put on a heavy, heavy tax, the availability of ammunition might not be as great. Whether or not that is true, you and I don't know, naturally.

Dr. FIELDING [continuing]. Let me answer, we have some good data from a couple of other areas that are being considered, revenue-raising opportunities from the smoking area. We do know that an increase in cigarette tax leads to reduction in teenagers who are starting and that is, by the way, where we stop making progress. We have a decline in teenage smoking, and it is pretty well stopped now, and one of the things that could contribute to much more savings is increasing that.

There is comparable data in the area of alcohol. When you increase alcohol taxes, you do reduce consumption. So I think it is realistic to assume that at some level tax on ammunition would have some impact on the availability of ammunition in times of domestic crisis or other things, but what impact that has, I would not be able to speculate.

Dr. WASSERMAN. I guess I don't think I would like to take on Senator Moynihan, but public health officials have no concern generally about the NRA. I think that——

Mr. KLECZKA. A bold statement.

Dr. WASSERMAN. I think when we made our presentation to our local board of health and our local association of health officials in the State of Maryland, we would support Governor Schaefer's assault weapon ban in any kind of control of handguns. As my training, like Jonathan's, is in pediatrics, and kids get hold of a weapon in the home, there have been multiple studies that show most of the time those injuries on guns at home injure the homeowners or their families and really don't help them and offer them certain safety and protection.

I might go one step farther than Senator Moynihan. I don't know the legal issues here, so I get my own legal consultation as to what to do, and I probably need political consultation as well, but certainly if you licensed handguns, or if you eliminated handguns and I am not—I don't think you have to worry about licensing rifles or anything to deal with people who legitimately hunt with those weapons, I support the second amendment—but I think that ammunition could be taxed, on the one hand, or you could license the ammunition for those people who already have the handguns.

So if you are talking about handgun ammunition, I might want to know who is getting the handgun ammunition because the argument is always made that you can't—if you take away the handguns, you will only take them away from the right-acting citizen and they will always be in the wrong hands. So if we license the ammunition or find out who is buying the ammunition for handguns that we want to diminish, it might be another alternative.

I guess, I see this purely as a public health issue. I often see—and in the conflict when there are individual rights against the public's rights, I think that we have to be looking at the denominator here: What is in the best interests of the American public?

And often, again, with prevention, in the long run, and I think in the short run as well, we have adequate proof and documentation that prevention, up-front dollars will save over the long haul.

Mr. KLECZKA. One quick question of commissioner Carey. In your testimony you indicate that the counties would like the option to be treated as corporate alliances availing themselves of the cap. My county and city have come to me with that same request. I think that is something we have to look at. Another portion of the bill requires the Federal Government to pay 80 percent of the health costs for early retirees age 55 to 64. Have the counties taken a stand on that?

Mr. CAREY. Not to my knowledge, at this point. I can get you a specific answer to that question from the counties association.

Mr. KLECZKA. Thank you, Mr. Chairman.

[The following was subsequently received:]

NATIONAL ASSOCIATION
of
COUNTIES

440 First St NW, Washington, DC 20001
202/393-6226

February 8, 1994

The Honorable Gerald D Kleczka
United States House of Representatives
2301 Rayburn House Office Building
Washington, D. C 20515-4904

Dear Representative Kleczka

During the Ways and Means Health Subcommittee hearing on February 4, 1994, you asked Moses Carey, Orange County, NC Commissioner if the National Association of Counties had a position on President Clinton's proposal to fund the employer share of early retiree health benefits

NACo supports the early retiree provision. However, there are more counties affected by their inability to continue to self-insure and the lack of a guarantee that no more than 7.9 percent of their total payroll will go towards meeting their share of the health premium. Benefits afforded to the private sector should also be available to public employers.

We hope to work with you to make the employer provisions equitable between the public and private sector. If you have additional questions on these issues or service delivery concerns, please have your staff call Tom Joseph, Associate Legislative Director, at 942-4230.

Sincerely,

Larry E Naake
Executive Director

cc: Moses Carey

Chairman STARK. I want to thank the panel for their contribution and call our next panel to which we will add Dr. William Richardson, president of the Johns Hopkins University; and including Merrill Matthews, Jr., the director of the Center for Health Policy Studies; James Stanton, president of the American Health Planning Association; Robert Gumbs, New York State Association of Health Planning Agencies; Arthur Stowe, president, Printing Industries of Maryland; and Marsha Radaj, vice president of operations of the Wisconsin Health Information Network, on behalf of Ameritech.

Dr. Richardson.

STATEMENT OF WILLIAM C. RICHARDSON, PH.D., PRESIDENT, THE JOHNS HOPKINS UNIVERSITY, AND CHAIRMAN, MARYLAND STATE HEALTH CARE ACCESS AND COST COMMISSION, ON BEHALF OF THE ASSOCIATION OF AMERICAN UNIVERSITIES, AND THE NATIONAL ASSOCIATION OF STATE UNIVERSITIES AND LAND-GRANT COLLEGES

Dr. RICHARDSON. Thank you, Mr. Chairman.

I am delighted to be here and I appreciate your courtesy in permitting me to join this panel. I am William Richardson, president of the Johns Hopkins University which, of course, includes the academic health center as well as many other parts of the university. I also serve as chairman of the Maryland Health Care Access and Cost Commission and so have a special interest in some of the issues you are discussing today.

I appreciate the opportunity to represent as I do today the Association of American Universities and the National Association of State Universities and Land-Grant Colleges. Together these two university associations represent the great majority of the academic health centers in the United States. These associations have established a joint task force made up of the presidents of several universities and some vice presidents for health affairs, medical deans and others to address the questions that health care reform will raise with respect to the well-being of universities and their academic health centers.

As we see it, members of the associations will be affected in four major areas. First, is universities as employers. Second, is our academic health centers as providers of care; third, our educational function; and fourth, the very important role we play with respect to university-based biomedical research.

I don't think I will say much about universities as employers this morning because we are virtually all large employers and understand the implications of both the administration plan as well as others that have been proposed.

We certainly will be alert to those impacts, but because of our size, I think we will not be affected differently than most large employers, with some differences between private and State institutions, of course. More important, I think, is for us to address the question of the overall impact of health care reform on academic health centers and therefore on universities as a whole.

It is true that many institutions find that their academic health centers, their medical schools and their teaching hospitals comprise major parts of the academic enterprise. They are fiscally interwoven and have a substantial impact on the university as a whole. It is more than an academic interest we have in the well-being of these health centers.

As to question of the continued successful operation of academic health centers under the legislation put forward and some of the other plans as well, one of the greatest concerns that we have is funding. Currently, there is a tremendous interweaving of revenues and sources of funds that support a very complex and interrelated set of missions, including the delivery of health care to low-income impacted populations in the areas around our health centers and special services that we provide on a regional basis and beyond.

We are concerned about the interrelated impact of changes in the sources of funding on both postgraduate and medical students' education. Also, as I noted earlier, there is a substantial cross subsidization of biomedical research. The impact that health care reform can have on our ability to conduct research is of special concern to us.

I should note that one of our concerns is the transition period that will take place almost without regard to what final form the action of the Congress may take. I say this because there is recognition within the Health Security Act of academic health centers, both in terms of the training of residents and other medical training and the training of other health professionals.

There is also recognition of the impact on academic health centers health care reform will bring. To whatever degree changes are phased in with recognition of possible shortfalls, pulling the financial rug out from under academic health centers is certainly a serious concern to the presidents of the universities within which these academic health centers are based.

If I could just say a word about medical education. I think there is wide acceptance—and indeed a movement towards—an emphasis on primary care. Whatever numbers are arrived at or whatever approach is taken, I think there is a strong commitment to move in the direction of training for primary care. We think it ought to be focused on the medical school where we can educate within the teaching hospital and in the community and physicians' offices and clinics.

We think second that it is important that different academic health centers be recognized as having different strengths and emphases and cultures. For example, in the preparation of primary care physicians of all sorts, we think that it is important to recognize that these will be done in different proportions and ways in our very diverse system of institutions.

Finally, I would note that it is increasingly important in our view that we look to other health professionals for the provision of primary care. Primary care providers in nursing and in a number of other health disciplines will be a key element of reform. Many of us have educational programs and research programs within our academic health centers to train and provide primary care services through other professional schools.

With respect to the issue of biomedical research, we are very concerned, I think it is fair to say, that the various sources of revenue—the mix of income that comes in to support the very complex set of missions that I have described—does, in fact, cross subsidize fundamental research that is done at our academic health centers in schools of medicine, public health, nursing, dentistry and other fields.

We feel that to the degree that we are in a competitive market and are competing with the rest of the health care system in our local and regional markets, that specific recognition needs to be made of the additional costs of research, both clinical research within our teaching hospitals and the uncompensated cost of research associated with our medical and other health professional schools.

These are very complex streams and again there is danger of pulling the financial rug out from under both biomedical research, the delivery of uncompensated care, and the education of medical students and other health professionals.

Mr. Chairman, I would be pleased to answer any questions.

Thank you.

Chairman STARK. Thank you very much, Mr. Richardson.

[The prepared statement follows:]

STATEMENT OF WILLIAM C. RICHARDSON, PH.D.
PRESIDENT, THE JOHNS HOPKINS UNIVERSITY
ASSOCIATION OF AMERICAN UNIVERSITIES
NATIONAL ASSOCIATION OF STATE UNIVERSITIES AND LAND-GRANT COLLEGES

Mr. Chairman and members of this Committee, my name is William C. Richardson, and I am President of The Johns Hopkins University. I also serve as the Chairman of the Maryland State Health Care Access and Cost Commission. I appreciate the opportunity to share with you the interests and concerns of universities regarding health care reform, particularly universities with academic health centers. I am here this afternoon on behalf of the Association of American Universities (AAU) and the National Association of State Universities and Land-Grant Colleges (NASULGC). Together, with some overlap in membership, the AAU and NASULGC represent the sizable majority of institutions with academic health centers.

The AAU and NASULGC have established a Task Force on Health Care Reform comprised of university presidents and chancellors, as well as medical school deans and vice presidents of academic health centers. Two senior university financial officers also serve on the task force. The task force is examining the key issues of interest to universities in health care reform in order to inform our membership and serve as a resource to the university community, as well as to the Administration and the Congress. The issues the task force is concentrating on include universities as providers of health care, as educators of health care professionals, as well as in our role with respect to university-based biomedical research, and finally, universities as employers.

Under the Administration plan, universities, like all employers, will be required to pay 80 percent of health care premiums and cover part-time as well as full-time employees. In addition to the other employer mandates required by the Administration plan, universities will need to make certain decisions similar to other large employers. For example, many private universities have 5,000 or more employees and could qualify for corporate alliance status. Private universities and colleges will need to consider the pros and cons of becoming a corporate alliance or joining a regional alliance. State universities and colleges will need to adapt university policies and procedures to comply with regional alliance decisions made by the states and localities.

The Administration's plan will affect several elements of current practice on campus. For example, some institutions offer retiree health benefits, while others do not. In still other instances, decisions will be made for us. If the Administration plan is adopted in its present form, Medicare coverage will be extended to all state and local government employees, including employees of state colleges and universities. At the present time, coverage of state and local government workers is limited to employees hired on or after April 1, 1986, and to state employees hired before that date pursuant to an agreement with the Secretary of the Department of Health and Human Services.

All of these choices and changes will affect university resources and, in many cases, significant changes will be required in the content and manner in which health care benefits and services are provided and paid for.

Of great interest to us under the Administration plan, and any other plan to reform the health care system, is that Congress recognize the essential role played by academic health centers and the importance of providing sufficient resources to support the multiple missions of these centers. While the Administration plan does identify academic health centers as integral to our health care system, we want to ensure that the funds essential to fulfilling the multiple missions of academic health centers are provided. Academic health centers educate health professionals, conduct world-class research, and provide care to many people, including a significant portion of those who now are uninsured and cannot afford to pay for services. At many academic health centers, a significant portion of the care provided is uncompensated. While the AAU and NASULGC appreciate the call for universal coverage, we know this guarantee of coverage will require a carefully considered transition period. We must not pull the financial rug out from under the centers that will continue to be relied upon to provide health care services to many people, with or without a health security card, in both the short-term and the long-term. We urge you and the Subcommittee to pay particular attention to the support that will be needed for academic health centers in any new health care system, particularly during the transition period from the current system to a new one.

The restructuring of our health care system will have a significant impact on teaching hospitals, such as The Johns Hopkins Hospital, that have traditionally served as the sites for care delivery, clinical research, and the education of health professionals in primary, secondary, and tertiary care services. Health care reform proposals will also change the various funding streams for our health education programs and world-class research programs. While there are clearly many reasons to reform our health care system, I urge you and the Subcommittee to assess carefully how each aspect of the reform proposals considered by Congress will affect the ability of academic health centers to continue to provide care, conduct research in medicine, public health, nursing and other fields, and educate health care professionals.

Let me turn for a minute to the issue of educating health professionals, a topic that has received a good deal of attention in the health care debate. The Administration plan calls for at least 55 percent of all medical residents to be enrolled in generalist training programs. As I understand it, generalists would include family medicine, internal medicine, pediatrics, and OB/GYN. Other proposals call for a 50-percent ratio, with mechanisms built in for determining the need for and allocation of residency positions over time. Mr. Chairman, we recognize that there is clearly a demand and need for more primary care providers in a new system that will rely heavily on primary care and prevention services. However, I raise three issues for your consideration in this area. First, whatever the final decision about primary vs. specialty residency training programs, the physicians of tomorrow will need to be educated in our medical schools. Some of the education process may be provided in the community, outside the medical school and the teaching hospital, but medical schools will and should continue to be the focus for quality medical education, whether a student is planning to be a primary care provider or a specialist Any changes in the funding level and mechanism for graduate medical education should be carefully considered for the impact such changes may have on academic health centers and schools of medicine and public health.

Second, universities and academic health centers around the country all have different histories, different cultures, and frankly, different strengths. I hope any proposal to increase the number of primary care providers will recognize and affirm the diversity of our institutions while we strive to meet certain national health care provider goals.

Finally, it is increasingly important that we look to many other health care professionals to serve as primary care providers in a reformed health care system. Nurses, dentists, physician assistants, to name just a few, will be needed to provide services, and sufficient resources will be needed to support education programs for these providers. While the Administration plan authorizes additional dollars for these programs, most of the money will need to be appropriated from an already severely constrained discretionary budget We could well find ourselves in a situation where we have created a system that relies on additional primary care providers (doctors and other professionals) before we actually have the providers in place to provide the services. It will take time for the 55/45 or 50/50 mix of generalists and specialists to be realized and, without sufficient resources, we will be unable to educate the other health professionals the system will need to succeed.

Another area of concern to many universities is the role of biomedical and related research in health care reform and, indeed, the impact of reform on our current investment in research. Of particular concern is the future of clinical research conducted at academic health centers around the country. As I indicated earlier, academic health centers have funded their various missions through multiple financing streams. Many of these financing streams have supported aspects of clinical care and research that are not covered by a research grant or other outside source. As we move toward a system that changes the way we finance graduate medical education, and the ways we finance clinical care and reimburse for services under Medicare and Medicaid, I urge that you remain diligent in preserving the kind of core support that enables academic health centers to conduct the research essential to the development of new and more cost-effective therapies and treatments.

I also urge that, in the debate on health care reform, we remember the importance of our current investment in biomedical research through the National Institutes of Health (NIH). The Administration plan calls for increases in the investment in research, specifically in prevention and health services research. We fully support these proposals and are appreciative of their inclusion in the Administration plan. However, as you know, these increases are not paid for under the Administration plan. The funds for this research will have to be appropriated out of the discretionary budget, the same budget that funds our current investment in research as well as many other vital domestic programs. Again, we urge your careful attention in this area to ensure that we do not shift the funding from one vital area of research to pay for another.

Even as we speak, market forces are at work which are driving our institutions to make changes, many of them long overdue. University presidents and chancellors across the country are taking a critical look at their institutions and thinking strategically about how to maintain quality programs with fewer dollars. Many universities, particularly those in your home state of California, are already experiencing the impact of the explosion of managed care programs and have begun to make institutional changes and adjustments.

Mr. Chairman, historically, universities have been problem solvers. We have taken on complex and difficult problems and have found solutions. Health care reform poses a significant challenge for the nation and for the university community. Changes are already occurring and clearly more are on the way. Many of these changes will not be easy, but the university community wants very much to work with you and with the President to make the kinds of changes that address the significant weaknesses in our current health care system while we preserve and support some of our greatest strengths, particularly academic health centers. My colleagues and I look forward to working with you as you address the challenges ahead.

Chairman STARK. Mr. Matthews.

STATEMENT OF MERRILL MATTHEWS, JR., PH.D., HEALTH POLICY DIRECTOR, NATIONAL CENTER FOR POLICY ANALYSIS

Mr. MATTHEWS. Mr. Chairman, I appreciate the opportunity to come and testify before the hearing today.

Two of the ideals and goals of the Clinton plan are to address the problem of the uninsured and at the same time to try to hold down health care spending, but I think the fear is that under the Clinton plan, health care spending will explode rather than decrease. And that is going to cause a great problem.

Let me explain to you by an analogy why it will explode.

Suppose you are the parent of a teenager and you go up to your teenager who needs a new pair of blue jeans. I will give you two scenarios. In the first scenario, you go to your teenager and you say "You need a new pair of blue jeans. Take this credit card of mine and get yourself a new pair of blue jeans. Let's call this a "blue jean security card." Take the card and go buy yourself a new pair of blue jeans, and whatever you get is fine. I don't care. Just please yourself."

In the other scenario, the parent goes up to the teenager and takes a $50 bill and gives it to the teenager and says, "You need a new pair of blue jeans. Take this $50, go out and buy yourself a new pair of blue jeans, but here is the catch: Anything you spend more than $50, you have to take out of your pocket. Anything you spend less than $50, you get to keep, and you can take that money and spend it however you like; I don't care."

Given those two scenarios, under which scenario is your teenager more likely to be a prudent shopper in the blue jean market place, and under which scenario is your teenager more likely to spend more money on blue jeans than you ever imagined a teenager could spend?

When I was growing up, I had the first scenario. My mother had a card and she used to give me the card to go out shopping, but she soon found she couldn't trust me to be a prudent shopper so she ended up going shopping with me. It seemed like whenever we went shopping, I always thought I needed "this" and she thought I needed "that." Since she was carrying the card, we always ended up with that.

Our concern is that under the Clinton administration proposal, the Federal Government is going to go shopping with us for health care, and in many cases we and our physicians may think we need "this," whereas the administration will think we need "that." Since the administration is doing the shopping and paying, ultimately we will decide on "that."

Under the blue jean scenario, the only thing at stake was my pride and sense of fashion. Under the Clinton administration proposal, what is at stake is my health and perhaps even my life.

Now, we know what the problem is. Virtually all health policy analysts agree that part of the major problem in spending is that somebody else is paying the bill. We are insulated from the bill. We know what the problem is and we know the direction the solution ought to take.

Now, we can approach that solution with a medical savings account proposal. A medical savings account is a tax-free account, one that would permit people to put money that they are now giving to the insurance companies, to put a portion of that money into the tax-free account to use for small health care expenditures and to purchase a catastrophic health insurance policy to pay for the major expenses.

Under the Clinton administration proposal, spending is going to increase. Under the medical savings account proposal, spending actually would begin to decrease. Under the Clinton plan with the card, the government is going to have to come in and take control of the system. Under the medical savings account proposal, we take control of the system.

Given the card, the insurance companies are going to get to keep all the money. With a medical savings account, we have the option to keep some of the money. Under the Clinton proposal, the government is going to end up making choices for us. With a medical savings account, we can make our own choices.

Chairman STARK. Thank you very much.

[The prepared statement follows:]

Your Money or Mine
Controlling Health Care Spending with
Medical Savings Accounts

Merrill Matthews, Jr., Ph. D.
Director, Center for Health Policy Studies
National Center for Policy Analysis

President Bill Clinton has identified two major problems in the American health care system: (1) that there are millions of Americans who are uninsured and (2) that total health care spending and medical inflation have been growing far faster than the economy as a whole. The President believes that his reform legislation will solve these problems.

But the truth is that under the President's proposal health care spending will explode, not decrease. Let me use an analogy to show you why.

Let's suppose that you are the parent of a teenager who needs a new pair of blue jeans. So you tell your teenager that you will provide the money for a new pair of blue jeans.

Two approaches:

In the first approach you bring out a card and you say to your teenager: "You need some new blue jeans. Take this card — let's call it a *Blue Jean Security Card* — and go out and buy whatever blue jeans you want. Money is not a problem. Just be sure that you are happy."

In the second approach you take out a $50 bill and you hand it to your teenager and you say: "Here's $50. You go out and buy yourself a pair of blue jeans — you need a new pair. But here's the deal. Anything you spend over $50, you have to pay for out of your own pocket. However, if you spend less than $50 on your blue jeans, you get to keep the difference, and you can take that money and spend it however you want. It doesn't make any difference to me."

Now, under which scenario is your teenager more likely to be a prudent, value conscious consumer? And under which scenario are you more likely to have to spend a whole lot more than you ever anticipated? Now I know that you know the answer to that. But what does the Clinton administration say? Give the kid a card!

My mother used to do this to me — she had a card, and she realized very quickly that she couldn't let me go out with that card by myself. Since she wanted to use the card instead of cash, she always went shopping with me. And whenever we went shopping, invariably I thought I needed "this," and she thought I needed "that." Since she was in charge of the money, we always ended up with "that," and I was never satisfied.

Under the Clinton proposal, you will have a security card. But the administration is going to find out very quickly that it can't permit you to go out and spend whatever you want. The government is going to go shopping with you for your health care. And I can assure you that in many cases you will think, and your physician will think, you need "this" while the government thinks you need "that." And since the government is providing the card, in most cases you will end up with "that."

Now, under the scenario with my mother, the only thing at stake was my fashion and my pride. Under the Clinton administration, what is at stake is your health and maybe even your life.

Mr. Chairman, we know what the problem is, and we know what the solution should look like. The solution is to remove the insulation most of us now experience in the health care marketplace and, as much as possible, return the money to the consumer of health care, the patient.

There is no mystery as to why health care spending is out of control. A primary reason is that most of the time when patients enter the medical marketplace they are spending someone else's money rather than their own. Economic studies — as well as common sense — confirm that we are less likely to be prudent shoppers if we believe someone else is paying the bill. All economists and most health policy analysts recognize this crucial fact. Nevertheless, most health care reform proposals — including the

President's — attempt to increase the role of third-party payers rather than diminish it. Because reformers know that increasing third-party payment will only increase spending, they want to hire a manager or government employee to look over the shoulders of the physicians and the patients to ensure no one is consuming too much medical care. Such proposals go in precisely the wrong direction, and they will never reduce health care spending without significant rationing — which the American people will never stand for.

As an alternative, why not give patients, rather than insurers and bureaucrats, more control over their health care dollars?

Last year, 180 members of Congress thought it would be better to empower patients rather than bureaucrats and cosponsored one of 12 different bills designed to create Medical Savings Accounts (MSAs).[1] Also called Medisave Accounts and Medical IRAs, Medical Savings Accounts are attracting growing support again this year, as new MSA bills are being fashioned in the current legislative session.

The advocates of MSAs span party lines and ideological divisions. They include Democrats and Republicans, liberals and conservatives. Medical Savings Accounts also have widespread support outside the Washington Beltway. The concept has been endorsed by such diverse groups as the American Medical Association, the American Farm Bureau, the National Association of Health Underwriters and the National Association for the Self-Employed.

Why have so many people, representing such diverse points of view, decided that Medical Savings Accounts are an essential element of health care reform? Because MSAs are better than any alternative in attempting to reach five important goals: (1) controlling health care costs, (2) maintaining the quality of health care, (3) getting more Americans covered by private health insurance, (4) making the market for medical care more competitive and (5) reforming Medicare, Medicaid and other government health care programs.

Under the current system, 250 million Americans find it in their self-interest to take actions that contribute to our nation's health care crisis. With Medical Savings Accounts, individual patients would become part of the solution instead of remaining part of the problem.

Establishing Medical Savings Accounts

In one sense, the establishment of Medical Savings Accounts for employees would represent only a small change in the tax law governing employer-provided health insurance. Yet this small change would give individuals an opportunity to take control of a substantial portion of their own health care dollars. If individuals took full advantage of this opportunity, there would be a major transfer of money and power from third-party-payer bureaucracies (employers, insurance companies and government) to individual patients. The result would be a radical transformation of the medical marketplace.

How Medical Savings Accounts Work. Medical Savings Accounts would be tax-free personal accounts used to pay medical bills not covered by insurance. Regular deposits could be made by individuals or their employers, but they would be the property of individuals. Money could be withdrawn without penalty only to pay medical expenses and health insurance. Money not spent would grow tax free and could be used for medical expenses after retirement, rolled over into an IRA or private pension plan, or would become part of the owner's estate at death.[2] MSAs would ensure that people would have money to pay small medical expenses, including expenses for preventive care, and to pay insurance premiums if they change jobs or become unemployed.

The Relationship Between Medical Savings Accounts and Health Insurance. Medical Savings Accounts represent a new way of paying for health care. Under

---

[1] The general case for Medical Savings Accounts is presented in John C. Goodman and Gerald L. Musgrave, *Patient Power: Solving America's Health Care Crisis* (Washington, DC: Cato Institute, 1992), p. 76. A shorter version of the argument may be found in John C. Goodman and Gerald L. Musgrave, "Controlling Health Care Costs With Medical Savings Accounts," National Center for Policy Analysis, NCPA Policy Report No. 168, January 1992.

[2] Some have suggested more liberal options for using the funds, including those that now apply to 401 (k) pension plans, which permit use when certain disabilities arise or for education expenses under conditions of financial hardship. Others have suggested that once the balance exceeds a certain level, account holders should be able to withdraw funds tax free — or at least without a penalty. Other proposals would restrict the use of MSA funds, for example, by limiting the amount that could accumulate in an MSA or by taxing the interest income.

traditional health insurance, people make monthly premium payments to an insurer (such as Blue Cross) and the insurer pays medical bills as they are incurred. Under the new system, people could confine health insurance to catastrophic coverage with deductibles of, say, $2,500 to $3,000, reduce their monthly insurance premium payments and make deposits to a Medical Savings Account instead. Under this arrangement, insurance would be used to pay for expensive treatments that occur infrequently, while MSA funds would be used to pay small bills covering routine services. MSA funds not spent would build up over time. Thus after a few years, most families would have MSA balances equal to, or greater than, the deductible on their catastrophic policy.

Why Government Action Is Needed. Under current law, every dollar of health insurance premium paid by an employer escapes, say, a 28 percent income tax, a 15.3 percent Social Security (FICA) tax and a 4, 5 or 6 percent state and local income tax, depending on where the employee lives. Thus government is effectively paying up to half the premium — a generous subsidy that encourages employees to overinsure.[3] At the same time, the federal government discourages individual self-insurance by taxing income that individuals try to save in order to pay their own future medical expenses. By subsidizing third-party insurance and penalizing self-insurance, federal tax law prevents employees and their employers from taking advantage of the opportunities that a Medical Savings Account option would create.

How Medical Savings Accounts Can Help Control Rising Health Care Spending

One of the most serious health policy problems we face is rising health care spending.[4] Over the past decade, health care expenditures grew about twice as fast as our gross national product. If that trend were to continue — which it cannot — we would be spending 100 percent of our income on health care by the middle of the next century.[5]

Why Third-Party Payment of Medical Bills is the Cause of the Problem. As mentioned earlier, a primary reason why health care spending is out of control is that most of the time when we enter the medical marketplace as patients we are spending someone else's money rather than our own. Although polls show that most people fear they will not be able to pay their medical bills from their own resources, the reality is that most of us pay for only a small portion of the medical care we receive. On the average:[6]

- Every time we spend $1 in a hospital, we pay only 5 cents out-of-pocket, and 95 cents is paid by a third party (employer, insurance company or government).

- Every time we spend $1 on physicians' fees, we pay less than 17 cents out-of-pocket.

- For the health care system as a whole, every time we consume $1 in services, we pay only 21 cents out-of-pocket.

Moreover, the explosion in health care spending over the past three decades parallels the rapid expansion of third-party payment of medical bills. The patient's share of the bill has declined from 48 percent in 1960 to 21 percent today.

---

[3] Given a fixed amount of total compensation, employers will tend to be indifferent about its makeup, i e,. how much is paid in wages vs. fringe benefits. The tax law, however, encourages employees to choose too much non-taxed health insurance and too little taxable wages. See Goodman and Musgrave, *Patient Power*, chapter 9.

[4] This problem is often described as the problem of rising costs. However, it is not clear that costs in the sense of average cost per treatment are rising. More importantly, the term "costs" encourages people to focus solely on the supply side of the market, when the fundamental source of the problem is on the demand side. See the discussion in Gary Robbins, Aldona Robbins and John C. Goodman, "How Our Health Care System Works," National Center for Policy Analysis, NCPA Policy Report No. 177, February 1993.

[5] See Goodman and Musgrave, *Patient Power*, p. 76.

[6] These estimates are based on National Health Accounts data for personal health expenditures adjusted for tax subsidies and include the administrative costs for private health insurance. See Robbins, Robbins and Goodman, "How Our Health Care System Works."

The Wastefulness of Third-Party Insurance. A great deal of the waste in our health care system is caused by people who have too much insurance. And one way in which people overinsure is through low deductibles or, in some cases, complete first dollar coverage. Low-deductible health insurance is usually wasteful for three reasons. First, low-deductible insurance encourages people to consume services they do not really need. That ultimately causes costs and premiums to rise for all policyholders. Second, low-deductible insurance discourages people from seeking low prices for the services they do consume. Third, using insurance to pay small medical bills leads to wasteful administrative expenses. For example, a $25 physician's fee can easily become $50 in total costs after an insurer monitors and processes the claim — thus doubling the cost of medical care.[7]

The Necessity of Choosing Between Health Care and Other Uses of Money. Most proposals to control health care costs turn out to be proposals to create a one-time reduction in health care spending. These proposals focus on ways of eliminating waste and improving efficiency. Yet even if they were successful, they would have no effect on the long-term trend. The long-run problem exists because people are rarely asked to choose between health care and other uses of money. As a consequence, they have an incentive to consume health care services as though they were costless. And, as long as people act on that incentive, health care spending will continue to soar.

How Medical Savings Accounts Would Help Control Spending. Given that someone must choose between health care and other uses of money, who will that someone be? Medical Savings Accounts give patients themselves the opportunity to make those decisions, after consulting with their physicians. Even though people would undoubtedly make mistakes, they would have the incentive to make good decisions rather than bad ones. And studies of actual patient behavior give us every reason to believe that empowering patients would lead to beneficial results. For example, Rand Corporation studies imply that families with a $2,500 deductible consume 30 percent less health care than families with no deductible — with no adverse effects on health.[8]

How Medical Saving Accounts
Can Help Maintain the Quality of Care

In an effort to stem the tide of rising costs, third-party-payer bureaucracies increasingly are imposing arbitrary rules and regulations on the providers of health care. Whereas it was once thought to be unethical for third-party payers to interfere with the doctor-patient relationship, today some of these bureaucracies are literally trying to dictate the practice of medicine. Although this trend is often defended on the grounds that it makes medicine more scientific, in practice it may substitute "cookbook" medicine for the judgment of trained professionals. With increasing frequency, physicians who want to admit a patient into a hospital or order a routine diagnostic test find that they must get telephone permission in order to do so. Permission is often given or denied, not by a professional, but by a clerk looking up symptoms in a manual.

How Third-Party Payers are Replacing Patients as the Real Customers of Providers. Because health insurance is the primary method of payment for the medical care Americans consume, in a very real sense it is the insurer rather than the patient who is the customer of medical providers. For example, when Medicare patients interact with the health care system, *what* procedures are performed — and *whether* a procedure is performed — increasingly is determined more by Medicare's reimbursement rules than by the patient's preferences or the physician's experience and judgment. Although this

---

[7] See the discussion in Goodman and Musgrave, "Controlling Health Care Costs With Medical Savings Accounts."

[8] The Rand Corporation, in a study conducted from 1974 to 1982, found that people who had access to free care spent about 50 percent more than those who had to pay 95 percent of the bills out-of-pocket up to a maximum of $1,000. A $1,000 deductible over that period would be equivalent to a deductible between $1,380 and $2,482 today. See Robert Brook et al., *The Effect of Coinsurance on the Health of Adults* (Santa Monica, CA: Rand, 1984); and Willard Manning et al., "Health Insurance and the Demand for Health Care: Evidence from a Randomized Experiment," *American Economic Review*, June 1987. The Rand study found no significant differences in the health status of people who had high and low deductibles. The one exception was vision care. See Joseph Newhouse et al., "Some Interim Results from a Controlled Trial of Cost Sharing in Health Insurance," *New England Journal of Medicine*, Vol. 305, No. 25, December 17, 1981, pp. 1501.07; and Robert Brook et al, "Does Free Care Improve Adults Health?" *New England Journal of Medicine*, Vol. 309, No. 23, December 8, 1983, pp. 1426.34.

phenomenon is more evident in government health care programs (Medicare and Medicaid), private insurers and large companies are increasingly copying the methods of government.

As a result, we are evolving not into a two-tier system of medical care, but into multi-tier system — in which the quality of health care a patient receives is increasingly determined by the third-party payer. The way medical care is now being delivered, Medicare patients may get one type of care, Medicaid patients another and Blue Cross patients yet a third.

How Medical Savings Accounts Could Make a Difference. The primary reason why third-party payers are interfering with the practice of medicine — denying people access to new drugs and new technologies — is that under the current system third-party payers are paying most of the bills. Since patients are encouraged to perceive health care as free at the time when they receive it, third-party payers must exercise the responsibility for choosing between health care and other uses of money. Third-party payers cannot be blamed for making these decisions. Given that people entrust their health care dollars to these institutions, they would be irresponsible if they didn't attempt to eliminate "unnecessary" procedures and substitute cheaper drugs for more costly ones when they judge the risk to be acceptable. The problem, of course, is that third-party-payer preferences toward risk may be very different from the preferences of patients. In fact, it could not be otherwise, since there are wide variations in the willingness to bear additional costs in order to avoid risks among patients themselves.

Medical Savings Accounts would give patients the opportunity to satisfy their own preferences. Rather than give all the money and power to a bureaucracy, MSA holders would control a substantial fraction of their own health care dollars and make important decisions for themselves. As a result, medical providers would begin to regard patients as their customers rather than employers, insurance companies and government. And if patients retained both the money and power to make decisions, they would receive a great deal of information that today they are denied.

How Medical Savings Accounts Would Increase the Number of People With Private Health Insurance

Like being unemployed, being uninsured is an experience that most Americans will probably endure at some time in their lives. But the experience is likely to be short-lived. Just as there are very few long-term unemployed, there are very few long-term uninsured.[9]

- Of the 37 million Americans who are uninsured this month, more than 50 percent will be insured 5 months from now.

- More than 70 percent will be insured within one year.

- Only 15 percent of the uninsured population will remain continuously uninsured for the next two years.

Moreover, contrary to widespread impressions, most of the 37 million people who are currently uninsured are healthy, not sick. Sixty percent of the uninsured are under 30 years of age and in the healthiest population age groups.[10] They have below-average incomes and few assets. As a result, they tend to be very sensitive to premium prices. Moreover, the primary reason why most of them are uninsured is that they have judged the price too high relative to the benefits. Less than 1 percent of the population is both uninsured and uninsurable.[11]

How Government Policy Causes People to be Uninsured. Government policy adds to the number of uninsured in three ways. First, federal tax policy encourages an employer-based system in a very mobile labor market. When people leave a job, they

[9] Katherine Swartz and Timothy D. McBride, "Spells Without Health Insurance: Distributions of Durations and Their Link to Point-in-Time Estimates of the Uninsured," *Inquiry* 27, Fall 1990.

[10] Jill D. Foley, *Uninsured in the United States: The Nonelderly Population Without Health Insurance* (Washington, DC: Employee Benefits Research Institute, April 1991), p. 16.

[11] Karen M. Beauregard, "Persons Denied Private Health Insurance Due to Poor Health," Agency for Health Care Policy and Research, Public Health Service, AHCPR Report No, 92-0016, December 1991.

eventually lose their health insurance coverage.[12] Second, government tax policy encourages people to remain uninsured while they are between jobs in which they will have employer-provided coverage. Currently, government "spends" more than $90 billion a year in tax subsidies for health care — mainly by allowing employer-provided health insurance to be excluded from the taxable income of employees. As a result, some employees receive tax subsidies worth 50 cents for every $1 of health insurance. Yet those who must purchase their own health insurance get no help from government and often pay twice as much aftertax for the same coverage. Those discriminated against include the self-employed, the unemployed and employees of small businesses that do not provide health insurance.[13]

Finally, state regulations are increasing the cost of private health insurance and pricing millions of people out of the market. For example, state-mandated health insurance benefits laws tell insurers that in order to sell health insurance in a state, they must cover diseases ranging from mental illness to alcoholism and drug abuse, services ranging from acupuncture to in vitro fertilization, providers ranging from chiropractors to naturopaths. These mandates cover everything form the serious to the trivial: heart transplants in Georgia, liver transplants in Illinois, hairpieces in Minnesota, marriage counseling in California, pastoral counseling in Vermont and deposits to a sperm bank in Massachusetts.[14]

By one estimate, one out of every four uninsured people has been priced out of the market by state-mandated benefits laws.[15] In addition to mandates, private insurance is burdened by premium taxes, risk pool assessments and other regulations. Ironically, most large corporations are exempt from these regulations because they self-insure.[16] As a result, the full weight of these regulations falls on the most defenseless part of the market: the self-employed, the unemployed and the employees of small businesses.

How Medical Savings Accounts Can Be Part of the Solution. One way to undo the harm caused by government policies is to change the policies that cause the harm. Thus we could end the practice of subsidizing an employer-based health insurance system, extend tax relief to those who purchase their own health insurance and repeal onerous state regulations. Even if these changes are not made, however, Medical Savings Accounts can make a big difference.

With Medical Savings Accounts, people would have a store of savings with which to continue their premium (COBRA) payments during periods of unemployment[17] or to purchase a new policy. And, because MSA contributions would be tax subsidized, the payment of insurance premiums with MSA funds would also be tax subsidized. Moreover, because MSAs would allow people to take advantage of high-deductible health insurance, they also would allow people to escape the most costly burdens of state-mandated health insurance benefits. Mandates have much less impact on the price of a $3,000-deductible policy than they do on the price of a $250-deductible policy.

How Medical Savings Accounts Would Help Make the Medical Marketplace More Competitive

In most American cities, patients cannot find out a hospital's charge for a procedure prior to treatment. When they get the bill, about 90 percent of the items listed on a hospital bill are unreadable. In only a handful of cases can patients both recognize what service was rendered and judge whether the charge is reasonable. Patients who try

---

[12] See the discussion in Stuart Butler and Edmund Haislmaier, eds., *A National Health System for America*, rev. ed. (Washington. Heritage Foundation, 1989).

[13] See Goodman and Musgrave, *Patient Power*, Chapter 9. The problem is exacerbated by the fact that the tax subsidies tend to go to people who least need help from government. Families in the top 20 percent of the income distribution get almost six times as much benefit from these subsidies, on the average, as families in the bottom fifth. See C. Eugene Steuerle, "Finance-Based Reform: The Search for Adaptable Health Policy," paper presented at an American Enterprise Institute conference, "American Health Policy" (Washington, October 3-4, 1991).

[14] John C. Goodman and Gerald L. Musgrave, "Freedom of Choice in Health Insurance," National Center for Policy Analysis, NCPA Policy Report No. 134, November 1988.

[15] Ibid.

[16] This is made possible under the provisions of the Employee Retirement Income Security Act, 1974

[17] Under the provisions of the Consolidated Budget Reconciliation Act (COBRA), employees are entitled to continue coverage for up to 18 months after they leave an employer.

to find out about prices prior to admission face another surprise. A single hospital can have as many as 12,000 different line item prices. For potential patients of the 50 hospitals in the Chicago area, there are as many as 600,000 prices to compare. To make matters worse, different hospitals frequently use different accounting systems. As a result, the definition of a service may differ from hospital to hospital.[18]

Hospital Bills for Patients Who Pay Their Own Way. There is overwhelming evidence that hospital prices are the result of a market dominated by bureaucratic institutions rather than any intrinsic feature of the services rendered.

Take cosmetic surgery, for example. In general, cosmetic surgery is not covered by any private or public health insurance policy. Yet, in every major city there is a thriving market for it. Patients pay with their own money and, despite the fact that many separate fees are involved (payments to the physician, nurse, anesthetist or anesthesiologist, hospital, etc.), patients are almost always given a fixed price in advance — covering all medical services and all hospital charges.[19] Patients also have choices about the level of service (for example, surgery can be performed in a physician's office or, for a higher price, on an outpatient basis in a hospital). Overall, patients probably have more information about quality in cosmetic surgery than in any other area of surgical practice.

The characteristics of the market for cosmetic surgery also are evident in other medical markets in which patients are paying with their own funds. For example, private-sector hospitals in Britain frequently quote package prices for routine surgical procedures. U.S. hospitals often quote package prices to Canadians who are willing to come to this country to get care that is being rationed in Canada. In many cities, Humana hospitals now advertise package prices for well-baby delivery to prospective parents. And although they rarely discuss it, many hospitals have special package prices and discount rates for uninsured patients who pay their own bills.

Why Medical Savings Accounts Would Make a Difference. Most patients already know that physicians will usually give them a better deal if they pay their own bill — especially at the time of treatment. Increasingly, the same is true of hospitals. By empowering patients and making patient payment a dominant force in the medical marketplace, the market will become increasingly competitive.

How Medical Savings Accounts Can Help Reform Government Health Care Programs

Most discussions of the problem of rising health care spending in the United States imply that the problem has been created by the private sector. Many who adopt this view are also inclined to believe that successful health care reform can disregard government programs such as Medicare (for the elderly) and Medicaid (for the poor). In fact, the primary source of the problem is government itself, not the private sector, and the primary way in which government is creating the problem is through direct spending programs.

The Size of the Public Sector. When federal tax subsidies for health insurance are combined with direct spending, government at all levels (federal, state and local) spends more than half of all health care dollars. Overall:[20]

- Direct government spending has increased from 24 percent of all health care spending in 1960 to 42 percent in 1990.

- When tax subsidies for health insurance are included, the government's share of health care spending has increased from 34 percent in 1960 to 53 percent today.

---

[18] See Goodman and Musgrave, *Patient Power*, pp. 52-58.

[19] To our knowledge, no one has studied the market for cosmetic surgery. That is unfortunate because most of what employers and insurers have unsuccessfully tried to accomplish for other types of surgery over the past decade has occurred naturally with few problems and little fanfare in the market for cosmetic surgery.

[20] Source: NCPA/Fiscal Associates Health Care Model.

Using Medical Savings Accounts to Control Costs in Government Programs. Since the primary reason why health care costs are rising is government subsidy and since 80 percent of spending generated by government is through direct spending programs — primarily Medicare and Medicaid — it follows that if health care spending is to be brought under control, Medicare and Medicaid must be reformed.

Medisave accounts could change incentives, and therefore behavior, in these programs. One way to change Medicare, for example, is to have government give each Medicare beneficiary catastrophic coverage with a deductible equal to, say, 10, 20 or 30 percent of their income. In return, the beneficiaries could deposit their current Medicare Part B premium, medigap insurance premiums and out-of-pocket money into a Medical Savings Account.[21]

Conclusion

Are Medical Savings Accounts the only reform we need? No. There are a number of needed reforms in the health insurance industry, the tax law and in malpractice law. But Medical Savings Accounts get at the heart of the problem: our tendency to overspend when we are using someone else's money.

Do Medical Savings Accounts solve the problem of the uninsured? Not entirely. Most of the uninsured are uninsured for a relatively short period of time. MSAs would provide a source of money for them to pay their insurance premiums while they are employed or in job transition. If we decide, as a public policy decision, to cover the chronically uninsured — usually low-income workers and the medically uninsurable — we can do so with a Medical Savings Account voucher.

But perhaps most importantly, Medical Savings Accounts will encourage people to make value-conscious decisions, just as they do in every other sector of the economy, which will reduce overall growth in health care spending. Reduced health care spending means reduced health insurance premiums. As a result, the number of uninsured will begin to diminish, since the primary reason why we have so many uninsured is because health insurance has become so expensive. For example, the reason most employers decide to cancel their health insurance plans is because they can no longer afford the premiums. By containing costs, MSAs will make health insurance more affordable.

Mr. Chairman, someone always must make the choice between health care and other uses of money. Most of the other health care reform proposals call on a manager or bureaucrat to make that decision. We at the National Center for Policy Analysis believe consumers should make that decision.

We have a choice in health care reform.

● With one option, health care spending will explode. With the other option, it will decrease.

● With one option, there will be increased taxes. With the other option, there will be no increased taxes.

● With one option, the insurance companies will get all of the money. With the other option, we will get to keep some of the money.

● With one option, the government will be in control. With the other option, we will be in control.

● With one option, the government will make choices for us. With the other option, we will make choices for ourselves.

The choice is clear, Mr. Chairman, we must have Medical Savings Accounts.

Dr. Merrill Matthews, Jr., is the health policy director of the National Center for Policy Analysis, a non-partisan, non-profit research institute based in Dallas, TX.

---

[21] See Milton Friedman, "Input and Output in Medical Care," Hoover Institution, 1992.

Chairman STARK. Mr. Stanton.

STATEMENT OF JAMES R. STANTON, PRESIDENT, AMERICAN HEALTH PLANNING ASSOCIATION, AND EXECUTIVE DIRECTOR, MARYLAND HEALTH RESOURCES PLANNING COMMISSION

Mr. STANTON. Thank you.

I am James R. Stanton, representing the American Health Planning Association as its president. For the record, however, I make my living as the executive director of the Maryland Health Resources Planning Commission. You have my testimony and I will not read that to you.

There are several points I believe that do need to be made, however. The first is that implicit within all health care reform proposals is planning. Planning occurs right now at the Federal, State and local level, whether that be done categorically or more generally. Planning is now happening and it will happen implicitly or explicitly within health reform.

We respectfully raise then the question not about whether or not health planning will occur, but rather what will that planning encompass, who will be responsible for it, whose interest will that planning serve, which values will be the foundation for planning, and how will accountability for that planning be assured?

We bring as an association a strong tradition of supporting accountable health planning. We know that health planning must be community based and that the planning that is done must reflect the community values, the concerns of the consumers, providers, payers and the needs of underserved population as best illustrated by problems within both the urban population centers as well as the rural ones.

We would like to make the point that the association does not believe that market forces alone will ensure that the broad community interest is served even when those forces are surrounded by a legislative framework.

In the written testimony, we have listed several items that we think are wrong with the current proposal. I won't go over those today in the interest of suggesting that health planning does have several functions. I think it more important to talk about the constructive than the criticism at this point.

The testimony lists key local planning functions, State functions, Federal functions, as well as those that have to occur across the country. Locally there must be identification of community health care needs and assisting of establishing priority in working the priority setting up through governmental levels. Local levels must assist in resource allocation decisions as well as evaluating the progress because the health care system truly is the fundamental piece of each our communities.

Key State level functions include developing State legislation and policy and respecting the fact in a 50-plus States or territories have different values as they approach these matters. States must be able to make resource allocation decisions and tie those to financing decisions and the State has a responsibility to help assure cooperative efforts in communities.

Federal planning functions include not only national health care priorities under which we can all function under an umbrella, but also assisting those areas underneath. Planning at all levels includes data as well as education and helping to solve problems.

Mr. Chairman, if you have questions, I would be pleased to respond.

Thank you very much.

Chairman STARK. Thank you, Mr. Stanton.

[The prepared statement and attachment follow:]

TESTIMONY BEFORE THE HOUSE WAYS AND MEANS HEALTH SUBCOMMITTEE
by
James R. Stanton, President
American Health Planning Association
February 4, 1994

Good Morning, Mr. Chairman and Members of the House Ways and Means Health Subcommittee.

My name is James R. Stanton and I am today representing the American Health Planning Association as its President. For the record, I am the Executive Director of the Maryland Health Resources Planning Commission, the Maryland state agency for health planning, health policy and regulatory activities.

Thank you for the opportunity and invitation to address you today on perhaps the most important issue of our decade-the reforming of our country's healthcare delivery system and the means by which each of us receive and have paid for his or her health care.

I believe it obvious that the health care delivery system is not only fundamental to each person, but is also fundamental to each community, state as well as the nation. Changes to the system, many of which are already occurring in anticipation of reform legislation by the President and the Congress, affect not only the physical well-being of each person, but also impact upon the social fabric, the economic fabric, the business and productivity fabric and the quality of life of every community across the nation.

The current health care debate focuses on proposals that address the financing of care and the provision of services primarily through the establishment of competitive systems, building in some ways on the basics of competition, enterprise and incentives that have characterized the development of our great country.

The American Health Planning Association believes that this focus must be expanded to ensure that health resources are allocated efficiently and appropriately and are commensurate with community needs.

Planning is inherent in all reform proposals. Budgets, by definition, imply that demands for health services are greater than available resources; allocation decisions are made after assessing needs and conflicting demands, then making judgements as to relative priority. Federal and state governments already fund disease and population-specific planning activities. Many states and communities are actively engaged in more comprehensive health planning and resource allocation efforts. It is not coincidental that two areas of the country often cited as examples of successful cost containment and access - Rochester, N.Y. and Hawaii, both have long traditions of community rating and community health planning. Reform proposals generally assume that planning and allocation of health resources will be vested in competitive economic institution/networks of providers and/or payers, each with its own interests which, in the aggregate, comprise the overall community interest.

Planning should be viewed as an organized process by which community participation is ensured, as an objective means by which to gauge the successes and limitations of reform and as a means to continually refine and shape future changes.

We respectfully suggest, therefore, that the question is not whether planning will occur in health reform, but rather: what will planning encompass? Who will be responsible for planning? Whose interests will planning serve? Which values will be the foundation for planning? and How will accountability for planning be assured?

AHPA strongly supports accountable health planning since health care is organized and provided locally in states and communities that vary in their needs and priorities. Broadly representative mechanisms to identify community needs, assess the capacity to meet those needs, allocate resources, and resolve conflicts are essential to health care reform.

These mechanisms must be based upon a public decision-making process which is sensitive to community values, the concerns of consumers/providers/ payers and the needs of underserved populations. There must be assurance that the supply and distribution of health care resources are commensurate with the needs of the population. Equitable ways to reduce or redirect excess capacity and to create new capacity are essential to successful, acceptable reformed health care system.

Without these mechanisms, many of the problems of our existing health care system, which are glaringly apparent in rural areas and inner cities, will continue.

AHPA believes that competitive market forces alone cannot and will not ensure that the broad community interest is served, even when those forces operate within a legislated policy framework.

* Changes in financing mechanisms are not sufficient to ensure access to services:

* Economic competition among networks does not provide a mechanism by which community values and priorities other than those that are economic can be articulated;

* Competition among networks does not necessarily provide either community decision-making or community accountability, both of which are critical when significant public policy is being determined; and

* Health service systems do not exist in a vacuum, apart from environmental and social factors that affect the health status of populations.

Given that the full community has a stake in the decision-making processes that will shape the framework and operation of a local health system, an objective and independent entity is needed to ensure that broad community input, needs, and values determine the overall design and direction of that system.

Key LOCAL PLANNING FUNCTIONS that must be integrated into any future health care system include:

o   Identifying community health care needs and helping establish priorities; Developing plans to help allocate health resources Assisting in resources allocation decisions; Monitoring and evaluating progress toward meeting community needs; and

o   Assuring that all sectors of the community participate in the planning and design of the health system.

Key STATE PLANNING FUNCTIONS that must be integrated into any future health care system include:

o   Developing state legislation and policy;

o   Makeing resource allocation decisions and tying them to financing decisions;

o   Coordinating and directing state activities, resource investment strategies, and quality of care monitoring functions; and

o   Assuring and supporting cooperative efforts in communities and among organizations.

Key FEDERAL PLANNING FUNCTIONS that must be integrated into any future health care system include:

o   Articulating and supporting in legislation national health care principles;

o   Undertaking health technology and complex service assessments;

o   Assisting financing health services; and

o   Supporting state and local planning infrastructure with data, technical assistance, and funding.

HEALTH PLANNING AT ALL LEVELS of governance in any future health care system must also include:

o   Compiling, analyzing, and disseminating technical information and data identifying statistical trends and gaps in services;

o   Promoting appropriate capacity investment and development;

o   Educating the public on health care issues; and

o   Solving problems, resolving conflicts, and building and maintaining consensus.

AHPA believes that incentives for planning must be specifically incorporated into reform if its goals for cost, quality, and access are to be achieved, and if health care is to remain a community affair.

Attached to this testimony is additional information about current planning and resources allocation activities at the state and local level. For more information contact, James R. Stanton, Executive Director, Maryland Health Resources Planning Commission, 4201 Patterson Avenue, Baltimore, Maryland, 21215.

American Health Planning Association

PRESIDENT'S OFFICE: 4201 PATTERSON AVE., PO BOX 2679-AHPA, BALTIMORE, MD 21512-2299

FOR INFORMATION   PHYLLIS E. KAYE, AHPA WASHINGTON, DC OFFICE
810 FIRST STREET NE, STE 300, WASHINGTON, DC 20002
TELEPHONE (202) 371-1515, FAX (202) 289-8173

STATEMENT ON HEALTH CARE REFORM (JANUARY 1994)

The American Health Planning Association (AHPA) is committed to the development of comprehensive community-oriented health systems designed to assure universal access to necessary, quality care at the most reasonable cost possible This goal requires fundamental reform of the supply, distribution, and utilization of health resources and services It also requires the creation of community-based systems of allocation and accountability

The current health care debate focuses on proposals that address the financing of care and the provision of services primarily through competitive systems. AHPA believes that this focus must be expanded to ensure that health resources are allocated efficiently and appropriately, and are commensurate with community needs

Planning is inherent in all reform proposals Budgets, by definition, imply that demands for health services are greater than resources, allocation decisions are made after assessing a variety of needs and conflicting demands, then making judgements as to their relative importance Federal and state governments, directly or indirectly, already fund disease- and population-specific planning efforts

The question is not whether planning will occur in health reform, but rather:

- What will planning encompass?
- Who will be responsible for planning?
- Whose interests will planning serve?
- Which values will be the foundation for planning?
- How will accountability for planning be assured?

AHPA strongly supports accountable community-based planning since health care is organized and provided locally in communities that vary in their needs and priorities Reform proposals generally assume that allocation of health resources in a community's health system will be vested in competitive economic institutions-networks of providers and/or payers, each with its own interests which, in aggregate, comprise the overall community interest. AHPA believes that competitive market forces alone cannot and will not ensure that the broad community interest is served, even when those forces operate within a legislated policy framework·

- Changes in financing mechanisms are not sufficient to ensure access to services, especially in high-need urban and rural areas;
- Economic competition among networks does not provide a mechanism by which community values and priorities other than those that are economic can be articulated,
- Competition among networks does not necessarily provide either community decision-making or community accountability, both of which are critical when significant public policy is being determined; and
- Health service systems do not exist in a vacuum, apart from environmental and social factors that affect the health status of populations.

AHPA President   **James R. Stanton**

Because health services are organized and provided on a local basis, broadly representative mechanisms to identify community needs, assess the capacity to meet these needs, allocate resources, and resolve conflicts are essential to health care reform. These mechanisms must be based upon a public decision-making process which is sensitive to community values, the concerns of consumers/providers/payers, and the needs of underserved populations. They must assure that the supply and distribution of health resources are commensurate with the needs of the population.

Without these mechanisms, many of the problems of our existing health care system, which are glaringly apparent in rural areas and inner cities, will continue. Equitable ways are also needed to reduce or redirect excess capacity, and to create new capacity as appropriate.

Given that the full community has a stake in the decision-making processes that will shape the framework and operation of a local health system, an objective and independent entity is needed to ensure that broad community input, needs, and values determine the overall design and direction of that system. Community-based health planning provides the mechanism for identifying those needs and resolving the conflicts inherent in the allocation of health resources.

Key LOCAL PLANNING FUNCTIONS that must be integrated into any future health care system include:

- Identifying community health care needs and establishing priorities;
- Developing plans to allocate health resources;
- Assisting in resource allocation decisions;
- Monitoring and evaluating progress toward meeting community needs; and
- Assuring that all sectors of the community participate in the planning and design of the health system.

Key STATE PLANNING FUNCTIONS that must be integrated into any future health care system include:

- Developing appropriate legislation and policy;
- Fostering coordination of state agencies and resources; and
- Supporting cooperative efforts in communities and among organizations.

Key FEDERAL PLANNING FUNCTIONS that must be integrated into any future health care system include:

- Articulating and supporting in legislation national health care principles;
- Undertaking health technology and complex service assessments;
- Financing health services; and
- Supporting the state and local planning infrastructure with data, technical information, and funding.

HEALTH PLANNING AT ALL LEVELS of governance into any future health care system must also include:

- Compiling, analyzing, and disseminating technical information and data identifying statistical trends and gaps in services;
- Promoting appropriate capacity investment and development;.
- Educating the public on health care issues;. and
- Solving problems, resolving conflicts, and building consensus.

AHPA believes that incentives for planning must be specifically incorporated into reform if its goals for cost, quality, and access are to be achieved, and if health care is to remain a community affair.

Excerpted from National Directory of Health Planning, Policy and Regulatory Agencies published by the American Health Planning Association, December 1993.

State Certificate of Need Review Thresholds (in dollars)

State	Capital	Equipment	New Service
Alabama	1,500,000	500,000	any
Alaska	1,000,000	1,000,000*	1,000,000
Arkansas	500,000 LTC	n/a	home health
Connecticut	1,000,000	400,000	any
Delaware	750,000	750,000	250,000
Dist. of Columbia	2,000,000	1,300,000	600,000
Florida	1,000,000	1,000,000*	any amount
Georgia	932,706	518,170	any
Hawaii	4,000,000	1,000,000	any
Illinois	2,157,820	1,118,272	any
Indiana	any LTC*	n/a	any LTC
Iowa	800,000	300,000*	300,000
Kentucky	1,545,000	1,545,000	n/a
Louisiana	any LTC/MR	n/a	any LTC/MR
Maine	500,000	1,000,000	155,000
Maryland	1,250,000	n/a	n/a
Massachusetts	8,175,000*	436,000**	n/a
Michigan	3M non-clinical	0	2M clinical
Minnesota	not reviewed	n/a	n/a
Mississippi	1,000,000	1,000,000	any
Missouri	600,000	400,000	any addtl. LTC
Montana	1,500,000	750,000	150,000
Nebraska	1,288,483	966,362	805,301
Nevada	4,000,000	1,000,000	n/a
New Hampshire	1,500,000*	400,000	any
New Jersey	1,000,000	1,000,000	any
New York	400,000	400,000	any
North Carolina	2,000,000	750,000	specified in law
North Dakota	750,000	500,000	300,000
Ohio	2,000,000	1,000,000	750,000
Oklahoma	500,000	n/a	any w/ beds
Oregon	not reviewed	1,000,000	500,000
Pennsylvania	2,000,000	n/a	n/a
Rhode Island	800,000	600,000	250,000¹
South Carolina	1,000,000	600,000	400,000
Tennessee	2,000,000	1,000,000	any w/ beds
Vermont	300,000	250,000	150,000⁻
Virginia	1M-2M	n/a	n/a
Washington	1,202,000	n/a	any
West Virginia	750,000	300,000	300,000

Chairman STARK. Mr. Gumbs.

STATEMENT OF ROBERT D. GUMBS, VICE CHAIRMAN, NEW YORK STATE ASSOCIATION OF HEALTH PLANNING AGENCIES, INC.

Mr. GUMBS. Good morning, Mr. Chairman. I am Robert Gumbs and I am the vice president of the New York State Association of Health Planning Agencies, a consortium of eight regional grassroots——

Chairman STARK. Do you have any relatives in Oakland, Calif.?

Mr. GUMBS. Not in Oakland, but I have one in San Francisco.

I am also the executive director of the Health Systems Agency for New York City, the largest one in the State of New York. I also serve as the chairman of the Service Delivery and Organization Committee of Governor Cuomo's Health Care Advisory Board, a board established to make recommendations to the Governor for reforming health care in New York State. You have my prepared statement.

For almost 20 years, HSAs have played a prominent role in efforts to improve quality, accessibility and cost effectiveness of health care services in New York State. HSAs have pursued these goals by functioning as a coalition that includes health care institutions, health care personnel, public officials, community and business leaders, labor and representatives of the State's diverse population.

HSAs strong ties with State and municipal government have resulted in their working with public officials to develop and implement major public policy initiatives in health care. HSAs strongly support the need for health care reform in the many areas being discussed. Universal coverage, insurance reform, standard benefit packages, innovative payment methods, global budgets, increased emphasis on primary and preventive care and the creation of a comprehensive health care network are among the measures that must be considered in developing an effective health care reform.

The problems of health care in America are complex and varied. Success in health care reform requires a plan that addresses systematically all the impediments of providing high quality, accessible and affordable care.

Deficiencies in the organization of health care services are the cause of many of America's most serious health care problems. Although health care includes a highly complex and specialized range of services, delivery systems are generally not structured to provide coordinated and comprehensive services in a way that effectively or efficiently meets patient needs.

One of the key goals of health care reform should be to reduce the financial burden resulting from a poorly organized health care delivery system. Unlike some aspects of health care reform, the difficult changes that will be required of providers to improve service delivery cannot be achieved by regulatory authority or market forces alone, nor can the process of change ignore very significant differences among communities throughout the United States.

The correction of deficiencies and the operation and organization of health care services is particularly difficult to address from the national perspective. Differences in regional and communities eeds, resource availability, cultural considerations and historical ractice trends vary widely throughout the United States. Means ust be found to recognize and take these differences into account. In my testimony, you have the equivalent of what the President's roposal refers to as a health plan. It is essentially an integrated etwork of services. These models do not exist in urban or rural reas of New York State, nor do they exist in many other parts of he country. A vehicle thus is needed to move the system from its urrent fragmentation to a more coordinated system. Planning is hat vehicle.

In New York State, we have had a long history of planning, and y testimony indicates some of the areas where I think we have een successful. The New York State Association of Health Planing Agencies believes that it is essential that the Federal health are reform bill ultimately agreed to by the President and Congress ust include provisions providing incentives for States to establish egional health planning programs.

We believe the key functions for planning bodies and implementng reform would include identifying community health care needs, stablishing health priorities and more importantly, strategies to ncourage appropriate network development consistent with an verall community health plan, as well as the unique needs of local ommunities; transition planning needed to assure continued proviion of needed services as States and localities implement individalized reform plans; assisting in regional allocation decisions with he goal of assuring the assessment of the adequate supply and disribution of health resources.

This would include a role in guiding and restructuring the health care delivery system, including reductions in excess capacity, building new capacity for needed services and shifting from institutional to ambulatory care and other means of achieving efficiencies; compiling, analyzing, publishing technical information and data for planning purposes by networks and for providers to increase consumer knowledge; negotiating contracts or exclusive franchises with provider networks to provide services to special populations, underserved communities and high priority program development; monitoring and evaluating progress by networks toward meeting community needs.

Many of these things we have been doing in New York State and again I have included some of that in my testimony. The chairman has generously let me continue to talk while the red light has been on. I will stop talking before he cuts me off.

Thank you.

Chairman STARK. Thank you.

[The prepared statement and attachments follow:]

STATEMENT OF ROBERT D. GUMBS
VICE CHAIRMAN
NEW YORK STATE ASSOCIATION OF HEALTH PLANNING AGENCIES, INC.

Honorable Pete Stark, Chairman, Subcommittee on Health and members of the committee, it is an honor and a privilege to speak before you today. My name is Robert Gumbs, I am the Vice President of the New York State Association of Health Planning Agencies, a consortium of the eight regional grass roots health planning organizations actively functioning in New York State (the Health Systems Agencies – HSAs), and the Executive Director of the largest of these organizations, the Health Systems Agency of New York City. I also serve as the chairman of the Service Delivery and Organization Committee of Governor Cuomo's Health Care Advisory Board, a board established to make recommendations to the Governor for reforming health care in New York State.

For almost twenty years, HSAs have played a prominent role in efforts to improve the quality, accessibility, and cost effectiveness of health care services in New York State. **HSAs have pursued these goals by functioning as a coalition that includes health care institutions, health care personnel, public officials, community and business leaders, labor and representatives of the state's diverse population.** HSA's strong ties with state and municipal government have resulted in their working with public officials to develop and implement major public policy initiatives in health care.

Recently, New York State government highlighted the importance of health care planning, using planning as the centerpiece of New York's hospital based reimbursement methodology legislation, called New York State Prospective Hospital Reimbursement Methodology or NYPHRM-V. The intent of the legislation states that health care planning and decision making at the regional level "is vital to the creation of an overall system to properly meet individual and community health care needs." Further, the Legislature notes that the emphasis on regional and local responsibility encourages flexibility, innovation, and cost-effective decision making and services.

The same legislation also establishes a stable mechanism for funding the eight regional Health Systems Agencies (HSAs) in the State, through a rate structure add-on to hospital inpatient rates, which will raise $5 million annually for the HSAs. The new law, which went into effect on January 1, 1994, also strengthens the roles and responsibilities of the HSAs.

HSAs strongly support the need for health care reform in the many areas that are currently being discussed. Universal coverage, insurance reform, standard benefits packages, innovative payment methods, global budgets, increased emphasis on primary and preventive care, and the creation of comprehensive health care networks are among the measures that must be considered in developing an effective program of health care reform. The problems of health care in America are complex and varied. Success in health care reform requires a plan that addresses, systematically, all of the impediments to providing high quality, accessible, and affordable health care.

Deficiencies in the organization of health care services are the cause of many of America's most serious health care problems. Although health care includes a highly complex and specialized range of services, delivery systems are generally not structured to provide coordinated, and comprehensive services in a way that effectively or efficiently meets patients' needs. This widespread fragmentation of functions and responsibility has contributed to many of the problems of America's health care: shortages of primary care services; restricted access to preventive care services; excessive emphasis on acute inpatient services; provision of unnecessary and inappropriate services; and lack of adequate attention to outcomes. These deficiencies have remarkably broad implications that lead to lack of access to basic service, uneven quality of care, and escalating costs. **One of the key goals of health care reform should be to reduce the financial burden resulting from a poorly organized health care delivery system.** Although savings can and should be achieved through a wide variety of measures, including changes in payment methodologies, insurance reform, global budgets, and more efficient handling of claims, the most substantial opportunities for cost savings may well come from improvements in the actual delivery of health care services.

Unlike some aspects of health care reform, the difficult changes that will be required of providers to improve service delivery cannot be achieved by regulatory authority or market forces alone. Nor can the process of change ignore very significant differences among the communities throughout the United States. This correction of deficiencies in the operation and organization of health care services is a particularly difficult issue to address from a national perspective. .**Differences in regional and community needs, resource availability, cultural considerations, and historical practice patterns, vary widely throughout the United States. Means must be found to recognize and take account these differences. These are issues that HSAs have given much attention and thought to over the years.**

Let me attempt to illustrate the case, borrowing one of the elements from the Health Security Act. The proposal calls for the establishment of certified health plans. As I stated earlier in my testimony, I also serve as a member of the Governor's Health Care Advisory Board, established by Governor Cuomo in 1991, to advise him on possible options for health care reform in New York State. The Board proposed, and the Governor has since adopted, a recommendation calling for the creation of community health networks. These are vertically integrated continuum of care models, providing both wellness and illness care for every resident of New York State. Figure 1 of my testimony provides a conceptual model of this community health network.

These community health, or preferred provider networks could have any number of organizational and governance models. They could be a single provider or a number of providers, with defined responsibilities and varying relationships assuring coordinated, comprehensive care.

These models do not exist in **urban or rural** areas of New York State. Regulation or market forces cannot actualize these models. A vehicle is thus needed to move the system from its current fragmentation to a more coordinated efficient system. Planning is that vehicle.

When the Federal government terminated its support of local health planning, in 1986 New York State, among a handful of other states, to their credit today, continued that planning.

Two examples illustrating the merit of State-wide and local planning activities are hospital occupancy rates and the spread of expensive high technology services. General community hospitals in New York, Maryland, and other states which sustained local and state-wide planning, despite a federal funding cut-off in early 1980s, are operating with occupancy rates in the high 70s to mid 80s. Whereas, hospitals in California, Arizona and other states which abandoned planning activities, are operating in the mid 50s to mid 60s. In other words, hospital beds built at a cost of half a million to a million dollars each, are lying empty because there was no planning structure to coordinate and consolidate these costly expansions or replacements.

Similarly, New York, Maryland and other states with active planning structures, have experienced the lowest, expansion rates of such expensive services as, cardiac surgery, MRIs, lithotripters, etc. California's cardiac surgical rates were, for example, as 27% higher than New York's rate in 1989, without any underlying reasons for this difference. In fact, California has a lower death rate for heart diseases than that for New York State. A recent Rand Corporation study, published in JAMA in 1993, determined that New York's cardiac surgical programs have a better success rate than the nation-wide average. The same study also determined that a higher proportion of coronary Artery Bypass Graft surgeries performed in New York are appropriate, compared to those in the rest of the nation.

I would also point out that a recent GAO Report on the Rochester experience with health planning. The January, 1993, GAO Report entitled Health Care: Rochester's Community Approach Yields Better Access. Lower Costs states:

"Extensive community-wide health planning is a major component of the health care system in Rochester. This planning has not been centrally directed by government; rather, business leaders, local government officials, health providers, health insurers, and health planners have worked cooperatively to develop and maintain a regional system to meet the health care needs of Rochester's residents. As early as the 1920s, Rochester's Community Chest Plan began to review requests for capital-fund drives. Since that time, community health planning in Rochester has enjoyed sustained attention."

The GAO report further notes that health planning was identified in a survey of Rochester community leaders as the most important factor in controlling costs and the second most important factor (after community rating) in ensuring access.

The New York State Association of Health Planning Agencies believes that it is essential that the a Federal Health Care Reform bill ultimately agreed to by the President and Congress include provisions providing incentives for States to establish regional health planning programs.

We believe the key functions for planning bodies in implementing reform would include:

o   Identifying community health care needs, establishing health priorities, and, more importantly, strategies to encourage appropriate network development, consistent with an overall community health plan, as well as the unique needs of local communities;

o   Transition planning needed to assure continued provision of needed services as States and localities implement individualized reform plans;

o   Assisting in resource allocation decisions, with a goal of assuring the assessment of the adequate supply and distribution of health resources.

This could also include a role in guiding the restructuring of the health delivery system, including reductions in excess capacity, building new capacity for new needed services, shifting from institutional to ambulatory care and other means of achieving efficiencies;

o   Compiling, analyzing, publishing technical information and data, for planning purposes by networks, and for providers to increase consumers knowledge;

o   Negotiating special contracts or exclusive franchises with other provider networks to provide services to special populations, underserved communities and high priority programs development;

o   Monitoring and evaluating progress by networks toward meeting community needs;

o   Educating the public on health care issues; and.

o   Problem solving, conflict resolution and consensus building.

Many of these tasks, the HSAs in New York State have already undertaken. Let me highlight two examples.

o   In New York State, primary care development and expansion in underserved communities has been a top priority. In NYPRM IV, New York City, between 1991 and 1993, received over $25.0 million in grant awards for primary care development. In NYPRM V, New York State's new health care financing legislation, New York City is expected to receive up to $45.0 million over two years. The basis for targeting these dollars and modeling services was based upon work my Agency performed over the past five years (Exhibit I – Health Status Index and Epidemic Health Status Index).

It is also being used as the basis for targeting up to $250 million in long term tax exempt bonds for primary care center construction, through the City's newly established Primary Care Development Corporation.

o   In 1990, in one medium sized rural county in Northeastern New York, only 11 primary care physicians and even fewer specialists provided significant levels of care to Medicaid clients. Today, following nearly a year long planning process conducted by the Health Systems Agency of Northeastern New York (HSA/NENY), local Department of Social Services and numerous community service providers, 30 primary care physicians and many more specialists are providing high quality accessible health care services to the Medicaid population in the program.

However, there are still many barriers to overcome there. There is an insufficient number of physicians in the community hospital and community based clinics are still not enrolling Managed Care clients; utilization of mid-level practitioners is far too low, and transportation services for clients in remote locations are needed. Through its ongoing participation in the county's Medicaid Managed Care Committee, HSA/NENY will provide the professional planning services and skillful community organization activities necessary to fully implement this vital new program.

I've also taken the opportunity to include a document on some of the recent activities of all of the HSAs in New York State that clearly demonstrate the contribution of local planning to reconfiguring services (Exhibits I and II).

CONCLUSION

In conclusion, I would reiterate, that local involvement in the **Implementation** of health care reform is essential. Health care delivery is a **local product**. Regardless of the paradigm used, a vehicle is needed to move the system from where we are to where we want to be. **Planning is that vehicle.** We urge your committee to include specific provisions for community based health care planning in the final Federal Health Care Reform legislation.

Thank You, Mr. Chairman I'll be happy to answer any questions that the Committee would like to ask me.

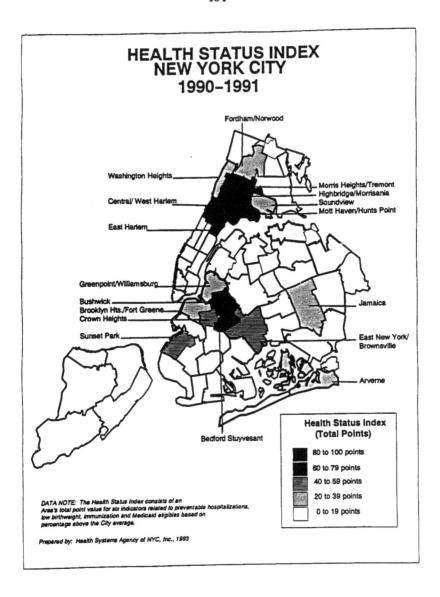

HEALTH STATUS INDEX
NEW YORK CITY
1990-1991

Fordham/Norwood

Washington Heights

Central/ West Harlem

Morris Heights/Tremont
Highbridge/Morrisania
Soundview
Mott Haven/Hunts Point

East Harlem

Greenpoint/Williamsburg

Bushwick
Brooklyn Hts./Fort Greene
Crown Heights

Jamaica

Sunset Park

East New York/
Brownsville

Arverne

Bedford Stuyvesant

Health Status Index
(Total Points)

■ 80 to 100 points

■ 60 to 79 points

▨ 40 to 59 points

▨ 20 to 39 points

□ 0 to 19 points

DATA NOTE: The Health Status Index consists of an
Area's total point value for six indicators related to preventable hospitalizations,
low birthweight, immunization and Medicaid eligibles based on
percentage above the City average.

Prepared by: Health Systems Agency of NYC, Inc., 1993

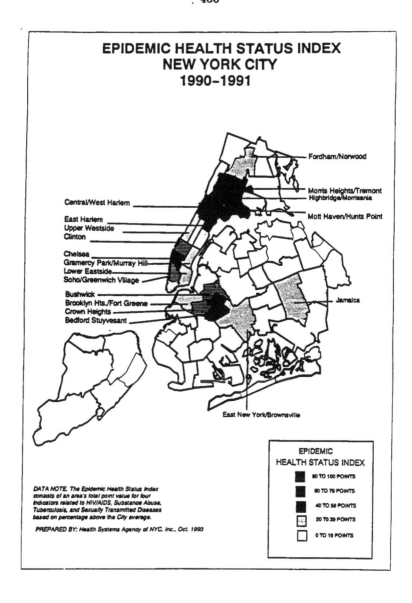

EPIDEMIC HEALTH STATUS INDEX
NEW YORK CITY
1990-1991

Fordham/Norwood

Morris Heights/Tremont
Highbridge/Morrisania

Central/West Harlem

East Harlem
Upper Westside
Clinton

Mott Haven/Hunts Point

Chelsea
Gramercy Park/Murray Hill
Lower Eastside
Soho/Greenwich Village

Bushwick
Brooklyn Hts./Fort Greene
Crown Heights
Bedford Stuyvesant

Jamaica

East New York/Brownsville

EPIDEMIC
HEALTH STATUS INDEX

80 TO 100 POINTS

60 TO 79 POINTS

40 TO 59 POINTS

20 TO 39 POINTS

0 TO 19 POINTS

*DATA NOTE. The Epidemic Health Status Index
consists of an area's total point value for four
indicators related to HIV/AIDS, Substance Abuse,
Tuberculosis, and Sexually Transmitted Diseases
based on percentage above the City average.*

PREPARED BY: Health Systems Agency of NYC, Inc., Oct. 1993

DEFINITIONS OF COMPOSITE INDICATORS FOR MEASURING OVERALL HEALTH NEEDS

HEALTH STATUS INDEX

The Health Systems Agency of New York City's Health Status Index (HSI) measures problems related to primary and preventive care. This Index represents an area's total point value, ranging from 0 to 100, based on percentage above the City average for the following six indicators:

1. **Ambulatory Care Sensitive (ACS) Index admission rate** — 35 points maximum.

2. **Change in ACS Index admissions** — 5 points maximum.

3. **Pediatric ACS Index admission rate** — 15 points maximum.

4. **Proportion of the Total Population that is Medicaid Eligible** — 20 points maximum.

5. **Low Birthweight (Less Than 2,000 Grams)** — 15 points maximum.

6. **Measles case rate** — 10 points maximum.

EPIDEMIC HEALTH STATUS INDEX

The Health Systems Agency of New York City's Epidemic Health Status Index (EHSI) is designed to identify the communities that are being hardest hit by several interrelated health epidemics. This Index represents an area's total point value, ranging from 0 to 100, based on percentage above the City average for the following four indicators:

1. **HIV/AIDS admission rate** — 30 points maximum.

2. **Substance Abuse admission rate** (opioid and cocaine) — 30 points maximum.

3. **Sexually Transmitted Disease case rate (syphilis and gonorrhea)** — 20 points maximum.

4. **Tuberculosis case rate** — 20 points maximum.

Prepared by Health Systems Agency of New York City, Inc., Oct. 1993

437

DEFINITIONS OF SELECTED HOSPITALIZATION INDICATORS

AMBULATORY CARE SENSITIVE (ACS) INDEX

The Health Systems Agency of New York City's Ambulatory Care Sensitive Index is the aggregated age and sex adjusted admission rate of the under-65 population for twelve conditions that are considered to be manageable at the outpatient level for patients in this age group. Except where otherwise indicated, the ACS Index includes admissions of persons between the ages of 0 and 64 for the following conditions:

1. Respiratory Infections/Inflammations
2. Chronic Obstructive Pulmonary Disease
3. Adult Bronchitis/Asthma (18 & over)
4. Adult Pneumonias (18 & over)
5. Adult Otitis Media/Upper Resp. Inf. (18 & over)
6. Congestive Heart Failure

7. Hypertension
8. Renal Failure and Dialysis
9. Kidney/Urinary Tract Infection
10. Diabetes
11. Cellulitis
12. Pelvic Inflammatory Disease

PEDIATRIC AMBULATORY CARE SENSITIVE INDEX

The Health Systems Agency of New York City's Pediatric Ambulatory Care Sensitive Index for the 0 to 4 population is the aggregated age and sex adjusted admission rate for the following five conditions that are considered to be manageable at the outpatient level for persons in this age group:

1. Pediatric Bronchitis/Asthma
2. Pediatric Pneumonias
3. Pediatric Otitis Media/Upper Resp. Inf.

4. Gastroenteritis/Volume Depl.
5. Convulsions

Prepared by Health Systems Agency of New York City, Inc., Oct. 1993

438

Ailing Grades

Measuring Health: The Total Health Status Index for each ZIP code in New York City. The index, with a score of 0 being the best and 100 being the worst, measures an area's total point value for six indicators of primary care-related problems.

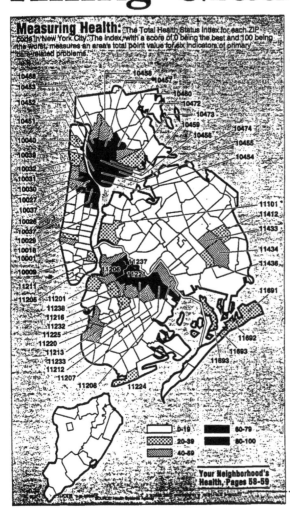

10456
10457
10455
10453
10480
10452
10472
10473
10451
10459
10040
10456
10474
10039
10455
10032
10454
10031
10030
10027
10037
11101
10028
11412
10057
11433
10029
10018
11434
10001
11436
10009
11237
1211
11108 11221
11205 11201
11691
11238
11216
11232
11225
11692
11220
11693
11213
11233
11691
11212
11207
11206
11224

0-19   60-79
20-39   80-100
40-59

Your Neighborhood's Health, Pages 58-59

Index shows need for more primary care

By Alison Carper
STAFF WRITER

At the age of 3, Denzel Moultrie Cox has visited the emergency room at Columbia Presbyterian Hospital Medical Center so many times that the doctors know him by name.

There was the broken arm before he was a year old, the burn on his hand a few months later and, at nearly every change of season — or when the wind over Harlem's North River sewage treatment plant wafts his way — there are the asthma attacks that block his tiny lungs and send his mother into a panic.

"I don't have any choice but to take him there," Denzel's mother, Cassandra Moultrie, said of why she rushes her son to the hospital instead of taking him to a family doctor.

Moultrie's predicament is a common one. According to a new Index measuring the overall health of neighborhoods in the city by ZIP code, poor areas — including West Harlem, where Moultrie and her family live — top the list of sickest communities. Indeed, the 10 ZIP codes in the city that score the worst on the new index are all in Harlem, the Bushwick and Bedford-Stuyvesant sections of Brooklyn and the South Bronx. And all are among the city's poorest.

Health-care professionals, who have long known that poverty and infirmity go hand in hand, blame a system that encourages the poor to rely on emergency, rather than preventative, care. (Minorities diagnosed more often with AIDS, Page 66.)

The new index, created by the nonprofit Health Systems Agency of New York City, is the first attempt to quantify communities' health care problems and needs. The index combines hospital admissions for 12 conditions that could have been treated on an outpatient basis, the incidence of low birth weight babies and four other factors to come up with a numerical score that reflects the overall health and medical needs of each neighborhood.

"The single measure is not an absolute value, but it's to try to give some framework of how communities, relative to one another, show some level of medical underservedness," said Robert Gumbs, director of the Health Systems Agency. "It's a basis for discussing where to put money on the basis of need."

A second index created by the agency measures the impact by ZIP code of the AIDS epidemic, tuberculosis and sexually transmitted diseases. Not surprisingly, it also shows poor neighborhoods like Harlem and the Morrisania section of the Bronx at the top of the scale.

The health index, while not prepared in anticipation of President Bill Clinton's health care reform plan, highlights the need for more physicians to serve as primary-care doctors. Gumbs says the Health Status Index offers a priority list of neighborhoods that need primary care physicians the most.

It also shows which areas are relatively healthy. Twenty-three of the

Please see HEALTH on Page 56

NEW YORK NEWSDAY, SUNDAY, OCTOBER 10, 1993

that can be managed at the outpatient level, including asthma, pneumonia, diabetes, hypertension and pelvic inflammatory disease (35 points maximum), Medicaid eligibles as of January, 1992, as a percentage of the total population (20 points maximum), the number of babies weighing less than 2,000 grams as a percentage of live births (15 points maximum); and the number of measles cases per 100,000 population (10 points maximum). The index' health data is from 1991, the most recent year available.

Borough, Neighborhood	ZIP Code	Total Health Status Index	Ambulatory Care Sensitive Index	% Medicaid eligible	% babies weighing less than 2,000 grams	Measles Rate
Q, Kew Gard./Richmond H.	11419	5	7.9	15.1	3.2	10.4
Q, Laurelton/Rosedale	11422	6	8.3	8.3	4.8	0.0
M, Downtown	10007	6	4.4	20.0	0.0	0.0
Bx., Kingsbridge/Riverdale	10463	5	11.3	14.2	2.9	9.7
M, Clinton	10019	5	10.9	7.5	3.5	2.4
Bx., Parkchester/Throgs Neck	10461	5	10.4	9.1	1.1	7.8
S I, Southshore	10309	5	10.2	8.8	1.7	0.0
S I, Westshore	10306	5	9.2	7.0	2.3	0.0
M, Lower East Side	10003	5	8.8	20.5	2.3	9.0
Q, Breezy Point/Neponsit	11697	5	8.4	1.9	1.7	0.0
Bk., Boro Park	11218	5	7.8	19.7	2.9	18.0
Q, Ozone Park/Howard Beach	11417	5	7.6	10.8	2.4	2.3
Q, St. Albans/Queens Village	11428	5	7.4	9.8	4.8	6.0
Bk., Bay Ridge/Bensonhurst	11214	5	7.3	13.9	1.8	10.1
Bk., Sheepshead Bay/Homecrest	11229	5	7.0	11.8	2.4	6.3
Q, Jackson Heights	11372	5	8.8	15.7	2.2	7.4
Bk., Boro Park	11204	5	6.4	14.3	1.6	14.9
S.I., Willowbrook	10314	5	6.3	6.0	1.8	1.9
Bk., Midwood	11230	5	6.2	16.1	1.9	3.2
S I, Southshore	10308	5	6.1	4.1	1.7	10.3
Q, Glen Oaks/Floral Park	11426	5	6.1	3.6	3.0	5.9
M, Soho/Greenwich Village	10014	5	5.9	3.2	1.8	4.3
Q, Kew Gard./Richmond H.	11415	5	5.9	9.0	2.7	8.0
Q, Flushing	11356	5	5.9	12.0	1.8	3.1
Q, Steinway/Astoria	11103	5	5.8	8.2	2.0	0.0
S.I., Southshore	10312	5	5.7	3.3	1.3	1.0
Q, Hillcrest/Jamaica Estates	11365	5	5.7	5.4	2.7	5.6
Q, Steinway/Astoria	11105	5	5.6	9.0	3.1	7.5
Q, Hillcrest/Jamaica Estates	11367	5	5.5	5.5	2.1	4.1
Q, Elmhurst	11373	5	5.5	13.1	2.2	5.9
Q, Long Island City/Woodside	11377	5	5.2	13.1	2.7	12.5
Q, Bayside/Douglaston	11361	5	5.0	5.6	2.7	2.2
M, Upper West Side	10025	5	4.9	8.3	1.4	5.0
Q, Glen Oaks/Floral Park	11004	5	4.9	3.3	2.2	0.0
Q, Forest Hills/Rego Park	11374	5	4.8	10.0	2.0	2.4
Q, Forest Hills/Rego Park	11375	5	4.1	6.5	2.6	2.8
M, Gramercy/Murray Hill	10017	5	4.1	2.5	1.8	2.5
Q, Bayside/Douglaston	11364	5	3.8	3.0	1.0	1.5
Q, Flushing	11358	5	3.7	3.9	2.7	5.1
M, Gramercy/Murray Hill	10022	5	3.5	1.5	1.4	5.0
Q, Glen Oaks/Floral Park	11040	5	3.2	12.4	0.0	0.0
Q, Hillcrest/Jamaica Estates	11366	5	3.2	7.7	1.8	4.1
M, Upper East Side	10021	5	3.1	2.0	2.1	1.4
M, Upper East Side	10128	5	3.1	2.5	1.9	0.0
Q, Bayside/Douglaston	11363	5	2.9	2.5	0.0	13.9
M, Downtown	10280	5	1.0	0.0	0.0	7.7
Bk., Coney Island/Gravesend	11223	4	9.1	16.4	2.5	9.2
Bk., Boro Park	11219	4	8.3	23.2	1.4	17.2
Bx., Woodlawn/Baychester	10469	3	9.8	14.9	4.2	11.8
Q, Breezy Point/Neponsit	11694	3	9.3	12.8	4.1	9.8
S.I., Southshore	10307	3	9.3	6.1	3.3	6.3
Bk., Woodlawn/Baychester	10470	3	8.8	6.6	4.2	0.0
Q, Ozone Park/Howard Beach	11414	3	5.6	4.1	3.6	4.3
Bx., Parkchester/Throgs Neck	10462	3	11.7	14.4	3.5	22.1
Bk., Canarsie/Mill Basin	11236	3	6.6	6.5	2.8	0.0
Q, Steinway/Astoria	11102	1	10.4	16.0	3.2	7.5
Q, Long Island City/Woodside	11106	1	9.3	12.1	3.3	6.6
S.I., Westshore	10305	0	11.7	9.5	1.5	11.0
Bk., E. New York/Brownsville	11239	0	10.3	18.2	2.5	5.3
Bx., Parkchester/Throgs Neck	10465	0	10.3	10.1	2.5	2.5
Bx., Co-op City/City Island	10475	0	9.9	7.7	3.3	5.1
Bk., Greenpoint/Williamsburg	11222	0	9.7	13.9	2.7	11.7
M, Sheepshead Bay/Homecrest	10010	0	7.2	6.6	3.0	5.4
Bk., Sheepshead Bay/Homecrest	11235	0	7.1	19.1	2.0	16.0
Q, Kew Gard./Richmond H.	11421	0	6.8	11.5	2.9	10.9
Q, Maspeth/Ridgewood	11378	0	6.7	6.3	2.7	13.6
Bk., Bay Ridge/Bensonhurst	11209	0	6.6	8.3	2.5	6.5
Bk., Bay Ridge/Bensonhurst	11228	0	5.6	6.1	2.0	2.5
Q, Flushing	11354	0	5.2	10.9	1.9	1.0
M, Upper East Side	10028	0	5.0	3.2	3.1	9.3
Bx., Kingsbridge/Riverdale	10471	0	4.9	8.3	3.0	0.0
Q, College Point/Bay Terrace	11356	0	4.8	8.5	1.5	9.7
M, Soho/Greenwich Village	10012	0	4.7	7.3	3.2	3.8
M, Downtown	10004	0	4.7	2.6	0.0	6.8
Q, Maspeth/Ridgewood	11379	0	4.6	6.4	2.4	13.6
Q, Glen Oaks/Floral Park	11001	0	4.1	5.0	2.9	15.1
M, Upper West Side	10023	0	4.1	7.0	3.1	4.5
Q, College Point/Bay Terrace	11357	0	4.1	3.2	1.1	1.4
Q, College Point/Bay Terrace	11360	0	3.3	1.7	2.7	5.5
Q, Bayside/Douglaston	11362	0	2.7	2.2	2.2	2.9

Not Ranked

Borough, Neighborhood	ZIP Code	Total Health Status Index	Ambulatory Care Sensitive Index	% Medicaid eligible	% babies weighing less than 2,000 grams	Measles Rate
M, Downtown	10005	n/a	156.6	47.1	6.3	0.0
M, Downtown	10008	n/a	39.2	1.8	0.0	0.0
Q, College Point/Bay Terrace	11359	n/a	3.0	3.5	12.0	0.0

SOURCE: Health Systems Agency of New York City

Minorities Often Hit By AIDS Infections

Struck more by fatal pneumonia

By Catherine Woodard
STAFF WRITER

Minorities account for three out of four city AIDS patients with a deadly but preventable pneumonia, according to activists sponsoring a six-month prevention campaign.

Too many blacks and Hispanics do not realize the need for preventive medicine for pneumocystis carinii pneumonia (PCP) or don't have adequate health care to obtain the medicine, according to the Gay Men's Health Crisis. GMHC, the nation's oldest and largest AIDS service organization, recently launched a six-month PCP prevention campaign with subway and radio advertisements.

"Many people with HIV have yet to be told that they can prevent one of the most debilitating and awful AIDS-related infections," said Steven Humes, director of AIDS prevention and training for GMHC.

Since 1992 more than 4,000 of the 5,444 cases of PCP AIDS cases diagnosed in the city were among minorities. Blacks and Hispanics also account for the greatest number of all new AIDS cases.

There is, however, encouraging news that all groups are benefiting from preventive medicine for PCP, one of many opportunistic infections that define AIDS. For all groups of men and women, the incidence of PCP has dropped in six years from nearly two-thirds to about a third of AIDS cases, said Dr. Pauline Thomas, the city's director of AIDS surveillance.

Community-based research demonstrated that aerosolized pentamidine and oral Bactrim are effective in preventing PCP, a leading killer of people with AIDS. In 1989, federal officials formally recommended prophylaxis, which dramatically decreases the likelihood of PCP and is often prescribed to those with HIV long before they have AIDS symptoms. PCP prevention is one of the main reasons that AIDS activists now encourage people at risk for HIV to think about being tested.

Phillip Coleman, 52, spent two months in the hospital when he was suddenly struck with PCP in 1989 but has avoided a recurrence by receiving monthly treatments of aerosolized pentamidine. Coleman, a black gay man, had never been tested for HIV, the human immunodeficiency virus, before the PCP attack. He thought he had avoided the virus because he had seemed healthy while he watched younger men die.

Black gay men are likely to avoid HIV testing and PCP prophylaxis because of homophobia, he said.

"People are still ignorant about it," said Coleman, a home health care administrator now on disability.

Through a state program, PCP medication is available free or at low cost for people who can't afford it and who aren't eligible for Medicaid. Information is available at (212) 807-6655.

The campaign, which will continue into early next year, was planned for the winter when susceptibility to respiratory illnesses increases. Every other subway car carries the posters — one quarter of them in Spanish. The campaign cost $116,000.

"We're doing what the government should be doing," said Daniel Wolfe, a GMHC spokesman.

440

New
York
State
Association of Health Planning Agencies, Inc.

submitted by: Edie Mesick
                 Executive Director
                 June 1993

HEALTH SYSTEMS AGENCIES IN NYS:
THEIR ROLE IN PROMOTING ACCESS AND COST CONTAINMENT
SUCCESS STORIES IN THE 1990s

Increasing Access To Cost-Effective Care

Lack of access to appropriate health services frequently results in poor health status, increased levels of disability, and the ultimate delivery of more costly services. Health Systems Agencies (HSA's) in New York State are routinely involved in a variety of activities which result in increased access to cost-effective services. Some recent examples are noted below.

•   In the Syracuse region, the Central New York HSA sponsored a planning effort to address the needs of hospitalized chronically ill children who are dependent on technologically advanced services (e.g. ventilator dependent). Specialized home care services were subsequently developed. As a result, the percentage of such hospitalized children decreased over a two year period from 43% to 24%; similarly the cost of care decreased as increased percentages were placed in home care settings, less costly then the acute hospital setting. Onondaga County was recently recognized as having the highest placement rate in the state for the "Care at Home" program.

•   Chenango, the only remaining county in the state without a Prenatal Care Assistance Program in the early 1990's, was unable to find a provider to sponsor the program. The NY-Penn HSA worked with Chenango County and local agencies to secure funding, and identify a local sponsor to establish and coordinate the program. Since its inception, the program has provided care for 273 low-income mothers with very positive results. Less than 2% of the babies born to these mothers were of low birth weight in comparison to 4% of the babies born county-wide. Since low birth weight is the major predictor of infant death as well as lifetime disabilities, the provision of these prenatal services not only results in improved outcomes, but significant future cost savings.

•   The HSAs in Buffalo and Rochester (the HSA of Western NY and the Finger Lakes HSA)jointly documented the long term care needs of veterans residing in the western quadrant of the state. This documentation resulted in a federal grant covering 65% of the capital cost for a veterans home to be located in Batavia (there has not previously been such a long term care facility available in the area). Savings in New York State Medicaid expenditures resulting from federal (V.A.) payments contributing to the cost of care at this facility are estimated at three quarters of a million dollars annually.

On Long Island (which has the highest numbers of suburban AIDS cases in the nation), the Nassau-Suffolk HSA conducted medical chart reviews of AIDS patients at the three AIDS-designated acute care centers. The study found that the annual cost of caring for these patients could be reduced from 25 million dollars to 19 million dollars if appropriate alternative services existed, e.g. long term care facilities and home. Through the efforts of the HSA, three long term care facilities have since been designated to serve AIDS patients. Additionally, the HSA worked with Nassau and Suffolk Counties to facilitate the provision and financing of home care services for this population.

Beginning this year, and for the first time in recent years, Putnam County medicaid clients will be able to receive primary care services within their county of residence. The Hudson Valley HSA, on behalf of local county government, worked with local providers to establish a medicaid managed care plan which will make these services locally available.

The Nassau-Suffolk HSA assessed the needs of the region's developmentally disabled population and determined that the outpatient diagnostic and treatment needs of this special population were not being appropriately met. Subsequently, the HSA involved consumers and providers in planning for the establishment of needed services. The result was the recent approval of a multi-site service to be operated by the Developmental Disabilities Institute which is expected to provide approximately 50,000 outpatient visits a year. These visits are expected to result in a net annual savings of 2 million dollars as inappropriate and more costly care is avoided.

The NY-Penn HSA played a lead role in designing and implementing a managed care initiative for the Broome County medicaid population. After 18 months in operation, the program has enrolled 15% of the eligible population. Moreover, those enrolled have gained significantly increased access to primary care physicians while their use of emergency rooms has decreased by 60% and their hospital admission rate has declined by 30%. Annual net Medicaid savings for the first year of operation are approximately $250,000. With the tripling of enrollment this year, annual savings are expected to reach $850,000.

- Additional physicians have recently been recruited to physician-short rural communities in Western New York. The recruitment of these physicians (and others over the years) has been facilitated by the research efforts of the HSA which led to the designation of these areas as federal health professional shortage areas. Such designation is a significant advantage to rural communities competing nationally for primary care physicians.

- In the Albany region, the HSA worked with a major medical center and rural health care facilities to form a partnership, the purpose of which was to strengthen rural health services in Warren, Washington, Essex, Clinton, Franklin and Hamilton counties. Over the past few years, that partnership has resulted in the expansion of primary care and prenatal care services in several of these counties as well as programs to support the recruitment and retention of health personnel.

Minimizing Duplicative Service While Enhancing Access To Needed Services

The existence of duplicative or excess health services influences cost, quality, and access. At best, services which are unnecessary, duplicative, and underutilized, result in higher overall cost to the community and the unnecessary consumption of resources that could be better used to provide other needed services. In the worst case, excess capacity provides a financial incentive for increased volume through inappropriate utilization, thus raising both cost and quality issues. HSAs typically are involved in a variety of activities to prevent duplication and development of services in excess of community need. Some examples are noted below.

- Because the Rochester area was considered to have a sufficient, if not excessive, supply of acute inpatient psychiatric beds, the Finger Lakes HSA disapproved a certificate of need application for establishment of an additional hospital-based unit. In doing so, however, it acknowledged that there were problems with the patients and physicians from the applicant hospital gaining access to the existing inpatient psychiatric facilities. A planning initiative that involved the facilities was initiated. As a result, the largest inpatient psychiatric facility (with an abnormally long length of stay) agreed to relinquish license of 1/4 of its beds so that the applicant hospital could develop its' own unit; and the hospital relinquishing the beds agreed to establish a specialized short stay program within its remaining bed compliment. Both services are now operational. Recent data indicates that an additional 750 inpatient admissions are now being accommodated without any increase in overall bed supply and the length of stay in the facility which relinquished beds has fallen to a level more comparable to the community average. Equally important is the fact that psychiatric patients receiving outpatient care at the applicant facility now have greater access to a full range of psychiatric services.

The Western NY HSA was approached by a licensed home care provider expressing an interest in establishing a hospice to serve terminally ill children. While noting that pediatric hospice services were not available, the HSA pointed out that the number of such patients was quite small and a free-standing hospice to meet their needs would be prohibitively expensive. The HSA suggested that the provider contact the existing hospice program serving adults and explore the possibility of a joint venture to serve children. Subsequently, a joint venture was developed. Pediatric hospice services are currently being provided with the two providers pooling their resources and thus significantly containing administrative and overhead costs.

The HSA of New York City identified two Staten Island neighborhoods in need of additional primary care services. Two major providers subsequently sought to develop additional primary care and preventative services in these areas through the submittal of three separate projects. The HSA's initial analysis documented the service duplication and waste of resources which would result from development of three separate programs to serve the same population. A series of meetings were held with both providers to encourage them to respond to the neighborhood's needs in both a collaborative and more cost-effective manner. These discussions led to the withdrawal of the competing proposals and the submission of a single joint application to develop coordinated primary care services. Annual operating cost savings achieved through this collaborative approach are estimated to be $2 million with an additional one time capital cost savings of approximately three quarters of a million dollars.

An Albany area hospital submitted a major renovation/construction project totalling approximately $42 million in capital costs. The project included a proposed increase in the number of operating room suites. At the time, the HSA of Northeastern New York was just completing a study of surgical capacity and utilization in the area. The HSA presented this information to the applicant who agreed to revise and down-size the project as it related to increased operating room capacity. Additional downsizing involved agreed upon changes in the scope of the project related to the community wide need for obstetrical services and neo-natal intensive care services. The project, as revised by the applicant and approved by the HSA, involved a capital cost of $26 million or $16 million less than originally proposed.

• The Nassau-Suffolk HSA collaborated with several area hospitals to eliminate excess acute care capacity and use the vacated space to provide services needed by area residents. In one instance, a hospital converted an underutilized medical-surgical service to a rehabilitation unit; in another, a facility converted a similar unit to an alcoholism treatment facility. In summary, the area's excess acute care capacity was reduced and needed new services were established at significantly less capital cost than would have been required by new construction, i.e. it is estimated that new construction would have required $40 million more in capital cost than was expended through utilizing the vacated space.

• In New York City, the HSA and the State Health Department worked with two major hospitals which were both preparing to submit major modernization projects with capital costs of approximately $1 billion each. Review of the facilities preliminary plans indicated an over-emphasis on acute care with fewer project resources be devoted to needed primary care services. As a result of the Agency and Health Department efforts with these facilities, their plans were revised to be more consistent with community needs and capital costs associated with there renovation projects were reduced by approximately $200 million at each facility.

Centralizing Expensive Specialty Services While Promoting Access

Certain specialty services are used infrequently and sometimes involve a high level of expensive technology. The cost-effective development of these services dictates that they be centralized, or shared by hospitals in order to achieve the economies of scale and quality assurance associated with a larger volume of clinical activity. However, centralization of such services necessitates consideration of access issues. Typically, HSAs promote collaboration among facilities so that these types of specialty services are both cost-effective and accessible. Some selected examples of HSA activity in this area are reported below.

• In Rochester, the HSA was faced with competing applications from four hospitals for the one additional cardiac catheterization laboratory that was needed. The successful applicant was the only one already performing open heart surgery and was preferred for that reason (both the State Cardiac Advisory Committee and the HSA have a policy preference for locating these services in facilities that have cardiac surgical backup). However, it was clear during the review process that access issues were in large part responsible for some of the hospitals continuing to pursue the further development of these services in the absence of community need. Therefore, planning was initiated to improve both physician and patient access to existing cardiac catheterization laboratory services. This was accomplished in one case through negotiating agreements whereby cardiologists on staff of one of the hospitals (without a laboratory) would have the right (and laboratory time assigned) to examine their own patients using the existing laboratory at a nearby area hospital. In another case, an agreement was reached between one of the inner city hospitals (without a laboratory) and a nearby hospital which operated two laboratories, an open heart surgery service and a teaching program. The teaching facility agreed to relocate one of its two labs to the inner city hospital while maintaining sponsorship of the service. These changes have resulted in more efficient use of existing resources as well as enhanced access to the service for the community's cardiologists as well as the minority and medicaid-eligible populations. And, importantly, this was achieved without the proliferation of additional laboratories.

At the suggestion of the HSA, three eastern Long Island hospitals initiated a joint magnetic resonance imaging (MRI) service. Since none of these hospitals alone would generate the minimum numbers of procedures to support efficient utilization of this service, a joint venture had the effect of providing patient and physician access to this service in a cost-effective manner. Since the average annual operating cost of an MRI unit is approximately $1.5 million, the joint venture makes the service available to all three hospitals while saving several million dollars annually in operating costs (which would be otherwise incurred if all 3 hospitals had individual services).

Chairman STARK. Mr. Stowe.

STATEMENT OF ARTHUR STOWE, PRESIDENT, PRINTING INDUSTRIES OF MARYLAND, ON BEHALF OF THE TRADE ASSOCIATION HEALTHCARE COALITION

Mr. STOWE. Thank you, Mr. Chairman.

Chairman STARK. This is Maryland. Congressman Cardin has all of his constituents and his friends in here today. He told me he is up in Annapolis working. Is Dick Heintz a member of the Printing Industries of Maryland?

Mr. STOWE. Yes, sir.

Chairman STARK. My neighbor.

Mr. STOWE. Thank you——

Chairman STARK. Go ahead. Did you enjoy your meeting with Ira Magaziner?

Mr. STOWE. Yes, sir.

Chairman STARK. Tell us what you learned.

Mr. STOWE. I will tell you later as developments occur whether we truly enjoyed it or not.

Thank you.

The Trade Association Health Care Coalition appreciates the opportunity to testify before the committee. I am Arthur Stowe, president of the Printing Industries of Maryland. Our association is a member of the Trade Association Health Care Coalition, and we are also appearing on behalf of the Association Health Plan Alliance.

As in our January meeting with the senior advisor to the President on health care, Dr. Magaziner, our theme today that we want to highlight is to describe the existing association group health benefits plans and point out their uniqueness. We would like to become an integral part of any future American health care system helping to secure comprehensive health care benefits for all Americans.

Until now, drafters of Federal and State legislation have not focused on and in some instances have not even recognized the existence of group health care benefits provided to small employers under the management of trade and professional associations. This is quite ironic because association plans have for 5 decades been the champions of small employer health plans when the group health needs of small employers were largely underserved or unserved.

The concept of aggregating small employers into professionally administered health risk pools is not new. The association plans have proved to be an effective and economic approach for small employers to provide their employees with access to group health insurance when it is otherwise unavailable.

The associations who belong to the Trade Association Health Care Coalition and the Association Health Plan Alliance are concerned about several aspects of the health care reform bills currently before Congress. If those bills become law they will jeopardize or completely eliminate effective and beneficial association small employer health programs, and will have a detrimental impact on the very groups the law is intended to serve.

Chairman STARK. Mr. Stowe, If I solve your problem, can I interrupt you?

Mr. STOWE. Certainly.

Chairman STARK. We had another person testify at a previous hearing about association programs and one of the things that compounds your problem, some associations, and rightfully so, like the Association on Health Care policies because they get members.

It is a sales tool to get people to join their association, which I think is fine. AARP is one of them. They sell a lot of insurance, they get a lot of people to sign up because they like it. I think that is a reasonable thing to do. I can see that the President's plan would put you out of business in that area. Not to worry.

First of all, insurance reform would probably put you largely out of business. In other words, if every insurance company in the country had to take any one of your members on open enrollment and community rating, you can't offer much of a price break except maybe the bookkeeping.

My guess is that there will always be a need for supplemental programs much as medigap is what is sold by AARP and it is a very good product. My mother buys it; it is worthwhile. So my guess is, while it is too early to predict what form the legislation will take, that there will be a market and/or a need, which creates a market often, for associations to be able to offer something special, if you will, to their members as both a reward for belonging or indeed an inducement for joining and allow you to use your collective purchasing power to get a little bit of a bargain for it.

I can't tell you what form that is going to take, but I can tell you the committee is aware of your concerns and I think that in the course of this legislation, they will be met. Fair grounds for interrupting?

Mr. STOWE. Fair enough.

Chairman STARK. All right.

Mr. STOWE. We have submitted full written testimony anyway. Thank you very much for listening.

[The prepared statement follows:]

STATEMENT OF ARTHUR STOWE
PRESIDENT, PRINTING INDUSTRIES OF MARYLAND
ON BEHALF OF THE TRADE ASSOCIATION HEALTHCARE COALITION

The Trade Association Healthcare Coalition appreciates this opportunity to testify before the Health Subcommittee. I am Arthur Stowe, and I am the President of the Printing Industries of Maryland. We are one of the member associations of the Trade Association Healthcare Coalition, but we are also appearing on behalf of the Association Health Plan Alliance. As in our January 11, 1994 meeting with the Senior Advisor to the President on Health Reform, Dr. Ira Magaziner, the theme of our comments today will be to briefly describe how existing association group health benefit plans are uniquely qualified to become an integral part of the future American health system helping to guarantee universal and secure healthcare benefits to all Americans.

Until now, drafters of federal and state legislation have not focused on, or in some instances, even recognized the existence of group healthcare benefits provided to small employers under the management of trade and professional associations. This is ironic because association plans have, for five decades, been the champions of small employer plans when the group health needs of these groups were largely unserved. The concept of aggregating small employers into professionally administered health risk pools is not new. Association plans have provided numerous number services and proved to be an effective and economical approach for very small employers to provide their employees with access to group health insurance, when it was otherwise unavailable.

The member associations who belong to the Trade Association Healthcare Coalition are very concerned about several aspects of healthcare reform bills currently before Congress. If those bills become law, they may jeopardize or completely eliminate effective and beneficial association small employer health programs and have a detrimental impact on the very groups the law is intended to serve.

In a concept very similar to what many reformers consider to be "reform", association plans have, for half a century, combined employers into health insurance pools of employees and provided the security of health care coverage to their families under a master insurance policy or association Trust.

Gaining leverage with insurers and health care providers through their combined numbers, association plans have given small employers the advantages of economy and scale, professional plan management and access to coverage for their employees and dependents. If it were not for these plans, these advantages would have been denied employees of small business and enjoyed only by those who work for large employers.

Recent estimates are that 4-6 million Americans are covered under association programs. In most instances, these programs have provided valuable health care benefits to small urban firms or in many cases, rural employers to which managed care networks, (HMO's, PPO's) are not available due to meager populations. Had it not been for the existence of association plans, the ranks of involuntary uninsureds would have been swelled a long time ago because of the prohibitive cost of obtaining health insurance for small businesses.

According to a national survey conducted in 1992 by the American Society of Association Executives, 779 responding associations reported 1,991 group premiums paid $6.2 billion. This amount is larger than the total health care premiums of Prudential, the largest health insurance carrier in the U.S.

Association plans have worked hard to keep up with large employers to manage care and to find new ways to deliver excellence in health benefits while slowing the increased cost of health care. Associations have been in the forefront of increasing access to their plans for those with pre-existing conditions, thereby reducing the number of involuntarily uninsured employed within their group membership.

These industry trade groups are not necessarily limited to select groups of low-risk individuals who are not likely to need health care. Since most of the trade groups are industry-wide, they include a mix of worker occupations such as mechanics, maintenance and construction workers as well as managers, accountants and clerical workers.

Most small employer plans are fully-insured by insurance companies and are not exempt from the state mandates as are large employers, most of which are self-insured. Thus, small employers unknowingly have had extra health costs piled onto them from their legislators through mandated benefits.

Much of the additional healthcare premium costs for small employers is attributable to state government mandates and premium taxes on small business plans that do not apply to self-insured plans of large corporations.

These bona fide trade and professional group programs have unfairly been confused with the bad publicity generated in the media by undesirable practices of some very aggressive small group insurance companies. The Trade Association Healthcare Coalition and the Association Health Plan Alliance want to distinguish our plans from those insurance companies who have profiteered through abusive tactics at the expense of small businesses, their employees and families.

We want to set the record straight and not be confused with those unscrupulous small group health insurer sales schemes which attempt to gain profits by limiting membership to low-risk employers and pick and choose among employees or even which, unfortunately, defraud insureds in a premeditated "hit and run" once an employee becomes seriously ill with a large claim. These practices and schemes should be eliminated.

While the media has publicized certain unscrupulous operators of small group insurance plans that load on as much as 40% for administration and sales commissions, large association plans and their insurers typically have total expense loads of under 15%, net of state premium taxes.

The "Managed Competition" concept being considered in Congress includes the creation of Health Alliances which are new federal agency entities acting as quasi-public regional purchasing groups. The purchasing groups offer Accountable Health Plans (AHP), which are approved by the federal government and contain a comprehensive standardized benefit plan.

The regional purchasing group concept envisions one health alliance in each region to buy standardized basic health insurance for all those not on Medicare. These government alliances would have such large numbers of insureds that they could negotiate prices to the medical community.

Legitimate trade and professional associations are by definition "true purchasing groups" and are in fact the forerunners to the proposed Health Alliances. Does it not make sense to expand upon those entities which have already proved to be successful (i.e. trade and professional associations as purchasing groups)? By leveling the playing field through the elimination of barriers to access and pre-existing restrictions, you return associations to their original purpose and further promote and encourage bona fide plans.

By contrast, the large businesses may go around the Alliance and can negotiate as a corporate alliance and obtain their own costs or insurance rates.

To be part of the managed competition system, Association Alliance plans should be "qualified" on a basis similar to that of qualifications set forth by the Internal Revenue Service for pensions. They would also need to satisfy the standardized basic plan requirements and provide complete access and portability of plans within their membership's limitations.

Qualified association plans are not taking the position of wanting to be "exempt" from the small group health benefit reform. Rather, they welcome the aspects of reform which will eliminate unscrupulous practices and offer choice and access to their membership. Association plans want to be a part of the future healthcare delivery system. They offer a track record which should be expanded upon rather than reinventing the wheel through quasi-governmental alliances.

The Trade Association Healthcare Coalition supports the goal of universal coverage. The evidence is clear that acute health care costs are shifted to those with insurance when uninsured individuals arrive at hospital emergency rooms for treatment. They receive treatment, but trigger a circle of cost shifting that impacts all of the stakeholders in the health care system. If all

450

Americans had healthcare coverage, the motivation for cost shifting would be greatly diminished.

Small businesses with less than one hundred employees are estimated to make up ninety-five percent of all employers. They employee more than fifty percent of the private sector labor force and are the greatest source of growth in new jobs in our economy.

Association plans of small employers could prosper under Universal Healthcare and their existence would encourage all potential participants to enroll in the association's multiple health care offerings.

We support the concept of associations as voluntary HIPC's to maintain and even expand the concept of healthy competition and quality health care delivery to the American people. We support the concept of rating based upon the unique association community. This modified form of internal community rating would be more effective than flat community rating. It would allow associations to manage their programs with factors such as geographic area, age, family composition and wellness factors within each association considered as its own community.

We also support the concept of freedom of choice, with the employees ability to select from a variety of health plans as offered by its association purchasing group. Options including traditional fee for service plans, PPO's and HMO's as available by geographic locale within a given association. Associations, like large employers, have extensive experience in dealing with insurance providers. Associations also have the organizational infrastructure with which to advise their members and employees on health care alternatives. In addition to being an information and data gathering center, associations have the staff available to monitor a plan's performance and communicate with members to achieve an improved health care financing and deliver system.

We are concerned, however, that any cap on contributions for employers with less than 75 employees, as included in the Administration bill, may prove to be transient. The financial impact to the individual businesses of mandated coverage of all employees, combined with as much as 80% premium payment by the employer, could drastically reduce the numbers of small businesses who could survive such costs.

Associations are uniquely structured to be a part of any new or revised health care delivery system. Because they are already structured to represent their members in other areas, they possess the infrastructure, administrative mechanisms and experience to unify employers and employees into effective consumers of health services. Employers who join purchasing groups or cooperatives organized by associations along industry lines can offer employees access to high quality private health coverage at lower costs, with an expanded number of options.

Associations should be organized to function as large employers or as purchasing groups. Such associations can offer a wide variety of approved health plans and managed care arrangements (insured arrangements, Blue Cross/Blue Shield, HMO's, self-insured) to employers and employees within an industry purchasing group. In this capacity, associations can also distribute information, provide price data and offer qualitative comparisons between health plans.\

Associations functioning as purchasing groups can also develop common statistical databases by major industry groupings for claims, premium contributions and utilization of health care services.

Association purchasing groups based on industry lines also offer the best opportunity to integrate coverage and provide statistical data for work related injury, offering a possible solution for the current and growing country wide Workers Compensation benefits crisis.

Such information could be made available for consumer education as well as to insurers for the purpose of risk management, rate negotiations, treatment guidelines, quality control and health plan selection.

In summary, qualified functional industry based associations have been successfully providing comprehensive health benefit programs, as well as many other services, to their Members for more than 50 years. The systems for administration, expertise in negotiation, data collection and communication are all in place and operational. It appears essential that the Congress take into consideration the positive purchasing successes of association programs and retain them as a viable part of the future health care delivery system.

Chairman STARK. Ms. Radaj.

STATEMENT OF MARSHA RADAJ, VICE PRESIDENT OF OPERATIONS, WISCONSIN HEALTH INFORMATION NETWORK, ON BEHALF OF AMERITECH

Ms. RADAJ. Thank you, Mr. Chairman, for the opportunity to be here today. I would also like to thank you, Congressman Kleczka, for the interest you have expressed——

Chairman STARK. You two know each other?

Ms. RADAJ. He had the opportunity to view the network. We appreciate not only his interest in lowering the cost of health care in the State of Wisconsin, but actually taking the time to see this network in operation.

I am not here today to solicit any appropriation or to make a statement about any of the legislation, but I am here to share with you what is going on in the State of Wisconsin and our efforts to lower the cost of health care through a private sector initiative.

I am vice president of operations of WHIN, the Wisconsin Health Information Network, which is the result of a joint venture between Ameritech, the Regional Bell Operating Co., and Aurora Health Care, which is the largest health care provider in southeastern Wisconsin.

WHIN is an electronic distribution channel over which health care-related information passes. We can connect hospitals with physicians, with payers, with utilization review firms. We were formed in 1992 and became operational in March of 1993. We are excited about what we have accomplished to date. We have nine of the major competing hospitals in the State of Wisconsin that have contracted with WHIN that are part of the network and we have over 600 physicians under contract.

We are working closely with physicians at the medical college to identify how to meet the needs of the rural community by using the capabilities of the system and by providing radiographic images through the network and their outreach program. We have been asked to work with the University of Wisconsin physicians to identify primary care physician reqiurements because the primary care physician has been identified as the gatekeeper in a managed care or managed competition environment, but the problem today in the health care environment is that so much of that information in a primary care physician's office is in paper form: It is inaccessible by a lot of individuals who need it.

So we are developing, along with University of Wisconsin physicians a prototype to show how medical information can be very easily automated, and how we can begin tracking it even at the point of contact with a patient in the exam room. We are also working closely with the Blood Center in the city of Milwaukee to design an inventory system with University Hospital in Madison.

We are very sensitive to security in this network. We worked with consultants who assisted the DOD in the design of the security system. My written statements have a more detailed description of all the security features that are built into the system.

Time does not allow me to expand on all the capabilities. However, we to date have demonstrated what we believe are significant cost savings not only in the administrative areas, but also in the clinical areas of health care. We have realized in 10 months over 150,000 transactions moving through our network. Each transaction equates to a minimum of 16 minutes that is being saved by a health care provider or someone who services that health care provider. That is 8 minutes on the part of the individual making a phone call for each one of those transactions and the person responding to the call. This equals to a phone call not being made and not being answered.

We believe that as a result of that, not only are we contributing to lowering the administrative costs, but we are also contributing to increasing the quality of care; because any time a phone call is used as the vehicle for communicating health-related information, the person that is receiving it is transcribing it on the other side, and that transcription can lead to a lot of inaccuracies and a lot of omissions.

We believe that by connecting hospitals with payers and with utilization review firms and with pharmacies, we are providing the right information to the right individuals or organizations at the time that they need it.

I know that I don't have time today to do a demonstration for you. However, I would like to invite each of you on the committee and anyone in the audience to room 1129 where I will be available to demonstrate the system for you. I sincerely hope that there is an interest on your part and that you have the time to visit and see how the network is working in the State of Wisconsin and to hear more about how we are lowering the administrative cost of health care by as much as 20 percent.

[The prepared statement follows:]

STATEMENT OF MARSHA RADAJ
VICE PRESIDENT OF OPERATIONS, WISCONSIN HEALTH INFORMATION NETWORK
ON BEHALF OF
AMERITECH

Mr. Chairman. Thank you for the opportunity to tell the Health Subcommittee about an exciting regional health information network in Wisconsin.

My name is Marsha Radaj. I am vice president of operations for the Wisconsin Health Information Network (WHIN). WHIN was developed jointly by Ameritech, the midwest regional Bell operating company, and Aurora Health Care, a regional health system based in Milwaukee, Wisconsin.

Incorporated in April 1992 and launched commercially in March 1993, WHIN is the nation's first fully functional health information service open to the entire community and dedicated to the electronic exchange of health care information. Aurora Health Care is WHIN's charter member and first user.

For Aurora, working with WHIN is part of a continuing effort to upgrade electronic communications among its hospitals and physicians.

WHIN uses the public switched network and state-of-the-art software to connect all parties -- hospitals, pharmacies, physicians, laboratories, insurers and employers.

To date, 9 hospitals with some 2,100 beds and more than 580 physicians have signed up for the WHIN service.

The health-care related transactions WHIN and other Regional Health Information Networks developed by Ameritech can handle today include hospital-physician links, physician referrals and claims submissions. Additional services anticipated include coverage eligibility, utilization reviews, teleradiology, and lab results.

WHIN enables its participants to exchange information swiftly and cost-effectively. By reducing the avalanche of paperwork currently required to track patient information, WHIN expects to cut the health care administration costs of its members by up to 20 percent. This figure includes Medicare and Medicaid administrative costs savings to participating WHIN members.

The current health care environment is filled with proprietary networks and access devices. Standards are not fully developed, and information currently is not easily accessed, modified or transported. Duplicate tests and procedures are often done because 30 percent of the information required at the time of the patient visit is not available to the provider.

One reason health care delivery is difficult today is because more than 20 different devices representing proprietary physician links, electronic labs, direct connections, claims processing systems are found in an individual doctor's office.

With WHIN, doctors begin to realize they can do all those activities at the same time. Those 20 different links can have one common user interface on a community network. A doctor's office needs only one input or PC per user.

A major issue for the health care infrastructure is the lack of information flow across the continuum of care. Providers, suppliers, payors, patients and employers are sometimes caught in the middle trying to comply with coverage rules and conditions.

No matter where you enter the continuum of care -- with the primary care physician, the specialist, the tertiary care hospital, employers, or pharmacies -- some common threads needed are data elements from clinical data, referrals, and electronic claims.

A Regional Health Information Network like WHIN facilitates the transport of the integrated collection of health information, and leverages the existing equipment investments throughout the community through computer and telecommunications capabilities.

Ameritech established the Ameritech Health Connections subsidiary in 1993 to serve the information needs of patients and the health care industry throughout the country. Ameritech Health Connections recently announced that, in addition to WHIN, two more Regional Health Information Networks are being established, with more coming on line soon. Baptist Hospital in Nashville, Tennessee, and Bethesda Hospital in Cincinnati, Ohio, are the first subscribers to these new Ameritech networks.

Ameritech also owns the subsidiary, Ameritech Knowledge Data, a clinical information systems company that offers specialized patient-centered information technology and services for the health care industry. For example, Methodist Hospital of Indiana, Inc. is using a clinical database developed by Ameritech Knowledge Data to help move the hospital from an acute, tertiary care model to a state-wide health care delivery system.

Regional Health Information Networks like WHIN

Unlike community e-mail systems, Ameritech has invested in a comprehensive information communications network. Improving information exchange may contribute more to solving health care delivery problems than improving systems and processes.

Our Regional Health Information Networks (RHINs) like the Wisconsin Health Information Network (WHIN) use community databases, comparative databases, and clinical databases. We can achieve cost savings by: lowering the community's cost of providing care; improving communication; eliminating duplication in the system; and leveraging the existing technology. For example, currently about 70 percent of hospital patient records are incomplete or inaccurate. Effective telecommunications applications can help cut down on these administrative problems.

Regional Health Information Networks can promote quality in the delivery of care by: giving knowledgeable consumer choices; supporting timely diagnosis and treatment continuity; and enhancing the ability to measure and compare healthcare.

Regional Health Information Networks can help improve access by: delivering patient information across the continuum of care; and linking all participants in a community-based healthcare delivery system.

Regional Health Information Networks do not create information that is not already available to doctors.

Regional Health Information Networks are designed to protect patients' privacy, an essential feature of the system. In fact, WHIN enhances the security its clients already have in place.

Centrally controlled user access, data encryption, frequent changing of passwords and constant monitoring of the system together ensure that only authorized users have access to WHIN. And users of the system will not have access to any patient information that would not otherwise be available to them.

Ameritech Health Connections and Aurora worked with SSDS, Inc,. a national consulting firm that has implemented systems for the Department of Defense, in the design of the security infrastructure for WHIN. The entry of a password and logon ID when entering the system is the foundation for the security system which includes:

- Data encryption for ALL information being transmitted across phone lines;
- Data encryption for user information stored in the "environmental data base;"
- Environmental Database which controls access to a hospital system;
- Virus checking when a workstation logs into the network;
- RAM signature upon logon with audit reporting; (WHIN knows if a user has added software to the requesting terminal since the last logon, if memory has changed, and if the request is coming from a workstation that the requester does not generally use.)
- Optional "Secure ID Card" with password changing every 30 seconds;
- Application control;
- Hardware control by providing the ability to disable an attached printer or disk drive during the life of a transaction;
- Host site authorization for each transaction request received, so that a hospital has responsibility for authorizing a request based on the status of the physician on the case. Implementation is determined by each participating hospital; and
- Audit reporting identifying which user is looking at what reports.

Ameritech's Regional Health Information Networks, like WHIN, do not store patient information, do not populate other databases, and do not maintain indexes pointing to the location of stored data. Regional Health Information Networks are enablers in the electronic highway facilitating the transmission of information between the requester and the provider. WHIN, for example, does not allow a user to peruse a database to collect research data. A physician cannot issue a request to search for all the occurrences of a specific diagnosis or outcome. The physician can only issue a request for specific data about his or her patients in hospitals participating in the regional network.

In addition to the security built into the system, we have also implemented PROCESS security. Before anyone is allowed access to the network, a letter of authorization must be on file from each of the hospitals. Logon is only allowed if authorization is approved in writing. We work closely with hospital staff in the implementation of a system to enhance the internal security systems already in place.

Unfortunately, in many hospitals today, an individual with a lab coat can approach a nursing station and review a chart. We are not able to eliminate the possibility of these problems occurring. We can, however, provide a facility to get the right information to the right person at the appropriate time. We strongly believe, Regional Health Information Networks, like WHIN, enhance the systems currently in place in the participating hospitals in the network, and in many instances, significantly surpass a hospital's ability to protect the confidentiality of patient data.

Telecommunications applications and health care public policy

Ameritech strongly believes that creative private sector telecommunications applications for effective delivery of care in the health infrastructure complements any health care reform legislative proposal. Whether the Congress agrees to concepts such as purchasing cooperatives, or regional and corporate alliances, or any other model, proper communications and information technology and systems will be a critical factor in administrative cost savings, access, and quality.

Regardless of whether it is patient identification, information access to records, standard interchange, outcomes measurement, best practices, a common data interface and exchange through information networks will be needed.

By maximizing use of the existing public switched network for health applications, scarce federal and state dollars can be devoted to other improvements in health delivery. The public network can be a vital resource for health infrastructure, making possible universal, high-speed transmission of voice and data.

The federal government should not own, deploy or manage this "Information Highway." Instead, the proper federal role is to stimulate development of computer and telecommunications applications through research and development, to support wider access to network resources, and to promote interoperable systems.

As the health care infrastructure moves from fee-for-service to a risk sharing, capitation model, communications and information systems will be key factors for successful delivery of care.

Telecommunications Can Cut Health Administrative Costs

Accessible clinical databases, regional health information networks like WHIN, health provider information exchanges and claims management -- these are but a few of the telecommunications applications that can reduce costs and improve access and quality of patient care.

The Bell companies have an historic commitment to universal service. Through our ubiquitous presence, the Bell companies offer telecommunications applications that give consumers, including those in rural and medically-underserved areas, the information they need to lead healthier lives. The health care delivery system is then improved, with reduced costs and improved access.

I would like to summarize for this subcommittee briefly studies that quantify how telecommunications can reduce the costs and improve the quality and accessibility of health care.

In 1992, Ameritech and several other telecommunications companies commissioned Arthur D. Little, Inc., the internationally recognized economic consulting firm, to assess how telecommunications technology could help address the national health care crisis.

A.D. Little's July 1992 study, "Telecommunications: Can It Help Solve America's Health Care Problems?" stated:

"America's health care bill can be reduced by more than $36 billion each year by applying selected telecommunications applications nationwide. These cost reductions in the health care industry will flow to patients, employers and government, who ultimately provide the source of funds."

Annual health care costs can be reduced by more than $36 billion (in 1990 dollars) through four telecommunications applications, according to the A.D. Little study:

1) $30 billion in savings by improving patient care through electronic management and transport of patient, clinical and diagnostic information;

2) $6 billion from electronic submission and processing of health care claims;

3) $600 million from electronic data interchange for materials and supplies; and

4) $200 million from videoconferencing for professional training and telemedicine applications such as remote medical consultations.

The A.D. Little study underscores that local telephone companies are vital partners in developing and deploying health care applications -- including home care, management and transport of patient information, claims processing, inventory control, video conferencing and health care professional telecommuting -- in urban, suburban and rural communities across the United States.

Furthermore, the A.D. Little study shows that government programs such as Medicare and Medicaid also can expect substantial administrative savings through effective use of telecommunications services.

Ameritech and other Bell companies are currently putting together specific proposals for Congress to save Medicare funds by promoting the use of telemedicine, and eliminating unnecessary hospital transfers and second admissions.

Unfortunately, government-imposed policy barriers significantly constrain the ability of seven major American telecommunications providers -- the regional Bell companies -- to contribute fully to solving the nation's health care crisis.

The consent decree that broke up AT&T back in 1984 barred the regional Bell companies from manufacturing telecommunications equipment and from providing information services and long-distance service.

Ameritech and the other regional companies were barred from providing health services like WHIN until the information services restriction was lifted by the federal courts in 1991.

To this day, the consent decree's long-distance ban prevents Ameritech from itself providing WHIN throughout the state of Wisconsin -- or across our entire midwest service territory or the United States.

Incredibly, Ameritech itself cannot even connect WHIN between Milwaukee and Green Bay, Wisconsin.

More precisely, the long-distance restriction prohibits Ameritech and the other regional Bell companies from providing phone service or transmitting information services across Local Access Transport Areas -- LATAs. In plain English, LATAs are service areas or boundaries that roughly correspond to metropolitan areas.

As a result of the long-distance restriction, Ameritech finds itself between a rock and a hard place whenever we are developing an information service product that contemplates the delivery of information across these service boundaries.

If Ameritech opts to construct a single central database and processing facility within a particular service area, information service customers located outside that area must themselves select a long-distance carrier and pay for the long-distance call.

Lifting the restriction and thereby permitting Ameritech both to select a long-distance carrier and pay for the long-distance transmission would benefit information service customers in two ways:

1) Ameritech could purchase long-distance time at bulk or high volume rates and pass these cost savings on to customers.

2) Ameritech could offer a package service including both the data sought by customers and the long-distance transmission of the information, a more convenient service for customers -- and one that our competitors already can offer.

Alternatively, to finesse the long-distance restriction, Ameritech could build complete data and processing facilities in every LATA or service area in which we want to offer the service.
But we would take this step not because there is any technical reason for multiple facilities, but only because they would be required by current legal fiat.

In this case, customers could access the service by placing a local call. But the tremendous costs of constructing redundant facilities in each service area ultimately would have to be passed along to customers in the form of higher service fees and charges.

The point is simple: Ameritech developed WHIN to deliver vital health information services in a cost-effective manner. The purpose of the system is to save money and cut costs spent on health care administration.

WHIN is just one example of how the nation's Bell companies are working to assist health consumers in their homes, providers in local clinics and hospitals and payors.

Each year the Bell companies invest billions of dollars in capital improvements for the telecommunications infrastructure, which supports health care, education, and rural development in the country.

By maximizing use of the existing public switched network for health applications, scarce federal and state dollars can be devoted to other improvements in health care delivery.

Ameritech's efforts to reduce health care administrative costs through WHIN are blunted by the long-distance restriction. That ban thwarts the regional Bell companies from fully competing in the health information industry, and it denies the public significant cost savings in the health care field.

In fact, the long-distance ban stands in the way of achieving a sizable portion of the $36 billion in annual health care cost savings that telecommunications applications can produce.

According to a second A.D. Little study commissioned by Ameritech and the other regional Bell companies and released in June 1993:

"American health care could experience annual cost reductions of more than $9.7 billion through enhanced use of [long-distance] services. In other words, more than a quarter of the $36 billion annual cost reductions identified by the previous study involve the use of health care applications that [entail long-distance service]."

The second A.D. Little study concludes:

"The ... long distance restriction precludes the Bells ... from developing applications which, to be most effective, need to be statewide, regional or national in scope. The Bell companies, in concert with health care providers, can bring together elements necessary for achieving the [$9.7 billion in] potential health care cost reductions identified by this [second] study only if the ... long-distance restriction is removed."

Besides the consent decree line-of-business restrictions, another ban hampers the ability of local telephone companies to help address health needs. Local telephone companies also are barred from owning and operating cable TV facilities in their local service territories.

We believe that allowing the regional Bell companies to offer long-distance service, provide cable TV programming, manufacture telecommunications equipment and remain in the information services business would substantially improve the nation's welfare.

Finally, Mr. Chairman, this subcommittee should know that Ameritech is so determined to be a full-service provider to its midwest customers, including health care providers, that we have submitted an historic proposal to the Federal Communications Commission, and we have requested a waiver at the Justice Department to offer a trial of long distance service in two of our states.

Under Customers First: Ameritech's Advanced Universal Access Plan, Ameritech proposes to open its local network fully to competitors in exchange for certain pricing and earnings regulatory reforms and the freedom to provide long-distance service.

Ameritech believes that this quid pro quo will yield the products and services our customers demand and deserve at competitive prices.

Ameritech also believes that our Customers First Plan is the way to make two-way movement of all forms of information -- voice, image, video or data -- as affordable and accessible as the telephone is today.

We strongly believe that the private sector developments to create a national health care information infrastructure must be a significant part of the solution of our nation's health care problems.

Mr. Chairman, Ameritech acknowledges your long-standing dedication to health issues. We appreciate the opportunity to appear before you today.

Thank you.

# # #

Chairman STARK. You get a prize if you can name 10 of the most famous public servants and legislators in the history of the United States whose families emigrated to Wisconsin and subsequently went on to great heights in leadership in public service. Who would be the first one you would name?

Mr. KLECZKA. Bob Lafollett. The chairman does hail from the State of Wisconsin, was born and raised in a burb outside Milwaukee. He was gracious enough to come to Milwaukee for a public hearing on this very same issue and embarrassingly knew more about the history of the great city of Milwaukee than I did, so he is not coming back any more.

Let me thank the panel and Marsha for coming forth with the program she has been instrumental in setting up and marketing in the State of Wisconsin. Part of the Clinton bill and part of the discussion on health care clearly has to include addressing the administrative costs that we are now bearing whether we like it or not. Most surprisingly, we have heard in this committee estimates of 20 to 25 percent of our health care costs go to shuffling papers and not providing one aspirin or any health care to anyone.

So let me encourage anyone that is interested to see the demonstration project. It is the wave of the future and is being implemented in Wisconsin already.

Marsha, as you look at the Clinton bill, is there anything in the legislation or any bills introduced on health care reform that would encourage or discourage the use of this type of system?

Ms. RADAJ. Not that I see. The opportunity afforded this system is opportunity afforded under any legislation that may pass. When you are in a managed care or managed competition environment, which we are slowly moving toward even before legislation is passed, there is—the term managed in and of itself indicates, the requirement for information. The network was put together to make that information in an accessible form available to the people who need it.

Mr. KLECZKA. Do you share the belief that this could be a model for other States and other networks to adopt?

Ms. RADAJ. I believe it can. Ameritech, because of the success of the pilot in the State of Wisconsin, is moving this, the regional health information network philosophy to other markets. Currently there are two, one which is already operational in Nashville, Tenn., at Baptist, and an initiative is beginning in Cincinnati.

Mr. KLECZKA. Let me turn to Dr. Matthews, the blue jean credit card guy of the panel. It seems to me that any time we have a social problem in this country we are going to resolve it by IRAs. In years past, we felt that people should be reserving more for their retirement so we instituted the retirement IRA; and subsequent to that enactment we have since restricted it because we found that the wealthy of society who clearly could afford retirement without an IRA were the ones taking advantage of it.

So we cut down on the deductibility for people in that situation. We also have a problem with educating our children in this country and it has been suggested that we have an education IRA. Then we have a problem with firsttime homebuyers. They don't have enough for a downpayment even though they can make the mortgage. So some propose a firsttime homebuyers IRA. Now we have before us this well-thought-out proposal called a medical IRA.

I have to ask you, Doctor, where do you think people are getting all this disposable income to slug away in these IRAs? Using your blue jean example, in a household with a couple of kids, a mortgage to pay at the first of every month. We are going to tell the person you can go without medical insurance, as long as you put in some money, not mandated, but as long as you put some money into an IRA.

This is disposable income and we are going to give you a tax break. That person, after paying the mortgage, tuition for the kids at the end of the month makes a choice between whether they can put money away in that medical IRA or buy blue jeans for their son or daughter.

What are the options the family will take? They will take care of the family first. But don't worry. We will get it next month and then the furnace blows, and in July the car goes flat. At the end of the year, there is nothing in the IRA because we couldn't find any income to put in there.

I will make a deal. Next year we will do it and then next year never comes and that person is involved in a catastrophe. They are driving a motorcycle down the road without a helmet. They are involved in a serious collision. They end up at not only St. Luke's Hospital, but they are also at Sacred Heart Rehabilitation Center for 3 years, and who pays for that? All of us, because they didn't have insurance.

But no, when they get out, they will open up an IRA and pay that back. Baloney. So it is a simplistic resolution to a serious problem which will never work. You know, it is pie in the sky, my friend.

Mr. MATTHEWS. We are suggesting that the money that is now going for health insurance, the average family policy now runs about $4,500 a year. In the current system, what happens is the employer pays most of that, half of it, employees part of it, most people are covered under that employer plan. But that money goes to the insurance company.

If you are healthy and don't use the money during the year, the insurance company keeps the whole thing. We are saying take the same money that is now going to the insurance company and give an individual an option to put the money into a tax-free account. If they want to do it the same way they are doing now with a low deductible policy that most people have, we have no problem with that.

If they want to take the money and go to a HMO, as many places do, I don't have a problem with that. But I think what most people would do is take part of the money, buy a catastrophic policy to cover a major medical expenditure, major accident, major illness, they have the policy there, and use the premium savings to pay for smaller health care expenditures.

Mr. KLECZKA. That all should be done on a voluntary basis?

Mr. MATTHEWS. According to whose bill it is.

Mr. KLECZKA. Instead of paying 20 percent of my policy, I now can keep the money, and that is the part that will never gets into the IRA.

What about the person who is permanently laid off from a decent-paying job with health care and is now working at the Target store as a security guard for $5 an hour? Where will that person scrape up enough money to provide for that IRA?

Mr. MATTHEWS. If we as a country decide we want to cover the working poor, which is what you are talking about there, you simply provide a voucher for those people. You could do it under several ways.

Senator Gramm has an option in his plan where you expand the money to the poor, provide a sliding scale subsidy to cover a catastrophic policy. We would like to see it be a larger subsidy so that if you provide a subsidy to those individuals, it is enough money to cover a catastrophic policy and leave money over in the account for lower health care—

Mr. KLECZKA. How does Senator Gramm fund that voucher program?

Mr. MATTHEWS. He does it through several ways. He has a savings element in there, plus it is going to cost more money.

Mr. KLECZKA. How does he propose raising it?

Mr. MATTHEWS. I don't recall that I have seen how he proposes doing that.

Mr. KLECZKA. You don't recall it because it is not in there. I think the fallacy in your testimony is that you flash this credit card around saying, "This is my health security card and today I have nothing to do so I am going to go down to Alexandria Hospital because I have this card that guarantees me anything."

I am going to walk in and say, "I am Jerry Kleczka and I am on a shopping spree. I have my security card. I have time for an MRI, serology workup and is x ray open today? Give me a couple of x rays, too."

That is foolishness, my friend. Don't say that they are going to have self-diagnosis and get anything they want. Are you a medical doctor?

Mr. MATTHEWS. Ph.D.

Mr. KLECZKA. The doctor and the health care professional will judge whether or not you need an MRI or a CAT scan. It is not going to happen because I have this Clinton security card. With more primary care doctors, we will get better screening on the front end so we can eliminate a lot of tests and unnecessary things.

Mr. MATTHEWS. Virtually all health policy analysts realize that the major issue here is that the consumer is insulated from the price of it.

Mr. KLECZKA. This bill and many other bills, not only the President's bill provides for copays and deductibles and through that mechanism we hope that we can stop some of the abuse and over utilization of the system.

Mr. MATTHEWS. The intent is to try to stop some of the overutilization. There are two ways to do that: Either increase the individuals share in it so they take a more value conscious look at it, or you have somebody looking over the shoulder of the patient or the physician to tell them what they can and can't have. That is the two different approaches that we have had.

Most proposals out there ultimately bring in somebody to look over somebody else's shoulder to say "This is too much," and this is the way insurance companies have been drifting for some time because of the problem of being insulated with the price. What you ought to do is bring in a deductible of $200, $250, and that should discourage me from getting needless care at least at the lower end ranges. For a poor family——

Mr. KLECZKA. If you want to go to a doctor every day, you have to reach into the pocket for $25 or so and that is a sort of a stopgap.

Mr. MATTHEWS. That first $250 can be a deterrent in many cases for poor people. That can be a significant part of your budget if you are low income. The medical savings account actually provides first dollar coverage for the first time you want to go to the doctor or you need preventive care.

The key, though, is that if you are prudent and value conscious you get to save the difference. Right now we are turning the money over to insurance companies and under this proposal we let individuals make a lot of those decisions themselves. They still have the catastrophic policy.

Mr. KLECZKA. It ain't going to work because the younger of our society are going to say "I am healthy and I will be healthy forever more and so I will start at age—I will start maybe at age 50 because that is when my dad had a little problem," and that individual won't put a nickel in and come age 50, there are other commitments and the kids are in college, so they don't contribute then.

The upshot is, under your swank proposal, that it is not going to work, people won't put money in and the public, all of us, will continue to cover them.

Chairman STARK. When the committee considers cold fusion and perpetual motion, we will bring this up again, Mr. Kleczka.

I would like to for a moment, Mr. Gumbs and Mr. Stanton, and Dr. Richardson—it is a matter of concern and I think Mr. Stanton and Mr. Gumbs you touched on it, the President's plan, for whatever other problems it may have, is fairly silent on the issue of resource allocation.

The great State of Maryland has done a very good job as has the Empire State of New York. It is to my shame that California kind of gave up on any kind of resource planning, and consequently it costs about twice as much for a procedure in California as it does in New York, and you would have a tough time convincing Dr. Richardson that our hospitals are twice as good as the hospitals in New York.

It is an interesting fact that we have about 50 percent occupancy. We are as close to 50 percent as you are to 100 percent occupancy in the State of New York.

I have always suspected in my simplistic approach that might have a little bit to do with the difference in costs and utilizations, but I have never been all that sure. I do think that we need at some point to interject, if we are going to be so extensive in this health care reform, dealing with a way to help communities find the proper resources, whether that is rural areas that are completely underserved or inner cities, Manhattan where there is an aging medical infrastructure, a medical care delivery infrastructure, and it 's a concern of this committee.

We haven't done much with it. That hasn't been really on our legislative agenda certainly since I have been on the committee. But the certificate of need—if it didn't have such a bad name in the world—people tend to look at that as the worst example of socialism—but I do think we are going to try and that to the extent where there is Federal money involved encourage the States to at least have a plan.

I don't know whether we will be able to enforce it, but to say before we are going to pony up with any Federal assistance you ought to have a plan, how many MRIs do you need and then if you are going to be a spendthrift and have more resources than you need, I don't know that we can prevent it, but I think we have to encourage it. Any kind of broad Federal guidelines that would work in Maryland and New York would be helpful for us.

I haven't spent a lot of time on that issue in this committee, but I do think we can't ignore it and your continued help in that arena—I think as long as we have this package before us I think it is an issue we should address.

I would say to Dr. Richardson also that we have a lot of trouble figuring out how this alliance thing could do anything but destroy teaching centers and that is not going to happen on this committee's watch. I am not sure that these regional alliances in a mandatory sense will ever come into being. But it is a concern and I know you know that, I know that Congressman Cardin has indicated that to you; but it is a concern for people in Minnesota and people in Texas and people in New York.

We have many great teaching centers around the country and it is not very likely that you get a lot of referral at Johns Hopkins from Kaiser Permanente in Oakland. I bet you get a few people coming there who have indemnity plans. Somehow I think we need to allow that to continue. I hope those comments will give you some reason for feeling that you didn't waste your time in coming here today.

I want to thank all the panelists for their contribution today, and we will call the next panel: Dr. Laurence Bouchard and Dr. Richard Nunnally. Dr. Bouchard is with the American Osteopathic Association. Dr. Nunnally is with the Colleges of American Pathologists. Dr. Edward Elliott is the past president of the American Optometric Association; Dr. Charles L. Jones is the president-elect of the American Podiatric Medical Association; and Kris Robinson is the executive director of the American Association of Kidney Patients.

Are any of you so miserably hungry that if I drink a little soup while you are testifying I will be exceeding the bounds of decency? The Chair is going to work through to accommodate the witnesses. Dr. Bouchard.

STATEMENT OF LAURENCE BOUCHARD, D.O., PRESIDENT, AMERICAN OSTEOPATHIC ASSOCIATION

Mr. BOUCHARD. Thank you for inviting me to testify on health care reform. I am Laurence Bouchard and I am an osteopathic family physician practicing in Narragansett, R.I. for the past 31 years. I am president of the American Osteopathic Association and with me is Douglas Ward, Ph.D., head of our Department of Education. Copies of my written testimony have been submitted for the record.

We agree that reform is needed and under reform patients must be able to choose the physician of their choice. Freedom of choice can only be guaranteed if Federal statutory language is written, one, to protect the role of osteopathic physicians on the current and future health care delivery mechanisms; and two, to ensure the continued viability of the osteopathic education training model.

The AOA is a national professional organization representing the Nation's 35,000 DOs. We are 5.5 percent of the Nation's physician manpower and are often the only physicians in rural and underserved areas and we are very proud of that.

Osteopathic physicians comprise more than 15 percent of all physicians in communities with populations of less than 10,000 people. According to HHS, osteopathic physicians serve approximately 1 out of every 7 Medicare and 25 percent of all Medicaid recipients in the United States. In fact, over 100 million patient visits are made to osteopathic physicians annually.

The patient demand for osteopathic services continues to grow in today's health care delivery system. Any reform must preserve this patient option. In addition, reform should include a global budget for national health care expenditures to reduce cost-shifting among the public and private payors and to control the rising health portion of GDP. We feel any uniform——

Chairman STARK. Repeat that last line.

Mr. BOUCHARD. In addition, reform should include a global budget for national health care expenditures to reduce cost shifting among the public and private payors and to control the rising health care portion of the GDP.

Chairman STARK. I thought that is what you said. That is very good.

Mr. BOUCHARD. We feel any uniform benefits package must include coverage of primary and preventive care and be made available to all Americans. We believe that health should be delivered through a system of managed competition and President Clinton's proposed system of alliances presents a good point to start the debate on delivery mechanisms.

Any delivery mechanism must provide the opportunity for all qualified physicians to participate.

Osteopathic physicians pursue training in osteopathic postgraduate training programs and become certified through approved osteopathic certification examinations. Many private payors are unaware of this separate process. Consequently, patients around the Nation today are being denied access to the provider of their choice, the osteopathic physician.

Congress needs to enact legislation which prohibits private insurers and delivery mechanisms from discriminating against physicians based on degree, postgraduate training and certification. Furthermore, we believe we have the model program that achieves appropriate national balance between primary and specialty physicians and this model has produced over 60 percent of primary care physicians. It must be protected.

The AOA has worked very closely with COGME and PPRC to advance the osteopathic training model. These groups well under-

467

stand the contribution of osteopathic medicine and both have recommended that the total funded residency positions be limited to the number of osteopathic and allopathic medical school graduates together, plus 10 percent.

The AOA is requesting that its training programs including internships and residencies be treated separately. Furthermore, the total funded osteopathic first-year internship and residency positions should be limited to the number of osteopathic graduates plus 10 percent.

Mr. Chairman and members of the subcommittee, thank you for the opportunity. Dr. ward and I will be happy to answer questions later.

Chairman STARK. Thank you.

[The prepared statement and attachments follow:]

STATEMENT OF LAURENCE BOUCHARD, D.O.
PRESIDENT
AMERICAN OSTEOPATHIC ASSOCIATION

Thank you, Mr. Chairman, for inviting me to testify on health care reform. My name is
Laurence Bouchard and I am an osteopathic physician who has practiced in family medicine
in Narragansett, Rhode Island for the past 31 years. I come before you today as the
President of the American Osteopathic Association (AOA). With me is Douglas Ward,
Ph.D., Associate Executive Director for Education of the Association.

I would like to begin by establishing the framework for debate of the health care delivery
system. That is - As the nation debates how best to deliver health care to the patients of
this nation, I believe we must remember the patients. With or without health care reform,
the needs of the patients do not change.

We as osteopathic physicians agree that reform is indeed needed. For reform to be
effective however, patients must be able to choose the physician of their choice, including
osteopathic physicians. This freedom of choice can only be guaranteed if federal statutory
language is written: 1) to protect the role of osteopathic physicians under current and future
health care delivery mechanisms; and, 2) to ensure the continued viability of the osteopathic
education training model.

The Osteopathic profession is no stranger to reform. We began as a reform movement.
Andrew Taylor Still, MD, was dissatisfied with the effectiveness of 19th century medicine
and began our profession over 100 years ago. He founded a philosophy of medicine which
focuses on the unity of all body parts and the body's innate ability to heal itself.

The American Osteopathic Association is the national professional organization representing
the nation's 35,000 osteopathic physicians who have chosen to learn, teach and practice Dr.
Still's philosophy. Doctors of Osteopathy (D.O.s) practice in all medical specialties, but the
overwhelming majority are primary care/generalist physicians who provide a complete range
of services to patients of all ages. Despite the fact that osteopathic physicians constitute
only 5.5 percent of the Nation's physician-manpower, they are often the only physicians in
rural and underserved areas, and we are proud of that. Osteopathic physicians in fact
comprise more than 15 percent of all physicians practicing in communities with populations
of less than 10,000 people and 18 percent of all physicians serving communities of 2500 or
less.

In addition, according to the U.S. Department of Health and Human Services, osteopathic
physicians serve approximately one out of every seven Medicare and 25 percent of all
Medicaid recipients in the United States. Osteopathic physicians also comprise 10 percent
of all physicians serving in the military. In all, over 100 million patient visits are made to
osteopathic physicians annually.

The osteopathic story has been written by the patients, who by their demand for osteopathic
services, have carved a vital niche for osteopathic medicine in today's health care delivery
system. To continue to meet this demand, the osteopathic profession recognizes the need
for reform of the current health care delivery system. This reform must include a global
budget for national health care expenditures to reduce cost-shifting among the public and
private payors, and to control the rising health care portion of the GDP.

Once a target is established, a uniform basic package of benefits, which includes coverage
of preventive care must and can be developed and made available to all Americans. As a
profession which was born based on the belief that the body has the intrinsic ability to heal
itself, the AOA wholeheartedly supports a greater reliance on preventive and primary care.

Once a basic benefits package is developed, a method on how best to deliver these benefits
must be determined. The AOA believes that a model which provides enough competition
to promote efficient health care delivery without sacrificing quality health care is the best
method to address the competing objectives of reducing costs while preserving quality. To
that end the profession supports a delivery system based on managed competition - that is,
an integrated system of financing and delivering health care through several types of health
plans. President Clinton's proposed system of alliances presents a good point from which
debate on delivery mechanisms should start.

Under a system of managed competition, or any other delivery system, however, patients should be able to receive care from the professional of their choice. Hence, any delivery system must provide the opportunity for all qualified physicians to participate. Criteria to determine who is qualified should not be based on degree granted or the organization which approves the graduate training programs or awards the certification. Rather, physicians should be judged on their ability to provide quality care at an appropriate cost. For example, osteopathic physicians hold a degree as a Doctor of Osteopathy (D.O.), pursue training in osteopathic postgraduate training programs, and become certified approved through osteopathic certification examinations. Although these valuative indicators are considered equal to similar allopathic indicators, many private payors are ignorant of this separate process. Consequently, patients around the nation today are being denied access to the provider of their choice -the osteopathic physician- because the private payer has not taken the time to understand the differences and the benefits that the osteopathic physician can bring to the patients.

It is because of this situation, that the AOA is before you today. In order for patients to truly have freedom of choice of provider, Congress must enact legislation which prohibits private insurers and delivery mechanisms from discriminating based on degree, postgraduate training and certification.

Congress also must act to protect the medical training programs which train individuals to provide appropriate care to the patient. The osteopathic profession is extremely proud of its unique educational model, which produces physicians who provide excellent primary and specialty care. As a matter of fact, the profession believes that it has the model program to achieve the appropriate national balance between primary and specialty physicians. This model has produced over 60 percent primary care physicians among all osteopathic physicians delivering care today, which is well in compliance with the federal initiative. Included in this model is a rotating internship which trains osteopathic physicians in generalist practice first and after which practically all choose to receive additional training whether it be in primary care or specialty residency programs. These internships and residencies are directed by both osteopathic primary care and specialty physicians. In order to retain this very successful training model, osteopathic training programs must be protected.

The AOA has worked very closely with both congressional advisory bodies of COGME and PPRC to advance the osteopathic training model. Both bodies understand well the contribution of osteopathic medicine. In an effort to address the aggregate number of training slots, however, both bodies also have recommended that the total funded residency positions be limited to the number of osteopathic and allopathic medical school graduates together plus 10 percent. Because of our smallness and community - based approach to teaching, the profession is very concerned that osteopathic programs could be absorbed if integrated rather than kept separate from the larger allopathic numbers. To prevent this from happening and to continue to provide patients with osteopathically trained physicians, the AOA is requesting that its programs be treated separately. That is, the osteopathic internship which is a requirement of all osteopathic trainees be additionally included in the eligible years of postgraduate training. Further, the total funded osteopathic first year residency positions should be limited to the number of osteopathic medical school graduates plus 10 percent while separately, the total funded allopathic residency positions should be limited to the number of allopathic medical school graduates plus 10 percent.

Mr. Chairman and Members of this distinguished Subcommittee, I hope that in this short time I have increased your awareness of osteopathic medicine and its unique and vital contribution to health care delivery in this nation. Additional details about my comments can be found in the written statement. In summary, though, the AOA is a balanced profession offering a majority of primary care physicians and an appropriate number of specialists. We believe that a health care crisis does indeed exist and as such support a global budget for health expenditures, a basic benefits package which includes primary and preventive care, and a delivery system based on managed competition.

We know that this crisis will only worsen if osteopathic physicians are prevented from delivering care because of the unique degree, training and certification they possess. Further, there will be no osteopathic physicians in the future if an appropriate number of our training programs are not recognized and funded.
Mr. Chairman that concludes my remarks. I would be happy to answer any questions of the Subcommittee.

STATEMENT OF LAURENCE E. BOUCHARD, DO
PRESIDENT
AMERICAN OSTEOPATHIC ASSOCIATION

I am Laurence E. Bouchard, DO, President of the American Osteopathic Association (AOA). As an osteopathic physician (DO), I have been in general practice for over 30 years in Narragansett, Rhode Island, a community of less than 10,000. I come before you to speak on behalf of the osteopathic medical profession. Osteopathic medicine is a separate and distinct school of medicine which was founded over 100 years ago as a reform movement in complete medical care. With this reform background, the profession has continued to today to provide the kind of health care which is essential to modern health care reform.

The osteopathic medical profession genuinely supports this health care reform effort and believes that the cornerstone of reform is concern for the patient. The osteopathic medical profession has for some time spoken out in favor of reform and is ready to make a contribution to the inevitable debate on this proposed legislation. Osteopathic medicine, with its commitment to primary care, preventive medicine and treatment of the whole person, and its history of providing care in under-served areas, is uniquely equipped to make a major contribution to this debate.

Today, I am here to focus on three areas: (1) the osteopathic medical profession; (2) discrimination against the osteopathic medical profession; and (3) preserving the osteopathic training system.

1. The Osteopathic Medical Profession.

There are two distinct branches of medical practice in the United States: osteopathic medicine and allopathic medicine. Osteopathic physicians start their medical careers by earning the degree of Doctor of Osteopathy (DO). The majority of the physicians in this country are allopathic physicians (MDs); however, doctors of osteopathic medicine constitute fully five percent of the physicians practicing in the United States, which translates into nearly one hundred million patient visits to osteopathic physicians each year. Significantly, osteopathic physicians serve approximately one out of every seven Medicare and one of every four Medicaid recipients. Clearly, by numbers alone, osteopathic physicians comprise an essential element in the network of medical services provided in this country.

There are some 35,000 osteopathic physicians in the United States today. Of these approximately 62% are primary care physicians (family physicians, general internists, general pediatricians, and obstetricians/gynecologists). The profession also trains and certifies specialists in all of the other medical specialties, such as surgery, anesthesiology, radiology, and psychiatry.

Of the 35,000 osteopathic physicians, 24,000 are members of the AOA. The AOA is the national osteopathic organization. The AOA is recognized by the U.S. Department of Education and the Commission on Recognition of Postsecondary Accreditation as the accrediting agency for osteopathic medical colleges. The AOA also accredits more than 140 hospitals and health care facilities in 26 states. Such hospital accreditation is recognized by the U.S. Department of Health and Human Services. Additionally, the AOA, in conjunction with various affiliated organizations, formulates general requirements for graduate medical education (internships and residencies) leading to specialty certification through the AOA's various specialty boards. The AOA also examines and approves osteopathic internship and residency programs in DO and DO/MD hospitals. The AOA conducts examinations for specialty certification following the completion of such training. Finally, the AOA administers an extensive program of continuing medical education which is required to maintain AOA membership, specialty certification and licensure in numerous states.

The profession grew out of concepts first developed in 1874 by Andrew Taylor Still, MD. Dr. Still's philosophy of medical care focused on "wellness," preventive medicine, and the body's ability to heal itself. Dr. Still studied the attributes of good health so that he could better understand the process of disease. He devised a philosophy which emphasized the unity of all body parts, particularly that of the musculoskeletal system, as a key element of health. The unique osteopathic manipulative treatment grew out of this philosophy. All of these principals -- "wellness," holistic medicine, osteopathic manipulative treatment, and emphasis on family/generalist practice -- have been essential elements of osteopathic medicine for over 100 years.

As of today, there are 16 accredited colleges of osteopathic medicine in 14 states.[1] The colleges enroll qualified

_____

[1]Chicago College of Osteopathic Medicine - Chicago, Illinois
    College of Osteopathic Medicine of the Pacific - Pomona, California
    Kirksville College of Osteopathic Medicine - Kirksville, Missouri
    Lake Erie College of Osteopathic Medicine - Lake Erie, Pennsylvania
    Michigan State College of Osteopathic Medicine - Lansing, Michigan

applicants that have graduated with four-year college degrees.
Last year 1,944 medical students were accepted out of a total of
28,557 applicants to these schools. Osteopathic medical schools
require for graduation the successful completion of a four-year
curriculum of basic sciences and clinical studies -- the same
subject matter taught in allopathic medical schools. Osteopathic
medical schools expose their students to clinical experience at
an early stage in their training, which is part of a larger
process of teaching all students to be primary care physicians
first and foremost.

The DO degree is fully equivalent to the MD degree. The DO
and MD degrees are the only recognized degrees leading to the
unlimited licensure for the practice of complete medicine and
surgery, including the prescription of medications.

Following graduation, osteopathic physicians generally
embark on a course of graduate medical education that starts with
an internship which requires rotations in internal medicine,
obstetrics and gynecology, general pediatrics, family practice
and surgery. Following internships, these physicians progress to
residencies in primary care and other specialties. This system
of graduate medical education creates a balanced profession in
which all facets of primary and specialty care are represented.

The proposed Health Security Act urges that more
encouragement be given to medical students to become

New York College of Osteopathic Medicine - Old Westbury,
New York
Ohio University/College of Osteopathic Medicine - Athens,
Ohio
Oklahoma State University/College of Osteopathic Medicine -
Tulsa, Oklahoma
Philadelphia College of Osteopathic Medicine -
Philadelphia, Pennsylvania
Southeastern University of the Health Sciences College of
Osteopathic Medicine - N. Miami Beach, Florida
Texas College of Osteopathic Medicine - Ft. Worth, Texas
University of Health Sciences, College of Osteopathic
Medicine - Kansas City, Missouri
University of Medicine & Dentistry of New Jersey, School of
Osteopathic Medicine - Stratford, New Jersey
University of New England, College of Osteopathic Medicine
- Biddeford, Maine
University of Osteopathic Medicine & Health Sciences
College of Osteopathic Medicine & Surgery - Des Moines, Iowa
West Virginia School of Osteopathic Medicine - Lewisburg,
West Virginia

family/generalist practitioners. As health care reform advances, medical systems will require increasing numbers of primary care physicians to realize the benefits of reform. With respect to primary care physicians it is important to note that:

1. 62% of osteopathic physicians practice primary care medicine which represents 9% of all DO/MD primary care physicians;

2. A recent Council on Graduate Medical Education (COGME) report reveals that DO graduates are significantly more likely to enter primary care (see chart appended as Exhibit 1); and

3. While comprising only five percent of the total number of practicing physicians, osteopathic physicians make up fifteen percent of the physicians practicing in communities of 10,000 or less, and eighteen percent of the physicians serving communities of 2,500 or less.

2. Protection from Discrimination Against Osteopathic Medicine.

The strength and independence of osteopathic medicine were not easily attained. While there has been a dramatic change in this attitude in recent years, there remain significant pockets of active discrimination. Also, it should be kept in mind that measured in numbers of physicians, osteopathic medicine represents only 5% of all physicians, who number in excess of 600,000. Consequently, where in many cases there may not be active discriminatory actions and attitudes, there may be a total failure to recognize the existence of the osteopathic profession, its training programs, certification and accreditation.[2]

---

[2]For example, the Social Security Act, as presently enacted, includes provisions regarding payments by the Secretary of Health and Human Services to the states in compensation for expenditures on physicians' services for children and pregnant women. Under the legislation, reimbursement is only provided if the medical services were provided by "physicians certified in family practice or pediatrics by the medical specialty board recognized by the American Board of Medical Specialties." 42 U.S.C. §1396(b)(i)(14). By including only specialties recognized by the American Board of Medical Specialties and excluding the medical specialty programs recognized by the AOA's medical specialty board, the legislation excludes reimbursement for medical services provided by osteopathic physicians

Notably, Senator Moynihan (D-NY) has proposed a bill which will amend the Social Security Act to allow for reimbursement to

The United States Government has recognized the equivalency of allopathic and osteopathic graduate training and certification in many areas.[3] Generally the courts have observed that such training and credentials are equal in terms of quality and requirements.[4] However, despite such recognition of equivalency, discrimination against DOs continues. For example, there are numerous cases of discrimination in hospital staff credentialing. A new form of discrimination is emerging with respect to acceptance of osteopathic physicians and osteopathic hospitals into managed care practice groups.

We view the practice of discrimination against osteopathic practitioners when granting hospital staff privileges as particularly dangerous. Such practice is accomplished by refusing to recognize osteopathic graduate medical education and certification by the AOA. This has the effect of preventing osteopathic physicians from admitting and caring for their patients in the hospital environment.

---

the States for osteopathic physicians' services. S. 1668, 103d Cong., 1st Sess. (1993).

[3]Medicare defines physicians to include osteopathic physicians (42 U.S.C. §1395x(r)); Hospital accreditation by the AOA is statutorily recognized (42 U.S.C. §1395bb(a)); osteopathic physicians are statutorily authorized to practice medicine in the Public Health Service (42 U.S.C.§209(d)), Medical Corps (10 U.S.C. §532(b)), Veterans Administration hospitals (38 U.S.C. §4105(a)(1)); or Federal Health Service (5 U.S.C. §7901(e)).

[4]See Stern v. Tarrant County Hospital, 778 F.2d 1052, 1060 (5th Cir. 1985), cert. denied, 476 U.S. 1108 (1986) (noting that osteopathic physicians and allopathic physicians have similar training and face identical testing and licensing requirements); Brandwein v. California Board of Osteopathic Examiners, 708 F.2d 1466, 1468 (9th Cir. 1993) ("At the present time the differences between the schools of osteopathy and allopathy are minor."); Weiss v. York Hospital, 745 F.2d 786, 792, 820-22 (3d Cir. 1984), cert. denied, 470 U.S. 1060 (1985) (noting at footnote 4 that an M.D. had testified as to the fact that there was no difference between graduates of allopathic and osteopathic medical schools in terms of medical training or ability to provide medical care, and at page 820 that the defendant hospital did not contend that osteopathic physicians are less qualified, nor did they offer any "public service or ethical norm rationale for their discriminatory treatment of D.O.s.")

For health care reform to be effective, patients must be able to choose their own physicians, including osteopathic physicians. This freedom of choice can only be guaranteed if federal legislation includes a global prohibition against discrimination against AOA-approved training, certification, and accreditation of colleges and health care facilities.[5] The AOA, as the representative of osteopathic medicine, will be following legislation as it emerges in order to point out instances where specific provisions are needed to achieve the goal of freedom of choice for patients.

3. Graduate Medical Education and the Health Security Act.

I would also like to discuss the specific proposals regarding funding of graduate medical education. We are concerned about the possibility of unintended discrimination arising in legislation such as those programs created by the proposed Health Security Act.

Before direct consideration of the Health Security Act, I would direct your attention to House Resolution 2436,[6] recently introduced by Congressman Lewis Payne (D-VA). This provision as drafted provides payments to hospitals for indirect costs associated with ACGME (Accreditation Council for Graduate Medical Education)-approved postgraduate training when such training occurs in non-hospital settings. While this bill is clearly in the best interests of the medical profession in that it provides funding for post-graduate training, the bill does not provide for payments to hospitals to defer the costs associated with AOA-accredited programs. As drafted, the proposed legislation does not recognize that allopathic and osteopathic internships and residencies are accredited by separate entities, and ignores the osteopathic branch of medicine by limiting funding to those programs which are accredited by the ACGME. That is, the bill provides assistance only to those interns and residents who participate in allopathic medical programs.

Keeping this example in mind, I would like to now direct your attention to the provisions in the Health Security Act that concern osteopathic physicians. In particular, I would like to address the Graduate Medical Education Provisions contained in

---

[5]Legislation in this spirit was recently introduced by Congressman James Barcia (D-Mich.). H. Con. Res. 173, 103d Cong., 1st Sess. (1993).

[6]H.R. 2436, 103d Congress, 1st Sess. (1993).

[7]H.R. 3600, 103d Congress, 1st Sess. §§ 3001 et seq. (1993).

Title III of the bill. As you know, this section of the
legislation is intended to increase the number of medical school
graduates, both allopathic and osteopathic, practicing in primary
care fields by limiting the number of individuals authorized to
enroll in non-primary care residencies. In addition, the
legislation establishes a systematic program of federal funding
for approved residency programs.

Under the proposed legislation, the limitation on the number
of non-primary care residencies will be established by a National
Council on Graduate Medical Education. While the legislation
notes that "school of medicine" includes both allopathic and
osteopathic medical schools and recognizes AOA certification of
residency programs, we are still concerned about the potential
for unreasonable limitations on osteopathic specialty
residencies. We hope that if the legislation is ultimately
approved, it will specifically protect the osteopathic profession
by requiring substantial osteopathic representation on the
National Council.

In addition, the National Council will be given the
authority to allocate the number of specialty residencies among
the various programs nationwide. The proposed Council will be
permitted to consider a wide variety of factors in developing a
method of allocation. Because the osteopathic profession has an
independent history and a separate system of specialty training,
we are concerned that any unified method of allocation could have
an adverse impact on the osteopathic training system -- a system
that has demonstrated record of producing significant numbers of
primary care physicians. In point of fact, our distribution
between primary care and other specialties currently reflects
national needs. Therefore, we urge that separate limits be
established for the number of allopathic and osteopathic
residencies.

Conclusions

While the debate about National Health Care reform
progresses, we urge you to not forget that practicing osteopathic
physicians are confronting and addressing vital concerns in their
medical practices. As you consider the various reform options,
please bear in mind that osteopathic physicians will play an
essential part in administering health care in the future. Their
background in primary care and orientation towards preventive
medical care makes them uniquely suited to participate in the
future of medical care. At the same time, osteopathic
physicians' willingness to provide medical services to otherwise
under-served communities requires that they be included in any
planning for the future of medical care.

As legislation progresses toward enactment, I would
anticipate that there will be numerous statutory and regulatory
provisions wherein it will be desirable to specifically recognize
the osteopathic medical profession and to specifically prohibit
discrimination against osteopathic accreditation, training and
certification. These provisions will preserve a profession that
for over 100 years has been preparing the kinds of physicians
required to address the health care needs of the nation.

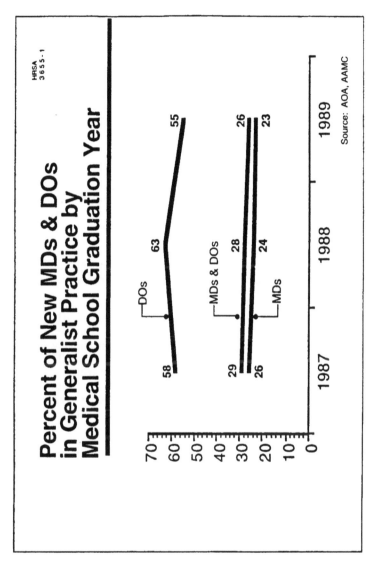

Percent of New MDs & DOs in Generalist Practice by Medical School Graduation Year

HRSA
3655-1

Source: AOA, AAMC

EXHIBIT 1

Chairman STARK. Dr. Nunnally.

STATEMENT OF RICHARD M. NUNNALLY, M.D., CHAIR, COUNCIL ON GOVERNMENT AND PROFESSIONAL AFFAIRS, COLLEGE OF AMERICAN PATHOLOGISTS

Dr. NUNNALLY. Thank you, Mr. Chairman.

I am Dr. Richard Nunnally, chair of the Council on Government and Professional Affairs and a Governor of the College of American Pathologists. The College appreciates this opportunity to appear before the subcommittee to discuss our views on health system reform and the President's Health Security Act.

The College supports universal coverage of basic health care for all Americans. Health system reform should build upon the strengths of the existing system and should include basic physical and mental health benefits, tax incentives, premium subsidies and other reforms to make insurance more affordable to small businesses and to individuals and are appropriate to ensure that universal coverage is achieved.

But the College is concerned that the degree of authority that would be granted a new National Health Board and regional health alliances under the Health Security Act would create an unnecessary new level of government bureaucracy.

Dr. NUNNALLY. Any such board or alliances should include physician representation and should not have such broad authority that micromanagement of health care decisions at the local level ensues. The National Health Board should not have the authority to establish price levels, set global budgets, or premium caps. The college strongly supports efforts to assure quality health care.

However, the extent of the Health Security Act's proposed Federal control and management of quality assurance programs such as practice guideline development and outcome and performance measurement is inappropriate. The college believes there should be formal recognition of private sector quality improvement, accreditation, and guideline development programs.

The college believes that the health system reform would be enhanced by requiring direct billing for all clinical laboratory services, including anatomic and clinical pathology.

There has been a direct billing requirement since 1984 for Medicare clinical diagnostic laboratory tests. Medicare payment can be made only to the entity that provides the test with an exception for referrals between laboratories that are independent of a physician's office.

Extending the direct billing requirement to all payers and all clinical laboratory services including both anatomic and clinical pathology services would be a positive contribution to the health reform process. Direct billing requires the laboratory performing a service to bill the patient or their insurer for the service. This would eliminate any real or perceived incentive to increased utilization of laboratory services and thus would help reduce costs.

The college opposes the imposition of a 20 percent coinsurance on Medicare clinical laboratory services. This will increase the costs of health care for Medicare beneficiaries and the costs of billing for laboratories without any reduction in utilization of services.

The proposed competitive bidding for Medicare clinical laboratory services will erode patient access to high-quality laboratory services in the whole area an eliminate local health care job opportunities. Any CLIA-certified laboratory that is willing to provide services to patients at the Medicare fee schedule amount should be allowed to do so.

The college opposes creation of distortions in the Medicare relative values to fund primary care initiatives. The proposal for reductions in nonprimary care relative values are arbitrary reductions outside of a formal RVS update and refinement process and are inappropriate.

In summary, Mr. Chairman, the College of American Pathologists supports health system reform that builds on the strengths of existing health care system and ensures universal coverage of basic health care for all Americans.

Overreliance on new bureaucratic entities that unnecessarily intrude on health care decisions at the local level should be avoided. A national mandate for direct billing of clinical laboratory services would be a positive step toward addressing laboratory cost issues. The College urges the inclusion of a direct billing requirement in health care reform legislation.

Thank you for the opportunity to appear today. I would be pleased to respond to questions.

Chairman STARK. Thank you, Dr. Nunnally.

[The prepared statement follows:]

STATEMENT OF RICHARD M. NUNNALLY, MD
CHAIR, COUNCIL ON GOVERNMENT AND PROFESSIONAL AFFAIRS
COLLEGE OF AMERICAN PATHOLOGISTS

The College of American Pathologists (CAP) appreciates the opportunity to appear before the Subcommittee on Health to discuss pathologists' views relating to health system reform and the President's *Health Security Act*. The College is a national medical society representing 14,000 physicians who are board certified in clinical and/or anatomic pathology. College members practice their specialty in community hospitals, independent clinical laboratories, academic medical centers, and federal and state health facilities.

The College supports universal coverage of basic health care for all Americans. Tax incentives, premium subsidies, and other reforms to make insurance more affordable to small businesses and individuals are appropriate to ensure that universal coverage is achieved. The College also supports extension and increase of excise taxes on alcohol and tobacco with funds ear-marked for health care, because alcohol and tobacco contribute significantly to medical costs. The College supports insurance reform including industry rating and underwriting practices that would ensure a non-discriminatory determination of health insurance premiums and coverage. Portability of health insurance is important to continued universal coverage.

The College of American Pathologists believes that health system reform should build upon the strengths of the existing health care system and should include basic physical and mental health benefits. While decreasing the rate of growth in health care costs is important, budget savings and health care economics can not be allowed to jeopardize the high quality of health care services that is currently available to Americans today. Similarly, pursuit of the most economically efficient health care provider should not be allowed to disrupt local patterns and networks of care that are best positioned to ensure high quality health care services to local enrollees.

Pathologists are responsible for the overall operation and administration of the laboratory and for ensuring that quality laboratory services are available. Pathologists must be involved in the determination of coverage and utilization of clinical and anatomic pathology services. Adequate resources must be allocated for the provision of laboratory direction, quality assurance, and other services provided by pathologists.

Market incentives are the most effective means of health care cost containment. Health system changes already underway and recent declines in the rising cost of health care support this position. The College opposes global budgets, federally mandated premium caps and other de facto price control initiatives.

National Health Board and Regional Alliances

The College is concerned that the degree of authority that would be granted a new National Health Board and Regional Health Alliances would create an unnecessary new level of government bureaucracy. Any such Board or Alliances should include physician representation and should not have such broad authority that micromanagement of health care decisions at the local level ensues. A National Health Board should not have the authority to establish price levels, set global budgets or premium caps, or in any other way establish de facto limits on health care expenditures.

The College is pleased that there is no limit to the number of fee-for-service plans that can be offered by a Regional Alliance. However, the provision in the percent of the weighted average premium may inappropriately limit patient choice and should be deleted.

Health plans should be required to accept any physician who agrees to provide services under an agreement with the plan. Limitations on the number of physicians who may provide services to plan enrollees will limit access to health care services and patient freedom of choice of physician and health care facility.

Quality Assurance and Health Reform

The College supports efforts to assure quality health care. However, the President's plan proposes extensive federal control and management of quality assurance programs such as practice guideline development and outcomes and performance measurement. The College believes there should be formal recognition of private sector quality improvement, accreditation and guideline development programs as an alternative to the proposed system of quality management.

There must be formal physician representation on any federal board or council that may be formed to address quality assurance. Similarly, any federal involvement in practice guideline development and outcomes and performance measurements must include explicit recognition of private sector initiatives.

Self-Referral Prohibition

The College supports extension of Medicare's prohibition on physician self-referral to all payers. We believe Medicare's current prohibition on certain physician ownership and referral arrangements has been effective in defining and discouraging situations where there may be incentives for increased laboratory utilization and costs.

National Direct Billing Mandate is Needed

The College believes that the President's *Health Security Act* would be enhanced by requiring direct billing for all clinical laboratory services (anatomic and clinical pathology) with an exception for referrals between laboratories that are independent of a physician's office. There has been a direct billing requirement since 1984 for Medicare clinical diagnostic laboratory tests. Medicare direct billing rules require payment be made only to the entity that provides the test, with an exception for referrals between laboratories that are independent of a physician's office. The College believes the Medicare direct billing requirement has been effective in helping to control laboratory costs and utilization.

Extending the direct billing requirement to all payers and all clinical laboratory services, including both anatomic and clinical pathology services, would be a positive contribution to the health reform process. Direct billing requires the laboratory performing a service to bill the patient or their insurer for the service. This would eliminate the practice by some physicians of purchasing and marking up services. The current system that allows physicians to bill for services they do not perform tends to lead to increased utilization and higher laboratory costs.

Medicare Savings Proposals

The College believes that the proposal to impose a 20 percent coinsurance on Medicare clinical laboratory services will increase the cost of health care for Medicare beneficiaries and the cost of billing for laboratories without any reduction in utilization of services. There is no evidence that utilization or total costs of laboratory testing would be controlled by reinstitution of the laboratory coinsurance provision that was deleted when Medicare adopted the clinical laboratory fee schedule methodology. Billing costs for laboratories would be very high to collect relatively small amounts per test. Laboratories accepted a reduced clinical laboratory fee schedule in exchange for eliminating copayments. It is unfair to reinstitute copayments.

The proposed competitive bidding for Medicare clinical laboratory services will erode patient access to high quality laboratory services in the local area and eliminate local health care job opportunities. Any CLIA-certified laboratory that is willing to provide services to patients at the Medicare fee schedule amount should be allowed to do so.

A more effective means of controlling laboratory test utilization would be to make payment for all clinical laboratory tests only to the provider of the service. A national direct billing requirement for all payers would contribute positively to the health reform process and should be included in health reform legislation.

The College opposes creation of distortions in the Medicare relative values to fund primary care initiatives. The proposals for a 10 percent reduction in non-primary care relative values and for development of "outlier intensity" relative value adjustments are arbitrary reductions outside a formal RVS update and refinement process. This undermines the methodology upon which the relative values are based.

Similarly, the College opposes the 3 percent reduction in the 1995 Medicare RVS conversion factor for non-primary care services. Medicare RVS fee schedule amounts are already too low in many instances. Continued erosion of the update factor will exacerbate this problem and ultimately lead to reductions in quality of medical care.

Medical Liability

The College supports enactment of medical liability reform to promote the basic goal of providing access to all necessary health care services, deter substandard or unethical practices and encourage improvements in the safety and quality of medical care.

A compensation system for medical injury should enhance, not impair, a cooperative relationship between patients and health care providers based on mutual respect and effective communication. Such a system should compensate patients injured by malpractice adequately and equitably, resolve claims promptly, encourage innovation in diagnosis and treatment leading to better care, and operate efficiently and economically.

Outcomes should be predictable with respect to findings of liability and amounts of awards. Specifically, the College supports the offset of collateral sources of patient compensation, sliding scale regulation of attorney contingency fees, limiting non-economic damage awards to $250,000, and providing for periodic payment for awards over $100,000.

Physician Workforce

Any changes in funding for graduate medical education must ensure that an adequate supply of pathologists is trained to meet the nation's needs during the upcoming century. Pathologists and other non-primary care physicians must be involved in any national board that may be established in efforts to address

483

Summary

The College of American Pathologists supports health system reform that builds on the strengths of the existing health care system and ensures universal coverage of basic health care for all Americans. Over-reliance on new bureaucratic entities that unnecessarily intrude on health care decisions at the local level should be avoided. When the national interest requires a federal oversight role, care must be taken to ensure that the private sector is explicitly included. There should be explicit provisions for physician membership in newly formed health system structures as well as reliance on private sector initiatives whenever possible - especially in attempts to evaluate and enhance health care quality. A national mandate for direct billing of clinical laboratory services, including anatomic and clinical pathology, would be a positive step toward addressing laboratory cost issues. The College urges the inclusion of a direct billing requirement in health care reform legislation.

Thank you for the opportunity to testify before the Subcommittee on Health.

484

Chairman STARK. Dr. Elliott.

STATEMENT OF L. EDWARD ELLIOTT, O.D., PAST PRESIDENT, AMERICAN OPTOMETRIC ASSOCIATION

Dr. ELLIOTT. Mr. Chairman, I am Ed Elliott, doctor of optometry from Modesto, Calif.

Chairman STARK. Welcome.

Dr. ELLIOTT. Your backyard. I am a past president of the American Optometric Association. On behalf of the Nation's 28,000 practicing optometrists, I appreciate the opportunity to present our views on reforming our Nation's health care system. You have my written statement, so in the interests of time, I would like to briefly summarize.

The AOA applauds the President for putting forth a comprehensive proposal to address the issue of universal coverage to health care. In addition, we believe the following principles must be included in any health care reform legislation. A viable fee-for-service option, primary eye care and disease prevention including periodic eye examinations, meaningful tort reform, quality care assurances, administrative cost controls, support for clinical education programs to train optometrists in primary care in community settings, protection of State laws designed to ensure proper access to care and providers, and most importantly, reasonable criteria to assure that health plans do not discriminate against any provider based on type, class, or profession of the provider.

We are pleased that the administration has clarified that the eye care component of the administration's benefit package includes routine periodic eye examinations, as well as the diagnosis and treatment of vision defects and eyeglasses and contact lenses for children under 18.

We would strongly urge the Congress to set forth a uniform benefits structure and to retain this important benefit as it considers health care reform.

Any benefits package should clearly cover symptom-related visits for acute problems, including eye health problems. The model for this coverage already exists at the Federal level with the Medicare program. In addition, to ensure early diagnosis of potentially costly and debilitating eye and systemic diseases, periodic preventive eye and vision care examinations should also be included in the package. The long-term savings to the health care system by early diagnosis of costly eye and systemic diseases will more than offset the cost of providing this routine preventive care.

Regular eye examinations are an essential preventive measure for the early diagnosis and prompt treatment of eye diseases which, if left undetected, result in serious personal loss and significant societal costs. A recent study by the Georgetown University Medical Center has concluded that nearly 100,000 of the new cases of blindness each year are curable or preventable through timely detection and treatment, leading to an estimated annual savings to the Federal budget of over $1 billion.

Finally, Mr. Chairman, we would like to express our concerns that managed care plans not be allowed to arbitrarily exclude entire classes of providers who are qualified to provide services covered in the benefit package.

While the administration proposal would allow doctors of optometry and other providers to deliver care on a level playingfield with their colleagues in medicine in the fee-for-service arena, the same is not true for managed care plans.

The administration proposal would preempt State nondiscrimination statutes and allow managed plans to limit the number and type of health care providers who may participate in the plan. To ensure access to a representative network of providers, it is imperative that any health reform plan contain a strong nondiscrimination provision to prevent exclusionary practices based on artificial barriers. In short, provisions prohibiting discrimination should apply equally for fee-for-service and managed care plans.

Again, I thank you for the opportunity to testify on this important issue and would be happy to answer any questions.

Thank you.

Chairman STARK. Thank you, Dr. Elliott.

[The prepared statement follows:]

STATEMENT OF L. EDWARD ELLIOTT, O.D.
AMERICAN OPTOMETRIC ASSOCIATION

Mr. Chairman, my name is Edward Elliott, a doctor of optometry from
Modesto, California. I am in private practice in Modesto and also teach
at the University of California at the Berkeley School of Optometry. I
am a past president of the American Optometric Association (AOA),
representing the largest eye care profession in the Nation with
approximately 30,000 optometrists and students of optometry.

I appreciate the opportunity to testify before the Subcommittee on behalf
of the American Optometric Association. Our association supports health
care reform that broadens access, controls costs and assures quality
care. Because AOA represents the providers of the majority of primary
eye care services in the Nation, we would like to discuss the direction
of health care reform and the inclusion of a comprehensive health benefit
package that includes primary eye care services.

The AOA applauds the President for putting forth a comprehensive proposal
to address the issue of universal access to health care. Besides the
concept of universal access for all Americans, AOA believes the following
principles must be included in any health care reform legislation: a
viable fee for service option, primary eye care and disease prevention,
meaningful tort reform, quality care assurances, administrative cost
controls, periodic eye examinations, support for clinical education
programs to train optometrists in primary care in community settings,
protection of state laws designed to assure proper access to care and
providers and most importantly reasonable criteria to assure that health
plans do not discriminate against any provider based on type, class or
profession of the provider.

While we have a number of concerns regarding the Administration's plan,
we certainly support the concept of a uniform benefit package, and agree
that eye care must be a part of such a package. We are pleased that the
White House has clarified in a memorandum to Congressional leaders that
the eye care component of the Administration's benefit package includes
routine periodic eye examinations as well as the diagnosis and treatment
of vision defects, and eyeglasses and contact lenses for children under
18. We would strongly urge the Congress to set forth a uniform benefit
structure and to retain this important benefit as it considers health
care reform.

NEED FOR EYE CARE

Vision and eye health problems are the second most prevalent, chronic,
health care problems in the U.S. population, affecting more than 120
million people. Undetected and untreated, they reduce the educability of
the child, hasten the loss of independence in the elderly and contribute
to the social isolation of the individual. Early detection and
appropriate treatment are essential to preserve performance and prevent
damage and consequent handicaps which can result from neglect. The two
age groups at highest risk for vision problems are children and the
elderly.

Children

Children are at high risk because of the impact of uncorrected vision
handicaps on their educational and developmental progress, including
visual and perceptual skills for language and learning. Since most
vision problems occur without pain, they may be completely unknown to
parents, teachers or even the child. The behavioral changes caused by
undetected vision problems in children are often erroneously attributed
to other unrelated causes, such as attention deficit disorder. Early
diagnosis and treatment can aid in preventing or correcting vision
conditions which can interfere with a child's learning and self image.

One example of how an undetected painless vision problem that could have
caused the loss of sight for an 8 year old girl was broadcast on the
TODAY show earlier this week. Through the AOA VISION USA program, low
income workers who are not covered by health insurance and meet a certain
income criteria are provided free eye exams during the month of March.
Last year an 8 year old girl from Rhode Island was detected as having a
detached retina by an optometrist providing services through the VISION
USA program. Because of this routine eye examination, a sight
threatening situation was avoided.

Elderly

The elderly, too, are at risk because of physiological changes which come with age. The elderly develop increasing incidence of systemic disease and a decline of sensory function. Vision and eye health problems increase significantly in frequency and severity with age and are more prevalent in those over 60. With the reduction in vision in the elderly, many times comes an increase in dependency. By providing regular eye care to the elderly, many times an independent life style can be maintained.

Equally important, regular eye examinations are an essential preventive measure for the early diagnosis and prompt treatment of eye diseases, which if left undetected, result in serious personal loss and significant societal costs. A recent study by the Georgetown University Medical Center has concluded that about 100,000 of the new cases of blindness each year are curable or preventable through timely detection and treatment, leading to an estimated annual savings to the federal budget of over $1 billion.

Mr. Chairman, it is significant to note that the health maintenance organization industry has long recognized the cost-effective nature of routine eye care. Data from the 1991 annual HMO Industry Survey conducted by the Group Health Association of America show that more than 90 percent of all HMOs cover routine eye and vision examinations on a periodic basis.

Another example of why routine eye care should be included in any health care proposal is illustrated again by the AOA VISION USA program. In 1993 more than 35,000 people, ranging in age from one to 96 were provided free eye exams. Nine out of 10 people receiving exams had eye health or vision problems.

Seven out of 100 patients had an eye health problem, the most common being cataracts and glaucoma. Nearly 7 out of 10 patients were given a new or updated prescription for eyeglasses.

The results of the VISION USA exams showed that 1,800 people had sight-threatening eye disease that, if left untreated, could force them on to welfare rolls or into tax-supported programs for the blind and visually impaired. The people that were provided services through the VISION USA program are just a small portion of the 38 million uninsured who would benefit from a comprehensive benefit package that included routine and eye health services.

OPTOMETRY'S ROLE

For many people, an eye examination is the entry point into the health care system since many Americans who postpone or avoid other forms of health care often continue to seek eye care. Optometrists performed 68 percent of the 78 million primary eye exams conducted in 1992. In a typical state, nearly two-thirds of all available eye care providers are doctors of optometry.

Optometrists are the most accessible of eye care providers, serving in 6,830 municipalities throughout the United States. In more than 4,100 of these communities, optometrists are the only primary eye care providers.

While approximately 70 percent of optometrists are in private practice settings, many others practice in multidisciplinary group practices, in hospitals, with the Veterans Administration, Public Health Service, and the Armed Services. Other optometrists participate in managed care plans such as HMOs, preferred provider organizations, and independent practice associations. In many of these organizations optometrists function as the entry point into the system for eye care.

As primary care providers, optometrists are an integral part of the health care team. They are specifically trained to diagnose, manage, and treat conditions and diseases of the human eye and visual system. As an entry point into the health care system, optometrists are positioned to serve a prevention role as an effective source of triage for not only eye health problems, but systemic health problems with eye manifestations as well.

ACCESSIBILITY

Because of their geographical distribution, optometrists provide services to patients that they may not have access to otherwise. This is especially true in rural areas. In many areas, an optometrist may be the only eye care provider available.

Increased accessibility for eye care from optometrists makes it easier for patients to receive prompt diagnosis and treatment. Prompt treatment of disease at the patient's first contact with the health care system assures patients of immediate symptomatic relief from pain. For many inflammatory and infectious diseases, the initiation of pharmaceutical treatment early in the course of the disease greatly improves the likelihood of effective treatment and lowers the risk of complications. Thus, total cost for an episode of illness is likely to be lower when full scope care is offered at the primary care visit in the optometrist's office.

Low income patients, often at high health risk, are very dependent on optometrists for their primary eye care services. In Oregon, a 1991 report found that over two-thirds of the care rendered to this high health risk population was provided by doctors of optometry. In Vermont, optometrists provide 90% of the eye care services provided in the Medicaid program and in the President's own state optometrists provide over 80% of the Medicaid eye care services. Historically, as a profession, optometrists have demonstrated a high participation rate in government programs serving disadvantaged communities.

COST EFFECTIVENESS

Besides being accessible, optometrists are also cost effective. Office fees and charges for visits associated with the treatment of eye diseases are on average lower for an optometrist than an ophthalmologist. National and regional surveys of professional fees and analysis of public health programs present significant evidence of the lower cost of eye care when provided by optometrists.

Managed care entities that utilize optometrists to provide primary eye care services recognize the cost savings such a delivery model can accomplish. InterStudy, a nationally recognized research firm, documented a potential 36 percent savings when optometric manpower was utilized to the full extent of their training and competence. "The most cost effective models are those where optometrists perform all routine examinations and also manage certain eye diseases and conditions," the study concluded.

COMPREHENSIVE EYE CARE BENEFITS PACKAGE

As I have stated previously before this Committee, it is important that a comprehensive eye care benefits package be included in any health care reform proposal. A comprehensive benefits package should include two components -- regular periodic preventive care for all age groups, and the more symptom-related diagnostic and treatment services currently covered under the Medicare program. In addition, the package should continue to provide ophthalmic materials for the Medicaid population.

We are pleased to note that the Administration's proposal embodies this approach to coverage through its health professional services section and its vision care section. The routine comprehensive eye exam serves the same preventive care role as the routine medical exam by primary care physicians. The Administration's routine eye care benefit promotes early diagnosis and management as a way to lower costs in the long run. The comprehensive eye care benefit can actually enhance the efficient operation of the health plan while expanding a desired service to their members.

NON-DISCRIMINATION BY MANAGED CARE PLANS

Mr. Chairman, we would like to express our concern that managed care plans not be allowed to arbitrarily exclude entire classes of providers who are qualified to provide services covered in the benefit package. While the Administration proposal would allow doctors of optometry and other providers to deliver care on a level playing field with their colleagues in medicine in the fee for service arena, the same is not true for managed care plans. The Administration proposal would pre-empt state non-discrimination statutes and allow managed plans to limit the number and type of health care providers who may participate in the plan.

Health care reform legislation should prohibit all health plans from denying participating provider status based on the type, class, or professional category of provider who provides covered services. A preliminary draft of the Administration's proposal had specified that each health plan would be "expected to provide a sufficient mix of providers and specialties to provide adequate access to professional services." However, this concept is not presently contained in the Presidents' bill, and absent strong legislative direction, the sufficient mix of providers referred to in the draft is not likely to occur.

To ensure access to a representative network of providers, it is imperative that any health reform plan contain a strong non-discrimination provision to prevent exclusionary practices based on artificial barriers. At a minimum, there should be criteria for provider eligibility in managed plans reflecting the needs of the plans' enrollees and their rights to choose from a diverse mix of providers of covered services. The volume, capacity and geographic distribution of health care providers within the network area should be considered to ensure appropriate representation. In short, provisions prohibiting discrimination should apply equally to fee for service and managed care plans.

BARRIER ELIMINATION

The Health Security Act also seeks to eliminate practice restriction and barriers in state law. However, there is no enforcement mechanism to insure that such barriers will in fact be eliminated. We recommend that state incentives be developed to insure that optometrists and other providers can provide full scope patient care based on skill and training and not be limited by artificial barriers.

ANTITRUST SECTION

AOA is also concerned with antitrust exemptions that are recommended by the Health Security Act and other health care proposals. The Health Security Act proposed that guidelines would be developed by the Department of Justice and the Federal Trade Commission to assist health care providers to determine whether their activity might subject them to antitrust enforcement. On September 15, 1993 DoJ and the FTC issued its first set of guidelines, "Statements of Antitrust Enforcement in the Health Care Area". The guidelines, as presently written, apply only to physicians. Although the FTC has given us assurances that non-M.D.s would be evaluated by the same standards as physicians, there needs to be some clarification as to whether the guidelines apply equally to all health professionals. The guidelines also fail to address whether exclusion of competitors would be considered a potential violation.

The other fear that is presented by the recommendation of antitrust exemptions is that physicians will use the exemptions to legitimately exclude competitors from participating in the system, ultimately to the detriment of non-M.D. health care providers and their patients. This is especially true when considering the AMA request of October 1993 that an antitrust exemption be permitted allowing groups of physicians, even when acting through state medical societies, to negotiate directly over fees, as well as other terms and conditions of payment and coverage.

Based on these reasons, AOA stresses that careful consideration needs to be given to providing antitrust exemptions. If exemptions are granted, protections should be provided that prevent the exclusion of health care providers authorized to provide the same or similar services.

CONCLUSION

Mr. Chairman, AOA strongly supports the concept of universal access to health care and a uniform benefit structure. The President has consistently stated that a comprehensive benefit package must be included in any health care reform package. The American Optometric Association urges the adoption of a comprehensive benefit package and opposes any attempt to delegate the development of the benefit package to a national board. As part of this comprehensive benefit package, AOA supports the

Administration plan which has rightfully recognized routine preventive eye care as an important component of the benefit package and we would urge the Congress to retain this benefit as it develops a reform plan.

At the same time, we would also urge Congress to address the critical issue of non-discrimination by managed care plans to ensure that each plan provides access to an appropriate mix of providers of covered services. Without the inclusion of non-discrimination language, many providers may be eliminated from the game. Without the inclusion of all providers qualified to provide health care services there cannot be competition and without competition, a cost effective, quality care delivery system cannot be reached.

Thank you again for the opportunity to testify on this important issue. I would be happy to respond to any questions.

1501F
2/2/94

Chairman STARK. Dr. Jones.

STATEMENT OF CHARLES L. JONES, D.P.M., PRESIDENT-ELECT, AMERICAN PODIATRIC MEDICAL ASSOCIATION, INC.

Dr. JONES. Mr. Chairman and members of the subcommittee, I am Dr. Charles L. Jones.

Chairman STARK. Do you know Paul Kay?

Dr. JONES. No.

Chairman STARK. He used to be in your association. He is my other neighbor.

Dr. JONES. I am president-elect of the American Podiatric Medical Association and a practicing podiatrist in Chicago, Ill. Our association appreciates this opportunity to once again appear and testify on the broad subject of health system reform.

On this occasion, I would like to focus attention to one area of the reform debate: The restructuring of graduate medical education financing and the vital interest podiatric medical education has in that subject.

Since 1973, Medicare has been authorized to make direct and indirect medical education payments to teaching hospitals with approved post-doctoral training programs in podiatric medicine and surgery. In 1993, we estimated that 120 hospitals with 400 residency slots in 27 States and the District of Columbia received Medicare payments for the direct costs of these programs.

Our present concern, Mr. Chairman, is that none of the major reform proposals pending in the Congress addresses the eligibility of post-doctoral training programs in podiatric medicine for continuing graduate medical education funding under reform. That benefit is limited in those proposals to plans in allopathic and osteopathic medicine.

The administration, we are pleased to note, has acknowledged that the omission of podiatric medical post-doctoral training programs in the Health Security Act, H.R. 3600, for graduate medical education restructuring was an oversight and would support a remedy to our problem. We would respectfully urge the subcommittee to do likewise as it crafts its own reform proposal.

We believe very strongly that podiatric medical residency programs must continue to have access to funding, including access to any new funding mechanism that might ultimately replace or supplement that which is currently in effect under Medicare. Among other requirements, completion of an approved residency program is now an essential component of the training of a doctor of podiatric medicine. A 1992 resolution adopted by the APMA House of Delegates makes clear that colleges of podiatric medicine should prepare their graduates for entry-level, post-graduate study, not for entry-level practice.

Very importantly, an increasing number of States require 1 year of post-graduate training for licensure. As of 1990, 32 States have such a requirement.

We are mindful, Mr. Chairman, that valid reasons exist to restructure graduate medical education financing. However, when the realities of podiatric medicine are considered along these reasons, we are confident that our graduate medical education objective is both sound and in the public interests.

First, proposed changes in the financing of graduate medical education rely on the fact that there are more allopathic medical residency positions than graduates in the U.S. schools of medicine with excess positions filled by foreign medical graduates. In the case of podiatric medicine, there were no foreign medical graduates and the goal has been to provide residency positions for all graduates of the U.S. podiatric medical colleges, a goal finally achieved in 1991.

The second premise is that there may be too many allopathic and osteopathic positions. However, no government body has determined that an excess of doctors of podiatric medicine is in the offing. In 1981, the U.S. Department of Health and Human Services established an ideal ratio of 6.2 DPMs per 100,000 population. But the actually 1991 ratio was only about 5.0. Moreover, DPMs provide the majority of foot care needed by Medicare beneficiaries, a population increasing by about 2 percent each year.

The third premise is that there are not enough primary care practitioners. As emphasized in the eighth report to Congress on Health Personnel in the United States, published September 1992 by the U.S. Public Health Service, and I quote, DPMs often serve as the entry point in the health care system for patients with systemic diseases that manifest themselves by symptoms in the foot, end of quote.

Further evaluation and management services accounted for about 24 percent of the Medicare allowed dollars paid to DPMs in 1991.

Finally, Mr. Chairman, APMA believes that post-doctoral residency programs in podiatric medicine and surgery must continue to merit graduate medical education funding, including any new financing schemes resulting from reform. This can happen by defining an approved physician training program to include those approved by the Council on Podiatric Medical Education of the American Podiatric Medical Association. It is equally important, we feel, that podiatric medicine be represented on any national council which might be charged to oversee the graduate medical education allocation process.

This concludes my statement. I would be pleased to respond to any questions you might have.

Thank you.

Chairman STARK. Thank you very much.

[The prepared statement follows:]

STATEMENT OF CHARLES JONES, DPM
PRESIDENT ELECT
AMERICAN PODIATRIC MEDICAL ASSOCIATION

Mr. Chairman, members of the Subcommittee:

I am Dr. Charles Jones, President-Elect, American Podiatric Medical Association, and a private practicing podiatric physician in Chicago, Illinois. The association very much appreciates this opportunity to once again appear and testify on the broad subject of health systems reform. But on this occasion I would like to focus primary attention in one area of the reform debate, the restructuring of graduate medical education (GME) financing and the vital interest podiatric medical education has in that subject.

GME, MEDICARE, & PODIATRIC MEDICINE
Since 1973, Medicare has been authorized to make direct and indirect medical education payments to teaching hospitals with approved post doctoral training programs in podiatric medicine and surgery. In 1993, we estimated that 120 hospitals with 400 residency slots in 27 states and the District of Columbia received Medicare payments for the direct costs of these programs.

Suffice it to say that we believe very strongly that podiatric medical residency programs must continue to have access to funding, including access to any new funding mechanism that might ultimately replace or supplement that currently in effect under Medicare. Among other things, completion of an approved residency program is now seen as an essential component of the training of a doctor of podiatric medicine. For example, a special consensus panel convened in March of 1992 by the Liaison Committee on Podiatric Medical Education and Practice concluded that "One year of 'postgraduate' training is necessary to enter either the private practice of or advanced specialty training in podiatric medicine." Further, a 1992 resolution adopted by the APMA House of Delegates makes clear that colleges of podiatric medicine should prepare their graduates for entry level postgraduate study, not for entry level practice. Finally, an increasing number of States have begun to require one year of postgraduate education or residency training for licensure as a doctor of podiatric medicine (D.P.M.). As of 1990, 32 States imposed such a requirement.

Our present concern, Mr. Chairman, is that none of the major reform proposals pending in the Congress addresses the eligibility of post doctoral training programs in podiatric medicine for continued graduate medical education funding under reform. That benefit is limited in those proposals to programs in allopathic (MD) and osteopathic (DO) medicine. The Administration, we are pleased to note, has acknowledged that the omission of podiatric medical post doctoral training programs in the **Health Security Act's** (HR 3600) GME restructuring was an inadvertent oversight; and it will support a remedy to our problem. We would respectfully urge the subcommittee to do likewise as it crafts its own reform proposal.

RATIONALE for RESTRUCTURING GME FINANCING
The basis for change in GME financing schemes begins with the well known fact that there are considerably more allopathic medical residency positions than there are graduates of U.S. schools of medicine, with these "excess" positions being filled by foreign medical graduates. For example, the Council on Graduate Medical Education (COGME) has suggested limiting the number of residency positions to 110 percent of the number of allopathic medical school graduates.

In the case of podiatric medicine, however, there are no foreign podiatric medical graduates, and hence the profession's longstanding goal has simply been to provide an adequate number of residency positions to accommodate all graduates of the seven U.S. colleges of podiatric medicine. This goal was finally achieved in 1991; but, as recently as 1988, there were only enough residency training positions to meet the needs of about 69 percent of podiatric medical college graduates. Thus, unlike allopathic medicine, there are no "excess" residency positions filled by non-U.S. graduates.

Assuring a match between the number of residency positions and the number of podiatric medical college graduates has been complicated somewhat, due to a decline in the applicant pool, by relatively recent fluctuations in first year enrollments in the nation's podiatric medical colleges. For example, while first year enrollments gradually rose throughout the first half of the 1980's to peak at 815 in 1986, the number of such students had declined to 561 by 1990. Of note, the Seventh Report to the President and the Congress on the Status of Health Personnel in the United States, March 1990, argued that one reason for the declining enrollments was "applicant awareness of an insufficient number of residency slots to accommodate graduates."

In the last few years, first year enrollments have returned to their previous levels. In 1992 and 1993, there were 802 and 829 first year podiatric medical students, respectively. Nevertheless, variations in graduating class size continue to pose a unique challenge to podiatric medical residency programs, especially given the fact that there are no foreign podiatric medical graduates to fill positions not occupied by U.S. graduates.

A second premise of the graduate medical education proposals developed by the PPRC, the Clinton Administration, and others is that there are too many allopathic and osteopathic physicians. The Council on Graduate Medical Education has spent considerable time and effort attempting to document physician supply and demand, and identify the types of allopathic and osteopathic physicians expected to be in under - or oversupply in the coming years.

In contrast, the Council on Graduate Medical Education has not examined the supply of, and demand for, podiatric physicians. In fact, no government body has determined that an excess supply of doctors of podiatric medicine is in the offing. In 1981, the U.S. Department of Health and Human Services established an ideal ratio of 6.2 podiatric physicians per 100,000 population. This ratio was developed as part of the Health Professions Requirement Model, a Federal econometric study. In comparison, the actual 1991 ratio was about 5.0 podiatric physicians per 100,000 population.

Much more recently, the Bureau of Health Professions of the U.S. Public Health Service contracted with the National Center for Health Statistics to obtain baseline data on foot care needs in the general population. This was done as part of the 1990 National Health Interview Survey. This survey of 46,476 households, comprising 119,631 individuals, found that one of every six Americans suffered from foot problems in the twelve months preceding their interview and one of every sixteen Americans deemed their problem serious enough to consider getting professional care. However, more significantly, only 55 percent of those who considered their foot problem serious enough to warrant professional care actually received such care. Of these, 47 percent were seen by a doctor of podiatric medicine for an estimated total of more that 14.5 million patient visits.

In comparison, podiatric physicians accounted for 4.5 percent of all the medical and surgical services provided to Medicare patients by all physicians in 1991. Doctors of podiatric medicine, in fact, provide the majority of footcare services needed by Medicare beneficiaries, and this population continues to increase by about 2 percent each year. For example, in 1991, doctors of podiatric medicine performed 98.5 percent of nail debridements, 82.3 percent of hammertoe operations, 72.5 percent of bunionectomies, and 55.4 percent of rear foot surgery required by Medicare beneficiaries.

The third premise underlying proposed changes in graduate medical education financing and related initiatives is that there are too many specialists and not enough primary care practitioners. While podiatric medicine is not included in the list of primary care specialties found in the Clinton Administration's health care reform proposal, the reality is that doctors of podiatric medicine "often serve as the entry point into the health care system for patients with systemic diseases that manifest themselves by symptoms in the feet," as emphasized most recently in the Eighth Report to Congress on Health Personnel in the United States, published September 1992 by the U.S. Department of Health and Human Services. Doctors of podiatric medicine also provide a large number of primary care services (as define in section 1842(i) (4) of the Social Security Act). In fact, evaluation and management services accounted for about 24 percent of the Medicare allowed dollars paid to doctors of podiatric medicine in 1991. Further, the Health Professions Reauthorization Act, enacted in November 1988, specifically authorized support for new primary care residency training programs in podiatric medicine. Ten such programs were funded, under which about 44 residents were trained each year. Finally, among the three recognized specialty boards in podiatric medicine is the American Board of Podiatric Orthopedics and Primary Podiatric Medicine.

In short, it would appear that the two premises underlying proposed changes in graduate medical education financing--excess number of residency positions and practitioner oversupply--do not apply to podiatric medicine. The third--the need for more primary care practitioners--may have unique implications in the case of doctors of podiatric medicine. We believe that policymakers should be mindful of these distinctions as they consider various health care reform proposals, especially those that would alter support for graduate medical education.

CONCLUSION

Finally, Mr. Chairman, APMA believes that post doctoral residency programs in podiatric medicine and surgery must continue to merit GME funding, including any new financing schemes resulting from reform. This can happen by defining an "approved physician training program" to include those approved by the Council on Podiatric Medical Education of the American Podiatric Medical Association. It is equally important, we feel, that podiatric medicine be represented on any national council which might be charged to oversee the GME allocation process.

This concludes my statement and I would be pleased to respond to any questions you might have.

Chairman STARK. Ms. Robinson.

STATEMENT OF KRIS ROBINSON, EXECUTIVE DIRECTOR, AMERICAN ASSOCIATION OF KIDNEY PATIENTS

Ms. ROBINSON. Thank you, Mr. Chairman.

Mr. Chairman and members of the Subcommittee on Health, I am pleased to be here today on behalf of the American Association of Kidney Patients, AAKP.

My name is Kris Robinson. I am executive director of AAKP. Moreover, I have been a dialysis patient and have currently been a kidney transplant patient for the past 7½ years. I want to preface my remarks by emphasizing that the membership of AAKP is very concerned about what will happen to Medicare's end-stage renal disease program in terms of the Health Security Act and health care reform in general.

As a national organization of kidney patients, it is our hope that Congress will ensure the continuation of the very successful ESRD program. This program has provided payment for renal replacement therapy including dialysis, transplantation, physician services and immunosuppressive drugs for more than 20 years.

As you know, dialysis is unique among high tech medical therapies. Without dialysis, death will certainly occur; however, with dialysis treatments, many patients can expect long-term survival allowing them to lead near-normal, healthy lives. There are several points we wish to make to the subcommittee.

First, AAKP hopes that the Medicare ESRD program under health care reform will continue as currently legislated. We are concerned about the Clinton plan requirement that kidney patients who work or who have a working spouse must remain in their health alliance plans instead of becoming Medicare ESRD patients. We are worried that this may lead to difficulties in maintaining the current level of care for these patients. It is our belief that undermining the Medicare ESRD program before a complete analysis of how the Clinton plan incorporates dialysis and transplant care could be detrimental to the more than 150,000 patients.

Second, we are concerned that quality assurance levels will be lower for patients choosing a health alliance plan over Medicare. As you are well aware, the Health Care Financing Administration—HCFA—currently sets certain quality standards criteria that are reviewed in the dialysis facilities by the ESRD Networks, thus assuring adequate patient care.

We recommend that the Clinton plan include the same quality assurance guidelines that are currently built into the Medicare program and these guidelines become mandatory for the alliances. ESRD Networks should be required to track Medicare and alliance kidney patients.

Third, discrimination is also a worry to kidney patients. AAKP is concerned that alliances will not be willing to enroll kidney patients even though they are prohibited from discrimination under the Clinton plan. We are concerned that if the plan's risk adjusted premium is not high enough to cover the cost of the dialysis, and/or transplantation, the plan will find ways to avoid covering kidney patients or only provide the services offered by the lowest bidder.

We also are concerned that alliance participants will have higher premium costs than Medicare participants, thus causing significant financial burdens to patients.

Fourth, AAKP is well aware that the Clinton plan emphasizes managed care and we wish to bring to your attention the numerous complaints we currently receive from kidney patients enrolled in HMOs. These complaints include difficulties in securing transplant services outside the HMO and the ability to choose dialysis facilities and physicians. We hope you will address these issues when you consider your health care reform legislation.

Last, AAKP supports various items in the Clinton plan and we are grateful for their inclusion. The expanded outpatient prescription drug coverage is very important and helpful to kidney patients who currently spend an exorbitant amount of out-of-pocket dollars on medications. We also support home and community based long-term care grant programs to the States as they will assist family members with the difficulties of both the financial and emotional burdens of caring for a loved one.

We are also very appreciative of the Clinton plan's $1,500 cap on out-of-pocket costs for individuals in the alliance plans and respectfully suggest that such a cap also be instituted in Medicare.

Mr. Chairman, we appreciate the opportunity to address your distinguished committee and I will be happy to respond to any questions or comments you may have.

Thank you.

[The prepared statement follows:]

STATEMENT OF KRIS ROBINSON
EXECUTIVE DIRECTOR
AMERICAN ASSOCIATION OF KIDNEY PATIENTS

MR CHAIRMAN AND MEMBERS OF THE SUBCOMMITTEE ON HEALTH, I AM PLEASED TO BE HERE TODAY ON BEHALF OF THE AMERICAN ASSOCIATION OF KIDNEY PATIENTS (AAKP). MY NAME IS KRIS ROBINSON. I AM EXECUTIVE DIRECTOR OF AAKP MOREOVER, I HAVE BEEN A DIALYSIS PATIENT AND HAVE HAD A KIDNEY TRANSPLANT FOR THE PAST SEVEN AND A HALF YEARS.

I WANT TO PREFACE MY REMARKS BY EMPHASIZING THAT THE MEMBERSHIP OF AAKP IS VERY CONCERNED ABOUT WHAT WILL HAPPEN TO MEDICARE'S END-STAGE RENAL DISEASE PROGRAM (ESRD) IN TERMS OF THE HEALTH SECURITY ACT AND HEALTH CARE REFORM IN GENERAL AS A NATIONAL ORGANIZATION OF KIDNEY PATIENTS, IT IS OUR HOPE THAT CONGRESS WILL INSURE THE CONTINUATION OF THE VERY SUCCESSFUL ESRD PROGRAM THIS PROGRAM HAS PROVIDED PAYMENT FOR RENAL REPLACEMENT THERAPY INCLUDING DIALYSIS, TRANSPLANTATION, PHYSICIAN SERVICES AND IMMUNOSUPPRESSIVE DRUGS FOR MORE THAN 20 YEARS. AS YOU KNOW, DIALYSIS IS UNIQUE AMONG HIGH-TECH MEDICAL THERAPIES. WITHOUT DIALYSIS DEATH WILL CERTAINLY OCCUR, HOWEVER WITH DIALYSIS TREATMENTS, MANY PATIENTS CAN EXPECT LONG TERM SURVIVAL ALLOWING THEM TO LEAD NEAR NORMAL, HEALTHY LIVES.

THERE ARE SEVERAL POINTS WE WISH TO MAKE TO THE SUBCOMMITTEE:

1. FIRST, AAKP HOPES THAT THE MEDICARE ESRD PROGRAM UNDER HEALTH CARE REFORM WILL CONTINUE IN THE SAME CAPACITY AS IT IS CURRENTLY LEGISLATED. WE ARE CONCERNED ABOUT THE CLINTON PLAN REQUIREMENT THAT KIDNEY PATIENTS WHO WORK OR HAVE A WORKING SPOUSE MUST REMAIN IN THEIR HEALTH ALLIANCE PLANS, INSTEAD OF BECOMING MEDICARE ESRD PATIENTS WE ARE WORRIED THAT THIS MAY LEAD TO DIFFICULTIES IN MAINTAINING THE CURRENT LEVEL OF CARE FOR THESE PATIENTS. IT IS OUR BELIEF THAT UNDERMINING THE MEDICARE ESRD PROGRAM, BEFORE A COMPLETE ANALYSIS OF HOW THE CLINTON PLAN INCORPORATES DIALYSIS AND TRANSPLANT CARE, COULD BE DETRIMENTAL TO THE MORE THAN 150,000 PATIENTS.

2. WE ARE CONCERNED THAT QUALITY ASSURANCE LEVELS WILL BE LOWER FOR PATIENTS CHOOSING A HEALTH ALLIANCE PLAN OVER MEDICARE. AS YOU ARE WELL AWARE, THE HEALTH CARE FINANCE ADMINISTRATION (HCFA) CURRENTLY SETS CERTAIN QUALITY STANDARDS CRITERIA THAT ARE REVIEWED IN THE DIALYSIS FACILITIES BY THE ESRD NETWORKS, THUS ASSURING ADEQUATE PATIENT CARE. WE RECOMMEND THAT THE CLINTON PLAN INCLUDE THE SAME QUALITY ASSURANCE GUIDELINES THAT ARE CURRENTLY BUILT INTO THE MEDICARE PROGRAM AND THESE GUIDELINES BECOME MANDATORY FOR THE ALLIANCES. ESRD NETWORKS SHOULD BE REQUIRED TO TRACK MEDICARE AND ALLIANCE KIDNEY PATIENTS.

3. DISCRIMINATION IS ALSO A WORRY TO PATIENTS. AAKP IS CONCERNED THAT ALLIANCES WILL NOT BE WILLING TO ENROLL KIDNEY PATIENTS EVEN THOUGH THEY ARE PROHIBITED FROM DISCRIMINATION UNDER THE CLINTON PLAN. WE ARE CONCERNED THAT IF THE PLAN'S RISK ADJUSTED PREMIUM IS NOT HIGH ENOUGH TO COVER THE COST OF DIALYSIS AND/OR TRANSPLANTATION, THE PLAN WILL FIND WAYS TO AVOID COVERING KIDNEY PATIENTS OR ONLY PROVIDE THE SERVICES OFFERED BY THE LOWEST BIDDER.

WE ALSO ARE CONCERNED THAT ALLIANCE PARTICIPANTS WILL HAVE HIGHER PREMIUM COSTS THAN MEDICARE PARTICIPANTS, THUS CAUSING SIGNIFICANT FINANCIAL BURDENS TO PATIENTS.

4. AAKP IS WELL AWARE THAT THE CLINTON PLAN EMPHASIZES MANAGED CARE AND WE WISH TO BRING TO YOUR ATTENTION THE NUMEROUS COMPLAINTS WE CURRENTLY RECEIVE FROM KIDNEY PATIENTS ENROLLED IN HMO'S. THESE COMPLAINTS INCLUDE DIFFICULTIES IN SECURING TRANSPLANT SERVICES OUTSIDE THE HMO AND THE ABILITY TO CHOOSE DIALYSIS FACILITIES AND PHYSICIANS. WE HOPE YOU WILL ADDRESS THESE ISSUES WHEN YOU CONSIDER YOUR HEALTH CARE REFORM LEGISLATION.

5. LASTLY, AAKP SUPPORTS VARIOUS ITEMS IN THE CLINTON PLAN AND WE ARE GRATEFUL FOR THEIR INCLUSION. THE EXPANDED OUTPATIENT

KIDNEY PATIENTS WHO CURRENTLY SPEND AN EXORBITANT AMOUNT OF OUT-OF-POCKET DOLLARS ON MEDICATIONS. WE ALSO SUPPORT HOME AND COMMUNITY BASED LONG TERM CARE GRANT PROGRAMS TO THE STATES, AS THEY WILL ASSIST FAMILY MEMBERS WITH THE DIFFICULTIES OF BOTH THE FINANCIAL AND EMOTIONAL BURDENS OF CARING FOR A LOVED ONE. WE ARE ALSO VERY APPRECIATIVE OF THE CLINTON PLAN $1,500 CAP ON OUT OF POCKET COSTS FOR INDIVIDUALS IN THE ALLIANCE PLANS AND RESPECTIVELY SUGGEST THAT SUCH A CAP ALSO BE INSTITUTED IN MEDICARE.

MR. CHAIRMAN, WE APPRECIATE THE OPPORTUNITY TO ADDRESS YOUR DISTINGUISHED SUBCOMMITTEE AND I WILL BE HAPPY TO RESPOND TO ANY QUESTIONS OR COMMENTS ANY MEMBER MAY HAVE. THANK YOU.

Chairman STARK. Thank you. Mr. Hoagland, did you want to inquire of any of the witnesses?

Mr. HOAGLAND. Well, I do, Mr. Chairman. I would just like to explore briefly the issue of whether or not the legislation should include a basic benefit plan or whether the legislation should create a national board of experts that would develop the plan.

And I know that Dr. Elliott, I think you addressed that directly in your statement. Didn't you come out in favor of Congress retaining the authority to develop a comprehensive benefit plan and not delegate that to a national board?

Dr. ELLIOTT. Yes. We feel very strongly about that. Optometry has had difficulties with boards of that nature primarily because they are all physicians, at least generally that is the way they are, so the discrimination factor that I mentioned in the testimony becomes very broad and very loud and creates a great deal of difficulty for access for the optometrist and the patients that we see.

Mr. HOAGLAND. If you set that issue aside, assume the legislation contains provisions prohibiting discrimination of that sort.

Dr. ELLIOTT. I think that kind of legislation could be written and antidiscrimination clauses could be broad enough to cover that. Our fear would be that they would not be and——

Mr. HOAGLAND. Why don't we set that issue aside for a moment. Don't you think the decisions could better be made by a board of experts than 535 Members of Congress?

Dr. ELLIOTT. I think they need the advice of experts. But I think that what is in law becomes the reality as opposed to what boards can do from time to time and so—you know, we have worked with boards and worked with them well, but our experience has been in the broad sense that it is often to the detriment of the patients that we serve.

So I can set it to the side with assurances that that issue would be covered and certainly we would like to be part and parcel of making sure that there would be language to prevent those kinds of discrimination policies from occurring and would feel much better if we were part of that process.

Mr. HOAGLAND. Well, thank you.

Dr. Nunnally, do you have any thoughts on this issue?

Dr. NUNNALLY. The college is currently studying the comprehensive benefit plan. We have not finalized our opinion. We are looking at it particularly in regard to pathology services such as the Pap smear but, as yet, we have not finished our study and don't have an immediate recommendation.

Mr. HOAGLAND. All right. I think the problem we have is that it is a lot easier for Congress to grant benefits than to deny benefits, and once benefits are granted, they are never taken away. That has been the history of our Medicare and Medicaid programs, anyway.

I wonder if we might not have a plan that is more affordable and more rationally based if it weren't left to the rough and tumble of the political process but instead delegated to a group of knowledgeable, fair experts operating in a nondiscriminatory fashion.

Do any of you have any opinions or thoughts on this issue? Sounds like not. OK. Well, thank you, Mr. Chairman. I have no further questions.

Chairman STARK. OK.

Mr. HOAGLAND. Mr. Chairman, I know they have thoughts on the issue, Mr. Chairman, by the way.

Chairman STARK. There were a couple of different opinions by the witnesses. Dr. Nunnally, I think you wanted to see direct billing, right—

Dr. NUNNALLY. Yes, sir.

Chairman STARK [continuing]. If I recall you, without going back to your testimony. But you probably, on the other hand, would oppose bundling the lab payments in the hospital under the DRG classifications. Certainly your colleagues in radiology and anesthesiology I think would resist that to some extent, so there is a problem there.

In other words, there are some of us who support direct billing as a way to prevent a primary care physician from marking up your services. On the other hand, direct billing when people unbundle procedures tends to cost us a little more money and we are trying to figure out, on the other hand, how to stop that.

Dr. Bouchard wants to make sure that they are included in procedures, and what I guess I am getting at with all of the different concerns—I will leave Ms. Robinson aside here for just a moment—if you had to pick one system today, I mean you have heard about the Cooper plan which is kind of a nothing sort of thing that everybody—it is like an Australian tag match or a greased pole race—and the President's plan which is highly structured and the single-payer plan that Congressman McDermott has introduced, is there any—as a compromise now, understanding that if you got to pick one plan and each of you might have a little bit different plan in mind, could you live with Medicare, Dr. Nunnally?

I am not suggesting the magnitude of the rates or the system. We will fight about the exact fee for each particular procedure, but could you live with that as opposed to a complete single-payer—it really is a single-payer plan, but it has a little more choice.

Dr. NUNNALLY. I really don't know if I have adequate information to answer that, Mr. Stark.

Chairman STARK. Let me just go down the line and see. I mean, Dr. Jones, you guys are all right under——

Dr. JONES. Well, there are problems with it with Medicare reimbursement.

Chairman STARK. Well, yes, there are problems, but you have got just as many problems with Aetna as you do with Medicare, don't you?

Dr. JONES. Yes.

Chairman STARK. I am just saying at some point, we have got to write a law and we can't write one for Dr. Bouchard and one for Dr. Jones and one for Dr. Nunnally. You guys are all going to be in the same box.

Dr. JONES. There is a potential that it would be satisfactory.

Chairman STARK. Dr. Elliott.

Dr. ELLIOTT. Looking over those same problems, the answer is yes, that Medicare would be an avenue that we could take. The one problem that I would bring forth is the preventive aspects that——

Chairman STARK. Look, I am just talking in terms here of reimbursement and choice, preventive choice.

Dr. ELLIOTT. Yes.

Chairman STARK. For Ms. Robinson, I think we solve your problems if we—do you remember something called catastrophic, Ms. Robinson?

Ms. ROBINSON. Catastrophic care?

Chairman STARK. In the Medicare chain some years—you are not old enough to remember that.

Ms. ROBINSON. Thank you.

Chairman STARK. There was an out-of-pocket cap; isn't that what you testified you wanted to have?

Ms. ROBINSON. Right, the $1,500 cap.

Chairman STARK. Some famous legislator, that law passed years ago, the $1,500 out-of-pocket cap for Medicare patients, only to watch the pharmaceutical manufacturers association spend billions a year later to feed it. But we are going to get that back to you and you will be happy, right?

Ms. ROBINSON. That is correct.

Chairman STARK. Or happier, correct?

Ms. ROBINSON. Happier.

Chairman STARK. I just don't know what to say in response to each of your valid concerns. My thought is that we will continue Medicare as it is, try to improve it. We have talked with all of you and your representatives over the years about minor changes relative to your own particular group of provider's concerns.

But the cost containment method for Medicare, I think, will continue as a way to assure the taxpayers that we just don't take the lid off. Some of you have objected, I think, to global budgets but, basically, that is what we have in Medicare and there are none of you who don't get paid under Medicare because we run out of money. You may not get paid enough, but there is nothing in Medicare that would force you to ration.

I think that it would make sense to me to use the same structure, not necessarily rates, on the private side, but I am getting to the point, as a variety of people calls us a variety of names for even mentioning that, to say, what the hell, if you guys want to cost shift to the private side, the private side will be back here in pretty short order asking us please to put cost controls back on you as providers, and so I thought maybe we ought to start right out from the beginning and let you help us write what those provisions are to be.

For instance, Dr. Nunnally, you practice in what State?

Dr. NUNNALLY. Baton Rouge, La.

Chairman STARK. OK. If we use California, Blue Cross-Blue Shield basically just went to the RVS system and the system that we wrote some years ago in this committee to reimburse physicians under Medicare. Let's assume that that becomes the structure.

Who in Louisiana would you be comfortable having negotiate the update for the private rates, understanding that Medicare will continue to set the private rates under the formula? Is there—the Louisiana State Medical Society? Who would negotiate for you and with whom?

Dr. NUNNALLY. Well, I think the medical society would be a logical choice, but there is a similar situation with Medicare now where the Blue Cross has a panel which includes representatives from not all specialties, but about 15 specialties, and then there are little panels that feed into the larger panel and they go to the RVS problems.

Chairman STARK. You are using a similar structure.

Dr. NUNNALLY. Yes, and I imagine that could be matched in the private sector.

Chairman STARK. Are you comfortable with that?

Dr. NUNNALLY. Sir?

Chairman STARK. Are you comfortable with that?

Dr. NUNNALLY. I don't know if we have enough experience thus far, Mr. Stark. We have some good things about the RVS and it is improving every year. There are still some things that need to be perfected with it.

Chairman STARK. I guess what I am thinking could happen is that we will, as you know, under the Medicare, we set some kind of a target for growth, not cutting rates, but just saying, look, we are going to let your growth be 8 percent, whatever we pick as a target.

My guess is that if we mean business about controlling costs, somebody is going to have to pick a target or an estimate or a budget, I don't care what you call it. We can't just say, well, we are going to try harder, thank you very much. That is what I used to tell my mother, but the grades never went up. I used to say next semester, mom.

So if we said, I don't care if it is 10 percent now, we say, gee, next year it can only be 8 percent, somebody is still going to have to fuss with how you all divvy that up in the medical or the health care delivery fraternity. I don't really care who that is if you are comfortable with it, and the process evolves so that there is some feedback, that you bargain in good faith and whomever is representing the purchasers bargains in good faith and then you can get about your business of dealing with cadavers or specimens or whatever you do and not be troubled with all this.

I think we are very close to getting there. I really sense that the medical care delivery community is beginning to say this. There is still a very much a distrust of us, but I would say on our behalf that we are the only ones that have kept their bargain all these years with the docs, this committee, of giving them the promised updates and bargaining. So I would hope we will earn our—at least your support that we can continue to bargain. Whether you use our procedure happily on the private side, I don't know.

But I would say that to all the rest of you. We try as best we can to stay out of your practice. We don't pretend to know what you are doing, but we are a payment operation. I think that is a fairly valid role for the government to play when we are spending taxpayers' money. If you are spending Blue Cross-Blue Shield's money, I could say relative to my legislative responsibility, I really don't care. I think that is not responsive.

I think the thing we are talking about is that overall costs are going too fast and we have to pitch in. I do not think that premium caps, for example, are going to do it. I think what they will do is cut services that you all can provide. When you have got an MBA telling an O.D. or an M.D. what they are doing, you have got a problem. And that is exactly what all this managed care business is all about.

And the horror stories that come out of it is somebody who is paid a big salary to keep patients from seeing you. That is a good way to make money, but it ain't a very good way to get health care. And I think somehow we are going to have to find an alternative.

We do all right in California, don't we, Dr. Elliott? We are getting there and I hope you will stay with us. The White House has had 1 year to fuss with this thing and they want us to do it in 6 weeks. So we are going to need a lot of help in the next 6 weeks and I appreciate your attempting to bring that to us here.

I sense, if you will, that there is room for us—you are all closer to suggesting that we recognize the problems that we face and we look forward to working with you.

Thank you very much.

Chairman STARK. Our final panel will consist of Eric G. Gustafson, the immediate past president of the Independent Insurance Agents of America, Inc.; Galen Barnes, the president of the Wausau Insurance Companies., who is accompanied by Hon. Donald C. Alexander, former commissioner of the Internal Revenue Service, one of the most loved positions in the United States, currently a distinguished member of the firm of Akin, Gump, Strauss & Feld; Kathelen V. Spencer, senior vice president, deputy counsel of the AFLAC, reading testimony prepared by Hon. Don Evans, one of the most outstanding lobbyists in the insurance community in the District of Columbia; Dean R. Kleckner, president of the American Farm Bureau Federation and probably has no members in the 13th Congressional District of California; and Karl C. Sommers, the vice president of corporate planning for the Mennonite Mutual Aid Society.

Mr. Gustafson, you are first on the list. Would you like to lead off.

STATEMENT OF ERIC G. GUSTAFSON, IMMEDIATE PAST PRESIDENT, INDEPENDENT INSURANCE AGENTS OF AMERICA, INC., AND CHAIRMAN, BLAKE INSURANCE AGENCY, PORTSMOUTH, N.H.

Mr. GUSTAFSON. Yes. Thank you, Mr. Chairman. Members of the committee, I am Eric Gustafson, the immediate past president of the Independent Insurance Agents of America and also chairman of the Blake Insurance Agency in Portsmouth, N.H.

Independent insurance agents have a unique dual perspective on the current health care system. As agents, we play an essential role in the delivery of all kinds of insurance and, as small businesses, we understand the profound difficulties of trying to provide coverage for our employees.

Mr. Chairman, IIAA is committed to health care reform, having adopted a policy position in 1991 that supports many reforms being advocated today. Like the President, IIAA supports guaranteed issue and renewal of coverage, insurance portability, limitations on preexisting condition clauses, and other small market reforms.

However, we have concerns about features of H.R. 3600. Specifically, we oppose the creation of government mandated exclusive alliances through which everyone except employees of firms of over

5,000 would be forced to purchase insurance. Alliances do not have to be mandatory to bring the purchasing power of big businesses to small employers and individuals.

It is often claimed that mandatory alliances are necessary to avoid risk selection. We believe that risk selection can be avoided in a voluntary alliance environment by using a risk adjustment mechanism and by incorporating the specific insurance reforms previously mentioned. This would guarantee a level playingfield and eliminate cherrypicking or risk selection by insurers.

A risk adjustment mechanism is necessary whether an alliance is mandatory or voluntary. My written testimony includes a study that IIAA completed at the request of the administration that fully explains how risk selection can be avoided within voluntary alliances. A——

Chairman STARK. Let's talk about that for 1 minute. Explain something. Does it explain how it can be adjusted for? I am looking at it here. If this really works, you are the first person in the world to have risk adjustment solved. Could we talk about that later? Do you tell us about it in the rest of your testimony?

Mr. GUSTAFSON. At the end or now?

Chairman STARK. Why don't we wait until the end because it is kind of detailed. There are a couple of pages of mathematical formula here and I won't trouble your colleagues at the witness table, but if that comprises—you want to skip over risk adjustment and we can come back to that in more detail.

Mr. GUSTAFSON. Yes.

Chairman STARK. Go ahead.

Mr. GUSTAFSON. A system of voluntary purchasing cooperatives would allow all consumers to organize in large groups to acquire even greater clout than large employers in negotiating with health plans. But unlike the President's monopolistic health alliance or the plan developed by the conservative Democrat forum, a market-driven model will foster efficiency and ensure that consumers have the power to demand high quality cost-effective plans.

Mandatory health alliances are untested. The six States that have authorized purchasing alliances have made them voluntary, not mandatory. Your State of California, Mr. Chairman, provides an example of a voluntary purchasing cooperative system that appears to be expanding coverage and keeping pressure on the entire system to hold down costs. Such competitive pressures would evaporate in a mandatory alliance. The California system has been in place for only 7 months and while no final conclusions can be reached from that experience, some trends are beginning to develop.

For example, despite the fact that employers are able to purchase coverage directly from the health insurance plan of California and avoid the costs associated with agents' commissions, 79 percent of the businesses participating in the HIPC chose to use agents to help them secure coverage. This indicates that small employers value the services of an independent counselor when selecting employee health benefits, so much so that they knowingly pay an additional cost for it.

In a reformed market, voluntary alliances will provide and array of choice and cause competition to focus on service and price. In a mandatory approach, where do the millions of Americans go if the system is ineffective? The current infrastructure will no longer exist.

The last thing I would like to discuss is the proposed merger of both the workers compensation and the auto insurance medical components in H.R. 3600. Title 10 currently coordinates these two insurance markets, but we believe that the proposed feasibility study is biased toward merger rather than coordination. IIAA believes that merging workers comp and auto will bring about many undesired changes to the system. It will increase costs and reduce safety incentives but provide no benefit to injured workers or employers.

Safe employers would subsidize unsafe employers and there would be no incentive to create safe working environments or speed the return of the employee to work. Lost wages, work, and productivity would certainly result. Many of the problems ascribed to the workers comp issue under the President's plan hold true for the proposed merger of auto insurance. The current relationship between driving behaviors and premiums would be eliminated. This would shift costs to the health plans and force good drivers to pay more, subsidizing bad drivers who would end up paying less.

Thank you very much for this opportunity to share our concerns. IIAA stands ready to assist the subcommittee. I will be happy to answer any questions.

Chairman STARK. Thanks.

[The prepared statement and attachments follow:]

507

STATEMENT OF ERIC GUSTAFSON
IMMEDIATE PAST PRESIDENT
INDEPENDENT INSURANCE AGENTS OF AMERICA

Good morning Mr. Chairman and members of the Committee. Thank you for the opportunity to appear before this subcommittee today to discuss health care reform. I am Eric Gustafson, the Immediate Past President of the Independent Insurance Agents of America, Inc and also Chairman of the Blake Insurance Agency in Portsmouth, NH.

IIAA is the nation's largest independent insurance agent association representing a network of over 280,000 independent agents and their employees. Its members offer all lines of insurance - property, casualty, life and health. Unlike other groups both within and outside the insurance industry, agents have an unique, dual perspective on the current system. As agents, we play an integral and essential role in the delivery of all kinds of insurance to millions of Americans, and, as small businesses, we understand the profound difficulties of trying to provide coverage for employees.

Mr. Chairman, IIAA is committed to health care reform. Our National Board of Directors adopted a policy position in 1991 that supports many insurance market reforms being advocated today We applaud the President for bringing to the table the same concepts we have supported for many years. Like the President, IIAA supports guaranteed issuance and renewal of coverage, insurance portability, limitations on pre-existing condition clauses, and other small market reforms. We believe that these reforms will greatly improve health care in the United States.

However, we have concerns about features of H R. 3600. Specifically, we oppose the creation of large, government-mandated exclusive alliances through which everyone, except persons employed by an employer with more than 5,000 employees, would be forced to purchase insurance.

In the broadest sense, the President's plan erects an enormously complicated bureaucratic structure that could undermine, not foster, an improved system. We believe that the structure of President Clinton's proposed Health Alliances is too regulatory, too centralized, and will quickly result in a politicized system of regional bureaucracies that will limit competition and hamper the efficiencies of a reformed market.

The theory underlying this concept of mandatory alliances is that a large pool of purchasers will have significant market clout to bargain for low-cost health care. However, alliances do not have to be mandatory to bring the health insurance purchasing power of big businesses to small employers and individuals. Every individual can receive the same insurance buying power as a large corporation if fundamental market reforms are enacted and enforced as a matter of Federal law.

Supporters of mandatory alliances claim that they are necessary to avoid risk selection. We believe that risk selection can be avoided in a voluntary alliance environment by using a risk adjustment mechanism and by incorporating specific insurance reforms. Eliminating pre-existing condition clauses, guaranteeing issuance and renewal of coverage, along with a risk adjustment mechanism, would guarantee a level playing field to individuals and small firms purchasing health coverage and eliminate any incentive for "cherry picking" or risk selection by insurers

A risk adjustment mechanism is necessary whether an alliance is mandatory or voluntary. All reform proposals call for open enrollment and rating restrictions and thereby disassociate the premium the carrier is allowed to charge from the costs the carrier expects to incur in serving a particular individual or group. With the enactment of market reforms and a risk adjustment mechanism, all health plans, whether or not they participate in the alliance, would have to play by the same rules so that neither the plans operating within the alliance nor those operating outside the alliance would receive an inequitable share of risk.

These reforms will lead to the elimination of risk-based marketing -- or at least make risk selection no longer a competitive factor. Carriers will compete on price, efficiency, quality of care and high service levels, and not on their ability to find low risks.

I have brought with me a study that IIAA completed at the request of Deputy Secretary for the Treasury Roger Altman that fully explains how risk selection can be avoided in a voluntary purchasing environment. It contains specific details regarding a risk adjustment mechanism and how it would work. I ask that it be entered into the record along with my testimony.

We believe that a system of voluntary purchasing cooperatives can accomplish exactly the same objectives as the quasi-governmental monopolies envisioned by the Clinton health reform plan, but with less regulation, less bureaucracy, more savings and minimal government intervention.

A system of voluntary purchasing cooperatives in each region will allow small firms and individual consumers to organize in large groups to acquire even greater clout than large employers in negotiating with health plans. But unlike the President's monopolistic Health Alliances, or the plan developed by the Conservative Democratic Forum, this market-driven model is distinguished by competition between purchasing cooperatives and health plans, which we believe will foster efficiency and ensure that consumers and businesses have the power to demand high-quality, cost-effective plans.

Mandatory health alliances are untested. The six states that have authorized purchasing alliances have made them voluntary, not mandatory, as proposed in H.R. 3600 and other legislation. Your state of California, Mr. Chairman, provides an example of a voluntary purchasing cooperative system that appears to be expanding coverage and keeping the pressure on the entire system to hold down costs. Such competitive pressures would evaporate in a mandatory alliance.

As you know, the California system has been in place for only seven months, so while no final conclusions can be reached from that experience, some interesting trends are beginning to develop. For example, despite the fact that employers are able to purchase coverage directly from the Health Insurance Plan of California (HIPC) and avoid the costs associated with agent commissions, 79% of the businesses participating in the HIPC chose to use insurance agents to help them secure coverage. This indicates to us that small employers value the services of an independent counselor when selecting employee health benefits -- so much so, that they knowingly pay an additional cost for it.

In a reformed market, voluntary alliances are able to compete, provide an array of choice, cause competition to focus on service and price, and put the individual consumer in the driver's seat. Voluntary purchasing programs will provide the opportunity to test various theories surrounding what value added services alliances can bring to the health care system, without gambling the security and future of health care coverage for all Americans in the process. In a mandatory approach, where do the millions of Americans go if the system is ineffective? The current infrastructure will no longer exist. And what provides the benchmark to see if this approach is better or more efficient than that which we would have under the fundamental reforms we have outlined?

The last thing I would like to discuss is the proposed merger of both the workers' compensation and the auto insurance medical components into the Accountable Health Plans (AHP) in H.R. 3600. Title X currently coordinates these two insurance markets, but calls for a feasibility study of merging workers' comp and auto. We believe that this study, consisting of appointees by the Secretary of Labor and the Secretary of Health and Human Services, is biased toward the will of some in the Administration to merge, rather than coordinate these two programs.

IIAA believes that merging workers' comp and auto will bring about many negative and undesired changes to the system. It will increase costs and reduce safety incentives -- but provide no benefit to injured workers or employers. Safe employers would subsidize unsafe employers. With no incentive to create safe working environments, more claims would obviously be filed. The incentive or impetus to return the worker to the workplace would be eliminated. Lost wages, work and productivity would certainly result.

Many of the problems ascribed to the workers comp issue under the President's plan hold true for the proposed merger of auto insurance. The current relationship between driving behaviors and premiums would be eliminated. This would shift costs to the AHPs and force good drivers to pay more to subsidize bad drivers who would end up paying less.

Again, Mr. Chairman, thank you for this opportunity to share our concerns with you regarding mandatory alliances and also portions of Title X. IIAA stands ready to assist the Subcommittee and full Committee in any way it can. I am happy to answer any questions that you may have for me.

Independent Insurance Agents of America
INCORPORATED

CAPITOL HILL OFFICE
SUITE 300
412 FIRST STREET S E
WASHINGTON, D C 20003
202/863-7000
FAX 202/863-7015

PREVENTING RISK SELECTION
IN A VOLUNTARY HIPC ENVIRONMENT

One of the items being discussed by the Clinton Administration and the insurance industry as they debate health care reform is the issue of mandatory versus voluntary health insurance purchasing cooperatives (HIPCs). The Clinton Administration's proposal requires almost all employers to arrange for their employees' health care through regional health alliances that would contract with health plans.

Many experts in health care policy fear that, because HIPCs have never been thoroughly tested, so comprehensive a restructuring of the health insurance marketplace would be very risky. On the other hand, a voluntary arrangement, giving employers the choice of using HIPCs or contracting directly with an insurer or health plan, would have considerable advantages: it would prevent the disruption that the wholesale severing of long-established insurance relationships would cause; and it would promote the competition that reduces costs and improves quality. Critics of voluntary HIPCs argue that, if insurers are allowed to market directly to employers, they will select only healthy groups, leaving HIPCs to cover high-risk groups and suffer adverse economic consequences. This paper explains how risk selection in a voluntary HIPC environment can be prevented.

Two kinds of initiatives can prevent or correct risk selection: (1) rules of market behavior that either prevent risk selection or make it difficult to practice and (2) a risk-adjustment mechanism, possibly combined with traditional reinsurance, that eliminates financial incentives to insurers to engage in risk selection and compensates plans that receive a disproportionate share of higher risks. These initiatives are described below.

RULES OF MARKET BEHAVIOR

1. Basic rules of accessibility (guaranteed issue, guaranteed renewability, no exclusion of employees from employment-based groups, elimination or limitation of pre-existing condition exclusions) apply to all employment-based health plans. The spirit of these market reform rules can be extended to individual coverage.

2. All carriers use the same rating methodology for all employers/employees eligible to use the HIPC, whether the carrier is selling through the HIPC or directly to employers or individuals.

   Note, however, that community rating, especially pure or flat community rating, creates strong financial incentives for carriers to select risks. One way to offset these incentives is through a risk-adjustment mechanism (see below). Another is to allow health plans and carriers to use rating factors such as geography, age, gender, family size, and industry (but not health status or claims experience) so that they can offer lower rates to demographically less risky groups

3. Minimum requirements for employers' contributions are consistent inside and outside the HIPC.

4. Employees must participate in an employer (group) plan, if eligible, rather than being issued an individual policy (inside or outside the HIPC).

    This rule prevents better individual risks from leaving the group. It also protects carriers who provide individual coverage against employers' attempts to expel high-risk employees into the individual market in order to improve the risk profile of their groups.

5. Marketing practices inside and outside the HIPC are reviewed according to the same procedures. This means that:

    o   Standard cost and quality data must be available, whether the plan is offered inside or outside the HIPC.

    o   Agents' compensation does not vary according to the claims experience of the cases that they write.

    o   The basic package(s) of benefits and cost-sharing inside and outside the HIPC is identical.

6. Self-insured employers who are HIPC-eligible are subject to the same market rules as insured plans, with limited modifications appropriate to self-insurance.

    o   Such employers must meet specified solvency requirements and participate in a risk adjustment mechanism on an equal basis with insured plans. This will protect the HIPC from the adverse selection that might occur if lower-risk groups chose to self-insure. It will also prevent insurers and self-insurers from profiting from risk selection and force them to focus on risk management.

    o   Alternatively, HIPC-eligible employers could be prohibited from self-insuring.

RISK-ADJUSTMENT MECHANISM

In a community-rated environment, it is essential that all health plans and carriers serving HIPC-eligible employers/employees be required to participate in a risk adjustment or risk pooling mechanism.

Attachment A outlines the steps in the risk adjustment process. Attachment B uses a simplified numerical example to show how the process would work. (These attachments, developed by the insurance industry, have previously been submitted to Congress).

The process is based on the assumption that there is a reliable method for assessing the relative risk (expected cost) of one health plan's enrollees versus another's. (The attributes of an acceptable risk assessment method include: accuracy, predictability, reasonable cost, comprehensibility, timeliness, and resistance to gaming).

Risk assessment methods based on readily available demographic information (area of residence, age, gender, family size, industry, etc.) could be implemented immediately, but demographic information alone may be an insufficient basis for estimating a group's future health care needs. Most reform proposals recommend that individual employees be able to choose their plans within HIPCs. Certain plans may attract primarily high-risk employees, such as those with existing medical conditions, from many or all employer groups. Under circumstances of individual employees choice, a highly refined risk adjustment mechanism will be needed. While this is being developed, interim policies may be needed to prevent health plans and carriers from failing owing to adverse selection. Options include:

o   using modified rather than pure community rating for HIPC-eligible employers/employees;

o   broad-based reinsurance to protect plans that include a disproportionate share of high-cost cases;

o   specifying that HIPCs enroll their members in health plans on an employer-group rather than an individual basis. It is easier to develop an effective risk assessment method in a group environment in which the higher risk of some members is offset to some extent by the lower risk of others.

ADDITIONAL CONSIDERATIONS

This paper has examined risk selection issues in a voluntary HIPC environment specific to the employed population. If the HIPC is used to provide health coverage to the non-employed, different subsidization issues arise since this population is, in general, less healthy, more costly, and less able to pay premiums. However, the non-employed can be treated as a separate rating pool, with a separate rate, within the HIPC. The total subsidy necessary to pay for their care can be easily calculated and the appropriate funding source determined.

Attachment A

How Risk Adjustment Might Work
in a Voluntary Purchasing Pool Environment

Steps in the Risk Adjustment Process

The following scenario illustrates one way in which "risk adjustment" [1] might work across all health plans in a market area. The example assumes that small employers may purchase basic coverage directly from health plans, or they may arrange for coverage through a purchasing pool (regional health alliance or HIPC). All health plans, whether selling to individual employees through a purchasing pool or to employers outside the pool, are subject to uniform rating requirements and other regulations pertaining to basic benefit coverage.

Additional assumptions include:

_Employers and employees are required to purchase coverage for the basic plan.

_Each health plan/carrier quotes a flat community-rated premium for basic benefit coverage which is the price each individual enrollee must pay. The community-rated premium could alternatively be calculated per employee (primary insured).

_For simplicity, we describe an annual risk adjustment process, assuming there is no entry into or exit from plans during the year. In reality, the adjustment process would take place more frequently to address differing enrollment periods and other enrollment changes during the year.

_This example addresses only risk selection issues within the employed population. The subsidies necessary to provide health coverage to non-employed individuals and families are essentially a separate issue.

In this example, the entity overseeing the risk adjustment process is simply called the "risk adjustment administrator" (RA Administrator). The function of overseeing the risk adjustment process could be performed by a state agency or board, a state or regional purchasing pool, a private-sector enterprise, or some other organization.

We first describe the sequence of events in the risk adjustment process. We then present a simplified numerical example of the rate adjustment and revenue transfer calculations which are part of the process.

---

[1] In the context of health reform, the term "risk adjustment" refers to a process of transferring (redistributing) premium income among health plans in a market area. Risk adjustment is needed in a reformed insurance market whenever rating restrictions prevent plans from charging premiums that reflect the expected costs the plans will incur.

Sequence of Events

p 1   **Health plans/carriers register with the RA Administrator.**

° Several months before enrollment begins, all health plans/carriers who wish to sell coverage for basic benefits in the market area in the coming year must register with the RA Administrator, and must indicate whether they plan to sell this coverage through the purchasing pool or directly to small employer groups.
° As a condition, they must agree to all market rules, including participating in the risk-adjustment process (discussed earlier).

ep 2   **The RA Administrator provides the information each health plan/carrier needs to develop its "standardized" community rate.**

The RA Administrator provides each plan/carrier with 3 standard pieces of information which the administrator will use in calculating revenue transfer amounts for each plan:

° definitions of the risk classification categories;

° the "relative risk factors" for each risk category; and

° the reference premium amount upon which the transfer amounts will be based. The reference premium could be last year's average premium in the community trended forward, or any another designated amount.

ep 3   **Each health plan/carrier develops its standardized community rate for the coming year.**

° Development of the plan's/carrier's "standardized" community rate starts with the community rate it would charge in the absence of a risk adjustment process. Adjustments are then made considering expected transfer payments and other contingencies associated with risk adjustment.
° Plans are free to use whatever method they choose to develop their standardized community rate. A plan may choose to use the information supplied by the RA Administrator (step 2) to calculate its expected transfer amount, and to adjust its community rate by the transfer amount. The rate would be adjusted upward if the plan/carrier expects to have to pay into the transfer pool, and downward if it expects to receive money from the transfer pool.

° Each plan/carrier may choose to further adjust its rate for pricing uncertainties associated with the risk adjustment process.

° The end result is the plan's "standardized" community rate, the rate enrollees (or their employers) will actually be charged for enrollment in the plan.

ep 4   **RA Administrator publishes rates.**

° The plans report their standardized community rates to the RA Administrator.
° The RA Administrator publishes the rates well before enrollment begins, together

with information about whether the plan/carrier is marketing inside or outside the purchasing pool.

| Step 5 | **Enrollment.** |

° Health plans/carriers market either directly to small employers, or to individual employees purchasing through the pool.

° Small employers evaluate options and decide to purchase coverage directly, or through the purchasing pool

° Individual employees (inside) and small employers (outside) choose their preferred plans.

| Step 6 | **Health plans/carriers report actual enrollment data to the RA Administrator.** |

° Plans/carriers selling inside the purchasing pool (HIPC) receive enrollment information from the pool administrator.

° All plans/carriers report to RA Administrator their total enrollment and distribution of enrollees by risk category.

| Step 7 | **RA Administrator calculates transfer amounts and administers revenue transfers.** |

° The RA Administrator calculates each plan's/carrier's revenue transfer amount, based on the plan's/carrier's actual enrollment, the relative risk factors and the reference premium.

° For plans/carriers which must pay into the transfer pool (plans/carriers with actual relative risk lower than the community average), the RA Administrator bills the plan/carrier for the transfer amount.

° The RA Administrator pays out the transfer amounts to the plans/ carriers which receive money from the transfer pool (plans/carrier which have actual relative risk greater than the community average).

° Theoretically, the risk adjustment process aims for a zero balance in the transfer pool in each period -- transfers in should equal the transfers out. In practice, neither the plans/carriers nor the RA Administrator have perfect knowledge, and there may be changes in total enrollment and enrollee distribution by risk class in the community during the year. To ensure that the transfer pool has sufficient funds (remains solvent), the transfer amounts could be adjusted, or another source of funds could be tapped to create a reserve upon which the transfer pool could draw if needed.

Attached (Attachment B) is a simplified numerical example of how this risk adjustment process would work in practice.

516

How Risk Adjustment Might Work
in a Voluntary Purchasing Pool Environment

A Simplified Numerical Example

NOTE: This example is intended solely to illustrate the steps in the risk adjustment process described above Other approaches to risk adjustment are possible. Further, the risk categories and assigned relative risk factors used here are arbitrary and purely illustrative.

Step 1   Health plans/carriers register with the RA Administrator.

Three health plans/carriers register with the RA Administrator: Plan A, Plan B, and Plan C. These are the only plans/carriers in the community (offering basic benefit coverage), and together they cover all 20,000 members of the community.

Step 2   The RA Administrator provides the information each health plan/carrier needs to standardize its community rate.

A. Risk categories.

The RA Administrator tells the health plans/carriers there are three risk categories:

Category Definitions
Category 1
Category 2
Category 3

B. Relative risk factors.

The RA Administrator tells the plans/carriers the relative risk factors for each category:

Relative Risk Factors
Category 1 - 0.6
Category 2 - 0.8
Category 3 - 1.6

C. Reference premium.

The RA Administrator tells the plans/carriers that the reference premium for calculating transfer amounts is $200. The reference premium can be fixed at any reasonable amount. One choice could be the RA Administrator's estimate of last year's average cost per person for the community as a whole, trended forward.

Step 3   Each health plan/carrier develops its standardized community rate for the coming year.

NOTE: Plans will in fact, use whatever method they choose to develop their "standardized community rate," which is the rate enrollees or their employers will actually be charged for enrollment in the plan. (We ignore here any mark-up the HIPC might add to fund its operations) This example illustrates one way the plans might approach developing their standardized community rates

A. Expected enrollment.

The three plans/carriers expect the following enrollment:

Expected 1994 Enrollment (number of enrollees)				
Plan	Category 1	Category 2	Category 3	Total
A	2000	5000	1000	8000
B	1000	3000	2000	6000
C	1000	2000	3000	6000
Whole Community	4000	10,000	6000	20,000

B. Unadjusted flat community rate.

Based on plan historical experience, expected medical inflation, etc, plan/carrier actuaries calculate the flat community rate the plan/carrier would charge in the absence of rating restrictions for the expected enrollment (expected risks). We call this the "unadjusted" community rate.

Unadjusted Community Rate
Plan A - $190
Plan B - $210
Plan C - $240

C. Plan/carrier expected relative risk (average risk relative to whole community)

Based on the enrollee category relative risk factors supplied by the RA Administrator, plan/carrier actuaries calculate the plan's expected relative risk. The average risk for the whole community is 1.00.

The expected relative risk is a weighted average of the category relative risk factors, where the weights are the proportion of enrollees expected in each category.

Plan A: (2000 (0.6) + 5000 (0.8) + 1000 (1.6)) / 8000 = 0.85000

Plan B: (1000 (0.6) + 3000 (0.8) + 2000 (1.6)) / 6000 = 1.03333*

Plan C: (1000 (0 6) + 2000 (0.8) + 3000 (1.6))-/ 6000 = 1.16667*

* rounded

Expected Relative Risk
Plan A - 0.85000
Plan B - 1.03333
Plan C - 1.16667

D. Expected transfer amounts per enrollee.

Each plan's expected per enrollee transfer amount is equal to:

(1 - plan's expected relative risk) (reference premium)

Plan A: (1 - 0.85000) (200.00) = 30.00

Plan B: (1 - 1.03333) (200.00) = - 6.67*

Plan C. (1 - 1.16667) (200.00) = - 33.33*

* rounded

Expected Transfer Amount
Plan A - $30.00
Plan B - ($6.67)
Plan C - ($33.33)

E. Developing standardized community rate.

Each plan's/carrier's standardized community rate equals its unadjusted community rate plus the expected transfer amount, further adjusted for other contingencies. In this example, we do not include an adjustment for other contingencies.

Plan A: $190 + 30.00 = $220.00

Plan B: $210 - 6.67 = $203.33

Plan C: $240 - 33.33 = $206 67

Standardized Community Rate
Plan A - $220.00
Plan B - $203.33
Plan C - $206.67

These are the rates that each plan/carrier charges per person enrolled.

Step 4   RA Administrator publishes rates.

Step 5   Enrollment.

Step 6   Health plans/carriers report actual enrollment data to the RA Administrator.

The plans/carriers report the following enrollment:

Actual 1994 Enrollment (number of enrollees)				
Plan	Category 1	Category 2	Category 3	Total
A	1000	3000	1000	5000
B	1500	4500	2500	8500
C	1500	2500	2500	6500
Whole Community	4000	10,000	6000	20,000

Step 7   RA Administrator calculates transfer amounts and administers revenue transfers.

A. Actual relative risk.

RA Administrator calculates each plan's/carrier's actual relative risk:

> *The actual relative risk is a weighted average of the category relative risk factors, weighted by the actual proportion of enrollees in each category.*
>
> *Plan A: (1000 (0.6) + 3000 (0.8) + 1000 (1.6)) / 5000 = 0.92000*
>
> *Plan B. (1500 (0.6) + 4500 (0.8) + 2500 (1.6)) / 8500 = 1.00000*
>
> *Plan C: (1500 (0.6) + 2500 (0.8) + 2500 (1.6)) / 6500 = 1.06154**

* rounded

Actual Relative Risk
Plan A - 0.92000
Plan B - 1.00000
Plan C - 1.06154

B. Transfer amounts.

The transfer amount for each plan/carrier is calculated according to the following formula:

Transfer Amount = (1 - plan actual relative risk) (reference premium) (# enrollees)

Plan A: (1 - 0.92000) ($200) (5000) = $80,000*

Plan B: (1 - 1.00000) ($200) (8500) = 0

Plan C: (1 - 1.06154) ($200) (6500) = ($80,002)*

* transfers do not add to $0 because of rounding.

C. Revenue transfers.

The RA Administrator instructs Plan A to pay into the pool $80,000. The RA Administrator then pays out $80,002 to Plan C. Plan B, in our example, transfers neither in nor out.

Chairman STARK. And now I see we have Mr. Barnes.

STATEMENT OF GALEN BARNES, PRESIDENT AND CHIEF OPERATING OFFICER, WAUSAU INSURANCE COMPANIES, AND MEMBER, BOARD OF DIRECTORS, ALLIANCE OF AMERICAN INSURERS; ACCOMPANIED BY DONALD C. ALEXANDER, AKIN, GUMP, STRAUSS & FELD

Mr. BARNES. Thank you, Mr. Chairman. My name is Galen Barnes, and I am the president and chief operating officer of Wausau Insurance. I am also a member of the board of directors of the Alliance of American Insurers and we appreciate this opportunity to be here. It is getting late in the afternoon, and if you will permit me to enter my comments into the record, I will try to make this very brief.

Chairman STARK. All right.

Mr. BARNES. The alliance has vital concerns about health care reform. Our organization supports health care reform. However, we have some significant concerns about title 10 of the act. Our concerns are several fold.

The States are now working on reform of workers compensation systems. We believe those reforms are working. We would hate to see the implementation of title 10 and its impediment to that progress. At the end of 1992, we experienced $122 of loss for every $100 of revenue. At the end of 1993, that ratio is down to $112. We believe that is significant evidence that health care—excuse me, workers compensation reform is working at the State level. We do not see the need for Federal intervention to slow the progress.

We are also very concerned about the adjudication process. Over the last 80 years, workers compensation adjudication process for conflicts at the State level have been resolved. Title 10 may replace and duplicate that and add significant costs.

We are also involved in the reform efforts in managed care for workers compensation. Our reading of title 10 would suggest that those managed care reforms will end. This gives us significant concerns. We believe that there are also incentives in title 10 to increase disability periods and one of our members has estimated that one day of additional disability will add $10 billions of cost annually to workers compensation. It does not seem to us to be appropriate to put that kind of cost pressure on a system that continues to need reform.

Our major concern with title 10 is the aspect of cost shifting. There will be new economics as a result of health care reform and we are very worried that the cost shifting to our products may occur in great degree.

We are also concerned that title 10 does not address the issue of duplicate medical payments under auto insurance. And we finally are very concerned that title 10 is likely to eliminate centers of excellence for the treatment of occupational injury and specialized care. All of these, we believe, will add to the costs.

The Workers Comp Reinsurance Institute estimates that the additional cost from title 10 to the workers compensation system may be approximately $7 to $9 billion a year, a solution that we do not find palatable.

We have several goals in the alliance. We would like to have access to the new health care delivery system. We would like to avoid cost shifting. We would like to have the States remain as our regulators. We would like to have employers and insurers stay within the managed care for occupational injury. And we would like to protect the exclusive remedy doctrine.

The one thing we would request as far as workers compensation is to make sure that we do not get discrimination in either patterns or the amount that we pay just because we happen to be a payer. We believe that if this process or practice would end, that significant cost pressures would come off the workers compensation and auto system.

I will close with one comment. The workers compensation and auto insurance systems are very complex. When the country is attempting to address, and we believe appropriately, health care reform, to have a discussion and a debate about a workers compensation system concurrently seems to be wasting the energy of the debate and we should focus in our judgment on health care reform and leave the workers compensation complexity to those that are best able to manage and understand the issues.

We appreciate the opportunity of appearing before you. We will be happy to provide any evidence and additional information that you might wish. And at the end of the session, we will be glad to answer any questions that you might have. Thank you.

Chairman STARK. Thank you.

[The prepared statement follows:]

STATEMENT OF GALEN BARNES
ALLIANCE OF AMERICAN INSURERS

I. INTRODUCTION

Mr. Chairman and members of the subcommittee, my name is Galen Barnes. I am a member of the Board of Directors of the Alliance of American Insurers. I am also President and Chief Operating Officer of the Wausau Insurance Companies. We appreciate this opportunity to express the views of the members of the Alliance on Title X of the Health Security Act (H.R.3600).

You will hear from a broad spectrum of organizations regarding this proposed legislation. The 214 member companies of the Alliance write nearly 18 percent ($5.8 billion) of the workers compensation insurance provided by all private carriers; about 6 percent of private passenger automobile insurance ($5.1 billion); and, over 8 percent ($1.3 billion) of commercial auto coverage. We administer the medical care component of these coverages in a manner to assure quality care given in a timely manner. We feel that we should continue to offer these products for two very basic reasons: we are efficient, and, through experience rating, we are able to match behavior and the economic consequences of that behavior.

While we support the need for responsible health care reform, we have major concerns about the impact which the Administration's proposal would have on existing state-administered and regulated systems of workers compensation and auto insurance. These programs offer a unique diversity in approach to compensation for injury which recognizes that one solution does not necessarily fit all localities. In recent years, states have been working effectively to curb increases in medical costs in workers compensation and auto insurance.

Property/casualty insurers have a keen interest in the current national health care reform debate because we are significant purchasers of medical care. Our total medical care bill equals some $25.3 billion annually. Exhibit 1, attached to this testimony, shows the medical costs paid by property/casualty insurers in 1992. While our portion represents a small percentage of the $700 billion total universe in health care costs, it includes about 47 percent of all workers compensation losses. Automobile and general liability medical costs range from 14 percent to 20 percent of total property/casualty losses.

For that reason, we commend this subcommittee for recognizing that workers compensation and auto insurance issues are very important to the overall health care debate and for taking time to examine the effect which the President's legislation could have on these complex systems. Medical care paid for by workers compensation and auto insurance is an important segment of this country's overall health care structure. But workers compensation and auto insurance also are much more than medical care delivery mechanisms -- they are disability management systems.

The Clinton Administration's Health Security Act seeks to remodel, in the name of "coordination," the medical care components of workers compensation and auto insurance. The 1,364 page bill is organized into 12 titles. Title X specifically addresses coordinating workers compensation and auto insurance with a new health insurance system. I will concentrate first on our concerns with Title X as it relates to workers compensation insurance, and then mention some specific points in the Act which would create problems for persons injured in auto accidents.

II. WORKERS COMPENSATION INSURANCE

Workers compensation is the oldest social program in the United States. The first enabling law was enacted in 1911. All 50 states and the District of Columbia have such programs, as does the federal government (through the Federal Employees Compensation Act). One hundred million Americans, or nine out of every ten workers, are covered by workers compensation insurance. Over the past decade, more than $128 billion in workers compensation benefits have been paid to over 16 million injured workers.

It is important to note that workers compensation insurance is a completely different product than first-party health insurance. The goal of health insurance is to return an individual to health. The twin goals of workers compensation are to quickly return an individual both to work and to health. Also, workers compensation provides unlimited first-dollar medical coverage at no cost to the employee, whereas health insurance draws upon individual employee contributions in the form of premiums, deductibles and co-payments. Because of these fundamental differences, merging the two systems without sacrificing the purpose and goals of the workers compensation system is a very complex task.

Workers compensation insurers have single claims in which the amount reserved for medical costs alone exceeds a million dollars. State statutes require that all reasonable and necessary medical care be provided to employees covered by workers compensation. That care can range from an aspirin to a multiple organ transplant. Medical coverage for injured workers is broader than that provided by most health insurance policies, and includes treatment provisions such as over-the-counter and prescription drugs, prostheses, long-term care, at-home care, home and vehicle modifications, custodial care and rehabilitation.

Workers compensation benefits are statutory, rather than contractual. Also, it is the state (rather than the employer or insurer) who ultimately determines the appropriateness of treatment and charges. In nearly half the states, workers compensation law gives the employer the right to choose a medical provider. In other states, the employee chooses. All covered employees, full-time or part-time, are entitled to workers compensation benefits even if an injury occurs the first hour on the job. In most jurisdictions, benefits extend from the time of injury through the remainder of the person's life, so long as medical care is needed.

The states take appropriate steps to correct problems with their workers compensation programs when they occur. We believe national health care reform should not undermine state programs that work. Yet the Health Security Act would pre-empt valuable state workers compensation law provisions, including those related to physician choice, changing medical providers, the number of providers, physical referrals, appropriate fee schedules, and other laws dealing with who can treat an occupational injury.

With our assistance, states are now making real progress in helping American businesses, large and small, to reduce workers compensation costs. Since 1989, 26 states have enacted legislation to update and strengthen their state-administered systems. Thirteen of those states (California, Colorado, Connecticut, Florida, Kansas, Louisiana, Maine, Massachusetts, New Mexico, Oregon, Pennsylvania, Rhode Island, and Texas) have seen, or will soon see, significant cost reductions as the direct result of reform.

Texas and Oregon serve as specific examples of reform progress. Medical cost containment initiatives enacted during 1989 in Texas have resulted in a 30 percent cost reduction to employers over the past three years. Reforms enacted in Oregon between 1987 and 1991 have brought a 30 percent reduction in disability claims, and a 34 percent reduction in workers compensation rates. A chart displaying estimated cost savings on a state-by-state basis is attached to this testimony as Exhibit 2. Any national health care reform plan should support, rather than hinder, this progress.

The Alliance of American Insurers suggests the following goals for workers compensation as it relates to national health care reform: 1) workers compensation insurers should be allowed access to all types of health care delivery systems; 2) cost shifting should be eliminated; 3) states should continue to regulate workers compensation; 4) insurers or employers paying for medical care should have substantial control over decisions relating to that care; 5) experience rating should be maintained; and, 6) the exclusive remedy doctrine should be preserved.

Our analysis of Subtitle A of Title X is that it clearly would undermine the second, third, and fourth goals listed above. If the medical care component of workers compensation is merged into the proposed health insurance system (and we think this is virtually a pre-ordained result flowing from Subtitle C), the fifth goal also would be lost and the sixth would be at risk. Title X also would create an unworkable system of regulation and administration, including health alliances engaged in price-setting (fee schedules), and unnamed state agencies controlling access to expert workers compensation medical care.

Let me amplify my concerns about cost shifting. Cost shifting occurs when medical providers price their services and tailor their treatment according to the source of payment. It also includes engaging in discriminatory treatment patterns, such as an excessive number of office visits and exams, again based on the source of payment for the medical care.

Workers compensation injuries tend to be trauma-related. A recent survey of trauma center and hospital reimbursement conducted by the American Association for the Surgery of Trauma (AAST) showed that in hospitals where workers compensation employers/insurers paid $1.32 for every dollar of medical care rendered, managed care payers (health insurers) paid at a rate of 97 cents; Medicare paid 93 cents; and Medicaid paid 85 cents. Another study, conducted by the Minnesota Department of Labor and Industry, found that for every dollar Blue Cross pays to treat an injury, workers compensation pays $2.04. This difference resulted from both price and treatment pattern discrimination.

Clearly, ending cost shifting would save millions of dollars for the workers compensation system and the employers who support it. Employers must have the tools necessary to manage care, including the tools to end cost shifting, so they can spend the savings on such things as investing in plants and equipment, and creating more jobs.

A key workers compensation element which must be preserved in any reformed system is the ability of the employer and insurer to manage disability. Medical treatment can reduce disability, but disability management speeds the worker's return to employment and can reduce the amount of medical care needed to achieve recovery.

The Clinton Administration's "coordinated" approach to workers compensation outlined in Title X is flawed because it requires, rather than allows, medical treatment for occupational injuries to be delivered through the employee's health insurance plan, leaving employers with no meaningful input into the choice of medical provider. Title X would shift case management of an injury away from the employer/insurer -- who has expertise in this area -- to the health insurance plan, where expertise would have to be developed. The requirement that each health plan provide a workers compensation case manager simply duplicates services presently provided by the payers for that care and moves this management function to the health plan, which bears no financial risk for medical care or disability.

In addition, Title X arguably prevents the employer and the state workers compensation agency from questioning whether appropriate medical treatment is being received by an injured employee. This would establish a prohibition that presently does not exist even in states where the employee has the right to initial selection of a physician.

Shifting medical management of an occupational injury from the employer/insurer to the health insurance plan is likely to increase the length of disability (lost productivity) and drive up disability costs. The parties paying for disability, who have a financial stake in an employee's swift return to work, would be restricted in directing treatment toward that optimal outcome. In contrast, a health plan, its providers, and case manager would have no financial incentive to speed recovery and return to work. This would work to the detriment of both workers and employers

Some workers compensation experts estimate that an increase in duration of disability of just one day of lost time will add $10 billion a year to the nation's cost of workers compensation. The Administration has estimated its plan will save, at best, $6 billion in workers compensation costs. So, if the Administration figure is correct, and if implementation of Title X coordination results in just one day of additional disability on average, we start off $4 billion in the hole.

A more recent quantitative analysis by the Workers Compensation Research Institute (WCRI) assesses the Health Security Act's probable impact on workers compensation costs. It estimates that the Administration's proposal would increase the cost to employers in regional alliances between $7 billion and $9 billion, with considerable leeway above and beyond that range.

On the other hand, workers compensation reforms undertaken at the state level are targeted at state specific cost drivers in order to control and reduce costs. Furthermore, state-based reform packages are beginning to include provisions allowing workers compensation carriers to have access to managed care arrangements. Such arrangements can substantially reduce medical costs. Currently, 22 states have authorized the use of, or experimentation with, managed care in workers compensation claims. In addition, in those states where employers have the opportunity to initially select the physician, managed care can be instituted without statutory change.

The use of managed care in the workers compensation system, in addition to specific state legislative initiatives, continues to grow. A recent study by Towers Perrin indicates that approximately 50 percent of employers/workers compensation insurers are using health maintenance organizations, preferred provider organizations, or other managed care networks. This is up from only 20 percent in 1991. Utilization review increased dramatically, from 28 percent in 1991 to 70 percent in 1993. Pre-certification of medical treatment tripled from 19 percent to 57 percent, and case management increased from 30 percent to 84 percent.

Unfortunately, Title X's pre-emption and voiding of state laws that restrict an employee's choice or provider payment would wipe out much of the improvement already achieved in several states through reform. This is especially true with respect to the application of managed care to occupational injury and disease.

In general, Title X imposes an entirely new operating structure on the state workers compensation system. In doing so, it fails to address fundamental, state-specific problems which currently are targeted for reform. In fact, it is clear Title X will result in additional costs for every state's workers compensation system. These costs will more than that offset the gains state-based reforms have achieved.

Finally, Title X would create a commission appointed from within the Departments of Labor and Health and Human Services to "study the feasibility and appropriateness of transferring financial responsibility for all medical benefits (including those currently covered under workers compensation and automobile insurance) to health plans." From statements made by Administration officials, it is clear that this commission is expected to recommend total integration of the workers compensation health benefits financing system into the national health insurance system. Such integration would seriously and adversely affect employer safety incentives by moving workers compensation from an experience-rated to a community-rated system. The public at large would then have to bear the cost of an employer's unsafe workplace.

This would be a giant step in the wrong direction. Integration would create the wrong financial incentives for health plans to provide the intense and special treatment intended to quickly return an injured employee to work. Also, integration would likely erode the exclusive remedy doctrine, thus flooding the courts with litigation, increasing delivery costs to employers and delaying payment of compensation to injured workers.

III. AUTO INSURANCE

The Wausau Insurance Companies are primarily concerned with workers compensation and other commercial insurance coverages. However, like most other Alliance members, we are affiliated with other companies which write auto insurance. In our case, we are part of the Nationwide group of companies based in Columbus, Ohio.

Title X of the Health Security Act, as currently drafted, would have a negative impact on our nation's auto insurance system. Each year, auto insurers pay out some $10.5 billion for medical treatment of those injured in auto accidents. In some cases, these payments are for first-party coverage, and in some cases, for third-party coverage. Twenty-six states have what is called "no-fault" insurance, where an individual's own insurer compensates their losses up to a statutory tort threshold, regardless of who may have been at fault in an accident. A good no-fault law is a proven method for reducing litigation.

The Health Security Act envisions that auto insurance medical coverage would be "coordinated" with the new health care system, (i.e., financing would remain with auto insurers, but delivery of medical benefits would come through the health insurance system). However, the approach which H.R. 3600 takes toward coordination is seriously defective. For example, the bill does not deal at all with the pressing problem of duplicate medical payments for the same injury from both an auto insurer and a health insurer, thereby increasing costs for everyone.

Auto insurers also should have access to all types of medical delivery systems, especially managed care. We know from experience that managed care can save our policyholders' money. For example, control of medical costs for persons injured in auto accidents is already underway in the state of Colorado, where premium reductions are given for those who participate in a preferred provider plan.

Medical damages serve as one of the key elements which determine the ultimate dollar value of a tort claim. Having ready access to medical care information through direct involvement in the claims process is a vital element of the auto claims settlement process. It is critical that the insurer's claims department have full and complete medical information at an early stage, in order to set aside sufficient funds (reserves) to meet future potential settlement obligations.

We think good, effective public policy for auto insurance as it relates to national health care reform, should embody the following principles: 1) auto medical insurance should continue as the primary source of payment for auto accident-related medical costs; 2) duplicate claims payments for auto injuries should be curbed; 3) auto insurers should be allowed voluntary, universal access to all types of health care delivery systems; 4) regulation of auto insurance, including medical coverages, should be left at the state level; and, 5) cost shifting should be eliminated.

IV. CONCLUSION

Before I conclude, I want to restate our concern that Title X signals the Administration's intent to fully merge workers compensation and auto coverages into the new health care system. The Commission called for under Subtitle C of Title X is to submit its finding to the President by July 1, 1995. This date is several years before the Health Security Act's deadline for states to implement health care reform. That time frame guarantees that there would be no time to test even the "coordinated" approach advocated by the Administration elsewhere in Title X. The Alliance believes that the formation of such a commission is premature, if necessary at all.

We believe -- and research seems to show -- that the Administration's plan to merge workers compensation and auto insurance into a new health insurance system would create more health care problems than it would solve. It also would increase costs for business. For instance, merger of auto health coverages would create a situation where individuals with good driving records would end up subsidizing bad, drunk and dangerous drivers. Also, approximately 11 percent of each driver's auto insurance premium (the portion due to medical coverages) would be shifted onto their employer.

In the case of workers compensation, merger would destroy the ability of employers and insurers to manage disability. Those who would integrate the medical coverages of workers compensation with the Administration's health care plan should ask themselves if states will want to retain any part of the system if the medical portion were to be stripped away. The federal government has had difficulty in dealing with total disability claims in the Social Security system. Imagine the problems which might occur, and the bureaucracy which would have to be established, if the federal government had to struggle with determination of partial disability benefits for workers compensation.

Placing the financing, as well as the delivery, of workers compensation health benefits into the national health system would inevitably federalize the entire system and call on the federal government to create a new bureaucracy to attempt to manage what the states have been handling well all these years. Even more significantly, it would eliminate the current system's incentive for employers to maintain safe workplaces. Is this in the public interest?

There is something that President Clinton and the Congress could do to directly benefit employers, workers and individuals who purchase workers compensation and auto insurance. Any health care legislation should contain "all-payer" language to deal with cost shifting and discrimination in treatment patterns.

The potential for cost shifting onto workers compensation and auto insurance increases if a reformed system holds down costs for health coverage either through government controls or market forces. If it is necessary to seek legislative protection against cost shifting in this circumstance, one approach would be to require that the new health care system guarantee that health care providers (whether or not they are in a network) only can charge casualty insurers what they charge health insurers for the same medical procedures. In addition, such legislation would need to contain language prohibiting discrimination in treatment patterns based on the payer of that treatment.

Mr. Chairman and members of the subcommittee, I would like to reaffirm the Alliance's commitment to achieving medical cost containment, without sacrificing the quality medical care and rehabilitation which victims of auto and occupational accidents now receive through the state-based auto insurance and workers compensation systems. We know that the system of health care delivery in this country needs to be improved. Our overall goal as an association is to actively participate in the debate, and to improve the state-based systems which have served the American public over the years.

Again, thank you for the opportunity to present our views here today. We would be happy to answer any questions you may have.

Chairman STARK. Ms. Spencer.

STATEMENT OF KATHELEN V. SPENCER, SENIOR VICE PRESIDENT, DEPUTY COUNSEL, AFLAC (AMERICAN FAMILY LIFE ASSURANCE CO. OF COLUMBUS)

Ms. SPENCER. Thank you, Mr. Chairman. Mr. Chairman and members of the subcommittee.

Chairman STARK. You wrote that testimony. Evans couldn't have written that good. I just looked at it.

Ms. SPENCER. I am sorry?

Chairman STARK. I said earlier that I thought Evans wrote that testimony. He is not that articulate. You must have written it. I will apologize.

Ms. SPENCER. We will have to take that up with him later, I think.

Mr. Chairman and members of the subcommittee, my name is Kathelen Spencer and I am senior vice president and deputy general counsel of AFLAC. AFLAC is the world's leading supplemental health insurance company. It sells supplemental insurance products in six countries with major markets in the United States and Japan. We are pleased to have the opportunity to testify before you today.

On behalf of AFLAC, I would like at the outset of my testimony to publicly commend President Clinton, Congress, and the Committee on Ways and Means, and in particular Chairman Rostenkowski, for having the courage to address what is clearly one of the most important issues we will face in our lifetime: How our country can best provide its citizens with adequate health care.

AFLAC would also like to commend the members of this subcommittee, and especially Chairman Stark and Mr. Thomas, for taking the lead and supporting efforts to formulate effective legislation to deal with this issue. We are appreciative of this opportunity to participate in the process, and we would hope that we can continue working with you throughout the consideration of this issue.

We have been asked today to comment on private supplemental health insurance and how it relates to health care reform and the President's health care reform proposal. Supplemental insurance, unlike comprehensive major medical insurance, is normally purchased by individuals for specific protection which they want or need and which goes beyond the protection provided for them by their regular health insurance policy.

AFLAC sells a broad range of supplemental health insurance products, including Medicare supplement, hospital indemnity, accident and disability, long-term care, cancer and hospital intensive care.

Our products are designed, priced, and marketed as supplements to comprehensive major medical type basic coverage. Consistent with both AFLAC's and the administration's view on health care reform, all of AFLAC's individually issued supplemental health products are guaranteed renewable for life, fully portable and community rated on a Statewide basis.

As we read the President's proposal, and other proposals, such as that of Mr. Thomas, people are not inhibited from purchasing most kinds of private supplemental health insurance policies. In fact, section 1421 of the President's proposal, which deals with the imposition of special requirements on supplemental insurance, specifically exempts certain kinds of voluntary private supplemental insurance policies from coverage. These include long-term care, specific disease policies, hospital or nursing home indemnification policies, and accident insurance. Mr. Thomas provides similar exemptions in his bill. These policies would, of course, remain subject to all existing State and Federal laws and regulations.

With the ongoing debate over how the final version of the health bill will look, there is predictably a certain amount of uncertainty on the part of the American people with regard to how their own individual insurance protection will be affected with any changes in the health care system. Wisely, the administration, as well as Mr. Thomas and others, have chosen to provide the American people with specific assurances that they will continue to have the right to purchase private policies.

Putting people on notice at the outset that they will continue to have the choice to exercise self-determination as to what they want and need is very important and is an integral part of the success of any reform.

Supplemental policies are not unique to our system. Last year, AFLAC commissioned a study by the Johns Hopkins School of Hospital Finance and Management and they studied the role of supplemental insurance in the United Kingdom, Japan, and Canada. We have attached a copy of that report to our written testimony and would be happy to supply further information.

Basically, the role—there is a role in the systems of comprehensive coverage where people continue to want cash benefits to provide assistance with both the uncovered medical charges as well as nonmedical costs of illness.

In closing, I would like to thank you for the opportunity to participate in this testimony. We look forward to continue to work with you closely. I will be happy to answer any questions.

Chairman STARK. Thank you.

[The prepared statement and attachment follow:]

STATEMENT OF KATHELEN V. SPENCER
SENIOR VICE PRESIDENT, DEPUTY COUNSEL
AMERICAN FAMILY LIFE ASSURANCE COMPANY OF COLUMBUS

Mr. Chairman, and members of the Subcommittee, my name is
Kathelen Spencer. I am Senior Vice President, Deputy Counsel for
AFLAC Incorporated whose worldwide headquarters is in Columbus,
Georgia.

By way of background, our Company, AFLAC, was founded in 1955,
and is the world's leader in supplemental insurance. We operate
in all 50 states, and sell a broad range of products, including
medicare supplement, hospital indemnity, accident and disability,
long term care, cancer, hospital intensive care and life
insurance. Our products are designed, priced and marketed as
supplements to comprehensive health benefit coverage. They are
designed to provide extra cash benefits to help the insured pay
for non-covered medical expenses, as well as the non-medical
costs of illness. AFLAC's benefits are payable directly to the
insured so they may use the money where it is needed most.

Through independent research we have confirmed a high level of
satisfaction on the part of our claimants, with over 90% stating
that they would recommend our insurance. The high cost of
illness, and the independent verification of our policyholders,
supports the fact that supplemental insurance can be a valuable
component in many individuals' insurance portfolios.

AFLAC insures approximately 38 million people worldwide with
international operations in Japan, Canada, and the United
Kingdom, each of which has a national health insurance program.
In fact AFLAC insures over 22% of all Japanese households. We
also have operations in Taiwan and Hongkong.

AFLAC has been designated as the safest insurance company in
America by Financial World Magazine for the last two years and is
rated A+ Superior by Best's Insurance Reports.

AFLAC believes that reforms are necessary to guarantee all
Americans the right to basic health care and to help control the
rise in medical costs. We are particularly supportive of reforms
with respect to universal coverage and portability. We also
believe very strongly that Americans should be guaranteed the
right to purchase the best medical services available and to
supplement their basic health care benefits with the amount of
insurance they judge to be appropriate to cover their financial
obligations. Consistent with AFLAC's and the Administration's
view on health care reform, all of AFLAC's individually issued
supplemental health products are guaranteed renewable, fully
portable and community rated on a state-wide basis.

On behalf of AFLAC, I would like at the outset of my testimony to
publicly commend President Clinton, Congress, and the Committee
on Ways and Means, and in particular Chairman Rostenkowski, for
having the courage to address what is clearly one of the most
important issues we will face in our lifetime: how our country
can best provide its citizens with adequate health care. AFLAC
would also like to commend the members of this Subcommittee and
especially Chairman Stark and Mr. Thomas for taking the lead and
supporting efforts to formulate effective legislation to deal
with this issue. We are appreciative of this opportunity to
participate in this process, and we would hope that we can
continue working with you throughout the consideration of health
care reform.

The purpose of my appearance before the Subcommittee is to
provide comment on supplemental insurance and how it relates to
health care reform and the President's health care reform
proposal.

With the ongoing debate over how the final version of the health
care bill will look, there is predictably a certain amount of
concern and apprehension on the part of the American people with
regard to how their own health insurance protection will be
affected when this bill becomes law. Wisely, at the onset of the
legislative process the Administration has chosen to provide the
American people with the assurance that its new health plan would

not interfere with their right to purchase private supplemental
policies. We certainly concur in this approach. The mere fact
that the American people will have the comfort of knowing that
they will continue to have the unimpaired right to keep the
supplemental cover they have -- or to purchase additional
coverage if they so choose -- will do much to allay any
apprehension they may have with regard to national health care
reform.

Mr. Chairman, preserving people's continual right to purchase
private supplemental insurance coverage is commendable for two
reasons, both of which I am sure are important to the members of
the Subcommittee -- (1) it is good public policy, and (2) it is
good politics.

Preserving the right to purchase supplemental insurance is good
public policy because people should have the right to purchase
additional coverage. It is good politics because people want the
right to purchase additional coverage. According to a survey
conducted by Opinion Research respondents reported they believe
supplemental insurance will be either as or more important in the
future given the proposed reforms to the health care system.
Eighty percent of all respondents said they oppose any limitation
of their ability to purchase this type of insurance.

Private supplemental insurance has developed in the United States
in order to meet the ever changing needs of Americans. These
policies are widely available on both an individual and voluntary
payroll deduction basis. Private supplemental insurance, unlike
comprehensive major medical insurance, is normally purchased by
individuals for specific protection which they want or need which
goes beyond the benefits provided for them by their regular
health insurance. Also, unlike comprehensive major medical
insurance, AFLAC's benefits are paid directly to the insured, so
they can use the benefits where needed most. Such areas might
include making up for lost income of a spouse that took unpaid
leave to care for the ill, private nursing, drugs, etc.

Private supplemental policies are not unique to our system. Last
year AFLAC commissioned a study by the Johns Hopkins Center for
Hospital Finance and Management on private supplemental insurance
in three countries which already have health care systems that
typify the general systems which have been frequently mentioned
as possible models to restructure the delivery system for the
United States -- the United Kingdom, Canada, and Japan. I have
submitted a copy of this study for the record.

The Johns Hopkins study noted that private supplemental insurance
is purchased in all three of these countries for various
purposes, including that of gaining access for services not
covered by the public system such as: certain procedures and
amenities; additional medical and medical related services; and
income maintenance during illness. Other purposes mentioned were
gaining access to providers not participating in the system and
avoiding compulsory system queues.

The Johns Hopkins Study also pointed out that in the United
Kingdom, as well as other countries, the concept of cash benefit
policies is rooted in a tradition of income protection during
times of illness or disability. It noted that this concept
actually pre-dates basic health insurance policies.

President Clinton's health care reform proposal establishes two
distinct markets for supplemental insurance: those sold within
the health alliance and those sold outside the health alliance.

The first market place would include cost sharing and additional
benefits policies. Cost sharing policies would be designed to
provide coverage for deductibles, co-insurance and co-payments
imposed as part of the comprehensive health reform package, much
like Medigap policies do with the medicare program today.
Additional benefits policies would cover benefits not provided
under the comprehensive package such as dental and vision care.

Both the cost sharing and additional benefits policies would be
sold through the health alliance to eligible individuals and
would be required to meet strict standards and guidelines.

The second market includes voluntary private supplemental
insurance (hereinafter referred to as private supplemental
insurance). Private supplemental insurance is designed to cover
a broad range of expenses which are not necessarily specifically
covered by any public or private health plan. Unlike cost
sharing and additional benefits policies whose benefits go
directly to pay for provider services, benefits from private
supplemental insurance are paid directly to the individual. In
addition to non-covered medical expenses, the money from these
plans can be used to cover the non-medical costs of illness as
well as compensate for wage and salary losses incurred during
hospitalization and illness.

Section 1421 of the President's proposal, which deals with the
imposition of special requirements on supplemental insurance
specifically exempts certain types of supplemental insurance from
regulation by the new legislation. Mr. Thomas provides similar
exemptions in his bill. These policies would, of course,
continue to be subject to existing Federal and state laws and
regulations. These policies include long term care, specific
disease, Medigap, hospital or nursing home indemnification, and
accident insurance. Currently AFLAC offers policies in each of
these categories. We support this approach.

Although the President's package does not propose federal
regulation of private supplemental insurance, our segment of the
industry is currently very tightly regulated by the states.
State regulation includes approval of policy forms, rates,
benefits, advertising and market conduct. With the exception of
Medigap insurance, which was found to have problems with
duplication and over selling by some unscrupulous companies, and
which were addressed in OBRA 1990, no significant problems have
ever been identified with these types of products.

Our interpretation of the President's proposal is that the bill
continues to guarantee individuals the continued right to
purchase any private supplemental insurance policies they need to
cover their financial obligations. For that reason AFLAC
endorses this principal as reflected in this portion of the
President's bill.

Mr. Chairman, and members of the Subcommittee, again I would like
to thank you for allowing us to participate here today and we
shall look forward to working with you throughout this process.

I will be happy to answer any questions that you may have for me
at this time.

JOHNS HOPKINS
HEALTH INSTITUTIONS

The Center for Hospital
Finance and Management
624 North Broadway / Third Floor
Baltimore MD 21205
410 955-2300   FAX (410) 955-2301

Private Supplemental Health Insurance

in the United Kingdom,

Canada, and Japan

Introduction

A wide variety of health care financing and delivery
systems has been developed in the world. While each country
has developed its own particular scheme, most health care
financing and delivery systems can be categorized into one
of three general systems:

   o National health service
   o National health insurance
   o Social insurance

The purpose of this report is two-fold: to explain the
variations in private supplemental health insurance in
general, and to explore the role of private supplemental
health insurance in each of these health care financing and
delivery systems. For each system, one country has been
chosen, and the role of private supplemental health
insurance in each country will be explored. Three countries
were chosen that typify the general systems and have been
frequently mentioned as possible insurance and delivery
systems for the United States to examine. The selected
countries are:

o United Kingdom
o Canada
o Japan

For each system, the basic principles that underlie the general health care financing and delivery system are presented, followed by a brief description of how the system operates in the selected country. The country description is followed by an explanation of the role of private supplemental health insurance in the country.

In this report's conclusion, we have attempted to generalize from the selected countries' experiences about private supplemental health insurance with respect to the following issues:

o When private supplemental insurance becomes available
o Why private supplemental insurance becomes available
o Who uses private supplemental insurance
o What services are covered by private supplemental insurance

Variations of Private Supplemental Health Insurance

When examining health care systems operating in the world, private supplemental health insurance can refer to several different forms of private insurance policies. One form of private health insurance is a comprehensive health insurance policy purchased as a substitute for national plans. Substitute health insurance coverage is available for purchase individually and through the benefits plans of larger employers.

A second form of private health insurance is an
additional health insurance policy puurchased to complement
the coverage of the government insurunce program. Two types
of health insurance policies are seen within this area of
insurance. The first type of policy is a "wrap around"
policy - one that provides coverage for health care and
health related services that are not included in the
government insurance program. The sseecond type of policy is
one that offers cash benefits in the case of hospitalization
or the onset of certain major diseasses.

National Health Service

Description

In countries that have adopted national health service
financing and delivery systems, the insurance system is
operated by the government. The govvernment typically
provides a minimum benefits package and controls health care
practitioners and facilities througzn annual salary and
budget negotiation processes. The gjovernment collects
revenues needed to pay for health caare services from general
taxation. Most of the facilities arre owned by the
government, and many of the practitzioners are salaried by
the government. Global budgets, diirect control over
individual providers, and other budzgetary methods are
commonly used to keep expenditures within a certain
budgetary target.

National Health Service in the United Kingdom

In 1990, 6.2 percent of the United Kingdom's gross national product (GNP) was spent on health care. In US dollars, $972 were spent per capita on health expenditures. About 84 percent of the dollars comes from public revenues (Schieber, 1992).

Since its creation in 1948, the guiding principle of the UK's National Health Service (NHS) system has been government-provided health care services for all inhabitants, financed by general tax revenues. The NHS provides comprehensive coverage of health services, including:

- o   Hospital services
- o   Physician services
- o   Preventive services
- o   Nursing home care
- o   Home health care
- o   Prescription drugs
- o   Limited dental care
- o   Eye care
- o   Paramedical services
- o   Psychiatric services (Citizen Action, 1992).

Under the NHS, a person is assigned to a general practitioner (GP) based on the person's residency (Schneider, 1992). Most of the physicians are salaried by the government, and most health care facilities are government owned.

Local government health administration organizations, known as District Health Authorities (DHAs), are allotted budgets by the national government to purchase health care

538

services. DHAs are managed by a collection of health care
practitioners, medical school representatives, trade union
representatives, and local government authorities. DHAs buy
health care services from competing "budget holders", which
are primarily large physician practice groups. Budget
holders contract with hospitals to provide services
(Iglehart, 1990a; Cuyler, 1989; Harrison, 1988).

Some hospitals have opted out of the public financing
system by applying to become "self-governing trusts". These
hospitals are permitted to compete for patients and generate
income by contracting with physicians, private insurance,
and other hospitals in the NHS. Such hospitals no longer
receive DHA funding (Iglehart, 1990a; Cuyler, 1989;
Harrison, 1988).

Private Supplemental Health Insurance in the United Kingdom

Private supplemental health insurance in the United
Kingdom mainly refers to comprehensive private health
insurance that subscribers may use as a substitute for their
NHS coverage, and to supplemental policies that pay
subscribers cash benefits during hospitalization. Private
insurance does not preclude subscribers from using the NHS.
About 12 percent of the UK's total expenditures is likely
private insurance expenditures. The remaining 4 percent of
all spending represents direct, out-of-pocket payments
(Schieber, 1992).

In 1982, about 7 percent of the British carried some
form of private insurance (Iglehart, 1983). Currently, over
15 percent of the population carries some form of private
insurance (Schieber, 1992). About 7 percent of the
population purchases private comprehensive health insurance.
This insurance is usually obtained through employers, and is

a very popular perquisite for business executives (Iglehart, 1983). Although private insurance usually is an employee benefit, some purchase this coverage individually.

Benefits covered by private insurance vary, however private carriers provide coverage for many services available through the NHS, particularly hospital and physician services. Private insurance coverage highlights coverage of relatively simple surgery with predictable costs, as well as services not provided in the NHS, such as private and semi-private hospital rooms furnished with televisions and telephones (Glaser, 1991).

In general, the British purchase private insurance in order to afford access to private physician and hospital services. Insurance for private physician and hospital services is purchased specifically to avoid queues, afford a choice of physicians, and to obtain greater patient amenities (Iglehart, 1984; Glaser, 1991).

Queues refer to the waiting time between an initial consultation and the date of undergoing a procedure. In 1987, about 690,000 patients were queued for specialist care, each waiting an average of four months. It is estimated that 40 percent of the waiting list receives their services within one month. Overall, about 83 percent of the waiting list receives their needed services within one year (Fowler, 1991). Queues are particularly long for services that are explicitly limited, such as renal dialysis and hip replacement (Schneider, 1992). In addition to queues for selected procedures, there are also long waiting periods for initial consultations with specialists (known as consultants). The average waiting time for a first visit with a consultant is twenty to thirty weeks (Fowler, 1991).

Private insurance also allows subscribers freedom of choice of health care providers. As previously noted, all inhabitants are assigned, based on residency, an NHS general practitioner (GP). The average GP has a patient list of about 2000 individuals (Schneider, 1992). GPs do not provide hospital care, which is provided in the NHS only by hospital based physicians. In contrast to the NHS, subscribers of private insurance may obtain services from a variety of office and hospital based physicians.

Private insurance coverage also allows patients to receive health care services in the more comfortable environment of private hospitals and private rooms of NHS hospitals. Although private and semi-private rooms are available in some NHS hospitals, the majority of the UK's private beds are located in private hospitals. In contrast, patients without private insurance are treated in the wards of NHS hospitals. Private insurance subscribers typically use private hospitals for treatment of relatively minor injuries and elective surgery. However, private insurance subscribers prefer NHS facilities for the treatment of severe or complex injuries and illnesses, where the care for such illnesses is generally considered superior.

A second form of private supplemental insurance that is purchased in the UK is the cash benefit policy (Schneider 1992). About 8 percent of the population purchases this type of supplemental insurance. Cash benefit policies are sometimes referred to as income payment or income maintenance policies.

Some cash benefit policies available in the UK pay a daily benefit for hospitalization. Subscribers can purchase this basic benefit, or may add optional benefits to their

policy. Options include additional benefits based on the
type of hospital stay (such as an intensive care unit stay)
or on a specified diagnosis. The more common disease
specific options in the UK include benefits for cancer,
stroke, and heart attack hospital stays. Although long term
care itself is a covered benefit in the NHS, cash benefit
policies are available for nursing home stays as well.

Private supplemental insurance in the form of cash
benefit policies typically is not purchased as a benefit
through employers. Instead, most policies are purchased
individually through life and accident insurance companies,
and even through bank and credit card companies. In the UK,
as in many countries, the concept of cash benefit policies
is in part rooted in a tradition of income protection during
times of illness or disability. In fact, disability based
income support predates actual health insurance in most
countries. In Britain, groups known as Friendly Societies
traditionally provided this support. Today, income support
is generally provided through the federal Social Security
system.

National Health Insurance

Description

In countries that have developed a national health
insurance model, governments typically mandate a minimum
benefit package and use revenues from general taxation to
finance health benefits. Unlike the national health service
model, the providers and facilities in a national health
insurance model are predominately private sector entities.
Hospitals tend to be non-profit facilities that negotiate

their budgets with the government. Although physicians
receive all or most of their revenues from the government
insurance program, they are typically private providers
receiving fee-for-service or capitation payment. Global
budgets and provider rate setting are often used to control
expenditures.

National Health Insurance in Canada

In 1990, 9.3 percent of Canada's GNP was spent on
health care. In US dollars, $1770 were spent per capita on
health expenditures. About 73 percent of the dollars comes
from public revenues (Schieber, 1992).

Canada's health insurance system closely approximates a
national health insurance model. The system is financed by
federal and provincial tax revenues, with an average of 62
percent of revenues coming from provincial sources. In many
provinces, individuals pay their provincial portion through
direct quarterly payments to the provincial programs, or
more commonly, through payroll deductions. In most
provinces, residents over age 65 are exempt from the
provincial payments (Iglehart, 1986b).

The ten provincial (and two territorial) governments
serve as the single payers and administrators of Canada's
insurance programs. Each province designs its own plan for
the residents of its region, and must meet five federal
conditions in order to qualify for federal contributions.
The Canada Health Act, passed in 1984, effectively banned
extra billing and hospital user fees, consolidated previous
health insurance laws, and reestablished the five conditions
to be met by the provinces in order to obtain federal
support. The conditions include:

o Government administration on a non-profit basis
o Comprehensiveness: provinces must cover all insured
  health services
o Universality: all provincial residents are
  insured
o Portability: residents can transfer coverage to
  another province if their residence changes, and the
  province will cover expenses incurred when traveling
  in other provinces
o Accesssibility: services are reasonably available to
  all residents with no deductible, copayments, or
  extra billing (US General Accounting Office, 1991a)..

When Canadian citizens obtain medical care, they
present their province-issued insurance card to their health
care provider. The card entitles the bearer to receive all
covered services, which, in most provinces, include the
following benefits:

o Hospital services
o Physician services
o Preventive services
o Limited nursing home care
o Home health care
o Limited dental care
o Paramedic services
o Mental health services (Citizen Action, 1992).

Other benefits vary by province. Ontario, for example,
Canada's most populous and influential province in terms of
setting trends, covers physiotherapy, and occupational,
speech, and audiological therapy as well (Iglehart, 1986)..
Individuals may elect to purchase private insurance to
supplement their provincial benefits.

Private Supplemental Health Insurance in Canada

In Canada, private supplemental health insurance refers
to additional, "wrap-around" policies that provide coverage
for amenities and services excluded from provincial
insurance coverage, and to policies that provide cash
benefits upon hospitalization. The 1984 Canada Health Act
prohibits private insurance policies from duplicating
services insured through the provincial programs (US General
Accounting Office. 1991a).

Twenty-seven percent of Canada's total health
expenditures represents private spending. The Canadian
Department of National Health and Welfare estimates that 20
percent of total health expenditures is paid out-of pocket
(Schieber, 1992). This estimate leaves 7 percent of total
expenditures likely to be paid by private insurance
payments.

An estimated 60 percent or more of all Canadians
carries some type of private supplemental insurance
(Schieber, 1992). Private insurance is commonly carried as
an employee benefit, and is sold through 182 insurance
companies. Companies in the market include Blue Cross
plans, numerous commercial firms, and some cooperatives as
well (Canadian Life and Health Insurance Association, Inc,
1992). Most private insurance policies purchased by
Canadians provide coverage for amenities and services not
offered through provincial plans, as opposed to cash benefit
policies. Services generally not covered by provincial
plans, and available for coverage through private plans,
include:

o Semi-private and private hospital room
  accommodations
o Private duty nursing
o Vision care, including eyeglasses and contacts
o Outpatient prescription drugs
o Crutches, braces and other appliances
o Periodic dental care
o Cosmetic surgery
o Non-emergency transportation services (Iglehart,
  1986b; U.S. General Accounting Office, 1991a).

The second type of private supplemental health
insurance available in Canada is insurance that provides
cash benefits upon hospitalization. Similar to these
policies in the United Kingdom, some cash benefit policies
in Canada pay a daily benefit for a hospital admission
regardless of cause. Subscribers can purchase this basic
benefit, and may purchase additional benefits as well.
Additional benefits may be based on the type of hospital
stay (such as an intensive care unit stay), the need for
home health care, or a specified diagnosis. In the mid
1980s, cash payment policies became available in Canada that
were targeted to the health and disability needs of small
business owners, professionals, and retirees. Many of these
policies are comparable to the cash benefits policies
written in the United States. Indeed, some US based
companies are licensed and marketing these policies in
Canada (Young, 1991).

Typical hospital benefits policies provide cash support
of about C$100 per day, up to usually C$10,000 per year.
Disease specific benefits typically pay a lump sum of C$3000
to C$4000. Preexisting condition exclusions generally
apply to the disease specific benefits.

Social Insurance

Description

In countries with social insurance systems, health
insurance is often financed through a payroll tax, and
employers provide health insurance to their employees and
their dependents. The self-employed, farmers, unemployed,
and elderly may receive insurance as part of a government
administered system. Typically the government mandates a
minimum benefits package, upon which employers and employees
may negotiate for more generous benefits. As in the
national health insurance model, the providers and
facilities in a social insurance model are typically private
sector entities. However, often the government plays a role
in negotiations between insurers and providers, and may
impose a global budget.

Japan, often mentioned as a model social insurance
system, developed its modern variant of social insurance in
1922. Japan patterned its system after the German social
insurance system, and has in turn beeen carefully examined by
South Korea, Taiwan, and other East Asian countries.

Social Insurance in Japan

In 1990, 6.5 percent of Japan's GNP was spent on health
care. In US dollars, $1171 per capita were spent on health
expenditures. Seventy-two percent of the nation's health
expenditures comes from public revennues (Schieber, 1992).
Health care in Japan is rendered by private physicians in
mainly private clinics and private, non-profit hospitals.
Most hospitals, and almost all clinics, are owned and
operated by physicians.

Japan's health insurance system is patterned particularly after Germany's social insurance system of health insurance. Japan's Health Insurance Law of 1922 provided the modern framework for the country's Health Insurance System (HIS). Incremental expansions occurred throughout the mid-century, and insurance coverage became universal in 1961. The entire population of Japan is insured through one of three HIS insurance programs. The Employee Health Insurance program covers about 56 percent of the population; the Community (sometimes referred as National) Health Insurance program covers about 34 percent of Japan; and the Health and Medical Services for the Aged program covers the remaining 10 percent of the population (Powell and Anesaki, 1990; Iglehart, 1988a).

Insurance in these three HIS programs is available through several public and private, non-profit plans, known as mutual aid associations, society managed health insurance plans, government managed plans, and national plans (Japan Ministry of Health and Welfare, 1988). About 1800 insurance plans serve the Employee Health Insurance program to provide coverage to employees. Employee plans are financed by income based premiums as well as by patient copayments. The Community Health Insurance program is operated by a conglomeration of local governments and private groups, and is financed by income based premiums, patient copayments, and national and local taxes. The program insures the self-- employed, including farmers, employees of small businesses, and the unemployed. The Health and Medical Services for the Aged program is a national plan insuring individuals over age 70 and bedridden people aged 65 through 70. The program draws revenues from Japan's other two insurance programs (Schieber, 1992).

In comparison to the United Kingdom and Canada, health insurance benefits are much more narrowly defined in Japan. HIS hospital coverage generally insures medical and surgical related hospital services, and excludes the hotel services, nursing care, and other health related hospital services. HIS insurance benefits required by law include:

- o Hospital services, as defined
- o Physician services
- o Prescription drugs
- o Partial income support (Japan Ministry of Health and Welfare, 1988).

Actual coverage varies among the three insurance programs and the many insurance schemes, since many schemes provide additional benefits. In general, however, the Community Health Insurance program is the least generous of the three programs. Its benefits include basically the medical and surgical related hospital services, physician services, pharmaceuticals, and some income support, as noted above. Both the Employee Health Insurance and Medical Services for the Aged program benefits are more generous. In addition to those services required by law, the Employee Health Insurance and Medical Services for the Aged programs generally cover services such as therapeutic appliances, nursing care, and transportation. Neither the Employee nor the Community Insurance programs provides explicit maternity services, preventive benefits, or general physical exams. However, the Employee Health Insurance program pays pregnant women an income-based lump sum cash benefit to cover maternity expenses (Iglehart, 1988a).

In addition to insuring different services, Japan's HIS programs, and the many plans operating within the three programs, require a range of coinsurance payments and

premium contributions and provide a range of out-of-pocket
ceilings. For example, the Employee Health Insurance
program requires a 10 percent employee copay, a 20 percent
dependent hospitalization copay, and a 30 percent dependent
copay for physician services. The dominant insurance scheme
in the Community Health Insurance program requires a 30
percent copay. Conversely, the Health and Medical Services
for the Aged program requires only very nominal copayments
(Japan Ministry of Health and Welfare, 1988).

Private Supplemental Health Insurance in Japan

In Japan, private supplemental health insurance refers
largely to cash benefit policies, and only recently to
private policies that provide coverage for specific services
excluded from public insurance coverage. An estimated 16
percent of Japan's health expenditures is likely private
insurance payments. The remaining 12 percent of all
expenditures is paid out-of-pocket (Schieber, 1992).

At least 20 percent of Japan's citizens has been
estimated to carry some type of private supplemental
insurance (Life Insurance Association of Japan, 1993). The
most popular type of private supplemental coverage in Japan
is the disease specific cash benefit policy, particularly
cancer benefit policies. Hospitalization policies are also
fairly popular (Takeda, 1993; U.S. General Accounting
Office, 1991b). Unlike cash benefit policies in other
countries, many Japanese policies traditionally have paid
out funds from the first day of hospitalization only if the
hospital stay exceeded 20 days. An unusual rise in 21 day
hospital stays was attributed to these policies. Insurance
firms corrected this incentive in contracts written after
1986 (Japan Ministry of Health and Welfare, 1992).

Cash benefits policies for specific diseases and for hospitalization have been available in Japan as stand alone policies since the mid-1970s. Before that, similar coverage was available in the form of riders to life insurance policies. High HIS copayment rates and the extent of uncovered services related to hospitalization in Japan are two major reasons for the relative popularity of cash benefits policies. However, as in the United Kingdom, the notion of cash benefit policies has a long tradition in Japan as well. Mutual aid societies, now a part of the HIS, predated the Health Insurance Law of 1922. Established in the 1800s, mutual aid societies provided income protection to their trade-based members during illness and injury. Today, income protection, and social support in general, is provided by Japan's federal Social Security System.

Policies providing coverage specifically for HIS copayment expenses or for services not provided by the HIS is the second type of private supplemental insurance purchased in Japan. These policies were introduced only recently in Japan, in early 1986. Popular additional benefits include coverage for private and semi-private hospital rooms, as well as coverage for nursing services during hospital and home confined stays (Japan Ministry of Health and Welfare, 1992). Additional dental services also are relatively popular benefits. A small but growing private benefit area is coverage for highly advanced technological services, such as laser procedures (Takeda, 1993).

Conclusions

Private supplemental insurance has developed in
conjunction with universal coverage in the United Kingdom,
Canada, and Japan, and fills an important niche in these
countries' health insurance systems. In exploring the
evolution and nature of private supplemental insurance in
these countries, specific trends can be identified
concerning the following issues:

      o When private supplemental insurance becomes
          available
      o Why private supplemental insurance becomes availablie
      o Who uses private supplemental insurance
      o What services are covered by private supplemental
          insurance

Private supplemental insurance for services not covereed
by national plans fills a niche in countries with a nationaal
health service, national health insurance, or a social
insurance system. In general, the nature of private
supplemental insurance in each country was defined at the
time the national health systems were created, and private
insurance evolved to meet health services needs not
satisfied by the national systems. The evolution of privazte
health insurance is heavily dependent on the scope of
benefits in the public programs and the restrictions placeed
on private insurers. For example, in Canada the growth off
private insurance was curtailed in the 1950s, when provincces
began enacting provincial hospital insurance plans. Privaate
insurance was further restricted in the 1960s, as provincees
enacted provincial medical insurance plans (Vayda, 1984).
Today, the private insurance industry in Canada is limiteed
to providing services and amenities excluded from the
provincial insurance plans.

Private supplemental insurance in the form of cash
benefit policies fills a niche in health insurance systems
that is distinct from that of additional health care
services. Predating modern health and social insurance
systems, the concept of cash benefits is rooted in craft
guilds and mutual aid societies, which provided income
protection to members during times of illness or injury.
Cash benefits, or income protection, have century-old
traditions in two countries, the United Kingdom and Japan,
and are a relatively recent presence in Canada.

Demand for private supplemental insurance in the form
of additional services exists in the three countries
examined because of the amenities that private supplemental
insurance provides its subscribers. Private insurance
facilitates immediate access to facilities and physicians
services, as in the case of the United Kingdom (Iglehart,
1984). Private insurance also provides for private and
semi-private hospital room accommodations, as is the case in
all three of the countries examined (Iglehart, 1984;
Iglehart, 1986b; Takeda, 1993). Private supplemental
insurance also fills a niche for providing additional health
services such as outpatient prescription drug coverage, as
in Canada (U.S. General Accounting Office, 1991). Demand is
growing in Japan for first dollar coverage, where
coinsurance rates are steep (Japan Ministry of Health and
Welfare, 1992).

Demand for private supplemental insurance in the form
of cash benefits is seen in all of the countries examined.
Cash benefits policies fill a niche for additional income
protection in these countries. Cash benefits compensate for
wage and salary losses incurred during hospitalizations and
illnesses, and provide funds that can offset any out-of-
pocket expenses experienced during illness.

The demand for different types of private supplemental
insurance appears to be related to income. Additional
services policies, as well as private system insurance in
the United Kingdom, are often viewed as status symbols and
as business executives' perquisites. These policies appeal
primarily to the most affluent (Iglehart, 1983; Canadian
Life and Health Insurance Association, 1992). Cash benefits
policies, on the other hand, are commonly sold individually
instead of through group or employer coverage. Subscribers
are relatively lower income individuals, and include
particularly the lower income self-employed and retirees.
In contrast, however, some cash payment policies have
entered the Canadian market designed to meet the needs of
relatively more affluent small business owners and
professionals Young, 1991).

The extent of additional services covered by private
supplemental insurance policies has been found to vary
chiefly with the laws of each nation. Canada, for example,
prohibits the private sale of benefits covered by its
provincial plans (U.S. General Accounting Office, 1991a).
The UK allows extensive benefits to be sold privately,
however the private system caters mainly to Britain's demand
for a prompt, comfortable elective surgery alternative to
the NHS (Iglehart, 1984). Finally, additional services
policies have only recently entered the Japanese market
(Japan Ministry of Health and Welfare, 1992).

The range of available cash benefit policies is less
delineated and restricted in the countries examined than the
range of available additional service policies. Private
cash benefit policies commonly pay a daily benefit during a
hospital admission. Cash benefit options available in the

United Kingdom, Canada, and Japan include additional
benefits based on the type of hospital stay (such as an
intensive care unit stay) or a specified diagnosis. Cancer,
stroke, heart attack, and Alzheimer's disease options are
common additions in the cash benefits field.

In sum, private supplemental insurance is typically
purchased in the United Kingdom, Canada, and Japan in order
to:

o Avoid compulsory system queues

o Access services not covered by the public system,
   for example:

   - certain high technology procedures
   - certain patient amenities
   - additional medical or medical related services
   - additional income maintenance during illness

o Access certain providers, such as

   - a provider of one's choice
   - a provider not participating in the public
     system.

REFERENCES - UNITED KINGDOM

Citizen Action. (1992) Comparison of National Health Care Systems. Nursing and Health Care 13(4): 202-3.

Cuyler AJ. (1989) Cost Containment in Europe. Health Care Financing Review Annual Supplement: 21--32.

Fowler E. (1991) Survey of the British National Health Service. Wichita, KS: Wesley Foundation.

Glaser WA. (1991) Health Insurance in Practice: International Variations in Financing, Benefits, and Problems. San Fransisco: Jossey-Bass Publishers.

Harrison S. (1988) "Great Britain" in Saltman RB (ed) The International Handbook of Health-Care Systems. New York: Greenwood Press.

Iglehart JK. (1990a) Reform of the British National Health Service: From White Paper to Bill in Parliament. New England Journal of Medicine 322(6): 4110-12.

Iglehart JK. (1983) The British National Health Service under the Conservatives. New England Journal of Medicine 309(20): 1264-68.

Iglehart JK. (1984) The British National Health Service under the Conservatives, part two. Neew England Journal of Medicine 310(1: 63-67.

Roemer MI. (1991) National Health Systems of the World, vol one. New York, NY: Oxford University Press.

Schneider M et al. (1992) Health Caree in the EC Member Countries. Social Science and Medicine 20(1 and 2):220-8.

Schieber GJ, Poullier JP, Greenwald LM. (1992) U.S. Health Expenditure Performance: An International Comparison. Health Care Financing Review 3(4): 1--88.

U.S. General Accounting Office. (1991b) Health Care Spending and Control: The Experience of France, Germany, and Japan. Washington, DC. Pub. No. GAO/HRD-92--9.

REFERENCES - CANADA

Canadian Life and Health Insurance Association, Inc. (1992) Canadian Life and Health Insurance Facts - 1992. Toronto.

Canadian Life and Health Insurance Association, Inc. (1991) Survey of Health Insurance Benefits in Canada - 1991. Toronto.

Citizen Action. (1992) Comparison of National Health Care Systems. Nursing and Health Care 13(4): 202-3.

Iglehart JK. (1986a) Canada's Health Care System (part one). New England Journal of Medicine 315(3): 202-8.

Iglehart JK. (1986b) Canada's Health Care System (part two). New England Journal of Medicine 315(12): 778-84.

Iglehart JK. (1986c) Canada's Health Care System (part three). New England Journal of Medicine 315(25): 1623-28.

Iglehart JK. (1990b) Canada's Health Care System Faces Its Problems. New England Journal of Medicine 322(8): 562-68.

Schieber GJ, Poullier JP, Greenwald LM. (1992) U.S. Health Expenditure Performance: An International Comparison. Health Care Financing Review 3(4): 1-88.

U.S. General Accounting Office. (1991a) Canadian Health Insurance: Lessons for the United States. Washington, DC. Pub. No. GAO/HRD-91-90.

Vayda E, Deber RB. (1984) The Canadian Health Care System: An Overview. Social Science and Medicine 18(3): 191-7.

Young JA. (1991) Disability Income in Canada. Disability Newsletter December 1991; 1,8,9,14.

REFERENCES - JAPAN

Citizen Action. (1992) Comparison of National Health Care Systems. Nursing and Health Care 13(4): 202-3.

Iglehart JK. (1988a) Japan's Medical Care System. New England Journal of Medicine 319(12): 807-12.

Iglehart JK. (1988b) Japan's Medical Care System, part two. New England Journal of Medicine 319(17): 1162-72.

Japan Ministry of Health and Welfare. (1988) Health and Welfare Services in Japan. Tokyo: Ministry of Health and Welfare.

Japan Ministry of Health and Welfare. (1992) Annual Report on Health and Welfare: 1991-1992. Tokyo: Ministry of Health and Welfare.

Life Insurance Asssociation of Japan. (1992) Summary of Life Insurance Business. Tokyo: Life Insurance Association of Japan.

Powell M, Anesaki M. (1990) Health Care in Japan. London: Routledge, Inc.

Schieber GJ, Poullier JP, Greenwald LM. (1992) U.S. Health Expenditure Performance: An International Comparison. Health Care Financing Review 3(4): 1-88.

Steslicke WE. (1982) Development of Health Insurance Policy in Japan. Journal of Health Politics, Policy and Law 7(1): 197-226.

Takeda T. (1993) Personal communication with Toshihiko Takeda, Director, Health and Welfare Department, Japan External Trade Organization (JETRO), New York.

U.S. General Accounting Office. (1991b) Health Care Spending and Control: The Experience of France, Germany, and Japan. Washington, DC. Pub. No. GAO/HRD-92-9.

Chairman STARK. Mr. Kleckner. Mr. Kleckner didn't show up. Do you want to represent the Farm Bureau today, pro bono?

Mr. ALEXANDER. No. Now that you have added that, Mr. Chairman, no.

Chairman STARK. Mr. Sommers. Would you like to represent the Farm Bureau?

Mr. SOMMERS. That is out of my league, I am sorry.

Chairman STARK. Without objection, because they did submit testimony, and I didn't mean to—and with the erratic schedule, without objection, the testimony of Mr. Kleckner, who is president of the American Farm Bureau Federation, will appear in the record today.

Mr. Sommers, you may proceed.

STATEMENT OF KARL C. SOMMERS, VICE PRESIDENT OF CORPORATE PLANNING, MENNONITE MUTUAL AID, GOSHEN, IND.

Mr. SOMMERS. Thank you. Mr. Chairman, my name is Karl Sommers. I am vice president of corporate planning for Mennonite Mutual Aid referred to here as MMA. MMA serves the Mennonite and related Anabaptist churches.

Approximately 600,000 persons belong to these churches in the United States today. MMA is responsible to lead Mennonites toward greater practice of the biblical principles of stewardship and mutual aid. Since the early 1950s, we have administered health insurance plans for our members as one form of mutual aid.

We provide comprehensive, high-quality medical plans to Mennonites emphasizing cost containment through managed care. We operate our business to reflect our Mennonite theology.

MMA is directly accountable to the general board of the Mennonite church. Our volunteer board is elected by the Mennonite membership. We manage our rating, underwriting, and renewal practices in order to maintain a long-term commitment to our members.

Our Mennonite beliefs govern and restrict how we invest our members' money. And we provide churches with first mortgage loans at reasonable rates in order to promote church growth. We keep our overhead costs low in accordance with our Mennonite beliefs about stewardship.

Now, not only do we offer and administer health plans for our members, we promote values which we believe are needed in helping to reform our health care system.

We do this with programs in two special areas. One is in financial assistance and the other one is in education. We offer financial assistance for our members who have unpaid medical expenses. We offer premium assistance for people who can't pay the full amount. We offer grants for congregations who want to reach out and help others in their local communities. We promote healthy lifestyles through our wellness programs.

We encourage the study of medical ethics and help members to establish advance directives for end-of-life decisions. We have a nurse-in-the-congregation program to help our members get information before they access the health care system.

We support the health care reform principles the President is calling for and we think universal access is of highest priority. We want to support government in bringing about reform.

Our concerns are focused on the requirements related to the regional alliances. Our theology and the practice of our beliefs for over 400 years has centered upon mutual aid in the community of faith. Our members would have a problem with being forced to join a large alliance with many people who don't share our beliefs and values.

If mandatory alliances were enacted, some of our people would refuse to participate and we believe the alliance could become a significant barrier for Mennonites connecting with the MMA health plan since we work primarily through our local congregations.

Health plans registered with the regional alliance will be available to everyone in the region. They must accept anyone who signs up. Such a requirement would directly contradict the very basis of MMA's health plan. Members of our health plans must first be members of a Mennonite or related Anabaptist congregation. Our market is, by necessity, a closed one, not open to members of the general public who don't share our beliefs and values.

In many of the proposals, including the Clinton's, exceptions are created but only for large groups in an employment relationship. The Clinton plan, for example, lets multi-State employers with more than 5,000 employees opt out of the compulsory alliances.

MMA is a multi-State organization with 47,000 members. We are subject to regulations as an insurer in every State where we transact business. We would respectfully request the ability to opt out of the regional alliances on the basis of the strong ties of religious faith which connect members with MMA.

As an alternative, MMA would like to operate as a closed health plan for members of the Mennonite and related Anabaptist faith community. MMA would remain subject to any State insurance regulation or any other requirements Congress imposes for health insurance coverage as long as these requirements are not in direct conflict with our beliefs.

Thank you, Mr. Chairman, very much for permitting me to testify on behalf of our people.

[The prepared statement follows:]

February 4, 1994

Introduction

Mennonite Mutual Aid (MMA) serves the Mennonite and related
Anabaptist churches. There are approximately 600,000 persons who
belong to these churches in the United States today.

MMA is responsible to lead Mennonites toward greater practice of
the biblical principles of stewardship and mutual aid. Since the
early 1950's we have administered health insurance plans for our
members, as one form of mutual aid.

MMA as a health insurer of Mennonites

MMA provides comprehensive, high quality major medical plans to
Mennonites, emphasizing cost containment through managed care.
We operate our business to reflect Mennonite theology:

- MMA is directly accountable to the General Board of the
  Mennonite Church. Our volunteer board of directors is
  elected by the Mennonite membership.

- MMA manages its rating, underwriting, and renewal
  practices to maintain a long term commitment to its
  members. For example, we provide health insurance for
  international missionaries who might not be insurable
  under a conventional policy.

- Mennonite beliefs govern and restrict how MMA invests
  members' money. We avoid investments in defense,
  alcohol, tobacco, and gambling industries. Instead, we
  invest in businesses that promote a better quality of
  life such as housing, food, transportation, and
  utilities.

- MMA provides churches with first-mortgage loans at
  reasonable interest rates to encourage church growth.

- Overhead costs are kept low in accordance with
  Mennonite beliefs about stewardship.

MMA promotes Mennonite values and beliefs

Not only do we offer and administer health plans for our members,
we promote values which we believe are needed for reforming our
health care system. We do this with special programs in two
areas -- financial assistance programs, and educational programs.

For example:

- We offer financial assistance for unpaid medical
  expenses when these costs would create a hardship.

- We offer premium assistance for persons who may be
  unable to pay the full amount.

- We offer grants for congregations who want to reach out
  and help others in their local communities.

- We promote health lifestyles through our wellness
  programs.

561

- We encourage the study of medical ethics, and help members to establish advance directives for end-of-life decisions.

- We have a "nurse in the congregation" program to help our members get information *before* they access the health care system.

MMA's Concerns About Health Care Reform

MMA supports the health care reform principles the President is calling for and we think universal access is of highest priority. We want to support government in bringing about reform. Our concerns are focused on the requirements related to the regional alliances.

Regional Alliances

Our theology and the practice of our beliefs for over 400 years has centered upon mutual aid in the community of faith. Our members would have a problem with being forced to join a large alliance with many people who do not share our beliefs and values. If mandatory alliances were enacted, some of our people would refuse to participate. We believe the alliance could become a significant barrier for Mennonites connecting with the MMA health plan.

Health plans registered with the regional alliance will be available to everyone in the region. They must accept anyone who signs up. Such a requirement would directly contradict the very basis of MMA's health plan. Members of our health plan must first be members of a Mennonite or related Anabaptist congregation. Our market is by necessity a closed one which is not open to members of the general public who do not share our beliefs and values.

Beliefs rather than employment bond Mennonites to MMA

In many of the proposals for health reform, including the Clinton's, exceptions are created only for large groups in an employment relationship. The Clinton Plan, for example, would let multistate employers with more than 5,000 employees opt out of the compulsory regional alliances.

MMA is a multistate organization with 47,000 members. We are subject to regulation as an insurer in every state where we transact business. We respectfully request the ability to opt out of the regional health alliances on the basis of the strong ties of religious faith which connect members with MMA. As an alternative, MMA would like to operate as a closed health plan for members of the Mennonite and related Anabaptist faith community. MMA would remain subject to state insurance regulation and any other requirements Congress imposes for health insurance coverage as long as these requirements are not directly in conflict with our beliefs.

Chairman STARK. Thank you, Mr. Sommers. Let me—and if this is information you feel is privileged, please don't hesitate to tell me so, but could—what I am curious to get at is if you know for the people who I am going to suggest you insure, if that is the proper terminology, if you have a ballpark average cost per year per person? Is that something you could do?

Mr. SOMMERS. I don't have that off the top of my head. I would be glad to supply it for you.

[The following was subsequently received:]

M   M   A

Mennonite Mutual Aid
1110 North Main Street
Post Office Box 483
Goshen. IN 46527

Toll-free: 1-800-348-7468
Telephone: 219 5339511
Fax: 219 533-5264

February 22, 1994

The Honorable Pete Stark
Chairman, Health Subcommittee
Committee on Ways and Means
U.S. House of Representatives
239 Cannon Office Building
Washington, D.C. 20515

Dear Mr. Chairman:

Thank you for inviting Mennonite Mutual Aid to provide testimony for your
Health Subcommittee on February 4. I agreed to supply you with some
additional information about the cost of MMA's health plans.

Most of our health plans purchased by persons under age 65 would be
classified as "Individual Health" by standards of the marketplace. For 1993,
the average annual price our members paid per covered person was
approximately $1,479. This figure covers a variety of comprehensive major
medical plans. The average annual price per person covered at the end of 1993
in our most recently issued comprehensive plan with a $250 calendar year
deductible, 80/20 coinsurance is $1,225.

Our administrative costs have been lower than others in the past. Over the
period of time from 1989 through 1993, total administrative and sales expenses
as a percent of health revenues averaged 15.6% for this block of business.
These costs also include expenses incurred to develop and implement new
forms of managed care.

I'm enclosing a graph showing administrative expense ratios from various
types of organizations for calendar year 1992. This information has been
reported to us from A. M. Best in the general insurance press, through our
consulting firm Milliman & Robertson, and from the *New England Journal of
Medicine*. The graph shows that expense ratios for individual and small group
carriers are in excess of 30%, large group carriers slightly under 25%, HMO's
at 15%, and hospitals at 25%. MMA's expense ratio of 15.1% for 1992 is noted
with the red horizontal line.

There are several factors which enable MMA to operate at lower overhead cost
levels. Salaries for management positions are significantly lower than for
commercial organizations. Members of our churches have a propensity to
purchase their coverage from MMA, making our costs related to sales lower.
MMA's staff and operations are located in a relatively low cost-of-living area.

The MMA staff has a strong work ethic. Much of this grows out of our heritage as a people. But it also relates to MMA's mission. As an organization accountable to the Mennonite Church, MMA is involved with a purpose that is much larger than itself. Many of our staff are willing to "go the second mile" to help with projects because they believe in MMA's vision of serving the church.

Service is a core value that we emphasize. We value serving one another and our customers with commitment, efficiency, and competence. Over the years we've developed efficient systems for running our business. In addition, we budget and evaluate expenses carefully before spending our members' money. This is an ongoing challenge -- to be good stewards in the midst of significant changes in the financing and delivery of health care.

Mr. Chairman, if I can provide additional information to assist you in your committee process, please let me know. Thank you for your sensitivity to our values and beliefs.

Sincerely,

Karl C. Sommers
Vice President, Corporate Planning

cc: Walter Vinyard

enclosure

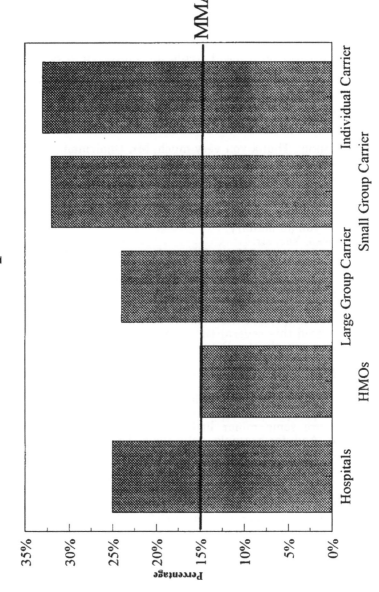

Administrative Expense Ratios

Chairman STARK. I am just curious. As I say, I am thinking of suggesting that you bid on the Medicare contract for the government and provide Medicare, if you would like to expand your operations a little. I like your philosophy.

And the only other thing I would say is that I think this subcommittee certainly, and I suspect the Congress, will be sensitive to your concerns. And if not, I would introduce you to counselor Alexander here who is an expert on first amendment cases, which I rather suspect you would qualify for immediately if you were in fact restricted under the plan.

So my guess is that we will try and work with you to see that you can continue to provide the fine service to your community that you do.

Mr. SOMMERS. Thank you very much, Mr. Chairman.

Chairman STARK. But in exchange, now, we ask for some advice on keeping overhead down and some of those other things. That is the quid pro quo. How is that? Fair exchange?

Mr. SOMMERS. Fair.

Chairman STARK. Thank you. I wanted to just kind of see—Mr. Barnes, are you an actuary?

Mr. BARNES. Yes, sir.

Chairman STARK. All right. Do you know, because Mr. Gustafson and I are going to have to discuss some of this. It is my understanding—I am not an actuary and I have the deepest respect for them. I can't understand what they do, but—or how they do it. I guess I know what they do.

But I don't think that there exists and the head of your actuary society has said this several times in testimony, a method for risk adjustment prospectively. Retrospectively, we can risk adjust, but that is just cost reimbursement, basically.

I know Mr. Gustafson has an outline which is attached to his testimony, but it has a couple of conditions that I am afraid don't let us get to what you want to do with it.

I have no quarrel that we need it, Mr. Gustafson, but you do suggest there are some minor little pieces of this that need to be worked out. And, for example, definitions of risk classifications and relative factors for each risk category and a reference premium.

And as far as I know, there is no—at this point, there is no plan of risk adjustment that we could put into operation that your principal or Mr. Barnes' company would sign on to and say we are willing to risk our stockholders' or our membership's money based on the fact that this is going to even out of a selection process against us.

I mean, is that fair that what you are talking about in your risk adjustment is an approach that could work if we had all the pieces completed? Is that a fair assessment of what you were testifying to?

Mr. GUSTAFSON. I think it absolutely is a fair assessment. I would like to say that, in my judgment, the real issue is not whether we have mandatory or voluntary alliances as it pertains to risk selection. Either way, as we see it, something has got to be done to take care of the potential problem where, even with mandatory alliances, some of the health providers are going to have different risks come to them for whatever reason, not through cherrypicking and not through actual attempted selection. So as we see it, that has to be dealt with either way.

Chairman STARK. That is only a problem if the—I mean, that problem diminishes as the pool gets larger.

Mr. GUSTAFSON. Well, again, as I understand it, though, the anticipation is there will be many approved providers within this thing, whatever we are going to call it, the purchasing alliance.

Chairman STARK. I am not at all sure, though, that those sorts of things will come into play. There is precious little—I would—we have yet to hear somebody testify that they want mandatory alliances.

We have heard an awful lot of witnesses. Now, we have heard a couple of Governors suggest that they would like alliances but both the Governors wanted different kinds of alliances and, of course, we are faced with one alliance for the whole country and already we have got a fight between South Carolina and Vermont. And California and New York and Illinois haven't even weighed in on that.

So my guess is that that is something that will be difficult to write in the next 6 weeks, so we may have to sort of put it aside, not to suggest that there won't be groups. California has a thing called CalPERS which the President often refers to except that his bill puts them out of business. It is kind of a—we have some minor details like that to work out.

So my guess is that a lot of this—the procedures and the relationships between providers and payers and insureds will continue, albeit reformed. I think you are going to get the community rating a little faster than you would like to. I don't think it will be overnight, but I don't think it will be 10 years. Five years? Maybe. Three, five, in that range, but I think you are going to get the community rating.

I think you are going to see a prohibition on medical underwriting. I think you are going to see a requirement for open enrollment. Those sorts of things I think are coming. They have been coming for a long time.

I think Mr. Barnes is going to see Federal regulation. I don't think it will replace State regulation, but I think it will set a standard for those States that don't have nearly the expert regulations that the State of the Wisconsin has. It is a leader in blue sky regulation. It has been a leader since 1911 in creating the type of insurance that Mr. Barnes' company makes so much money writing.

Who wrote the bill, Mr. Barnes, in 1911?

Mr. BARNES. Who wrote the bill?

Chairman STARK. Yes.

Mr. BARNES. In Wisconsin?

Chairman STARK. The Soldiers Sailors Relief Act of 1911, if my memory serves me right, who wrote it?

Mr. BARNES. I am not sure. I was not there.

Chairman STARK. Oh, Wausau does not have a bust statue and a portrait of which great Wisconsin legislator? Robert M. La Follette, who wrote the soldiers—without which there would be no workman's compensation. Don't ever forget that.

Mr. BARNES. I will not.

Chairman STARK. Heavens. Mr. Alexander knew that.

Mr. ALEXANDER. One of my better years was 1911, Mr. Chairman. But as we all know, one of the signs of decrepitude is a failing memory and I can't remember.

Chairman STARK. Another problem that I am surprised you didn't address, but why don't we address it, because I don't know whether there is a solution that the independent agencies would like is you guys are out of business in the President's bill.

You were very gracious, but the fact is that there would be no more insurance salesmen. Did you overlook that or were you just——

Mr. GUSTAFSON. I appreciate you bringing that up, Mr. Chairman. As a matter of fact, obviously, we are aware of some of those implications and we feel, for not just that reason by any means, that if we allow the purchasing alliances to be voluntary, if we allow free choice, if people can do business with where they want to, all of those things will reach their own level.

I have been in the business as an independent agent now for 36 years and never in that time have I ever asked my government or anybody else has asked them to guarantee me a job or guarantee me commissions.

But at the same time, never in that 36 years has my government ever said, we are going to pass a law that makes it illegal for you to even offer those services.

Chairman STARK. If you can't pass the exam——

Mr. GUSTAFSON. The law that we are discussing today could have that effect.

Chairman STARK. I recognize that. What I would suggest to you is that, at the worst, you may be limited in the range of products you have available, and other than that I don't believe this is a political statement—it is one of the reasons I don't believe you will ever get the mandatory alliances passed.

With all due respect to the insurance agents, we don't hear from them because they don't spend a lot of time lobbying us there. The States do and there are few State capitals, I think, that could pass an alliance bill over the objection of the agents. I suspect that you will be in business—you were kind enough not to raise it, but——

Mr. GUSTAFSON. I appreciate those comments.

Chairman STARK. We would like to work with you. I am not suggesting for 1 minute that risk adjustment wouldn't be a useful tool for us. It really would. I am sure that the Federal Government would be glad to fund any kind of reasonable responsible research to get there.

We have been working on it in the administration, in fact HCFA, under Republican and Democratic administrations for some years; and we have a real use for it in the Medicaid-Medicare programs, but we find that we come up against a blank wall. I suspect that maybe we were being shown a tablet today that we hadn't seen before.

Mr. Hoagland.

Mr. HOAGLAND. I would like to ask a question about the voluntary alliance proposal. Mr. Gustafson, how do you protect an alliance against adverse risk selection? You know, New York right now has voluntary alliances with a must-issue requirement.

Mr. GUSTAFSON. Well, I think obviously we would have to be concerned about two things. On the front end, we would have to make sure that we didn't have some kind of under-the-table risk selection going on. There have to be rules of market conduct, guaranteeing accessibility, not allowing insurance companies or agents to use preexisting conditions and other things like that to favorably preselect.

So those rules have to be enforced, and they are there for everybody. Once companies and agents cannot preselect and therefore offer a better price, no one will be able to select best risks. We are determined that it must be that way.

The other problem is, what happens if there is adverse selection that takes place without anybody trying to make it happen? Or the other way, what happens if good selection takes place? That is the issue that I spoke to that somehow that has to be dealt with.

I don't think there is that much difference between having voluntary or mandatory alliances as it pertains to risk selection. It may well be that it needs to be a retrospective adjustment. Clearly, there has to be a way to effectively spread those costs across all of the plans.

Mr. HOAGLAND. If you have a health alliance that has contracts with four health providers and one has cancer specialists and draws all the cancer patients, and another health provider has some family practitioners known for keeping people healthy, and for some reason, draws the healthy patient, there has to be an adjustment among the health plans.

Mr. GUSTAFSON. That is right.

Mr. HOAGLAND. So as long as we have strict rules governing those insurance companies that would issue basic indemnity policies that play across the board, a voluntary health alliance system could work?

Mr. GUSTAFSON. That is right.

Mr. HOAGLAND. These statistics you prepared spell that out?

Mr. GUSTAFSON. We attempted to do that. I am not a mathematician or lawyer or actuary. That is to my benefit maybe. That was the attempt. It does leave unanswered the question of, where do you come up with this information to know what these risk selection factors should be; and yet it has to be done.

Mr. HOAGLAND. Thank you.

Ms. Spencer, from the point of view of a company that issues supplemental insurance, AFLAC issues exclusively supplemental?

Ms. SPENCER. Yes.

Mr. HOAGLAND. The legislation—the administration's legislation and the Cooper legislation—is written in such a way as not to interfere with your operations?

Ms. SPENCER. That is my understanding, yes.

Mr. HOAGLAND. You have no objections with the way those two pieces of legislation are drafted?

Ms. SPENCER. We are interested in our focus on the ability of the American people to be able to exercise choice and purchase additional coverage, because that is preserved under the plans. As we understand them, we will leave the debate about which plan to companies with more of a vested interest in that.

Mr. HOAGLAND. As far as a single-payer plan, does that interfere with your operations?

Ms. SPENCER. Based on our experience in foreign countries where there is a form of national insurance, there is still a need for supplemental policies to provide cash for expenses of illness. There is a role, and we feel there would continue to be a role for our type products.

Mr. HOAGLAND. Thank you.

Chairman STARK. I want to thank the witnesses and note that Mr. Kleckner has arrived. I will excuse the witnesses.

Mr. Kleckner, did you bring a note from your mother?

Mr. KLECKNER. Mr. Chairman—

Chairman STARK. We will forgive you just this once.

We did make your testimony a part of the record. Perhaps you would like to summarize for me. Let's talk about a couple of things that kind of stood out in your testimony, because I was reading it, and you can add any other things you want.

You want to see that health insurance regulation remains a State government responsibility; and you oppose a Federal minimum benefit plan and Federal regulation of health insurance plans. I think you have come into conflict with most every bill introduced, except perhaps the Gramm bill.

I think most of us want Federal legislation. You oppose the State governments' having the option to impose single-payer plans, and I know the rest of my committee members here would have real problems because while many of us are not wedded to mandatory sorts of alliances, we are all pretty bound and determined that a State be allowed, if it meets other standards of nondiscrimination and stays within some kind of budgetary outlines, that if it chooses a single-payer plan—let's say Vermont is kind of leaning that way—we are not very inclined to deny that State that opportunity.

You have a lot of members in Vermont. Why would you and the Governor be at cross-purposes on that?

I don't mean that in a pejorative sense, because I am a cosponsor of the single-payer plan. It will be on the ballot in California. You have a lot of members there. What is your concern with single-payer?

STATEMENT OF DEAN R. KLECKNER, PRESIDENT, AMERICAN FARM BUREAU FEDERATION

Mr. KLECKNER. I was sitting here this morning. When I left to have lunch you were on the second panel. It proves to me that government can move rapidly when you have to. I do apologize. You have my testimony, and thank you for putting it in the record.

[The prepared statement and attachment follow:]

STATEMENT OF THE AMERICAN FARM BUREAU FEDERATION
TO THE HEALTH SUBCOMMITTEE OF THE
WAYS AND MEANS COMMITTEE
UNITED STATES HOUSE OF REPRESENTATIVES
REGARDING HEALTH CARE POLICY REFORM

Presented by Dean R. Kleckner, President
American Farm Bureau Federation

February 4, 1994

Mr. Chairman, thank you for this opportunity to present the views of the
American Farm Bureau Federation (AFBF) regarding health care policy reform.

The American Farm Bureau is the Nation's largest general farm
organization representing all 50 states and Puerto Rico with a membership of 4.2
million member families.

At our January 1994 annual meeting in Ft. Lauderdale, Florida, our voting
delegates adopted policies in regard to health and nutrition. A copy of those
policies is attached to this statement.

We are particularly interested in these hearings and in the work of your
subcommittee because health care and the financing of that care are of direct and
pressing concern to our membership. We believe you and your subcommittee are
serving the public interest by holding these hearings now in anticipation of major
public decisions that will be made in the months ahead.

Farm Bureau Goals

Farm Bureau policy establishes six broad principles that should guide
reforms.

We believe that health care is primarily the responsibility of the individual.
We strongly support efforts to improve the present health care delivery system.
Future health care policy changes should embrace the following principles:

(1) Promotion of personal wellness, fitness and preventive care as basic
health goals;

(2) Minimal government intervention in decisions between providers and
receivers of health care;

(3) Federal tax policies that encourage individuals to prepare for future
health care needs:

(4) Direct government financial assistance for those who are economically
unable to pay for health care needs;

(5) Government programs like Medicare and Medicaid properly compensate
providers; and

(6) Every possible effort to affect cost management while providing
accessible, high quality health care.

In our approach to this complex issue, we believe there are three areas
which need emphasis, understanding and support. These deal with the role of the
individual receiver of care, the role of providers of care and the role of the
government. All three of these roles are, of course, interwoven totally into the
health care profession and the health care delivery and information system.

At the core of any kind of health structure stands the individual.

Farm Bureau Concerns

We have reacted, along with all other Americans, to some of the positive suggestions in one or more of the half dozen or so major plans being presented by the President and by various groups of Representatives and Senators.

We fully support, for example, the President's and other's inclusion of a 100 percent deduction against income for income tax purposes for health insurance premium costs for the self-employed.

We also share the President's goals for improving rural health care delivery systems and encouraging young doctors and other health professionals to serve rural areas.

We, likewise, support many of the provisions of Senator Gramm's proposal, especially the "Medisave" tax-free accounts, which would broaden the choices for all of us when it comes to our own health care.

Likewise, the Michel bill, the Chafee bill and the Cooper-Grandy bill each contain positive ideas, such as malpractice liability reforms.

On the other hand, we find fault with several key suggestions pending before your subcommittee.

In the Presidential plan, we cannot support employer mandates. These will hit farm employers hard, forcing many out of businesses. Employer mandates shift health care financing responsibility from the individual to the employer.

There are several other aspects of the Administration's plan that we believe are unwise.

- We oppose the loss of the choice of physicians and hospitals that will be the natural results of forced creation of large health care provider networks.

- We oppose the creation of a federal bureaucracy to decide how much health care should be delivered and who should deliver it.

- We oppose the federal government limiting how much money individuals can spend on health care through the creation of a global budget.

- We oppose the federal government's control of health care financing through the creation of health alliances with vast regulatory and financial control powers, including price controls on health care plan premiums and fines and imprisonment for doctors and patients who try to conduct private medial transactions.

- We oppose a federal minimum benefit plan and the federal regulation of health insurance plans. Health insurance regulation should remain a state government responsibility.

- We oppose state governments having the option to impose single payer plans.

- We oppose granting state governments the power to set prices under fee-for-service arrangements.

We believe that the Administration's proposal does make important positive changes in suggesting that medicare recipients should have more choices in health care beyond passive acceptance of the one-size-fits-all medicare plan. We believe the idea of moving medicaid recipients into the mainstream of the health care system, with assistance to buy the same plans as offered other people, is also sound.

At the same time, we find no reason to adopt a single-payer system. Individuals lose control of health care financing decisions. Citizens lose the opportunity to receive specialized medical treatment as services must be limited to meet increasingly severe budget shortfalls. Rural areas will be particularly shortchanged under a single-payer system because they do not have the political influence to gain control of limited resources.

While the Cooper-Grandy managed competition approach avoids employer mandates, we feel it should be modified to be more market oriented. By definition, the term "managed competition" is internally inconsistent. We know what government "management" is, and we know about market competition. The Cooper-Grandy plan is long on government "management" and short on competition. The Cooper-Grandy plan suffers from many of the same federal regulatory control problems as the Administration's proposal. It will set the stage for a further growth of federal government control and rationing of health care in future years.

The various Republican plans likewise contain several attractive features, but need more work. The Republican plans propose that more federal regulations and controls and more federal spending will solve the real health care problems we face. We believe that the current level of federal control over health care is part of the problem and want to move more decision making back to individual providers and receivers of care.

In summary, Mr. Chairman, we look forward to working with you, the subcommittee, the full Ways and Means Committee and the several other House and Senate committees that are crafting this important legislation.

Our guiding star will be to improve the current system that is market based while providing more security and choice to individuals and families.

We prefer this approach because it will allow steady and progressive improvement in health quality, access and costs.

Attachments

Policy 159. Health:

We believe that health care is primarily the responsibility of the individual. We strongly support efforts to improve the present health care delivery system. Future health care policy changes should embrace the following principles:

(1)   Promotion of personal wellness, fitness and preventive care as basic health goals;

(2)   Minimal government intervention in decisions between providers and receivers of health care;

(3)   Federal tax policies that encourage individuals to prepare for future health care needs;

(4)   Direct government financial assistance for those who are economically unable to pay for health care needs; and

(5)   Government programs like Medicare and Medicaid properly compensating providers.

We support:

(1)   Every possible effort to affect cost management while providing accessible high quality health care;

(2)   Legislation to allow 100 percent federal income tax credits or tax deductions for those who self-finance their health insurance;

(3)   Greater use of non-physician providers to help relieve personnel maldistribution in the medical profession;

(4)   Efforts of medical schools to train additional qualified family physicians who intend to practice medicine in rural areas;

(5)   A program whereby Medicaid would assume nursing home expenses for a person whose net worth has been reduced to $20,000;

(6)   Economic inducements at state and local levels to encourage doctors to practice in rural areas and the restoration of equitable Medicare payments to rural hospitals and physicians;

(7)   State and federal government policies that provide incentives for medical and mental health services in rural areas;

(8)   Residency programs to provide postgraduate family physician training away from major metropolitan-based medical training centers;

(9)   Privately funded optional care delivery systems such as health maintenance organizations;

(10)   Efforts to reduce medical malpractice insurance costs;

(11)   Programs, including education, which support efforts to eradicate sexually transmitted diseases;

(12)   Legislation to require the use of the generic as well as the trade name on prescription drugs;

(13) Closer working relationships between organizations of family physicians, medical societies and health agencies;

(14) Teaching of balanced diet including foods from all four food groups--meat, milk, breads and cereals, and fruits and vegetables;

(15) Efforts by state Farm Bureaus to seek state legislation to certify nutritionists;

(16) Education of physicians, teachers and other health professionals to include the clinical application of sound nutritional principles;

(17) Recognition by USDA and FDA of studies and research in nutrition which are based on published standard research criteria whether funded by producer groups or other recognized research groups:

(18) Funding of nutrition research on relationships between agricultural products and coronary heart disease and cancer;

(19) A requirement that drug manufacturers label all inert as well as active ingredients contained in medicines;

(20) Third-party payer recognition for payment of outpatient treatment and preventive measurers;

(21) "Certificate of need" funding legislation to curb the over-building of hospital rooms;

(22) Research leading to a cure for AIDS;

(23) The belief that AIDS is a health issue and should not become a civil rights issue;

(24) Federal government incentives to the private sector for providing long-term health care; and

(25) Allowing veterans to receive medical care at local hospitals, to lessen costs of the services to the veteran and family and increase local hospital funds;

We oppose:

(1) Federal government interference with private enterprise by subsidizing professional medical services;

(2) Legislation or regulations that would jeopardize present volunteer emergency medical technician (EMT) systems;

(3) Federal guidelines that would close the obstetric wards in hospitals that do not meet annual requirements for number of births;

(4) Compulsory national health insurance and a national health plan in any form;

(5) Anyone dictating which foods should and should not be eaten. We deplore the use of taxpayers' money for the purpose of legislating or controlling the diets of American people; and

(6) Legislation which calls for employees to provide employees with health insurance throughout the calendar year of their employment."

Policy, General Labor Issues (in part):

"...We oppose legislation that would mandate health insurance to be provided by employees;"

We had mainly there the six broad principles that we think should guide all reforms. To your questions concerning Federal Government, State government and so forth——

Chairman STARK. Let me suggest that that might just be your membership's overall concern with the Federal Government, and much preferring State government in general, and I would accept that as a response; but if there is more to it, that is what I would really like to know.

Mr. KLECKNER. We, by policy, are opposed to a single-payer. My own feeling is that if it has to be a single-payer system, say there is no option better, let the State experiment with it. However, the studies that we have looked at and the personal experience that some of our people have had with relatives in Canada and other countries show us that rural parts of those countries have less access to health care, even though that is not—that is not in the title or that is not in the body.

Chairman STARK. You are right. Let me try and change your mind, though.

Medicare is a single-payer system, and your members who are over 65 wouldn't have insurance anyway, because most of them, if they are not California members, don't work for big corporations, and so most don't have a retirement plan. Their retirement plan is a free and clear form, and most don't have a retirement plan that is going to pick up insurance even if it existed for them after retirement. The only thing they have is Medicare.

In Susanville, Calif., there is a lot less access for the Medicare beneficiaries than there is in Oakland; but that is the same access problem whether you have got Blue Cross or Medicare or whatever you want.

I would hope that we could work together on the access issue, which is as important to me as an inner-city Representative as to my colleagues here who represent rural areas. Remembering that while we have a pretty good system, Medicare needs a lot of improvement; but there would be nothing for those of your members over 65 if we didn't have it.

All I am saying is that if a State like Vermont does it, as long as you can get the access thing solved, I am not so sure—this is free advice, worth what you pay for it—that single-payer becomes the enemy of your members. I will rest my case——

Mr. KLECKNER. You make a valid point with Medicare. My mother is still alive, and at age 84, soon to be 85, in good health in northern Iowa, obviously has Medicare.

Chairman STARK. And she can go if she chooses to Minnesota, to Rochester, to Mayo's; she could come to California, if she could afford the transportation, or to Ames, to a medical center there, or sign up for an HMO if she chose. You know, it ain't bad is all I am saying.

Mr. KLECKNER. Medicare, and I am not the expert on Medicare or health care that you are, Congressman, but Medicare has been around now for a good many years and has, I believe, taken the place of private health care in large part for those citizens over 65.

So I am not so sure that I agree with your earlier statement that they have no other health care available.

Chairman STARK. If we read the history, the reason they did it is because insurance companies quit insuring people as a policy once people got to be 60 or 65 years old; before 1968, you couldn't buy it, all the health insurance available in this country ended.

Mr. KLECKNER. That would be a concern today if we went back to that system.

Let me say that a couple of the areas that we will agree with, most of the current plans, as I understand them—moving toward portability, continued coverage for preexisting conditions—which, I believe, would take care of the age discrimination were we starting again. However we are not starting again.

Chairman STARK. Get that for all your members, because I agree we need portability and elimination of preexisting conditions. But those things, I don't think you are going to get voluntarily. We have them in a couple of States—New York has it to some extent, Hawaii has it.

Mr. KLECKNER. Portability?

Chairman STARK. Portability within the States. But I don't think you are going to get it unless the Federal Government says to all the States, you must have it.

Mr. KLECKNER. That is where we agree that in a bill—if we get one, and you probably will—portability needs to be a part of it.

Chairman STARK. OK.

Mr. KLECKNER. But we just have concerns about what we see in nations that have single-payer systems. Maybe we could do it better than they can. We think we have learned from their mistakes, but we have great concern about the results we see in a single-payer system.

You bring up the example of Medicare.

Chairman STARK. That is American. I am just saying that if that is the level of guarantee, and then you say OK, do what you want, you live in Iowa. There is a huge insurance company in Ames, Farmers.

Mr. KLECKNER. Principle Insurance is in Des Moines.

Chairman STARK. And you guys want to bid, provide a base system for the uninsured in Iowa and let them operate it for the States. I don't care. There has to be a minimum benefit, so if your mom moves from Iowa to California, you know she will have the same benefits available to her. That is all we ask.

Mr. KLECKNER. It has to be the Federal Government that does that.

Chairman STARK. We have got to set the standards. We need your help, because you speak with a great deal of authority in the other bodies. The farm States have many more votes percentage wise in the Senate, and if we are going to help everybody in this country, we are going to need a lot of support. We need yours.

Mr. KLECKNER. In this area of Medicare-Medicaid, one of the things that we have been concerned with over the years is the difference in payment levels between rural and urban areas. I think there cannot be a rational case made for that, or at least to the degree of difference there has been.

When I look at the President's plan, which in my opinion is the plan to look at. I know the Cooper bill has gotten oxygen lately. As I remember, and I listened to the President in the car when he spoke last September, and reading about it later, he commented that he was going to pay for part of his new plan by taking some money away from the Medicare area, some millions of dollars.

We see that if that happens—politically, it may not happen—we will already then be hurting rural America which because of age——

Chairman STARK. Let me tell you, I wrote the EACH, the essential access bill, and we wrote the RPCH stuff, the rural assistance. We wrote it because we recognized that there are problems. Now, there are political problems. There are probably a lot of little rural hospitals that should consolidate, a 3- or 5-bed hospital—but there isn't a—not one of my colleagues wants to go home and tell the small rural town, I closed your hospital. They aren't going to do this.

When they consolidated schools—we had 6 million football teams until we decided to consolidate high schools. There was a hell of a fight as to who got the consolidated school. Somehow we have to find a way politically to bring this access to rural America, and I think the President is committed to do that. I am not sure that this bill just automatically does it; but not only politically do we have to do it—it is because it is the right thing—there should not be any individual who doesn't have access to an insured plan and there shouldn't be anyone who doesn't really have access to good care. I think we are committed to do that.

We have to bring a lot of groups together, and you are right, we will start with the President's plan, that is what we are working on; and I don't know what is going to happen.

Mr. KLECKNER. Well, we don't disagree at all with the effort that you are making, that your committee is making—the President or the minority party or anybody on the issue. It needs to be addressed.

As I get around the country, I give a lot of speeches. I gave 104 formal speeches in 1993 in all parts of the country and a few overseas. I didn't make health care a part of all those speeches, but it was a part of a good many of them. After meetings, Farm Bureau meetings, urban or rural, if I talk about health care, often there will be a few people waiting to talk to me afterward; and it seems to me that the main issue in rural America that people are complaining about is the cost.

At this point, it is only 25 percent tax deductible for our insurance. In Iowa with our Farm Bureau group, it is a Blue Cross group, age rating, and my wife and I are toward the upper age, our five children are grown and married; with a Cadillac plan it, is now costing between $12,000 and $14,000 a year.

Chairman STARK. For the two of you?

Mr. KLECKNER. For the two of us, yes. But I would say for many farmers in the country that it is running from $5,000 to $10,000 a year, some under, some over. Some toward the $5,000 end per year, and only 25 percent tax deductible. You are still talking about a fairly hefty deductible and a good copay. What I am hearing from farmers and ranchers all over is not a concern about qualities by and large. There are always those who are left out.

One concern is cost. The second one the availability. Beyond that, yes, there are isolated instances et cetera, but nothing big. Then the employer mandates issue—when I was in South Dakota, I heard—you don't think about South Dakota being a dairy State.

Chairman STARK. Not when you come from Wisconsin.

Mr. KLECKNER. It was a dairyman with 150 or 175 cows with 2 full-time employees, and his response as we talked about this was, if I am forced to pay—he said, I would like to pay my employees' health insurance. I can't afford it today. If I am forced to do it, even at a reduced level, my cows are going to town the next day and I am going to revert to crop farming on my farm.

That is a concern.

Chairman STARK. What he is going to have to do is look at less than a buck an hour, maybe 70 cents for every hour he pays those hands, just like he withholds Social Security.

Now, he—in 1990, 1991 he got hit twice with 45-cent-an-hour wage increases. So he went up 90 cents in those 2 years, and he is still milking. He needs to look forward to that, and the hands will be covered by a State or Federal plan, and he won't have a responsibility. For him, we will have to put a minimum charge to the small business person or small farmer who has occasional employees.

Seasonal employees, we deal with that differently. For somebody who has periodic part-time or minimum-wage employees, we are going to have to have some kind of a minimum charge. But I think it would be more of that nature. He ain't going to like it, but I don't think it will break him either. Otherwise, I don't think we get a bill.

If it makes that member feel any better, I think that is about the level that we are thinking about. The committee is sympathetic to understanding that. Many of the small business entities or professional entities that don't provide insurance really aren't—don't have a lot of cash income, and we have to get those people in as well. So I would tell you that I don't think you are going to see a situation that would force that option to take place.

Mr. KLECKNER. The feeling that I am picking up, is that not every farmer and rancher in the country, is an employer with hired employees. Many are private entrepreneurs as I am on my farm in northern Iowa.

In California, many, many farmers would be employers of labor. Some of those would be—many probably in your State would be providing health insurance now, but not all. That is a concern.

My first comments are, the big concern I hear is cost; we have got to do something about the cost. Folks are not unhappy with the care that they are getting. This country has the best care in the world or nobody any better, probably. Second, if you live out in the middle of nowhere, it is availability of hospitals and doctors.

Chairman STARK. We may address it differently, but the President says the same thing. We cannot, whether it is just pointed at high-cost policies like you are faced with, because you can't be part of a group or whether it is an overall cost of the economy, $953 billion in 1993, we are looking forward to $1 trillion this year. That is just—in 3 years, that is the national debt.

I mean, that is one whole—there is no bigger business in the world than what this country spends on medical care. So from a two-pronged approach, first, to stop that rate of growth, or the country is going to be broke; and second, for groups like yourself, you should not have to pay $7,000 a head for insurance.

I know many people do. My wife and I, the government picks up ours, but it is probably more than $3,600 apiece, of which we pay a portion and the government pays the balance. That is Blue Cross—not Cadillac, but Blue Cross low option.

There is no reason that your insurance should cost $7,000 and mine should cost $3,500. It doesn't make any sense. Somehow we have got to even that out, and that is what we hope to do. Stick with us; we will try and get a bill out, and we won't do it without hearing from you.

Mr. KLECKNER. Mr. Chairman, again I appreciate being here and representing Farm Bureau. You do have our complete statement. In it are the policies that our members adopted at a national meeting in mid-January. And our farmer voting delegates are all farmers, and there were eight or nine from your State, 10 from my State, based on membership; and I think you know something about that. It was debated and we did adopt I think, basically, principles in our policies that will fit to some degree probably some of the six or seven bills that have been introduced to date, but we have got some problems with parts of all six or seven bills that have been introduced to date and probably you do too.

Chairman STARK. You are not alone. Let's get a chance to reason again, when we get a little closer, which one of those bills we are going to have.

Mr. KLECKNER. We want to work with you and the committee and the administration and the whole Congress on this, because health care costs—I would say health care insurance costs are for many farmers either the highest or among the two or three highest expenses that they have.

On my farm it would be—it would probably come—it is probably at the top. I have a 350-acre farm. It is a corn-soybean farm. We are going to raise hogs. I think our health insurance costs are the number one costs that I pay above fertilizers, above chemical and seed costs. Health care is number one. So it is major.

Chairman STARK. Thanks very much.

Mr. KLECKNER. Thank you.

Chairman STARK. The committee is adjourned.

[Whereupon, at 2:35 p.m., the hearing was adjourned.]

[Submissions for the record follow.]

581

Testimony to the

Health Subcommittee

of the Committee on Ways and Means

on the Mental Health Provisions of HR 1757

The Health Security Act of 1993

December 8, 1993

Submitted by   American Academy of Child and Adolescent Psychiatry
American Association for Marriage and Family Therapy
American Association for Partial Hospitalization
American Association of Children's Residential Centers
American Association of Pastoral Counselors
American Association of Psychiatric Services for Children
American Association of Private Practice Psychiatrists
American Counseling Association
American Family Foundation
American Occupational Therapy Association
American Psychiatric Association
American Psychiatric Nurses Association
American Psychoanalytic Association
American Psychological Association
American Society for Adolescent Psychiatry
Anxiety Disorders Association of America
Association for the Advancement of Psychology
Bazelon Center for Mental Health Law
Children and Adults with Attention Deficit Disorders
Child Welfare League of America
Cult Awareness Network
Family Service America, Inc.
Federation of Families for Children's Mental Health
International Association of Psychosocial Rehabilitation Services
National Association for Rural Mental Health
National Association of Counties
National Association of Homes and Services for Children
National Association of Psychiatric Treatment Centers for Children
National Association of Protection and Advocacy Systems
National Association of Social Workers
National Association of State Mental Health Program Directors
National Community Mental Health Care Council
National Depressive and Manic Depressive Association
National Federation of Societies for Clinical Social Work
National Foundation for Depressive Illness
National Mental Health Association
National Organization of State Associations for Children
Society for Education & Research in Psychiatric-Mental Health Nursing

For further information, call: Joe Manes, Bazelon Center, (202) 467-5730.
Peter Newbould, American Psychological Association, (202) 336-5889

TESTIMONY TO THE

HEALTH SUBCOMMITTEE

OF THE COMMITTEE ON WAYS AND MEANS

ON THE MENTAL HEALTH PROVISIONS OF HR 1757,

THE HEALTH SECURITY ACT OF 1993

DECEMBER 8,1993

Chairman Stark. Mr. Thomas. Members of the Subcommittee:

The undersigned mental health organizations are pleased to present our views on mental health provisions in the Health Security Act. Thank you for making our views part of the record of the hearing you held on October 26.

The hearing permits us to examine the mounting evidence that mental health benefits are a sound investment in the healthcare of our nation and to correct erroneous notions about the cost and effectiveness of mental health treatment. It also provides us the opportunity to evaluate HR 1757. the Administration bill introduced on November 20, from the viewpoint of people who need mental health services.

We commend the President and Hillary Rodham Clinton for their leadership in bringing healthcare reform to the fore. And we want particularly to acknowledge the valiant efforts of Tipper Gore. who headed the work group on mental health and has been an ardent and eloquent champion of mental health services from the beginning.

Our Position on Mental Health Benefits in Health Care Reform Legislation

Our position is clear and explicit: mental health care must be an integral part of healthcare reform. Some of us may emphasize one element of the overall benefit and some another. according to the needs of our particular constituencies. But we stand united behind the following principle: **Mental health benefits must be provided through a system of organized care, with a full continuum of services, and must not be subject to arbitrary limits in amount or duration of services which are not imposed on other healthcare benefits.** The position has found significant support in Congress. Over 218 members of the House and 18 Senators have endorsed concurrent resolutions calling for parity and the inclusion of a comprehensive mental health benefit within any healthcare reform initiative.

Without a comprehensive flexible array of mental health services, the basic benefits package will neither serve the essential needs of the population nor be cost effective. We ask you to soundly reject the spurious reasoning that argues against comprehensive mental health coverage. Much of it is based on conditions which no longer exist and assumptions that are badly outdated. This coverage is far too important to our nation and to the millions of people who suffer from mental disorders to allow it to be buried under the dust of antiquity.

The Positive Elements in the Health Security Act of 1993

The Clinton plan has many broad features that are clearly in the best interests of the general public as well as people with mental disorders. Most importantly, it assures universal coverage to all lawful residents regardless of income and job status. In disproportionate numbers people with serious mental illnesses now are without health coverage at all because they are not in the work force.

Further. the proposal eliminates annual and lifetime dollar limits on healthcare services. abolishes pre-existing condition exclusions. includes coverage for assessment. diagnosis and crisis intervention. creates a new community-based long-term care program. and stresses prevention and early intervention. These aspects of the plan are tremendously important to our constituencies We also recognize the significant value of the overall benefits package to the populations for which we advocate. After all. individuals with mental illnesses get other illnesses too

The Administration s proposal makes mental health services an integral part of t benefits package. It clearly articulates the principle of parity between the treatment of illness and other illnesses by committing to full comprehensive benefits without arbitrar on January 1 2001. three years after the onset of the program However. until full e achieved. the interim mental health benefits in the plan contain severe limits on amc duration and excessive copayments which substantially interfere with their accessibility b; with mental illness. Eligibility for mental health services should be determined on the medical or psychological necessity, not by overly restrictive criteria like life endangerme discuss the problems with the interim benefit in more detail below

Our Objectives for Healthcare Reform

As the deliberations around healthcare reform unfold. there are key objecti organizations and the people they represent want Congress to pursue:

♦ Congress should endorse and enact the Administration's commitment to full c for mental health services to begin on the date of initial implementation of the plan rat in 2001.

♦ Congress should remove the discriminatory barriers to access for low-incom(with mental disorders caused by copayments and inadequate subsidies.

♦ Congress should add incentives to assist the integration of public and privat(health providers to end the two-tier system of care prevailing today.

♦ Congress should assure that each health plan permits maximum consumer c provider selection and participation in treatment planning, confidentiality of records process procedures.

♦ Congress should require that quality assurance standards and access to serv supported by monitoring mechanisms to assure that consumers receive the amount and care they need.

Why Equity Now

The Clinton plan for health care reform contains a firm unequivocal commit comprehensive mental health services in 2001, three years after the effective c implementing the Act. The date is not dependent on any other factor such as approva state plan for integrating mental health services or cost savings in the interim peric appreciate the Administration's commitment to eventual equity. However, we urg treatment for mental and physical disorders when the overall program goes into effect We agree with Senator Wellstone. who reminded us in his Roll Call article that "those cannot wait until 2001 for the phase-in."[1]

There are compelling public policy reasons for making comprehensive benefits a from the start rather than 2001. The absence of a comprehensive benefit will pe unnecessary national crisis for mental illness, both within and outside the health care Coverage for a full continuum of mental health services is essential to ensuring access in the most appropriate and cost-effective setting. Until the phase-in occurs, care will be by the services covered rather than the services the patient needs. The imbalance car mental health care costs over the short term and thereby fuel the arguments of some wh that mental health services are too expensive.

The societal payoffs of effective services for people with severe mental illness ar increased earning power. less dependency on public programs of support. reduced pre' the correctional system. fewer social problems. Individuals and their familie reintegrated and their personal satisfaction enhanced. Experts even project ar

Wellstone P.. "Mental Health Care is a Right for All, Too. But Clinton Plan Relies T Treatment. May Make Cost Too High to Afford " Roll Call Health Care Reform Polic' 1993 reduction in general health care costs, as proper mental health care will reduce use of the general health system.[2]

The three year period between enactment of the plan in 1994 and implementation in 1998 is sufficient time for providers to develop the management capacity and procedures to properly administer a comprehensive plan. Artificial limits on care are not only costly to the consumer but unnecessary as well. The limits create disincentives to move toward a truly flexible comprehensive benefit in 2001.

Finally, we are fearful that 2001 may never arrive for those suffering from mental disorders if full implementation is delayed. The goal may be made hostage to the achievement of cost savings or other considerations that could excuse the Administration and Congress from the promise of equitable coverage.

Deficiencies in the Plan for People with Mental Illness

The President's interim plan for mental health services raises a number of serious problems for people with mental illness which demonstrate why a limited benefit is unworkable. We have divided our concerns into two sections, the first relates to the mental health benefit provisions; the second, to problems in other parts of the bill which have serious consequences for people with mental illness.

A. Defects in the Interim Mental Health Benefit

1. Limitations on Inpatient/Residential Services

The plan permits extension of inpatient/residential services beyond 30 days only on the basis that the patient is a threat to himself or others, needs drug regimen adjustment or requires somatic therapy. These limited bases represent interference with the patient's ability to obtain appropriate treatment. Medical and psychological necessity should be the criteria for determining length of stay. The trade-off features in the benefit compound the problem. For example, after drawing down 30 inpatient days to use the first 60 days of the intensive nonresidential benefit, individuals may find they have "lost" access to the inpatient benefit because of the overly strict criteria for obtaining additional days.

2. Restrictions in Intensive Non-residential Treatment

The intensive non-residential benefit offers a bold and progressive approach to treating people with serious mental illness. However, it contains conditions which make the services difficult to access. The initial 60-days are available only on the basis of trade-offs for inpatient care. This arrangement forces individuals whose illnesses are often unpredictable to relinquish their inpatient safety net to utilize community based intensive services. The choice places an inappropriate decision burden on people with mental illness. Their conclusion is likely to be based on fear rather than clinical appropriateness.

To use the second sixty days, an individual must pay both a one-day deductible and 50% copayment. Even in the low-copay plans, using the 60 days will cost the individual $1500, none of which counts toward the out-of-pocket limit on the individuals total health expenditures.

Further, while the benefit specifies four "treatment purposes", it also permits plans to employ their own criteria for determining who can receive services. This discretion can result in plans choosing the narrowest treatment purpose, thus further limiting access.

The combination of trade-offs and high co-payment requirements diminishes the value of this innovative approach as an alternative to more expensive inpatient care. Only if these services are fully available will consumers have a true choice to utilize the least restrictive environment.

---

[2]See p 12. In 16-19 For example, Strain, J.J., Lyons, J.S. and J.S. Hammer, "Cost Offset from a Psychiatric Consultation-Liaison Intervention with Elderly Hip Fracture Patients." American Journal of Psychiatry. Vol 148 (8) August 1991

585

3.   Confusion on Psychotherapy Substitution

The bill attempts to offset a totally inadequate 30-visit benefit with a provision that allows health plans the discretion to substitute four outpatient psychotherapy visits for one day of hospital care to reduce or shorten hospitalization. It is unclear whether the plan's discretion applies to determining the individual situations where the substitution is applicable or the availability of substitution entirely. If the latter. the provision can create serious adverse selection problems. as discussed below. Patients who reach maximum limits on outpatient psychotherapy (as with other limited services in the bill) are faced with the same difficult and, in some cases. life threatening situation: no coverage for needed services. Unlike any other health benefit, individuals suffering from a mental disorder are forced to accept arbitrary and discriminatory limits on care vital to their recovery.

4.   Inadequate Incentives to Integrate Public and Private Systems

At the present time, there are two tiers of mental health services: the publicly funded state system which serves as a safety net for the most seriously ill: and the private system which relies on multiple funding sources. including a significant percentage of private pay patients. Together with the President, we support the integration of these two systems. Under an integrated approach. the role of the public system undoubtedly will change--probably by moving away from acute service delivery toward emphasis on support services, quality assurance and innovation. Congress should assist the process by creating incentives for states to integrate their system with the national plan while protecting those vulnerable populations who will be at risk if state mental health service dollars are diverted into other purposes. In addition, we recommend that Congress authorize the states. applying Federal standards. to designate publicly supported mental health and substance abuse programs as *essential community providers* to ensure that people in low income areas will have access to services and promote the integration of the public and private systems.

5.   Cut-back on Collateral Services

The latest revision to the plan reduces the mental health benefit by including collateral services for family members within the already inadequate 30-visit limit on psychotherapy. In the October 27 draft bill, 30 visits for collateral services were in addition to psychotherapy. Visits with family members are often highly effective means for treating the individual with mental illness.

6.   Barriers to Services for Children

The interim benefit creates barriers and disincentives to services for children. The requirement that the individual pose a threat to himself or others to receive residential treatment beyond 30 days is wholly inappropriate for children. Similarly, having to substitute home-based, behavioral aide or day treatment services for residential care will leave parents with seriously ill youngsters with fewer future choices. They may forego effective community treatment in order not to lose their residential safety net. The high copayments may be a particular barrier for children who are dependent on others to gain access to needed treatment.

Instead of building barriers and disincentives, public policy should actively encourage early identification and intervention for childhood problems. The Clinton plan endorses this approach for conditions other than mental illness. The failure to do so for our children only results in devastated young lives and higher future costs as untreated problems worsen into disability.

7.   Inappropriate Services for People with Dual Diagnoses

People with substance abuse disorders and mental illness are particularly at risk of undertreatment because the limits on services apply to both conditions. The needs of a dually diagnosed individual may quickly exceed the limits in the interim benefits package. The effect will be that people with substance abuse disorders and mental illness will be forced to obtain care in the overburdened public system much sooner than others not so seriously impaired. We recommend that Congress recognize the special situation of the dually diagnosed population. Only a comprehensive benefit would accurately respond to their needs.

B. Other Weaknesses of Particular Concern to People with Mental Illness

1.   Caps on Premium Subsidy

The plan contains premium subsidies to low income individuals and small businesses. If the subsidies required in a given year exceed the estimates for the year, an additional appropriation is needed. We believe the failure to make the subsidy payments automatic potentially threatens guaranteed access to care. If Congress fails to enact additional revenues, the plans can pare back benefits. Given the historic stigma associated with mental illness and substance abuse, we fear these benefits will be cut first when shortfalls occur. We recommend that the legislation contain guarantees that no one can be denied any benefit under the plan because of insufficient funds for subsidies.

2.   Unaffordability of Services

The poorest and the sickest among us become even more vulnerable when access to care is contingent on payment of deductibles and coinsurance. For many Americans living in the shadows of economic despair even the most minimal copayment can be prohibitive. We believe that individual responsibility is a valuable principle, but it should not become a mantra invoked to legitimize continued discrimination against low-income citizens, regardless of their disability or diagnosis. Requiring 50% copayments for outpatient psychotherapy and intensive non-residential services and one-day deductibles, for example, represent excessive cost-sharing requirements which will inhibit access to critical services by people with mental illness.

We support a sliding scale for copayments to help low income people, with adequate subsidies to prevent premiums, deductibles, and coinsurance from becoming barriers to appropriate care. In addition, we believe all copayments and deductibles for mental health services should be counted toward the out-of-pocket limit, just as they are for all other benefits in the plan.

3.   Inadequate Quality Standards for Delivery of Services

Individuals with chronic illness, both mental and physical, are at risk of being denied essential services in managed care settings. The experience with HMOs in limiting care to people with severe mental illness demonstrates that providers operating under capitated premiums have strong incentives to undertreat high cost patients.

Health care reform legislation should not create a culture in which clinically necessary services are inappropriately denied or are approved too late. Instead the legislation should emphasize early intervention, quality assurance standards and effective monitoring to assure that consumers receive services in the amounts and settings appropriate to their conditions.

4.   Potential for Adverse Selection

We anticipate that some health plans will provide their enrolles with better mental health care either by offering four additional outpatient psychotherapy visits for one inpatient day if the additional treatment would prevent or reduce hospitalization, or by providing more effective or higher quality mental health services overall. Other plans may begin to move toward the 2001 goal of comprehensive benefits earlier. The "better" plans will naturally attract more people with mental illness. However, the Clinton proposal would penalize these plans because of the vague rules on risk adjustments for plans who have higher costs. We recommend that plans which have higher costs because of the flexibility of their benefits or the quality of their services be clearly eligible for cost adjustments.

5.   Strictness of Long-Term Care Eligibility Criteria

We are pleased that the proposed eligibility criteria for the home and community-based long-term care benefit reflects an understanding of the need to use different approaches to determining eligibility for physical and mental disabilities. However, the eligibility criteria are set at a level of severity that permits only people with extreme dysfunction of a chronic nature to receive services. The eligibility rules do not recognize the cyclical nature of the active symptoms of mental illness. We recommend that the criteria recognize that people with serious, persistent mental illness may need long-term support services on an intermittent basis.

These are serious problems areas for people with mental illness. They represent challenges to the Congress to correct the significant flaws in the Administration's plan, to enrich it and move it to the next level where true parity between mental health and physical health can be realized.

The Magnitude of the Mental Illness Problem in the United States

An enormous number of people are affected by mental health problems and will benefit from comprehensive mental health coverage. An estimated 41.4 million adults have had a mental disorder at some time in their lives[3] and about 7.5 million children suffer from mental and emotional disturbances such as depression, autism and attention deficit disorder.[4] We also know that about one-fifth of those afflicted with AIDS will develop AIDS-related cognitive dysfunction and two-thirds will develop neuropsychiatric problems.[5] These are people who often cannot obtain mental health services under the current system. Only about one-third of the children and adolescents who need treatment ever receive it.[6] Among adults, one out of six individuals with serious mental health problems gets needed care.[7] And one need only look under the nearest bridge to see homeless persons with mental illness with no access to mental health services. Persons with significant mental health problems are legion within the ranks of the uninsured and the underinsured. And even those fortunate enough to have insurance coverage too often find their treatment limited by lifetime or annual limitations, discriminatory copayments, and other cost containment devices that eke financial savings out of the mental torment of the afflicted.

We cannot afford to write off so many of our people by excluding or only minimally covering mental health services in the reformed health care system. It is a matter of justice and it makes good economic sense to assure access to needed mental health treatment.

Untreated Mental Health Problems Exact a High Price

Consider for a moment the costs currently borne by society because mental health coverage is so woefully inadequate. Nearly a third of the nation's homeless persons have a severe mental illness.[8] A majority of the 30,000 suicides in America each year can be attributed to a mental or addictive disorder.[9] Major depression accounts for more bed days (people out of work and in bed) than any impairment except cardiovascular disorders.[10] Persons with job-related stress, anxiety and depression miss an average of 16 work days per year. Persons with untreated mental illnesses consume almost twice as much medical care as the average individual.[11] Add to the mix the thousands of persons with mental illnesses who are denied treatment, but instead languish in high-cost prison and jail cells. Add in the costs of unfulfilled human promise, education not pursued, work not obtained, contributions to society

---

[3]Bourbon, K. H.; Rae, S., Locke, Z., Narrow, E.; and Regier, D., "Estimating the Prevalence of Mental Disorders in U.S. Adults from the Epidemiologic Catchment Area Survey," *Public Health Reports*, Vol. 107, No. 6, November-December, 1992.

[4]U.S. Congress, Office of Technology Assessment. *Children's Mental Health: Problems and Services—Background Paper*, OTA-BP-H.33 (Washington, DC. U.S. Government Printing Office, December, 1986).

[5]Detmer, W.M. and F.G. Lu, "Neuropsychiatric Complications of AIDS: A Literature Review," Intl. Psychiatry in Medicine, Vol. 16 (1) 1986.

[6]U.S. Congress, Office of Technology Assessment, op. cit.

[7]Manderscheid, R et al., "Congruence of Service Utilization Estimates from the Epidemiologic Catchment Area Project and Other Sources," Arch of Gen. Psychiatry, Vol. 50 February, 1993.

[8]Interagency Council on the Homeless, *Outcasts on Main Street: Report of the Federal Task Force on Homelessness and Severe Mental Illness.* (ADM) 92.1904. Washington, DC 1992.

[9]National Center for Health Statistics, Public Health Services, U S. Dept. of Health and Human Services 1993. Unpublished data from Division of Vital Statistics.

[10]National Advisory Mental Health Council, Health Care Reform for Americans with Severe Mental Illness: Report of the National Advisory Mental Health Council, Rockville, Maryland: National Institute of Mental Health 1993

[11]Borus, J.F , Olendski, M C., et al., "The Offset Effect of Mental Health Treatment on

not made. These human costs are monumental: even in hard dollars and cents. they are staggering. The costs associated with SSI. SSDI. welfare programs. incarceration. and divorce are equally enormous--estimated at $74.9 billion in 1990.[12] These costs are being paid every day, by people like you and me. They are being paid out in the human tragedies wreaked on families and their relatives with mental illnesses. Coverage limits so prevalent in private insurance today can shift catastrophic costs onto families. forcing many into bankruptcy or long term indebtedness. Lack of options can force persons into hospitalization. when broader coverage could permit them to be more appropriately and more cheaply treated in the community. Or worse. lack of comprehensive benefits delays needed treatment until a crisis occurs.

<u>The Effectiveness of Mental Health Treatment</u>

All relevant research tells us that mental health treatment is effective. A whole new armamentarium of interventions available for treatment has emerged since President Kennedy launched the community mental health movement in 1963. Medications like lithium and clozapine have worked miracles for some patients, while others have experienced dramatic success through psychotherapy, psychiatric rehabilitation programs, residential treatment, partial hospitalization, crisis intervention, day treatment, and in-home services. For most persons, the days are gone when long-term hospitalization and custodial care were the only services utilized. Today, most mental disorders can successfully be treated without hospitalization. Community based intensive treatment programs and services, such as psychiatric rehabilitation and partial hospitalization, have been shown to have a positive long term effect of significantly reducing hospital utilization, increasing the level of functioning and improving the individual's quality of life. Nearly 80% of patients with manic depression can be restored to essentially normal lives. Outpatient treatment for anxiety disorders is both effective and relatively inexpensive. Most schizophrenia symptoms can now be controlled, significantly reducing the relapse rate of patients.[13] And companies around the nation are also discovering that relatively minimal mental health interventions can dramatically increase worker productivity and reduce absenteeism.

<u>Mental Healthcare is a Good Investment</u>

Mental healthcare is not as expensive nor are the costs rising as rapidly as many other sectors of health care. Three independent studies between 1971 and 1985 found that mental health costs have remained relatively constant over the last 20 years, ranging from 9-11 percent for total treatment costs.[14] When combined with substance abuse treatment, mental healthcare ranks 25th in the factors influencing the increase in health care costs.[15]

Good mental healthcare is also a good deal because it can help reduce other physical healthcare costs. One investigator found that untreated persons with panic disorders mimicked heart patients and were often misdiagnosed and subjected to needless, ineffective, and expensive treatments.[16] Other studies have shown that general inpatient medical care can be cut by as much as 70% following mental health treatment, and outpatient utilization can be lowered by 20%.[17] In a study of the Federal Employees Health Benefits Plan, patients with chronic medical diseases who received psychotherapy used 56% fewer medical services than those who

[12]National Advisory Mental Health Council, op. cit.

[13]Ibid.

[14]Ibid. See also, Rice, D.P., Kelman, S., Miller, L.S., et al., Economic Costs of Alcohol and Drug Abuse and Mental Illness: 1985, DHHS Pub. No. (ADM) 90-1694, Rockville, Maryland, ADAMHA, 1990; Harwood, H.J. and Napolitano, D.M., et al., Economic Costs to Society of Alcohol and Drug Abuse and Mental Illness: 1980, Research Triangle Park, North Carolina, Research Triangle Institute, 1984; and Cruze, A M., et al., Economic Costs to Society of Alcohol and Drug Abuse and Mental Illness, 1977, Rockville, Maryland, ADAMHA, 1981.

[15]Modern Health Care's compendium of Cost Factors: Coddington.

[16]National Institute of Mental Health, Memorandum from Alan Leshner, Deputy Director, Concerning cost-effectiveness of mental health services, Rockville, Maryland, 1993

[17]Mumford, E., and H I Schlesinger, et al. "A New Look at Evidence About Reduced Cost of Medical Utilization Following Mental Health Treatment." American Journal of Psychiatry, Vol. 141 (10) October,

589

did not receive psychotherapy.[3] The National Institute of Mental Health has estimated that general medical costs could be reduced by as much as $1.2 billion through the use of associated mental health treatment.[19] These savings make mental healthcare a sound investment--especially when mental health services are well managed.

Managed Care and Mental Health

Managed care is an area in which the mental health community has substantial experience, both good and bad. An estimated 48 percent of people with health insurance are already enrolled in some type of managed behavioral health program.[20]

We appreciate that care management is a central feature of the cost containment strategies in the healthcare reform plan. As we describe above, we are concerned that care be managed properly so that consumers receive services in amounts and settings appropriate to their conditions. We know this can be done.

Many large businesses (like Honeywell, Chevron, Pacific Bell, and IBM) now know that managed care techniques are as effective--and often more effective--than the imposition of arbitrary and discriminatory limits on mental health care. For example, McDonnell Douglas Helicopter Company realized a decline in per capita costs of 34% under a managed mental health benefit, including a 50% reduction in psychiatric inpatient costs. First National Bank of Chicago removed its mental health coverage limits and also reduced inpatient costs by 50% over five years under a managed care approach.[21] We believe the Congress should take notice of such experiences and build upon their successes by removing all discriminatory barriers to mental health services once and for all.

Seize the Moment Before It Passes

Skeptics might question whether it is feasible to improve upon the President's benefit package at a time when cost considerations are so prominent. But we assert that it is not only feasible, it is also prudent. The availability of a broad array of community based mental health services can produce the offset in costs indicated by research. The sooner these services become fully available, the sooner the savings will be realized. Major businesses have achieved significant offsets and savings by eliminating discriminatory features in the plan design and permitting the mental health benefit to be managed on the basis of medical necessity. Their experience should weigh heavily in your judgments, because it reflects a broader reality than a narrow technical perspective dominated by arcane rules for "scoring" savings. The offsets demonstrated through research and real-world application have greater validity than conjectural and abstract mathematical calculations.

The time to fix flaws and address known problems is now. With the House Working Group on Mental Health/Mental Illness and its Senate counterpart, and the members of this subcommittee, the mental health community is fortunate indeed. We look forward to working closely with all of you and your colleagues in helping to shape the mental health benefit to serve the needs of our people.

[18]Schlesinger, H.J., Mumford, E., Glass, G.V., et al., "Mental Health Treatment and Medical Care Utilization in a Fee-For-Service System: Outpatient Mental Health Treatment Following the Onset of a Chronic Disease." American Journal of Public Health, Vol. 73 (8) April, 1993

[19]National Advisory Mental Health Council, op. cit

[20]Open Minds. Managed Behavioral Health Market Share in the United States, Gettysburg, PA, 1993.

[21]McDonnell Douglas Corporation. *McDonnell Douglas Corporation Employee Assistance Program Financial Offset Study: 1985-1989.* St. Louis, MO: McDonnell Douglas Corporation and Alexander

 AMERICAN CHIROPRACTIC ASSOCIATION

1701 Clarendon Boulevard, Arlington, Virginia 22209   (703) 276-8800
FAX (703) 243-2593

STATEMENT SUBMITTED TO

THE COMMITTEE ON WAYS and MEANS

SUBCOMMITTEE ON HEALTH

U.S. HOUSE OF REPRESENTATIVES

ON

THE PRESIDENT'S "HEALTH SECURITY ACT"

H.R.3600 and S.1757

FEBRUARY 4, 1994

On behalf of the American Chiropractic Association's 23,000 members, and the millions of Americans who regularly benefit from their care, I would like to thank you, Mr. Chairman, for the opportunity to submit this testimony.

First, I want to stress ACA's desire to work with Congress in addressing the central issues of health care reform· high health care costs and the lack of access to basic health care services for millions. We welcome the opportunity to work with Congress toward systemic reforms that will guarantee access to affordable health care for all Americans regardless of their income; will help contain health care costs; and will guarantee consumers the freedom to choose their health care provider. ·ACA has called for reforms of this nature for many years and our resolve remains as strong today as ever. We are anxious to help tackle the health care crisis which has left far too many Americans exposed to the great physical and economic risks associated with their inability to obtain appropriate health care services.

While we applaud President and Mrs. Clinton for elevating health care reform to the top of the national agenda, the ACA remains deeply concerned with certain aspects of President Clinton's Health Security Act (H.R.3600/S.1757). First, the "comprehensive benefits package" to which all Americans would be entitled does not guarantee that chiropractic services will be available to consumers. Because these services are not specifically enumerated in the benefits package, the health plans envisioned under the legislation would be free to include or exclude them at their discretion. Managed care plans -- presumably similar to the plans that would form under H.R.3600 -- historically have not adequately covered chiropractic services. Our fear is that chiropractic services would continue to be excluded from these plans in the absence of a statutory requirement that they be covered.

We are also concerned about the plan's potential impact on the entire community of non-allopathic health care providers. By relying so heavily on managed care health delivery plans, the legislation would permit unfair limitations on opportunities for health professionals to participate in the provider networks that would be established. This could vastly reduce the ability of non-allopaths to treat the millions of patients they currently serve and could also impede any future consumers who may wish to avail themselves of their care. Unless the plan is amended to "level the managed care playing field" for all licensed providers, the participation of D.C.s and others will remain a hollow promise. In the cost control environment envisioned under H.R.3600, dominant health provider groups will guard the "turf" they perceive as theirs even more jealously than they do today. Unless managed care plans are prohibited from engaging in exclusionary and discriminatory practices, the likelihood of having a range of providers available through these plans will remain small and both providers and consumers will suffer for it.

COVERAGE OF CHIROPRACTIC BENEFITS

Once again, our foremost concern is that chiropractic services are not covered under this plan. The "comprehensive benefits" package does not specifically list chiropractic services as a guaranteed benefit, and while theoretically covered as a "health care professional service," decisions of whether to cover chiropractic care would be left entirely to health plans. In other words, there would be no guarantee that consumers would have access to chiropractic care even if they specifically requested it. This would not only be unfair to the country's 20 million current chiropractic patients, but it would also establish a system that failed to guarantee consumer access to one of the most cost effective forms of care available.

National health care reform should encourage the use of cost effective care, not discourage it. This is especially true of chiropractic care, which has proven to be the most effective treatment for low-back pain -- the health care condition most prevalent among working-age Americans.[6] As a new study commissioned by the Ontario Ministry of Health reveals, "there is an overwhelming body of evidence indicating that chiropractic management of low-back pain is more cost effective than medical management." In fact, the renown health economists who conducted the study were so impressed with chiropractic care, they recommended that government policies actively encourage patients with low-back pain to visit D.C.s as the first course of treatment. Furthermore, the report recommended that chiropractors serve as "gatekeepers" for patients with these conditions.[7] (It is interesting to note that the study's recommendation for chiropractic "gatekeepers" came after ACA made a similar recommendation in testimony before the House Ways & Means Subcommittee on Health in April of 1993. At the time, many viewed such an assertion as extraordinary, but the Ontario study should persuade all but the most bias critics that the proposal has merit.)

Chiropractic care is covered extensively under most fee-for-service insurance plans, but, as stated above, coverage dramatically declines under managed care arrangements. According to one recent survey, 85% of employers provide coverage for chiropractic services under their fee-for-service health care plans.[8] However, this contrasts sharply with the fact that nationwide, only 16% of HMOs provide chiropractic care.[9] Since the most economically attractive incentives in H.R.3600 would lead consumers toward low-cost sharing HMO-type plans, one can understand the anxiety with which chiropractic practitioners and patients view the proposal. If today's HMOs evolve into tomorrow's "low cost sharing plans", the historical pattern of denying consumers access to chiropractic care may very well continue.

This is why we are so adamant that chiropractic services be specified in the benefits package. Without such specific assurances, we have little doubt that managed care plans will continue to discriminate against chiropractic care. As a non-invasive, non-pharmaceutical form of holistic health care, chiropractic is the leading "alternative" to traditional medicine in this country. As such, it is sufficiently unique from other health care approaches that one cannot assume that a benefits package includes it unless these services are definitively listed. In light of this, it is clear to ACA that without specific guarantees of coverage, millions of chiropractic patients will have their access to these unique services jeopardized by a system that is dependent upon managed care plans.

We understand that, in addition to HMO and PPO style health plans, H.R.3600 would provide consumers with the choice of a fee-for-service plan and a "point-of-service" option. Both of these avenues, however, would entail significantly higher costs to consumers, and thus, the legislation would erect economic barriers to health plan options where choice of provider is more extensive. We believe that regardless of the type of plan a consumer selects, they should be free

---

[6] Mason, James, M.D., *Press Release*, Agency for Health Care Policy and Research, U.S. Department of Health and Human Services, April 20, 1992.

[7] Manga P, et al, *The Effectiveness And Cost Effectiveness Of Chiropractic Management Of Low-Back Pain*, Pran Manga & Associates Inc. Ottawa Ontario, August 1993.

[8] Beresford L., "Is It Time To Back Chiropractic?," *Business and Health*, December 1991.

[9] *Marion Merrill Dow Managed Care Digest*, HMO Edition, 1993.

to choose chiropractic care if they desire it. Since we have seen how managed care plans consistently deny patients coverage of these services, we are convinced that the most effective way to ensure access to them is to specifically enumerate "chiropractic services" as a covered benefit under any benefits package approved by Congress. Specific language to amend H.R.3600 in this way is contained in the attached set of amendments.

ANY WILLING PROVIDER

Even if chiropractic services are explicitly covered under a comprehensive benefits package, as ACA recommends they should be, H R 3600 still provides no guarantee that consumers would enjoy the freedom to select the health care provider of their choice for covered services. While the bill would permit consumers to choose among three different types of plans -- and while this may represent more choice than many Americans now have -- we feel that truly effective health care reform should provide consumers with a low-cost option that provides access to a range of state-authorized health providers. We propose to do this by establishing a requirement that every American be offered at least one "any-willing-provider" health plan.

These types of plans are conceptually simple. If a state licensed or authorized health provider is willing to meet the operating terms of a health plan -- such measures as fee discounting, utilization review, and adherence to quality standards -- he or she should be permitted to participate in that plan. Under such an arrangement, costs can be adequately controlled through the mechanisms mentioned above, through beneficiary cost sharing or through a combination of both.

We are well aware that "any-willing-provider" provisions are not *en vogue*, but in our judgment they are the best way to ensure that consumers enjoy both the low-costs associated with managed care plans and genuine choice of provider. Again, suggested amendatory language is contained in ACA's attached proposal.

HEALTH CARE PROVIDER ANTI-DISCRIMINATION

In addition to an "any-willing-provider" provision, Congress should ensure a broad range of consumer choices through enforceable health provider anti-discrimination language. Non-allopathic health providers care for hundreds of millions of Americans ever year and consumers want assurances that they will continue to enjoy access to highly valued professionals such as chiropractors, psychologists, optometrists, nurses, podiatrists and others.

Amendatory language to help ensure the availability of these providers has been developed by the ACA after consultation with a dozen other national health provider organizations. The proposed language would prohibit health plans from excluding providers from provider networks based solely on the "type, class or license" of that professional. Such a proposal would guarantee that all state-recognized health professionals have an equal opportunity to compete for participation in managed care delivery systems, regardless of whether those systems are HMOs, PPOs or some other arrangement. ACA's anti-discrimination amendments are also contained in the attached material.

Prohibitions against health professional discrimination should be bolstered with tough enforcement measures. ACA proposes to make such discriminatory practices subject to the civil monetary penalties outlined in Section 5412 of H R.3600. Additionally, to ensure that health plans engage in pro-active efforts to include a range of health care providers, they should be required to provide sufficient advance notice to the providers in the region they serve. By giving health professionals the opportunity to compete to participate in these plans, this provision would help ensure that plans are responsive to consumers' preferences.

We believe that these "anti-discrimination" amendments represent a reasonable approach to ending exclusion of chiropractors and other non-M.D. providers. The language does not mandate managed care plans to contract with any specific provider group or any particular provider. To the contrary, plans would remain free to select providers based on other appropriate criteria. The language merely ensures that all providers will have an opportunity to participate by outlawing "blanket" exclusions of certain types of providers. Unless the concepts embodied in these anti-discrimination amendments are adopted, we will continue to witness health plan discrimination against non-M.D. providers and the reduction in consumer choices that results.

The three areas outlined above comprise ACA's primary recommendations to H.R.3600. In addition, we have developed other amendments that would further protect consumer access to chiropractic and other non-allopathic care. These amendments would: change the definition of "health professional services" to clarify that it includes the services of all state-authorized health professionals; provide for representation of non-allopathic health providers on health alliance advisory boards; guarantee the right of patients to go outside of health plans to contract for health services from the provider of their choice; ensure that claims review of chiropractic or specialty services are performed by a professional within the same branch of the healing arts; and ensure that individuals retain the right to choose their initial treating provider under the workers' compensation and automobile insurance portions of the program.

ACCESS TO CHIROPRACTIC UNDER EXISTING FEDERAL PROGRAMS

The ACA understands that the process of enacting health care reform will be fluid and that no one can accurately predict the content of the final legislation that Congress will adopt. While we remain hopeful for the passage of meaningful health reform that will correct the system-wide problems associated with access, costs, and consumer freedom of choice, we also urge Congress to remedy the many problems within existing federal sector health programs.

We have identified myriad federal programs and policies where barriers to chiropractic services have been erected or where bias against the chiropractic profession exists. To rectify these problems, the ACA has drafted the "Federal Chiropractic Patient Anti-Discrimination and Access Act." These amendments are also attached for your consideration.

Our proposal aims to "level the federal playing field" for D.C.s and their patients by providing federal beneficiaries full coverage of chiropractic services under Medicare and other major federal health insurance programs; by expanding chiropractors' eligibility for health training and student loan repayment programs; by according D.C.s the same status as other health professionals under the U.S. Public Health Service; by establishing chiropractic care as a basic health service of federally qualified HMOs; and by prohibiting ERISA health benefit plans from discriminating against chiropractic patients.

From discriminatory coverage restrictions under Medicare, to exclusion from the National Health Service Corps, the federal government has consistently denied the chiropractic profession the degree of recognition and status that it deserves. It is well past time for our federal institutions to fully recognize the chiropractic profession as a valuable and viable part of the country's health care delivery system. Our proposed amendments would take the profession an important step in that direction.

CONCLUSION

For too long, the American people have had to tolerate barriers to chiropractic care. Perhaps the most glaring and inequitable of these barriers have resulted from a mean-spirited and illegal boycott of the chiropractic profession by the American Medical Association. From the early 1960s to the late 1980s, the AMA engaged in illegal efforts to "contain and eliminate" the chiropractic profession as a competitive force through the establishment of ethical restrictions on professional association between medical physicians and D.C.s.

In the landmark case Wilk v. AMA,[10] a federal District Court found that the AMA had violated federal anti-trust laws in an effort to economically destroy the chiropractic profession. While the purpose of AMA's boycott was many-fold, its primary objective was to prevent any cooperation between the medical and chiropractic professions in the delivery of health care. This is not ancient history. The final resolution of this case came just recently when the U.S. Supreme Court upheld the Wilk decision in 1992. It is important that Congress understand the impact of AMA's actions as it enters into the task of reforming our country's health care system. The opinions of the medical profession's elite were shaped during the boycott. Today, many

---

[10] Wilk v. AMA, 895 F 2d 352 (cert.den. 110 S.Ct.2621, June 11, 1990.)

of these individuals enjoy positions of power and influence within the health care establishment and regularly contribute to decisions about public and private policies on health care delivery. That is precisely why we are insisting that Congress place consumer access to chiropractic care and patient freedom of choice of provider among its top health care reform priorities. If selfish interests are allowed to dominate health care delivery in the future, our profession and its patients will be put at risk.

The amendments we have developed would help end the inequities that chiropractors and their patients have faced as a result of past professional discrimination. To help begin the process of alleviating these problems, we urge Congress to take this historic opportunity to enact health care reform legislation that incorporates our recommendations.

-- End --

595

ACA AMENDMENTS TO
H.R. 3600/S.1757
"THE HEALTH SECURITY ACT"

(All amendatory language is underlined)

A.   BASIC BENEFITS PACKAGE AND COVERAGE

1.   Service of Health Professionals [p. 38]

Title I, Subtitle B, Section 1112(c)(2) is amended to read as follows:

(2)   Health Professional Services. The term "health professional services" means professional services that:

(A)   are lawfully provided by a physician; or

(b)   are lawfully provided by an individual who is licensed or otherwise authorized by the State to deliver health services in the State in which the individual delivers services.

Explanation: The existing definition of health professional services is defined in terms of "physician services." Because Title I of the legislation leaves the term "physician" undefined, the existing language could be construed to mean that only the services of medical doctors or doctors of osteopathy are to be considered "health professional services."

The new language is virtually identical to that which appeared in the September 7, 1993 Working Group Draft of the President's plan. It is preferable because it makes clear that the services of State licensed and authorized non-allopathic health professionals are meant to be covered in addition to the services of physicians.

2.   Chiropractic Services [p. 32]

Title I, Subtitle B, Part 1, Section 1101(a) is amended after paragraph "(10)" by adding a new paragraph "(11)" to read as follows:

"(11) Chiropractic services (described in section 1121)."

and by renumbering each subsequent paragraph beginning with "(12)."

Explanation: The legislation enumerates eighteen items and services covered under the "comprehensive benefits package." This new language simply adds chiropractic.

3.   Description of chiropractic services [p. 67]

Title I, Subtitle B, Part 1, Section 1121 is amended to read as follows:

Sec. 1121. Chiropractic Services.

(a)   Coverage - The items and services described in this section are chiropractic services performed by licensed doctors of chiropractic as those services are defined by each State or other jurisdiction in the United States."

and by renumbering each subsequent section beginning with the number "1122".

Explanation: This new section defines chiropractic services as those doctors of chiropractic are licensed to perform in their state or other jurisdiction.

4.   Medical Necessity [p. 90]

        Title I, Subtitle B, Part 4, Section 1141(a),
"Exclusions" is amended to read as follows:

        (a)   Reasonable and Necessary Services - The
        comprehensive benefits package does not include -

                (1) an item or service that is not reasonable and
                necessary or appropriate; or

                (2) an item or service that the National Health
                Board may determine is not reasonable and
                necessary or appropriate in a regulation
                promulgated under section 1154.

        Section 1154 is amended to read as follows: [p. 94]

        "Sec. Establishment of Standards Regarding Reasonable and
        Necessary Services.

        The National Health Board may promulgate such
        regulations as may be necessary to carry out section
        1141(a)(2) (relating to the exclusion of certain
        services that are not reasonable and necessary or
        appropriate)."

        Explanation: The current bill excludes certain items and services from coverage
        under the comprehensive benefits package including those deemed "not medically
        necessary." If read strictly, the term "medically necessary" could be construed to
        mean that only the services of medical doctors are "necessary." The criteria
        applied by M.D.s are not always appropriate for services rendered by non-allopathic
        health professionals. Medical criteria that do not take into account the legitimate
        practice methods and techniques of State authorized, non-allopathic health
        professionals can be used to deny coverage of such care.

        The new language would replace the term "medically necessary" with the term
        "reasonable and necessary" in order to eliminate any possible confusion of this
        nature. The term "reasonable and necessary" is the current standard utilized under
        the Medicare program and is completely appropriate and sufficient in this context.
        (See Section 1862(a)(1) of the Social Security Act.)

B.   HEALTH PROFESSIONAL ANTI-DISCRIMINATION

        1.   Health Plan Requirements Relating to Enrollment and
Coverage [p. 228]

        Title I, Subtitle E, Part 1, Section 1402(c)(2) is
amended by adding a new paragraph, "(C)", to read as follows:

                (C) based on the type, class or profession of a
                provider authorized by state law to provide health care
                services."

        Explanation: Under this new language, when selecting providers for their
        networks, health plans would be prohibited from discriminating against a provider
        based solely on his or her professional type, class or license. Current language
        prohibits discrimination against providers based on their race, national origin,
        gender, language, age or disability only.

2. **National Health Board's Role Relating to Health Plans** [p. 92]

Title I, Subtitle B, Part 5, Section 1151 (b) is amended as follows:

"(b) Flexibility in Delivery - The regulations or guidelines under subsection (a) shall permit a health plan to deliver covered items and services to individuals enrolled under the plan using the providers and methods that the plan determines to be appropriate to the extent that such regulations or guidelines are consistent with the requirements of section 1402(c) of this title."

Explanation: Section 1151 gives the National Health Board the authority to promulgate regulations for health plans. Under the current language, these regulations must grant health plans the flexibility to use "appropriate providers and methods to deliver covered services" -- language which would permit plans to exclude certain types of providers.

By referring to section 1402(c) as amended, the new language would not allow these regulations to permit health plans to discriminate against providers based on their professional type, class or license.

3. **State Responsibility Relating to Health Plans** [p. 101]

Title I, Subtitle C, Section 1203(a)(2) is amended to read as follows:

"(2) Requirements - Such criteria shall be established with respect to -

(A)   the quality of the plan,

(B)   the financial stability of the plan,

(C)   the plan's capacity to deliver the comprehensive benefits package in the designated service area,

(D)   the plan's compliance with section 1402(c) of this title."

And redesignate the subsequent subparagraphs.

Explanation: The amendment adds a new subparagraph that requires States to certify only those health plans that conform with section 1402(c), i.e., only those that do not discriminate against providers based solely on their professional type, class or licensure.

4. **Provider Representation on Purchasing Alliance Advisory Boards** [p. 120]

Title I, Subtitle D, Part 1, Section 1303 is amended to read as follows:

"Sec. 1303. Providers Advisory Boards for Regional Alliances.

Each regional alliance must establish a provider advisory board consisting of representatives of health care providers and professionals who provide covered

services through health plans offered by the alliance.
Appointments of providers to such boards shall be
consistent with section 1402(c) of this title."

Explanation: Each regional alliance must have a provider advisory board. The new
language will prohibit regional alliances from discriminating against providers when
making appointments to advisory boards.

5. Preservation of State "Freedom of Choice of Providers

Title I, Subtitle E, Part 1, Section 1407(a) is amended
read as follows:

"(a) Laws Restricting Plans Other Than Fee-For-Service
Plans - Except as may otherwise be provided in this
section, no State law shall apply to any services
provided under a health plan that is not a
fee-for-service plan (or a fee for service component of
a plan) if such law has the effect of prohibiting or
otherwise restricting plans from -

(1) except as provided in section 1203, limiting
the number of health care providers who
participate in the plan.

Explanation: Current language in H.R. 3600/S.1757 would preempt State laws that
prohibit health plans from limiting the number and type of health providers allowed
to participate. The new language would not permit preemption of the latter.
Therefore, state laws prohibiting health plan discrimination against certain types
or classes of health professionals would be preserved.

"ANY WILLING PROVIDER" PROTECTIONS

1. Offerings of Regional and Corporate Alliances [pg. 133

Title I, Subtitle D, Section 1322(b) is amended by
moving the period at the end of paragraph (1) and inserting new
nguage to read "and at least one health plan that is not
e-for-service sub'ect to an willi rovider re irements as
; and by inserting a new paragraph 3 at
e end of subsection (b) to read as follows:

(3) "Any Willing Provider" Requirements Defined
- A health plan that is not a fee-for-service plan is
deemed to be subject to "any willing provider"
requirements if no health care provider willing to meet
the terms and conditions of plan provider agreements or
arrangements is excluded from participation in the plan.

Title I, Subtitle D, Section 1382(b) is amended by
moving the period at the end of paragraph (2) and inserting new
nguage to read, "and (3) at least one health plan that is not
e-for-service sub'ect to an 'll' rovider re irements as

Rationale: These changes would offer a new option requiring Alliances to provide
at least one managed care plan with "any willing provider" access and protection.

FREEDOM TO CONTRACT OUTSIDE OF HEALTH PLAN

1. Prohibition Against Balance Billing [p.236]

Title I, Subtitle E, Section 1406(d)(1) is amended by
serting language at the end of the subsection, to read as follows:

"**Nothing in this title shall be construed to invalidate or limit an enrollee's right to contract with a provider of his choice for the provision of covered and non-covered items and services independent of health plan arrangements.**"

Explanation: This new language guarantees the right of any patient to go outside of any health plan in which he or she is currently enrolled and contract for the provision of health care services from the doctor of his choice. Currently under Medicare such independent contracting by Part B beneficiaries is prohibited. The current HSA language would extend this prohibition to plan enrollees.

E.   QUALITY AND CONSUMER PROTECTION

1.   **National Quality Management Council**

Title V, Subtitle A, Section 5002(c)(4) is amended by inserting "**all classes of licensed**" before the term "health care provider".

Explanation: The Council should reflect the views of all providers in the health delivery system. This amendment assures such representation.

2.   **Academic Health Center Definition**

Title III, Subtitle B, Section 3101(c)(1) is amended by inserting a new subsection (D) to read:

"**(D)   Operates a school of chiropractic medicine accredited by the Council on Chiropractic Education.**"

Rationale: Academic health centers are operated by chiropractic institutions of education accredited by an agency recognized by the U.S. Department of Education. These institutions should be recognized under the HSA and afforded an opportunity to participate in quality management.

3.   **Evaluation and Reporting of Quality Performance**

Title V, Subtitle A, Section 5005(c)(1) is amended by deleting the phrase "if the available information is statistically meaningful" on line 10, and inserting in its place the phrase:

"**and such report shall include a breakout of all classes and types of health care provider services so performance can be analyzed.**"

Rationale: The change will permit a closer analysis and comparison of the effectiveness of provider services.

4.   **Health Information System**

Title V, Subtitle B, Section 5101 is amended by inserting a new subsection (e)(7) and renumber subsection (e)(7)(8)(9)(10)(11) accordingly. The new language to read:

"**(7) a list of all classes and types of health care providers who are not members of provider networks of the plans and the reasons for their lack of inclusion.**"

Rationale: This provides the opportunity to identify what types of providers are not being included in the plans.

5.   Additional Requirements for Health Information System

      Title V, Section B, Section 5102 is amended by
inserting the phrase "such as state and national professional
associations" after the word "providers" in subsection (E)(6).

> Rationale: The review of chiropractic or specialty services should be performed
> by a professional within the same branch of the healing arts.

6.   Additional Requirements for Health Information System

      Title V, Subtitle B, Section 5102 is amended by
inserting a new subsection(b)(5) to read:

> "(5) such data shall be in a form that shall allow a
> breakout of different state licensed health care
> providers and their services."

> Rationale: This provides the data base for information related to the provision of
> services by different providers.

7.   Health Plan Claims Procedure

      Title V, Subtitle C, Section 5201 is amended by
deleting Subsection (b)(4)(C) and inserting in its place the
language:

> "shall include a review by a qualified peer of the same
> specialty or class of licensure of the provider who
> provided the service if the resolution of any issues
> involved requires medical or professional expertise."

> Rationale: The review of chiropractic or specialty services should be performed
> by a professional within the same branch of the healing arts.

8.   Qualified Specialist

      Title V, Subtitle D, Section 5303 is amended by
inserting the phrase "is qualified by state licensure in" after the
word "of" in subsection (c)(1).

> Rationale: This assures that licensure will be included to determine whether or
> not a provider qualifies as a "specialist."

9.   "Health Care Provider"

      Title V, Subtitle A, Section 5002 is amended by
inserting the phrase "under the license" after the word "that" in
subsection (j).

> Rationale: This addition would clarify the need for all health care providers to
> be licensed as such by the applicable state board."

10.   Civil Monetary Penalties

      Title V, Subtitle E, Section 5412 is amended by
inserting a new subsection (a)(4) and renumbering the remaining
(c)(4) and (c)(5). The new subsection to read as follows:

> (4) Discrimination Against Providers - The engagement
> in any practice that would reasonably be expected to
> have the effect of discriminating against an individual
> health care provider based on his or her type or class
> of state licensed profession.

> Rationale: This provision provides an effective civil monetary penalty mechanism
> for Section 1402(c)(3) anti-discrimination language.

F.   PRESERVATION OF CHOICE OF TREATING PHYSICIAN UNDER WORKERS
     COMPENSATION INSURANCE AND AUTOMOBILE INSURANCE

1.   Workers Compensation

a.   Title X, Subtitle A, Section 10001 is amended by
inserting the language "such injured worker may initially select a
health care provider to provide professional services" after the
last sentence in subsection (a)(2).

> Rationale: This assures an injured worker the right to select the initial
> treating provider under the plan.

b.   Title X, Subtitle A, Section 10012 is amended by
inserting the language "Nothing in this subtitle shall be construed
as preempting or limiting any state law that may provide for the
initial selection of a treating health care provider by an injured
worker." after the last sentence in subsection (a).

> Rationale: A worker's right under state law to select his or her initial treating
> physician is preserved and clarified by this amendment.

2.   Automobile Insurance

Title X, Subtitle B, Section 10112 is amended by
inserting phrase "or the right to initially select his or her
treating health care provider."

> Rationale: This permits the initial choice of provider to be retained by an
> injured individual if provided for under state law.

1876u

FEDERAL CHIROPRACTIC PATIENT
ANTIDISCRIMINATION AND ACCESS ACT

Section 1.   SHORT TITLE: TABLE OF TITLES AND SUBTITLES

    (1) Short Title - This Act may be cited as the
"Federal Chiropractic Patient Antidiscrimination and Access Act".

    (2) Table of Titles and Subtitles in Act - The
following are the titles and subtitles contained in this Act:

Section 2.   FINDINGS

The Congress finds as follows:

    (1) Under the current health care system in the
United States:

    (A) Individuals covered under Federal health
care programs and Federal worker's compensation who select
chiropractic health care are discriminated against because of their
selection;

    (B) While State scope of professional practice
laws recognize a wide variety of health care services provided by
chiropractors, Federal programs recognize only one service, i.e.
manual manipulation of the spine to correct a subluxation
demonstrated by x-ray to exist;

    (C) Because of this limited recognition,
individuals choosing chiropractic services under Federal programs
are denied otherwise covered benefits and denied the ability to
utilize State recognized reports and opinions prepared by his or
her chiropractor;

    (D) Quality and effectiveness in the health
care system can be enhanced by the full participation of doctors of
chiropractic and the availability of chiropractic and the
availability of chiropractic services in all Federal health care
programs.

Section 3.   PURPOSES

The purposes of the Act are as follows:

(1)   To guarantee that patients of chiropractors have equal treatment and access under all Federal health and worker's compensation programs consistent with State scope of professional practice laws.

(2)   To guarantee that patients of chiropractors are not discriminated against in all Federal programs based simply upon their selection of their licensed health care provider.

(3)   To ensure greater quality and effectiveness in Federal in health care programs through inclusion of chiropractic services.

TITLE I - CHIROPRACTIC PATIENT EQUALIZATION AND ANTIDISCRIMINATION

SUBTITLE A - MEDICARE

Section 1001.   Definition of Physician. Title XVIII of the Social Security Act is amended by striking the language in subsection (r)(5) of Section 1861 and inserting in its place new language to read:

(5) a chiropractor who is licensed as such by the State (or in a State which does not license chiropractors as such, is legally authorized to perform the services of a chiropractor in the jurisdiction in which he performs such services) and who meets uniform minimum standards promulgated by the Secretary, but only with respect to the functions which he is authorized to perform by the State in which he performs them".

This change would redefine chiropractors as full fledge "physicians" limited only by State law.

SUBTITLE B - MEDICARE HMO/CMP PROGRAM

Section 1001. Definitions, Requirements. Title XVIII of the Social Security Act is amended by striking language "(as defined in Section 1861 (r)(1))" in subsection (b)(2)(A)(i) of Section 1876, and inserting in its place new language to read "(as defined in Section 1861 (r)(1) and 1861 (r)(5))".

This change would require HMO/CMP Medicare plans, at a minimum, to provide physician services provided by medical doctors and chiropractors within confines of State law and outlined in Section 1861(r)(5).

Section 1002. Enrollment in Plan, Duties of Organization to Enrollees. Title XVIII of the Social Security Act is amended by inserting the language "and without discrimination against any class of licensed health care professionals or persons in the provision or referral of services" at the end of subsection (c)(2)(A) of Section 1876 prior to the listing of subparagraphs (i) and (ii).

This amendment would prohibit Federal payment to an HMO or CMP that discriminates against any class of licensed health professional in the provision or referral of Medicare covered services.

SUBTITLE C - MEDICAID

Section 1001. Chiropractic Expenses. Title XIX of
the Social Security Act is amended by striking the language in
subsection (g)(2) of Section 1905 and inserting in its place "(2)
services which the chiropractor is authorized to perform by the
State".

This would grant full scope recognition under Medicaid for chiropractors in
those States which choose to include chiropractors in their State programs.

SUBTITLE D - FEDERAL WORKERS COMPENSATION

Section 1001. Definitions. Chapter 81 of Title 5 of
the United States Code is amended by deleting the second sentence
in subsection (2) of Section 8101 and the second sentence in
subsection (3) of Section 8101. .

These changes will remove existing limitations and will include full range of
chiropractic services as defined by State statute under Federal worker
compensation. These changes will also address the limited recognition and
limited authority that chiropractors currently experience in terms of acceptance
of reports prepared for their patients. This would place chiropractors in
exactly the same position that podiatrists, dentists, clinical psychologists and
optometrists currently enjoy under the program.

SUBTITLE E - FEDERAL HMO ACT

Section 1001. Health Professionals. Title XIII of
the Public Health Service Act is amended by inserting the word
"Chiropractors" after the word "optometrists," in subsection
(b)(3)(D) of Section 1301.

This amendment would add chiropractors to the definition of a health
professional along with physicians, nurses, podiatrists and optometrists.

Section 1002. Basic Health Service. Title XIII of
the Public Health Service Act is amended by inserting a new
subsection (1)(I) to read "(I) chiropractic care" to subsection (1)
of Section 1302.

This amendment would include chiropractic care as a basic health service of
federally qualified HMO's.

Section 1003. Supplemental Health Service. Title
XIII of the Public Health Service Act is amended by inserting the
word "chiropractor" after the word "psychologist" throughout in
subsection (2) of Section 1302.

The amendment would enable chiropractors to provide supplemental health
services along with optometrists, dentists, podiatrists and psychologists in
federally qualified HMO's.

Section 1004. Antidiscrimination. Title XVIII of
the Public Health Service Act is amended by inserting a new
subsection (6) at the end of Section 1302 to read:

605

A health maintenance organization shall not discriminate against any class of State licensed health profession for the provision of basic and supplemental health services within such health professions State scope of professional practice in either (a) the contracting for such services, or (b) the referral of members for such services.

This amendment would prohibit discrimination by an HMO against any class of licensed provider in the treatment or referral of a patient.

SUBTITLE F - ERISA

Section 1001. Prohibited Transactions. Section 406 of the Employee Retirement Income Security Act of 1974 is amended to add a new subsection (d) at the end of Section 406 to read as follows:

d. Transactions with welfare benefit plans that discriminate. A fiduciary with respect to a welfare benefit plan shall not cause the plan to engage in discrimination against any class of State licensed health care practitioners in the provisions of services and benefits to plan participants. The fiduciary shall assure that plan participants shall be free to select and shall have direct access to all classes of State licensed health care practitioners without supervision or referral by another health care practitioner, except if, or to the extent that such supervision or referral is required under State or local law, or regulation issued thereunder.

This proposes a fiduciary obligation on an administrator of an ERISA welfare benefit plan (both insured and self-insured) to assure the plan refrains from discriminating against chiropractors and guarantees direct access of a participant to a chiropractor.

TITLE II - CHIROPRACTIC PATIENT ACCESS TO FEDERAL PROGRAMS

SUBTITLE A - HEALTH SERVICE PROGRAMS

Section 1001. Authorized Professional Services. Chapter 79 of Title 5 of the United States Code is amended by inserting the words "and chiropractors" after the words "osteopathic practitioners" in subsection (e) of Section 7901.

This amendment will enable chiropractors to deliver services within scope of practice to Federal government workers under health service programs established by Federal agencies.

SUBTITLE B - FEDERAL EMPLOYEE HEALTH INSURANCE

Section 1001. Contracting Authority. Chapter 89 of Title 5 of the United States Code is amended by revising subsection (K) of Section 8902 as follows:

(a) in paragraph (1), by inserting "(except if, or to the extent that, any such supervision or referral is required under State or local law, or regulations issued thereunder, as described in subsection(m)(1)(B)" after "practitioner"; and

(b) by striking out paragraph (a) and inserting in lieu thereof the following:

(2)(A)   When a contract under this chapter requires payment or reimbursement for services which may be performed by a health practitioner referred to in subparagraph (B), an employee, annuitant, family member, former spouse or person having continued coverage under 8905a of this title covered by the contract --

(i)   shall be free to select, and shall have direct access to, such a health practitioner without supervision or referral by another health practitioner (whether of a type referred to in subparagraph (B) or otherwise), except if, or to the extent that, any such supervision or referral is required under State or local law, or regulations issued thereunder, as described in subsection (m)(1)(B); and

(ii) shall be entitled under the contract to have payment or reimbursement made to him or on his behalf for the services performed.

(B)   This paragraph applies with respect to --

(i)   a chiropractor;
(ii) a marriage and family therapist; and
(iii) a mental health counselor who is licensed or certified as such under Federal or State law, as applicable.

(3)   When a contract under this chapter requires payment or reimbursement for services of a health practitioner covered by paragraph (2), the terms and conditions governing such payments or reimbursement shall be the same as the terms and conditions generally applicable under contracts under this chapter requiring payments or reimbursement for services of health practitioners covered by paragraph (1).

This is a version of the existing proposed Federal Employees Health Freedom-of-Choice Act and would add concepts of freedom of choice and "insurance equality" into all Federal health benefits plans. Chiropractic patients who are Federal workers would have equal access to chiropractic health care.

SUBTITLE C - VOCATIONAL REHABILITATION SERVICES

Section 1001. Scope of Vocational Rehabilitation ces; Individual Services. Title 1, Part A, of the ilitation Act of 1973 is amended by inserting a new subsection n Section 103 to read as follows:

(G) diagnosis and treatment of physical disorders by a chiropractor licensed in accordance with State laws.

This amendment would include chiropractic services along with medical, surgical, optometric, and psychological services to be provided to an individual under the Vocational Rehabilitation Program. It would place chiropractic patients on an equal footing in terms of obtaining chiropractic care. Currently they may obtain optometric and psychological care under this program.

SUBTITLE D - LONGSHOREMEN'S AND HARBOR WORKERS'
COMPENSATION ACT

Section 1001. Medical Services and Supplies.
Chapter 509 of the Longshoremen's and Harbor Workers' Compensation
Act is amended by inserting the word "chiropractic" after the word
"surgical" in subsection (a) of Section 7 and by inserting the
words "or chiropractic" after the word "medical" wherever the word
appears in subsection (b) of Section 7.

This would specifically grant an injured worker full access to chiropractic
care under this program in the same way workers under most other workers'
compensation programs have such access. Currently patients of chiropractors have
limited access to services through regulations adopted by the Secretary. This
change would provide full scope of practice coverage by statute.

SUBTITLE E - VETERANS BENEFITS

Section 1001. Medical Services. Chapter 17 of Title
38 of the United States Code is amended by adding the word
"chiropractic" after the word "optometric", in subsection (6)(A)(i)
of Section 1701.

This amendment would include chiropractic into the definition of "medical
services" available to Veterans. Currently, such services include dental,
optometric, podiatric and mental health care but not chiropractic.

SUBTITLE F - PUBLIC HEALTH SERVICE

Section 1001. Appointment of Personnel. Chapter 6A
of Title 42 of the United States Code is amended by inserting the
word "chiropractic" after the word "nursing" in subsection(a) of
Section 209.

This amendment would permit the appointment of chiropractors as officers in the
Public Health Service.

Section 1002. National Health Service Corps
Program. Chapter 6A of Title 42 of the United States Code is
amended by inserting the word "chiropractor" after the word
"dentist," by inserting the word "chiropractic" after the word
"dentistry" or the word "dental" wherever such words appear in
subsection (b) of Section 254d, in subsection (e) of Section 254 f,
in subsection (a)(3) of Section 254f-1, in subsection (f)(1) of
Section 254h-1, subsections (a)(1) and (b)(1) in Section 2541,
subsections (a) and (b) of Section 2541-1, and subsection (s) in
Section 254m.

These changes would place chiropractors and their educational institutions on
an equal par with medical physicians, osteopathic physicians, dentists, certified
nurse practitioners and other providers and their educational institutions in the
National Health Service Corps Program. These changes would also provide for
access by chiropractic students to Scholarship and Loan Repayment Programs under
the Corps program.

SUBTITLE G - NATIONAL ARTHRITIS ADVISORY BOARD

Section 1001. Board Composition. Title IV of the
Public Health Service Act is amended by inserting the word
"chiropractors" after the word "physicians" in subsection (c)(4) of
Section 442.

This amendment would require the inclusion on this prestigious board and with
it lend the expertise and knowledge of chiropractic in the treatment of patients
with arthritis.

1875u

608

Statement of the American Dance Therapy Association
Submitted by Susan Kleinman, President, ADTA
to
the Subcommittee on Ways and Means
House of Representatives

Hearing on
The Congressional Budget Office's
Analysis of the President's
Health Care Reform Proposal
February, 1994

The American Dance Therapy Association is pleased to have this opportunity to offer the views and recommendations of our Association concerning the needs of the people we serve. We estimate that over three million people in the United States currently receive dance/movement therapy services.

We therefore recommend that you, as you carefully explore the varied approaches which have proven successful in our present health care system, consider including identification of dance/movement therapy services in any health care reform act.

History and Overview

Dance/movement therapy came into existence in 1942 during the health care crisis of World War II. Marian Chace, a dancer with 25 years of performing, choreographing and teaching experience pioneered dance/movement therapy in Washington, DC at St. Elizabeths Hospital at the request of DC area psychiatrists. Psychiatric problems hampered the military effort; a staggering 1 3/4 million men were rejected for military service and 3/4 million more were discharged because of emotional problems. Mental health facilities simply could not treat the scores of returning veterans. This problem cried out for new approaches. New approaches were also needed to treat the severely mentally ill patients including those who could not be released from restraints. Drastic measures, such as insulin, electroshock and lobotomy were no longer the only solutions. Chace accepted the challenge and her use of dance/movement therapy with groups proved to be able to reach the physically and emotionally isolated patients and address the stress of trauma of the returning veterans. She became known world wide for her innovative and effective methods and received several honors, such as the St. Elizabeths Hospital Award for Outstanding Service (1954) and the Oveta Culp Hobby Award (1955). In 1956 Chace received an award for outstanding service from the U.S. Department of Health, Education and Welfare.

Range of Clients & Settings

Today, in addition to the those with severe emotional disorders, people of all ages and varying conditions receive dance/movement therapy in accredited facilities. Examples of these are:

- those with eating disorders
- adult survivors of violence
- sexually and physically abused children
- dysfunctional families
- the homeless
- autistic children
- the frail elderly
- substance abusers

Health service providers in general medical hospitals acknowledge that a patient's emotional state and mental health contributes to the recovery of illness. Dance/movement therapy used for disease prevention, chronic conditions and health promotion has become an evolving area of specialization. Many innovative programs provide dance/movement therapy services to patients with:

- cardiovascular disease
- hypertension
- chronic pain
- Traumatic Brain Injury
- amputees
- the well elderly
- caretakers

Dance/movement therapy accomplishes the following:

- alters moods and creates the emotional intensity
  necessary for behavior change
- organizes cognitive process and actions
- reduces isolation, establishes rapport and group
  cohesion
- increases the endorphin level inducing a state of well
  being
- stimulates functioning body systems: circulatory,
  respiratory, digestive, and neuromuscular
- activates muscle and joints and reduces body tension
- facilitates expression of a wide range of feelings

Research has been undertaken on the effects of dance/movement therapy on specific illnesses with the following populations: Children and adolescents who are: learning disabled, emotionally disturbed, sexually abused, depressed and suicidal, mentally retarded, asthmatic, substance abusers, visually and hearing impaired, and autistic.

Adults who are: psychotic, depressed, mentally retarded, alcoholic, imprisoned, homeless, physically and sexually abused, anorectic and bulimic, and those with physical problems, such as amputations, arthritis, chronic pain, heart disease, diabetes, AIDS, head injured, Alzheimers, stroke and cancer.

Professionalism

The American Dance Therapy Association (ADTA) was founded in 1966 by 73 charter members in only 15 states. The Association has grown to nearly 1,200 members in 46 states and 20 foreign countries. Dance/movement therapy like other health disciplines is a profession which has an ethical code, standards of practice, professional credentialing, scientific theories, a body of knowledge and specific training requirements. The ADTA maintains a dance/movement therapy registry which insures a high level of standards for consumers.

The Dance Therapist Registered (D.T.R.) title is granted to entry level dance/movement therapists who have a masters degree which includes 700 hours of supervised clinical internship. The advanced level of registry, Academy of Dance Therapists Registered (A.D.T.R.) is awarded only after dance/movement therapists have completed 3,640 hours of supervised clinical work (two years), post masters, with additional supervision by an A.D.T.R. In addition, the individual must successfully pass examination by the ADTA Credentials Committee.

The Association also has established standards for professional practice, education and training and these are reflected in the Code of Ethics. Dance therapy academic programs stress course work in dance therapy theory and techniques, movement observation and analysis, human development, psychopathology, group process and internship seminars concurrent with supervised internship in clinical settings. The ADTA established an approval process in 1979 for the purpose of evaluating these masters programs on an ongoing basis.

The American Dance Therapy Association sponsors an annual national conference and supports the formation of chapters and regional groups which hold conferences, seminars and workshops. In addition, the ADTA publishes the American Journal of Dance Therapy (semiannually), the ADTA Newsletter (quarterly) and timely monographs and bibliographies for its members and allied professionals.

Federal Recognition

Recommendations at a federal level have for many years promoted greater use of innovative treatments such as dance/movement therapy. For example

A. Dance/movement therapy was recognized nationally by the Task Panel on the Arts & Environment of the President's Commission on Mental Health during the Carter Administration.

B. Dance/movement therapy was also listed among related services in Public Law 94-142 (1978).

C. Dance/movement therapy was included in the publication of the fourth edition of the Dictionary of Occupational Titles. (1991)

D. On June 18, 1992, the U.S. Senate Special Committee on Aging held a hearing on Dance/Movement Therapy and Art Therapy. Testimony was provided attesting to the benefits of both therapies with older people.

E. Dance/movement therapy was included and defined in federal legislation when the amendments to the Older American Act, P.L. 102-375 became law on September 30, 1992. We are pleased that more older Americans will receive the benefits of dance/movement therapy and that for the first time, dance/movement therapists can now obtain state funds from the Older Americans Act through Title III grants to provide their services.

Current Research

The Senate Appropriations Committee report accompanying H.R. 5677 awarded funds earmarked for research in dance/movement therapy, music therapy and art therapy through the Administration on Aging. We are grateful to Senator Harry Reid for requesting the Subcommittee on Labor, Human Resources, Education and Related Agencies that $825,000 be identified within the funds appropriated for fiscal year 1993 for extramural grants to study these therapies under Title IV of the Older Americans Act.

The American Dance Therapy Association has recently received word that our proposal entitled, "Dance/Movement Therapy With Older Individuals Who Have Sustained Neurological Insult" has been funded.   A proposal from Hebrew Rehabilitation Center for Aged in Boston has also been funded and will study, "Dance/Movement Therapy With Older Individuals With Evidence of Distressed Mood or Social Withdrawal" which will include persons with dementia.

The National Institutes of Health recently funded a project to study dance/movement therapy with victims of Cystic Fibrosis. These research projects will further advance understanding of the specific effects of dance/movement therapy.

Quality of Service

In institutional settings dance/movement therapists work in capacities as administrators and clinicians.   One full time dance/movement therapist leading three (3) groups per day can easily provide over 7,000 patient contact visits per year. As administrators of therapeutic programs they frequently supervise other disciplines including therapeutic recreation workers, other creative arts therapists and physical and occupational therapists.

As a member of the treatment team, the dance/movement therapist provides invaluable insights regarding patient progress by participating in staffing reviews of treatment goals and objectives. Dance/movement therapists, because of their training, are able to look at the patient's behavior from a movement perspective which is not only different from other disciplines, but is often a barometer for emerging behaviors and possible problems of concern such as suicidal ideation, disorientation and physical deterioration. Vital information is provided through movement, because it emerges spontaneously and because it is common for people to conveniently mask feelings through intellectualization and verbalization.

Dance/movement therapists are experts in facilitating non-verbal expression and developing this expression into meaningful group interaction. For this reason, dance/movement therapists are frequently called upon to lead group process seminars and inservice programs to improve group work and observation skills of others providing patient care.

Prior to the discovery of phenothiazine medications and before it was thought to be possible to work with schizophrenics in groups, dance/movement therapists worked effectively with people considered unreachable, uncommunicative, and undesirable. Today, dance/movement therapists continue to work effectively with many people that others cannot reach. What occurs in dance/movement therapy is the unfolding of spontaneous movements and behaviors which are developed into expressive feelings, communications and interactions through the dance dialogue, a process facilitated by the dance/movement therapist. Material surfacing in this process often is not accessible through verbalization. Because of these powerful and effective processes, dance/movement therapy is prescribed by physicians in many settings.

Although our services are recognized by CHAMPUS and the Joint Commission on Accreditation of Health Care Organizations, our advanced clinicians (ADTRs) are often excluded from sitting for state licensure exams. Such licensure would make dance/movement therapists eligible for reimbursement and thus able to serve those in need not treated in clinical settings.

It is of deep concern to administrators of programs across the country that dance/movement therapy services may be lost to their health programs, not because of ineffectiveness, but because these services are not reimbursable. In the present system, type of care is based on whether it is reimbursable and whether or not it meets the minimum requirements of the facility for accreditation. Health care services, including dance/movement, art, music, drama and poetry therapies and psychodrama are at risk because for the most part they have not been reimbursed by insurance companies. Services such as physical therapy and occupational therapy are reimbursed under Medicare and Medicaid. Medicare and Medicaid would be a likely place to also include services such as dance/movement therapy.

We believe it is imperative that the healing role of the arts be recognized within our health care structures.

Recommendations

The American Dance Therapy Association recommends that the following be considered for inclusion in National Health Care Reform:

1) Lists of authorized providers should be expanded to include services whose modalities have proven successful in our present system.
2) Opportunities for new modalities to prove their efficacy should always exist.

3) Research should be supported as a critical means of evaluating promising newer treatments.

4) Development of new approaches should not be hampered by defining services too narrowly.

5) The varied approaches to health care now being used by countless numbers of our citizens should be supported and allowed to continue to provide beneficial treatment.

6) Dance/movement therapy (and other Creative Arts Therapies - art, music, drama, poetry, psychodrama) should be identified and named along with occupational therapy, physical therapy, recreational therapy, social work, counseling, and psychology in managed care plans. Inclusion of a broad variety of services can offer a richness of beneficial treatment for our citizens.

7) The frequency of expensive one on one services may often be diminished through greater use of group services.

8) Provisions should be made to include inpatient partial hospitalization programs and outpatient follow-ups to help deter re-hospitalization as well as to permit those who are able to return, where possible, to productive functioning.

The American Dance Therapy Association thanks the Subcommittee on Ways and Mean for this opportunity to give our views and recommendations regarding health care reform.

References

Fisher, A.C. with Stark, A. (1992) Dance/Movement Therapy Abstracts: Doctoral Dissertations, Masters' Theses and /Special Projects Through 1990. Columbia Md. The Marian Chace Memorial Fund of the American Dance Therapy Association.

Fledderjohn, Heidi; Swickley, J. (1993) An Annotated Bibliography of Dance/Movement Therapy 1940-1990. The Marian Chace Memorial Fund of the American Dance Therapy Association.

Kleinman, S. (1992) Dance is Life-Written testimony submitted to U.S. Senate Special Committee on Aging Hearing, "Aging Artfully: Health Benefits of Art and Dance".

Sandel, S, Chaiklin, S., Lohn, A., Editors (1993) Foundations of Dance/Movement Therapy-The Life and Work of Marian Chace. The Marian Chace Memorial Fund of the American Dance Therapy Association.

Schmais, C. (1985) "Healing Processes in Group Dance Therapy". American Journal of Dance Therapy, Vol. 8.

Schmais, C. (1974) "Dance Therapy in Perspective: FOCUS on Dance VII. American Association for Health, Physical Education, and Recreation.

THE AMERICAN DIETETIC ASSOCIATION
216 WEST JACKSON BOULEVARD
CHICAGO, ILLINOIS 60606-6995
312/899-0040

DIVISION OF GOVERNMENT AFFAIRS
1225 EYE STREET, NW #1250
WASHINGTON, DC 20005
202/371-0500

TESTIMONY OF
SARA C. PARKS, MBA, RD,
PRESIDENT
THE AMERICAN DIETETIC ASSOCIATION
on the

STANDARD BENEFITS PACKAGE
in

HEALTH CARE REFORM LEGISLATION
before the

SUBCOMMITTEE ON HEALTH
of the

HOUSE COMMITTEE ON WAYS AND MEANS

February 28, 1994

Chairman Stark and Distinguished Members of the Subcommittee:

Thank you for the opportunity to comment on the standard benefits package in health care legislation pending before your Subcommittee. We respectfully request that our comments be included in the Subcommittee's public hearing record.

It is well understood that nutrition plays a key role in preventing disease. Surveys of the American public show that people know that "eating right" prevents heart disease, diabetes, high blood pressure, and cancer. In contrast, little is known about the vital role medical nutrition therapy plays in treating disease.

For example, medical nutrition therapy is key in the treatment of:

•   Kidney (renal) disease, for which reduced liquid, protein, potassium and sodium intake, along with adequate caloric intake, can delay and reduce the need for dialysis;

•   Cancer, in which nutrition therapy helps prevent the weight loss associated with cancer treatments, thereby increasing patient responsiveness to treatment, and enhancing patient tolerance of chemotherapy and radiation therapy;

•   Heart disease, for which a specialized diet and exercise program helps reduce serious risk of further damage to the cardiovascular system and heart, often avoiding expensive surgery;

- Diabetes, for which aggressive nutrition counseling, combined with frequent monitoring of blood sugar levels, prevents the need for insulin (for individuals with Type II diabetes) and reduces the occurrence of diabetes-related health problems.

- AIDS, where maintaining body weight and scientifically pursuing nutrition evaluation allows patients to more successfully combat opportunistic infections, prevent complications and live longer, more productive lives;

- Prenatal Care, for pregnant women at high risk of premature labor or other complications, where aggressive dietary therapy can achieve a balanced nutritional status and appropriate weight gain which reduces the incidence of cesarean section and low-birth weight;

- Pediatric Care, in which infants suffering from failure to thrive syndrome have lower hospital utilization when progressive nutrition therapy is applied; and

- Geriatric Care, for elderly home health and nursing home patients whose conditions make digesting and ingesting difficult, and specialized nutrition therapy can help prevent or treat complications like decubiti (bed sores) when they are able to maintain their nutritional status.

Medical nutrition therapy is further defined in the attachment.

MEDICAL NUTRITION THERAPY IS RARELY COVERED BY HEALTH INSURANCE

Health insurance plans seldom cover medical nutrition therapy. If they do, it often requires extensive requests, vigorous follow-up, documentation of medical necessity and personal pleas by the patient, physician and dietitian.

Health insurance plans typically follow the coverage rules adopted by the Medicare program created in 1965, well before the major advances in medical nutrition science that the program has never been updated to reflect. Medicare covers medical nutrition therapy only when patients are hospitalized and the hospital chooses to provide this service as part of its overall inpatient treatment plan. Medical nutrition therapy is generally not covered on an outpatient or ambulatory basis, the most cost-effective setting for its provision.

The vast majority of non-hospitalized patients must pay for medical nutrition therapy out of their own pockets. Those who cannot pay for the services of a registered dietitian or qualified nutritionist are more likely to be hospitalized or have surgery to treat their conditions. Furthermore, physicians are less likely to recommend or prescribe medical nutrition therapy because it is not a covered benefit in the vast majority of health insurance plans.

MEDICAL NUTRITION THERAPY SAVES MONEY BY PREVENTING SURGERY AND HOSPITALIZATIONS

THE MONEY SAVED CAN BE USED TO FUND THIS NATION'S HEALTH CARE SYSTEM

Our current health care system spends millions of dollars needlessly because nutrition therapy is NOT routinely covered and provided when medically necessary. Research shows that **for every $1 spent on medical nutrition therapy, over $3 are saved** in later medical care costs. This represents the minimum savings from over 450 actual case studies collected by ADA members over the past six months. Savings frequently ranged up to $600 saved for every $1 spent on medical nutrition therapy.

To achieve the savings in hospital and treatment costs which medical nutrition therapy offers, health coverage must encourage the provision of these services before complications or disease progression occurs. Medical nutrition therapy must be accessible to patients in:

• ambulatory and outpatient treatment settings;

• home health care treatment settings;

• long term care facilities; and

• inpatient treatment settings.

Providing comprehensive nutrition therapy coverage to all patients with conditions or illnesses for which nutrition services are recommended would require approximately $638 million in **new** spending for coverage of the ambulatory and outpatient treatment, the setting for which coverage is currently not provided. This investment in outpatient and ambulatory care medical nutrition therapy would help prevent hospitalizations and reduce treatment for disease progression, **saving almost $2 billion in health costs.** (Source: Report prepared by George J. Nielson, *Technical Report, Analysis of Costs Associated with Clinical Nutrition Services,* June 1993.)

MEDICAL NUTRITION THERAPY IN HEALTH CARE REFORM LEGISLATION

ADA urges you to support coverage for medical nutrition therapy in the standard benefit package. Almost 17 million people are treated each year for conditions or diseases that respond to medical nutrition therapy. These individuals should be eligible for medical nutrition therapy upon the recommendation of their primary care provider when medically appropriate and necessary. This coverage would produce net health care cost savings by helping to prevent surgeries and hospitalizations.

The Health Security Act (H.R. 3600), introduced at the request of the Administration, marks a major breakthrough in the recognition of the value of nutrition in health care. The Health Security Act includes several provisions related to the standard benefit package:

- The Administration's bill intends to cover medical nutrition therapy as a basic benefit in "health professional services."

- Clinical preventive services specifically include nutrition counseling. This is in line with the recommendation of the U.S. Preventive Services Task Force in its *Guide to Clinical Preventive Services: An Assessment of the Effectiveness of 169 Interventions.*

- Nutrition counseling is singled out as an example of health education and training that health plans are allowed to cover.

- Home infusion therapy—the administration of drugs or nutrients through a tube or intravenously for those unable to swallow or digest--is covered.

We applaud the above proposal for its recognition of the importance of medical nutrition service to improve the health of the nation and to lower health care costs.

However, ADA recognizes that several health care reform proposals in addition to President Clinton's plan are before this Subcommittee for consideration. Several do not specify a standard benefit package, and propose to establish a national health board outside Congress to do so. We want to ensure that coverage of medical nutrition therapy is not ignored or forgotten as it has been until this point.

RECOMMENDATIONS TO CONGRESS

If Congress decides to define the standard benefit package in legislation, ADA requests inclusion of medical nutrition therapy when medically necessary and appropriate upon the referral of a primary care provider.

On the other hand, if Congress establishes a Health Care Standards Commission or other form of national health board to recommend a benefit package, ADA urges that criteria be established in health care legislation to ensure that insurance coverage will keep pace with scientific medical advancements that offer cost-effective, efficacious treatment -- criteria that require coverage of treatment recommended by practice protocols and outcomes research. Medical nutrition therapy, which has advanced so rapidly over the last decade, would then have a fair opportunity to be covered when medically appropriate.

CONCLUSIONS

Despite the overwhelming evidence that professionally delivered medical nutrition therapy results in more cost effective and quality health care, treatment is received by only a portion of the 17 million patients per year who are at risk. The reason is that current Medicare reimbursement policy—which many insurers copy—discourages its use.

A federal problem requires a federal solution.

It is critical that any health care legislation approved by Congress discontinue the discriminatory treatment for medical nutrition therapy in present health insurance plans. ADA strongly urges this Subcommittee to ensure that the final bill acknowledges the scientific advancements of medical nutrition science by providing coverage of medical nutrition therapy, or if the benefit package is developed outside Congress, by establishing clear criteria regarding its eligibility for coverage.

We look forward to working with this subcommittee in the development of important health care legislation and would be pleased to respond to any questions you may have.

618

Attachment

MEDICAL NUTRITION THERAPY IN DISEASE TREATMENT

Based on clinical research and experience, medical professionals ---physicians, dietitians, and nurses---identify specific nutrition services that may be necessary to treat illness and injury. Nutrition assessment and nutrition therapy, the two key components of medical nutrition therapy, involve:

Assessment of the nutritional status of patients with a condition, illness or injury that places them at high risk of malnutrition. The assessment includes review and analysis of medical and diet history, blood chemistry laboratory values, and anthropometric measurements to determine nutritional status and therapeutic modalities.

Therapy ranging from diet modification to administration of specialized nutrition support, which includes intravenous medical nutrition products as determined necessary to manage a condition or treat illness or injury. Components of nutrition therapy are:

- Diet Modification and Counseling: For many patients, key components of nutrition therapy are intervention and counseling leading to the development of a personal diet plan to be followed to achieve nutrition goals--such as reduced blood sugar levels, reduced protein intake, or increased caloric intake. For example, patients with diabetes can often control their blood sugar levels without medications or with reduced levels of medication after counseling and diet modification intervention from a registered dietitian.

- Specialized Nutrition Support: Professional assessment may identify special nutrition needs that must be met by specialized nutrient supplementation using medical foods, by enteral nutrition delivered via tube, or by parenteral nutrition delivered via intravenous infusion. For example:

     ----Supplementation with medical foods would be appropriate for patients with pressure ulcers, chronic obstructive pulmonary disease and muscular dystrophy; for surgical patients with low biochemical values; and for patients unable to digest adequate nutrients through food intake.

- ---Enteral nutrition delivered via tube feedings would be appropriate for patients unable to ingest or digest, such as is the case for some stroke victims and for patients with head or neck injuries.

----Parenteral nutrition delivered via intravenous infusion would be appropriate for patients with severe burn injuries---where hydration, electrolyte balances, and adequate caloric intake are vital to recovery and to preventing secondary infections---and for patients with gastrointestinal disorders that prevent normal absorption of nutrients.

STATEMENT OF THE AMERICAN FERTILITY SOCIETY

The American Fertility Society (AFS), an organization of more than 11,400 physicians and scientists specializing in reproductive medicine, is pleased to have this opportunity to comment on health care reform proposals before the Subcommittee on Health. The AFS believes that meaningful health revision requires an emphasis on coverage for health maintenance and disease prevention as well as for the diagnosis and treatment of illness, including infertility.

An essential part of significant heath care reform is coverage for reproductive health services. These services include prevention of unintended pregnancy, sexually transmitted disease, infertility, gynecologic cancer, osteoporosis and cardiovascular disease. The services also include safe and effective treatment for infertility and other reproductive disorders.

The AFS applauds the President's decision to include coverage of reproductive health services in the Health Security Act. Family planning services are low-cost and cost-effective, and coverage should include counseling, contraception and sexually transmitted disease screening and treatment. We believe health reform must cover other essential preventive services like mammography and pap smears, the benefits of which have been well documented. The health plan for this country should provide coverage for pregnancy diagnosis, prenatal care, nutrition counseling, prescription drugs, labor and delivery and postpartum evaluation and services. We emphatically assert that these services should also include the diagnosis and treatment of infertility.

Infertility is a disease which affects the human reproductive system and can lead to an inability to have children. It affects one in every 12 couples. It is defined as a disease in which there is abnormal function of the reproductive system of either the male, female or both partners which requires indicated, not elective, treatment. The disease can be traced to medical problems in the female roughly a third of the time, medical problems in the male a third of the time, and a combination in both partners for the remaining third. We believe that any benefits package should include medically necessary and medically appropriate therapy for these infertile couples.

Left untreated, some infertility conditions can lead to serious health risks which will be more costly to treat down the road. For example, pelvic inflammatory disease can lead to scarring of the fallopian tubes, which can lead to the life-threatening condition of ectopic pregnancy.

Most infertility -- 85 to 90 percent -- is treated with conventional medical and surgical therapy, from drug treatment to surgical repair of reproductive tract structures in both men and women. The majority of infertile couples require relatively low-cost conventional methods of treatment. Other treatment options include assisted reproductive technologies, standard clinical procedures which require the use of a laboratory to process human sperm and eggs. In vitro fertilization (IVF) is the most well-known of these techniques, although fewer than five percent of infertile couples who seek therapy are actually treated with IVF and other assisted reproductive technologies. The national health plan should provide coverage for both the conventional and assisted reproductive technologies.

In a letter to AFS from Dr. Judith Feder of the Department of Health and Human Services, she states that "appropriate infertility diagnosis and treatment will be covered under the Health Security Act although they are not explicitly identified in the legislative language...The plan covers all services that a clinician has determined to be medically necessary or appropriate unless specifically excluded. The only infertility service excluded from the plan is in vitro fertilization." Although this letter is reassuring that conventional infertility services are covered in the Clinton health care plan, they are not specifically mentioned and we would like to see the word "infertility" included in the bill.

The AFS is grateful that the diagnosis and treatment of infertility are now covered under the proposed Health Security Act. However, we are very concerned about the specific exclusion of in vitro fertilization services. We strongly believe that this exclusion should not be in the statutory language for the following reasons:

♦ Exclusion will displace the medical decision-making process for medically necessary and appropriate procedures from physicians, patients, and the informed consent process.

♦ Exclusion will cancel present IVF coverage provided to individuals in the states of Arkansas, Hawaii, Illinois, Massachusetts, Maryland and Rhode Island, and other individuals who have coverage for this benefit. Practitioners estimate that 30 to 40 percent of IVF cycles are partially or completely covered at this time.

♦ Exclusion will deny access and availability to those in need, and will shift infertility management back to less effective and frequently more invasive and more costly procedures.

♦ Coverage would add minimal costs to the benefits package. For example, mandated fertility coverage in Massachusetts accounts for four-tenths of one percent of the cost of the family package. In vitro fertilization services account for one-tenth of one percent of the package. There would be additional cost savings as a result of the reduction in the number of less-effective infertility services presently performed because they are covered by insurance.

In sum, providing benefits for reproductive health services is a vital part of any meaningful health system reform. Disease prevention -- via mammography and other screening -- clearly saves both lives and dollars. Family planning services are fundamental to preventive health care for women, since the ability to control the timing and spacing of pregnancy directly relates to the health and well-being of women. Moreover, the desire to parent is among the most fundamental desires of the human race, and is essential to the sustenance of society and the human spirit. Coverage for pregnancy-related services - including infertility diagnosis, treatment and in vitro fertilization will be an integral part of any health reforms enacted.

AFS is eager to help the Subcommittee on Health determine what will be appropriate revision of the health care system. We applaud your involvement in this matter of great importance, and we thank you for the opportunity to comment.

Submitted by:
Robert D. Visscher, M.D.
Executive Director
American Fertility Society
1209 Montgomery Highway
Birmingham, AL 35216-2809
(205) 978-5000

STATEMENT OF DEBRA T. BALLEN
AMERICAN INSURANCE ASSOCIATION

PROFILE

The American Insurance Association is a full-service trade organization of casualty insurance companies. In its present form, the association combines three earlier organizations. One of those, the former National Board of Fire Underwriters, was organized in 1866, making it one of the oldest trade associations in the nation.

The various departments provide members with up-to-date intelligence on legislative, regulatory, judicial and technical developments relating to our industry. The AIA also maintains liaison with insurance regulators, federal and state lawmakers, other state and federal government officials, insurance and non-insurance industry groups and media—supplying information and assistance on issues of mutual concern.

A countrywide system of regional offices and local legislative counsel ensures prompt and rigorous attention to casualty insurance matters. At the same time, technical specialists from disciplines as diverse as law, economics and engineering educate members and outside publics on developments that may affect the industry and its services to the insurance-buying public.

U.S. HOUSE OF REPRESENTATIVES
WAYS AND MEANS COMMITTEE
SUBCOMMITTEE ON HEALTH
HEARING ON H.R. 3600
FEBRUARY 4, 1994

AMERICAN INSURANCE ASSOCIATION

The American Insurance Association is a trade association of approximately 250 property/casualty insurance companies, writing about 25% of all such insurance sold in the United States. AIA has a vital interest in the relationship of national health care reform to our two largest lines of business--workers' compensation and automobile insurance. We believe that your Subcommittee has an important role to play in determining the applicability of national health care reform legislation to our industry.

According to the Insurance Services Office ("ISO"), total incurred medical costs for the property/casualty insurance industry totalled approximately $29 billion in 1992. While this is a relatively small share (approximately 4%) of total medical expenditures in the United States, the decisions you will be making in these areas will have profound implications for millions of claimants and policyholders.

Overview of Current Systems

Workers' compensation and automobile insurance are proven systems that have been developed, administered, and refined by the states.

Workers' compensation is one of the oldest social insurance mechanisms in the country, providing "no fault" coverage for work-related injuries and illnesses. Benefits include complete medical care without deductibles, copayments, dollar limits, or time restrictions, as well as income support, rehabilitation, and burial expenses. These benefits are intended to cover all of the economic losses associated with a workplace injury or illness. But workers' compensation is more than a benefit delivery system. It is a disability management system, the purpose of which is to facilitate prompt return to meaningful employment. In this regard, medical treatment decisions are heavily influenced by the need to maximize medical recovery as quickly as possible.

Automobile insurance provides compensation for injuries to people and losses to property that result from automobile accidents. When payments are provided through first party coverage, an injured person receiving medical care files a claim directly with his or her insurance company. This is the case in states with no fault laws and, on a more limited basis, in other states through the purchase of "medical payments" coverage. When payments are provided on a third party basis, the injured person must prove that another driver was "at fault." The settlement of successful liability claims often involves payments for both economic (e.g., lost wages and medical treatments) and non-economic (e.g., pain and suffering) losses.

Both workers' compensation and automobile insurance are heavily regulated by the states with respect to the coverages supplied to policyholders, the rates charged by insurers, and the claims settlement services provided to claimants. Most states have mandatory purchase requirements, and all states have public or private residual markets which guarantee availability to all policyholders, regardless of prior claims experience. Both workers' compensation and automobile insurance utilize rating systems which reflect both the risk profile and individual claims experience of each policyholder. And, employees who change jobs or retire from employment remain fully covered under workers' compensation, without regard to pre-existing conditions. It is interesting to note that many of the goals of national health care reform--such as universal access, comprehensive coverage, and portability--are already built into the workers' compensation and automobile insurance systems.

I do not mean by this brief description to suggest that either system is perfect. Over the past decade, both the workers' compensation and automobile insurance systems have experienced rapidly escalating costs, driven by a number of factors, including: the accelerating cost of medical care; greater claims frequency; increased incidence of litigation; and expansion of the scope of injury the system is called upon to compensate.

Fortunately, there has been progress, as well. In the past several years, a significant number of states have taken affirmative steps to address these problems, targeting medical cost containment as an important area of focus, particularly for workers' compensation. For example, in early November, Florida, one of the nation's largest workers' compensation systems, enacted comprehensive workers' compensation legislation that included extensive medical reforms.

While AIA's role is to focus on legislative/regulatory reform, we are also aware that, over the past several years, our member companies have individually taken affirmative steps to increase the use of managed care in workers' compensation and have registered some impressive cost savings through the use of managed care networks, utilization review, bill audits, and other cost containment measures.

Relationship to National Health Care Reform

AIA believes that national health care reform offers the potential for further streamlining the medical care component of workers' compensation and automobile insurance. We support the careful "coordination" of new federal health plans with the compensation systems under the stewardship of our industry. A well-designed coordinated system, along the lines I will describe, provides the greatest promise for both improving medical care for our claimants and reducing costs for our policyholders.

By contrast, we strongly oppose the "merger" approach, which would wreck existing workers' compensation and automobile insurance systems by severing their medical component and "merging" them into the new health care system. This approach would increase costs and reduce safety incentives--but provide no benefit to injured workers or employers in the case of workers' compensation, or motorists, passengers, and pedestrians covered by the automobile insurance system. Moreover, if workers' compensation and automobile insurance medical benefits are brought into the restructured health care system, Congress will have to find a way to finance more than $40 billion in benefits that are currently provided through alternative compensation systems and have not been factored into current revenue estimates for the President's plan. Our opposition to the merger approach is shared by important members of the business community, including the National Federation of Independent Business, the U.S. Chamber of Commerce, and the National Association of Manufacturers. Each of these groups has released member polling data or position statements strongly critical of the merger approach.

Some of the health care reform bills introduced to date have taken a third approach, which is to exclude workers' compensation and automobile insurance, either explicitly or implicitly. This, in fact, is the approach taken by every major health care reform bill introduced in this Congress, with the exception of the Clinton plan, and one deserving of serious consideration. However, we are concerned about the potential cost shifting implications of such an exclusion, particularly if the health care delivery system is redesigned in a manner that creates new incentives and opportunities for providers to shift costs to property/casualty insurers. We are in the process of studying H.R. 3600, as well as alternative bills, in order to better understand these cost shifting implications.

H.R. 3600

H.R. 3600 adopts a coordination framework and provides the building blocks for an optimal system for the delivery of medical care to injured workers and motorists. However, we believe that the proposal needs to be significantly improved if it is going to work well and achieve savings. In its current form, the bill represents a step backward from the progress in managed care that is being made both through state legislation and individual carrier efforts.

The primary area for improving the proposal relates to the extent to which workers' compensation insurers and self-insured employers can manage the care of workers' compensation patients. As currently drafted, the plan requires employees generally to receive all non-emergency occupational medical treatment from the same health plan they have selected for their other health care needs. Insurers and self-insured employers would be prohibited from channeling injured employees to appropriate providers and from instituting "hands on" claims management. AIA believes that such limitations will result in increased costs for medical care, doctor-shopping designed to increase the dollar "value" of the wage loss portion of claims, and the lengthening of time before an employee returns to a productive life.

Many states recognize the value that insurers and self-insured employers bring to the claims management process. About half of the states authorize the insurer/employer to make the initial choice of provider, and a number of traditional "employee choice" states have recently enacted legislation which allows insurers and self-insured employers to designate a certified managed care organization to provide the care to injured workers. The bill explicitly preempts these state laws which have sought to balance the needs of employers, injured employees, and insurers alike.

The proposal attempts to compensate for the absence of insurer/employer involvement in claims management through the use of various controls--fee schedules; certification standards; designated coordinators; and reporting requirements. While well-intentioned, these controls will be of limited value and some could add new costs to the system. They are no substitute for true managed care by the workers' compensation insurer or self-insured employer.

Fee Schedules: Workers' compensation fee schedules are an effective cost containment tool when they are set at the right level (neither too high or too low), enforced by a regulatory authority, and coupled with strict utilization controls. As currently drafted, the proposal contains none of these features. Moreover, the bill appears to give states and Regional Alliances the unilateral authority to substitute alternative payment methodologies, creating an enormous potential for cost shifting against property/casualty insurers.

Although the bill also allows negotiated agreements between health plans and workers' compensation carriers, it does not establish a level playing field for such negotiations. Since workers' compensation insurers and employers will not be able to influence the employees' selection of a health plan, there will be little incentive for the plans to negotiate terms that are fair for the workers' compensation carrier.

State Certification: In order to obtain state certification, a health plan would be required to demonstrate its ability to arrange for workers' compensation medical care, including rehabilitation and long-term services. While the certification requirement is an effort to address quality concerns, experience tells us that such regulatory standards are seldom effective in the absence of a market incentive to provide the highest quality care. Moreover, since total workers' compensation medical payments (through private insurance, state funds, and self-insurance) constitute less than 3% of medical expenditures in the United States, it is hard to believe that state certification of health plans will depend heavily on the plans' ability to service the needs of workers' compensation patients.

Designated Coordinators: The health plans also would be required to designate a "workers' compensation case manager" to coordinate care. This could duplicate case management already being provided by workers' compensation insurers and self-insured employers and thus add costs to the system. Moreover, because the plans will be under enormous pressure to reduce administrative expenses, they will not have an incentive to invest heavily in workers' compensation case management and coordination.

Reporting Requirements: Information related to provider and health plan performance in treating work-related injuries and illnesses (including return to work) is to be included in reporting information provided by the plans to regulatory authorities (and ultimately the public at large). Unfortunately, the workers' compensation insurer will have no opportunity to act on such information, given the constraints on provider selection I previously described.

In short, AIA does not believe that the controls set forth in the plan will be nearly as effective in containing costs as insurers and self-insured employers can be, if granted a role in the selection of the provider and the on-going management of the claim. Within this construct, we support reasonable safeguards to assure that injured workers are comfortable with the quality of their treatment. Such safeguards should be consistent with the on-going role of the state workers' compensation agencies, which provide informal assistance to injured workers and a forum for resolution of disputes should they arise.

I also would like to call the Committee's attention to the Commission which would be created to "study the feasibility and appropriateness" of transferring the financial responsibility for all medical benefits (including those now covered under workers' compensation and automobile insurance) to the new health system, as well as to provide a detailed plan as to how such a merger might be achieved. The Commission is to be appointed and staffed by the Administration and report to the President, with no apparent Congressional role. We are concerned that this commission will not engage in objective analysis but will be predisposed to recommending the merger approach. Recent statements by First Lady Hillary Rodham Clinton, as well as documents published by the White House, reveal that this conclusion has already been reached--according to an October 8 briefing book to Congress, for example, "in the long run, a federal commission will develop a detailed strategy to fully integrate the financing of workers' compensation benefits."

We are confident that a neutral analysis of the issues demonstrates the fundamental weaknesses of the merger approach. However, an analysis that is preprogrammed to ignore the adverse cost and safety implications will make recommendations that do not make sense. If a Commission is established, Congress should be involved in the process to assure a full and objective review of the issues.

Guidelines for a Well-Coordinated System

We believe it is possible to design a coordinated system that meets the needs of all participants in the workers' compensation and automobile insurance systems and that is consistent with President Clinton's and Congress's goals for national health care reform. With this in mind, we offer the following suggestions:

(1)   The health care system should be coordinated with workers' compensation and automobile insurance, not merged with them;

(2)   Workers' compensation and automobile insurers should be able to select managed care networks and have a role in critical treatment decisions that may affect the speed of recovery;

(3)   Consistent with points (1) and (2), state laws should govern the resolution of disputes over medical treatment and the use of a particular physician or health care provider;

(4)   Workers' compensation insurers and automobile insurers should have explicit authority to engage in utilization review, use medical treatment protocols, prescribe generic drugs, use centralized pharmaceutical services, and adopt other cost containment measures;

(5)   Cost shifting to workers' compensation and automobile insurance for medical treatment should be explicitly prohibited; and

(6)   With regard to automobile insurance, specifically, duplicate recovery of medical costs should be eliminated by requiring that the proceeds from a liability award (through a tort action or the settlement of a case) be used to reimburse a health care provider for the costs of the medical treatment rendered in relation to the injury.

Conclusion

Your decisions with respect to the treatment of workers' compensation and automobile insurance by national health care reform legislation will have profound implications for the millions who depend on those systems for benefits and protection. We believe it is possible to design a "coordinated" system that meets the needs of all players and is consistent with the broader goals of health care reform. Such a system should build upon existing state efforts, and not displace them.

STATEMENT OF THE AMERICAN OCCUPATIONAL THERAPY ASSOCIATION

Chairman Stark, Representative Thomas and Members of the Subcommittee:

The American Occupational Therapy Association, Inc. (AOTA) appreciates the opportunity to submit testimony to the Subcommittee on Health to share our views on proposed changes to the health care delivery system under President Clinton's reform plan.

The Association established in 1917, represents the professionals interests of 48,000 occupational therapists, occupational therapy assistants and students of occupational therapy. As health and rehabilitation professionals, our members provide services to people of all ages disabled by illness, injury, psychological congenital or developmental impairment. The goal of occupational therapy is to enable individuals to achieve a maximum level of independent functioning in their everyday lives. Occupational therapy services include, but are not limited to, providing for the development, improvement or restoration of sensori-motor, oral motor, perceptual or neuromuscular functioning or emotional, motivational, cognitive or psychosocial components of performance; and interventions directed toward developing, improving, or restoring daily living skills, work readiness or work performance skills. These services may require assessment of the need for, design of, and training in the use of assistive technology.

Occupational therapy practitioners provide services to millions of people each year in acute care and rehabilitation hospitals, nursing facilities, freestanding clinics, psychiatric facilities, school systems, homes, offices of independent practitioners and other community settings.

The President's health care reform initiative presents the opportunity to reform our health care system in a comprehensive manner to improve the availability of health care to all Americans. It challenges us to create a system of care with participation by all health care providers to ensure access to quality care while encouraging cost containment and real competition. Comprehensive reform can enable us to examine health care with a wide lens, encompassing a view of health which addresses the needs of an individual to lead a full and productive life. It offers the opportunity to solidify gains made possible by new knowledge in areas such as assistive technology, and to refine and redirect trends such as managed care to better meet the health care needs of Americans.

However, a comprehensive revamping of the health financing and delivery system brings with it potential for unintended consequences and adverse effect. Our testimony targets initiatives envisioned in President Clinton's plan that we believe will create barriers to appropriate care and serve to undermine a comprehensive system of care that accurately reflects actual care provided and needed, particularly for more vulnerable underserved populations.

The Association believes revising our health care delivery system to ensure consumer health care needs are met requires:

- designing managed care systems with adequate safeguards that allow access to necessary care when deemed appropriate by qualified gatekeepers, through a range of accessible practice settings;

- ensuring an adequate health workforce, particularly for underserved populations, by allowing all health professionals access to graduate medical education, Medicare shortage area bonus payments, and opportunities related to essential community providers and manpower shortage areas under the Public Health Service Act;

- guaranteeing a level playing field for all health care professionals by requiring health plans to include all types, classes and categories of health care professionals as qualified providers, and eliminating other existing barriers to practice.

ACCESS TO QUALITY CARE IN MANAGED CARE PRACTICES

President Clinton's cost containment initiatives raise real concerns about the prospect of underservice, particularly as it relates to specialized non-physician services that are dependent on gatekeeper or primary care provider referral. Under the President's proposed cost containment strategies, health plans are likely to be compelled toward stricter payment and service volume controls. Under such a scenario all consumers will be at risk, but individuals with chronic conditions or disabilities will be particularly vulnerable. Experience within the current managed care environment, where examples of financial incentives to restrict access and questionable quality are too common, are not encouraging. Strong quality assurance mechanisms, developed with participation by a full range of health professionals, as well as strong grievance procedures, is critical to ensuring quality care while attempting to contain health care costs.

The Association has endorsed the managed care safeguards articulated by the Consortium for Citizens with Disabilities (CCD) Health Task Force, a copy of which is attached for the Subcommittee's review. Specifically, these recommendations address problems such as financial incentives used to restrict access, the lack of an array of comprehensive services needed particularly by children and adults with disabilities, the lack of adequate quality assurance mechanisms and effective grievance policies to ensure access to appropriate care; and the lack of expertise and training on the part of gatekeepers to determine the needs of individuals, particularly the specialized needs of individuals with disabilities, and access to specialists and specialty care.

The gatekeeping function is of particular concern when determining the rehabilitation needs of an individual. Creating a gatekeeping process that can ensure individuals have access to appropriate care, whether it be rehabilitative or other specialty care, must recognize a single gatekeeper's limited expertise in these specialty areas. Managed care plans should not be permitted to arbitrarily select one health discipline to be the gatekeeper for all individuals, and in effect, control and possibly limit the range of services available. Information on the health needs of the individual, as well as information on current and appropriate practices, must be sought from a variety of sources, including the health professional whose service is under review. A multidisciplinary team approach can be required where a combination of opinions are solicited, including the opinion of a specialist licensed and trained specifically to provide the service being evaluated.

ENSURING AN APPROPRIATE RANGE OF PRACTICE SETTINGS

Under a revised health reform plan, consumers should have access to a full range of practice settings from hospital-based care to community-based settings and offices of private practitioners. The President's plan does not require alliances or health plans to ensure consumer access to services in a full range of practice settings. In fact, under Sec. 1407(a)(6) of the Health Security Act, all health plans that are not fee-for-service plans would be exempt from state laws prohibiting a single source supplier for services. This has serious implications for ensuring accessibility to needed care, particularly for consumers in rural and underserved areas. We urge the Subcommittee to examine this issue closely as it proceeds.

ENSURING AN ADEQUATE HEALTH WORKFORCE

The appropriate shift envisioned under health care reform to primary, preventive and rehabilitative care requires an examination of the supply of both physicians and non-physician health professionals to ensure access to a comprehensive range of care.

Physicians do not provide all of the nation's health care. We believe it is important to recognize that manpower shortages exist across all health care professionals. Opportunities to participate in education and training programs should be available to all health care professions proportionate to their manpower shortages. Additionally, the same incentives, such as loan forgiveness and bonus payment programs, should be offered to non-physician health professionals to encourage them to work in underserved areas and with underserved populations. These health professions also must have access to the same opportunities to increase enrollments of students from culturally diverse backgrounds.

The President's plan is unbalanced in its support for funding of a broad range of health professional education programs needed to serve these shortage areas. Health care reform efforts should focus on providing access for consumers to high quality health practitioners by supporting activities which would provide greater numbers of these professionals.

The President's plan lacks the clarity necessary to ensure that a broad range of essential providers will be available to serve vulnerable populations in both rural and inner city areas. Health care reform must recognize that there is a wide array of health professionals critically important to our nation's ability to meet the health care needs of millions of Americans. Particular types of providers are essential to certain special populations. Rehabilitation services are critical to enabling an individual to achieve a maximum level of independent functioning, and are often the vital link to an individual's ability to lead a full and productive life.

The Association believes that compelling evidence exists documenting a serious and continuing shortage of occupational therapy practitioners throughout the country. Based on the Association's own research, we estimate there is at least a 25% shortage of occupational therapists nationwide. The shortage of occupational therapy assistants is even higher. Although the current supply of occupational therapists and occupational therapy assistants is at an all time high (46,357 occupational therapists, 12,000 occupational therapy assistants) the demand for occupational therapy services far outstrips the supply of trained professionals.

Several factors have contributed to the need for additional occupational therapy services. The aging of the our nation's population has placed additional strains on the health care system. Technological advances have allowed injured and disabled individuals to survive conditions that in the past would have proven fatal. A recognition of rights of the disabled population has also increased the demand for rehabilitation care. Finally, increasing numbers of occupational therapists are moving into nontraditional practice settings, including private practice.

Ample evidence from independent sources corroborate the Association's contention of widespread personnel shortages. Included among them:

- The American Hospital Association reports vacancy rates at 3,100 hospitals for full time occupational therapists in 1991 at 14.2 percent nationwide - the second highest health professional vacancy rate reported. This percent is up from 13.6 percent reported by the AHA in 1989.

- The U.S. Department of Health and Human Services' annual Report to the President and Congress on the Status of Health Personnel in the United States has consistently noted that critical personnel shortages within a number of health professions is a growing problem, and has identified occupational therapy as one of those professions.

- In a landmark study of allied health professions, the National Academy of Sciences' Institute of Medicine expressed serious concern over the supply of occupational therapists and future demand.

The U.S. Bureau of Labor Statistics projects the field of occupational therapy among the twenty top growth professions for the 1990s. Of the five fastest growing health professions, occupational therapists rank number four and occupational therapy assistants rank number five. The supply of occupational therapists is expected to increase by 55 percent from 1990 through 2005, or a need for 20,000 additional therapists. Demand for occupational therapy assistants will grow by 5,000 or 57 percent during the same period (*Monthly Labor Review*, U.S. Bureau of Labor Statistics).

Despite the severe overall shortage of occupational therapists (the overall ratio of occupational therapists to the population is 12.6 per 100,000) the shortage is even worse in some rural areas and in particular states. States with especially low ratios of occupational therapists to state population include West Virginia (3.8 per 100,000), Mississippi (3.9), Kentucky (6.8), South Carolina (6.6), Tennessee (5.7), Nevada (7.4), Georgia (7.7), Idaho (7.2), Utah (6.0), Oklahoma (7.3), Puerto Rico (2.5), and the Virgin Islands (2.0). Occupational therapy assistants are relatively scarce in Idaho, Utah, Nebraska, southern states, the Appalachian region and Puerto Rico.

Other evidence for the severity of the shortages is the fact that new graduates of educational programs for occupational therapists and occupational therapy assistants are receiving between 3 and 4 job offers each. Most find jobs within a month of graduation and sometimes accept scholarships from employers in exchange for employment agreements upon graduation.

Lastly, the shortage is severe enough that employers are increasingly looking oversees for therapists to fill positions in the United States. Evidence comes from the numbers of foreign-trained occupational therapists who are applying to take the national certification examination offered by the American Occupational Therapy Certification Board (AOTCB), which is used as a qualification standard by most of the 49 States which license or otherwise regulate the profession. The number of approved foreign applicants for the examination increased from 185 in 1986 to 509 in 1992. Actual applicants approved for 1993 totaled over 900.

The enrollment of students from ethnically diverse backgrounds in occupational therapy education programs is also low. Only 9.8% of the students enrolled in programs to train occupational therapists and 15.3% enrolled in programs to train occupational therapy assistants are from ethnically diverse backgrounds.

GUARANTEEING A LEVEL PLAYING FIELD FOR ALL HEALTH CARE PROFESSIONALS

Assuring appropriate access to necessary health care services and making our system more cost-efficient will require broad provider participation in the health plans among which consumers will choose. The President's health care reform proposal does not require any health plan to include any particular type of health professional. In earlier drafts of the President's proposal, explanatory language was included which indicated that health plans were expected to have a sufficient mix of providers and specialties to assure adequate access by consumers. The Association was concerned at that time that an "expectation" was insufficient to assure the desired outcome. Barriers continue to exist in the health care marketplace that prevent non-physician health professionals from practicing within the scope of their professionally recognized education and training. Now the final version of the President's plan has even eliminated any reference to an "expectation." In fact, Sec. 1407 of the legislation exempts health plans from many state laws, including state freedom-of-choice laws.

Legislation must ensure that non-physician health professionals have equal opportunity to participate along with physicians and hospitals in forming health plans and that non-physician health professionals are proportionately represented in health plans. Limited fee-for-service plans and HMO point-of-service options with higher premiums and additional copays do not go far enough to offer a level playing field for all qualified health care professionals.

Barriers to practice are always anticompetitive because they restrict the ability of a group of health professionals to compete in offering and providing services to consumers. A variety of restrictions exist in both current federal and state law and practices. Privately imposed barriers to practice may be violations of the antitrust laws, as well, especially if they are imposed by competitors of restricted or excluded health professional groups. Examples of barriers experienced by occupational therapists and other non-physician health professionals include:

- supervision by physician requirements and physician referral rather than direct access to a non-physician professional:

- denial of clinical/hospital privileges and criteria for participation in a health plan tied to hospital privilege requirements;

- subjective or arbitrary insurance reimbursement policies, such as denial of a reimbursement for services performed within the scope of any licensed provider's practice if there is coverage of the service provided by the physician;

- inability to obtain malpractice insurance for anticompetitive reasons not related to competence;

- limitations on scope of practice more restrictive than justified by skill, education and clinical training as stated by the profession;

- joint state licensing board jurisdiction over certain non-physician health professionals by the state medicine board as well as the licensing board of the particular profession;

- limitations in the use of billing codes that reflect the scope of services furnished by non-physician providers; and

- exclusion from participation on managed care panels, and limited referrals when on panels.

Health care reform provides the opportunity to remove such barriers, while achieving other important reform goals of access and choice.

The Association is concerned that state licensure, certification and registration requirements and national certification standards and practice guidelines as recognized by the various professional organizations continue to be respected under health care reform. The President's proposal would override restrictive state practice laws: "No state may, through licensure or otherwise, restrict the practice of any class of health professionals beyond what is justified by the skills and training of such professionals" (Sec. 1161). We applaud the President's effort to eliminate barriers, but we are troubled that this language, as written, may give states the right to weaken the use of state credentialing requirements as the criteria used to ensure that services are provided by qualified professionals.

Additionally, the President's proposal discusses the use of "national standards" in various sections of the health care plan when discussing services, practice guidelines and health care professionals. Any national certification standards should reflect existing education and clinical training programs, as well as the accreditation requirements, certification standards and practice guidelines recognized by each professional association. We believe the health care plan should clarify the importance of referring to these standards for each health profession when identifying the appropriate national standards that should be used.

We urge the Subcommittee to incorporate provisions into health care reform legislation that would prohibit purchasing cooperatives and health plans from denying any type, class or category of health care professional who provides covered services from participating as a qualified provider. Additionally, it is important that reform legislation recognize non-physician health professional qualifications under state licensure, certification and registration laws and guarantee that these professionals can perform patient care activities within their professionally recognized scope of practice.

In addition, national health care reform should ensure an appropriate and sufficient representation of all health professionals, including occupational therapists, on the national, regional, and state health boards, including similar representation and participation in the Quality Management Program data collection system envisioned under the plan. Non-physician health professionals should participate in the development of practice guidelines and the clinical effectiveness of services of these professionals should be studied.

ANTITRUST EXEMPTIONS

The Association is concerned with the antitrust exemptions in the President's plan. We believe that such exemptions will further exacerbate inherent disparity in bargaining power, resulting in continuous and increasing control by hospitals and physicians. Among other exemptions, under Sec. 1322(c) the President's plan would allow alliances to negotiate with providers before setting fee schedules, and allow providers to collectively negotiate.

The President's plan also proposes that guidelines would be developed by the Department of Justice and the Federal Trade Commission to assist health care providers determine whether their activity might subject them to antitrust enforcement. On September 15, 1993 The Department and the Commission issued a first set of guidelines entitled, "Statements of Antitrust Enforcement in the Health Care Area". The guidelines, as presently written, apply only to physicians and hospitals. Although the FTC has given us assurances that non-physician health professionals would be evaluated by the same standards as physicians, there needs to be additional formal clarification as to whether the guidelines apply equally to all health professionals. The guidelines also fail to address whether exclusion of competitors would be considered a potential violation.

AOTA believes that all health care professionals should have equal bargaining power with health plans. Health care reform legislation should create an environment of good faith bargaining where monopolistic practices, competitor collusion or discrimination by physicians, hospitals and health plans toward non-physician health professionals will not be tolerated.

The Association appreciates the opportunity to submit this testimony, and we look forward to working with members of the Subcommittee as the health care reform debate moves forward.

TESTIMONY OF

THE AMERICAN ORTHOTIC AND PROSTHETIC ASSOCIATION

SUBMITTED TO U.S. HOUSE WAYS AND MEANS COMMITTEE

SUBCOMMITTEE ON HEALTH

ON THE ISSUE OF NATIONAL HEALTH CARE REFORM

AND ITS EFFECTS ON ORTHOTIC AND PROSTHETIC PRACTITIONERS

November 29, 1993

Introduction

Thank you for this opportunity to introduce the American Orthotic and Prosthetic Association (AOPA) and to discuss national health care reform. AOPA commends the President and Congress for their diligence in the health care reform debate. AOPA is honored to be included in the debate on health care reform to achieve, quality, accessible, and comprehensive coverage for all Americans. AOPA would like to thank the President for following AOPA's recommendation and clarifying the language in his health care reform bill, The American Health Security Act, to include coverage of "customized" orthotics and prosthetics.

The American Orthotic and Prosthetic Association is the national membership organization representing the approximately 1,200 facilities that provide orthotic and prosthetic (O&P) patient services to the physically challenged throughout the United States. Practitioners employed by AOPA members design and fit orthoses and prostheses (braces and artificial limbs) that enable physically challenged individuals to overcome often serious and crippling injuries and return to productive lives. Most of our patients return to their homes, work, schools, or active retirement.

The expectation of health care reform gives America an opportunity to maximize the quality and productivity of its citizens' lives by strengthening the role of rehabilitative services in the delivery and financing of health care in our nation. In this cooperative spirit, the following points should be addressed regardless of the health care model ultimately passed by the Congress.

National Health Care Reform Recommendations:

Coverage: Basic   health   care   benefits   legislation   should
incorporate universal access to care, comprehensive and quality
health   care   services,   and   consistency   in   coverage/cost-
effectiveness. Any legislation designed to reform the current
health care system should recognize O&P as an essential ingredient
of any basic health care benefits package. The patient's freedom
of choice must be preserved in the national health care plan or
during any modification of the present system. Finally, any
legislation designed to reform the current health care system
should emphasize preventive care as a priority.

Separate Status from Durable Medical Equipment (DME):   To
accomplish the goals of reducing health care expenditures tomorrow
by providing assistive technology today, such as quality orthotics
and prosthetics, it is crucial that O&P:

    1.   be recognized by Medicare as **distinct** and
separate from the vending and renting of durable medical
equipment; and,

    2.   is provided by qualified board certified practitioners.

Despite the fact that a legislative separation of O&P and DME has
been secured by Omnibus Budget Reconciliation Act of 1990,
confusion over the differences between these two disciplines
continues to exist within Congress and the federal agencies. To
clarify this confusion, the organized field of O&P is strictly
defining orthotics as "braces" and prosthetics as "artificial
limbs", and proposes that Congress do the same.

Orthotics and prosthetics are radically different from durable
medical equipment in that O&P health care "services" are highly
individualized to specific patient needs, and are as much a
professional "service" as a "product". The "product" element of
the O&P practice is only part of the total package of treatment
provided by an O&P practitioner, and reimbursement for the service
element is specifically included in O&P's Medicare reimbursement
codes.   O&P devices are generally custom-fabricated and custom-
fit for each individual patient, unlike DME products, which are
reusable and rentable by other individuals.

The approximately 2,700 certified practitioners provide artificial
limbs and braces that are designed in response to a physician's
prescription and meet the unique needs of individual patients. O&P
patient care services include evaluation, consultation, design,
individual fabrication, fitting and patient orientation training.

Furthermore, the O&P medical field is completely different from DME in that O&P has a defined body of technical knowledge, a core of certified practitioners, and a well-established post-baccalaureate education program offered at eight major American universities.

Medical Necessity Criteria: The application of medical necessity criteria must be fair and consistent and make extensive use of practitioner input. It is appropriate and necessary to include functionality as a valid medical necessity criterion. And the continued exemption from completing certificates of medical necessity is appropriate for O&P.

In addition, President Clinton's plan recognizes the importance of "functional necessity." Rather than medical necessity, determination of the effectiveness of O&P devices and services should rest on functional necessity. "Function" should be critical when measuring health status. AOPA supports the concept of "functional necessity" and supports using it as an alternative to "medical necessity". The definition of health should be broad enough to include the ability of a person to function effectively in everyday life. A new definition of health implies that levels of functioning should be used as measures or indicators of health status. Long term, cost effective treatment including rehabilitation of a patient should be the primary consideration for both clinicians and policymakers.

Reform Insurance Practices: Pre-existing conditions should not exclude anyone from obtaining comprehensive insurance. In addition, claim form uniformity would save significant time and cost, for both practitioners and insurers, thus reducing the cost of health care. Regarding malpractice insurance reform, AOPA supports limitations on jury awards for pain and suffering, and guaranteed coverage of all allied health practitioners with a system to accommodate high-risk specialists.

The Health Security Act: AOPA is supportive of the language in President Clinton's plan which states, "leg, arm, back and neck braces, artificial legs, arms and eyes" including "replacements if required due to a change in physical condition" are included as standard benefits. The fact that training for the use of prostheses and orthoses is also included in the standard benefit package, which is an extremely important aspect of O&P care, only serves to emphasize the importance President Clinton is placing on rehabilitative care. In addition, the Health Security Act includes "accessories and supplies used directly with a prosthetic device to achieve the therapeutic benefits of the prosthesis or to assure the proper functioning of the device." AOPA strongly supports this language and President Clinton's deep commitment to rehabilitation and comprehensive health care.

Other health care proposals need to recognize the importance of rehabilitative care and O&P's contribution to returning individuals to productive, self-sufficient lives, most often to the level of functionality they enjoyed previous to the loss of their limb. The expectation of health care reform gives America an opportunity to maximize the quality and productivity of its citizens' lives by strengthening the role of rehabilitative services in the delivery and financing of health care in this nation. In this cooperative spirit, the contribution orthotics and prosthetics make to rehabilitative care must be addressed regardless of the health care model ultimately passed by Congress.

Conclusion

It is our hope that this testimony has demonstrated that the organized field of O&P has acted responsibly with respect to the delivery of health care and has not contributed to spiralling health care costs, and more specifically, has not contributed to cost spirals that result from fraud and abuse. For example, it is important to note that the O&P field: **CAN'T** market artificial limbs and braces through unsolicited telephone calls; **CAN'T** sell unneeded artificial limbs and braces; **CAN'T** engage in carrier shopping; and, **CAN'T** provide unnecessary tests to bilk Medicare. In short, O&P has not used these tactics to gouge and abuse Medicare. It is critical that O&P be recognized by lawmakers and the public as being separate from the vending and renting of durable medical equipment.

Another concern is that O&P services might be "capped." Although this option is tempting to those wishing to curb what they see as "runaway" costs, O&P services can mean the difference between a patient who is active and contributing to society and one who is confined to a hospital or nursing home. Increases in medicare reimbursement for O&P practitioners over the last 10 years have totaled less than 12 percent and have never increased more than 5 percent annually. This record was achieved despite the fact that O&P practitioners have no control over the cost of their components.

No one can deny rehabilitation improves people's lives and their productivity. Furthermore, rehabilitation services are cost effective. Studies show that for every dollar spent on rehabilitation, at least $11 are saved. AOPA supports a team approach: the physician, prosthetist/orthotist and therapist, as well as the patient, making decisions together. This continued call for awareness will enable the nation's lawmakers to make wise decisions regarding every American's access to O&P skills.

February 28, 1994

SUBJECT: Health Care Reform

TO: The Honorable Daniel Rostenkowski, Chairman
            House Ways and Means Committee
            United States House of Representatives
            Washington, D.C. 20515

FROM: *[signature]*
            Miles L. Appleton
            R.R. # 2 Box # 2172
            Berwick, Pennsylvania 18603
            717-675-1101 Extension 291 (Days - Work)
            717-784-1012 (EVenings - Home)

I sit down to write my feelings and recommendations on Health Care Reform at the
request of my Congressman, Paul E. Kanjorski. Congressman Kanjorski has oVer the
last ten years been of great help to me with my chronically ill son Daniel. I feel
that I must first try to make you and your committee understand my situation, so
in turn you can more effectiVely deal with Health Care Reform. I must also say that
I wish you had choosen me to personally testify in front of you committee. I
sincerely hope that you will call upon indiViduals like me to testify, and not
haVe business as usual, with only Special Interest Groups getting the opportunity
to present testimony on this Vital national issue. You would be doing President
Clinton a great diservice by only hearing from Special Interest Groups, such as
Physcians, Hospitals, Insurance Companies, Drug Manufacturers, Health Care
ProViders and National Advocacy Groups, such as the Americen Heart Association,
American Cancer Society, and other such groups with special Vested interest in
Health Care Reform You must, and I say must, hear from what our history refers
to as the "Common Man", for if you do not, Health Care Reform is doomed to certain
failure, or worse than that, you will totally devistate our nation and make the
situation with health care worse than it is already. It is in my opinion imperatiVe
that the citizens of this great nation hear from their peers, for the current
feelings that driVes public opinion is either based on trust or distrust of what
they perceiVe as business as usaul in our federal goVernment. I can guarentee
you that the general public will not look kindly on the testimony of Special
Interest Groups, who haVe Vested financial interest in health care reform and
the general public is also Very skeptical of their elected officiasl in Washington,
D.C. So you see it is vital that if you are to generate public support for Health
Care Reform, you must present testimony that is both personal and can be related
to eVery private citizens situation. IndiViduals like myself who have the ability to
speak with authority, and haVe the personal experiences, to be belieVed by the general
public, will be perceiVed as believeable by the "Common Man", and without broad
based support Health Care Reform will remain only a dream. We must make the issue
of Health Care Reform, "A personal issue to every person in this great nation."
The only way to make this happen, is by balancing the testimony of Special Interest
Groups with equal amount of testimony by indivduals who the public can sympathize
with and relate personally with. I haVe always said that if I could speak to
someone and make them cry, I could at the same time make them understand the
importance of Health Care, so in order to succeed, we must make eVeryone feel
the pain, then only then will we haVe the support to succeed.

Ten years ago this month, as I sat at my then 9 year old sons hospital bed as
he was sleeping, but I could not sleep knowing tha within hours the surgeons would be
cutting into his brain to remoVe a rare brain tumor, that this surgery could kill
him or foreVer impair his life, I was crying at his bedside, and my son awoke,
and said to me "Daddy don't cry, I know everything will be alright, then he
looked up at me and said, but daddy just in case everything is not OK DADDY
PROMISE ME THAT YOU WILL MAKE IT OK. I looked down at my child in amazement,
hearing that wisdom from one so young, and that night I promised my son that I would
make everything OK and that promise has foreVer changed my life, for I keep that
promise near to my heart everyday, and try to make everything alright for my son
and even more try to make everything alright for all the children and parents who
have not the energy or ability to get appropriate health care for their children.
By what I write in the following testimony I am keeping that promise made so
long ago and will continue to do so as long as I liVe. In January 1993 I filed
for bankruptcy because of enormous medical bills, but I must say I would do it
all oVer again, for I will get my child treatment no matter the financial cost,
or the emotional cost. When it comes to loVe you cannot count the cost.

"HEALTH CARE REFORM - POINTS OF VIEW"

Democratic View: President Clintons Plan is mandatory 100% Basic Health Care
CoVerage for all Americans. This would be accomplished by
fees on both employees and employers to fund Health Alliances.
Health Alliances would then contract for Health Insurance
by region. A National Health Board would oVersee the whole
process and set regulations on health care. President Clinton
indicates that their is a National Health Care Crisis.

Republican View: Republican respone has been to say "Their is no Health Care Crisis".
They feel there is a problem, but it can be addressed on a small
scale with existing programs, and with tax incentiVes for health
care. They also feel that President Clintons plan would set up
yet another expensiVe bureaucracy, and create more deficits and
would mean tax increases, which would hurt the economy.

My View: I belieVe the truth and need are somewhere between the aboVe
two Views. There may not be a Health Care Crisis, for the
United States has the best health care in the world. But what
we do haVe is a "Crisis in Access and Ability to Purchase Health
Care Insurance. Health Care Reform must be fair and equitble
to eVeryone and must not impair our national economy. I will
in the following pages detail what National Health Care Reform
must address and make recommendations on how finance and implelment
such reform.

"THE ISSUES OF HEALTH CARE REFORM"

1. Financing Health Care Reform, how and who pays.

2. Dealing with Pre-Existing Conditions.

3. Maintaining insurance if one becomes unemployed or if one wishes to change
   employers.

4. The Medicare and Medicaid Programs.

5. Chronic illness and long term care.

6. Physcian choice.

7. Managed health care or standard health care.

8. Health Insurance Premium cost.

9. Hospital Cost.

10. Mental Illness CoVerage.

11. Prescription Drug Cost and Coverage.

12. Health Insurance Coverage for those whose employer does not proVide program.

13. PreVentiVe Medical SerVices.

14. Consumer Choice.

15. Socailized Medicine or Free Market Insurance.

16. Abuse of Insurance and Medicare/Medicaid.

17. Health Insurance Coverage for those who are disabled and unable to afford coverage.

638

"THE ISSUES OF HEALTH CARE REFORM"
(CONTINUED)

18. Physcian Training and Practices.

19. Consumer Awareness and Education.

20. Special Interest Groups and the Polictical System.

21. Federal Regulations and Requirements that Increase Health Care Cost.

22. Childrens Immunization Programs.

23. Health Insurance Coverage for Non U.S. Citizens.

24. State or Federal Control of Health Care Programs.

25. Hospital and Physcian Acceptance of Insurance Programs.

"RECOMMENDATION ON ABOVE ISSUES"

It is my recommendation that we not create one national health insurance agency. But instead create a National Health Care Policy that realistically deals with rising and inflationary cost of health care, and creates National Health Insurance for those who cannot obtain insurance, or who's employer does not offer health insurance. I will below list specific recommendations for each of the twenty-five major issues listed above. These recommendations embody the spirit of President Clintons initiative and I feel would be acceptble to Congress and the American people. This compromise recommendation would be equitable to both employee, employer and providers, and should stimulate the national economy.

Issue # 1 - Financing Health Care Reform.

A. Employees whose employer pay for employees health care insurance should pay federal income tax on the amount of employer contribution, and these funds should be directed to a National Health Insurance Fund, this fund to provide insurance for those who are either indigent, disabled and unable to work, or for those who work and employer does not provide insurance. In addition those employees who contribute for their health insurance should be able to deduct the total amount paid for health insurance directly off of their gross income. Additionally tax law should be modified to allow individuals to save money for health care and long term care and give individuals who do tax incentives.

B. Employers who do not provide health care benefits to their employees must enroll their employees in the above stated National Health Insurance program, premiums should be structred 50% Employer and 50% Employee, and the premiums should be set' so that employers are not unduly burden, as to cause layoffs of personnel, or jeopardize employers viability.

C. Individuals who are on Unemployment Compensation, Workmens Compensation, will have these income compensation surcharged at .05% and this amount to forwarded to the National Health Insurance fund.

D. Individuals who are on Public Welfare will have this supported income surcharged at .05% and money to be forwarded to the National Health Insurance Fund. Individuals who are able to work will be encouraaged to seek employment and health insurance will continue until either employment with insurance is found or employment is found which utilizes the National Health Insurance Program. Individuals deemed able to work, but do not seek or find employment will have their surcharge share increased at a rate of .05% per month until employment is found or total Public Assistance Income will be used to pay for health care. Penalty surcharge will start after 12 months of Public Assistance.

E. That all Physcians, Hospitals, Pharmacutical Companies, and other health care proViders of services and equipment shall haVe .005% of taxable income set aside and forwarded to the National Health Insurance Fund, or contract with the National Health Insurance Fund to proVide serVices to indiViduals who have National Health Insurance at a discounted rate.

F. Insurance Companies selling health care insurance shall agree to proVide insurance to the National Health Care Insurance Fund at discounted rates. Insurance companies who fail to work with the National Health Insurance Fund, shall be surcharged at a rate of .005% of sales payable to the National Health Insurance Fund.

G. That .10% of all Federal Taxes on Tobacco, Beer, and other alcholic beVerages be set aside and forwarded to the National Health Insurance Fund.

H. That .10% of all Federal Taxes collected on Automobile or Automobile products be forwarded to the National Health Insurance Fund.

I. That .10% of all Federal Drug confications money and sales of property confisciated be transferred to the National Health Insurance Fund.

J. That .10% of all Federal Gasioline Tax collected be forwared to the National Health Insurance Fund.

K. That all monies now proVided to state for health care, be forwarded to the National Health Insurance Fund.

L. That .005% of all monies collected for National Charities be forwarded to the National Health Insurance Fund.

M. That the general public, and other persons and charities be allowed to make charitable contributions to the National Health Insurance Fund, and that these contributions be tax dedcutibele.

Issue # 2 - Dealing with Pre-Existing Conditions.

A. Persons with Pre-Existing Conditions, who cannot purchase Health Insurance shall be enrolled in the National Health Insurance Plan. Premiums should be based on ability to pay. Additionally Insurance Companies should be compelled to enroll a percentage of persons with Pre-Existing Conditions after a 12 Month Waiting Period, and during this waiting period the indiVidual will be coVered by National Health Insurance Fund.

B. Parents who haVe a child who is covered by Health Insurance, but has a Pre-Existing Condition and coVerage will end at age 18 should haVe the option to pick up premiums of priVate insurance, or seek coVerage under the National Health Insurance Fund. Insurance companies should be made to offer this coverage at a premium that is comesurate with indiViduals ability to pay.

C. Federal law in hiring should preclude discrimination in hiring individuals with Pre-Existing Medical Conditions.

Issue # 3 - Maintain insurance if one becomes unemployed or if one wishes to change employers.

    A. Insurance companies must be mandated by law to offer affordable coVerage to persons who lose their job and their employer health care plans, until such time as individual can obtain employment.

    B. Persons should have the option of continuing their preVious coVerage at reasonable rates, or picking up National Health Insurance until they obtain employment.

Issue # 4 - The Medicare and Medicaid Programs

    A. The federal goVernment must reduce the burden of paperwork cost to Hospitals, Physcians and other health care proViders, thereby freeing money for health care.

    B. The federal goVernment must reduce waste in bureaucacy and in fraud in these programs.

    C. The federal goVernment must giVe the states more flexibility in using and waivering these money so that these moneies can be used more efficeintly and let states utilize these funds based on their geographic needs.

Issue # 5 - Chronic Illness and Long Term Care.

    A. Congress must pass legislation to allow indiViduals to saVe money designated for Illness and Long Term Care, and make doing so a positiVe situation with tax incentiVes.

    B. Chronic Illness must be addressed, current situation for families with chronic illness is becoming more and more prevelant. Health Care Cost For Chronic Illness, must haVe some type of tax credit program similar to Tax Credits for Child care.

Issue # 6 - Physcian Choice.

    A. Any National Health Care Policiy must allow for consumer choince in choosing physcian for treatment.

Issue # 7 - Managed Health Care or Standard Health Care.

    A. These options should both be available to consumers, so that whichever plan would be more appropriate for there situation is available to them.

Issue # 8 - Health Insurance Premium Cost.

    A. Health Insurance Premiums should not be controlled by federal goVernment, but some broad guidelines should be in place if Insurance Companies do no find ways to be more cost effective.

    B. National Health Insurance Premiums should be reviewed yearly.

Issue # 9 - Hospital Cost.

    A. Hospital cost could be reduced by reduction of federal paperwork requirements and by haVing National Health Insurance for those who now do no pay, but would pay under National Health Insurance loses would be less, therefore prices should stablize or come down, if they do not, the borad based reguations should be contemplated in the future.

Issue # 10 - Mental Illness Coverage.

    A. Mental Illness CoVerage should be included, as if we can treat
Mental Illness Early on the chances are good that a majority
of persons with Mental Illness, would be able to work and pay
taxes and therefore not be a burden of the goVernment.

    B. Federal funding for Mental Illness and Mental Retardation should
focus on Community Programs and treatment. Federal Regulations
should be changed to giVe states more flexibility in utilizing
these funds.

Issue # 11 - Prescrpition Drug Cost and CoVerage.

    A. Drug Manufactures should make aVailable at discount cost to the
National Health Insurance Plan, prescription drugs at a discount
rate. Manufacturers should also when possible make prescription
drugs avaiable at no cost, and be able to take these expenses
as a tax deduction.

    B. Orphan Drugs, which are so expensive should be subsudized by the
Federal GoVernment.

Issue # 12 - Health Insurance CoVerage for those whose employers does not proVide program.

    A. Employers of these indiViduals should be compelled to provide insurance
thru the National Health Insurance Program at discounted rates.
Employers and Employees paying 50% Equal Shares. The premiums
should be set as to not adVersely affect company Viability, or
cause massiVe lay offs.

    B. Employees should haVe options of more than one choice, preferablly
a choice between Managed Care Program, or Standard Insurance
Program.

Issue # 13 - PreVentiVe Medical SerVices.

    A. Both priVate and national health insurance must proVide preVentiVe
medical care especially for children. Early interVention reduces
long term medical cost.

Issue # 14 - Consumer Choice.

    A. Both Employer and National Health Insurance should proVide for
choice in both Managed or Standard Insurance and espeically in
Physcian Choice.

Issue # 15 - Socialized Medicine or Free Market Insurance.

    A. My recommendation is for separate PriVate Insurance and
National Health Insurance Fund. Free market is preferable,
but National Health Insurance is a necessity for those who
are indigent, unemployed, disabled, or who employer does not
provide coVerage.

Issue # 16 - Abuse of Inssurance and Medicare/Medicaid.

    A. The federal government must educate the public about abuse of
our health care system, and those who do must have the responsibility
of those health care expenses taken out of their pocket.

Issue # 17 - Health Insurance CoVerage for those who are disabled and unable to afford coVerage.

    A. Health Insurance for the disabled should be proVided by the National Health Insurance Plan, and Medicare/Medicaid. But The federal goVernment should work to help these indiViduals oVercome their disabilites, and prejudices of employers, so that these indiViduals can become contributing members of our society. Meaningful job training for the disabled is a must.

Issue # 18 - Physcian Training and Practices.

    A. We as a society View our physcians as only after the money. But I belieVe that part of this problem of haVing caring family physcians, is what we put physcians thru before they can begin practice. The many years of school, graduating with educational bills in the 10 or 100's of thousands of dollars. Then we put them thru residency programs where they 100 to 150 hours a week. Then we expect them to be caring physcians. We need a way to help pay for their medical education, and reform residencey programs, so that they will be what we want. If a federal program was available to help defray medical education expenses, with a requirement that the physcian do a certain amount of community family medicine practice, we would be trainig physcians who will be needed in the future.

Issue # 19 - Consumer Awareness and Education.

    A. The federal goVernment and our local schools need to haVe education and consumer awareness taught in our schools. Adults also should have health care education and consumer awareness a more informed consumer, will be healthier and be more cost concious in using our health care system.

Issue # 20 - Special Interest Groups and the Polictical System.

    A. The federal government must take the lead in reducing the impact of special interest groups on legislation. IndiVidual citizens should have more access to the legislatiVe system. We are based as a nation in serving the good of the common man, and I say the common man has more sense of our needs that someone who has a financial incentiVe in who legislation is drafted.

Issue # 21 - FederalRegulations and Requirements that Increase Health Care Cost.

    A. Medicare/Medicaid paperwork requirements and reporting requirements has a drastic impact on health care cost.

    B. Better management of the Federal GoVernments checks and balances in waste and fraud in federal programs needs to be oVerhauled.

Issue # 22 - Childrens Immunization Program.

    A. All Health Care Insurance both priVate and federally funded, must include proVision for childhool immunization programs.

Issue # 23 - Health Insurance CoVerage for Non U.S. CItizens.

    A. Under no circumstances should health care be provided for Non U.S. Citizens.

Issue # 24 - State or Feder Control of Health Care Programs.

    A. It is my recommendation that the federal goVerment supply health care money to the states and that indiVidual states control health care programs within their states.

Issue # 25 - Hospital and Physcian Acceptance of Insurance Programs.

    A. All hospitals and physcians and other related heath care proViders must accept the National Health Care Insurance, but they may choose not to accept insurance reimbursements as payment in full.

Additional Issues To Be Addressed:

Malpractice and Tort Reform - It must be noted that without meaninful
Reform in Malpractice Insurance and Tort Reform, health care cost will
continue to suffer. Legislation must control malpractice insurance
cost, and reform of the legal tort system is manadatory to reduce
frivilious law suits.

Welfare Reform - Welfare reform is the next step in controlling the
cost of health care, and spiraling cost of our mandated programs
dealing with Mental Illness and Mental Retardation. Without
meaning welfare reform, health care reform will not work.

Abortion and AIDS Issue - Two major issues, AIDS coverage must be
included in health care reform, both treatment and education.
On the abortion issue, I belieVe that abortion coVerage should be
included, but should be modeled after the Pennsylvania Plan.

Additional Funding Issue - If as I haVe recommended states are given
the responsibity for Health Care, additional funding which is already
in place and financed with state money would naturally be included
in setting federal contributions to state health care programs.

Additional Resosurces - It might be possible to use Military
Hospsital Facilities and personnel in some situations as a supplement
to other treatment programs.

Self Insurance - If the recommendation of leaVing present employer and
self pay insurance options, Self Insurance by persons with incomes over
$100,000.00 would be permitted, but at that indivuals on risk, and
that if self insurance is chosen, that indiVidual could only change
to another insurance option eVery twelVe months.

"CLOSING STATEMENT"

There are many issues and recommendations I would like to make, but because of the
restrictions of ten pages of testimony, I can only outline the whole issue briefly.
I again must say that I wish I could come before your committee and testify, but
I haVe not been choosen, but I must insist that this Congressional Process include
a balance of special interest groups and by individuals and families like mine,
otherwise this whole matter of Health Care Reform is doomed to failure. The
American people are not sheep, who must be lead and taken care of because we
cannot think for ourselVes, we are the backbone of this country and we have as
much initative and thought to be part of developing Health Care Reform. It
seems to me that over the years our elected officials haVe developed the ideology
that they and only they haVe innovative ideas and they alone should decide the
course and future and direction of this country. Our forefathers said this should be
the land for the people, and that our elected officials should listen to the common
man. Please listen to us.

I believe that eVery citizen in this country should be part of our political process
and that every citizen should do and participate in public service to our goVernment.
In 1966 during the Vietnam War Era, as has been my families history, I did not wait to
be drafted, nor did I run away from service to my country, I enlisted in the Regular
Army and gave my country three years of serVice. When I was Honorable Discharged in
1969, I married and had a son born in 1975, when my son became ill in 1984, I was
devasted, by my sons courage has inspired me to again take service to my country in
the Health Care Issue. My sons has severe brain damage, an auto-immune disorder,
payhypothyroidisim, Diabetes Insipidus, Bleeding Disorder, but this fate has not
destroyed me, it has strengthen me, my sons has been so many hospitals It would
take pages to list them, his medical bills over the last ten years are in the
multi-millon dollar range, prescription drug cost are tens of thousands of dollars per
month. My son is in a rehab facility in New Hampshire and I can only see him once a
month, but his strength givesme and my wife the strength to go on to keep that
promise I made to him so long ago. Shortly after my sons illness a friend sent me a
poem, it dealt with "What is Success in Life", I won't quote it all, but it says
Success is not Riches or Power or Glory or Prestige, Success in life can only be
achieved if when you pass from this life it is said of you that because you haVe
lived if only one child or person has breathed or liVed better because of what you
have done in your life by your words and deeds then and only then can you say that
that you haVe been successful in life, I would like that to be said of me, and I
hope that it can also be said of all of you who are working on the Issue of Health
Care Reform. I challenge you to be successful in this endeaVor.

February 28, 1994 ATTACHMENT # 1

Sherry, Danny and Miles Appleton discuss Danny's problems in finding assistance

Catastrophic illnesses

Family learns state has little to offer

By David DeKok
Patriot-News

Danny Appleton and his parents are forcing state government to deal with two realities it might rather avoid.

One is that doctors are saving children who have diseases that not long ago were fatal.

The other is that Pennsylvania has little help to offer the survivors, who often need rehabilitation and 24-hour care beyond the resources of loving but overburdened families.

Danny, 12, is like a machine that needs daily tuning to run properly. Most human bodies run themselves just fine. Danny's does not, a regrettable but necessary outcome of the brain surgery in 1985 that saved his life.

Danny with his medicine

The Columbia County youth's fluid intake and outgo must be carefully monitored. He is prone to severe nosebleeds that could be fatal if no one is around to help him. Someone must make sure he takes the eight drugs he needs to survive.

Danny's body no longer knows if it is too hot or too cold. His brain can no longer control his thirst or appetite.

Worst of all, he is prone to sudden and sometimes violent emotional outbursts. The surgery took away the control most humans have over their emotions. Often, his outbursts center around food or drink.

Despite his many problems, Danny has a relatively normal intellect. He can be friendly, even charming, and displays a lively interest in art.

His doctors believe his out-

See APPLETON — Page A14

A14—Sunday Patriot-News, Harrisburg, Pa., Sunday, December [illegible]

Appleton

From Page A1

bursts could be limited if he underwent intensive behavior modification in tandem with education by teachers who fully understand his special needs.

But he has not attended school full time since the operation in March 1985. School district and intermediate unit officials in Berks and Columbia counties have tried, with little success, to fit him into the existing public and private education structure in Pennsylvania.

Last January, Danny was rejected as a resident student by Elwyn Institute in Media, the last private school in the state for mentally handicapped children that might have helped him.

Intermediate unit and state Welfare Department officials began to look outside Pennsylvania for a place to treat and educate Danny. They quickly learned that the state had no way to pay for such an arrangement.

That prompted an initiative — to place Danny in a state institution for the mentally retarded — that left Miles and Sherry Appleton, his parents, angry and bitter.

Welfare Secretary John White is considering a new proposal that would place Danny in a group home with two other children with similar intellects and disabilities. However, no one is certain if DPW has authority to fund it.

Danny is neither mentally ill nor retarded, and if the state or federal government has any aid to offer disabled children at all, it is usually earmarked for children with those conditions or obvious physical handicaps.

The Appletons do not have the funds. Their struggle with Danny's enormous medical expenses, and their efforts to create a state catastrophic-illness fund for children, were described in a Patriot-News story in November 1987.

Danny's plight tests the ability of state government to respond creatively to a social problem that did not exist 10 years ago. Doctors say more and more children will survive once-fatal diseases, and will need help from the state.

* * *

Danny had a craniopharyngioma, a relatively rare form of brain tumor. Two or three children per 100,000 develop brain tumors, according to Dr. Roger Packer, a pediatric neurologist at Children's Hospital in Philadelphia.

Only about 10 percent of all brain tumors are craniopharyngiomas, said Packer, who once treated Danny and is helping complete a study of what factors affect curing brain tumors in children.

Almost all children survive the surgery, he said, but their quality of life afterward can vary from relatively good to poor. Some eventually die of their complications.

Packer said the best result after craniopharyngioma surgery is usually a partial loss of hormones that can be treated by replacement therapy. At the other end of the spectrum are children like Danny, whom he said make up about 10 percent of craniopharyngioma victims.

The advent of the operating microscope and the surgical laser made it possible for surgeons, in the past decade or so, to save children with craniopharyngiomas that once might have been deemed inoperable because of their location in the brain.

Asked if any state or any country had a good program for helping children like Danny, Packer called it "a worldwide problem."

Children who don't have "an arm that drops or an eye that doesn't work" have few programs to help them, Packer said.

"We have no program to deal with emotional disorders," he said. "Danny doesn't fit any of the categories."

A particular concern is when children like Danny grow older, toward adulthood and independence. They become physically more imposing, he said, and more of a threat when they fly into a rage.

"We don't know how to make people [craniopharyngioma survivors] emotionally more stable," Packer said. "Or control their eating and drinking. It winds up being laid back onto the families, which is a 24-hour a day job."

To focus only on a rare case like Danny Appleton, he said, risks ignoring the many other children who have survived once-fatal ailments like cancer, were scarred by the cure, and need help from the state.

"The numbers [of children] are staggering," Packer said. "They have a variety of impairments ... Danny is just the tip of the iceberg. It's the iceberg we have to really worry about."

* * *

In the spring of 1988, the Department of Public Welfare became actively involved in the Danny Appleton case. It had not been invited to do so by the Education Department, but did so in part because of the strain of Danny's illness on his parents.

DPW officials would have no more success than anyone else in finding a solution to Danny's problems.

Gary Boone, central region community program manager for DPW, had met the Appletons after a hearing in November 1987 on a proposed piece of state legislation that would create a catastrophic-illness fund for children.

He had talked frequently with Miles Appleton in the weeks after the meeting. Boone said Appleton wanted his son to undergo behavior modification as well as be educated. That made sense to him as well.

"In other words, it couldn't just be a special school placement," Boone said. "[Not with] all the other kind of medical needs that he had. It had to be [a] very special and unique kind of placement."

Doctors and psychiatrists had been saying that ever since Danny's first psychiatric evaluation a few months after his operation in 1985.

The Appletons worried that Danny's teachers and their administrators did not take his medical and emotional problems seriously enough, were not properly trained, and did not have sufficient resources.

Danny attended a class at Central Columbia Middle School for learning disabled students on a half-day basis this year. The class was taught by a teacher from Central Susquehanna Intermediate Unit.

PRESS-ENTERPRISE/Tuesday, July 21 1987

Boy still suffers from effects of brain surgery

Tumor left youth unable to control emotions, hunger

By SUSAN BROOK
Press-Enterprise staff

BERWICK — Danny Appleton sometimes feels hungry or aggressive, like other 12-year-olds, but brain damage has taken away his natural controls. As a result, he has episodes of violent aggression, says his mother, and he now bears 185 pounds on his 4-foot frame.

Yet, "When he's feeling well, he's touched almost everyone he's met," said his father.

For Miles and Sherry Appleton of Berwick R.D.2, every day in the life of their chronically ill child is focused on emotional, medical and money problems.

Danny had surgery for a rare brain tumor two years ago in Pittsburgh. He escaped the blindness and paralysis that could have resulted, said Sherry, but other problems have developed.

Danny is now a patient at a Virginia children's hospital, where he is being evaluated for his physical and behavioral problems.

During brain surgery, the pituitary gland, which regulates growth, was removed. Sherry said the hypothalamus was also damaged; that part of the brain controls appetite, thirst, aggression and emotion in general.

Doctors are trying to find the right medication to control extreme mood swings, which have recently provoked violent episodes, said Sherry, 37.

The surgery also left his brain unable to regulate the body's temperature. His fluid intake must be watched constantly by his parents, and he takes medication to help regulate body fluids. He can run a fever in summer, and his body temperature can drop so low in winter that he must be hospitalized.

His brain cannot properly regulate his appetite, and he wants to eat constantly, said his mother. At home, they must lock the cabinets and refrigerator; otherwise, Danny will overeat.

Their only child's condition is a constant worry, the parents said, and paying for doctors and medications worries them, too.

The family has been helped by a special fund at St. John's Lutheran Church, Espy, which staged a

Sherry and Miles Appleton, Berwick R.D 2, hold a get-well card from the Yankees baseball team for their son Danny, whose picture sits in the center of the table surrounded by other snapshots of him with famous friends. Danny is in a Virginia children's hospital, being evaluated for problems stemming from a brain tumor removed two years ago

breakfast to raise money for Danny's treatment. The local effort was matched two for one by funds from a Lutheran fraternal organization, bringing the total to $7,000.

"We plan to continue to do that," said the Rev. Michael Schelp. "It sounds like a lot of money, but when you consider their expenses, it's very little," the minister said. "They aren't poor enough to get public aid and not rich enough to meet all their bills."

Miles Appleton, 40, is a guard at the state prison at Dallas. Sherry has been needed at home because Danny requires nearly constant care.

Miles' insurance includes hospitalization coverage, but even with that, the costs are high, he said.

"I'm a state employee and everyone thinks you've got insurance, it pays it all," he said. "But it pays 95 percent. And 5 percent of $200,000 is a lot of money," he said.

Miles describes his son as a likable child who made drawings of Garfield and Odie, the comic-strip cat and dog, to give to workers in the blood laboratory at Geisinger Medical Center in Danville.

The parents miss their child terribly when parted from him. Visiting him in Virginia will mean nine-hour drives and extra spending on housing, gas and restaurants.

The Appletons are beginning to feel a residential school may eventually be the only suitable facility. They always wanted him to attend public school and live as normally as possible, they said. A few times in the year he's lived here, he's been able to serve as an acolyte at church and meet others through a youth group, said Schelp.

When he lived in Allentown, school authorities refused to admit him to public school because of the amount of physical care required each day. Danny attended a day school, but the drive from home took more than two hours, and the ride exhausted him, his mother said.

Central Columbia schools were more receptive and helpful to Danny when the family moved here after a job transfer, they said. But he has been absent a great deal because of hospital stays, making it hard to adjust to the new environment. The parents credit Geisinger doctors, schools and social workers with searching to find the right combination of palliative measures to help them cope with their child's chronic problems.

Miles says he doesn't want anybody to support him, but he's worried about being able to afford medication that might give the child a chance at a more normal, peaceful life. "We've basically used our life savings to get him treated," said Miles.

At Geisinger, doctors experimented with different medications, finally hitting on something that controls one side effect — a form of hepatitis believed to have been contracted as a result of blood transfusions. When he left for the Virginia hospital, Danny was taking nine medications, his mother said.

February 28, 1994   ATTACHMENT # 2

Sunday Patriot-News

Volume 11 · No. 19   HARRISBURG PA. DECEMBER 14 1989   Price $1.00

Upstate couple's struggle to help son yields happy ending

By David DeKok
Patriot-News

FAMILY — Sherry, Danny and Miles Appleton in November 1987.

THE WHITE HOUSE
WASHINGTON

December 8, 1993

The Appleton Family
Route 2, Box 2172
Berwick, Pennsylvania 18603

Dear Sherry, Miles, and Daniel:

Thank you for writing me about my health security plan. My plan is designed to fix our badly broken system before it is too late. Currently, 37 million Americans are without health care. If we do nothing, one in four Americans will lose their health coverage at some point over the next two years, and skyrocketing health care costs will continue to threaten our families and businesses.

The plan I have proposed would give Americans the peace of mind they deserve and help secure a better future for our children and grandchildren. It would guarantee a comprehensive package of benefits that could never be taken away even if you move, lose your job, or become ill. In addition, it would simplify the system and save tens of billions of dollars now spent on health care. Under my proposal, one standard insurance form would be used and everyone would receive a health security card to speed record keeping and processing. The plan would reduce costs by encouraging competition among health plans, emphasizing prevention, reducing excessive paperwork, and cracking down on waste and fraud. The plan also emphasizes consumer choice and would give Americans the ability to choose their health plan and their own doctor. Our plan will build on the quality health care many now enjoy by creating report cards on health plans, so that consumers can reward the highest quality health care providers with their business.

For reform to be both successful and lasting, everyone -- starting with those who profit from the current system -- must take responsibility for being part of the solution. We must have the courage to embrace this new direction and produce a health care system that is built to provide for all Americans now and in the future. I hope I can count on your support.

Sincerely,

Bill Clinton

THE WHITE HOUSE
WASHINGTON

Thanks so much for your ideas on health care reform. They will be carefully considered. My Administration is committed to bringing costs under control and offering quality coverage to every American. No family should face bankruptcy when a parent or child becomes ill or disabled. I appreciate your input in that effort.

Bill Clinton

646

Statement of
The Association of Minority Health Professions Schools
Submitted to the
House Committee on Ways and Means Subcommittee on Health
Record for the February 1, 1994
Health Care Reform Hearing

Thank you for this opportunity to present the views of the Association of Minority
Health Professions Schools (AMHPS) on the training of health professionals within the
context of health reform. As an organization comprised of the eleven historically black
health professional schools in our country, AMHPS is critical to any efforts to reform
the health care system. Our schools train, to an extraordinary extent, the providers
who are dedicated, and particularly competent, to serve the health needs of
traditionally underserved communities. Our schools have trained :

> 50% of the nation's black physicians
> 50% of the black dentists
> 75% of the nation's black pharmacists
> 75% of the black veterinarians

within the context of a health reform that seeks to expand access to health care for *all*
americans, this becomes particularly important because our graduates consistently
choose to work in the underserved inner-city and rural sites that are so critical to any
notion of universality of health care coverage.

However, as important as are the *numbers* of health professionals that we train, and
where they practice, *how* they are trained is also critical to reform. Over our many
years of teaching and providing care on the front lines of America's health care
battleground, (battleground that are in part defined by the disgraceful reality of 75,000
excess premature deaths experienced by African-Americans each year), we have
learned a great deal about how to more **cost effectively and efficiently** provide
comprehensive, and **multidisciplinary,** quality health care to people suffering from
overwhelming and inter-related health and socio-economic challenges.

Our experience has made us passionate about the importance of **community
oriented primary care** and the necessity of providing preventive, diagnostic and
therapeutic health services to the whole population of people from which our individual
patients arise and will return. Each day our faculties and students experience new
insights and develop new knowledge about how to provide health care that
appropriately controls costs while enhancing quality in challenging populations.

Our experience is a national treasure that ought to be more fully realized. But to do
so, we must have the opportunity to survive and to *expand* our capacities as we enter
this exciting new era.

Mr. Chairman, we are **very** enthusiastic about the real possibility, at long last, for
meaningful health reform. We urge urgent action because we understand that each
new day delivers more premature autopsies in our communities. From our vantage
point, it is inconceivable that anyone could think that we do not have a national crisis
in health care.

Despite our enthusiasm, we do have four issues concerning some potential
implications of health reform that could impede our opportunity to fulfill our missions.
They are:

1. *Issues regarding fair competition*

Academic Health Centers require an adequate number and mix of patients with whom
to collaborate in teaching and research activities. Also, an adequate patient base is
essential to the financial survival of our institutions. As a result of our dedication to
working in and with poor communities, our institutions have been significantly
financially disadvantaged. Universal health insurance that is provided through ever

traditional patient base *suddenly* becomes attractive to entrepreneurially minded, well financed enterprises. The competitive playing field ought to be a level and fair one. Those of us who have done the right thing and played by the rules of compassion and equity require and deserve capital and technical support that allows our hospitals, ambulatory clinical facilities, and faculty practice plans to compete, to survive and to serve the needs of our communities and of our nation.

2. *Financial support for community oriented primary care*

While we are pleased to observe the groundswell of support for primary care, we are greatly concerned about the availability of the **financial** support necessary for faculty to teach our students in these new community oriented health care settings. In addition, we are concerned about how this support will be coordinated between medical student education, graduate student education, continuing medical education and with other health care discipline training programs. Graduate and undergraduate medical education reimbursement must be sufficient in amount, and distributed in a manner, that facilitates the efficient and coordinated education of the health professional of the future.

We are also concerned about sustaining our ability to develop new innovations in health care delivery and health services research in community environments, particularly as federal research budgets are held level or increases limited to traditional bio-molecular disciplines. We urge you to make available specific funding, including requirements that all payors contribute to the costs of medical education, to support teaching and research in academic centers generally and in inner-city and rural community oriented primary care settings in particular. Support for the development of more efficient and effective relationships between health professional disciplines working in these communities and between academic health centers, community and migrant health centers, public health facilities and other essential community providers is strongly recommended.

3. *Inequities in the availability of physician specialists*

Our daily experiences remind us that our communities suffer from inadequate numbers of **all** types of health professionals and medical specialists, not just primary care providers. Despite the relative national oversupply of specialists, there are precious few minority physicians of **any** kind. We urge you to be sensitive to our responsibility and requirements for support in training the full spectrum of professionals necessary for comprehensive health systems in our communities. National strategies need to be sensitive to the historical inequities that plague the physician workforce of today and that jeopardize the health of vulnerable communities.

4. *Adequate support for the "pipeline" of future minority physicians*

We embrace the goal of the Association of American Medical Colleges to have 3,000 minority medical students in training by the year 2,000. We were pleased that this goal was included in the president's health reform legislation. Our schools have pioneered the development of "pipeline" programs that begin in early childhood, continue throughout high school and college, and that occur after school, on weekends and during summer vacations. We have learned the value of these programs and strongly urge you to provide the resources necessary for them to grow and to survive. As the President said last night in his state of the union address "it's time to take away our children's guns and give them more books."

In conclusion Mr. Chairman, many of these recommendations are contained in the Council on Graduate Medical Education Third Report's recommendations for increasing the numbers of underrepresented minorities in medicine. We would encourage your committee to strongly consider these recommendations and our statement as you proceed to set the legislative policy that is so critical to realizing effective health reform.

Thank you for this opportunity.

STATEMENT OF IRLE L. BRIDGE
BRIDGE INSURANCE & PROFESSIONAL SERVICES

To serve our 2,000 clients and 100 Corporations, we have offices at 169 N. Peru, Box 768, Cicero, Indiana 46034 and 8888 Keystone Crossing, Suite 1500, Indianapolis, Indiana 46240.

My daughter Cindy Watson has been with me 17 years and the Health and Life Business is called the Bridge/Watson Agency.

We hope by now you have read the articles that I wrote on the National Health Issue in 1988 and 1991.

Before I give you my solution to the National Health Issue, I feel a brief back ground on myself will add validity to my comments. I was born in Ft. Wayne, Indiana in 1933. We lived on $5.00 a week my father brought home during the Depression. He worked at International Harvester 42 years, 22 years a member of UAW and AFL and CIO, Called "Red" Bridge in the Union. My father was a Republican, my mother a Democrat, maiden name was Schinbeckler. President McKinney's mother was a Bridge and part of the families heritage all from Ohio, orginally. 1951 I gave up a Basketball Scholarship to Ball State and went to Purdue for Ag instead. Got a B.S. from Purdue in 1955. 1956 got my M.S. from Purdue and worked on my PHD till 1959. I had the pleasure to teach Vo-Ag and Science from 1956-61. 1961 became a Jr. High Principal till 1962. Started my Life and Health Business in 1962. In 1965, went to Tipton to be a Jr. High Principal. 1968 went back to full-time Life and Health Business. You can tell with this background I have written and enclosed that I have earned and accomplished in the good old fashion American way; hard work, honesty, trust of my clients and self discipline.

Since President Bush's committee did not see fit to listen to me in 1988 and 1991, I appreciate the opportunity to present my solution to the Health Issue.

Dan Burton and Andy Jacobs Congressman have been helpful, along with Chairman Dan Rostenkowski.

It has reinforce my belief that the system still works. Even though I do not agree with President Clinton and his wife Hillary on most of his Health Proposals, I do give him credit for bringing it to a head.

In getting to a solution for the Health Issue,
you must address the following:

    1.) 5 Trillion Dollar National Debt.
    2.) Greed.
    3.) Do you want complete Government
       control?

My answer to the preceding 3 statements;

    1.) Debt - Present Health Ideas increase
      debts - Medicare in the 60's what
      does it cost today?

        a.) What's wrong to increase
           Capital gains?? (7% of business
           people who have the money will
           either add jobs or keep their
           money.)
        b.) Since when does more Police
           cut down crime? Got to start at
           the source: Homes and a lax
           legal system.
        c.) How to pay California's Disaster?
        d.) Entitlements.
        e.) When does the new Tax Bill cut
           the debt today? Or three years
           from now?
        f.) Pork Barrel Funding!

My ideas will not increase the debt.

    2.) Greed - This has been here since
      Adam and Eve. Greed will never be
      changed unless everyone becomes
      "God" fearing people on where we
      will spend eternity instead of 26%
      of the population today.

    3.) Philosphy - Do we want complete
      Government control that President
      Clinton and wife Hillary are proposing
      or good old free Enterprise that I
      feel can still work.

Reason for this in my Professional opinion of
32 years, (in the Health and Life Business) and 40 years
in the people business, that the majority of Americans
want continued good Health Service. (We have the best
in the world and no complete Government control.)

Based on the preceding Philosphy and presented
in December 8th, 1988 (article enclosed), I offer you
the solution that will work and maintain the best
Medical Service in the world.

Even though some people in Washington, D.C. feel
that the Insurance Companies are the only problem this
is not true.

Because of "greed" the consumer, Hospitals, Doctors,
Insurance Companies, and the Government all play a
part.

It is important that we protect all people when
they change or transfer jobs. Pre-existing conditions
are of concern to all people.

Government will have to take care of the 10-15
Million who can't or won't get coverage.

Would consumers buy more groceries if they didn't
have to pay for them? The 3,000 Savings Plan to have
individuals pay part of the bill. (No free lunch anymore.)
Some ideas the Industry and Congresmen have already
presented are good.

Hospitals to cut Administrators and merge services.
Hospitals in most cases have been poorly managed. Doctors
will have to follow local schedules for Surgery and ,
adjust their charges. Insurance Companies and Agents
will have to provide more service on claims and service
to all clients over 65. Get rid of people in Home Office's
and Insurance Field force who are not doing their job.

Also allows individuals to take off 100% (like
Corporations) instead of 25% from their taxes.

In conclusion: I believe very strongly that this
is "One nation under God", that people do not want to
wreck the best Medical System in the world, that they do
not want complete Government control and do not want to
raise the National Debt.

I am also a realist!! If the suggestions I have made are not applied as soon as possible, then by the turn of the Century we will have a complete National Health Program.

I would like to feel that "Free Enterprise will always work and when you get to crunch time that proper decisions are made."

As I said in 1988, 1993 was crunch time. It still is!! (IN 1994.)

I again thank the Chairman and Congresman Jacob and Burton for getting me the opportunity to present a Small Businesman's viewpoint.

I hope and pray you put a Health Bill that will take care of the needs of Americans and preserve "Free Enterprise."

SUBMITTED BY:

IRLE L. BRIDGE
LIFE AND HEALTH
AGENT SINCE
1962

Heights Herald

Thursday, December 8, 1988   Serving Cicero, Arcadia and Atlanta   Vol. 8, No. 5

Health care: A possible time bomb

Insurance Scene

The national debt is not the time bomb waiting to go off in the next five years. It is the cost of health services.

Now that we have your attention, it is time to point out what kind of health coverages you now have. You will find that it is the finest in the world. We know that you do not want these benefits cut whether you are young or old. The problem has been that everyone wants first-class coverage, but they are only willing to pay third-class rates or none at all.

We have three types of people: those who cannot afford any coverage, those who have individual policies, and those who are under group coverage and Medicare. Because of this mixed bag we need to have the hospitals, doctors, insurance companies and the people to be insured to get together.

Some readers will disagree with us. Washington is not the sole answer. In 1979, we visited Europe where they have national health insurance. The hospitals were dirty, doctors were on set pay and the rich were going to private hospitals. In other words, for most of people it is a disaster.

To help you visualize the problem we have here, let me give you some facts.

Total health services next year will cost $500 billion. Medical care inflation is running at a higher rate than overall inflation. People are living longer because of the advances in medicine but it has a price. Part of the 10-30 percent increase in cost is partly due to the government and the hospital and doctors adding to everyone else's bill to make up the difference in Medicare cuts. Start adding the cost of AIDS and you see we have a problem.

As you know, the average cost per family is around $2,200 per year and people do get sick and have accidents.

So that we don't wait till the

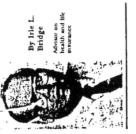

By Irle L.
Bridge

Advisor on
health and life
insurance

bomb goes off, we have some suggestions that will help the problem.

First, select an agent who works for an A.M. Best listed company with an A+ (superior) rating and provide service that will reduce costs.

Secondly, get all hospitals to hire administrators who are excellent budget people.

Get doctors to charge rates that apply to the county they are working. For example, the cost of coverage is cheaper in Tipton County than Marion County.

Insurers that have coverage in Tipton or Hamilton counties should not go to Marion County unless it is a condition that cannot be covered in your county.

We must control costs and the premiums. If you want to have the fine services you are now getting and a premium not be beyond what the employer or an individual can pay, all parties will have to get together before the bomb goes off and you get a national health program.

Remember, if it happened in Europe in 1979, it can happen here.

Remember, the bomb is ticking! In my opinion, you have five years at the most.

Our next article will be on the "Medicare Catastrophic Protection Act: A Trojan Horse."

Consortium for Citizens with Disabilities

The Consortium for Citizens with Disabilities Health Task Force is a coalition of over 65 national organizations working to enact comprehensive health care reform that will meet the needs of persons with disabilities and chronic illnesses, and their families.

TESTIMONY ON BEHALF OF

THE CONSORTIUM FOR CITIZENS WITH DISABILITIES

HEALTH TASK FORCE

RESPECTFULLY SUBMITTED TO

THE U.S. HOUSE OF REPRESENTATIVES
WAYS AND MEANS SUBCOMMITTEE ON HEALTH

FEBRUARY 28, 1994

ON BEHALF OF

Aids Action Council
American Academy of Physical Medicine and Rehabilitation
American Association on Mental Retardation
American Association for Respiratory Care
American Association of University Affiliated Programs for Persons
    with Developmental Disabilities
American Congress of Rehabilitation Medicine
American Council of the Blind
American Counseling Association
American Foundation for the Blind
American Network of Community Options and Resources
American Occupational Therapy Association
American Psychological Association
American Speech-Language-Hearing Association
American State of the Art Prosthetic Association
Amputee Coalition of America
Association for Education and Rehabilitation of the Blind and Visually Impaired
Association of Academic Physiatrists
Association of Maternal and Child Health Programs
Autism National Center
Bazelon Center for Mental Health Law
Center on Disability and Health
Council for Exceptional Children
Disability Rights Education and Defense Fund
Epilepsy Foundation of America
Federation of Families for Children's Mental Health
Higher Education Consortium for Special Education
International Association of Psychosocial Rehabilitation Centers
Joseph P. Kennedy, Jr. Foundation
Learning Disabilities Association of America
National Association of Developmental Disabilities Councils
National Association of Medical Equipment Services
National Association of Private Schools for Exceptional Children
National Association of Protection and Advocacy Systems
National Association of School Psychologists

Continued...

National Association of State Directors of Developmental Disabilities Services
National Association of the Deaf
National Center for Learning Disabilities
National Community Mental Healthcare Council
National Consortium for Physical Education and Recreation for Individuals with
Disabilities
National Council on Independent Living
National Easter Seal Society
National Head Injury Foundation
National Mental Health Association
National Multiple Sclerosis Society
National Parent Network on Disabilities
National Spinal Cord Injury Association
National Recreation and Park Association
National Rehabilitation Association
National Transplant Support Network
NISH - Creating Employment Opportunities for People with Severe Disabilities
Paralyzed Veterans of America
Research Institute for Independent Living
RESNA - An Interdisciplinary Association for the Advancement of Rehabilitation
and Assistive Technologies
Spina Bifida Association of America
Task Force for Health Care Parity for the Environmentally Ill
The Arc
United Cerebral Palsy Associations, Inc.

For additional information, please contact the CCD Health Task Force Co-Chairs:

Kathy McGinley 202-785-3388
Janet O'Keeffe 202-336-5934
Peter Thomas   202-659-2900

The Consortium for Citizens with Disabilities (CCD) is a working coalition of over
100 national consumer, advocacy, provider and professional organizations, which
advocates on behalf of people of all ages with physical and mental disabilities and
their families. Since 1973, CCD has advocated for federal legislation, regulations, and
funding to benefit people with disabilities. This testimony is presented on behalf of
the undersigned members of CCD.

People with disabilities include individuals with physical and mental impairments,
conditions or disorders, and people with acute or chronic illnesses, which impair
their ability to function. The 49 million Americans with disabilities have an
enormous stake in the current health care reform debate. Access to adequate health
care coverage is a critical issue for many persons with disabilities and chronic
illnesses, who have experienced first hand the myriad problems with the current
system.

The U.S. health care system provides high quality care, but it is overly expensive,
often wasteful, and does not assure adequate health care coverage for all Americans.
Escalating and uncontrolled costs make insurance unaffordable for an increasing
number of Americans, and discriminatory practices by insurance companies exclude
millions more Americans who need health care. Current health insurance is also
biased towards acute care and fails to cover necessary services for persons with
chronic illnesses and conditions. For many persons with disabilities, lack of access to
comprehensive health care undermines the promise of the Americans with
Disabilities Act for inclusion, independence and empowerment.

Persons with disabilities and chronic illnesses are disproportionately represented
among both the uninsured and the under-insured in the current system of private
health insurance. As it operates today, the U.S. health insurance system fails persons

with disabilities and chronic conditions in fundamental ways:

- It excludes many persons with disabilities and chronic conditions as "medically uninsurable" or offers them insurance only with pre-existing condition exclusions. In a recent Census Bureau survey, 43 percent of persons with severe disabilities reported that they did not have private health insurance.

- It often charges prohibitive rates to persons with ongoing health needs, making insurance unaffordable for many.

- It does not pay for many necessary health-related services, including adequate rehabilitation, assistive technology, and long-term services and supports.

- It places annual and life-time limits on health care services.

- It often fails to provide protection against catastrophic health care costs.

- It allows insurers to terminate insurance coverage when a person becomes ill.

For all these reasons, CCD strongly endorses the need for far-reaching and comprehensive reform of the American health care system. When evaluating the adequacy of a health system reform proposal, whether the needs of persons with disabilities and chronic illnesses are met is an essential litmus test. It is our strong belief that a health care system that meets the needs of persons with disabilities and chronic illnesses will meet the needs of all Americans.

Concerns About Managed Care

As noted in the Subcommittee announcement for this hearing, health insurance plans that utilize managed care arrangements have become increasingly common, with enrollment increasing from 10 million to over 80 million in the last twelve years. The disability community has very serious reservations about the ability of managed care plans, particularly staff model Health Maintenance Organizations, to meet the needs of persons with disabilities and chronic illnesses who require specialized health services, who require a wide range of closely coordinated services, or who have physical or mental impairments that necessitate more time-intensive services.

To assure that a reformed health system will meet the specialized needs of persons with disabilities and chronic illnesses and conditions, CCD recommends several refinements to the provisions of the Administration's Health Security Act related to managed care. It is important to note that while these recommendations relate specifically to the Health Security Act, *the problems they address are not problems with the bill per se, but problems with the current health system that must be adequately addressed in any health reform legislation that the Congress enacts. At the same time, the positive aspects of the current system must be retained.*

1. Reducing Financial Incentives to Underserve

The continuation of a multi-payer system of health insurance as proposed in the Health Security Act will reduce the extent to which risk and associated health care costs are spread. Therefore, individual health insurance plans will continue to be at risk for insolvency if they incur catastrophic costs. This situation and the need to contain costs generally create a variety of financial incentives to underserve persons with extensive or special health care needs. These incentives exist throughout our current health care system but are particularly problematic in capitated managed care plans.

As an example, certain types of managed care plans place individual physicians at financial risk when they serve persons with a need for intensive, ongoing services. This is a problem particularly for non-salaried physicians who receive a capitated payment for each person enrolled. In one such plan, a family whose child was born with multiple disabilities had great difficulty finding a pediatrician in their health plan who was willing to accept the child as a patient, because the physicians stated they would lose money if they accepted responsibility for the child, because he would require too much care. Other managed care plans pose similar problems of access and under-service. Some managed care plans attempt to pass on risk to providers in the form of financial incentives that seem especially likely to lead to underservice. These include bonuses or penalties to providers related to meeting or exceeding utilization limits and policies requiring physicians to assume the cost of out-of-plan specialty care. A recent GAO report concluded that the more risk is shifted to physicians, the greater the potential for inappropriate reductions in services. *Therefore, CCD RECOMMENDS:*

1. *Contractual provisions in managed care plans that shift financial risk to physicians and other health care providers should be strictly prohibited.*

2. The Need for Time-Intensive Services

Another incentive to underserve is related to the time-intensive treatment needs of some persons with disabilities. If providers are not adequately reimbursed for their time (e.g. volume and time-based services), particularly in non-salaried, capitated care, or fee-for-service arrangements, or if salaried physicians are penalized for not seeing a set number of patients in a given time period, they may be reluctant to provide services to persons with particular disabilities who require more time-intensive service. For example, a gynecologist may be reluctant to treat women with severe cognitive impairments because they may require considerably more time than is usually allotted for a given procedure. While there has been no systematic research on this issue, there is a large amount of anecdotal evidence documenting the problem.

Managed care plans that specialize in the treatment of certain health conditions such as AIDS, report that they need to assign a far smaller caseload to individual physicians because persons with certain conditions need both more services, and more time-intensive services. This need has been recognized by the Physician Payment Review Commission (PPRC), which has proposed a plan to compensate doctors for the time they spend with persons who have disabilities. In its annual report to Congress in 1991, the PPRC endorsed the use of special modifier that would increase payment by a fixed percentage for visit with patients who have communication barriers, disabling cognitive or physical impairments, or an unusual need for counseling or coordination of care.

Risk adjustment formulas consider aggregate utilization and expense, but do not take account of the need for more time-intensive services by some persons with disabilities, who may or may not be high-users of care. *Therefore, CCD recommends*

1. *The presence of physical, mental, and communicative functional impairments must be added to the list of factors used to calculate risk adjustment formulas.*

2. *Reimbursement formulas for all health professionals must include adjustments that take into account the need for more time-intensive services by some persons with disabilities.*

3. *Financial practices in managed care health plans that penalize physicians and other health providers for not seeing a pre-determined number of patients in a particular time period should be prohibited.*

657

3. Assuring Choice of Providers in all Managed Care Plans

As health care costs have continued to rise at double digit rates, insurers and employers have searched for ways to control costs. One response has been a growth in managed care plans of many different types. These include staff-model Health Maintenance Organizations (HMOs), Individual Practice Associations (IPAs), and Preferred Provider Organizations (PPOs). The number of people enrolled in managed health care plans has increased dramatically. Today, there are very few fee-for-service plans that do not employ "managed care" techniques, such as utilization review and pre-admission certification for non-emergency hospitalizations.

Apart from a few well-established HMOs, such as Kaiser in California, the development of many managed care entities is a relatively recent phenomenon and there are serious concerns about some of the financial practices they employ to control utilization. CCD is concerned that while there are incentives in these plans to keep people healthy and decrease inappropriate utilization of expensive services, many plans offer financial incentives to decrease *appropriate* utilization. For example, some plans will withhold a percentage of a provider's income (15 - 20 percent) if they have exceeded a targeted number of referrals to specialists and hospitalizations. To address these concerns, *CCD RECOMMENDS:*

1. *The Point of Service option for managed care plans must be maintained.*

2. *There must be strong provisions to assure that physician referrals to physician and non-physician specialists are financially neutral and based solely on the health needs of the patient. Just as physicians should not receive payment for referrals, so they should not receive payment for denying referrals. The legislation must expressly prohibit financial penalties for making referrals and bonus payments for not making referrals.*

3. *There must be a prohibition against balance billing for medically necessary services obtained outside a network.*

A.   Single Source Contracting

The Health Security Act currently preempts state laws that prohibit health plans from contracting with a "single source" to provide all of the services for a particular aspect of health care. For instance, under the HSA, health plans would be able to contract with one orthotic and prosthetic practitioner to provide all of the orthopedic braces and artificial limbs prescribed by physicians in the health plan. Similarly, one home medical equipment supplier could be chosen to service all of the home equipment needs of the plan's beneficiaries.

This approach is undesirable in a number of respects. First, qualified providers will be prevented from gaining access to and competing in the health care market. Monopolies of providers of particular types of services will be encouraged by this policy, thereby decreasing competition and eventually driving up prices. Some qualified providers could be forced out of business. The combined effect of allowing single source providers and decreases in the number of qualified providers in a given area will reduce the service options available to consumers. Consumers will be prevented from choosing a health care provider with whom they may have developed a long-standing relationship or one who is conveniently located.

The quality of care may also be compromised when managed care plans contract with a single provider for a specialized service. As an example, in the area of orthotics and prosthetics (O & P), many certified O & P practitioners specialize in different aspects of orthotic and prosthetic care. One may specialize in advanced upper limb prostheses and another in orthopedic braces for the management of spinal conditions such as scoliosis. Other providers may specialize in advanced fitting techniques and material applications. In an area like O & P, where "one size does *not* fit all", allowing a plan to contract with a single provider severely restricts access to providers with expertise in a given area, and has to potential to seriously undermine the quality of care that a persons receives. Consumers must be given a real choice of providers for all services covered under a health plan. Therefore, *CCD RECOMMENDS:*

1. *The legislation must include incentives for health plans to contract with as many providers as necessary to meet the health care needs of their beneficiaries, particularly persons with disabilities and chronic, disabling illnesses.*

2. *No health plan should be allowed to engage in practices that have the effect of discriminating against any type or category of provider, or within a category of providers, as long as the provider is authorized under state law or regulations to provide health and mental health services. This will allow the consumer to have a real choice when selecting a health professional for a particular condition. This freedom of choice is particularly important for persons seeking mental health services, where interpersonal variables are important factors in treatment success.*

B. Gatekeepers

While the Health Security Act enables choice of providers outside of a managed care network, it does so at a substantial cost to the enrollee of at least 20 percent of the cost of the service, and there are no provisions to address the problem of balance billing for "out-of-network" services. In addition, in managed care systems, neither the person with a chronic condition or disability, such as severe spinal or head injury, stroke or cancer, nor the generalist gatekeeper are necessarily aware of the services available and needed. To remedy these problems, it is necessary to give individuals who need ongoing specialized services for their particular condition, a right to choose his or her gatekeeper physician, including an appropriate specialist for the condition involved. Each health plan would be obligated to create panels including specialists dealing with the major disabilities.

The National Health Board would define the conditions requiring specialized, ongoing care and would issue guidelines to assist plans in determining appropriate specialties to be represented on such panels. For example, specialists in physical medicine and rehabilitation would be relevant for managing spinal cord injury or head injury or stroke; specialists in neurology would be relevant for managing stroke, epilepsy, multiple sclerosis, and Alzheimer's disease; specialists in oncology would be relevant to managing cancer.

This right to choose one's main and primary physician is very important and particularly important to a person with a serious health problem. This right is all the more significant in managed care where the main or primary physician has gatekeeper functions. A specialist often is the main or primary physician in terms of personal contact and management for people with disabilities, and would generally be the best informed and competent manager of resources and services for persons with chronic disease or disability. However, managed care systems often prohibit the use of specialists in such roles. To address this problem, *CCD recommends the following change to Section 1402:*

Requirements Related to Enrollment and Coverage by Health Plans

"(h) Any health plan which utilizes a gatekeeper or similar process to approve health care services prior to their provision, shall provide each enrollee who has a chronic condition or disability likely to require substantial health care services over a

prolonged period of time, a choice of his or her gatekeeper physician from a panel of physicians which shall include specialists in the medical management of the condition. The National Health Board shall develop and publish a list of the chronic conditions and disabilities that are likely to require substantial specialized health care services over a prolonged period of time. The National Health Board is authorized to develop guidelines to assist health plans in determining which physicians are specialists in the medical management of the conditions or disabilities defined by the Board under this section. A health plan shall annually establish panels of physicians who agree to serve as gatekeeper physicians, including specialists in the medical management of chronic conditions or disabilities such as specialists in physical medicine and rehabilitation, and neurology.

Suggested Report Language:

Individuals with chronic conditions or disabilities of a certain type including spinal cord injury, head injury, or stroke will often need ongoing medical management of a specialist in medicine. This person will often be the primary physician of the patient in terms of the amount of contacts with the patient and the decision making about his or her condition. Individuals with such conditions and disabilities generally desire to have a physician who specializes in the condition they have manage their care in managed care systems. This amendment provides that such individuals have a right to annually select a gatekeeper physician from a panel that shall include specialists in the conditions defined by the NHB as being of such a nature to require specialists case management rather than generalist case management. Many organizations representing persons with disabilities have urged that persons with disabilities be empowered to select a specialist as their gatekeeper case manager. Conditions which lend themselves to better case management by specialists are usually severe disabilities, for example spinal cord injury, multiple sclerosis, head injury, or AIDS. These conditions often affect many body systems and require a comprehensive approach to medical management and rehabilitation services. Specialists in treating such conditions are trained to understand such complex conditions and to be knowledgeable about the resources available to manage such conditions effectively. Physical medicine and rehabilitation specialists are trained and experienced in handling the comprehensive rehabilitation needs and most general medical problems of persons with severe physical disability of the neuromuscular and musculoskeletal systems. Specialists in neurology are trained and experienced in the diagnosis and medical management of persons with neurological conditions such as epilepsy, stroke and Alzheimer's disease.

C.   Access to Academic Health Centers and Centers of Excellence

Academic health centers are entities operated by or affiliated with a school of medicine or osteopathy or a teaching hospital. It is through such centers that many specialized treatments are available, including treatments for rare diseases and disorders, and for unusually severe conditions. A major issue of concern to persons with disabilities and special health care needs is whether persons in managed care settings will be able to receive services at specialized treatment centers. The Health Security Act says that a state "may" require alliances to assure that at least one accountable health plan has a contract with a "center of excellence." This provision does not adequately address the concerns of persons with special health needs. .
Additionally, we are concerned that persons with disabilities will be financially penalized for receiving medically necessary, specialist services outside the network if these services are not provided in the network. Given that a large percentage of the population is currently enrolled in managed care plans, and this percentage is expected to increase, it is essential that final legislation includes provisions to assure access for all Americans to academic health centers and centers of excellence. Therefore, *CCD RECOMMENDS:*

1.   *Regional and corporate alliances must ensure that all health plans have*

sufficient contracts with eligible academic health centers and centers of
excellence so their enrollees can receive specialized treatment services.

2. *There should be effective quality assurance mechanisms in managed care plans*
    to ensure that people with disabilities and chronic conditions who need
    ongoing specialized services have appropriate access to these services, and
    should not be financially penalized when their medical condition requires
    specialty services.

4. Consumer Involvement and Protections

To ensure that the health care needs of persons with disabilities are met, CCD
RECOMMENDS:

1. *An advisory committee under the auspices of the National Health Board*
    should be established to address the needs of persons with disabilities and
    chronic illnesses.

2. *There must be a formal process for the incorporation of consumer input in the*
    development of "report cards" for health plans. Additionally, these report
    cards must assess not only the quality of care delivered to the "average"
    person, but must include assessments of the quality of care delivered to
    persons with disabilities and chronic health needs.

Additional Concerns and Recommendations

The CCD has developed a document listing four major problem areas in managed
care and our recommendations to address them. This document is included as an
addendum.

Closing

In closing, we would like to state that CCD is committed to working with both the
Administration and Congress to enact comprehensive health care reform in 1994.
With the exception of President Clinton's plan and the Single Payer Plan introduced
by Senator Wellstone and Rep. McDermott, all of the other bills currently being
considered in the 103rd Congress fail to address the needs of persons with disabilities
in fundamental ways. We strongly urge the Subcommittee to reject those proposals
that do not guarantee universal coverage for comprehensive benefits, protection from
catastrophic costs, and cost containment measures that will slow the growth in health
care costs so that comprehensive benefits remain affordable. We also urge the
Subcommittee to support the proposed home and community-based long-term care
provisions of the Health Security Act. Health care reform must include provision to
address the need for long-term services and supports by persons with disabilities and
chronic illnesses.

As you proceed with your work on health reform legislation, we would like you to
remember one point: "In the long-term, the success of the health care system must be
judged less on its success in serving the majority of the population, most of whom
have few or simple medical care needs, and more on how effectively it addresses the
needs of those with serious and persistent disabling illness, who depend on the
health system for their functioning, perhaps even for their lives. To the extent that
the reforms address their needs successfully, they are likely to serve us all well."[1]

1. Mechanic, David. Mental health services in the context of health insurance
reform. *The Milbank Quarterly*, Vol. 71(3), 1993.

Consortium for Citizens with Disabilities

The Consortium for Citizens with Disabilities Health Task Force is a coalition of over 65 national organizations working to enact comprehensive health care reform that will meet the needs of persons with disabilities and chronic illnesses, and their families.

THE CONSORTIUM FOR CITIZENS WITH DISABILITIES HEALTH TASK FORCE

PROBLEMS AND SAFEGUARDS FOR
PEOPLE WITH DISABILITIES IN MANAGED CARE

The CCD Health Task Force "Principles for Health Care Reform from a Disability Perspective" were developed to assess the ability of various major health care reform measures to meet the needs of people with disabilities. Since many reform proposals utilize some form of managed care, the CCD has applied these principles and identified a number of major problems in managed care.

This document identifies these problems and makes recommendations to improve the ability of managed care systems to better meet the needs of people with disabilities. The CCD believes that it is critical for health care policy makers to recognize that there are at least 43 million Americans with disabilities and a large number of others with special health care needs. This includes individuals of all ages with physical and mental impairments, conditions or disorders, that are severe, acute, or chronic and limit or impede their ability to function.

Problems with/Recommendations for Improvement

I.   Managed care systems often include financial incentives to restrict access, limit or deny care, or provide poor quality care. This is especially detrimental to children and adults with disabilities and those with special health care needs.

   A.   Capitated managed care systems must have the flexibility necessary to permit primary care physicians to refer participants with disabilities to specialists without being financially penalized.

   B.   Primary care physicians in managed care plans must be adequately compensated and not placed at inordinate financial risk.

   C.   Methods for ensuring the financial solvency of managed care entities, particularly capitation models, must be considered. These may include financial solvency requirements for HMOs, mandatory reinsurance, state reinsurance for Medicaid managed care programs, stop-loss coverage, and mandatory capitalization requirements.

II.   Managed care systems often do not include the array of comprehensive health related services needed by children and adults with disabilities.

   A.   Managed care programs must offer a comprehensive benefits package that meets the needs of people with disabilities and special health care needs. This includes such basic benefits as prescription drugs, rehabilitation services, durable medical equipment, such as wheelchairs and other assistive technology, and mental health services.

   B.   Managed care programs must not include disincentives, financial or otherwise, to the provision of services in home and community-based settings when appropriate.

   C.   Specific services should be provided not only to treat acute and chronic conditions but also to promote and maintain health and optimum functioning and prevent deterioration and secondary complications.

III. Managed care systems often have limited experience in providing comprehensive services to children and adults with disabilities because of a systemic emphasis on primary care. This leads to limited access to needed specialized services, delays in services, and a lack of continuity of care needed by children and adults with disabilities.

   A.   Managed care systems must offer people with disabilities and special health care needs the option of having a specialist as their "gatekeeper" in the system. This specialist would provide both necessary specialized care (at the specialized rate) and primary care (at the lower primary care reimbursement rate).

   B.   Managed care entities must have specific limits on waiting times for first appointments and for speciality referrals. To assure geographic accessibility of services, there must also be established standards on travel times and distances to both primary and specialized services.

   C.   Managed care systems must be structured to ensure continued, appropriate access to health and health-related services for children and adults with disabilities.

IV. Managed care systems lack adequate quality assurance mechanisms, as well as effective grievance policies and procedures designed to ensure access to appropriate health services.

    A. Managed care systems must provide participants with clear information on policies, procedures, and grievance mechanisms and must ensure consumer participation in the establishment of such procedures. All reviews must be conducted in a timely manner. An independent ombudsman program should be required.

    B. Managed care systems should be required to provide health care service in accordance with nationally accepted prevention and treatment protocols, e.g. protocols for prenatal care, well-baby care, and childhood immunization schedules.

    C. Managed care systems must have in place timely procedures for obtaining independent second opinions when covered benefits are denied for any reason, including a judgement that they are not "medically necessary" or when a consumer challenges the appropriateness of a proposed treatment. These second opinions must be considered in any grievance review.

    D. Managed care systems must include the option to disenroll for those participants who are not receiving adequate and timely services.

    E. Managed care programs must have strict quality assurance provisions that require internal and external audits by independent assessors and the results of these audits should be available to consumers to assist them in choosing a managed care program. Outcome reviews should be a component of this process.

    F. Additional protections which must be included are satisfaction surveys of enrollees and disenrollees, including current and former providers.

STATEMENT OF LES FIELDS
COST CONTAINED HEALTH INNOVATIONS
BEFORE THE WAYS AND MEANS COMMITTEE
SUBCOMMITTEE ON HEALTH
November 23, 1993

Mister Chairman and Members of the Committee:

My name is Les Fields. For the past 21 years, I have been involved in assisting companies, large and small, to provide benefits, especially health benefits to their employees. As a reinsurnace consultant, our most important job is to provide our clients and their employees with clear information about the health care benefits market. That information will allow them to select or construct a health care plan that is affordable and meets the needs of their workers.

For the past several years, an increasing number of our clients have been choosing to self fund their insurance. Companies, large and small, put funds aside in a trust account arrangement, which is subject to all relevant ERISA regulations and protections. The monies in the fund are used to pay typical claims. The company will usually purchase "stop loss" coverage to protect its own savings in the case of larger than average claims in the plan.

The small businesses we work with consistently choose self funding because it is an excellent combination of a company specific plan and financial predictability. And as the plan administrators, we are closer to the employees and more responsive than a large bureaucracy in a far off location.

We are presenting this statement to your committee because we are particularly concerned that the Clinton proposal will effectively outlaw this self funded approach which has worked so well for our clients. The Clinton plan would require every company that has less than 5,000 employees to join a regional health alliance. The alliance will be responsible for picking and choosing what kind of health plans our employees can select, and we will have to pay for. Neither we nor our clients will have any control over what plan may or may not be acceptable to the alliance. And we will have no control at all over the price we will have to pay to buy that coverage.

In the long run, perhaps the worst part of the President's proposal is that it completely removes our employer clients from any ability to manage or control health care expenses. If we lose any stake in the cost of the system as a whole, it makes sense that many of the careful cost control techniques pioneered by employers over the years will go by the wayside. If our employees no longer can connect that extra doctor visit with an increase in our company's costs, then no one, outside the bureaucrats in Washington or the state capital, will have any direct interest in keeping cost under control.

Clinton's plan could be modified in a number of ways without throwing out the self funded option that works for our clients. First, the threshold for opting out of the health alliances should be reduced to 50 employees. Many small companies who offer health insurance (60 percent by one survey) utilize self funding. It just makes no sense to favor large companies who self insure, but not to allow smaller firms the same advantage. IF the alliances are all that they're cracked up to be, many companies will join them anyway. Why not let the market decide instead of restrict choice.

We have no problem with reasonable minimum benefits. Any self insured employer should meet whatever the appropriate standards are. We have no problem with the sorts of "small group" reforms we have heard discussed, guaranteeing insurance to all employees and eliminating restrictions based on pre-existing conditions. If the Congress believes some sort of "adjustment" based on health risk is necessary, we believe a simple system could be applied to self funding. We are not interested in shirking our responsibilities.

But we strongly object to being forced to abandon the one approach to health care access which has worked for our clients. Self funding with stop loss coverage is a financially sound system that serves thousands of companies and employees. We believe that if the President really knew the extent of success of self funding, especially in small and medium sized firms, he would not have so completely foreclosed it from his "reformed" system.

We would be happy to provide you and any other Members of Congress with additional information about how our system of providing health care access to our employees. With an emphasis on individual company savings, local claims and case management, and employer and employee flexibility with benefits, we think the health care reform "experts" have a lot to learn from our system.

JOHN LEWIS
5TH DISTRICT GEORGIA

CHIEF DEPUTY MAJORITY WHIP

COMMITTEES

WAYS AND MEANS

SUBCOMMITTEES:
HEALTH
OVERSIGHT

COMMITTEE ON
THE DISTRICT OF COLUMBIA

SUBCOMMITTEES:
GOVERNMENT OPERATIONS AND
METROPOLITAN AFFAIRS
JUDICIARY AND EDUCATION

Congress of the United States
House of Representatives
Washington, DC 20515-1005

WASHINGTON OFFICE:
329 CANNON HOUSE OFFICE BUILDING
WASHINGTON, DC 20515-1005
(202) 225-3801

DISTRICT OFFICE

THE EQUITABLE BUILDING
100 PEACHTREE STREET, N.W.
SUITE #1920
ATLANTA, GA 30303
(404) 659-0116

January 18, 1994

The Honorable Fortney Pete Stark
Chairman
Subcommittee on Health
U.S. House of Representatives
1114 Longworth
Washington, D.C. 20515

Dear Mr. Chairman:

I am enclosing testimony that I would like included as
written testimony in the February 1, 1994, hearing on health care
reform. Ms. Donna Espy of Marietta, Georgia, has a very
compelling story to tell about her brother Robert who had cystic
fibrosis and died at the age of 27. Robert Espy was working
full-time, living independently and paying taxes. Unfortunately,
he then lost his health care coverage, which may have delayed him
from seeking appropriate care. The consequences of that delay
were fatal. I believe you will find Ms. Espy's testimony both
instructive and moving.

I appreciate your attention to this request. If you have
any questions, please contact my Legislative Assistant, Deborah
Spielberg.

Sincerely,

John Lewis
Member of Congress

Written Testimony for Congressional Record Regarding Health care Reform

Dear Congressional Leaders:

My name is Donna Espy and I reside in Marietta, Georgia. I am sharing this testimony to tell you the story of my brother, Robert, who died on July 17, 1992 at the age of 27. I believe my brother would be alive today if there would have been a national health care program available to him like the ones under consideration presently.

Bobby was born with Cystic Fibrosis, a genetic lung disease with no known cure presently. For 27 years, he was on my father's insurance coverage through his employer. But, suddenly, in March of 1992, Bobby received a letter stating he would be dropped from his insurance coverage effective immediately. The reason? He was working and making too much money to stay on the policy. Why the sudden change? A new insurance carrier had been chosen and all policies were under review. With no notice, they dropped Bobby and didn't offer him an individual policy.

My brother was a general manager for a construction company in Marietta for almost four years. He moved to Georgia nine years ago and had enjoyed very good health during the entire time, except for one hospitalization for a stomach operation. He was self supportive and held down a full-time job, lived independently in an apartment, and just needed some help when he was hospitalized. He was very distraught about this drop in coverage, because he knew he could never get health insurance on his own with a pre-existing condition like Cystic Fibrosis -- even if he could afford to pay the premiums.

Two months later, around the first part of June, Bobby became ill. He was coughing, losing weight and just feeling awful. We urged him to go to the doctor, but he decided to try to get better in bed at home with his usual regimen of medicines. After about a week and a half, my mom took him down to Emory University Hospital in Atlanta, where his CF doctor took a look at him and, unbelievably to us, sent him home with oral antibiotics. Two days later, barely able to breathe, he drove himself to the emergency room and was admitted with severe pneumonia.

Would Bobby have gone to the doctor sooner if he would have had insurance coverage? Did the doctor at Emory Hospital not admit him because he was uninsured?

These questions will haunt us forever, but why should anyone in this country be put in that position? Why are people punished for wanting to be independent instead of living off the government? Our health care system often rewards people for lying. My brother could have lied about his income, about having a job at all, and about living on his own, but his pride and self-esteem wouldn't let him. But it probably would have allowed him to stay on my father's insurance.

Bobby's disease was not a result of smoking, bad eating habits, sexual misconduct or drug misuse. He was just born with a bad disease -- and he seemed to be punished for it. Why can't we help other Americans help themselves with their health care needs -- no matter what the reason for the need?

Bobby was transferred to Emory University Hospital so his Cystic Fibrosis doctors could take over his treatment. Throughout his two-week fight at Emory, the respiratory therapists who worked day and night to save his life said they were amazed that a 27-year-old CF patient could hold down a full-time job and live alone.

My brother was not an exception to the rule -- he was the only one who would admit it. Other CF patients have had to become dependent upon their parents for living arrangements, and turn down jobs when indeed they were able to work -- just to meet the criteria to get insurance coverage for their medical needs. Did my brother's pride and high self-worth kill him? You tell me.

In the past year, I have urged both state and national political leaders to work together to pass a health plan that would include persons with pre-existing medical conditions. Bobby was blessed with good health so he could work, but what about those who can't work? Does our federal government offer programs to take care of them, or does the family have to bear the burden?

There are good people in this country who, through no fault of their own, have serious medical problems and "fall through the cracks" when it comes to health care programs needed to aid in catastrophic illness and major hospitalizations.

I miss my brother very much, but I'm very proud of him. Proud of his courage to be independent and to enjoy working and earning an honest living. He paid his taxes and believed in hard work. He also believed in getting the chance to live a long, normal life. He didn't get that chance. I hope in the future we can give it to someone else's brother.

Thank you.
Sincerely,

Donna Espy
2444 Sewell Mill Road
Marietta, GA   30062
404/977-7004
Fax - 404/509-9162

STATEMENT OF HEALTH INDUSTRY DISTRIBUTORS ASSOCIATION

I. INTRODUCTION: HIDA

The Health Industry Distributors Association is the national association of health and medical products distribution firms. Created in Chicago in 1902 by a group of medical products business people, HIDA now represents over 800 wholesale and retail distributors with nearly 2,000 locations. This statement is submitted on behalf of these members in all 50 states and the District of Columbia.

HIDA members include a broad range of medical products distributors — billion dollar, multi-location, national companies, and neighborhood stores, chains, and independents. HIDA members provide critical, value-added distribution services to virtually every hospital, physician office, nursing home, clinic, and other health care site in the nation, and for a growing number of patients directly for use in their own homes.

II: THE VALUE OF MEDICAL PRODUCTS DISTRIBUTORS AND HOME MEDICAL EQUIPMENT SUPPLIERS

Ensuring that the right products arrive at the right places, in the right quantity, at the right times, in the right condition — all at the least cost — is the challenge that faces health care distributors, manufacturers, and providers. However, distribution involves more than just moving medical and surgical products — from cardiac catheters to hip implants to wheelchairs — from the point of manufacture to the point of use in the hospital, nursing home, physician's office, clinic, patient's home, or wherever health care is provided.

HIDA members are the traditional pipeline through which medical supplies and equipment flow to the final users in all segments of health care. They handle the process of "materials management" which includes the storage, handling, and transportation activities at each location in the chain. Distributors also conduct the billing and collection for hospitals, nursing homes, and home care patients. Nationwide, distributors are financing hospitals for 45 to 60 days on average, and up to six months in some parts of the country. Value-added services such as equipment repair and maintenance, product in-service, training, and installation are routinely provided by distributors.

But the value of distributors does not stop there. Distributors continue to squeeze costs out of the health care system by investing in systems and technology that utilize EDI (electronic data interchange) paperless transactions, maximize fill-rates, reduce handling costs, and control excess inventory. Through value-added services such as product bar-coding, distributors have also helped providers reduce their costs in tracking inventory use for patient care and develop more efficient patient charge systems.

Distributors are also responsible for asset management programs such as consignment, "Just-In-Time," and "Stockless" which are helping hospitals, nursing homes, and other providers convert inventory assets to cash, and warehouse space into patient care facilities. These asset management programs have also helped medical facilities realize that their health professionals should not spend their valuable and expensive time processing supplies and related paperwork. As a result, some of these functions are being assigned to distributors who already perform them more efficiently.

And the value of distributors continues. It goes beyond the walls of health care facilities and into the homes of patients who need continued care. HIDA members who sell medical products directly to patients in their home provide an extremely high level of much-needed service.

The home medical equipment (HME) supplier is responsible for implementing the physician's medical determination of a patient's equipment needs, training the patient and family in the use of the equipment, servicing the equipment through the period of need, and retrieving the item when it is no longer needed. Full realization of the potential of home medical equipment services can achieve significant cost savings, as well as improve patient satisfaction. (See Attachment A., *Economic Analysis of Home Medical Equipment Services* Lewin/ICF May 1991.)

It is apparent how distributors and HME suppliers improve the efficiency of the supply chain, while at the same time reducing overall costs. Yet despite all that is being done, HIDA believes there is even more to do.

III. NATIONAL HEALTH REFORM

The Health Industry Distributors Association supports an effective, affordable, free enterprise solution to the health care crisis facing the nation. Problems of cost and financing have limited access to quality health care for the millions of Americans without health care coverage; and they jeopardize future access for the additional millions of Americans whose insurance coverage is at risk due to rising costs.

HIDA applauds the President for his efforts to improve our nation's health care delivery system and supports provisions to increase small market reforms, reduce administrative burdens, reform malpractice laws, and eliminate pre-existing condition regulations. These incremental issues are the common elements upon which advocates of reform agree and should be included in the final package. The results of such policy changes can even be gauged by reviewing the progress of states which have already implemented similar revisions in their health systems. We can learn by their mistakes and successes.

In addition, medical products distributors are in a unique position to see another side of the health care system. This vantage point has enabled HIDA members to observe benefits, as well as areas of concern regarding the President's proposal. To help paint a broad picture of the issues at hand for the President, the Task Force on National Health Care Reform, and Members of Congress as they finalize the reform package, HIDA is presenting its position on various elements of the Health Security Act.

A. Utilize Private Sector Cost Efficiencies

HIDA urges Congress and the Administration to utilize the cost-efficiencies of private sector distribution in any national health care reform plan and to augment the role of the private sector in eliminating administrative waste. HIDA is wary of the direction of the Clinton plan to increase the role of the federal government in health care, which will only fail to reduce costs and improve the health care system. In fact, the current trend within various arms of the government is to utilize the private sector for its distribution needs. For example, commercial medical products distributors are currently providing substantially lower warehousing and distribution service costs to the Departments of Defense and Veterans Affairs than the existing federal depot/distribution system.

According to a report issued by the General Accounting Office (#NSIAD-92-58), the Department of Defense will save millions of dollars by increasing the use of commercial inventory management practices at military medical facilities. The GAO study found that military hospitals held about 30 to 45 days of inventory, warehouses held inventory which would last from 36 to 95 days, and the Defense Logistics Agency stores additional supplies that would last another 250 days. In contrast, civilian hospitals have greatly reduced inventories and costs through improved ordering and delivery systems, standardization of supplies, and better communication with vendors.

The Secretary of the Department of Veterans Affairs (VA) recently announced the VA's plans to convert its current centralized storage and distribution system to a commercially-based distribution system. The Secretary said the VA plans to use 'innovative and cost-competitive" national contracting methods and distribution strategies such as just-in-time, prime vendor, volume-based Federal Supply Schedule pricing, consignment, direct vendor delivery, leasing, and value-added services.

The Defense Personnel Service Center awarded its first prime vendor contract on June 11 for the National Capital Region. The prime vendor program, which the Department of Defense initiated last year, is in the process of establishing a prime vendor distributor of commercial "brand-specific" medical supplies for groups of military hospitals in 22 geographic regions nationwide.

These experiences demonstrate ability of private sector distribution to meet the needs of the government more efficiently and cost effective than the government itself.

B. Home Care — A Vital Component
The Home Care Coalition, of which HIDA is a member, is an organization of consumer groups, health professionals and provider organizations which are involved in home care. In January 1993, the Home Care Coalition submitted a position paper to the President's Task Force on National Health Care Reform which recommended the inclusion of a home care benefit in any standard benefit package. That paper (Attachment B.) showed the cost effectiveness of home care versus institutional care and urged the Administration to change the language in the Medicare statute from "Admit to Hospital" to "Admit to Home." Home care is a leading example of desirable and patient preferred health care, and is a critical component of a system which provides appropriate and cost effective health care. The aging population will continue to grow, and medical technology advances will allow more and more patients, both the elderly and the disabled, chronic and acute, to lead more productive lives outside traditional institutional settings.

1. Home Care Is Cost Effective
Allowing patients to recover and rehabilitate at home, and allowing disabled patients to reenter the mainstream with the support of home care equipment, supplies, and services, is cost effective. In a study entitled *Economic Analysis of Home Medical Equipment Services (May 1991)*, Lewin/ICF analyzed three case examples: Hip fracture, Amyotrophic Lateral Sclerosis (ALS) with pneumonia, and Chronic Obstructive Pulmonary Disease (COPD). The study concluded that savings of up to $2,2330 per patient episode could be achieved, with annual savings potential of up to $575 million when home medical equipment is used following inpatient hospital treatment.

There are numerous other studies which support the cost-effectiveness of utilizing home care as opposed to institutional care when treating such conditions as infant breathing and feeding problems, neurological disorders with respiratory problems, nutrition infusions, bone marrow infections, AIDS patient care, and cancer chemotherapy. The studies report that the percentage of savings ranges from 40 percent to 98.9 percent. (See Attachment C.)

Patients being transferred to another facility spend days waiting for a space or waiting for the appropriate paperwork to be completed. For patients returning home, the only waiting time is that which is required to develop a plan of care; to teach the patient's family or responsible person how to care for the patient; in some cases to teach the patient self-care; and to work with the home health agency staff. The HME staff participate in the preparation of the plan to send the patient home, and continue to work with all parties involved for the duration of care. (It must also be noted that some patients and families become independent in the necessary care and the HME staff may be the only health care professionals providing services to the patient in his or her home.)

2. Patients Prefer Home Care
A large and diverse population relies upon home care for a wide variety of medical reasons, and when given a choice, patients prefer to have their health care administered in the home. These are the results of a Consumer Research Study conducted by National Research, Inc.

The existing support services that are incorporated into the Medicare home medical equipment services benefit are absolutely essential to assure the timely availability of quality home care services. These support services include: timely delivery, set-up, and education for the beneficiary and family in their home; technical, logistical and paperwork support for the hospital discharge planner and prescribing physician to achieve more cost effective delivery of care at home; and the supplier's inventory availability of the wide variety of products patients need in the home. These are services the beneficiary cannot afford to lose.

3. Financing — Medicare and Medicaid Cuts
Medicare has borne many cuts in the last decade to reduce the deficit. HIDA believes it cannot also bear the level of cuts recommended by the President. HIDA believes that further Medicare and Medicaid cuts are not appropriate for financing health care reform. HIDA opposes a Medicare competitive bidding program for HME because it would limit patient access to quality HME servcies, and the long term administrative costs of establishing a competitive bidding program would exceed any program savings that might result. Competitive bidding would limit

access, increase prices and result in high infrastructure costs. HIDA also opposes the President's proposal for mandatory assigment.

4. Preserving Market Access and Consumer Choice

HIDA strongly believes that any change in our nation's health care system should promote competitiveness — not regulation — and should enhance consumer choice of their provider rather than restrict it.

Perhaps the most significant feature of President Clinton's proposal is the extent to which government regulation will replace market competition. The Clinton proposal would allow states to grant antitrust immunity to hospitals and other institutional providers if they establish "a clearly articulated and affirmatively expressed policy to replace competition with regulation and actually supervise the arrangement." (p. 171 of description in 239-page document).

A health reform plan that permits the destruction of competition through the establishment of "health plans" that monopolize health care within particular regions will lead inevitably to a fully regulated system in which all providers will lose their autonomy. There can be no meaningful consumer choice without market access by truly competing providers of care.

HIDA believes that the following provisions must be included in any health reform plan:

1. There should be a clear statement that no provision in a health reform plan is to be construed as permitting monopolization, attempted monopolization, conspiracy to monopolize or other restraint of trade which is prohibited under the Sherman Act, the Clayton Act, or the Federal Trade Commission Act.

2. Health reform proposals which call for the establishment of "health plans" or "AHPS" must provide for competition at the provider level, as well as at the plan level. Accordingly, providers in health plans must be selected by a competitive process which utilizes objective criteria including quality, price, services, and patient satisfaction.

3. A description of any competitive selection process and the criteria to be used must be published and made available to interested providers upon request sufficiently prior to the selection determination to permit all interested providers a fair opportunity to participate.

4. There should be periodic evaluations of participating providers and an "open season" at least every two years in which new providers have an opportunity to demonstrate that they can fulfill the selection criteria better than participating providers.

5. Consumers should be given a choice of providers, and providers should honor that choice.

6. A state may not limit or prohibit competition among providers to participate in a health plan by any antitrust exemption or otherwise.

7. No provider or integrated health system will be permitted to acquire or maintain market power (more than 20% of the business) in a particular health care product and geographic market unless it demonstrates initially, and periodically thereafter, that there is no alternative which preserves competition.

8. Providers and other health care organizations seeking the protection of "safe zones" under guidelines published by the Department of Justice and the Federal Trade Commission must contemporaneously publish a notice in a local newspaper of general circulation generally describing the nature of the project.

The rationale for the foregoing principle is two-fold:

(a) those seeking an exemption from the public policy expressed in the antitrust laws should be required to provide at least some notice of the public, and

(b) interested parties should have some minimal opportunity to alert the Department of Justice and the Federal Trade Commission to local market conditions which may be material to their determination.

IV. CONCLUSION

HIDA commends the President for his efforts to improve the nation's health care delivery system, as the time for reform is long overdue. However, there are numerous aspects of the health care system which must be examined before any change occurs. The ramifications of ignoring these areas of concern could be disastrous for the American public that the President is trying to help. HIDA is happy to work with Congress and the Administration to achieve a cost-effective health care delivery system that utilizes the cost efficiencies best produced by free market competition.

[ATTACHMENTS ARE BEING RETAINED IN THE COMMITTEE FILE]

673

KIM EUGENE HILL
601 BRENTWOOD STREET
TILTON, IL   61833
217-446-8029

Dear Members of Congress:

My name is Kim Eugene Hill. I am a 35 year old citizen of this country who is greatly concerned about the health care issue being discussed before my nation's Congress and I wanted to address my personal concerns on the matter to you directly. Not because I am a professional lobbyist for insurance corporations, health professionals, or any other group, but because I am someone who lives each and every day with the high cost of health care! Since I was not an invited guest to stand before you, I pray that you hear my words as they are spoken from who ever reads this to you, because the words I have written can be echoed by millions of other citizens of this country just like myself.

Does this country need a national health care policy? YES!

I have diabetes. A disease that affects over 13 million people in the United States alone. This disease is the leading cause of blindness, amputations and kidney failure. The complications brought on by the disease are one of the major causes of disability in this country, and is a world leader for most pre-mature deaths. Treating the conditions brought on by the disease are most costly. I know this to be true because I have read the documents with all the statistics and because I am disabled today from these complications.

When I first became a diabetic, my wife and I spent some $500 per year on diabetes medical supplies. But because I did not qualify for health insurance at the time, and also had the normal responsibility of household expenses and taxes, we had to make cutbacks in my diabetes disease management. Where my physician wanted me to have checkups every three months, I saw him every six. Where I was told to take 5 glucose tests of my blood per day, I took two. Where I was told to visit my health care nurse and educator every 4 months, I saw them every six. This was all done because we, like so many others, could not afford the cost. The result of making these cutbacks caused me to lose control of my diabetes and disabled me to where we now have to spend some $9000 a year for my diabetes care. Considering that with my wife's employment and my Social Security we make only $17,000 a year, I believe my medical costs put us below the poverty level.

I do not entirely blame the disease for the troubles I am having today. I also blame the fact that I did not have the health insurance that was needed to allow me access to my diabetes medical professionals and the medications that I needed to control this disease. And I blame the way most insurance corporations are allowed to use "pre-existing" condition clauses to either flat out deny us insurance, or give us premiums so costly we cannot afford them. My personal experience dealing with insurance corporations and government agencies has taught me that the current policies work against people with major health problems instead of allowing us to get help in treating the conditions that could cause our deaths.

I thank "God" for the election of President Clinton, because he has opened the door for me to ask my congressmen for help to change all of this.

You, my country's leaders, have the power to save millions of lives and on behalf of all people with diabetes in this country, that is what I am asking you to do. By creating a national health care policy and ensuring that the policy has provisions so people with diabetes have access to the medical professionals and prescriptions we need, we can stay one step ahead of this disease.

The provisions I am asking you to consider in your health care reform were created by people who know diabetes the best -- the American Diabetes Association. The provisions are endorsed by seven other leading diabetes organizations as well as thousands of us who have diabetes or who are related to people with diabetes. The provisions I am asking you to include in the health care policy are in the ADA's "Statement of Principles on Health Care Reform" pamphlet.

The pamphlet includes four basic principles:

1.   Ensure universal access to quality diabetes treatment.

I believe that any health care policy that does not have this principle as part of the package will not guarantee that I have access to the type of health care physician that I need to control my illness. Three endocrinologists first labelled me as disabled due to my diabetes. They stated that if I continued to work, it would mean brain damage or death. These three physicians are all specialists in diabetes treatment and considering the hell I went through, I had no reason to doubt them.

But I also have nothing against a second (or correctly a fourth) opinion. When the Social Security Administration sent me to another physician of their choice to see if I qualified for disability, I could not believe that they sent me to a family practitioner. Though I had nothing against this physician, I felt that by all rights, the Social Security Administration should have sent me to a physician who was as qualified as the physicians I was currently seeing.

By adding principle number 1 in the policy, people with diabetes could be seen by physicians and other health care professionals who are specially trained to take care of them. It would also allow us to see diabetes educators who could teach us how to better take care of ourselves so we could prevent diabetes-related complications from happening. Since preventive care is much cheaper than immediate care, the government would save money that would be spent on such emergency diabetes services.

This country currently spends some $24 billion a year on diabetes-related emergency medical services. Much of this cannot be paid by the patient because he or she has to use most of their income to pay for diabetes supplies and normal household expenses. If this principle is added it could drop that emergency figure down to around $8 or $9 billion per year.

2.   Prohibit pre-existing condition exclusions.

Diabetes is one of the United States most common "pre-existing" conditions that is used to deny health care insurance. Those of us who have diabetes do have a "pre-existing" condition, but it is not the only illness that we will face in our lifetime. By being labelled with this "pre-existing" condition clause, an insurance corporation could, in a sense, keep a person with diabetes from receiving help in a life threatening matter that has nothing to do with his or her diabetes. Without insurance to help them meet the cost, they would not be able to afford the cost of the operation or medical service needed to treat that non-diabetic related matter.

3.   Provide coverage for prescription drugs and insulin, diabetes-related supplies, equipment and education.

By adding this principle to any health care package, the cost of diabetes health care will go down because you would provide people with diabetes the tools they need to prevent the complications that cost this country billions of dollars. This is a principle that needs to be included because I know first hand its importance.

I wear an insulin infusion pump and have Medicare as my only health insurance. This agency of the government would not help me with a $375 prescription that I needed for syringes and infusion lines to supply my insulin through the pump. Because of this, I had to use contaminated syringes, which clogged my infusion line. The same agency that denied me help had no trouble with paying the 80% of the $8,000 hospital bill that was caused by my not getting help with the $375 prescription.

Medicare follows policies that discriminate against me on the basis of my disease. This insulin infusion pump I wear is not for convenience. I was placed on it because after twelve years of taking the traditional injections (or as the Health and Human Service Department calls it -- Standard Therapy), my body quit responding to long acting insulin. I became very ill and nearly died. The physicians at the hospital found that for some reason my body would now only respond to quick acting insulin. This meant that I would have to have insulin injected into me on a twenty-four hour a day time schedule if I were to live. This meant that I would need a machine to supply this insulin since there was no way that I could stop and inject myself with insulin every ten minutes for the rest of my life. My doctor stated that I would die from the multiple injection wounds or from lack of sleep. The physicians then connected me to an insulin infusion pump that delivers insulin on a timed basis. Though it could not reverse the complications that caused my disability, it has kept me alive for the last four years.

This machine can be used by cancer patients, AIDS patients and people with throembolic and iron diseases, as well as people with diabetes, but the only disease that Medicare does not provide coverage for the pump or its supplies is diabetes. They state this is because information supplied to them by the Public Health Service and current medical literature does not clearly indicate that there is a medical advantage to using controlled continuous insulin infusion (via infusion pump) rather than multiple daily injections. I have several medical documents stating just the opposite. I am also living proof of the PHS being wrong.

With Medicare not giving me and other people with diabetes the same access to this machine as the other diseases, they are in turn causing my wife and I to spend an even greater amount of income in the line of diabetes care. This is because I have to decide on what medical prescriptions I need the most since we have other household bills and cannot afford to spend all of our income on my medical needs. Because of the lack of these prescriptions, I become sicker and have to depend upon Medicare to help pay for the trips to the hospital. I also feel that this office of the government is discriminating against diabetics. If there is no medical advantage to us using it for insulin, why is there an advantage to a cancer patient using it? Cancer medication can also be used through a standard syringe.

Medicare would be saving money by allowing those who depend upon it to get help with their diabetes medications (insulin, glucose sticks, etc.) because in the long run, helping with these supplies would prevent major medical cost from ocurring at hospitals. The same would hold true in any national health care plan.

4.   Mandate for community rating.

This principle is needed because many insurance premiums are based on the likelihood of its use by the individual. A person labelled "diabetic" is automatically presumed to be a person likely to use this insurance. That is why many are given insurance premiums too costly for them to pay for. Though we diabetics share a common disease, diabetes affects each of us differently. Some of us will experience difficulty with it, but as we are all different, there will be individuals who will live with no problems. The are nine diabetics on the block of my street alone and only two of us are having trouble. Don't base the premiums of the other seven on my medical claims.

Members of Congress, I am sure that since the start of this health care matter you have talked with many lobbyists on this matter. I am now asking on behalf of millions of diabetics for you to work with the American Diabetes Association as the group to represent our needs. My personal experience has taught me that they are the best and only organization that could ensure that people with diabetes are finally given equal access to the health care we need to survive.

I am asking all of you to apply the "Statement of Principles on Health Care Reform" in any national health care policy.

I feel strongly that President Clinton's stand on this issue is too late to help me since I can no longer afford the health care I need to fight this disease and its complications and I truly don't believe that I will be alive at the end of his term. I am writing you because I believe that my personal experiences with both the state and federal government offices prove that changes must be made. Organizations that know us best can help the government see to our urgent needs. I am not alone in this pursuit.

Your actions towards adding the "Statement of Principles" would not only save this country money, but it would save the lives of thousands of diabetics who die for the plain and simple fact they cannot afford the medications and health care services they need.

Thank you,

Kim Eugene Hill

HOUSE WAYS AND MEANS SUBCOMMITTEE ON HEAL
QUALITY CONTROL PANEL ON ADMINISTRATIVE SIMPLIFICATION
February 1, 1994

Testimony of
Congressman David L. Hobson and
Congressman Thomas C. Sawyer

BIPARTISAN HEALTH CARE REFORM:
HEALTH CARE INFORMATION MODERNIZATION AND SECURITY ACT

Mr. Chairman, we want to thank you for convening this panel today. As Congress works toward serious health care reform, it has become clear that the success of any reform is dependent on maintaining and measuring high quality health services. It is imperative that we have reliable, comprehensive data in a form that can be used by the consumers, providers, administrators, researchers, and policy-makers.

With these issues in mind, we introduced H.R. 3137, the Health Care Information Modernization and Security Act of 1993. In the Senate, Mr. Bond and Mr. Riegle introduced this legislation as S. 1494. You will recall that Senator Bond testified before your committee last year on this bill. Our bipartisan, bicameral bill reduces excessive paperwork and administrative waste in our health care system by facilitating the development of an electronic health care data network.

BACKGROUND

The paperwork burden in our current health care system -- which has grown to staggering proportions -- impacts everyone. We pay for this burden in higher insurance premiums and medical bills that consume as much as 10 cents of every health care dollar.

But the cost is greater than dollars. Just ask the person on Medicare who must suffer the anxiety of filling out confusing forms, or the physician who is forced to spend less time with patients and more time completing paperwork. President Clinton was correct when he said, "A hospital ought to be a house of healing, not a monument to paperwork and bureaucracy."

The technology exists today to move away from a paperwork system and toward an electronic health care data network. But there are no uniform standards to allow this technology to fully develop. To make this work, a hospital in Ohio must be able to communicate with an insurance company in Chicago, which then must be able to contact Medicare in Baltimore. Today, these providers often speak a different electronic language.

The Health Care Information Modernization and Security Act removes the barriers that have slowed the development of an electronic health care data network. It adopts standards for health care data and ensures patient privacy and confidentiality of medical records.

HEALTH CARE DATA PANEL

Our bill establishes a Health Care Data Panel that is responsible for adopting data standards and strict privacy and confidentiality standards. The Panel (this section of the bill currently is being revised) includes government officials and private sector experts who represent different professions, geographic areas, federal or state government health programs, applicable standard-setting groups, and consumers of health care services. The Panel makes recommendations to the Secretary of HHS, who in turn promulgates regulations.

DATA STANDARDS

The Panel develops data standards so providers, insurers and others can communicate in the same, standard electronic language. When possible, the data standards must reflect existing, widely-adopted standards.

The data standards are implemented according to an aggressive timetable. Within nine months after enactment of this bill, financial and administrative transactions must be standardized; within twelve months, an initial quality indicator data set must be standardized; and within two years, a comprehensive clinical data set must be standardized.

The data standards are enforced using civil penalties. There is a one-year grace period during which penalties do not apply. In the case of the more complicated clinical data set, there is a two-year grace period. There are waivers for small and rural hospitals.

PRIVACY AND CONFIDENTIALITY REQUIREMENTS

Strict patient privacy and confidentiality of medical information are fully protected according to the following principles: Information should be collected only to the extent necessary to carry out the purpose for which the information is collected; information collected for one purpose should not be used for another purpose without the individual's informed consent; information should be disposed of when no longer necessary to carry out the purpose for which it was collected; and individuals should be notified (in advance of the collection of information) whether furnishing the information is mandatory or voluntary, what the record keeping practices are concerning the information, and what uses will be made of the information. Recommendations for criminal fines and penalties will be submitted to Congress.

IMPACT

The benefits of reducing excessive paperwork and administrative waste in our health care system are significant. Conservative estimates indicate an electronic health care data network would save $4 billion annually in administrative costs. It would save $20 billion annually by providing medical researchers, physicians, and hospitals with the clinical data they need to reduce unnecessary and costly medical procedures. And by reducing health fraud it could save as much as $150 billion annually.

These savings are significant, but in achieving these savings -- in computerizing all of these various health transactions -- we also create a system capable of much more than just paperwork simplification.

Today, fragmented information makes it difficult to reform our health care system. We create the information infrastructure necessary to provide the comprehensive data needed to enact effective reform. Our plan can be enacted as a stand-alone bill, or as the foundation for comprehensive reform. It is consistent with insurance market reform, managed competition, and single-payer.

Today, information on cost and quality among hospitals and benefit plans is not available to consumers. We create a system that provides the data consumers need to compare the value of insurance plans and health services. Our plan allows consumers to make the smart choices that are necessary to make competition work.

Today, information on the effectiveness of medical procedures is either unavailable or scattered among providers in an unusable form. We create the tools needed for outcomes research to improve the quality of care. Our plan provides medical researchers, physicians, and hospitals with the clinical data they need to reduce unnecessary and costly medical procedures.

And today, the confusing, disjointed paperwork system provides cover for the consumer or provider who wants to cheat the system. We make it possible to expose fraud in ways that are impossible to do under the paperwork system we have today.

Mr. Chairman, thank you again for convening this panel. We believe that our bill can contribute in a meaningful way to the discussion on administrative simplification, and appreciate this opportunity to testify. Much of the support for our bill comes directly from the businesses and associations that make up the health care information industry -- some of whom are testifying here today. We want to reinforce their message, and to assist in their efforts to develop uniform health care data standards and health information networks.

STEVEN R. HOFER
ATTORNEY AT LAW
4475 ALLISONVILLE ROAD, SUITE 820
INDIANAPOLIS, INDIANA 46205-2466 NOV 1 1993
(317) 545-5753

Fax (317) 545-5852
E-Mail (Internet) Conslaw@aol.com

Admitted in Indiana
and Florida

October 26, 1993

Rep. Andy Jacobs Jr.
49 E. Ohio Street
Indianapolis, Indiana   46204

    Re: Health Care Proposals and Internet

Dear Congressman Jacobs:

        President Clinton's healthcare package is far from perfect, but it
is a concrete proposal which, even if only halfway successful, will be
preferable to the system we have now.   For this reason, I urge you to
actively support healthcare reform, and Clinton's package is a
reasonable choice.

        The strength of Clinton's plan is it's guarantee of universal
coverage.   The weaknesses are a continuation of a employment-based
coverage, and doubtfulness about the plan's effectiveness at controlling
costs.   The "Cooper" plan as I understand it, though similar, is
inferior to the Clinton plan because it relies not only on employment as
a conduit to coverage, but also as a source of coverage.

        Enclosed is an article from the Wall Street Journal, October 25,
1993 which discusses problems with employer-provided heath care.   As one
of only three attorneys in the Indianapolis Yellow Pages under the
heading "Insurance Law" I receive a lot of calls from consumers with
horror stories about non-payment of claims by their health insurance
companies.   The reason more attorneys don't pursue this business is
because the insurance companies wrote the policies and make the coverage
determinations also wrote the laws.   Market forces don't work because
the employer who is the "insured" under the plan would rather keep costs
down than make sure employees are paid for bills incurred.

        Right now there is a consensus that we must do something about our
out-of-control healthcare costs, but there is not a consensus about the
best method to do so.   If we adopt the Clinton plan as is, many possible
alternatives may never be tried.   The Clinton plan comes at a time when
many states have alternatives on the blackboard, but have not
implemented them.

        Although I have heard some talk that the Clinton plan is only the
default plan, I don't know to what extent that's true.   States should be
able to opt in or opt out of the Clinton plan.   If they opt out, they
must have an alternative plan which guarantees universal coverage.
Strengthening the state opt-in/opt-out provisions could be the basis of
a political compromise where advocates of a single-payer plan, and those
of health insurance savings accounts (the Republican plan) can endorse
the system without undue political delays.   Alternative systems can be

tried out in the crucible of federalism. Over time we can evaluate the strengths and weaknesses of the various approaches.

My perspective on these issues comes from my personal experience and my experience as a consumer lawyer. As a consumer lawyer, I have battled the "pre-existing condition", "usual and customary charges", "medically necessary", "and pre-admission authorization problems". I have talked to people who have lost their coverage when they became disabled, and couldn't work in the job that provided them their insurance. Personally, I have worked for two different companies which said they were covering their employees, but stopped paying the insurance premiums without notifying the employees.

My preference would be for a single payer system. Only with a single payer system can we eliminate the tie between the employer and the insurance, a tie which makes no logical sense and is merely the result of a historical accident. Market forces do not work well for health cost decisions because the underlying assumptions of efficient markets, rational decision making and zero information costs, do not apply.

It is highly unlikely that a single payer plan will receive a majority vote. The support for such a plan is spread-out. For this reason, a middle of the road plan which allows states to experiment with single payer systems is a reasonable compromise. In the meantime, we should not abandon the people who need immediate help, because we have at least five years of transition ahead of us.

I realize these issues are complex. If there is a way I could donate my time to assist your staff in looking into and reporting on healthcare issues, including drafting legislation, please have someone get in touch with me. If you tie into the new house Internet e-mail system, you can reach me at Conslaw@AOL.com. Thanks for your time.

Very truly yours,

Steve Hofer

Enclosure

681

Livingston W. MacCracken
12 MacCracken Road
W. Cornwall, CT 06796
Post Office Box 3

November 2, 1993

On behalf of myself, Livingston W. MacCracken with the
support of past Honorary Mental health Chairperson, Mary Field
Burnham MacCracken, I comment to introduce, without petition,
Learning Disabilities, to the Mental Health Program to be covered
within the National Health Care Program.

Learning Disabilities is of a neurological, physiological
base, with discrepancy between intellectual ability and
performance.

I recommend a Livingston W. MacCracken statement to support
a Mary MacCracken clause stating Learning Disabilities is a
Mental Health problem to be covered in the National Health Care
Program.

To include an initial diagnosis of neurological,
physiological base followed by a once or twice a week, nine month
September-May remediation program, and vacations exempt. This is
to be within 2 three year ceiling with a final diagnosis and
recommendation.

Sincerely,

Livingston W. MacCracken

Livingston W. MacCracken

Statement of
Kenneth McLennan
President
Manufacturers' Alliance for Productivity and Innovation (MAPI)
to the
Subcommittee on Health
House Committee on Ways and Means
Concerning
The President's Health Care Reform Proposals

I am Kenneth McLennan, President of the Manufacturers' Alliance for Productivity and Innovation. The Alliance is pleased to submit this statement as part of the Subcommittee's hearings on national health care reform. The Manufacturers' Alliance is a nonprofit policy research organization which for 60 years has published studies and conducted seminars on the full range of national issues affecting the manufacturing sector, U.S. competitiveness, and the strength of the U.S. economy. Approximately 500 companies are affiliated with the Alliance and represent numerous manufacturing sectors: aerospace, automotive, electronic, computers, telecommunications equipment, chemicals, heavy industrial machinery, oil and oil-related equipment; farm and construction machinery, and primary and fabricated metals.

Over the last few years, the Alliance has aired its views on U.S. health care policy in a series of reports.[1] The most recent publication was released in December 1993 and concludes that, as it stands, President Clinton's health care reform proposal is a policy choice we cannot afford either financially or medically. This statement reflects the findings of our December report.

Overview

With health care in the United States consuming 14 percent of the Gross Domestic Product (GDP) in 1992 and projected to jump to 19 percent of GDP by the end of the decade under a business-as-usual scenario, we all must be concerned that the escalation of health care spending in the United States is increasingly crowding out other funding priorities, including investments in the type of activities essential to productivity growth and continued improvement in the standard of living of future generations of Americans. Everyone has a stake in securing a successful outcome to the policy debate.

Unquestionably, the key areas of cost, access, and quality must be dealt with simultaneously in order to achieve a workable balance. **The best health care strategy is one that builds upon the strengths of the current system, relies to the greatest extent possible on market principles, and minimizes government intrusion.** The Administration's scheme could achieve universal insurance coverage, but we have grave doubts about its ability either to contain costs or to improve quality. The President's plan succeeds in providing an expansion of the current employer-based insurance coverage; however it would vastly increase government involvement and would fail to marshal competitive forces.

MAPI concludes that the Clinton proposal is the wrong cure for the ills confronting the U.S. health care system—and our difficulties with the plan extend to its most fundamental theoretical underpinnings. Indeed, the Administration has not chosen the right goal for health care reform. By aiming to provide "health care that is always there," the President has defined his objective to be a **strategy to purchase health care**, and thereby seeks to cure the wrong disease. Instead, the goal of our health care system should be **keeping people healthy.** This is not a trivial nor merely semantic divergence; it means that our answers to some of the most important questions concerning health care reform differ markedly from those of the President. These questions include, "What are we buying for our health care dollars?" and "What is the relationship between those expenditures and health?"

The Clinton proposal is problematic because of its complexity, its lack of reliance on market incentives, its promise of a new government bureaucracy that almost certainly will lessen competition, its potential effects on jobs and the economy, its use of premium caps for cost containment, its emphasis on changing health care inputs rather than outcomes, and its concealment of the real costs of medical care from the largest group of health care decision makers—consumers. In addition, much of the new spending in the proposal is done with dollars that will not yet have been saved by its cost-containment measures.

But perhaps the plan's most serious flaw is the generosity of the "basic" benefit plan that would be guaranteed to everyone. That single well-intentioned feature, in its current form, calls in question the package's ability even to slow the growth of health care costs, let alone to reduce future spending to levels below current expenditures as a percentage of GDP and to use net savings to lower the federal deficit, as the Administration promises. By devising a system that is at the same time a defined contribution and a defined benefit plan, President Clinton avoids answering important questions about U.S. health care priorities, beginning with how best to allocate a finite amount of resources.

---

[1]*The Clinton Health Care Reform Proposal A Policy Choice We Cannot Afford To Make*, PR-127, MAPI, December 1993, *The Oregon Health Plan—A Process for Reform*, PR-126, MAPI, August 1993; *Critical Components of Responsible Health Care Reform in the United States*, PR-123, MAPI, May 1993; *Canadian Health Care Is It the Right Approach for U S Reform?* If Not, Are There Better Alternatives?, PR-119, MAPI, February 1992; *Ethical Issues in Terminating Medical Treatment Implications for the Business Community*, PR-118, MAPI, January 1992; *Crisis in the U S Health Care System How Should Government and Industry Respond?*, PR-108, MAPI, May 1989.

Choosing an Approach to Health Care Reform

A key point in the political debate concerning the President's reform proposal has become whether or not there is now a health care crisis in the United States. The Alliance does not believe policymakers should waste any more effort defining "crisis." There is a broad consensus that in general the U.S. health care system is the best in the world. There also is widespread agreement that there are problems with the existing system—problems of escalating cost and access to affordable insurance, for example. It is time now to end the unproductive debate over the issue of a "crisis" and to focus instead on what to do about the problems of the existing health care system.

The Clinton Approach Is
Too Radical

The Manufacturers' Alliance questions the necessity of so far-reaching a reform package as President Clinton's, which threatens to "fix" more than is "broke" and does so in a way that increases government regulation and intrusion into the workings of our free market system. It is a gamble with one-seventh of the U.S. economy that could lead to serious misallocations of resources and other unintended results that would be difficult to correct.

A more prudent path would seem to be immediate action by the Congress on reform aspects common to both the President's plan and the leading congressional proposals and about which there seems to be little disagreement. These could include:

- 100 percent deductibility of insurance premiums for the self-insured;
- administrative reforms, including moving to a standard claims form and electronic billing;
- malpractice reforms to help lower the cost of malpractice insurance and decrease the tendency to practice defensive medicine;
- antitrust reform, including legislation to allow greater cooperation among providers;
- Medicaid reform, including more state flexibility, and
- insurance reform to ensure that individuals do not lose coverage or are confronted with unaffordable premium increases.

Incremental changes such as these would allow modifications on the basis of experience, and could provide for greater flexibility through experiments by states, health plans, or providers in much the same way as individual companies have been trying various methods to increase efficiency and contain their health care costs. Narrowing the scope of reform also would lessen dislocations and allow the system more time to adapt to change. Some proponents of drastic change may favor that approach, at least in part, because they fear that success in tackling the problems of the health care system would incrementally lessen the impetus for radical reform.

The above steps constitute a sensible regimen that would go a long way toward achieving some of the cost, quality, and access goals without requiring major disruptions in the health care sector or huge outlays of new funds. Moreover, as the above changes are completed, other worthy reforms could be financed from savings realized from these initial actions.

Having said that MAPI would opt for a more measured approach, we recognize the paradox of stating in the next breath—as we are about to do—that the Clinton plan does not go far enough. But we believe that, having chosen the "go for broke" approach, the President errs in not pushing to include more in his reform program; for example, by folding into the package those people currently covered under the Medicare and Veterans Affairs programs. Beyond its role as policy maker, the government is a key player as the largest purchaser of health care; responsible reform cannot be achieved if all those for whom the government purchases coverage are not included in a reorganized system.

Manufacturers' Alliance Comments
on Specific Aspects of the
President's Proposal

The President's Proposal Is Antithetical
to Managed Competition

The Alliance has often stated in the past that we favor managed competition as an innovative approach to health care reform and that it has the potential to improve the U.S. system in all three key areas—cost, access, and quality. At the same time we have maintained that our ability to realize that potential hinges entirely on how any managed competition scheme is put in place. For example, devising a standard benefit package under managed competition that is too broad or too generous would seriously limit the ability to contain costs. Marshaling competitive forces by giving individuals a sufficient financial stake in choosing the least costly plan that is appropriate to their needs must be a key aspect of managed competition.

President Clinton has said that his plan represents "managed competition," although that term is not used in the legislation he forwarded to the Congress. He claims that his scheme is an expansion of the managed competition model originally proposed by the Jackson Hole Group, whose intent was to establish a system of health plan purchasing cooperatives that would pool groups of small employers and individuals so that they could buy insurance on the same terms as large employers. Risk would be spread over a large population, achieving economies of scale in marketing and administration. The Jackson Hole arrangement also would ensure a choice of health plans, which would compete with one another within the cooperative on the basis of price and quality. **By contrast, the health alliances proposed by the Administration are monopolistic, regulatory government agencies that would neither offer more choices to most consumers nor would increase competition in health markets.**

The Clinton proposal presupposes that if health plans must offer a specified package of benefits with standardized deductibles, copayments, coinsurance, and out-of-pocket limits for premiums whose yearly increases are controlled by the government, the plans' only choice will be to improve quality in order to keep their customers. By placing limits on so many of the variables and by establishing a premium cap that will end up being the amount by which all premiums will rise, the Administration instead would create a system for delivering captive customers to health plans that have no incentive for more efficient operations.

The President's plan restricts consumer choice.—The Clinton plan demonstrates a lack of confidence in the ability of individuals to make wise decisions on health care because while the plan promises greater choices it wants those choices locked in a regulatory straitjacket designed by the government. Apparently, President Clinton thinks that government works best; experience shows, however, that competitive market forces can be much more effective.

The Clinton proposal includes some incentives to help individuals in making wise health care decisions. Nonetheless, much more could be accomplished through such changes as

— increasing the availability of health care plans to consumers by allowing them to choose from outside the regional alliance;
— stimulating competitive forces by giving health plans a free choice in devising deductibles, copayments, and coinsurance amounts;
— allowing alliances to compete with one another on the basis of cost and quality rather than granting each one monopoly status;
— tying employer contributions not to the average but to the lowest-cost health plan in an alliance area, and
— trimming the required benefit package in order to give teeth to the provision to include in taxable income the value of health care that goes beyond the comprehensive package;

Success can best be attained not by the government intruding further in health care markets, but by providing the proper incentives that allow individuals and institutions to alter their behavior. The regional health alliances should not be run as state-authorized monopolies, which inevitably have few incentives to find ways to operate more efficiently. Consumers should have the choice of buying coverage from within the risk pool or from plans outside the alliance, and more than one alliance should be permitted in each region. Health alliances should succeed because they are the best game in town—not the only game in town.

Achieving Universal Coverage Must Be Balanced With Other Goals

In spite of the high levels of national spending on health care, 37 million Americans currently are uninsured. **The access problem in the United States is not one of access to health care, but of access to health insurance.** The uninsured are able to receive care, but often it is in an emergency setting where medical intervention is least effective and most expensive. The U.S. health care system would realize some cost savings through providing those who are now uninsured with coverage for basic needs, such as preventive care, which is far less costly than emergency service and would allow medical interventions before routine cases require critical care

Another aspect of gaps in insurance coverage is that the availability of services provided to those who are underinsured leads to the cost of their uncompensated care being shifted by providers to those who do pay. One study found that the average rate paid by private insurers was 30 percent above hospital costs in 1991. Another estimate claims that cost shifting accounted for 28 percent of 1991 health care costs in the manufacturing sector.

Universal insurance coverage is a desirable goal, but it is feasible only if we are able to distribute the costs of health care fairly and contain costs over time. The Clinton plan succeeds in broadening access to health care insurance but does so in ways that will make it impossible to meet the President's own goals for containing costs.

The President's "Cadillac" Basic Benefit Plan Is Unnecessary And Unaffordable

The most serious flaw in the Clinton health care reform proposal is the extravagance of the comprehensive package of benefits that would be available to all citizens and legal aliens. The specified benefit package, which is far more generous than the current average insurance coverage, goes far beyond the needs of basic comprehensive care It is a "Cadillac" plan that the nation cannot afford and does not need.

Once specific benefits are granted, it will be politically difficult to limit or end them should such action become desirable or fiscally necessary. A wiser course of action would be to make the comprehensive benefit package truly a **basic** one. If sufficient savings from reform measures result, immediately or eventually, other benefits could be added easily when the nation is able to afford them.

People need to be protected against substantial losses, but they do not need to be absolved of any and all financial responsibility for their actions. The purpose of health insurance, whether it is through a private insurer or a government agency, is to provide risk-sharing, not to pay all medical expenses. Indemnification should not be "front-end loaded," that is, it should be targeted more toward the last dollar of coverage than the first.

Responsible limits are necessary on high-cost services that have low probable success rates.—All countries ration health care as a way of containing cost. The United States rations health resources by limiting not *what* is covered, but *who* is covered. Most people have access to all the health insurance they can use, while others are underinsured or have no insurance at all.

A better approach is to increase access to health insurance by following the innovative approach being taken by the state of Oregon. In order to broaden the base of coverage there, the state will limit the services available to individuals Oregon has made an explicit decision to ration scarce resources by limiting not *who* is eligible for insurance coverage, but *what* is covered, and to choose which medical services will be made available according to what it makes sense to do from a health standpoint.

To choose the components of its comprehensive benefit package, the state created a commission to prioritize health services in the form of condition/treatment pairs (such as an appendectomy for acute appendicitis) from the most important to the least important, in terms of health produced, as judged by a consideration of clinical effectiveness and social values. The final priority list was given to an independent actuarial firm which determined the cost of delivering each element on the list through capitated managed care. Then the list and actuarial data were given to the legislature, which determined how much could be funded from available revenues and what additional revenues would be needed to fund the basic care package, thus providing a direct link to fiscal limits. This mechanism allowed the legislature to look at health care expenditures in the context of other demands for state funds, rather than creating an entitlement whose future financing demands would be difficult to predict or contain.

The resulting basic benefit package in Oregon covers all effective preventive medical care (including physicals, mammograms, and prenatal care); doctors' visits for diagnosis of any condition and follow-up treatment for most conditions; the costs of hospitalization; psychological treatment for a range of conditions; gynecological care; noncosmetic surgery, including most organ transplants; prescription drugs; and hospice care for the terminally ill. It does not cover cases where treatment is judged to be ineffective (e.g., the common cold); no more effective than a home remedy; cosmetic; or futile. This means that even though the treatment is for a noncosmetic condition and medical intervention may improve the chances of recovery, if the probability of survival is less than 5 percent in the five-year period commencing with diagnosis, the condition will not be treated under the Oregon plan; e.g., if cancer has spread extensively to major organs or if a stroke is so severe that there is less than a 5 percent chance of recovery, the illness will not be treated under the plan.

Adopting a system of priorities for determining what treatments would be provided under basic health insurance plans avoids the dilemma of devoting health care resources to high-cost procedures that have extremely low success rates and permits these resources to be invested instead in procedures that produce much higher social benefits. For example, more resources would be available for preventive services, such as prenatal and well-child care, and for sophisticated medical procedures that promise long-run improvements in the quality of life.

The components of the Oregon plan present a reasonable, well-thought-out strategy for allocating health care resources while broadening access to insurance coverage. This strategy for choosing the components of a basic benefit package is far superior to the mandated benefit approach in the Clinton legislation because it is fiscally responsible and allows explicit and transparent decisions to be made on the basis of health outcomes.

Proposed Insurance Reforms Are Overly Complex and Untested

Changing the insurance system is a needed component of U.S. health care reform. Individuals should be assured of the portability of their coverage; affordable insurance should be available to the self-employed and those who become unemployed; coverage should not be denied due to preexisting conditions; and coverage should not be cancelled nor premiums increased when illness or injury strikes. The Administration's plan accomplish these reforms; unfortunately, it also includes some aspects regarding insurance that are questionable.

The Clinton proposal places operation of the health insurance industry on a community-rating basis, with a mechanism designed to adjust for utilization and cost deviations from expected or average levels. The risk adjustment method chosen by the Administration is untested; it remains to be seen whether it will be effective in judging per capita spending for alliance eligible individuals. It also will be important to devise a system that differentiates between health plans whose costs are low because they have an efficient operation and those that benefit from a healthier set of enrollees. Everyone benefits from an insurance industry that remains vital and competitive.

The Proposed Employer Mandate Will Restrict Employment Growth

An employer mandate for health care insurance coverage has definite drawbacks, and seems justifiable only if an Oregon-type mechanism is used for designing a standard benefit package.

A Congressional Budget Office report on health care costs found that "(a)lthough employers initially pay a significant portion of employer-provided health insurance, in the long run employers shift most of their costs to workers in the form of lower wages or less generous nonmedical benefits. * * * Rising health care costs have absorbed much of the growth of employees' real compensation over the last 20 years."[2]

A mandatory employer premium contribution based on the number of employees or the total value of payroll will result in companies reducing employment, not hiring additional employees, or decreasing wages and foregoing future pay increases. This will adversely affect some workers, especially those for whom the health care premium is large relative to their current wage. Employers of the lowest-paid workers obviously will not be able to pass along their higher costs by reducing wages and may resort to cutting some of these jobs.

Over the past two decades competition in most industries has increased as markets have become global. Consequently, even companies with high-skilled, high-wage workforces will have difficulty passing on to their customers the increased cost of higher premiums for a generous basic health care plan. As a result these new mandated costs will slow down employment growth throughout industry.

The employer mandate as designed by the Clinton Administration could deliver a major blow to employment in what has been, at least when compared with other post-recession periods, a jobless recovery. The U.S. economy is remarkably resilient, but the reform plan hits the sectors that historically have shown the highest job growth—small business and the service industries. And the persons most severely impacted will be individuals in low-paying jobs and those seeking entry-level positions.

Predictions of potential job losses due to the health reform plan differ greatly. The Administration estimates that the effects of the health care plan would be equivalent to raising the minimum wage by between $0.15 and $0.35; others estimate the difference to be as much as $1.67 an hour and point out that, while a

---

[2]"Economic Implications of Rising Health Care Costs," Congressional Budget Office, Washington, DC, October 1992, pp. 5 and 8.

686

rise in the minimum wage is eroded over time by inflation, the cost of health benefits will not be affected in the same manner. One analyst asserts that 2.2 million workers are so close to the minimum wage that they could be priced out of the labor market.[3] Two health care experts put the loss at 3.1 million jobs nationwide, with a few industries such as restaurants, retail trade, and agriculture bearing a disproportionate burden of the job loss.[4]

The structure of the employer premium discount for small businesses will mean that the advantages of each dollar of increase in compensation and each potential expansion in the size of the workforce will be weighed against the disadvantage of moving up another notch and losing money to increased insurance premiums. Capping the premiums at between 3.5 percent and 7.9 percent of payroll will cause firms to make future "raises" in nonsalary form in order to minimize payments in premiums and other payroll taxes. That, in turn, will reduce the government's ability to capture through the income tax system money that the Clinton Administration says firms will "save" due to efficiencies resulting from the health care reforms.

Proposed treatment of early retirees' health insurance would create inequities among industries.—Employers currently have a $412 billion liability for retiree medical benefits, up from $227 billion in 1989. This includes $8.6 billion annually to provide health insurance for 2.5 million early retirees. The provision in the Administration's proposal calling for the federal government to pick up the employer portion of the premium cost for those who retire prior to achieving Medicare eligibility would be a boon to employers who now cover retiree health care as well as to future retirees who otherwise might face reduced or canceled benefits.

Whether this provision would result in massive new early retirements and an accompanying drain on federal government resources is one of the more unpredictable aspects of the plan.

Employer-paid benefits above a truly basic health care plan should be included in individuals' taxable income.—A primary cause of the high cost of U.S. medical care is that health insurance is structured in such a way as to insulate consumers from the cost of service. The strength of a free market lies in informed decision making. **Isolating health care consumers from information about the costs and consequences of their choices effectively nullifies these market forces, contributing to over-consumption of services and escalating costs.** It follows that some portion of employer-paid health benefits should be included in taxable income, since the current tax exclusion simply subsidizes those who have employer-provided health insurance. Also, elderly persons of means should be asked to bear a greater portion of the cost of the Medicare system

The Clinton proposal would include in taxable income for employees the value of employer-paid premiums for coverage beyond the basic benefit package, but the inclusion would be delayed until 2003. The ability of that provision either to raise revenue or to contribute to cost-consciousness on the part of health care consumers is postponed by the delay and is lessened substantially by the generosity of the comprehensive benefit package.

Business-led efficiencies would no longer be realized under the President's proposal.—Another disadvantage of the Clinton proposal is that it removes business from the part it has played in health care policy Industry has been a driving force in finding innovative ways of cutting health care costs, which is reflected in the slowing of the growth of private sector medical costs versus government expenditures. Under the Administration's plan, businesses serve mainly as premium payers who will have little motivation to become involved in the health care choices their employees make

Based on Experience, Controlling Costs
Through Price Controls Would Be
Ill-Advised

Government-imposed spending controls would lead to distortions in the way medical services are provided and in care usage patterns, would freeze in position all the inequities of the current system, and could block changes designed to reduce inefficiencies. Furthermore, the rate of innovation in medical technologies, procedures, and new drugs could be irreversibly harmed. Innovation must be encouraged and companies allowed to see returns from significant research investments because these factors lower total treatment costs and improve medical outcomes. In addition, any strategy for meaningful market-based health care reform in the United States should be given ample opportunity to work before a decision is made to impose more stringent and more onerous mechanisms such as price controls or spending caps.

Capping premiums would lead to distortions in how care is provided and may not control costs.—A principal method of cost control in the Clinton proposal is the imposition of caps on the increase in insurance premiums. **Regardless of their makeup, these ill-advised caps will lead to distortions in care-usage patterns and in the way medical services are provided.** Some Medicare spending controls now in place have led to increases in the use of certain diagnostic tests and of medical procedures as health care providers attempt to make up in quantity what they have lost in unit price. Many physicians have stopped treating patients who rely on government-funded programs.

Cost controls that are more explicit than those embodied in the proposed Health Security Act already exist for the 40 percent of medical services reimbursed by the government for the poor and elderly. They have been largely unsuccessful in containing overall spending, and in the case of Medicare and Medicaid, account for a significant portion of the cost-shifting that currently plagues the U.S. health care system. Health expenditures by all levels of government grew 17.9 percent in 1992, compared with a 9.3 percent increase for employee health care spending in private industry.

[3]"Analysts Say Health Care Mandates Are Likely To Lead To Lower Wages," *Daily Report for Executives*, Bureau of National Affairs, Inc., Washington, DC, October 20, 1993, p A-36.
[4]June E O'Neill and Dave M O'Neill, "The Impact of a Health Insurance Mandate on Labor Costs and Employment: Empirical Evidence," Center for the Study of Business and Government, Baruch College, City University of New York, New York, NY, 1993, p i

The Clinton premium caps, which will hurt the ability of providers to recoup their costs, will lead to rationing and a poorer quality of care, including delays in treatment, reduced availability of high-technology procedures, and a slower rate of medical innovation. The combination of universal coverage and price controls in Canada has led to explicit limits on access to health care resources—queues for advanced diagnostic and therapeutic equipment and for costly procedures, lengthy delays for tests that are considered routine in the United States, longer hospital stays with less intensive care, less efficient operation of hospitals, and delays in the introduction of new drugs and medical innovations.

Another potential problem of premium caps is that a "ceiling" quickly will become a premium "floor" for each health plan in the absence of sufficient competitive pressures.

Proposed cost savings from Medicare and Medicaid are unrealistic.—The Administration's cost-cutting estimates rely on $65 billion in savings from the Medicare program and $124 billion in savings from the Medicaid program. Two sources account for the expected Medicaid savings: the near elimination of uncompensated care and the fact that the growth of alliance premiums paid by Medicaid on behalf of cash recipients will be constrained to grow at the same rate as private sector premiums. The Medicare cost reductions are the result of about two dozen policy changes affecting payment rates to providers, program utilization, and premiums for high-income beneficiaries. Administration officials say these changes will reduce the rate of growth in Medicare from its current annual rate of 11 percent per year to around 8.4 percent by the end of the decade, even while adding new coverage for prescription drugs, estimated to cost $66 billion per year.

It is difficult to imagine that the Administration will succeed in reductions of this magnitude in these two entitlement programs; indeed, holding the growth in Medicare costs to the current growth rate while adding the costly new drug benefit would be an impressive result. The promised additional savings seem particularly questionable in light of the $56 billion cut in Medicare and the $7 billion reduction in Medicaid made as part of the Omnibus Budget Reconciliation Act of 1993, signed into law in August. Moreover, further cuts in Medicare payments to doctors, which already are 30 percent lower than private sector rates, are bound to affect the quality and availability of service to Medicare beneficiaries.

In practice, the subsidy ceilings in the President's proposal would not control spending.—The Clinton proposal would place a ceiling on the overall amount that could be paid out as subsidies to low-income people and to small businesses. In the absence of such a cap, making a commitment to pay these subsidies would create an expensive new category of entitlement whose future cost would be difficult to predict and impossible to control. Inclusion of a cap, however, means only that the Administration would seek additional appropriations from the Congress or would reduce benefits. Given that choice, it is highly unlikely that the Congress would opt for cutting benefits for those who "need it most." The subsidy ceilings, thus, are a sham introduced only to mollify those worried about the potential cost of the Clinton package.

A crackdown on fraud and abuse would not produce significant savings.—Fraud and abuse are worthy and attractive targets for health care reform; however, there are limits on how much fraud and abuse can be wrung out of the system and how much money can be saved doing it. This is particularly true considering the incremental cost of rooting out each additional dollar's worth of wrongdoing beyond current compliance efforts. That is not to say that more should not be done in this regard, but only to suggest that caution must be exercised in claiming that large net savings will result from a fraud and abuse crackdown

Savings From Information and Administrative Reforms May Be Swamped by Higher Costs From New Bureaucracy

Devising standard medical forms would be a major improvement over the current system, as would the issuance of a health security card to provide individual identification and enrollment information. Legislation to bring about these reforms was transmitted to the Congress by President Bush but neither House acted on it. Other aspects of the Clinton proposal regarding administration and new reporting requirements seem overly complicated and redundant. The burden of the new reporting requirements may well outweigh the simplicity brought about by form standardization.

Designers of the Jackson Hole Group approach believe their health plan purchasing cooperatives could provide administrative services for a cost of approximately $15 per employee, which as a percentage of total employer costs is similar to the administrative costs for large employers. Inclusion in the Clinton bill of an administrative assessment for each health alliance enrollee of up to 2.5 percent of premiums means that individuals could pay $48.30, and families up to $109, to cover administrative costs. This figure does not reflect administrative costs of the national boards or the regulatory bureaucracies in the 50 states or the increased reporting costs of individual health plans and corporate alliances.

Malpractice Changes Do Not Go Far Enough

Although liability insurance and defensive medicine add about 15 percent to physicians' bills in the United States, the Clinton plan does little to address this cost driver. A nationwide cap on monetary awards for noneconomic damages in malpractice suits is needed. Several bills that have been introduced in the Congress include a $250,000 ceiling on noneconomic damages as a way of discouraging frivolous lawsuits.

Doctors should be held accountable for malpractice in instances where the service delivered clearly falls short of recognized professional standards. However, the current tendency of the U.S. court system toward excessive malpractice awards in cases where there is an adverse outcome, even if the doctor performed in an acceptable manner, must be reversed.

Administration's Proposed Quality Provisions Could Be Improved

Americans receive the highest quality of health care in the world, although some key statistics appear to paint a different picture. Data on life expectancy and infant mortality, for example, show the United States lagging behind a number of industrialized nations. It should be remembered, however, that these figures are negatively affected by matters other than medical inadequacy, such as violence, crime, drug use, and teenage pregnancy--problems that reflect social ills. Creative experiments in linking health care information and quality of services are being performed by such private sector groups as the Cleveland Health Quality Choice Coalition and the Pennsylvania Health Care Cost Containment Council; both groups are making available statistics on clinical outcomes in selected local medical facilities. Focused programs of this sort should serve as a guide to further quality efforts. In contrast, the Clinton proposal would establish a National Quality Management Program and require extensive reporting by the health alliances and health plans regarding quality. Although market efficiency scarcely can exist without material information, one need not create a new bureaucracy for the purpose, and the program might more effectively be conducted at the state and local levels even if federal guidelines are used for basic uniformity.

Quality cannot be mandated. We believe that quality would better be enhanced by assuring the maximum possible level of competition in the delivery of health care.

The Administration's Cost Estimates
Do Not Seem Credible

Deputy Treasury Secretary Roger Altman has said that if the President's health plan were fully implemented by 2000, annual U.S. health care expenditures should be only about 10 percent of GDP, thus freeing up some $1 trillion per year for other investments early in the next century. Treasury Secretary Lloyd Bentsen has estimated that by the end of the decade, total business spending on the services covered by the proposed Health Security Act will fall by $10 billion. Other Administration officials have predicted that increased efficiency and competition from health care reform will result in medical inflation being brought in line with general prices by 2000. In addition, the Administration says that higher wages—due to savings produced by health care reform—will yield $14 billion a year for the federal government in the form of higher income tax payments.

There is ample evidence to demonstrate the government's inability to predict future program costs and its consistency in erring on the side of underestimation. In the 1960s, it was predicted that Medicare would cost around $12 billion in 1990, but the actual cost was $107 billion; the End-Stage Renal Disease program was projected in 1977 to cost $250 million annually, but 1991 costs were $6.6 billion; in the 1980s, the government's vision care turned out to cost twice the original estimate and skilled nursing facilities to cost three times the original estimate; two baseline estimates of Medicare and Medicaid spending between 1992-1996, one made in 1991 and the other in 1993 by the Congressional Budget Office, differed by a total of $151 billion

The public is told that the great expansion of health care services called for in President Clinton's proposal can be accomplished while saving billions of dollars, regardless of what reform vehicle is chosen and the efficiencies it may bring about. However, no one can be sure—to cite one variable—how newly insured individuals and those whose covered benefits would be expanded by enactment of the legislation will react. Because the cost issue is so central to the reform debate, the proponents of the Clinton plan claim fiscal responsibility, but their estimates are seriously in doubt.

Concluding Comments

In order to evaluate the likely effect of President Clinton's plan, one must separate the rhetoric of the reform campaign from the reality of the proposal's provisions. The Manufacturers' Alliance does not believe the Administration's package is the right approach for U.S. reform, nor is it superior to some of the other proposals that have been introduced in the Congress.

The reform proposal and the promotion surrounding it seem to have been carefully crafted to disguise elements that might otherwise have been unpalatable spending is contained not by the federal government through the establishment of overt price controls, but by premium caps imposed on insurance companies which must then pass on cost restrictions to providers; employers are not charged a payroll tax, but rather a mandatory premium contribution; the federal government trims its direct spending while requiring that others pay the cost of expanding coverage; each state directly regulates health alliances, rather than by a more visible expansion of the federal bureaucracy; government-sanctioned monopolies are created in the name of competition, new administrative complexities and reporting requirements are created, while the Administration claims simplicity as a nonnegotiable goal Further, by not calling employer-required premiums a payroll tax, President Clinton is able to keep the tax "off-budget," which means that future tax increases would receive less congressional scrutiny and the true costs could more easily be hidden from the public.

In addition, it is regrettable that individuals in the Administration are attempting to structure the reform debate in "us-versus-them" terms by criticizing certain players in the health care sector, including some of those who have been responsible for developing innovative procedures, breakthrough drugs, high-technology diagnostic equipment, and other advances that have led to the high quality of U.S. medical care. There is plenty of blame to go around, care must be taken that steps designed to correct the problems of the health care system do not discourage continued innovation in this vital sector of the U.S. economy.

The Clinton Reform
Principles

The President's plan is based on six principles, which he has said are not negotiable: the security of never losing health coverage; a guarantee of comprehensive benefits; controlling costs; simplifying the system; improving quality; and increasing choice. In MAPI's view, the Clinton plan fails to meet four out of six of his own principles for reform The proposal would succeed impressively in providing comprehensive benefits and ensuring that those benefits never can be taken away. However, it would not control health care costs; it would lead to poorer quality of care; it actually would decrease the choices available to most consumers, especially when the plan is compared with competing reform proposals; and the simplification realized by instituting a standardized claims form would be swamped by the regulatory and bureaucratic morass the proposal layers on top of the current health care system.

There is no question that several features of the current U.S. health care system should be reformed and that universal coverage should be phased in over the next several years. However, the Clinton proposal is so radical in its introduction of bureaucratic intervention in the delivery and insurance systems that, if it is adopted, society would lose much of what is commendable about U.S. health care. Indeed, the private sector itself through employer-initiated reform of individual health plans already has a better track record on reducing cost escalation and quality improvement than anything the Clinton proposal is likely to achieve.

Who Benefits, Who Pays?

Certainly, many people would benefit, at least in the short term, from the Clinton reform proposal, including those who are self-employed, workers locked in jobs because their benefits are not portable and individuals who cannot afford coverage. In addition, those who now pay for coverage could profit as universal coverage works to lessen cost-shifting and spread costs more evenly. Numerous provisions in the plan were designed specifically to attract the political support of some groups, such as the addition of prescription drugs and long-term benefits to Medicare recipients; the 10-year continuation of the current federal income tax exclusion for workers' supplemental benefits; the government take-over of most of the burden of covering early retirees; maintaining a separate health care system for veterans; the 7.9 percent cap on employer premiums; allowing large companies to opt out of the regional alliance system; and premium discounts to small businesses.

Although the constituency for health care reform has grown and the Clinton plan in its current form is receiving considerable attention, persons who would be affected ought not support a measure that is detrimental to the long-term health of the U.S. economy simply because it provides some short-term gains to their businesses or to their sectors of the population. Regardless of the structure of the funding mechanisms in the Clinton plan, which carefully hide the proposal's costs, everyone would end up paying much more, if not directly through higher overall health care costs and higher taxes to pay for them, then indirectly through lost jobs, lower wages, higher budget deficits, and foregone future consumption—or through poorer quality of care, delays in treatment, reduced availability of high-technology procedures, and a slower rate of medical innovation.

No country can afford to buy all the "best" health care for all of its citizens. Everyone would like to have the finest medical care available at the least possible cost. But while these goals are not mutually exclusive, the fact is that we cannot reach the ultimate in quality, in access, and in cost all at the same time. President Clinton has yet to make the hard decisions necessary to achieve an acceptable balance among the three.

If the United States is to succeed in providing high quality care and making health insurance coverage universal, responsible limits on what services are available will be not only necessary but judicious to keep health care costs from consuming an ever-increasing portion of our national income and crowding out the prospects for achieving other vital U.S. public policy goals. As it stands, the Clinton proposal is a policy choice we cannot afford either financially or medically.

690

2605 Stanford Ave.
Boulder, CO 80303
November 6, 1993

The Honorable Chairman Dan Rostenkowski
House Ways and Means Committee   Room 1102 LHOB
Washington, D. C. 20515

Dear Chairman Rostenkowski:

I have read President Clinton's booklet on Health Security and I have become most insecure. My wife and I urgently seek your help in protecting our earned health and annuity rights from cutbacks and even destruction of long standing programs. I served the U. S. Government for 33 years. My wife and I have now been under the Federal Employees Health Benefit Program (FEHBP) for some 33 years. It is one of the best health insurance programs in the U. S.

President Clinton's health reform plan as outlined in the White House booklet proposes to discontinue FEHBP for retirees. Instead of retaining the security of our earned benefit rights under a Federal program we would be forced to go under some kind of "alliance" which our State would create. The report on the ColoradoCare plan being developed by a task force under the Governor proposes basic health benefits costing $4.5 billion in contrast with existing health outlays in Colorado of $9-10 billion a year. Even so, the special interests here do not want an employer mandate to finance the new plan and have stirred up a big fight on financing health care here. We need guaranteed benefits.

President Clinton's plan provides for the continuation of Medicare for retirees who have earned this social insurance coverage. I have read that the Office of Personnel Management is supposed to develop a Medigap plan to supplement Medicare. Is that true? But the Health Security booklet states that for people with higher incomes the Medicare premium would be tripled. This crude "means testing" in effect abrogates much of the earned Medicare rights for which people worked and paid HI tax. (See p. 107 of White House booklet.)

In the budget program for 1994-98 the Clinton administration put through big cuts in Medicare, Medicaid, and veterans programs, deferred Civil Service COLAs, and increased tax on Social Security benefits. But several hundred billion of additional reductions in Medicare and Medicaid outlays are envisioned to reduce the budget deficit. (See Mid-Session budget Review, pp. 21-22 and Wall Street Journal, 9/9/93, pp. A3,A10.) Trust fund programs for the elderly people are being cut in disregard of Federal Government obligations.

The Clinton administration reductions in entitlements for the elderly are unjust for three reasons: First, the bulk of entitlements are paid from earmarked payroll taxes and contributions into trust funds. Second, the increases in general fund deficits which boosted the gross public debt by $3 trillion from 1980 to 1992 resulted in roughly even shares from (1) the doubling of defense outlays, (2) the 1981 and 1986 tax cuts for the rich and the corporations, and (3) growing interest on the debt due to the two prior causes. Third, in shaping its 1994 budget program the Clinton administration increased taxes on the very rich top one percent of households by a scant $25 billion a year. But data in the 1991 and 1993 Ways and Means Committee "Green Books" show that the net worth of this group grew by $2.3 trillion from 1983 to 1989, approximately $383 billion a year. The logical and socially just place for the Clinton administration and the Congress to look for money to reduce the budget deficits is not at the ordinary elderly, disabled, and survivors who are living on pensions, but at the previously favored rich group where the big money is. "Hold harmless" the benefit rights of Federal retirees.

Please let us know what you can do to help protect our earned benefits.

Respectfully,

Michael S. March, Ph. D.
303-494-4871

TESTIMONY TO
THE
WAYS & MEANS COMMITTEE
by
Linda Gantt, Ph.D., A.T.R. (Registered Art Therapist)
Acting Chair,
National Coalition of Arts Therapies Associations
February 1994

Mr. Chairman and Committee Members:

Thank you for the opportunity to submit some remarks on behalf
of our coalition about the pending health care reform legislation.
The National Coalition of Arts Therapies Associations (NCATA)
represents the following 6 professional membership organizations:

American Art Therapy Association
American Association for Music Therapy
American Dance Therapy Association
American Society for Group Psychotherapy and Psychodrama
National Drama Therapy Association
National Association for Poetry Therapy

Collectively, we have approximately 8,000 members and we estimate
that there are some five thousand more like-minded practitioners
across the country. Like the larger and better known groups
representing such professions as social work, psychology, nursing,
or occupational therapy, each of our organizations has an ethical
code, standards of practice, professional credentialling,
scientific theories, a body of knowledge, and specific training
requirements.

Each of the associations developed independently as the result of
people with a special interest and background in various art forms
and processes working with groups and individuals in special
settings. The types of facilities where we work include:

General and psychiatric hospitals	Schools
	Day treatment programs
Nursing homes, extended care facilities	Community mental Health centers
Group homes, sheltered workshops	Forensic programs
	Substance abuse centers
Rehabilitation programs	

Programs using the creative arts therapies can be found in some of
the most innovative hospitals and agencies in the country
including Chestnut Lodge, the Menninger Clinic, the Cleveland
Clinic, St. Elizabeths Hospital, Walter Reed Army Medical Center,
Sheppard-Pratt Hospital, the Rusk Institute, Cedars-Sinai
Hospital, and a number of Veterans Administration hospitals. The
Institute for Therapy Through the Arts based in Winnetka,
Illinois, provides the services of various creative arts
therapists to agencies serving the blind, emotionally disturbed
children and adolescents, the elderly, multiply handicapped, and
the chronically mentally ill. Similar programs exist in New York
City and Boston.

Major Issues
There are several issues which we feel are important for the
Ways & Means Committee to consider as it reviews the various
proposed health care bills:

• **Innovation in treatment should be preserved,
especially for the hard-to-reach and difficult-to-treat
individuals.**
We are gathering growing evidence to support the contention
that nonverbal therapies (art therapy, dance/movement
therapy, and music therapy) and arts-based treatments based
on specific artistic processes (poetry therapy, psychodrama,
and drama therapy) are effective ways to work with patients
who are difficult to reach. (See the appendix for some
recent articles and books which report a variety of

692

applications and research studies using these therapies).
In the past, most of our work has been done in psychiatric
hospitals and special education settings but we have been
expanding our services to a wide range of agencies and
community programs because we can demonstrate our
effectiveness in treating people who do not respond to more
conventional approaches.

Medical patients also respond to our methods. The creative
arts therapies are being used with patients who have:

Somatic complaints	Spinal cord injuries
Cystic fibrosis	Cardiac problems
Muscular dystrophy	Aphasia
Cancer	Traumatic injuries
Parkinson's disease	

These innovative approaches should be recognized in Federal
legislation so that they may be provided for those who can
benefit from them.

• **Funding for milieu treatments should be preserved.**
The fee-for-service model is an expensive way of paying for
certain types of milieu therapies which are usually provided
for groups of patients within a structured program. We urge
Congress to consider specifying certain services including
the various creative arts therapies which may be included in
the day rates for particular programs such as inpatient and
outpatient psychiatric and substance abuse programs, partial
hospital programs for the chronically mentally ill, and day
treatment programs for patients with dementia. The
regulations for CHAMPUS already provide the language for
such inclusion and we ask Congress to give consideration to
including similar language in the final version of any
health care reform legislation.

• **Non-invasive treatments should be emphasized in any
health care reform.**
A front-page article in the *Wall Street Journal* (January 13,
1994) described a special unit of Meridian Healthcare Inc.,
where "demented residents are given 40 hours a week of
structured activities [which are based on the arts]. In
these 'special care' units, just 3% of the residents require
psychoactive drugs to manage their behavior, compared with
between 40% and 60% of Meridian's other residents." Given
that many elderly patients have other health problems which
are complicated by the use of psychotropic medicine it is
important to use non-medical treatments whenever possible.
By using behavioral interventions instead of tranquilizers
care we can avoid some of the serious side effects of
certain medicines. The creative arts therapists have
specific therapeutic techniques which can be used with a
variety of patients who have behavioral problems.

• **Preventive programs should be stressed, particularly
those which engage the participants in such a way as
to head off episodes which require hospitalization.**
Depression is a serious condition for many people with
chronic physical and psychiatric illnesses. Programs based
on the creative arts therapies involve participants in an
active rather than a passive way and thus provide a method
for dealing with depression. In community-based programs,
the creative arts therapies are used to keep people
functional for a longer period of time thus avoiding
hospitalization. Loss, abandonment, loneliness, and
isolation are counteracted by the arts-based therapies.
The creative arts can also be used as a means of assessing
a person's psychological state or compliance with
treatment regimens.

• **Federal programs should recognize a broad range of
reimbursable services which can be selected according
to the specific needs of patients.**

Creative arts therapists typically work in
multidisciplinary teams providing group services as part
of a structured program as well as individual treatment.
Generally, we are given referrals for special work by the
team leader or physician. By permitting health care
professionals a range of permissible treatments we can
assure that individual treatment plans can take advantage
of any effective techniques. The arts serve as a catalyst
for achieving specific therapeutic goals.

When President Carter convened a President's Commission on
Mental Health in 1977, he included a Task Panel on "The
Role of the Arts in Therapy and the Environment." One of
the recommendations of the task panel was that when
"considered part of the therapeutic regimen prescribed for
the patient, the services of arts therapists should be
considered as a reimbursable service. And, the panel
added, "future funding, including a national health
insurance program, should also include these
considerations."

Increasing Recognition

The contributions of the creative arts therapies are getting to be
better known both by the general public and legislators. In 1991
and 1992, the Senate Special Committee on Aging had hearings on
music, art, and dance/movement therapy. As a result of these
hearings amendments were added to the reauthorization of the Older
Americans Act which included these therapies and provided money
for research and demonstration grants. This past fall, the newly
created Office of Alternative Medicine (OAM) in the National
Institutes of Health awarded research grants to study the use of
music therapy to aid psychosocial adjustment after brain injury
and the use of dance/movement therapy for patients with cystic
fibrosis.[The response to the request for applications (RFA) for
the OAM money brought in 452 proposals. The two creative arts
therapies grantees were up against rather stiff competition.]

We ask that the creative arts therapies be considered reimbursable
services and that creative arts therapists be included in any
Federal listing of health providers so that patients may benefit
from a wide range of effective treatments.

The issues pertaining to health care reform are extremely complex
and we are appreciative of the committee members who must work out
the myriad details in this legislation.

APPENDIX

A. A Representative Bibliography on the Creative Arts Therapies

Barker, L. (1991). The use of music and relaxation techniques to reduce pain of burn patients during daily debridement. In: C. Maranto (Ed.), Applications of Music in Medicine. Washington, DC: National Association for Music Therapy.

Baron, P. (1989). Fighting cancer with images. In: H. Wadeson (Ed.), Advances in Art Therapy. New York, NY: John Wiley & Sons.

Bright, R. (1988). Music Therapy and the Dementias. St. Louis, MO: MMB Music.

Cousins, N. (1987). Confronting Cancer Through Art. Los Angeles, CA: Jonsson Comprehensive Cancer Center, University of California.

Crystal, H., Grober, E., & Masur, D. (1989). Preservation of musical memory in Alzheimer's disease. Journal of Neurology and Psychiatry, 52, 1415-1416.

Davila, J., & Menendez, J. (1986). Relaxing effects of music in dentistry for mentally handicapped patients. Special Care in Dentistry, 7, 18-21.

Durham, L, & Collins, M. (1986). The effect of music as a conditioned aid in prepared childbirth education. JOGN Nursing, May-June, 268-270.

Epstein, L. (1974). Music feedback in the treatment of tension headache: An experimental case study. Journal of Behavior Therapy & Experimental Psychiatry, 5, 1, 59-63.

Fleming, M., & Cox, C. (1989). Engaging the somatic patient through art. In: H. Wadeson (Ed.), Advances in Art Therapy. New York, NY: John Wiley & Sons.

Grob, H. (1993). Use of music and paraverbal techniques in degenerative diseases with focus on Huntington's disease. In: F. Bejjani (Ed.), Current Research in Arts Medicine. Pennington, NJ: A Capella Books.

Guzetta, C. (1989). Effects of relaxation and music therapy on patients in a coronary care unit with presumptive acute myocardial infarction. Heart and Lung, 18, 609-616.

Hanser, S. (1985). Music therapy and stress reduction research. Journal of Music Therapy, 22, 193-206.

Johnson, D. (1990). How the arts are used in therapy. In: Health and Medical Horizons. New York, NY: Macmillan.

Kaempf, G., & Amodei, M. (1989). The effect of music on anxiety. American Operating Room Nurses Journal, 50, 112-118.

Kaufman, G. (1981). Art therapy with the addicted. Journal of Psychoactive Drugs 13, 4, 353-360.

Kent, R. (1989). Genesa: An adjunct to art therapy in the treatment of drug and alcohol abuse clients. In S. Einstein (Ed.) Drug and Alcohol Use: Issues and Factors. New York, NY: Plenum.

Locke, S., & Colligan, D. (1987). The Healer Within: The New Medicine of Mind and Body. New York, NY: Mentor.

Locsin, R. (1981). The effect of music on the pain of selected post-operative patients. Journal of Advanced Nursing, 6, 1925.

Lyon, J., & Sims, E. (1988). Drawing: Its use as a communicative aid with aphasic and normal adults. Clinical Aphasiology Conference.

McKinney, C. (1990). Music therapy in obstetrics: A review. Music Therapy Perspectives, 8, 57-60.

Mitchell, J. (1987). Dance/movement therapy in a changing health care system. American Journal of Dance Therapy, 10, 4-10.

Moore, R. (1983). Art therapy with substance abusers: A review of the literature. Arts in Psychotherapy 10, 4, 251-260.

Pallaro, P. (1993). Culture, self and body-self: Dance/movement therapy across cultures. In: F. Bejjani (Ed.), Current Research in Arts Medicine. Pennington, NJ: A Capella Books.

Palmer, J., & Nash, F. (1993). Humanizing the health-care environment: Models for a new arts-medicine partnership. In: F. Bejjani (Ed.), Current Research in Arts Medicine. Pennington, NJ: A Capella Books.

Perowsky, G. (1993). Dance therapy with the orthopedic patient.
In: F. Bejjani (Ed.), Current Research in Arts Medicine.
Pennington, NJ: A Capella Books.

Plevin, M. (1993). Working with Dionysus: Dance/movement therapy
with recovering substance abusers in a therapeutic community
setting. In: F. Bejjani (Ed.), Current Research in Arts
Medicine. Pennington, NJ: A Capella Books.

Rossi, E. (1986). The Psychobiology of Mind-Body Healing. New
York, NY: W.W.Norton.

Sacks, O., & Tomaino, C. (1991). Music and neurological disorder.
International Journal of Arts Medicine, 1, 1, 10-12.

Saperston, B. (1989). Music-based individualized relaxation
training: A stress-reduction approach for the behaviorally
disturbed mentally retarded. Music Therapy Perspectives, 6, 26-
33.

Saperston, B. (1993). Music-based models for altering
physiological responses. In: F. Bejjani (Ed.), Current Research
in Arts Medicine. Pennington, NJ: A Capella Books.

Standley, J. (1986). Music research in medical/dental treatment:
Meta-analysis and clinical applications. Journal of Music
Therapy, 22, 56-122.

Thompson, G., & McMahon, D. (1988). Music and analgesia. Problems
in Anesthesia, 2, 3,376-385.

Troupe, E. (1986). Training severely aphasic patients to
communicate by drawing. Annual Convention of the American
Speech-Language-Hearing Association.

Unruh, A., McGrath, P., Cunningham, S., & Humphreys, P. (1983).
Children's drawing of their pain. Pain, 17, 385-392.

Updike, P. (1990). Music therapy results for ICU patients.
Dimensions in Critical Care Nursing, 9, 39-45.

Zimmerman, L., Pierson, M., & Marker, J. (1988). Effects of music
on patient anxiety in coronary care units. Heart & Lung, 17,
560-566.

February 25, 1994

Hon. Pete Stark, Chairman
House of Representatives Ways & Means
 Health Subcommittee
239 Cannon House Office Building
Washington, D.C. 20515

Dear Congressman Stark:

As the Summit County (OH) Executive and President of the National Council of Elected County Executives, I would like to express support of, on behalf of my county and the members of my bi-partisan organization, the concept of universal health insurance. The debate of course is how to pay for the cost of implementing such an ambitious program.

It is an honor to have the opportunity to explain the dilemmas confronting our nation's county leaders to this subcommittee regarding the most aggressive social program in our nation's history since the implementation of Social Security under President Franklin D. Roosevelt.

The National Council of Elected County Executives represents the chief elected executive in a county, or a consolidated city/county in over 400 counties throughout the United States. Although the county executive form of government is practiced in only 12 percent of our nation's counties, these officials represent approximately 30 percent of the nation's total population

The county executive form of government is represented by County Executives, County Judges, County Mayors and Parish and Borough Presidents. The county executive is also the fastest growing form of government in the United States.

As the federal government and state governments continue to experience diminishing resources there is a growing need for a centralized authority at the local level to not only formulate and implement public policy, but to also distribute property tax dollars. Not an official appointed by a Board of Commissioners, or a Board of Freeholders, but one individual directly elected by the taxpayers, who can be held accountable at the polls on election day.

Our concerns regarding universal health insurance are the financial implications directed upon us by the federal government and our individual state governments. The terms for this cost-shifting of course are mandates, and namely, unfunded state and federal mandates, which are already an extreme burden on county government operations. We fear that the implementation of universal health insurance will result in even more unfunded mandates.

Specific areas of concern mentioned by the NCECE General Membership at past meetings of our organization include the following:

• The most glaring and crucial aspect of President Clinton's National Health Security Act affecting local government leaders, and for that matter, government employers, is the term "salary cap." While the private sector has a salary/payroll cap of 7.9 percent of the gross salary/payroll, there is no such cap on the public sector. If adopted as is, the National Health Security Act could devour limited public sector funds if the health care plan exceeds projected annual costs. Again, I stress to the entire subcommittee, this stipulation as is could be ruinous to state and local government operating expenditures.

• Medicaid - in states such as New York, New Jersey and Wisconsin, counties are required to pick up the costs of "maintenance of effort" services. State budget burdens are becoming more and more exacerbated by Medicaid services and as a result, costs are passed off onto counties If states are allowed, under the Clinton plan, to operate their own Medicaid system, how are counties to prevent this continuing cost-shifting (mandates) when other components of the plan necessitate county expenditures such as providing care to the incarcerated population? Under a national health care system, we would prefer some type of federal government control over the state government regarding Medicaid expenditures placed upon local governments.

NCECE members would like the federal government to place a cap on the growth of Medicaid due to the unpredictability of projecting Medicaid rates into annual county budget forecasts. I know many of our members would prefer that escalating rates be met by a conditional reimbursement formula so as not to cause budget crises.

Medicaid needs to be "attacked" through a two prong strategy - i.e. health care and welfare overhaul. However, we want to be fair in protecting those that this historic program was designed to assist. We applaud the Congress's initiative regarding the extremely complex issue of Medicaid reform, which we feel is an integral component of both health care and welfare reform.

• Incarcerated population - county governments are responsible for overseeing a number of public safety initiatives including the maintenance of county jail facilities. If universal health insurance is adopted, what happens to this coverage when a person is arrested, tried, found guilty and incarcerated? Does the person remain enrolled, or does the county assume the costs of providing insurance after the fact? With exploding crime rates and hence, prison populations, county executives are distressed about the cost implications of assuming health care costs for our incarcerated populations.

• Counties would like the federal government to pick up the health care costs of early retirees. In times of serious budget constraints, offering early retirement incentive packages to county employees is most beneficial and would be even more helpful if the federal government took on the expenditure of picking up early retiree's health care costs.

• Home & Community Based Care - in order to alleviate the astronomical cost of long term nursing home care, counties are beginning to utilize home and community based care in providing quality of life services for our aging population. With the World War II generation of which I am a member, approaching retirement in the near future, long term care will become a critical budgetary issue if we do act now in implementing a national program to service our elderly. Again, a cap on home and community based care is a practical matter due to the unpredictability of the growth of such services.

• Long Term Care - it is our understanding that citizens in county nursing home facilities will remain our responsibility. We hope that adequate funding of home and community based care will be a fair financial trade-off under a national health care insurance program.

Medicaid, incarcerated population, home and community based care, and long term care are just some of the critical areas that affect a county executive's governing ability; it is the difference between having a rotating county executive every four years and stable government.

NCECE is in the process of educating our national leaders about the duties and responsibilities of the county executive form of government. We certainly did not view health care as an issue in which our goal was to be accomplished, but health care reform and the concept of universal health insurance will have dramatic effects on the local level, especially among elected county executives.

As NCECE continues to become recognized on Capitol Hill as the vehicle for promoting the agenda of elected officials representing over 30 million constituents, we look forward to becoming more involved in the national public policy discourse.

On behalf of the National Council of Elected County Executives I would like to thank Chairman Stark and the members of the subcommittee for the opportunity to verbally express the view of our nation's County Executives, County Judges, County Mayors and Parish and Borough Presidents.

Sincerely,

Tim Davis
Summit County (OH) Executive
NCECE President

cc: Michael G. Griffin
        NCECE, Executive Director

February 24, 1994

Congressman Pete Stark
Chair, Health Subcommittee
  Ways & Means Committee
239 Cannon House Office Bldg.
Washington, D.C. 20515

Dear Congressman Stark:

As Dane County Executive, I know that national health care reform **now** is essential for the well-being of our citizens in Dane County and Wisconsin. Of course, the provision of basic health care is fundamental to the well-being of every citizen throughout the country. Beyond this, a cost-effective health care system is critical to the strength of our private sector economy and to the maintenance of vital public services which are being strained by growing health care costs.

During December, 1993, I put together a group of 27 Dane County citizens who have interest and knowledge in the health care system: medical care providers; University experts; representatives of community organizations serving people with special needs; public health representatives; and, others. With the help of this discussion group, I have reviewed health care reform proposals before the Congress. This letter has been improved by edits I received as a result of sending the first draft to all 27 citizens engaged in these discussions. I believe the final product is a consensus of the group. (Attachment 1 is a listing of the members of the group.)

The most basic conclusion that I want to emphasize is this: The worst choice for our county is to do nothing to change the current system.

We strongly support the passage of health care reform legislation in 1994.

I recognize the challenges you face as legislators in addressing the complex and difficult choices inherent in health care reform. Despite this complexity and difficulty we should not lose sight of the need to take action. No plan will be perfect, but we must improve on the current situation.

From a strictly financial standpoint, the current system is a budget breaker for the federal, state, county and local governments as well as a drag on the private sector economy. Comparisons with other countries show we have the most expensive system, yet it is one of the few systems among developed countries that does not offer basic coverage to everyone.

Based on my discussions with a range of knowledgeable Dane County citizens described above, let me suggest some more specific elements of reform that will benefit our county and state the most.

1. Key policies that should be enacted in health reform:
    - universal coverage is fundamental (not just universal access). Some 84% of Wisconsin citizens share this view with 58% saying they would pay $1,000/yr more in taxes; [1]
    - if there must be a phase-in process for some components, other than universal coverage, the timetable for implementation should be aggressive; and
    - it is appropriate to maintain states' flexibility to design specific systems ranging from single payor to managed competition/cooperation models, within a national framework of consistent coverage and benefits along the lines recommended by the President.

2. States and counties have a strong interest in:
    - providing coverage for everyone, including a clearly defined minimum package of coverage that cannot be decreased by states;
    - controlling costs for the good of the economy as well as for savings at all levels of government;
    - making sure the needs of special populations are met in an appropriate, cost-effective manner; and
    - accommodating the fact that each local area has different resources which requires authority for local modifications that maintain flexible, innovative, coordinated, methods of meeting citizen health care needs.

3. The program needs to be realistically funded:
    - legislation should achieve savings in Medicare & Medicaid, along the lines recommended by the President;
    - consistent national benefits can streamline insurance administration costs;
    - increased Medicare premiums based on ability to pay are acceptable;
    - user co-payments are reasonable as long as they are lidded by a total out-of-pocket cost cap. Mental Health/Alcohol & Drug Abuse co-pays should be subject to the cap also although a phase-in period might be acceptable, particularly if some link to ability to pay is put into place.
    - increased taxes appear to be an inevitable part of a total package. . "Sin taxes" are an appropriate source of support although the total burden should not fall solely on users of tobacco. Appropriate increases in alcohol excise taxes should also be considered.

---

[1] Report Dec. 3, 1993 Wi Survey Research Laboratory see attachment 2.

- the design needs to allow care management for cost-effective care which includes making sure benefits are "medically necessary and appropriate" (although mechanisms for this assurance could be defined by each state); and
- for cost reasons, I would support some limits on MH/AODA coverage in the short term. However, these benefits should not be excluded from the overall package totally because appropriate care in these areas can save health care and other social costs long-term.

I realize taxes are a substantial political concern of many people, but I think some "sin taxes" ought to be acceptable if they finance a real improvement in our health care system for the general public's benefit. In fact, I would suggest referring to these as "users fees," as those who engage in tobacco and excessive alcohol use are consistently shown to use health care to a greater extent than the balance of the population.

4. The traditional health care system has not worked well to meet the needs of special populations. State and county governments have developed systems and programs to meet these needs; in Wisconsin, our programs are largely organized through county human services delivery systems.

We have learned, over time, the best way to care for frail elderly and disabled people, and others with special needs, is to combine social and health services in a comprehensive "wrap around" system; to serve people as much as possible in their homes & communities; and to provide quality care with cost restrained through using expertise of a range of staff including paraprofessionals and, within limits, volunteers. We have put together programs that creatively combine health care financing with other public and private financing sources to meet people's needs and to control government costs.

Currently, we have a public human service system working with the private medical system. When we do national health care reform it is important we build on what we have learned in these efforts, and not lose ground. There is a risk that "health care reform" will inadvertently lead to worse public service and ultimately higher costs as a result of "over-medicalizing" problems and emphasizing late rather than early intervention.

Examples of excellent programs developed in Dane County and Wisconsin that should be preserved are:

- Children Come First, serving children with Severe Emotional Disturbance in the Community. This is funded by a mix of capitated Medical Assistance diversion funds (saving psychiatric inpatient dollars) via use of a State Option in MA regulations 1915 a, and county funds for Child Caring Institutions and Corrections placements. The program keeps children in the community at the same or cheaper cost/month as compared to institutional care. (Savings on capital costs for not having to build more institutions is an additional plus.)

- Community Options Program, retain frail elderly and disabled citizens in the community, saving nursing home costs; this is funded by a mix of county, state, and federal MA dollars.

- Community Integration Program, integrating disabled citizens in the community from more expensive specialized residential treatment facilities and nursing homes, again funded by a mix of county and federal MA dollars.

- MA case management dollars, accessed as part of the funding strategy for a host of programs operated by senior centers and other organizations serving the frail elderly and disabled.

-- Community Support Program that integrates adults with severe and persistent mental illnesses in the community from very costly institutional and residential settings. Dane County pioneered this Assertive Community Treatment program resulting in our county spending less of our mental health budget on inpatient services costs (33% vs 50+% for most counties.)

- A capitated managed care arrangement for a very needy group of general assistance consumers where the U-CARE HMO from the University of Wisconsin-Madison Medical Center provides excellent services while the accept most of the risk for costs beyond a low negotiated rate.

Specific recommendations to avoid the potential loss of valuable programs which are clearly cost-effective and combine medical, health and social services are:

- make sure all current MA-funded programs of this type, including not only formal "waivers" but options for managed care such as Children Come First and the use of MA case management dollars for approved programs, are maintained at least for a several year phase-in period (5 years?); and

- require state plans for implementing innovative programs to combine social, health, and medical care services for special needs populations to be in place by the end of the phase-in period.

5. Long Term Care for the elderly and disabled is a major social need, and cost. The program in the President's plan is a good start which should be maintained and expanded over time. We recognize that this is a topic that often defies compromise and can lead to unhealthy conflict. However, we urge that Wisconsin's experience with nursing home diversion programs such as COP and CIP be kept in mind: We have proven beyond any doubt that consumers prefer to stay in their homes and communities, and that home and community care can be substantially cheaper than nursing homes for many persons who need long term care. Whatever system is authorized should not perpetuate a nursing home/institutional bias.

For individuals whom nursing home placement is necessary and cost effective, we support a system under which public and private dollars are available to assure that the increasingly complex direct care needs of each resident are met and quality of care safeguards are in place.

For Community Based and Nursing Home care, the legislation could negate divestment with a co-pay based on a reasonable rate, not an all or nothing approach as we have now.

A percentage of income based on a realistic sliding co-pay scale will allow the lower income/asset person to be a part of the care giving, without being impoverished, and the higher income/asset person to pay a much higher portion of the care without having recourse to divestment.

6. County public health agencies have a long tradition of providing high quality, low cost preventive health services and health education directed toward maintaining a health population. Typically funding for local public health services has lagged far behind health services directed towards "sick care" rather than "health care." This has been particularly true in Wisconsin.

National health care reform should not perpetuate this pattern. A greater investment in health education and preventive health care, through local public health services, can pay great dividends in a healthier population which will demand fewer costly secondary and tertiary health interventions.

In order to achieve this end, health care reform should foster a wider range of preventive care services.

In part, this can be achieved by assuring public health representation on the Regional Health Alliances.

I would note that the Dane County experience with Health Maintenance Organizations has proven that employees will choose managed care when their contribution to premiums will be less, and that HMO's can save money in the delivery of care while providing quality care. [2]

---

[2] Dane County experience under HMO's has shown an annual adjusted premium increase between 10.5% & 10.8% vs a national trend of 14% from 1987-91. Comparing Madison, Milwaukee, and Minneapolis/St Paul all with 29% + HMO subscribers against similar cities Ann Arbor, Portland Maine, and Rochester N.Y. hospital beds per/1,000 persons dropped from averaging about 5/1,000 to 3.5/1,000 from 1981-1990 while the other three cities stayed at 5/1,000 in both years. On average the three high HMO cities admissions/1,000 population dropped about 17% while the other three cities dropped about 7%. Dane summarization of report from: Steven C. Hill, Barbara Wolfe, "Testing the HMO Competitive Strategy" Working Paper # 22, September 1993, The Robert M. La Pollette Institute of Public Affairs 1225 Observatory Drive, U. W. Madison, 53706.

In summary, I want to reiterate our concern that the time for national health care reform is now; and that meaningful, fundamental reform should be supported. I encourage you to consider our position on behalf of Dane County.

If you have any specific issues you would like us to review, please feel free to communicate them to me directly, or to Helene Nelson, Director, Dane County Human Services Department, 1202 Northport Drive, Madison, Wisconsin, 53704 (Phone 608-242-6419).

Sincerely,

Richard J. Phelps
Dane County Executive

RJP:gh

cc: Tim Davis, President, NCECE
     Earl Wells, Griffin Media Group

WRITTEN STATEMENT OF PAUL HOUGHLAND, JR., EXECUTIVE DIRECTOR,
OPTICIANS ASSOCIATION OF AMERICA ON HEALTH CARE REFORM
LEGISLATIVE PROPOSALS

SUBMITTED TO THE SUBCOMMITTEE ON HEALTH, COMMITTEE ON WAYS AND
MEANS, FEBRUARY 28, 1994

The Opticians Association of America is pleased to have this
opportunity to present its views on health care reform
legislation to the members of the House Ways and Means Committee.

OAA represents approximately 40,000 dispensing opticians
throughout the United States. Our membership consists of both
individual and firm members. Individual members may work for
another optician, an ophthalmologist, an optometrist, or one of
the large chains which dispenses eyewear. Firm members are small
businessmen who own their own independent optical firms and
compete with medical doctors(ophthalmologists), optometrists, and
the chain stores in dispensing eyewear, both spectacles and
contact lenses. The principal issues examined in this statement
reflect the concerns of the small, independent firm owner, the
heart and soul of our association.

Because we represent independent small businesses, we believe
that freedom is the paramount issue. Allowing consumers freedom
to shop for eye glasses and contact lenses at stores of their
choice is a cardinal tenet of the optician's credo and must be
recognized in the final health care reform legislative package.

OAA's Board of Directors has adopted three principal objectives
with regard to any health care reform plan adopted by Congress.
First, any health care plan which includes vision services must
recognize opticians as providers AND at the same time contain
strong anti-self referral provisions similar to the prohibitions
included in HR 345 introduced by Ways and Means Health
Subcommittee Chairman Stark and cosponsored by Representative
Levin, a member of the Ways and Means Health Subcommittee.

We are very pleased that significant portions of HR 345 were
included in the Omnibus Budget Reconciliation Act of 1993, and
strongly support the inclusion of strong anti-referral language
in health care reform legislation. With respect to vision care we
strongly support extending and improving the ban on self-
referrals to prohibit both ophthalmologists and optometrists from
making referrals to health care providers with which they have a
financial relationship.

Maintaining a level playing field within the vision care field
requires the passage of strong language banning self-referrals.
We encourage every member of this committee to support the
extension of the Stark anti-referral language as the best way
to assure the preservation of the kind of competition which will
lead to the lowest cost for vision care services to consumers.

Second, any alliances, voluntary or mandatory, must recognize
opticians as providers. We recognize that the mandatory alliances
found in HR 3600, the Health Security Act, the Administration's
health care reform proposal do not command much support in the
Health Subcommittee, and we accept that fact. In fairness to the
interests of our members, however, we must retain a pragmatic
approach to this matter. If the alliances, in either voluntary or
mandatory form, remain in the legislation being considered by
this committee, we insist upon the inclusion of opticians as
providers within these alliances.

Finally, we support the preemption of anti-competitive state laws
with regard to allied health professionals(opticians). Our
objective here is keeping health care costs to the consumer as
low as possible. Studies have shown that where competition with
regard to spectacles and contact lenses does not exist, prices
for these commodities increase, sometimes sharply.

We recognize much merit in HR 1200, the American Health Security
Act of 1993, sponsored by the Honorable Jim McDermott of
Washington, a member of this subcommittee, and HR 2610, the
Mediplan Act of 1993, introduced by the Honorable Fortney Stark,
chairman of the Ways and Means Health Subcommittee, particularly
the extensive benefits provided in both plans and the
universality of coverage.

However, we prefer an approach which would provide generous
benefits, including vision care and universal coverage, while
preserving the existing structure of private insurance. We
believe significant health care reform can be achieved within a
system that relies upon private health insurance sold by private
companies competing within the free enterprise system. OAA will
back health care reform bills that encourage small businesses to
stay in business, and our association will strongly oppose plans
which, in our judgment, cripple the entrepreneurial spirit.

We are very supportive of the concept of small business pooling
of health insurance purchases. OAA members who are firm owners
would benefit greatly from plans to enlarge the purchasing pool
for health insurance premium purposes.

As a representative of small businesses, the OAA strongly
supports paperwork reduction and standardization of forms used by
private health care providers and commercial carriers. It is high
time that health care providers spend their time delivering
health services not filling out complicated, duplicative forms.

While the Opticians Association of America recognizes the
motivation of those who would streamline the provision of health
services by amending the antitrust laws, it wishes to urge
extreme caution in crafting these modifications. Antitrust
exemptions designed to help hospitals and clinics in rural areas
share expensive equipment must be written in **very precise
legislative language.**

Unfortunately, opticians have suffered from anti-competitive
practices, sometimes sanctioned by legislation, in many states.
For example, opticians are excluded from providing vision care
services within health maintenance organizations in some states.
Other states prohibit opticians from fitting contact lenses
despite evidence cited by a Federal Trade Commission study which
found no significant difference in quality between opticians,
ophthalmologists, and optometrists in the fitting of contact
lenses. Therefore the OAA approaches any modification of existing
antitrust law with great trepidation.

Finally, the Opticians Association of America objects to the
inclusion of an entire subtitle in HR 3600 which would change the
status of independent contractors not only for health care
purposes but also for employment tax purposes. Section 7301 would
permit the Internal Revenue Service to issue regulations on
"employment status." Section 7302 would increase penalties on
businesses who fail to issue accurate Form 1099's. Section 7303
would amend Section 530 of the Revenue Act of 1978 concerning
safe harbor provisions. The issues raised by the independent
contractor subtitle would do serious damage to productive
business arrangements which opticians currently have with certain
other vision care providers. Many OAA firm members hire
optometrists, contact lens technicians, and other providers in
which the independent contractor status is the key element of the
relationship. Approval of these IRS proposals would have a
serious impact on these relationships. Therefore the OAA strongly
opposes these provisions.

STATEMENT
OF
DR. KEN FOX
PRESENTED TO THE
HOUSE WAYS & MEANS COMMITTEE
ON THE
PRESIDENT'S HEALTH SECURITY ACT
H. R. 3600

Thank you, Mr. Chairman, for allowing me to deliver some remarks to the Committee on matters related to the President's health care initiative and how it may affect leading edge medical technologies such as laser angioplasty. PILLCO, of which I am CEO, holds the key patents in the United States and in some foreign countries related to the current treatment method which utilizes a pulsed ultraviolet excimer laser. The procedure is FDA-approved and uses these lasers to vaporize atherosclerotic plaque and restore normal blood flow to arteries of the heart. The fact that ours is a pulsed laser -- which utilizes carefully selected energy parameters -- permits the physician to vaporize plaque without thermal harm to surrounding arterial tissue. Needless to say, this innovative method is a revolutionary approach to cardiac disease mitigation.

The FDA approved these technologies for commercial use in 1992 after many years of evaluation. Presently, two companies are licensed to manufacture these lasers in the United States: Advanced Interventional Systems and Spectranetics. Dr. A. Arthur Coster and I began working on these advances in the late seventies, and I can tell you without bias today that the list of difficulties in bringing this technology to fruition in American hospitals for human benefit would easily, as a popular song once noted, fill the entire Royal Albert Hall. Any changes to our health care system should address the dual matter of bringing life saving and quality-enhancing technologies safely and efficiently to the marketplace in its opening legislative clauses.

Technology drives our health care system as well as our entire economy. The advent in the later 1970's of 'balloon angioplasty' gave interventional cardiologists a tremendous advantage. However, balloon angioplasty is primarily effective in a smaller number of cardiac patients. The balloon can be effectively used when the lesions (plaque blockages) are simple, and changes in personal diet may provide additional success. When the disease gets more complex and includes long lesions, diffused lesions, heavily calcified lesions, and other difficult blockages the pulsed laser is undeniably the best angioplasty method. Obviously the best method of eradication of the most difficult plaque lesions will also be the best method for attacking the smaller and simpler lesions. The net benefit of this thesis statement becomes more apparent when surgery rates for failed balloon angioplasty are taken into consideration. The resultant expense of open heart and bypass surgery is well documented. Announcements in the news this month that the national cost figure for coronary artery bypass grafting (CABG) is approximately $9 billion a year was astounding! Both the Bureau of National Affairs and the Health Care Data Information Center have jointly claimed in a study that CABG has inflated our national health costs without a correlating enhancement in our national health status. Their study also suggested that we should quantify our projected financial savings in relation to real changes in our medical practice patterns. I believe this would be helpful, too.

Another interesting facet in this debate is that the pulsed laser advance in angioplasty technology can be less expensive than other angioplasty remediations including balloon. For ease of reference, attached to my statement is a comparative hospital reimbursement and length of stay survey we developed via interviews with hospital administrators for the three major cardio vascular procedures. While the initial hospital investment in the excimer laser technology may appear substantial, the vaporization of the plaque via these lasers provides dramatic cost efficiencies and time savings when the survey results are compared. Although many reasons exist for this, the major ones are:

1. People are out of the hospital sooner that after surgery or balloon,
2. Patients are back to work faster,
3. Laser angioplasty offers lower mortality rates than bypass,
4. Plaque is vaporized via laser versus being compressed against the arterial wall by balloon angioplasty, and
5. Surgery is risky, expensive, and the recurrence of plaque is a familiar result.

The Wall Street Journal on February 4, 1994, reported on a U.S. Centers for Disease Control and Prevention study in an article entitled "Coronary Disease Poses Risk to 82% of Americans, Despite Lifestyle Changes." The study points out that we should not ignore the risk factors: obesity, lack of exercise, high blood pressure and cholesterol, diabetes, and cigarette smoking (which was defined as having smoked at least 100 cigarettes in one's lifetime). The CDC's Cardiovascular Health Studies Branch notes that physical activity and diet changes do help reduce one's risk but do not erase the disease altogether. Contrary to popular understanding, coronary heart disease is America's greatest health threat today. In response, Medical Laser Marketplace '93 quotes 1992 Arthur D. Little Co. statistics which project a 25% penetration of lasers in cardiovascular surgery by 1995. The trend is established, and it is based on medical success and the positive cost-benefit ratio of lasers in cardiovascular treatment.

President Clinton's concern for access to good medical care for all Americans is an honorable goal for our nation. I want to amend that goal with the thought that access to medical care must include access to effective medical care for all Americans. Biotechnology has been an engine of growth for our economy and must remain a locomotive of growth for the continued enhancement of our national health. Everyone should have access to the best medical procedures when warranted. We cannot ignore costs in this equation, and, at the same time, we cannot ignore medical success either. Coronary artery disease cuts across both socioeconomic and geographic boundaries in our country. Our hospitals must be adequately reimbursed for advanced, efficient, and effective procedures like laser angioplasty. If they are not, the companies that develop and supply these and related technolo ies cannot survive. In a directl related manner our national health status will falter. The resultant macro-economics and macro-politics of this potential turn of events should be evident.

Thank you, Mr. Chairman, for allowing me to provide you some details related to a very complex medical arena. In closing, I wish to point out that we at PILLCO are not opposed to managed care in the heath industry. What kind of managed care is the important issue. We must provide for the American people a health care system which takes advantage of advances in technology and requires the advances to pay back solid dividends in terms of a longer and better quality of life for all Americans.

COMPARATIVE HOSPITAL REIMBURSEMENT FIGURES

(AVERAGE)

BALLOON ANGIOPLASTY
Length of Hospital Stay	5.7 Days
Amount Charged By Hospital	100 %
Percentage of Charge Paid by Carrier	47.3 %
Hospital Cost as Percentage of Charge	48 %
(average hospital loss on procedure is .7%)	
Amount Charged Compared to Charge for ELCA (laser)	102 %

CORONARY ARTERY BYPASS GRAFTING (CABG)
Length of Hospital Stay	13.5 Days
Amount Charged By Hospital	100 %
Percentage of Charge Paid by Carrier	45.2 %
Hospital Cost as Percentage of Charge	40.3 %
(average hospital profit on procedure is 4.9%)	
Amount Charged Compared to Charge for ELCA (laser)	308 %

EXCIMER LASER CORONARY ANGIOPLASTY (ELCA)
Length of Hospital Stay	4.6 Days
Amount Charged By Hospital	100 %
Percentage of Charge Paid by Carrier	47.1 %
Hospital Cost as Percentage of Charge	46.7 %
(average hospital profit on procedure is .4%)	
Amount Charged Compared to Charge for ELCA (same)	100 %

Note: In the past, hospitals have made a profit from bypass procedures. This has been outweighed by the costs to American health status, however, by long hospital stays and higher morbidity/mortality rates, as well as other medical complications.

Princeton Task Force on National Health Care

204 WITHERSPOON STREET
PRINCETON, NEW JERSEY 08540
809-921-6752

INTRODUCTION:

We represent ourselves in our capacity as private citizens of the United States, with no axe to grind, with no particular political affiliation.

PURPOSE OF TASK FORCE:

To objectively study, analyze and propose for these United States the best possible National Health Care System.

Result is substantial agreement with President Bill Clinton, the NEW YORK TIMES Lead Editorial Feb. 22, 1994; the American College of Surgeons, the House of Delegates of the American Medical Association on their Dec. 7, 1993 Resolution; the Presbyterian Church (U.S.A.), the National Conference of Catholic Bishops, the true wishes of the national labor union leaders.

MAJOR RECOMMENDATIONS:

1) A free enterprise, private insurance, privately-run single-payer national for-profit public utility stock insurance company chartered by Congress; charter can be revoked or amended, giving Congress the ultimate "oversight" power.

This health corporation shall have the entire legal population of the United States as one UNITED STATE community-rated pool.

Absolutely the same free choice of health care providers by patients whether employed or not; the same free choice of patients by health care providers as at present.

Mandatory that all legal residents purchase a combination ID/Insurance Card, reading as follows (or equivalent):

```
!_____!
!              _____NAME_____                 !
! is afforded insurance for all health care needs !
!         at all authorized locations.           !
!      Policy No. XXX-XX-XXXX dated 02/28/94      !
!_____!
```

2) PHYSICIANS PAID BY NEGOTIATED ANNUAL CONTRACT FEE WITH BONUSES

3) HOSPITALS TO RETURN TO PER DIEM CHARGE

4) USERS/PATIENTS COVERED FOR ALL HEALTH CARE NEEDS INCLUDING:

SUBSTANCE ABUSE, LONG TERM NURSING HOME CARE, Health related ABORTIONS. NO NEED TO CONTINUE MEDICAID or MEDICARE.

5) ESTABLISHMENT OF GENERALLY ACCEPTED MEDICAL PROCEDURES TO CONTROL "HEROIC" EFFORTS, FRAUD.

6) JOB REDUCTION/ELIMINATION: NATURAL MIGRATION OF CURRENT EXPERIENCED HEALTH ADMINISTRATIVE PEOPLE TO NEW HEALTH CORPORATION.

RESULT

COST REDUCTION OF ESTIMATED $512 BILLION.......6% of GDP

Canada = 7.3%, Germany = 7.3%, Japan = 6.8%, Britain = 5.3%

Current U.S. = 14% '93, Est. 23% '97 CLINTON PLAN = 17% Est. '97

NO "BILLING" PAPERWORK, NO COLLECTIONS HASSLE, NO NEED FOR COORDINATION OF BENEFITS, NO NEED FOR EMPLOYER HEALTH BENEFIT DEPARTMENTS

Princeton Task Force on National Health Care

206 WITHERSPOON STREET
PRINCETON, NEW JERSEY 08540
609-921-6753

NAMES, FULL ADDRESSES AND TELEPHONE NUMBERS

OF WITNESSES IF ORAL TESTIMONY DESIRED

(All in their private capacity as citizens of the United States)

* Dr. Forrest C. Eggleston, M.D., P.O. Box 1098
  Mechanicsburg, Pa. 17055   Tel. 717-691-9518

* Luther Slifer, 7023 Dolphin Road
  Lanham, Maryland   20706   Tel. 301-552-1761

* Dr. Jack Minnis, M.D., 724 Arastradero Drive
  Palo Alto, Calif. 94306   Tel. 415-493-5528

* Gordon Douglass, 26 Library Place
  Princeton, N.J.   08540   Tel. 609-497-0082

* Dr. Nancy Block, M.D., 87 Cromwell Court
  Berkeley Heights, N.J. 07922   Tel. 908-322-9665

* Dr. Robert Carman, M.D., 3334 Eden Drive
  Bloomington, Indiana 47401   Tel. 812-332-6883

* Dr. Birch Rambo, M.D., 526 Painter Road
  Media, Pa.   18063   Tel. 215-KNOCKER

* Dr. Eugene Betts, M.D., 108 Rock Rose Lane
  Radnor, Pa.   19087   Tel. 215-687-5633

* Dr. Horst Weinberg, M.D., 2983 West Pembroke Loop
  Fresno, Calif.   93711   Tel. 209-224-2500

* Dr. James Hastings, M.D., 15 Tyson Lane
  Princeton, N.J.   08540   Tel. 609-924-2799

* Atty. Andrew Sapiro, 7605 S.W. 142nd Street
  Miami, Florida   33158   Tel. 305-252-8651

* Susan Swavely, RN, Star Route, Box 12-22-A
  Jim Thorpe, Pa.   18229   Tel. 717-325-2558

* Irene Teyssier, RN, 8 Fern Road
  Turnersville, N.J. 08012   Tel. 609-582-6049

* Heidi Anderson, 132 Holder Hall, Princeton University
  Princeton, N.J.   08544   Tel. 609-258-9428

* Rebecca Kosloff, 234 Henry Hall, Princeton University
  Princeton, N.J.   08544   Tel. 609-258-7432

* Judith Wells, 324 Maple Avenue
  Haddonfield, N.J. 08033   Tel. 609-427-4446

* Dr. Jon Scopes, M.D., 3 Chestnut Avenue
  Hampton, Middlesex, United Kingdom Tel. 011-44-81-979-6933

712

Princeton Task Force on National Health Care

206 WITHERSPOON STREET
PRINCETON, NEW JERSEY 08540
609-921-6752

INTRODUCTION

We thank you for this opportunity to present our views as well as to thank those unknown persons who have made this opportunity possible.

WHO WE ARE - WE HAVE NO AX TO GRIND. WE REPRESENT NOBODY BUT OURSELVES. WE HAVE NO KNOWLEDGE OF THE POLITICAL PARTY AFFILIATIONS OR POLITICAL VIEWS OF OUR MEMBERS.

\#   We would bring the joy of medicine back to the practice of medicine.

\#   We are the only group proffering a plan with real,measurable cost reductions.

        from '93 $900 billion,   14% of GNP

        to   ' 95 $ 478 billion, 7.3% of GNP

        SAVING $ 422 billion

\#   We are proffering a "MODEL BILL", almost verbatim to that enabling COMSTAT. Thus it has already been reviewed by Congressional Committees, its legal staff, the Congressional Budget Office, and passed by the House and Senate. (Copy upon request)

(It only needs revisions to remove language that only pertains to relations with foreign countries.)

PURPOSE OF THE TASK FORCE

\# To objectively study, analyze and propose for these United States the best possible National Health Care System. Drawing on worldwide resources from Jan - June '92, we issued a "white paper" July '92

In the Declaration of Independence, that incomparable,precious heritage of our Nation, it reads,

> " We hold these truths to be self-evident, that all men are
> created equal, that they have been endowed by their creator with
> certain unalienable rights, that among these are life, liberty
> and the pursuit of happiness "

We affirm that the plan we are about to propose will further these rights.

We agree with President Bill Clinton that our eventual goal is:

Legislation " that .... guarantee(s) every American private health insurance that can never be taken away." (NYT editorial 2/22/94)

We agree with the progressive New York Times' lead editorial Feb 22, 1994 that " Health Tinkering Is Not Reform," that "the solution is to make insurance mandatory" (as is Social Security) to "insist that insurers provide an identical set of health benefits"

We agree that "every American ought to have coverage that is portable, community-rated and guaranteed. Operating through a system that is fair, dependable and free of loopholes."

We affirm that this insurance can best be provided by one single-payer, for-profit public utility stock company chartered by Congress,as is COMSAT and others.

We affirm that this insurance should have the entire population of legal residents as its community-rated pool (Americans are well know for their mobility)

        Health care is the last unmet basic essential life-sustaining
        human need.

WE ARE:
- Representative of the American Missionary family overseas,
\ particularly in India,

- Representative of the view of the White House, as spoken by
Jeff Eller, "While we believe the guarantee should be for private
insurance (our position and proposal), we share many of the
goals of single-payer advocates, like universal coverage, cost
control and administrative simplification." (WSJ 2/11/94)

We are pleased that Hillary Rodham Clinton chose the name of our
group, substituting "White House" for "Princeton".

We would be pleased if you choose our proposal: for a free enterprise, private insurance, privately-run single-payer national
for-profit public utility stock insurance company chartered by
Congress; charter can be revoked or amended, giving you oversight: substituting our free enterprise MODEL BILL for the
federal government/state government/2,000 insurance company CLIN-
TON PLAN.

- representative of the view of the American College of
Surgeons who endorsed a national "single-payer" health system at
a Capitol hearing. (David Murray, chairman of the college's
board of regents as quoted in the WSJ 2/11/94)

"We absolutely must get the insurance companies off the doctor's
backs in order to practice medicine.

"The best people are no longer applying to medical school".

- Dr. James Hastings, Surgeon, Princeton, N J.

- representative of the view of the House of Delegates of
the American Medical Association (AMA) voting Dec. 7, 1993

"The concept of individually required and individually owned
health insurance"

and   "to bring about universal access and universal coverage"
- Dr. J William Cox, Calif (NYT 12/8/93)

[our mandatory requirement that all legal residents possess a
combination ID/insurance policy card (babies to receive automatically along with their birth certificates); and pay for it

A very simple combination ID/Insurance Declarations Page:

```
!_____!
!                                         !
!            _____NAME_____                !
!                                         !
! is afforded insurance for all health care needs !
!        at all authorized locations.     !
!                                         !
!    Policy No. XXX-XX-XXXX  dated  02/28/94   !
!_____!
```

(Plastic, magnetized, with halogram protection)

- Representative of the 70 Million main-line Protestants,plus
several Jewish viewpoints,

- Representative of the views of the Presbyterian Church (U.S.A),

- Representative of the views of the National Conference of
Catholic Bishops,

- Representative of the views of the 230 million middle-class, -
upper middle-class Americans.

- Representative of the true wishes of the national union
leadership, who prefer a single-payer plan. (NYT, 1/13/94)

- Representative of the views of some of the health care
providers such as Physicians,Medical School Professors, Nurses,
Hospital Administrators, Ethical Drug Company Middle Management,
Lawyers specializing in workers compensation, as well as users of
their services, members of our task force.

List of Witnesses

If you see merit in our giving oral testimony, our witnesses
would each be speaking in their private capacity only: they could
be:

* Dr. Forrest C Eggleston, M.D. Medical Missionary to India.
Currently with Medical Benevolence Foundation,Mechanicsburg, PA.

(1) * Luther Slifer, Space Craft Power Engineer, NASA,Goddard
Space Center, Maryland, representing himself and Dr Mary Slifer,
M.D. Nationally-known Obstetrician, Tuckerton, N J.

Princeton Task Force on National Health Care

(1) * Dr Jack Minnis, former Professor, Stanford University
Medical School - salaried staff,currently,practicing surgeon,
Kaiser Permanente, Polo Alto,CA.-expertise-salaried physician.

* Gordan Douglass, Chairman, Health Task Force Committee, General
Assembly, Presbyterian Church (U.S.A.)Princeton, N.J.

* Nancy Barrand, Staff, Robert Wood Johnson Foundation.Princeton.
N.J.

(1) Dr. Nancy Block, Professor, Univ. of Medicine & Dentistry
Newark. N J. Practicing Psychiatrist, Berkeley Heights, N.J

(1) * Dr Robert Carman, Medical Missionary to India,Vellore
Medical Center. India.Practicing Radiologist, Baptist Hospital,
Bangalore,India.

(1) * Dr. Birch Rambo, Medical Missionary, Zaire None: Medic,
PA General Practitioner- went to the Mission field 40 years ago
with only one functioning kidney(son of Dr Victor Rambo,
World-famous for Pioneer work on Cataract Surgery and former
Medical Missionary to India)

(1) Dr Eugene Betts, Anesthesiologist Children's Hospital,
Philadelphia Radnor. PA

(1) (Dr. Horst Weinberg, Holocaust Refugee,Surgeon,Fresno,
Calif.

* Dr James Hastings, Surgeon, Princeton, N.J. expertise, dealing
with insurance companies.

Atty Andrew Sapiro, Specialist, Workers Compensation insurance.
Miami, Florida

* Daniel Shongo, Lawrenceville, N J. Manager, Merck & Company
Pro-Bono work, River eye sickness, Africa

(1) Susan Swavely, RN, Lehighton Hospital, Lenighton, PA.

Irene Teyssier, RN, Cooper Medical Center, Camden, N J.
Turnersville. N.J.

Heidi Anderson, Rebecca Kosloff, Premed students, Princeton
University, Princeton, N J

Judy Wells, Director, MIS, Germantown Hospital, Phila.
Haddonfield, N.J.

(1) * Dr. Jon Scopes, M D , Surgeon, London, England (95% of its
doctors approve the salaried British National Health Service)

* may be out of the country
(1) Graduates, Kodaikanal School, India

(Now called Kodaikanal International School, and is partially
funded by Congress through the "Aid to American Hospitals and
Schools Abroad" program)

LIFE

"LIFE" is the most precious gift we have been given, and
universal coverage for all needed health care services from
prenatal to expiration for all legal, resident Americans will
provide for healthier Americans, more productive and longer
lives.

LIBERTY

"LIBERTY" has been preserved in the private sector by free
enterprise and

a) Preserving freedom of choice of Doctors, Hospitals,and other
providers,

b) Preserving freedom of choice of Doctors to limit patient load,

c) Saving substantial dollars and putting us in line with our
Major Trading Partners and other Global Competition

d) Preserving the free enterprise business component

e) Eliminating government bureaucracy

f) Reducing overall National Health Care Costs to 7.3% G.D.P.
from 14%

g) There is wide Bi-Partisan and public support for above a)& b)

HOW

* A free enterprise, for-profit stock public utility chartered by
Congress,

* A free choice of patients by all physicians and personal
health care providers will best promote the Liberty of All.

PURSUIT OF HAPPINESS

With Life, Good Health and Liberty; The American people will be
freed for their pursuit of HAPPINESS.

And Congress, for its part, will have promoted the General
Welfare of the people, and strengthened the Economy for Global
Competition.

Princeton Task Force on National Health Care

715

MAJOR RECOMMENDATIONS

1) For-Profit National Stock Public Utility like AT&T
(former Bell System)

* Was crown jewel of achievement of the American people before
break-up by courts

* The momentum of its success has continued through its successor
regional operating companies for ten years.

* AT&T stock traded at $54 1/4 at the close 2/17/94, with a
yield of 2.4% on a Price/Earnings Multiple of 18, paying a
quarterly divided of $1.32, and 2 volume of 17, 275,000 shares.

* Regulated since 1934 by the Federal Communications Commission,
AT&T has been a stable capital investment, paying good,
consistent dividends, providing reliable, good-paying technical
union and non-union jobs; providing excellent, reliable telephone
and other services world-wide

Reliably supported countless thousands of widows, millions
of retirees, and sent hundreds of students to college on AT&T
dividends and stocks.

Its record of achievement has only been marred by its court-
mandated breakup. (Ditto for IBM)

With the able and gracious assistance of Robert Allen,
Chairman, AT&T, and President Bill Clinton; and the resources of
this great nation, we are confident that the PRINCETON PLAN could
be implemented by early 1995.

(the Author Project Manager, TWX, for Western Union, New York,
N.Y.'67-'69 successfully dealt with both AT&T Headquarters and
its Operating Companies)

This would provide universal coverage insurance for the
entire legal American population, one community rating, the most
efficient, economical, fraud-free and personally
responsible:($5-10 co-payments to curb abuse), creating a United
'State' (federal) of America for community rating.

$2,227 Annual Premium per person for full coverage prenatal to
expiration with our proposed cost reductions,(less when
co-payment experience is actually factored into premium rate)
See cost reduction table below.

$2,227 Annual Premium Per Person subject to negotiations
between employers and unions, government, business competitive
decisions as at present, as to % to be paid by employer, % paid
by employee.

Affordability to others set by policies of public utility
and proposed National Health Care Commission, as is currently
the case with electric, gas, water and telephone utility
companies.

Individual premium assistance or waivers from this public utility
charge would NOT be based on 'class entitlements, like' all
unemployed', 'all MediCaid'. 'all welfare recipients', 'persons
over 65', etc.

Medicaid alone as a 'class' entitlement costs $75 billion(NYT,
2/11/94), and would be a federal and state budget/ tax
elimination under our plan.

It has been said, through not recently, that a large
proportion of your legislative office's duties --- and
expense --- is in responding to your constituents requests
for help in dealing with the Federal Bureaucracy.

Do you really want to add to that burden with passage of the
Clinton plan, or a Government-run single payer plan ?

At the very least, you would need to add more staff, rent or
build more office space, then furnish the office and provide
communication facilities.

SINGLE-PAYER GOVERNMENT-RUN: SINGLE-PAYER PRIVATELY-RUN:

Bad weather -- closed 2/11/94   open
Union, Civil Service Workers   Probably non-union
Bureaucratic   Responsible to customers
Union Government Hours   Hours convenient to public
Not responsible   Responsible
Not motivated by efficiency   Motivated for efficiency
No goals   Goal to make a 6-8% profit on
                                      equity
No motive to reduce fraud   Profit motive to reduce
                                      fraud,also pressure from
                                      Health Commission

Princeton Task Force on National Health Care

Insurance companies have had 200 (Blue Cross/Blue Shield 50)
years to offer non-cancellable insurance policies covering
comprehensive health care benefits without exclusions to a
nationally community-rated pool without applicant rejection.

(2) PHYSICIANS PAID BY NEGOTIATED ANNUAL CONTRACT FEES.

(Lump annual fee; not fee for service. Very similar to German
system, i.e., could have national contract, with %age variations
for job skills, experience, and regional living costs.)

Also similar to corporation annual contingency contracts with
corporate Law firms.

No need for doctors to "cost-shift" anything.

3 1/2 times average earnings of blue collar workers(currently 7
times)

If physicians can't live very well on 31/2 times the earnings
of their blue collar patients(this would be hefty raise for
rural & reservation doctors) something is wrong with the
physicians.

Current doctor's incomes coming right out of the pockets of the
people, businesses and governments.

The New England Journal of Medicine let the cat out of the bag.

" The best way to control costs and preserve quality is to have
the physicians do it. The whole health-care system is built on
the behavior of doctors, and that behavior is greatly influenced
by the way health care is organized."

--- Dr. Arnold S. Relman, former editor, The New England Journal
of Medicine (NYT, 3/18/93)

" In medical school we were taught that the way to set our fees
was to first determine how much money we wanted to make, and then
divide that amount by the number of patients we expected to see."
--- Dr. Robert Carman, M.D. Currently Medical Missionary to
India, 40 years.

" On the application form for the college of Radiology, I was
required to sign a statement that I would never work for a
salary, except for the government, and I would always charge fee-
for-service."
--- Dr. Robert Carman, M.D. Currently Medical Missionary to
India, 40 years.

QUESTION: WHAT DOES FEE-FOR-SERVICE HAVE TO DO

WITH QUALITY CARE FOR PATIENTS ?

(Physicians control all medical costs, which include their income
levels)

" The bedrock is the careful selection of doctors who share the
group philosophy and are happy to work for a salary. Since they
are not paid piecework, they make decisions with no direct
financial interest at stake."

" We look for a different type of physician, one who still looks
at medicine as a profession, not a business."
--- Geisinger, Danville. PA.(NYT, 3/18/93)

" The reason the home-care companies want these relationships
with doctors is because the patient goes with it. Tnat way they
have a lock on the referral, and when you have a lock on the
system, you can charge higher prices and not worry about
service."

" Providing doctors with these kinds of financial incentives is
wrong. We can't afford these kinds of abuses anymore."
--- Dr. Jean Mitchell, Georgetown University (NYT, 3/19/93)

" I don't like to think that greed in the marketplace was that
strong but I guess I was wrong. It is also one thing when an
investor is willing to take a risk but there is no risk here."
(doctors being sole eligible investors in home-care companies)
--- Dr. Bruce Feinberg (NYT, 3/19/93)

The AMA wrote us that 65% of Americans physicians are on salary.
Therefore, it shouldn't be too much of a difference to change to
annual contract fee plus ability to earn bonuses in lieu of
salary.

May, 1990 General Anesthesia, DDS, Surgical oral extraction $150
Dec, 1992 General Anesthesia, DDS, Surgical oral extraction $150
Feb, 1993 General Anesthesia, MD, Thyroidectomy $1200
          (Co-chairman's actual bills)

Princeton Task Force on National Health Care

\# Credit a physician's account with the lowest cost procedure performed during a visit.

Physician earns an annual bonus for performing more procedures than needed to qualify for earning the annual contract fee.

\# Malpractice threats leads through fear to defensive medicine. which inflates medical costs.

Malpractice suits curbed through adoption of GENERALLY ACCEPTED MEDICAL PRACTICES.

Reducing need for "heroic" medical procedures for dying patients, usually the most costly period of medical treatment

"Everyone wants to live forever, and they can't "

"Often family and friends insist on continuing the heroic measures, even though the doctor and they know it is hopeless"

        - Susan Swavely, RN, Lehighton, Pa Hospital

H FRAUD (and overbilling) would be greatly reduced under our single-payer public utility plan According to the General Accounting Office, there is 10% fraud in our present insurance company/government based system, costing $90 billion in '92.

"If someone comes up with a new scam, it takes months for the bureaucracy to catch up with them"
--- Richard Kusserow, Former Inspector General,Dept. of Health & Human Services (Courier-Post, Somerville, N.J. 2/12/94)

AT&T has had an outstanding record of low fraud over its 60 years under the FCC of the highest standards of integrity and service; and a single-payer for-profit public utility has the best chance of continuing such a record.

Hospital paid a flat per Diem. Hospitals are currently regulated by unregulated doctors, who in turn enjoy an unregulated monopoly, like the medieval guilds.

H The Federal Government to offer FULL SCHOLARSHIPS to cover all medical school expenses This would eliminate medical school indebtedness, and would promote both racial, ethnic and geographic diversity.

HOSPITALS

& Flat per diem covering room and board and lab tests, X-rays fee-for-service.

\# Return management to the communities who paid for and built them in the first place with community fund drives, often supple_ mented by federal dollars.

\# In most cases, no need for vice-president of community relations, vice-president of publicity, vice-president of sales, vice-president of marketing, vice-president of advertising, vice_ president of development, along with their attendant department directors, managers, supervisor and staff.

\# No need for slick, glossy "puffery" mailings to community.

NATIONAL COSTS OF DENTISTRY, NURSING AND ETHICAL DRUGS ARE AFFORDABLE

Dentistry	- .6% of Natl Health costs ('91), .004% of GNP
Nursing	- 1% of Natl Health costs ('91), .004% of GNP
Ethical Drugs	- 1% of Natl Health costs ('91), .004 of GNP

USERS / PATIENTS

& UNIVERSAL, COMPREHENSIVE COVERAGE WITH LONG TERM NURSING CARE

\# Mandatory enrolment for all legal residents.

\# We have no answer to the problem of the millions of poor

people, homeless people, legal immigrants and others who do not sign up for the benefits to which they are entitled. Even the census admits to undercounting. (NYT 2/16/94)

Hawaii has made a commitment to see that all of its residents have health insurance through strict requirements for its employers. Yet "3% of Hawaiians still lack coverage"
--- Dr. John C. Lewin, State Health Director.

The Census Bureau estimated that 6.8% of Hawaiians were uninsured in 1990-92. (NYT 2/16/94)

- A free choice of doctors by patients.

- No need to change doctors or treatment if person changes jobs.

g A national community-rated pool.

No need for hospitals to "cost-shift" anything

No need for physicians to 'cost-shift' anything

Can't compare taxpayers, patient population, and urban needs of states like New York, New Jersey and California with rural needs of states like Wyoming, Utah and South Dakota.

The poor and sick have flocked to the cities for succor and medical treatment in all times and in all locales for millenia.

Present MEDICAID system totally unfair to taxpayers of New York, Pennsylvania, Texas, California, etc., expecting them to bear the burden alone of poor and sick immigrants to their states.

SUBSTANCE ABUSE VS DIET

Persons are concerned about coverage for Substance Abuse, feeling that such people are responsible for their own health problems.

Heart disease is the number one cause of death in the U.S., and has very costly treatments, striking all ages

Heart disease is mainly caused by an irresponsible population ignoring doctors on diet, and continuing to gorge on hamburgers, red meat, french fries, fatty milkshakes, fried chicken, other fried food, junk food, potato chips, rich desserts, etc.

AIDS treatments vs. treatment for other sexually transmitted diseases.

We see a "draw" here on finger-pointing, and affirm full coverage for all "health" procedures.

LONG TERM NURSING HOME CARE

Need not confined to the elderly.

My Kodai classmate, Richard Harrison, Lawrenceville, N.J., 59 years old at the time an impatient 18 year old kid crossed the double-yellow line and ran into his car head-on, putting him into an awake, speechless coma within a healthy body, has been in a Plainfield, N.J. long term nursing home for the past 6 years, and is still there. 65 years old; how many years to go?

Somebody is paying the bills.

The same thing can happen to any of us at any moment in a blink of the eye

Total long term nursing care cost $53 billion in '90, or $215 per capita.

New Jersey disability insurance costs each employee $77 annually.

New Jersey unemployment insurance costs each employee $96 a year.

Including long term nursing home care is no biggy in the total scheme of things

ABORTIONS

Not being Solomon, we assay a Solomon-like response.

All "health-related" procedures, like threat to the life of the mother, pregnancy caused by rape, would be covered.

All "medical" procedures used to affect an abortion would not, but would be for the account of the parties involved

Irresponsible intercourse, which leads eventually to its natural conclusion, pregnancy, is not a responsibility of the responsible people of America in the health plan.

OTHER

65% of total health care costs are incurred by patients over 65. Thus an inordinate share of the cost burden is being borne by those under 65 who are paying for the entitlement benefit of MediCare; and its beneficiaries which is a recent benefit, have hardly paid into the MediCare Trust Funds for their own care.

Princeton Task Force on National Health Care

The Nation's Governors at their August, 1991 meeting declared that the MediCaid system is broken, and called upon Congress to revise it or produce a new system.

We affirm that these are reasons enough that MediCare and MediCaid should be TERMINATED.

MediCare, and or MediCaid though invaluable and well intentioned, are flawed both in its limits and many exclusions, as well as being a bureaucratic headache for both users, heath providers and its bureaucrats, and an enormous drain on state budgets with their mandated share of its expense.

\#   Elimination of duplicating coverage and payments by working husbands and wives.

H   Employer & Employee Federal and State tax reductions:

Elimination of MediCare portion of FICA $59 billion
(monies freed could go toward paying new health insurance premium)

Elimination of MediCaid

\#   Fraud reduction $90 billion

A significant "cost-shifting" is MediCare, where those employed, mainly those under the age 65, are paying with their payroll deduction of 2.90% (FICA) and federal and state income taxes, etc., for this entitlement for all those over 65, whether they need this entitlement not.
                        or
Thus, average cost of health insurance per employee was $3,781 in '93, whereas per capita costs, even with our cost reductions, would be $2,227 for full, comprehensive coverage prenatal to expiration. (NYT, 2/15/94)

The employed are paying by their federal income taxes $2,207 per tax-payer, $1,450 into FICA(1.45% each, employer/employee), and $376 in state taxes which, plus the above $3,781, total $7,814 to pay for the health costs of the residents of America (legal and illegal).

JOB REDUCTION / ELIMINATION

Concern has been rightfully expressed over the administrative and other jobs that would be lost in a re-structuring of the health care sector.

Many of these experienced workers would be hired by the new for-profit public utility corporation.

Concern has been rightfully expressed over the blue and white collar jobs lost in manufacturing, over the white collar jobs lost in the service sector, over the garment workers jobs lost, over the defense jobs lost, over government jobs lost

No concern has been expressed over the banking, brokerage and insurance jobs lost in their down-sizing.

Every sector of the economy is cost-cutting except the health "industry", which is industriously increasing its costs

We know unemployed executives who used to earn $400,000 who lost their jobs to mergers or down-sizing.

But with our national commitment to "free trade and free competition", we have allowed this to occur.

Down-sizing our bloated health care industry to the 7-8% of GNP world standard is a necessity of free "global" competition.

Actually, it would enhance our competitiveness, as health care dollars going to the providers would be returned to the pockets of the patients and Federal and State governments.

And the elimination of all health care expenses by the federal and state governments would mean a reduction in taxes and/or their deficits, in this case benefitting both providers and patients.

If our major industrial trading partners can maintain their National Health Costs within a range of 6-9% of GNP, so can we. And we must in order to compete.

2% of the U S population are physicians, and they are running a fee-for-service system costing nearly thrice the British sala-ried system, 14 cents out of every dollar and rising---and 14% of Americans aren't even covered

(500,000 doctors to 250 million patients)

Princeton Task Force on National Health Care

COST REDUCTIONS TABLE

```
TOTAL HEALTH COSTS     '93 cost, $900 billion    ^ SAVINGS

1) ADMINISTRATION  20% to 3% '93 cost, $180 billion  - $153 billion

"Program Administration & net
cost of private health insur-
ance" ('94 World Almanac) '91 cost, $ 44 billion    - $ 44 billion
                                                    ---------------
                                                    - $197 billion

2) PHYSICIANS 18.9% to 10%  '93 cost, $170 billion   - $ 89 billion
   (From 7.3 times workers to 3.5 times)

3) HOSPITALS 38.4% to 34 6% '93 cost, $346 billion   - $ 31 billion Est

4) ALL MEDICAL COVERAGES REMOVED FROM
   OTHER INSURANCE POLICIES' LIABILITY,
   WORKERS COMPENSATION, AUTO, HOME-
   OWNERS, ETC   .... ... .....  $ 66 billion Est.  - $ 66 billion Est

5) FRAUD (General Accounting Office)  $ 90 billion  - $ 70 billion Est.

6) ELIMINATION OF EMPLOYER/EMPLOYEE
   MEDICARE PORTION OF FICA (2.9% of
   national payroll)  ... . .....  $ 59 billion Est. - $ 59 billion Est
                                                    ---------------

                  TOTAL SAVINGS  .............. - $512 billion Est.

   NET COST EQUALS  6 % of GDP  .....................  $388 billion
```

COMPARISION: U.S.A. and other MAJOR INDUSTRIAL COUNTRIES

\# Canada has 12 different provincial plans with fee-for-service,
     total cost: 7 3% of GNP '90

\# Germany has 1.147 different insurance plans, with 17 state-
   cepped regional annual contract mark pools for each group of
   fee-for-service physicians, to be divided among themselves as
   equitably as possible, with members watcning the others to see
   that nobody gets too greedy,
     total cost: 7 3% of GNP '90

\# Japan has 5,400 different insurance plans, a "uniform national
   'point-fee' schedule for all doctor and hospital services',
     total cost: 6 8% of GNP '90

\# Britain has one single-payer government-run "National Health
   Service" with health services paid by taxes,
     total cost: 5.3% of GNP '90

\# CLINTON PLAN has one federal government plus 50 state governments, plus ??? regional alliances and 2,000 insurance
   companies collecting premiums, fee-for-service physicians,
     total cost: 17% of GNP '97 est.

\# Princeton Plan has one single-payer privately-run "Healthcare
   Corporation" with health services paid by individual premiums.
     total cost: 7.3% of GNP '93

   [MODEL BILL, either legal or letter size available on request]

\# U.S.A Present system Federal Government est '97 23% of GDP

SELECTED WORLD HEALTHCARE EXPENSES
as a Percent of Gross National Product

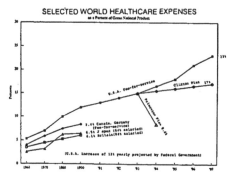

Princeton Task Force on National Health Care

Coverage: Health Care Plans Compared

Clinton Plan

White House's proposed legislation

GOAL Universal coverage by 1998.

APPROACH All citizens and legal residents would have to obtain a comprehensive health benefits package. Most people would get coverage through large purchasing cooperatives called health alliances.

FINANCING Businesses would be required to pay at least 80 percent of premiums for their employees. Small companies, early retirees and people with incomes below certain levels would get Federal subsidies.

Single-Payer Plan

Sponsored by Representative Jim McDermott, Democrat of Washington, and Senator Paul Wellstone, Democrat of Minnesota

GOAL Universal coverage by 1995.

APPROACH All citizens and legal residents would be automatically enrolled in a national health insurance program established by the Federal Government and administered by the states.

FINANCING Private insurance premiums would be replaced with a combination of payroll taxes on employers (4 percent for small companies and 8.4 percent for larger ones), a 2.1 percent tax on individuals' taxable income and new or steeper taxes on tobacco, handguns and ammunition.

Cooper Plan

Sponsored by Representative Jim Cooper, Democrat of Tennessee

GOAL Universal access to coverage. Sponsors say that with insurance more affordable, 80 percent of the uninsured would voluntarily get coverage.

APPROACH Relies on a voluntary program to cover all American citizens and legal residents through insurance reforms, the creation of insurance purchasing cooperatives and subsidies for the poor.

FINANCING Would pay for subsidies by reducing Medicare and Medicaid spending. Would cap tax deductions that employers make for contributions to employee health plans.

Chafee Plan

Sponsored by Senator John H. Chafee, Republican of Rhode Island

GOAL Universal coverage by 2005.

APPROACH All citizens and legal residents would have to buy coverage through a qualified health plan. All employers would be required to offer their employees enrollment in a qualified plan but would not have to pay for it. Subsidies would be available for low-income individuals.

FINANCING Would pay for subsidies by reducing Medicare and Medicaid spending.

Single-Payer Plan - Private APPROACH All citizens and legal residents would be automatically enrolled at birth in a national health insurance program run by a for-profit public utility stock company chartered by the Federal Government, and supervised by a Federal Health Commission like the FCC.

FINANCING All citizens would pay their health insurance premiums in the same way that they now pay their other insurance and utility bills.

Special needs for those unable to pay would be subject to arrangements with the health public utility in the same manner as works for public utility gas & electric companies.

Employer-employee splits of premium, and/or payroll deduction of premium would be subject to the same negotiating process currently in effect between government and business employers and employees; or part of benefits package preferred by employers of non-union workers.

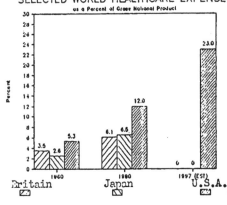

SELECTED WORLD HEALTHCARE EXPENSES
as a Percent of Gross National Product

Britain   Japan   U.S.A.

98% Salaried   64% Salaried   Fee-for-Service

Author: Harrison A. Moyer
Project Manager, MIS, Monroe Systems for
Business, Morris Plains, N.J.

Home: 1424 Chippewa Drive, Allentown, Pa.!
Telephone: 215-395-2711   18104

CO-CHAIRMAN

Princeton Task Force on National Health Care

STATEMENT OF DIANE ARONSON
EXECUTIVE DIRECTOR
RESOLVE

Mr. Chairman and Members of the Subcommittee, RESOLVE is pleased to submit this testimony on behalf of its 25,000 members and the 5.3 million Americans who suffer from the disease of infertility. We are very supportive of your efforts to reform this nation's health care system which currently discriminates against the infertile by frequently denying them coverage for medically appropriate treatment. I will use this opportunity to provide the Subcommittee with some important information about infertility and to urge the Subcommittee to include comprehensive infertility diagnosis and treatment in any benefit package enacted as part of national health care reform.

RESOLVE is a national, nonprofit organization established in 1974 to provide support, education and advocacy for infertile couples. Today we have 56 chapters across the country. Our national HELP LINE receives hundreds of calls annually from people needing information about various treatments or clinics and those seeking help with the emotional trauma of infertility. Our local chapters offer support groups run by trained therapists, educational seminars on infertility developments and treatments, information on adoption and child free living, and advocacy efforts at the state and federal levels.

RESOLVE's membership is very pleased that the Clinton Administration has included most infertility treatment in the benefit package of the Health Security Act (HR 3600). I have attached a letter from Dr. Judith Feder, Principal Deputy Assistant Secretary for Planning and Evaluation at the Department of Health and Human Services, which specifies that "...appropriate infertility diagnosis and treatment will be covered under the Health Security Act although they are not explicitly identified in the legislative language." We are dismayed, however, that Dr.

Feder goes on to state, "The only infertility service excluded from plan coverage is in vitro fertilization." RESOLVE strongly believes that totally excluding in vitro fertilization (IVF) from coverage is medically and fiscally irresponsible since it is the most medically appropriate and cost effective treatment for some forms of infertility. I will return to the subject of in vitro fertilization later in this testimony.

First I would like to give you some important facts about infertility, a disease of the reproductive system that is greatly misunderstood by the general public because, unless faced with this condition, most people have given it little thought. Media stories have helped to create misperceptions by attempting to sensationalize a real and tragic problem. Numerous stories printed or aired recently have been poorly researched and contained erroneous information. Following is factual information that I hope will enhance your understanding of infertility which is a serious medical condition that exacts an enormous toll on those who suffer from it, their families and friends, and society as a whole.

Definition and Scope of Infertility

- *Infertility is a disease or malfunction of the male or female reproductive system.* A specific medical problem can be identified in eighty percent of all cases of infertility. The other twenty percent includes cases in which a combination of problems are present or the cause of the infertility cannot be isolated. The reproductive system is one of the major systems in the human body. Diagnosis and treatment of reproductive problems should be covered by health care insurance just as problems with the digestive system, respiratory system or muscular system are covered. Infertility is **not** a life style choice; medical treatment for this disease is **not** elective.

- *Infertility affects 5.3 million Americans, or approximately 10 percent of the reproductive age population.* This means that one out of every six couples in this country will face an infertility problem of one kind or another.

• *Men and women suffer equally from infertility.* Male factor infertility accounts for fifty percent of identifiable problems (low sperm count, poor sperm motility, hormonal imbalances, deformities in the reproductive organs, and other abnormal functioning). Female factor also accounts for fifty percent of identifiable difficulties (ovulation problems, fallopian tube damage or disease, hormonal imbalances, ovarian tumors or cysts and other abnormalities). These conditions can be diagnosed and medically appropriate treatments, ranging from simple drug therapy to corrective surgery or in vitro fertilization, can be used with successful outcomes, that is, pregnancy, possible about half the time. According to a federally funded study published in July 1993*, more than 98 percent of people with infertility can be treated by conventional drug and medical/surgical procedures; only 1.2 percent use IVF.

• *Infertility affects a very broad range of people. It knows no boundaries of race or socioeconomic status.* For example, the children of mothers who took DES (diethylstilbestrol) have an increased incidence of infertility. Adult males who contract mumps may become sterile. Some asthma sufferers take a drug that can cause infertility. Environmental pollutants can adversely affect reproduction. No group or individual is immune from the possibility of not being able to create a biological family on their own.

Rationale for Including In Vitro Fertilization

IVF is a proven, nonexperimental, medically appropriate and necessary treatment for some forms of the disease of infertility. The procedure has been used for fifteen years, has produced over 23,000 babies in the United States alone and is considered a standard part of the continuum of infertility treatments. Covering infertility treatment but excluding IVF -- the only specific medical protocol on the

* Use of Fertility Services in the United States, Lynne S. Wilcox, MD, MPH, and William D. Mosher, PhD., Obstetrics and Gynecology, Vol. 82, No. 1, July 1993.

exclusion list -- is like covering heart disease through a triple bypass, but excluding coverage if a quadruple bypass is needed. Excluding IVF is unfair and will result in the two tier system of health care that President Clinton is trying to avoid by making it available only to those who can afford to pay for it privately. It is also not justified by the facts and experience of IVF treatment over the past decade:

- *Fewer than two percent of people suffering from infertility use IVF; more than 98 percent are treated with more conventional therapies. For this group of patients, however, IVF is medically appropriate and necessary. In some cases it is the only treatment available.* IVF is most commonly used to treat women with blocked, damaged or absent fallopian tubes. For these women IVF is the simplest, most successful and most cost-effective treatment. It allows the physician to remove the eggs from the ovary, inseminate them in a petri dish (the term "test tube" baby is incorrect), and place any resultant embryos directly into the woman's uterus thus bypassing the absent or destroyed tubes. Sometimes women with this problem choose to undergo one or several tubal surgeries which is more expensive, riskier to the patient and less successful in terms of pregnancy outcome. It is often the only choice, however, because most insurance will pay for tubal surgery but not for IVF. *IVF is the cost-effective and more medically appropriate alternative.*

- *IVF has a good success rate.* The rate of success for IVF is 15-20 percent per cycle. For women whose primary diagnosis is fallopian tube problems, the success rate is even higher. When compared to the 20-30 percent chance that a reproductively healthy couple has of achieving a pregnancy in any given cycle, the IVF pregnancy rate is quite good.

- *IVF is self-limiting.* IVF is self-limiting because of the rigorous emotional and physical nature of the treatment. Each woman, with her husband and physician, must decide what her most appropriate course of treatment is, but covering IVF will not result in uncontrolled expenditures.

- *Excluding IVF will result in a loss of benefits currently available in states that now mandate infertility coverage.* Ten states now have mandates that require insurance companies to cover or offer coverage of infertility treatment. In addition, some employers voluntarily offer infertility coverage to their employees. If the national benefit plan specifically excludes IVF, some residents of these states will lose benefits that they already have. President Clinton has stated many times that no one should be worse off under his plan than before it. That would surely not be the case if IVF remains on the exclusion list.

• _Legislating the exclusion of IVF, a specific medical protocol, is neither good medicine nor good public policy._ A piece of legislation that will be law for several decades, if enacted, is not the place to determine which specific protocols doctors may use. In vitro fertilization is one of many treatments for infertility and is appropriate and necessary for certain cases. No medically appropriate treatment for the disease of infertility should be excluded from the benefit package.

In recent months the media have reported extensively on a number of new ideas in the field of reproductive endocrinology. We have read about attempts to "clone" embryos (not really what the experiment was about), about women having babies beyond their reproductive years, about the potential of using fetal eggs as donors. All of these procedures or potential procedures would require the use of IVF technology. RESOLVE's position on these developing technologies is that insurance need not cover any experimental procedure. But these extreme instances of IVF usage should not be allowed to deprive hundreds of couples in their childbearing years who might achieve the goal of biological parenthood through IVF from having access to it.

The Cost of Infertility Treatment

The cost of infertility treatment varies greatly from patient to patient depending on the diagnosis and the treatment required. For those needing only a mild hormone drug the cost will be minimal, while those needing tubal surgery will have a significantly higher bill. Couples who remain in treatment for many months or who pursue treatments like IVF can expend tens of thousands of dollars on the quest for a biological family.

The critical point as you deliberate about health care reform, however, is what is the cost to the U.S. health care budget. Perhaps the best laboratory we have to study what potential costs will be is to look at the experience in the state of Massachusetts. Since 1986 Massachusetts has mandated that all insurers cover comprehensive infertility diagnosis and treatment including unlimited cycles of IVF. In a letter to RESOLVE dated June 4, 1993 Nancy C. Turnbull, then First Deputy Commissioner for the Division of Insurance of the Commonwealth of Massachusetts, stated that all infertility coverage accounted for "four-tenths of one percent of the total monthly family premium." Factoring out the cost of IVF based on fewer than two percent of patients means that the cost attributable to IVF would be in the hundredths of a single percentage point.

In short, there is no justification based on experience to exclude IVF because of cost. In fact, it is fiscally unsound since some patients are undergoing more expensive, less effective procedures because they cannot afford to pay privately for IVF. There would be a definite savings from less tubal surgery is IVF were covered by insurance.

Summary

Our society places great value on families and there may be no greater instinct in the human species than to create wanted children. When a diagnosis of infertility is made it is a shock to a couple and shakes one of the most basic assumptions we all grew up with: that one day we would become parents. An enormous emotional toll is exacted by infertility as the rollercoaster ride of hope and disappointment goes on for months and even years. In addition to the often arduous rigors of the physical treatment and the emotional upheaval, infertile Americans should not also have to struggle with the financial burden of treatments that are arbitrarily omitted from insurance coverage for no reason based in fact or experience.

We have been told that infertility is not life threatening. But nor are most of the reasons people seek medical care. What people are concerned about is the quality of life and the relief of pain. The quality of life for an infertile couple can be just as severely impaired as that of someone suffering from back pain or requiring arthroscopic surgery or any one of thousands of non-life threatening conditions covered under the national benefit package. The pain of infertility is real and consuming. There is nothing elective about infertility. It is insulting to infertile people to see in vitro fertilization listed with cosmetic surgery and private room accommodations on the exclusion list.

RESOLVE supports health care reform. We believe that all Americans should have access to the medical care they need. The Administration's bill is a step forward where infertility coverage is concerned, but the exclusion of IVF mars our enthusiasm. Medical technology can now offer people who suffer from infertility a chance to have a family. It is unreasonable and unnecessary to restrict access to IVF treatment for those who can benefit from it. Any national benefit package should include all non-experimental infertility services including IVF. It will not add significantly to the cost of the package, but will add immeasurably to the lives of those wishing for a child.

I thank the Subcommittee for its interest and hope that we can count on you to include comprehensive infertility treatment, including IVF, in whatever health care plan is passed by the Subcommittee and enacted into law.

729

 DEPARTMENT OF HEALTH & HUMAN SERVICES   Office of the Secretary

Washington D.C 20201

NOV 1 6 1993

Ms. Diane D. Aronson
Executive Director
RESOLVE
1310 Broadway
Somerville, Massachusetts 02144-1731

Dear Ms. Aronson:

Thank you for writing regarding RESOLVE's concern over coverage
of infertility services in the comprehensive benefits package of
the Health Security Act.

I understand from your letter that you are concerned that the
wording of one category of covered services in the comprehensive
benefits package, "Family Planning and Services for Pregnant
Women," may result in the exclusion of infertility services.

Please be assured that appropriate infertility diagnosis and
treatment will be covered under the Health Security Act although
they are not explicitly identified in the legislative language.
The comprehensive benefit package under the Health Security Act
has broad definitions that will assure coverage for services not
itemized in the Act, such as infertility services. The plan
covers all services that a clinician has determined to be
medically necessary or appropriate unless specifically excluded.
The only infertility service excluded from plan coverage is *in
vitro* fertilization.

The Health Security Act lists "Family planning services and
services for pregnant women" as a distinct category of services
in the comprehensive benefit package to emphasize the importance
of family planning and perinatal care within the plan. This
benefit distinction does not signify the prohibition of other
services that do not fall within the category.

Thank you for expressing your concerns and for your interest in
the Health Security Act. We appreciate your support of President
Clinton's health reform plan.

Sincerely,

Judith Feder
Principal Deputy Assistant Secretary
for Planning and Evaluation

**STATEMENT OF COL. FRANK G. ROHRBOUGH, USAF RETIRED
DEPUTY DIRECTOR OF GOVERNMENT RELATIONS
THE RETIRED OFFICERS ASSOCIATION**

MISTER CHAIRMAN AND DISTINGUISHED MEMBERS OF THE COMMITTEE

This statement was prepared by Colonel Frank G. Rohrbough,
USAF, MSC, Retired, Deputy Director of Government Relations
(Health Affairs) for The Retired Officers Association (TROA),
which has its national headquarters at 201 North Washington
Street, Alexandria, Virginia. Our association has a
membership of more than 396,000 active duty, retired, and
reserve officers of the seven uniformed services. Included in
our membership are approximately 60,000 auxiliary members who
are survivors of former members of our association.

First, we would like to thank the Chairman and other
distinguished members of the House Ways and Means Committee's
Subcommittee on Health for allowing us to submit for the
record our views on health care reform and its impact upon
military members and veterans and their families. Further, we
applaud you for holding hearings on the various health care
reform bills that have been introduced by members of this
committee and other members of Congress. All of these bills
recognize the need for reforming the way health care is
financed and administered in both the government and private
sectors. Our concern is that reforms needed to improve the
delivery of health care services for all DoD beneficiaries and
veterans, especially those who are Medicare-eligible, are
made.

TROA is concerned that the "MediPlan Health Care Act of 1993
(HR 2610) and other plans presented before this committee do
not address the retention of the Military Health Services
System (MHSS) and the Department of Veterans Affairs (DVA)
Health Care System as separate entities. We feel strongly
that the MHSS and VA Health Care System must continue under
national health care reform to assure that DoD and DVA can
continue to meet their medical readiness and contingency
support missions and to honor the long-standing commitments
made to those who have served this great country.

Further, there are critical elements required to strengthen
the MHSS and the DVA. These include:

  • **Guaranteed access to quality health care
services.** This can be accomplished through either the MHSS
for all military beneficiaries, including retirees of all
ages, or the DVA for all veterans. The benefit package must
be uniform, comprehensive and affordable for all

- **Adequate funding for the MHSS and the VA health delivery programs.** Although the military has been downsizing, the workload for the MHSS has not and will not decrease appreciably because much of the drawdown includes many active duty personnel who are retiring. DoD must still provide medical care through either the military treatment facilities (MTFs) or under the Civilian Health and Medical Program for the Uniformed Services (CHAMPUS). Likewise, the VA's patient workload will not diminish since its population is aging and, therefore, requires more medical care.

President Clinton's "Health Security Act (HSA)" has addressed the needed reforms for the Military Health Service System (MHSS) and the needs of its 8.5 million beneficiaries as well as the reform needed for DVA and its 27 million veterans. Included in President Clinton's plan is the blueprint for military health care called the "Military Health Plan (MHP)" (Section 8001) and for veterans care called "Veterans Health Plans" (Section 8002). Significantly, this proposed legislation preserves the Military Health Service System (MHSS) and the DVA Health Care System so they can meet their worldwide contingency and peacetime health care missions. Most appropriately, it allows the DoD and DVA to develop and manage their own health plans, but within the broad guidelines of "managed competition". Specifically, the proposed legislation provides all DoD and VA eligible beneficiaries, including those 65 and older, access to quality health care in military treatment facilities (MTFs) or DVA medical facilities, as appropriate, or through a network of contracted civilian providers.

One of the most critical provisions of President Clinton's plan, a long-standing goal of TROA's, is a provision that allows Medicare-eligible military beneficiaries freedom of choice to enroll in DoD's Military Health Plan or DVA's Health Plan, but with Medicare paying a predetermined amount (a capitated payment) to DoD or DVA for those who enroll. Simply stated without Medicare reimbursement neither DoD or DVA have the funding nor the financial incentive to treat beneficiaries 65 and older and no statutory authority to receive payment for Medicare-eligible retirees who enroll.

The "Medicare Subvention" Imperative

For some time, TROA and The Military Coalition - a consortium of 25 military and veteran organizations representing 3.75 million members of the uniformed services (active, reserve and retired) plus their families and survivors - have advocated

implementation of a reimbursement concept called "Medicare
Subvention", that is, Health Care Financing Administration
(HCFA) reimbursement to DoD or DVA for care provided to
Medicare-eligible beneficiaries in military treatment
facilities (MTFs) or in Department of Veterans Affairs (DVA)
medical treatment facilities. The singular purpose of
subvention is to save money for DoD, DVA, HCFA and ultimately
the taxpayers.

Currently, DoD has no financial incentive to provide access to
care through the MHSS for military Medicare-eligible retirees,
and they are frequently the first group of beneficiaries to be
denied care when budget shortfalls force cutbacks in care.
With the President supporting "Medicare Subvention", DoD and
the DVA have proposed to HCFA that Medicare reimbursement be
80 percent of the capitation rate now use by HCFA for their
Medicare "At Risk" contracts with civilian plans. **This will
save HCFA and taxpayers money every time a Medicare
beneficiary is treated by the DVA or DoD.** We believe
that subvention would facilitate maximum use of federal
medical facilities without calling for additional appropriated
funds. The hard cold reality without subvention, when health
care reform evolves, Medicare-eligible military beneficiaries
will be shunted to the private sector to the financial
disadvantage of HCFA. Accordingly, we strongly recommend that
this critical concept be incorporated into any compromise
legislation.

DoD and DVA have some facilities, which are similar to those
in the private sector in at least one significant respect -
they are not operating at maximum constructed capacity. This
phenomenon results from a seemingly controllable factor --
lack of physicians, nurses, ancillary personnel or necessary
high-tech equipment. The staffing and equipment problems
could be solved by an infusion of more funds into the DoD and
DVA budgets. The desired result is to motivate MTF commanders
and Directors of VA hospitals to increase patient load knowing
that the reimbursement they receive would help them expand the
capability of their facilities and be competitive in the local
community.

The premise underlying interagency reimbursement or
"subvention" is that care in federal facilities, especially
MTFs, is less costly than care at private medical facilities
and therefore will result in savings for Medicare. A closer
look at military medicine reveals that health care provided by
DoD would be cheaper for Medicare than the same care provided
in the private sector and billed to Medicare. In a
Medicare/military treatment facility pilot project conducted

at U.S. Naval Hospital, San Diego, between November 1988 and March 1990, significant savings were realized by HCFA.

The program provided for the treatment of DoD beneficiaries who were eligible for Medicare. Under this project the Navy authorized two private Medicare certified physicians to perform inpatient and outpatient services at the military hospital. The Navy negotiated the rate with the physicians. HCFA authorized the waiver of the Medicare co-payment and the Naval Hospital provided the facility at no cost to Medicare. Over the test period, 75 coronary artery bypass grafts were performed in the Naval Hospital at a conservatively estimated savings of $17,000 per procedure, with a total savings over the period of $1.3 million.

When such savings are possible, it is clear that maximum use should be made of MTFs. This is further supported by a GAO Study directed by the House Armed Services Committee. The GAO report (GAO/HRD 90-131) dated September 7, 1990, indicated that in 1988 military hospitals had an overall occupancy rate of 45 percent of designed capacity. At the same time approximately 70 percent of the CHAMPUS costs were being incurred near military hospitals. The GAO concluded that by adding staff and equipment at military hospitals to treat more patients rather than paying for their care under CHAMPUS, DoD would reap substantial savings. The same logic applies to treatment of Medicare-eligible beneficiaries in MTFs.

Based on a review of six hospitals, GAO estimated savings ranging from $18 million to $21 million in CHAMPUS funds. If Medicare-eligible beneficiaries were included, the savings to the Government would be substantially greater. The estimates showed that military hospital care would cost from 43 to 52 percent less than care by private providers.

By authorizing reimbursement by HCFA for treatment of Medicare-eligible DoD beneficiaries, additional funds would be available to expand care, make greater use of hospital space and thus obtain even greater savings.

The authority to use the additional funds to hire or contract for additional medical personnel and purchase necessary equipment is an essential underpinning of the program. Without it, the ability to expand in-house care would not be realized. Further, since the rates charged by the military facility would be less than the prevailing local provider rate, the HCFA Regional Director would have an incentive to use the less expensive MTF facilities, thus creating a win-

win-win situation for the patient, HCFA, DoD and, of course,
the tax payer.

Currently, care for Medicare-eligible military retirees in
MTFs is provided at no cost to HCFA; thus, Medicare now reaps
a windfall for every Medicare-eligible beneficiary treated in
an MTF. HCFA, until now, has been concerned that should
subvention funding be allowed, it could increase Medicare
outlays. Conversely, Medicare costs would, arguably, increase
to a greater extent if Medicare-eligible retirees were turned
away from military health care and forced to receive care in
the private sector through Medicare. This phenomenon is
precisely what is happening today. The President recognizes
that and has offered a way to fix it in his legislative
proposal as contained in Section 8001 for DoD and Section 8002
for DVA.

Today, current budget practices financially penalize MTF
Commanders and VA Medical Directors for providing care to
Medicare-eligible retirees. A simple example helps illustrate
the problem. Consider that a MTF Commander is faced with two
retirees who need hospitalization. One retiree is less than
sixty-five years of age and eligible for CHAMPUS; the other
is sixty-five and eligible for Medicare. By law, both
military retirees are eligible for care on a space-available
basis in military hospitals. But when care is not available
due to limited staffing or equipment shortages, the Army,
Navy, Coast Guard or Air Force has to pay the CHAMPUS bill
when retirees get civilian health care. On the other hand,
military medical resources are conserved when Medicare-
eligible retirees obtain care from civilian sources.
Therefore, the more patients that military facilities "shift"
to Medicare, the more bed spaces and other resources are freed
up for CHAMPUS users. So, if all other things are equal, the
military commander has an incentive to treat the CHAMPUS
retiree and to refer the Medicare-eligible retiree for
civilian care -- so Medicare can pay the bill. As the number
of Medicare-eligible retirees increases over the next decade
to almost double what it was in 1987, the commander's
incentive to turn away Medicare-eligible retirees will be even
greater.

As proponents of subvention, we realize that total care may
not be possible or even workable at all installations. The
key is that there has to be underused capacity that can be
utilized to increase patient loads if more resources are
infused into the facility. Also, the discounted rates for
HCFA must reflect the substantial savings Medicare now

realizes because Medicare-eligible retirees now receive care in MTFs at no cost to HCFA.

TROA's Position

Subvention will save millions of taxpayer dollars because treatment in military and DVA medical facilities generally is less costly than from comparable civilian sources. Another plus is that military retirees and veterans would receive treatment in medical facilities of their choice and in a system they know.

The use of Medicare "risk contracts" to provide health care services on a capitated basis, now used by HCFA, has great potential, if similar risks were assumed by DoD and DVA. The bottom line is that subvention will save money for everyone -- Medicare, DVA, DoD, patients and taxpayers. We strongly petition this committee to endorse Sections 8001 and 8002 in the President's plan to provide payment by Medicare to whatever plan the member chooses to enroll. This freedom of choice is critically important to our members and as it is to all Americans.

CLOSING

MR. CHAIRMAN, THANK YOU FOR ALLOWING US THE OPPORTUNITY TO PRESENT THE VIEWS OF THE RETIRED OFFICERS ASSOCIATION ON THIS VERY IMPORTANT ISSUE OF HEALTH CARE REFORM. WE WILL BE PLEASED TO ANSWER ANY QUESTION THAT YOU OR ANY OTHER MEMBER OF THE COMMITTEE MIGHT HAVE.

STATEMENT OF STATE FARM MUTUAL AUTOMOBILE INSURANCE
COMPANY ON THE AUTOMOBILE INSURANCE PROVISIONS OF
TITLE X OF THE HEALTH SECURITY ACT (H.R. 3600)

State Farm Mutual Automobile Insurance Company
appreciates the opportunity to submit its views to the
Subcommittee on the automobile insurance coordination
provisions in Title X of The Clinton Administration's
Health Security Act (H.R. 3600). As the largest
automobile insurer in the nation, insuring more than
35 million automobiles, State Farm has a major stake in
reforms affecting the medical component of automobile
insurance.

Title X of the Health Security Act would directly
alter the current mechanisms for delivery of health care
covered by automobile insurance through a new
"coordinated" system. State Farm supports the basic
principles underlying the Title X automobile insurance
coordination plan, but believes certain modifications to
and clarifications of the Title X language are necessary
to ensure that it serves the Act's fundamental goals of
efficient and effective health care delivery and medical
cost management.

A. Background: Health Care Paid
By Automobile Insurance

The automobile insurance system currently
finances health care for injuries sustained in
automobile accidents in two principal ways: (1) direct
payment to an injured individual under such individual's
automobile insurance policy, and (2) indirect payment to
an injured individual under the insurance policy of
another person legally responsible for causing the
accident in which the injuries were sustained. The
total industry costs covered by both types of payments
amount to approximately $12.5 billion per year.

As Congress well knows, the costs of health care
have rapidly escalated. Problems specific to the
automobile medical insurance system, however, are
fueling cost increases for auto accident-related health
care that go beyond the general cost-escalation trend.
Principal among these problems are duplicate payments
for auto accident-related health care, unwarranted
expenditures on such care, and shifting of general
health care costs to automobile insurers. Health care
reform legislation that fails to address these problems
could seriously exacerbate their cost-inflationary
effects.

1. Duplicate Payments

Duplicate payments for auto accident-related
health care are prevalent. According to current
estimates, duplicate payments for such care amount to
approximately $5 billion per year. This represents
about 40 percent of the total of $12.5 billion of health
care costs annually paid by automobile insurers.

Some duplicate payments for auto accident-related
health care occur because of overlapping health and auto
insurance coverages held by a single individual. Even
more, however, are the result of laws applied in auto
accident liability cases that permit an injured
individual to recover from the driver responsible for
the accident (i.e., the driver's automobile liability
insurer) the costs of medical care already paid for by
insurance. In some instances, the existence of both
overlapping health and automobile medical insurance and
the ability to recover medical expenses through
automobile liability insurance results in three separate
payments for a single medical expense.

When 37 million Americans have no health
insurance coverage at all, it seems unthinkable to allow
such duplicative payments. Any responsible plan for
health care reform should include provisions to ensure
that there is only single payment for medical expenses;
this is at the heart of the "coordination" goal.

2. Artificial Cost Inflation

Under the current automobile insurance system,
there is no effective way for automobile insurers to
manage the extent and cost of health care provided for
most automobile accident-related injuries. Because most
automobile insurance health care payments are made under
liability policies for treatment of persons other than
the insured, automobile insurers are not in a position
to manage the types and extent of treatment they pay
for. Unlike health maintenance organizations and
preferred-provider network insurers, automobile insurers
-- whose payments for health care are almost always on a
fee-for-service basis -- generally cannot, for example,
require that the medical treatment they cover under
liability policies be subject to utilization review or
specific fee limits. As a result, automobile insurers
have little ability to ensure that the costs charged for
auto accident-related medical care are reasonable or
that the services provided were medically appropriate.

The lack of cost management for auto accident-
related medical services creates perverse incentives for
over-utilization of such services. In some cases, these
incentives lead to abuse and even fraud. Any health
care reform legislation that aims to curb health care
costs overall should include measures to eradicate these
incentives and their adverse results.

3. Cost Shifting

Closely related to the problem of uncontrolled
automobile accident-related health care expenditures is
the problem of cost shifting. To some extent, all
private insurers of medical care are the victims of cost
shifting, as providers seek to compensate for government
caps on reimbursement under Medicare and Medicaid. The
problem is particularly acute for automobile insurers.

Health care reform legislation has the potential
to create a more equitable and rational system by
applying uniform cost management techniques to medical
care covered by all types of insurance, including
automobile insurance. This is the approach of the
Health Security Act: under Title X, the fee schedules
to be established under the Act would apply to
automobile accident-related health care as they do to
other types of health care. State Farm strongly

supports this aspect of the Act, which reflects
recognition that if cost controls, such as fee
schedules, do not apply uniformly to health care for
injuries caused by auto accidents and injuries otherwise
sustained, cost shifting to automobile insurers will
amplify, rather than eliminate, existing cost-allocation
distortions.

B. The Title X Coordination Plan

Title X prescribes a system for coordinating
automobile medical insurance with the proposed new
health care system. Specifically, Subtitle B of Title X
provides that (1) an individual injured in an automobile
accident shall receive treatment for the injury by or
through such individual's health plan and (2) automobile
insurers responsible for payment of medical expenses
shall make such payments directly to the health plan.

The basic elements of the Subtitle B coordination
plan are sound. They would retain the benefits of the
current system of financing auto accident-related health
care through automobile insurance -- internalizing the
costs of auto accidents and thereby encouraging auto
safety -- while providing a mechanism for more efficient
delivery of and payment for such care. If appropriately
implemented, the Subtitle B plan could represent a vast
improvement over the current system.

Subtitle B fails, however, adequately to address
certain of the problems cited above, including the
problem of duplicate payments. The Health Security Act
expresses a general intent to eliminate duplicate
medical insurance payments (see, e.g., sections 1422(a)
and 2324(f)), but Title X contains no provisions to
carry out this intent with respect to payments for
automobile accident-related health care. State Farm
believes that the inclusion of such provisions is
critical.

To address the duplicate payments problem,
Subtitle B should be amended to state that,
notwithstanding current liability rules, there shall be
no payment for auto accident-related health care
expenditures except to the health plans and in
accordance with the Act's coordination scheme. This
amendment would ensure that the health plans, and only
the health plans, receive payment for the auto accident-
related medical services they provide. Absent such
amending language, Subtitle B will merely perpetuate
inequity in the health care insurance reimbursement
system.

In order to address the cost management problems
discussed above, further amendments should be made to
the current Subtitle B language. Specifically, there
should be provisions that expressly extend to auto
accident-related medical care the Act's general
requirements that medical services provided by health
plans be (i) limited to "medically necessary or
appropriate" services (Section 1141(a)) and (ii) subject
to "reasonable restrictions" (as described in Section
1322(b)(2)(B)). Such provisions, coupled with the
existing Subtitle B language regarding application of
the Act's medical services fee schedules to auto
accident-related services, would represent very
substantial steps toward management of auto accident-
related health care costs.

C. The Subtitle C Commission

Subtitle C of Title X calls for a Commission on Integration of Health Benefits, to be charged with studying the feasibility and appropriateness of transferring financial responsibility for all medical benefits, including those currently covered under workers' compensation and automobile insurance, to health plans. State Farm believes that there is no need for such a study, because there is ample evidence that financial "merger" of automobile insurance with the health care system would be unwise.

Financing auto accident-related health care through the automobile insurance system has sound public policy justifications. First, it is fair: it avoids imposing auto accident-related costs on persons who do not contribute to those costs (i.e., non-drivers). Second, it makes drivers accountable for the risks they pose, and thereby encourages safer driving. Finally, it provides incentives for automobile insurers to promote increased auto and highway safety -- incentives that have proved highly instrumental in advancing new highway and auto safety legislation, regulations, and other initiatives. Given the importance of preventive mechanisms for reducing health care costs and the substantial financial burdens the government must assume to improve other aspects of the health care system, it would seem futile, at best, to consider whether automobile medical insurance should be "merged" with the health care system.

Accordingly, State Farm would suggest that the proposed commission not study -- or at least not exclusively study -- the possibility of transferring financial responsibility for auto accident-related health care to the health plans. State Farm believes that if there is to be a study, it should broadly address possible ways of improving the delivery of and payment for auto accident-related medical services.

State Farm also firmly believes that no commission should be charged with studying both automobile insurance and workers' compensation insurance. There are significant ways in which automobile insurance differs from workers' compensation insurance, which counsels against any commingling of decision making with respect to each system. Recognition of these differences should be made both in considering the role of the proposed Subtitle C commission and the benefits of the auto insurance coordination provisions of Subtitle B, as opposed to the workers' compensation provisions of Subtitle A.

With respect to workers' compensation, there are important questions relating to the employer's responsibility for the course of treatment for disabled workers under workers' compensation that are not relevant in the automobile insurance context. For example, the extent to which employers should control the type and extent of care provided under workers' compensation insurance, and the role of state and or federal regulators in monitoring such control, are critical issues with respect to possible reform of the workers' compensation system, but they have little bearing on the automobile insurance system.

Likewise, there are questions about automobile insurance that have no corollary in the workers' compensation context. Most obviously, issues relating to automobile liability insurance are not relevant to workers' compensation. Critical questions, such as how to remove impediments to efficient resolution of automobile liability insurance claims, should be addressed when considering automobile medical insurance reforms, but need not be addressed with respect to workers' compensation reforms.

Accordingly, State Farm would suggest that, if there is to be a commission charged with studying automobile medical insurance, it have no responsibilities relating to workers' compensation insurance. Consonant with this suggestion, State Farm believes that the members of any such automobile insurance commission should not be appointed by the Secretary of Health and Human Services and the Secretary of Labor, as Subtitle C currently provides, but rather by the Secretary of Health and Human Services and the Secretary of Commerce.

Finally, State Farm believes that any Subtitle C commission should have more time to complete its study, in order that it have an opportunity to evaluate the experience of the new Subtitle B coordinated system before recommending any changes to it. State Farm would suggest that the deadline for submission of the commission's report to the President should be postponed until two years after the effective date of Subtitle B.

*   *   *

In summary, State Farm strongly supports adoption of a properly coordinated automobile medical insurance system, under which drivers would remain accountable for the health care costs associated with auto accidents. Such a system could result in a more rational health care delivery system with increased efficiencies, including the elimination of duplicate auto accident-related medical payments and uniform management of auto accident-related and other health care expenditures. These efficiencies, in turn, can help to make health care and automobile insurance more affordable for all Americans. State Farm believes that, with appropriate amendments, Title X of the Health Security Act has the potential to achieve these important goals.

ISBN 0-16-046334-3

90000

9 780160 463341